HISTORY OF THE
PERSIAN EMPIRE

GATEWAY TO ALL LANDS

A. T. OLMSTEAD

HISTORY OF THE
PERSIAN EMPIRE

PHOENIX BOOKS

THE UNIVERSITY OF CHICAGO PRESS

This book is also available in a clothbound edition from
THE UNIVERSITY OF CHICAGO PRESS

THE UNIVERSITY OF CHICAGO PRESS, CHICAGO 37
Cambridge University Press, London, N.W. 1, England
The University of Toronto Press, Toronto 5, Canada

Foreword

A BOOK—to its author—is a living, pulsing entity through every phase of its creation: through manuscript, galley proof, and page proof. Constantly it needs to be changed: words must be altered, thoughts rephrased, arguments re-worked, or conclusions redrawn.

Unfortunately, A. T. Olmstead did not live to see this book through its later stages, and the task had to be undertaken by a few of his colleagues on the faculty of the University of Chicago.

Obviously their revision could by no means be as extensive as the author's would have been—or as they themselves sometimes desired it to be. They, however, were not assuming full responsibility or editorship, for so eminent a scholar as A. T. Olmstead was clearly entitled to express his own point of view in his own way. As his colleagues they have performed their work as a last gesture of friendship.

Professor Olmstead's daughter, Cleta Olmstead Robbins Boughton, has chosen the illustrations, read the page proofs, and prepared the indexes.

GEORGE G. CAMERON

Preface

EIGHTY years have passed since George Rawlinson, Camden Professor of Ancient History in the University of Oxford, published the first edition of his *Five Great Monarchies of the Ancient Eastern World*. During these eighty years ancient history has been made over completely. It has been publicly stated by a great modern historian that the most significant feature in the historiography of the last forty years has been the emergence of the ancient Near East into the full light of history. The other ancient monarchies of Rawlinson have long since been hopelessly antiquated; it is all the more strange that his *Fifth Monarchy* still remains our one full-length history of the Achaemenid Empire, for its place has not been taken by later though less detailed sketches. So strange a phenomenon would have appeared inexplicable did not more mature reflection supply reasons which may explain, if they do not excuse, the neglect.

The most obvious is the fact that Rawlinson possessed virtually all the sources even now available for the general narrative and for the culture in general. He had already shown himself a master of classical studies by his magnificent translation of Herodotus and by a wealth of annotations we still value. For us, likewise, Herodotus remains our one main source written in Greek. Rawlinson enjoyed a wide acquaintance with other sources composed in Greek and Latin; to his list, few indeed have been added, even from "fragments" of earlier authors quoted by later writers. His brother, Sir Henry Rawlinson, had deciphered the Behistun Inscription; today the autobiography of Darius is still our one long piece of literature composed in Old Persian. The Avesta, the Bible of the Persians, had been known for nearly a century. Our own Bible was available.

In addition, the impressive ruins on the Persepolis platform had often been visited and had been described fully by well-known and thoroughly competent travelers. Rawlinson was a historian who understood the value of archeology long before "scientific" archeological method had been evolved, and his interpretation and analysis of architecture and art in the light of his written sources was a model for his successors to follow.

Neglect of the Achaemenid history was intensified by the lack of spectacular new discoveries. Why should the Orientalist waste his time in threshing over the old straw when excavation after excavation in other and more favored countries was every year pouring forth new treasures to astonish the world and when many periods of Near Eastern history were now becoming better known than those of the once more famous Greek or Roman or even early medieval times? New cultures were being recovered in hitherto unknown languages; new literatures cried out for decipherment, publication, and interpretation. To be sure, now and then an Egyptian or a Babylonian document from this period was recovered; but how could this interest scholars who were fortunate enough to deal with the glories of the Babylon of Hammurabi or of Nebuchadnezzar, of Assyrian Nineveh, or of Egyptian Thebes? The majority of the available sources on Achaemenid history were in Greek. They were adequately dealt with by outstanding historians trained in the classics; more and more the Orientalist, in the press of his own work, had lost familiarity with Greek. Why should not this uncongenial task be left to those best fitted to undertake it? The natural consequence was that the history of the mighty Achaemenid Empire was presented as a series of uncorrelated episodes which found unity and significance only when inserted into the story of the little Greek states.

Despite this somewhat stepfatherly attitude, significant gains have been made in our knowledge of the Empire. New and sounder texts of the Greek authorities are available. A few works of major importance have been recovered from the papyri, and with them numerous fragments of minor works. Authors and dates of our Greek sources are more precisely established, and their data have been more carefully tested. Archeology has almost usurped the place of literature in classical studies. Excavations in Greek lands, within the Achaemenid Empire as without, have afforded a wealth of Greek statues and reliefs, not to speak of innumerable objects of everyday life. Investigation of Greek coins has become a science. Another science is epigraphy; the corpus of Greek inscriptions must be at the elbow of every historian of antiquity. Nowhere in the ancient field has the result of its use been quite so revolutionary as in the Greek world of the fifth and fourth centuries before our era, and not a few texts throw their gleam of light on Greek relations with Persia. Historians by profession now write the history of Greece; by long tradition, ancient history has always recognized the supreme importance of literature and art, and the professional historian needed only to emphasize administration, economics, and social movements to bring classical history to at least the levels of the more modern fields. Only if viewed from the Greek point of view can even one portion of Achaemenid history be considered up to date, and that is the relationship of Greece to Persia.

Not all Orientalists had completely ignored the Achaemenid Empire. One small but able group, students of Indo-European philology, subjected the few Old Persian inscriptions to the most intensive scrutiny ever undergone by so scant a literature. Some of them went on to an examination of the Avesta, which through their labors was made intelligible. A few Old Testament scholars have realized the significance of this period as background for the understanding of a good half of our Bible.

The past few years have witnessed a dawning realization on the part of other Orientalists that the period has too long been neglected. Discovery of the archives from a Jewish mercenary colony near the first Egyptian cataract was truly sensational. Here were the closest parallels in language and in style to the Aramaic of Ezra. Rescripts from Persian kings were cited in Ezra; Old Testament critics had declared them unauthentic, but now there was ample proof that the critics themselves were in the wrong. For comparison with these once-disputed decrees, there was now still another, where a later monarch enforced compliance by these distant Jewish heretics with the recently promulgated Passover law. Other rescripts came from the satrap or from church officials; the inner life of the community was laid bare by their business documents. Most wonderful of all the discoveries was the autobiography of Darius himself, now no longer known only from the inscriptions in the three cuneiform writings, for these Jews possessed a well-worn copy in their own Aramaic language!

Scholars had read since modern times the Wisdom of Ahiqar in the "original" Greek and in various oriental and Western translations. A few had suggested that the true original must have been in Aramaic; now that Aramaic original was found in the archives. Old Testament scholars were quickly convinced that a new era had begun for Aramaic studies. New discoveries of contemporary papyri and of inscriptions were constantly being made, and the belief grew that large sections of the Jewish apocrypha and pseudepigrapha were also of Aramaic origin. Then Aramaic originals were suggested for the very Gospels. Professional New Testament critics remained adamant to the suggestion, but the challenge led only to the recovery of more early Aramaic literature, including the Aramaic Targums of the Hebrew Bible, whose original forms could be traced back almost to the latest Achaemenid period. By that time, professed Orientalists were sure that Aramaic was the normal language of the Achaemenid chancellery.

So long as they were invited to consider mere translations of the Old Persian inscriptions into Akkadian, Assyriologists remained uninterested. When, however, thousands of cuneiform tablets from the later periods were acquired, something had to be done about their publication and interpretation. Once the craze for Greek papyri was well under way, Egyptologists were obliged to study contemporary papyri in demotic writing and contemporary inscriptions in hieroglyphics. No longer could Egyptian history be properly closed with the last dynasty of the Empire, leaving later centuries up to Saite times for an unwelcome appendix. The Saite period, it was now realized, marked rather the beginning of a new era, when Greeks and Egyptians first became intimately acquainted. That acquaintance ripened throughout the whole Achaemenid period until Alexander came to introduce Hellenistic civilization.

A new epoch in the recovery of the ancient Near East opened when the director of the Oriental Institute of the University of Chicago, the late James Henry Breasted, dispatched a party to conduct minor "clearances" preliminary to a definitive publication of the well-known edifices on the Persepolis terrace. These "clearances" quickly turned into regular excavations under the direction of Professor Ernst Herzfeld and were then successfully brought to conclusion by Dr. Erich F. Schmidt. Results have been spectacular beyond the wildest hopes. The world held its breath in amazement when a hundred yards of magnificent reliefs, for the most part as unscratched as on the day they were carved, were unearthed after twenty-two centuries of concealment. Other reliefs of almost equal beauty quickly followed. Buildings whose very existence was hitherto unguessed were excavated, among them the barracks of the palace guards and the treasury of Darius and Xerxes. The harem of these monarchs was laid bare and restored as the excavation house; visitors might sleep in the rooms where the queens and their attendant ladies once resided under the watchful care of eunuchs.

Traces of the fires set by Alexander's drunken orders yet marred the ruins, the burning beams having left their marks where they fell. His soldiers had looted the treasures of precious metals and had smashed the objects of art they were unable to carry away. Fortunately they

left for us the greatest treasure of all, a statue which, despite the barbarous mutilation of head, hands, and limbs by these supposed car-
riers of Hellenic culture, still leaves the torso of a supremely beautiful
woman, carved by a Greek master in the years when Greek sculpture
was at its very height.

They left also thousands of tablets for whose full decipherment
many years must elapse. The inscriptions are regularly in Elamite,
though some are in Aramaic; a few in Phrygian and one in Greek are
also known. All these deal with the building activities of Darius and
Xerxes while they were erecting these very structures. We may learn
the names of the workmen and the countries from which they came,
the work which they did, and the salaries they were paid. We learn,
too, of a new daughter of Darius named after a mother whom we knew
already, and of a gift with which she was provided. From the royal
treasury come the archives of Xerxes, dealing with the routine procedures of administration. The seal impressions of Darius, Xerxes, and
their higher officials open up a new and hitherto undreamed school of
art. To the evidence long since derived from the reliefs, we may add
much new information on the life of king and nobles; from the minor
archeological findings and from the tablets, we obtain for the first
time some idea of the life of the common people.

Work at home in the quiet of the Oriental Institute building in Chicago has kept pace with the excavation at Persepolis. As they have
been discovered, the newly found inscriptions have been incorporated
into an up-to-date card-catalogue dictionary of Old Persian. A similar
dictionary of Elamite made possible the more rapid decipherment of
the thousands of Elamite tablets. In like fashion, reading of the
Aramaic written in ink on tablet and stone is facilitated by a third dictionary in that language. A fourth dictionary is devoted to Phoenician,
in which many inscriptions were written in this period. The great
Assyrian dictionary, now virtually complete, has a separate section
in which more than ten thousand administrative and business documents from the Chaldaean, Achaemenid, and Seleucid periods are arranged in chronological sequence year by year. Other young scholars
are working on the Egyptian texts in demotic, hieratic, and hieroglyphic script which come from the later centuries. Our Old Testament students are more and more interested in the later half of the
Bible. Our photographic Archeological Corpus of some three hundred
thousand cards is now almost complete; included is all the scattered
cultural material from the various countries which formed the

Achaemenid Empire, together with what is needed from earlier centuries for its proper understanding. A considerable proportion of the valuable historical information which has come from these various investigations is already in print and will be cited in the ensuing pages; even more surprising results may be expected in the years to come.

In this renaissance of later Near Eastern history, it would be inevitable that a professor of oriental history should play his part. Fortunately, the author has always been fascinated by the history of this crucial era when Persians and Greeks came into contact and so profoundly influenced each other. In his student days he prepared for his future task by numerous courses in ancient history, Greek and Latin literature, archeology, epigraphy, and paleography, as well as in oriental languages and literatures. For twenty years at the universities of Missouri and Illinois, his general courses were in ancient history, while advanced courses and seminars were held regularly in fields where East and West came together. Since his arrival at the University of Chicago, nearly half of the lectures in his elementary course have been devoted to this later ancient oriental history, and his seminars have almost without exception been given over to problems of the same period.

Through these years a new picture of the Achaemenid Empire has gradually emerged. As a result of recent excavations, the prehistoric cultures of the Iranian plateau are now known; one of the most important excavations, that near Persepolis itself, was the work of the Oriental Institute, and the final synthesis of the results of all these excavations was made here by my most recent candidate for the doctorate. Another candidate has brought together the written documents for the pre-Achaemenid history of Iran. Thus we now possess a fairly adequate background for the special period to which this book is to be devoted.

Through these years also the oriental sources for the Achaemenid period have slowly been pieced together. Their contribution is especially valued because they redress the balance so heavily weighted until now in favor of the Greek writers. From these authors we have become well acquainted with many famous Orientals; now we learn their true names, and at the risk of boring the reader we must tell what they were. We hear of other activities at home which the Greeks did not know and which turn out to be quite as interesting and as important as their relations with the western frontier.

These sources are by no means all Persian. Egypt wrote almost as

much under Persian rule as she did when independent. During most of
the fourth century, the land of the Nile went her own way under native monarchs, some of whom deserve quite as much space in our history as the great kings of Persia. Because of Egyptian records, it is
possible to know the Egypt of these later dynasties quite as well as
that of their better-known predecessors.

Since their writings are preserved in our own Old Testament, the
comparatively small Jewish tribes will always have a special interest.
The great flood of light that Achaemenid history throws on the sacred
record has been revealed in another volume; here it must suffice to indicate that the Old Testament throws as much light on the history of
Persia. From their own inscriptions, the Phoenicians, too, add no
small amount of information. Asia Minor has its native records also,
and through Lydian, Lycian, and Aramaic inscriptions we learn of
new figures, new peoples, and new customs.

It is Babylonia, however, which yields the most information.
Many of its satraps are known to us by name. Rebels against Persian
authority can be added to our narrative. But the great debt we owe
to the Land of the Two Rivers is for the amazing picture of the culture.

The honest seeker after historical truth must in a detailed study present the names of many individuals who are of little interest in themselves but who belong to the general picture. For those who are not
specialists, they may be treated as anonymous. Narrative history is
often dull, and as it is unfolded there are inevitably many points on
which not all minds will agree. This volume was itself preceded by a
number of articles on controversial subjects. But the essential truth
behind any individual problem rests with the manner in which the so-
lution fits into the over-all picture. Hence the historian need not, in a
narrative history, interrupt the continuity of his story by detailed
arguments for the soundness of the views which he presents, for the
resulting picture will itself prove them sound or unsound.

The real purpose of the book, however, will be exposition of culture—or rather, of cultures, for Achaemenid history presents a fascinating picture of various civilizations at different stages of evolution
and all in the process of intermingling. No more illuminating and instructive picture of such a mixture can be found in the whole of world
history. We have known something of this blending during Hellenistic times, and we have vaguely realized that it was going on some
years before. The fact that this series of changes was proceeding at an
accelerated pace a century and more before Alexander is a more recent

discovery. We have realized that there was mixture between Persians and Greeks; recovery of the oriental sources has shown how universal was the process.

From these sources we have confirmation of what Herodotus says about Persian administration, but now we can describe the system in minute detail and with numerous illustrations. We know how heavily taxes were levied and how overtaxation hastened the decline of the Empire. We have stories, comic and tragic, to show official graft and attempts of the higher authorities to check it. We can trace the career of the victim, of his oppressor, and of amusing rascals.

We know how the common man lived in the various satrapies of the Empire. We can tell what he ate and what he paid for his food, his drink, his clothing, his medicine, his rent, or his house. Throughout the period we can see his expenses increasing without adequate rise in his income, and we can sense his increasing misery until relief comes by death. With him, we rejoice at his weddings, deplore his divorces, or attend his funeral. We witness his contracts and testify at his trial under the new imperial law code. For every phase of his daily life we have a document for testimony.

The common man's life was dominated by the temple. There he might at festival time witness gorgeous processions; there he might worship his gods. But to the majority of the Empire's inhabitants, the temple (represented by its priests) was an unpleasant institution. The common man was its serf or renter, and to it went most of the hard-earned returns on his labor. Religion was rarely indeed a cause of joy in the ancient Near East.

But we have also the story of the wonderful religion preached by Zoroaster, greatest of Aryan prophets. We may tell of the Aryan paganism from which it grew and of the partial paganism into which it soon relapsed. We tell also the story of more primitive Magism, though its dire results on the still later Zoroastrianism fortunately lie beyond the bounds of the present volume. During our period, Judaism developed into something nearer the Judaism of today, though with various excursions along side paths which are not without interest. Other religious movements may be more dimly glimpsed, but all were proceeding along syncretistic lines which were to produce the mystery religions of the Roman Empire. During this period also a remarkable science, astronomy, was developing—the science which so profoundly influenced that of the Greeks and so that of our own day.

By this time we realize how incomplete was our knowledge of the Empire when observed through the eyes of Greek writers only, even when aided by the best of modern historians. Throughout the greatest portion of the period, the Orient lived by and to itself. Toward the end, the higher classes may have taken over some aspects of Greek culture, but the imitation was superficial. Greek mercenaries in the pay of the court, of rebels, or of rival kingdoms were not the best of missionaries, for they created more antagonism against than adherence to their culture.

We realize as never before that Greece was at no time a serious political threat to the Empire, because there was no Greece as a political entity; there were only Greek states. Soon after its origin, the Empire conquered the greatest, most wealthy, and most enlightened of these Greek states, and for the most part they remained within the Empire. Recent excavations have shown that they continued completely under Persian rule and that their life was thus profoundly affected. We can see how Darius and Xerxes should have conquered what little remained of the free Greek states, but we may also analyze the Persian blunders which saved a few. As the free states grew in power, though constantly weakened by internal wars, we can trace the process by which Persia declined in military effectiveness, but at the same time improved in diplomacy. This continued despite the internal decay and rampant revolt of satraps and native kings, until bribes by Persian "archers" gave Persia the envied position of dictator to what was left of a free Greece.

The dawn of a Hellenistic age is sensed in the increasingly deeper penetration of the Empire by Greek mercenaries and merchants, by utilization of Greek physicians, athletes, sculptors, and cooks, by visits of Greek philosophers, literary men, and scientists. When Alexander destroyed the Empire by a military invasion, the Orient for a short time lost its place in the world; how the Orient quickly recovered much of its dominance must be the subject for another volume.

A. T. OLMSTEAD

ORIENTAL INSTITUTE
UNIVERSITY OF CHICAGO
October 18, 1943

Table of Contents

Maps

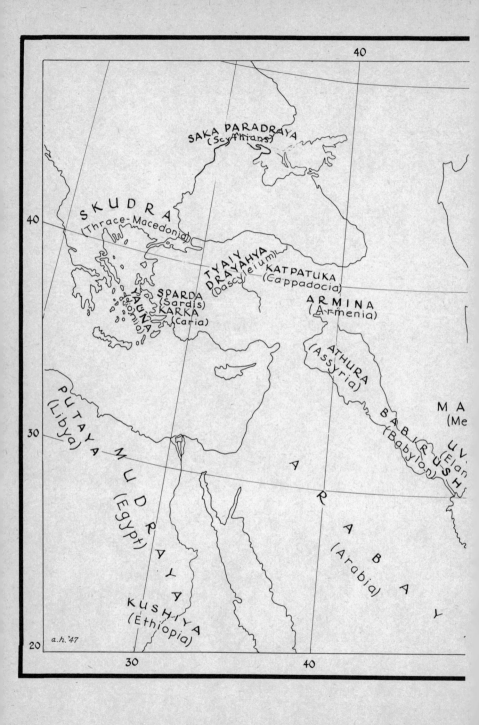

SAKA PARADRAYA
(Scythians)

S K U D R A
(Thrace-Macedonia)

TYAIY
DRAYAHYA
(Dascyleium)

KATPATUKA
(Cappadocia)

SPARDA
(Sardis)

KARKA
(Caria)

YAUNA
(Ionia)

ARMINA
(Armenia)

ATHURA
(Assyria)

PUTAYA
(Libya)

MUDRAYA
(Egypt)

BABIRUSH
(Babylon)

MA
(Me

UV.
(Elan
USH

A

R

A

B

A

Y
(Arabia)

KUSHIYA
(Ethiopia)

40

40

30

30

20

40

30

40

a.h. '47

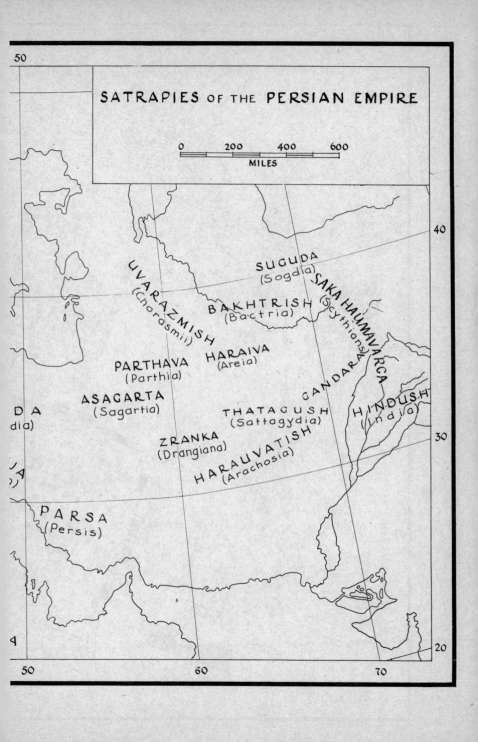

SATRAPIES OF THE PERSIAN EMPIRE

0   200   400   600
MILES

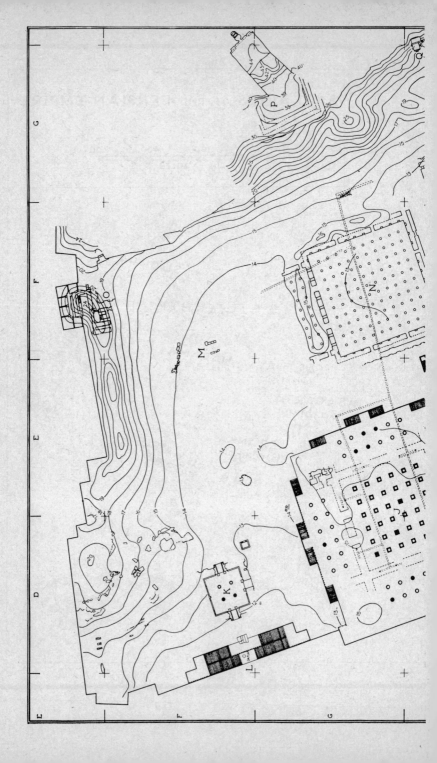

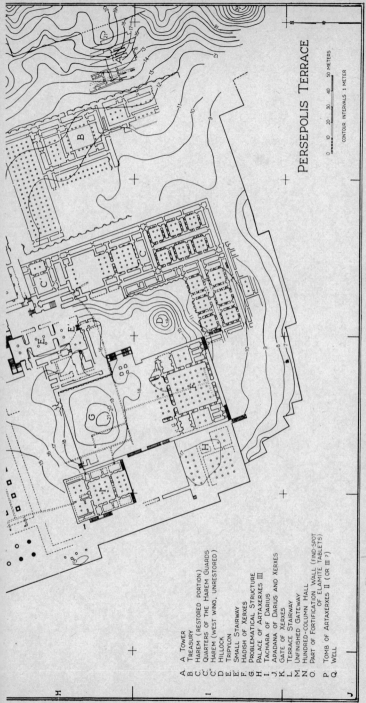

A A TOWER
B TREASURY
C HAREM (RESTORED PORTION)
C' QUARTERS OF THE HAREM GUARDS
C" HAREM (WEST WING, UNRESTORED)
D HILLOCK
E TRIPYLON
E' SMALL STAIRWAY
F HADISH OF XERXES
G PROBLEMATICAL STRUCTURE
H PALACE OF ARTAXERXES III
I TACHARA OF DARIUS
J APADANA OF DARIUS AND XERXES
K GATE OF XERXES
L TERRACE STAIRWAY
M UNFINISHED GATEWAY
N HUNDRED-COLUMN HALL
O PART OF FORTIFICATION WALL (FIND-SPOT
      OF ELAMITE TABLETS)
P TOMB OF ARTAXERXES II (OR III ?)
Q WELL

PERSEPOLIS TERRACE

0 10 20 30 40 50 METERS

CONTOUR INTERVALS 1 METER

Plan of the Terrace of Persepolis, showing structures uncovered by the end of 1937. Surveyed and drawn by John S. Bolles,
with additions by Eliot F. Noyes and R. Carl Haines. Scale, 1:2,000

Plan (courtesy, Erich Schmidt)

PERSEPOLIS

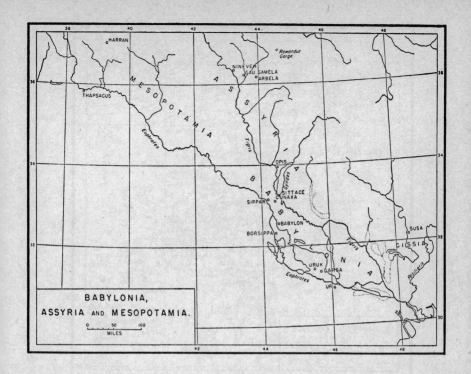

BABYLONIA,
ASSYRIA AND MESOPOTAMIA.

0   50   100
MILES

HARRAN

MESOPOTAMIA

Rowandut
Gorge

NINEVEH
GAU GAMELA
ARBELA

ASSYRIA

THAPSACUS

Euphrates

Tigris

OPIS

Gyndes

SITTACE
CUNAXA

SIPPAR

BABYLON

BORSIPPA

BABYLONIA

SUSA

CISSIA

URUK

LARSA

UR

Euphrates

Tigris

Pasitigris

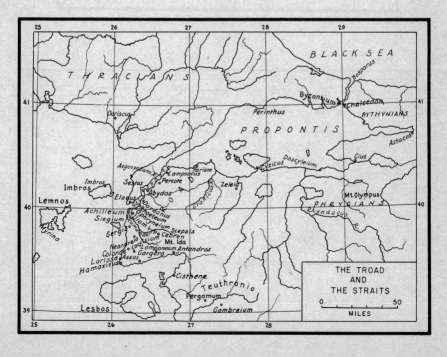

THE TROAD
AND
THE STRAITS

0   50
MILES

BLACK SEA

THRACIANS

Bosporus

Byzantium
Chalcedon

BYTHYNIANS

Doriscus

Perinthus

PROPONTIS

Astacus

Cius

Aegospotami

Lampsacus

Parium

Cyzicus

Dascyleium

Imbros

Sestos

Abydos

Zeleia

Imbros

Elaeus

Percote

Granicus

Mt. Olympus

Lemnos

Rhoeteum

PHRYGIANS

Achilleum

Ophryneium

Ilium

Rhyndacus

Siegium

Cebren

Scepsis

Gergis

Mt. Ida

Karina

Neandrea

Cocylium

Antandros

Colonae

Assos

Larissa

Lamponeum

Gargara

Hamaxitus

Cisthene

Teuthronia

Lesbos

Pergamum

Gambreium

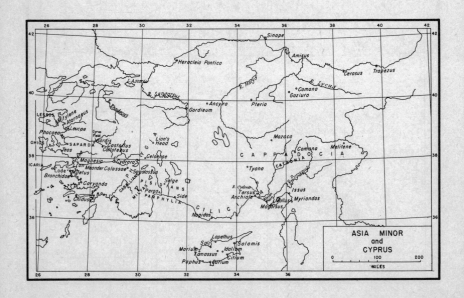

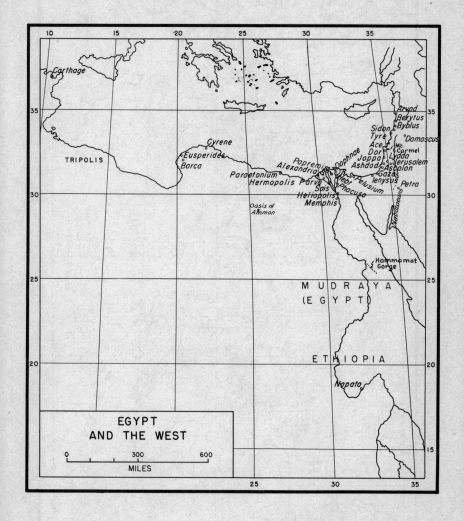

EGYPT
AND THE WEST

0   300   600

MILES

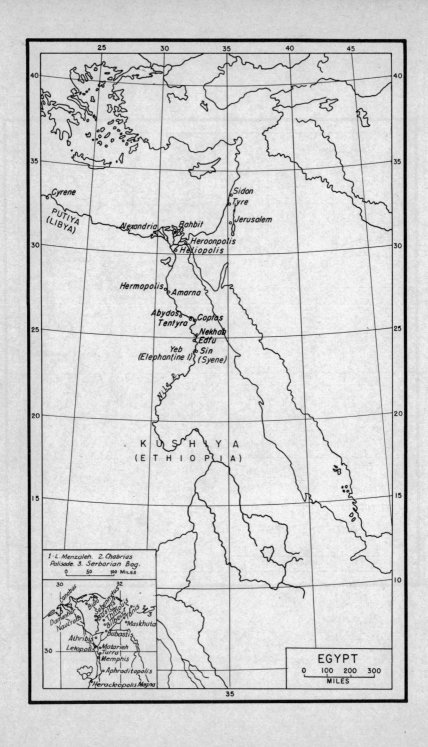

25　　　　30　　　　35　　　　40　　　　45

Cyrene

**PUTIYA
(LIBYA)**

Sidon
Tyre

Alexandria　*Bahbit*　*Jerusalem*

Heroonpolis
Heliopolis

Hermopolis　*Amarna*

Abydos　　*Coptos*
Tentyra

Nekhab
Edfu

Yeb　　*Sin*
(Elephantine I)　*(Syene)*

Nile R.

K U S H I Y A
(E T H I O P I A)

1 - *L. Menzaleh.* 2. *Chabrias*
Palisade. 3. *Serborian Bag.*

0　　50　　100 MILES

30　　　　　32

Canobus
Buto
Damanhur　*Sebennytus*
Naucratis　*Busiris*
Tamuis
Bilbeis　*Tanis*
Maskhuta
Bubastis
Athribis
Letopolis　*Matarieh*
Turra
Memphis

Aphroditopolis

Heracleopolis Magna

EGYPT

0　100　200　300
MILES

35

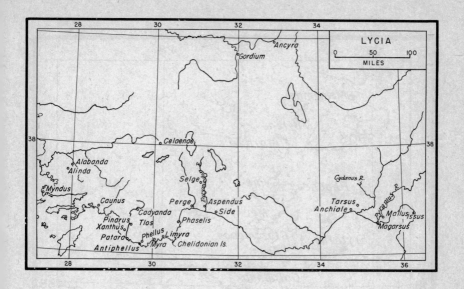

LYCIA

Ancyra

Gordium

Celaenae

Alabanda
Alinda
Myndus
Caunus
Cadyanda
Pinarus
Xanthus
Tlos
Patara
Phellus
Antiphellus
Myra
Selge
Perge
Phaselis
Limyra
Chelidonian Is.
Aspendus
Side

Cydanus R.

Tarsus
Anchiale
Mallus
Issus
Magarsus

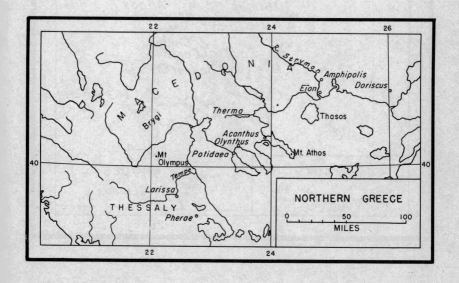

NORTHERN GREECE

Strymon
Amphipolis
Eion
Doriscus
Thasos
Therma
Acanthus
Olynthus
Mt. Athos
Potidaea
Brygi

Mt
Olympus
Tempe
Larissa
THESSALY
Pherae

MACEDONI

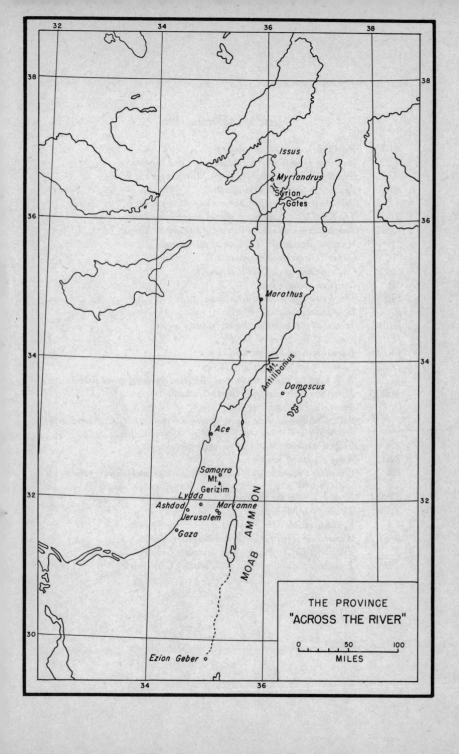

Issus

Myriandrus

Syrian
Gates

Marathus

Mt.
Antilibanus

Damascus

Ace

Samarra
Mt.
Gerizim
Lydda
Ashdod   Mariamne
Jerusalem
Gaza

MOAB AMMON

Ezion Geber

THE PROVINCE
"ACROSS THE RIVER"

0   50   100
MILES

List of Abbreviations

AJA	*American Journal of Archaeology*
AJSL	*American Journal of Semitic Languages and Literatures*
AMI	ERNST HERZFELD, *Archäologische Mitteilungen aus Iran*
AS	*Annales du Service des Antiquités de l'Égypte*
ÄZ	*Zeitschrift für ägyptische Sprache und Altertumskunde*
BE	*The Babylonian Expedition of the University of Pennsylvania*
BRM	*Babylonian Records in the Library of J. Pierpont Morgan*, ed. A. T. CLAY
CH	HARPER, ROBERT F. *The Code of Hammurabi*
CIG	*Corpus Inscriptionum Graecarum*
CIS	*Corpus Inscriptionum Semiticarum*
CP	*Classical Philology*
FHG	*Fragmenta Historicorum Graecorum*
IG	*Inscriptiones Graecae*
JAOS	*Journal of the American Oriental Society*
JEA	*Journal of Egyptian Archaeology*
JNES	*Journal of Near Eastern Studies*
JRAS	*Journal of the Royal Asiatic Society*
JS	A. J. JAUSSEN and R. SAVIGNAC. *Mission archéologique en Arabie*
MDOG	*Mitteilungen der deutschen Orient-Gesellschaft*
OLZ	*Orientalistiche Literaturzeitung*
PW	PAULY-WISSOWA. *Real-Encyclopädie der classischen Altertumswissenschaft*
RA	*Revue d'assyriologie et d'archéologie orientale*
RES	*Revue des études sémitiques*
RT	*Recueil de travaux relatifs à la philologie et à l'archéologie égyptiennes et assyriennes*
SPAW	*Sitzungsberichte der preussischen Akademie der Wissenschaften*
TAM	*Tituli Asiae Minoris*
VS	*Vorderasiatische Schriftdenkmäler*
WZKM	*Wiener Zeitschrift für die Kunde des Morgenlandes*
ZA	*Zeitschrift für Assyriologie und verwandte Gebiete*
ZDMG	*Zeitschrift der deutschen morgenländischen Gesellschaft*

Chapter I

ANCIENT HISTORY

WHEN Cyrus entered Babylon in 539 B.C., the world was old. More significant, the world knew its antiquity. Its scholars had compiled long dynastic lists, and simple addition appeared to prove that kings whose monuments were still visible had ruled more than four millenniums before. Yet earlier were other monarchs, sons of gods and so themselves demigods, whose reigns covered several generations of present-day short-lived men. Even these were preceded, the Egyptians believed, by the gods themselves, who had held sway through long aeons; before the universal flood the Babylonians placed ten kings, the least of whom ruled 18,600 years, the greatest 43,200.

Other peoples knew this flood and told of monarchs—Nannacus of Iconium, for example—who reigned in prediluvian times. The sacred history of the Jews extended through four thousand years; modest as were their figures when compared with those of Babylon and Egypt, they recorded that one prediluvian patriarch almost reached the millennium mark before his death. Greek poets chanted a legendary history which was counted backward to the time when the genealogies of the heroes "ascended to the god." Each people and nation, each former city-state, boasted its own creation story with its own local god as creator.

Worship of the remote national past was a special characteristic of these closing days of the earlier Orient. Nabu-naid, last independent king of the Chaldaeans, rejoiced when he unearthed the foundation record of Naram Sin, unseen for thirty-two hundred years—or so his scholars informed him. His inscriptions are filled with references to rulers long since dead, from Ur Nammu and his son Shulgi, founders of the Third Dynasty of Ur, through the great lawgiver Hammurabi and the Kashshite Burnaburiash, to the Assyrian conquerors of almost his own day—a stretch of at least fifteen centuries. Ancient temples were restored, ancient cults revived with their ancient ritual, and his daughter consecrated to an ancient temple office.

Nabu-naid was not the only "antiquarian." More than one of his temple restorations had been commenced, and more than one of his

1

cult reforms initiated, by Nebuchadnezzar, who sought in vain early building records his more fortunate successor uncovered, and whose own inscriptions were purposely archaistic, imitating in style and in writing those of the famed Hammurabi.

The cult of antiquity became a passion when the Twenty-sixth (Saite) Dynasty seemed about to restore the Asiatic empire of the Eighteenth Dynasty. Ancient texts were copied and new texts composed on their model—even to style and form of hieroglyph. Contemporary Saite art was a softened copy of Eighteenth Dynasty sculpture. The god Amon, upstart of less than fifteen centuries, lost his place of honor to Neit, the aged mistress of Sais, and almost forgotten deities were again worshiped. Officials borrowed pompous titles from the Old or Middle Kingdom and were buried with ancient ceremony in tombs which repeated the plans, reliefs, and pyramid texts of the Fifth and Sixth dynasties some two thousand years before.

Like forces were at work among the lesser peoples. Josiah's reform was a national declaration of independence, but its basis was a legal code attributed to the ancient lawgiver Moses. Hope for an immediate deliverance was found in the story of how the national God had saved his people from Egyptian bondage. Revival of the past was the theme of Exilic prophecy and the dream of the Second Isaiah. High as was the degree of literacy, the majority could neither read nor write—but they could listen. By word of mouth, Jewish fathers taught their sons about the Exodus from Egypt, the conquest of the Promised Land, and that Davidic rule which some bright day would return; by word of mouth, legends of Sargon, Moses, or Khufu filtered down to the common people. Vague as might be the details, all the peoples of western Asia were conscious of a past whose glories shone the brighter as they faded into the remote distance. Conquest by rulers increasingly alien only intensified this worship of the past.

What these peoples thought of their past is a vital element of our history; what that past actually was must form the background of the picture. In essentials their account was true. We may prove that scholars placed in succession dynasties which were actually contemporary and that the beginnings of written history came a thousand years later than they supposed. We no longer believe that gods and demigods ruled through aeons far greater than the span of life today. But we need only substitute for the demigods the unnamed heroes of proto-history to recognize how much of truth is dimly remembered in the legends; for the reign of the gods we substitute prehistory and realize how these men twenty-five centuries ago experienced the same awe we feel in recalling the long ages since man first strode the earth. True man is first discovered in the Near East. Before the first period of intense rainfall and glaciation, he had begun to chip flints. By these flint implements, we may trace his progress through the second, third, and last of these wide swings of climate, each of enormous duration counted in our years; at the close he was still at the paleolithic, or Old Stone, level of culture. During these long ages he had done more than improve his stone or bone technique: he had evolved the family, which he supported by hunting; he had made a cave home; he propitiated or averted the dangerous "powers" by magic; and he hoped for life beyond the grave.

Near the end of the paleolithic period, men of our own species were inhabitants of the Near East. Cattle, sheep, goats, and pigs were domesticated; barley, wheat, and flax were cultivated. Thereafter the inhabitants of the Near East were divided, some as wandering nomads, some as settled villagers. While the nomads remained essentially the same, civilization grew in the villages. Walls were built to protect the prosperous from the less fortunate or from the nomads, and a "king" was chosen to lead the village levies in war. Specialization of function increased as life became more complex. That the soil might give freely its products, there was worship of the powers of fertility, which became defined as true gods and goddesses, of whom the greatest was Mother Earth in her varied manifestations.

To the early and inferior Eurafrican, other races were added. Around the great inland sea the dominant race was Mediterranean—long-headed, slim, of moderate height, with clear olive complexion. Sub-races developed: the Egyptian in the Nile Valley, the Semitic in the North Arabian Desert. South of Egypt were Negroids, to the west were Libyans (in whom some would find the earliest Nordics), and in the northern highlands were Armenoids, tall and stout, with sallow complexions and extraordinarily round heads.

Caucasian, spoken today only in the nooks of the Caucasus, was perhaps the basal language of the Near East. Until the first pre-Christian millennium, Elamite was spoken in western Persia; Haldian appeared in Armenia, Hurrian or Mitannian in northern and western Mesopotamia, and Hittite, Carian, Pamphylian, Lycian, and Lydian in Asia Minor. The original Semitic was confined to North Arabia. Some six thousand years ago the first great outpouring of nomads brought a near-Semitic language to Egypt, introduced the Canaanites and Phoenicians to their historic abode, and led the speakers of Akkadian to Babylonia. Into Babylonia also descended the Sumerians, whose use of the horse and chariot, physical characteristics, and agglutinative "Turanian" speech suggest a Central Asian origin.

Man had learned to hammer pure copper. Later, he discovered that copper might be smelted from ore; soon gold, silver, and lead were secured by the same process. Metal implements made agriculture more fruitful and industry more productive and assured the basis for a more advanced technology. Clay for the hitherto crude pottery was cleansed, while a primitive wheel permitted more regular forms, and slips and paint gave further ornament. Medicine men added to their charms and incantations a knowledge of wild herbs.

A more complicated civilization expanded villages into cities and these into city-states which constant fighting gradually welded into larger units. Royal power increased as more complex living conditions demanded more efficient government.

Toward the close of the fourth millennium, writing was invented in Babylonia and in Egypt. Each started with simple picture-writing, in which the sign meant the word. Each quickly took the next step, employed the sign for any word of like sound, and evolved a purely phonetic writing by syllables. The Babylonians indicated the vowels; the Egyptians did not, but in compensation they worked out a consonantal alphabet to supplement the ideographic and syllabic characters. Egypt retained its picture-writing for monumental inscriptions, while a conventionalized script—the hieratic—grew from the pen and papyrus. Babylonia passed rapidly through a linear form to the cuneiform, best impressed by the stylus on clay tablets.

Writing made possible a narrative history, written when kings of Egypt or Babylonia engaged in war with other peoples. Through their records we may glimpse these cultures, which are still more evident in the material objects they left behind. In essential elements, the picture is identical. Everywhere we find the city-state, an urban center with its surrounding villages and fields. At the head is the king, vicegerent on earth of the local god, and as such partaking of the divine essence. He has direct access to the gods, but there are also priests who perform a ritual prescribed from dim prehistoric times. The land is owned by the divine king who presents the usufruct to his earthly deputy, the actual ruler; tillers of the soil therefore pay the deputy rent and not taxes. A king's first duty is to protect the god's worshipers. Success in war is the victory of the local god over his divine rivals; the subjugated gods become his vassals just as the subjugated kings become the vassals of his deputy. In this fashion, city-states gradually merge into kingdoms.

Despite the long narrow Nile Valley in its desert trough, where the only political boundaries must of necessity be upstream and down, at the date writing appeared there were but two kingdoms in Egypt, and Menes quickly united both in the Egypt of history. In Babylonia the whole process of unification, which the elaborate canal system demanded, can be followed in written documents. North Babylonia was occupied by illiterate Semites. The south was the home of Sumerians, advanced in material culture but with lives overshadowed by fear of innumerable malignant spirits whose attacks could be warded off only by a vast magical literature. To the east was the Iranian plateau, where painted pottery showed to perfection the abstract art which was always to dominate these lands. Near the close of the period Elam borrowed Sumerian signs for its language and with them many another element of culture. Mesopotamia proper was in the Babylonian sphere of cultural influence, as was North Syria, which, however, also exhibited peculiar characteristics stemming from Asia Minor. Canaanites and Phoenicians were in closer contact with Egypt; so also were the future Greek lands, already an essential part of the Near East.

With the beginning of the third millennium, the picture becomes clearer. Egyptian and Sumerian tombs alike show an amazing outburst of a fresh vigorous art and an equally amazing use of the precious metals, but everything is devoted to the dead king and his court, whose members, ritually slain, accompany their lord to the afterworld. The cult of the dead king reached its climax in the Egyptian pyramid, which exhausted the land in order that one man might remain ever living. To accomplish this end, the kingdom was overadministered, but, even with this handicap, documents prove that business flourished.

Parallel with the development of administration and business went the beginnings of science. Business and administration demanded reckoning, and this was carried out by the decimal system in Egypt, by a combination of decimal and sexagesimal in Babylonia. Arithmetical problems were solved, and the survey of fields resulted in elementary geometry.

Men so close to the soil, whose outdoor life compelled minute observation of the heavens, could not fail to realize the influence of the celestial bodies. Day and night were distinguished by the sun- and moon-gods; waxing and waning of the moon-god gave the next calendar unit, the month; the sun-god, by his northern journey and return, afforded a still larger unit, the year. Soon it was recognized that sun- and moon-gods did not agree in their calendar, for the sun did not return to his starting-point in twelve of the moon-god's cycles. Adjustment of the lunar to the solar year was made quite differently by the two peoples. The Egyptians had early learned that the sun's year is approximately 365 days; they therefore added to the twelve months of thirty days five extra days to form a year whose deviation from the true solar year would not be discovered for several generations. The Babylonians were content to retain the year of twelve months, intercalating a new month when it was observed that the seasons were out of order.

There were other needs to be met, equally practical to the Oriental. Every action might be ominous; data were collected from the activities of the most minute insect, the movements of the stars, the misbirths of women or animals, or from the livers of the sacrificial sheep. Men organized these into elaborate "sciences," rigidly logical in classification and interpretation once their postulates were assumed, and so prepared the way for true science. Cosmological speculation was to answer practical questions such as why man, evil, and death came into the world, or why man cannot remain immortal; it resulted in stories of the creation which were deeply to influence later thinkers. Evil spirits or the gods themselves inflicted sickness; hence the medicine man must be invoked. Naturally, he employed spells from hoar antiquity in whose efficacy he half-believed; as a practical psychologist he knew their effect on the minds of his patients, but accumulated observation had given him certain knowledge of the medicinal properties of plants, animal substances, and minerals.

Toward the close of the third millennium, Sargon of Agade united the Babylonian alluvium and extended Semitic control far beyond its natural limits. Sumerian cuneiform was adapted to the phonetically different Semitic Akkadian, and Semitic literature began. Sumerian continued as the sacred language, alone intelligible to the older gods, alone of avail to drive off the evil spirits. Business formula likewise retained the ancient tongue, and so Akkadian was filled with Sumerian loan-words. To meet new needs, scribes prepared interlinear translations, sign lists, and phrase books, and practical grammar was born. Through the impact of the two cultures, thought was stimulated, new ideas came into the world, and there was a fresh outburst of artistic genius.

Then the ancient cultures began to disintegrate, as enemies threatened the borders, and new problems compelled men to think more seriously. Egyptian monarchs realized that mere weight of pyramid could neither assure personal immortality nor protect their poor corpses, and written magic superseded physical bulk in the pyramid texts of the Fifth and Sixth dynasties. Hope of a true immortality cheered the common man. The wise vizier Ptahhotep collected aphorisms from earlier sages and gave instruction in a practical morality. As disintegration increased, Ipuwer meditated on social and economic changes which horrified his conservative soul, dreaming of days to come when the god Re himself would reign in justice. Babylonia, likewise, reconsidered the problem of evil, why the gods are angered, why man does not live forever, and why the just reformer Urukagina met an unjust fate.

Complete disintegration split Egypt into warring local kingdoms which suffered Asiatic invasion; the Guti conquered Babylonia in the first northern folk wandering. Questionings of earlier sages culminated in a tremendous wave of pessimism, represented by the Egyptian's dialogue with his soul or by the Babylonian Job, where the complaint of the just man unjustly punished is treated with sympathy, yet the conclusion is submission to an all-powerful deity whose will may not be questioned.

Babylonia recovered first under the Third Dynasty of Ur. Ur-Nammu and Shulgi reunited the alluvium and added foreign territory to north and east. The kings were Semites, but the royal inscriptions, the administrative and business documents, and the formal literature almost without exception were in Sumerian. Although this was the last great period of Sumerian literature, it was far from classic; the language showed marked signs of degeneration. Trade flourished, great buildings were erected, and a somewhat conventionalized art was in vogue. The dynasty fell and Elam entered upon its own career of conquest and cultural development, while Babylonia was divided into petty states always at war under newly arrived Amorites.

From the welter emerged Babylon as the capital of the able administrator and lawgiver Hammurabi. Henceforth this upstart city represented to foreigners the Babylonia to which it gave its name. Marduk, its local divinity, was saluted king of the gods; the ancient religious literature was translated from the dying Sumerian and re-written to honor Babylon's divine lord as creator and king.

Hailed in almost messianic terms by "predictions" of alleged ancient prophets, Amenemhet reunited Egypt and founded the Twelfth Dynasty. Like Babylon, his capital Thebes was an upstart whose ram-god Amon secured lordship of the land through identification with the sun-god Re. Popular worship turned rather to the old fertility deities, Osiris and his consort Isis, while coffin texts show the first dawning of a belief that men must deal justly on earth if they would be happy in the world to come. Justice in politics was considered of great importance. A king just prior to Amenemhet had improved the older "admonitions" into an "Art of Ruling" for his son Merikere. Amenemhet prepared a Machiavellian tractate on kingship for his son Sesostris and another tractate for his vizier; he stressed the isolation of those in positions of responsibility with an equally emphatic—if thoroughly unsentimental—insistence on official regard for the welfare of the ruled. Canaan was made a dependency, and the Phoenicians became willing subject allies. Egyptian art, technically excellent but hardening through convention, found new life among Phoenician merchant-princes.

Minoan Crete was at its prime, its navy swept the sea, and its trade brought enormous wealth; this wealth was devoted to objects of art whose motifs are often borrowed from Egypt but whose perfection makes strong appeal to our modern taste. Writing was in general use; the idea of representing words by pictographs was suggested by Egypt, but the clay tablet was derived from Assyrian merchant colonies in eastern Asia Minor.

This was the great period of scientific advance. Egypt and Babylonia contended for supremacy in mathematics, The Egyptians employed a decimal system and expressed fractions by continuous subdivision. To the decimal system the Babylonians added the sexagesimal for the higher units and broke up the complex fractions into subdivisions of sixty which made easier computation. Egyptians knew squares and square roots and solved in textbooks complicated problems of proportion and arithmetical progression. Babylonians prepared handy reference tables for multiplication and division, squares and cubes, square and cube roots.

It was in algebra and geometry, however, that the most spectacular advances were made. Babylonians discovered the theorem for the right-angled triangle we name from Pythagoras, as well as two simpler methods which result in only a slight error. They had learned that similar right triangles have the sides about the right angles proportional; they had divided the triangle into equal parts; they could compute the areas of rectangles, right-angled triangles, and one form of trapezium. More irregular surfaces were broken up into forms they were able to calculate. They had found the area of a circle chord and approximated pi as three. Without the aid of algebraic formulas, they solved problems by methods essentially algebraic, and each step can be represented by a modern formula. They employed the equivalent of the quadratic equation and stopped just short of the binomial theorem.

Like the Babylonians, the Egyptians divided the triangle and calculated its area as they did the trapezium with parallel sides. Their approximation of pi as eight-ninths of the diameter (or, as we should say, 3.1605), was more accurate than the Babylonian, and with it they secured the areas of circles and the volumes of cylinders or hemispheres. They calculated the frustrum of a square pyramid, and what we call simultaneous quadratic equations they solved by false position.

Babylonian astronomers, not yet sufficiently freed from astrology to utilize the new mathematics, were nevertheless making observations and preparing a terminology. Often the constellations bore names familiar today: the Twins, the Snake, the Scorpion, the Lion, the Wolf, the Eagle, the Fish, Capricorn. Orion, the "True Shepherd of Heaven," kept to their paths the "wandering sheep" (the planets), each identified with a god or goddess. The path of the sun-god was charted through the twelve constellations which were to give their names to our zodiac. His eclipses were ominous, but those of the moon-god were more numerous and more often observed; the four segments of the moon's face were assigned to Babylon and to three neighbor-states, and eclipse of the appropriate segment portended evil to that land.

Other omen collections also contributed to coming science. More than by the stars, the fate of kings and nations was determined by the liver of the sacrificed sheep; models and drawings of the liver can be described only by the Latin terminology of modern anatomy. Long lists, roughly classified, were prepared of animals, plants, and stones. Plant lists begin with the grasses, then the rushes, then other groups closely corresponding to our families; we may distinguish species and varieties through the careful listing of the various parts. Sex in the date palm had long been recognized, and the terms "male" and "female" were applied to other plants. Classification systems employed such headings as "men," "domesticated animals," "wild animals" (including serpents, worms, frogs, and the like), "fish," and "birds."

Lists of plants were prepared generally for medical use. In the medical texts proper, there remain plentiful traces of magic, but there is also empirical knowledge. Symptoms of disease are carefully described in regular order from head to feet; we can identify the majority of the diseases. Poulticing, hot applications, massage, suppositories, and the catheter are employed. Drugs are usually taken internally; mercury, antimony, arsenic, sulphur, and animal fats are often prescribed, but in general the same plants are drawn upon that we find in the modern pharmacopoeia. Egyptian medical texts were much the same, but in a surgical textbook the attitude is quite scientific. Each case is given careful diagnosis, even if no cure is possible; if the case can or may be cured, suggestions for treatment follow. Wounds are probed by the fingers; cauterization is by the fire drill. In his treatment, the Egyptian surgeon uses absorbent lint, linen swabs and plugs, bandages and splints; wounds are brought together by tape or stitching. He describes the various parts of the body in such a fashion that we can see he is still working out his terminology, but he has made astonishing discoveries. He has recognized the brain and its convolutions, he knows that brain and spinal cord control the nervous system, and he suspects localization of function in the brain. He knows the heart is a pump; he takes the pulse; he has almost discovered the circulation of the blood.

Meanwhile, all unnoticed by the cultured peoples, a rude half-nomad Semite at the Egyptian mines in Sinai had introduced an invention of infinite promise for the future. Too ignorant to learn the complicated hieroglyphic of the Egyptians, but knowing that they employed a consonantal alphabet to supplement the syllabic and ideographic signs, he wondered why no one had realized the beautiful simplicity of a purely alphabetic writing. To a few common Egyptian signs he gave a name in his native Canaanite and took the first consonantal sound as its phonetic value. He scratched a few short sentences in his Canaanite dialect on the rocks of Sinai, and the consonantal alphabet was in use.

During the third millennium there lived on the broad plains of southern Russia a group of Nordics who spoke a primitive Indo-European language. At the head of each tribe was a king, chosen from the god-born family and assisted by the council of elders, although important decisions—war, peace, and the choice of a new ruler—

were acclaimed by the fighting men, the people in arms. While to a degree they cultivated the soil, they were essentially half-nomads whose chief delight was in war. Their horses allowed free movement on their raids; their families were carried in the ancestor of the "covered wagon." They settled, not in open villages, but in camps surrounded by quadrangular earthen ramparts. A highly developed technology and no mean art was devoted especially to weapons.

Before the end of the millennium, they began to move out—west, south, and east. While Achaeans entered Greece, other Aryans were on their way to Italy, and a brilliant metal culture appeared in Hungary and Bohemia. Asia Minor was overrun, and the former individual states gradually coalesced into a mighty Hittite empire. No Hittite king bore an Indo-European name, which is mute witness to incorporation of the immigrants with older elements whose native language persisted in the sacred ritual. In an adaptation of the cuneiform, we may read the first Indo-European language to be written. Mitanni was conquered by an aristocracy with Indo-Iranian names, though they took over the local language of their subjects; they worshiped such Indo-Iranian gods as Mithra, Varuna, Indra, and the Nasatya twins. Egyptian tomb paintings show them to be pure Nordics, whose descendants remain as Iranian-speaking Nordic Kurds. Other Indo-Iranians penetrated Syria and Canaan and ruled as petty kings over cities to be made famous by our Bible. Hammurabi's descendants were supplanted by Kashshites, who perhaps spoke a Caucasian language, though names of men and gods suggest an Aryan element. Soon they adopted the native Akkadian, and with it Babylonian culture, their only innovation being a feudal regime with charters of immunity, imposed on the older manorial system.

Aryan elements were discovered among the Hyksos, who founded a great empire in Syria and for many years held Egypt. The effort to expel them led the Eighteenth Dynasty into Asia and to the establishment of an empire. To original Mediterranean and Semitic elements, Syria had already added many from the Nile and the Euphrates; Egyptian cultural influence now grew much stronger. Anatolian elements entered with the Hittite conquest of North Syria, but the Akkadian of Babylonia was employed as the international language of diplomacy and commerce throughout the Near East. Civilization had become international in character.

The way was prepared for Ikhnaton, with his gospel of a loving god whose fatherly care extended to all peoples, and also with his in-

tolerant monotheism. All thought was in flux. Talented artists hailed
release from century-old shackles of convention and produced works
of outstanding power and beauty; the mediocre artist turned out
freakish "modern" caricatures.

Immersed in glorious dreams of universal religion, Ikhnaton permitted the empire to disintegrate. Under the influence of selfish Amon
priests, the boy Tut-ankh-Amon restored the older cults and condemned the gracious teaching of the "heretic," but the Egyptian Empire in Syria was not restored. Seti and Ramses II of the next dynasty
recovered part of the loss, but the wars against the Hittites ended with
Syria being divided between the rivals. Even the small portion thus
far retained was soon lost, and Egypt ceased to be reckoned a first-
class power. More and more the land fell into the hands of the priests,
who ultimately secured the kingship and made Egypt a true theocracy.

New peoples once again appeared on the scene. From the North
Arabian Desert came Aramaeans, who settled the whole border from
Canaan to Babylonia. As a rule they continued to speak Aramaic, but
a part of them—the Hebrews—learned the "lip of Canaan." At first,
the Hebrews were divided into numerous small warring tribes, but, as
they gradually conquered the Canaanite cities, they absorbed something of the attenuated Canaanite culture which had survived their inroads. Acquisition of material culture was good; not so pleasant was
the adaptation of their narrow, barbarous, but relatively pure desert
religion to the degenerate cult of the fertility powers.

Pressure from new peoples in central and southeastern Europe was
driving on fresh hordes of Aryans. Dorians were pushing south the
older Indo-European-speaking Greeks and breaking up the far-flung
Mycenaean empire which had renewed Minoan relations with Egypt.
The last Minoan remnants were destroyed. Achaeans were pressed to
the west coast of Asia Minor, where they met the Hittites and also the
Phrygians, Aryans who had crossed the Hellespont and chosen the
well-watered, well-forested uplands in the west-central interior. Other
Achaeans reached Cyprus, to find half the island already colonized by
Phoenicians. A last desperate effort of Mycenae captured Phrygian
Troy, whose epic was to inspire later generations to fresh conquests
in Asia; but the effort destroyed the empire. Ionians followed and
married Anatolian wives. The once mighty Hittite empire disappeared in a chaos of tiny states.

Bands of homeless men, whether of Minoan or of Aryan tradition,
united, and the wave rolled on over the sea or through Syria to Egypt,

where Merneptah and Ramses III broke its force. Achaeans returned home or sailed away to Cyprus, while Silicians and Sardinians transferred their names to western islands; Etruscans brought to primitive Italians a rich oriental culture which was strongly to influence Rome; and Philistines settled that Palestine to which they gave their name.

Crushed between invaders from sea and desert, the Canaanites lost their freedom. For the moment, the Philistines were all-powerful; then foreign pressure and prophetic urging brought union to the Hebrew tribes. Saul's kingdom was a failure, but David made good the union, and Solomon expanded it into a small empire whose administration copied the greater empires and whose royal shrine was equally foreign. His death marked the division into Israel and Judah; Israel was the greater and often held Judah as vassal, while Jerusalem and its temple were in ruins.

Sidonian traders invaded the Aegean and exchanged goods and words with the backward Greeks. They brought also a more precious gift: the alphabet, which the Greeks improved. Since the alphabet as borrowed had no characters to represent the vowels, the Greeks used some of the consonantal signs which stood for sounds not present in their tongue to write the important Indo-European vowels. In turn, the alphabet was transmitted to Asia Minor; the Greek alphabet had no problems for the Indo-European Phrygians, but Lydians, Lycians, and Carians found it necessary to invent new characters for native sounds. As the Greeks regained sea power, the Phoenicians abandoned the Aegean, and a race for the Mediterranean began, ending with Phoenician control of northern Africa and Spain.

Through long centuries Assyria had remained a second-rate power, often subject to Babylonia or Mitanni. In the general decline toward the end of the second millennium, Assyria extended its boundaries. After two periods of weakness—the second of which permitted the Jews to establish the Davidic kingdom—it was now the great world empire. Babylonia was definitely a vassal, Syria was invaded, and Jehu of Israel was forced to submit. In the wars with more important states, a few punitive expeditions against Parsua and the Medes passed with little notice.

For a few years Assyria was checked by Haldia, which enjoyed brief pre-eminence as the great world power. The moment of respite gave opportunity for a remarkable development in Hebrew religion. In essence, it was a reaction of the desert elements against civilization. The preaching of Elijah and Elisha culminated in the bloody reforms of Jehu, and thereafter Israel acknowledged no national god but Yahweh. The methods of the reform and its unsavory results could not satisfy finer spirits, and a noble company of prophets protested against Canaanite elements in the cult; with equal fervor, they protested against social injustice. Amos preached unmitigated doom, Hosea proclaimed the loving-kindness of Yahweh, but Isaiah again predicted destruction—which was, indeed, fulfilled for Israel. Sennacherib's invasion opened the eyes of Isaiah, who henceforth proclaimed the inviolability of Jerusalem, Yahweh's temple. However, Judah remained an Assyrian dependency.

The rise of Assyria marked a new era in the government of dependencies. Predecessors had been content with vassal states, controlled at best by a "resident" and a few soldiers; Assyria reduced the conquered areas to provinces whose administrators were kept in close touch with the central government by means of frequent letters. Rebels were transported to far-off lands where their future welfare depended on loyalty to their new masters; the provincials were united in worship of the national god Ashur and of the divine king.

Though based largely on the Babylonian, Assyrian culture was thoroughly eclectic in character. In the great cities, whether royal capitals or cities free by charter, a varied life of great complexity might be seen. Phoenicians and Aramaeans utilized to the full the trade opportunities of a wide empire, and "Ishtar heads" were employed as coins. Royal libraries were crammed with copies of ancient Babylonian tablets, but the royal annals were original productions of Assyrian historians. Alongside the cuneiform, Aramaic with its more convenient alphabet was coming into use. Scientific advance is indicated by a textbook on glazes, by letters from astronomers who await lunar eclipses at the full moon and solar eclipses at the new, and by a nineteen-year cycle of intercalated months, probably from the era of Nabu-nasir. Assyrian reliefs present battles, palace life, and the hunt most vividly, and their representations of animals have seldom been surpassed.

Babylon revolted under the Chaldaeans, and Assyria fell to an alliance of Chaldaeans and Medes. There were now four great world powers. Egypt had found new life under the Saites, who ruled by the aid of Greek and Carian mercenaries and allowed Greeks to live their own lives in their own city of Naucratis. Phrygia's successor, Lydia, rich in Pactolus gold, reduced the Greek coastal cities. The merging of seaboard and inland trade was mutually profitable, and, with the wealth thus secured from Egypt and the Black Sea, the Ionians laid the basis for the first brilliant flowering of Greek civilization. Nabopolassar reconstructed Babylonian administration and business practice to such effect that his reforms dominated the country as long as cuneiform remained in use. Babylon was rebuilt by Nebuchadnezzar and became the world's metropolis. Jerusalem was destroyed and the rebels led into exile as Jeremiah and Ezekiel had foretold; Judaism came into being.

Hitherto there had been many changes in dynasty and many shifts in dominant peoples, but throughout there had been definite interrelation of cultures, and cultural evolution had followed much the same pattern in each segment of the Near East. If the Orient had repeatedly been invaded from without, it had always stamped its own characteristics upon the newcomers. To contemporaries, Iranian Media might appear only the fourth great oriental empire, and the inquisitive Greeks might seem, like their Minoan and Mycenaean predecessors, mere students of the ancient oriental cultures. But events were soon to prove that, with the appearance of Iranians and Greeks on the stage, the Near East had entered its modern history.

Chapter II

IRANIAN ORIGINS

LONG before the great plateau was called Iran, it was well populated. Obsidian flakes have been found under the alluvial deposits from the last glacial period, while men of the late Stone Age left their crude flint implements in the open. By the fifth pre-Christian millennium, numerous tiny hamlets sheltered a peaceful agricultural population, which satisfied its aesthetic instincts through fine wheel-made pots decorated with superb painting; an elaborate though lively conventionalization of native flora and fauna betrayed more interest in beauty of design than in exact representation and set the pattern for all subsequent art on the plateau. Burned settlements and changes in pottery styles indicate population shifts.[1] Only Elam on the west affords us writing and, therefore, history,[2] though tablets from the middle of the plateau inscribed in Elamite pictographs[3] suggest that the same language was spoken there as at Susa, Elam's most important city.

For further information on these early peoples, we turn to the Videvdat, the "Antidemonic Law." Although its form as it appears in the Avesta was written down shortly before our own era, it still retains the essential features of this prehistoric culture.[4] At first view, it is a pleasant world in which we meet the house master richly endowed with cattle, fodder, hound, wife, child, fire, milk, and all good things, with grain, grass, and trees bearing every variety of fruit. Waste lands were irrigated by the underground *qanat*, and there was increase of flocks and herds and plenty of natural fertilizer. But to obtain these blessings hard work was demanded: sowing and planting

---

[1] Donald E. McCown, "The Material Culture of Early Iran," *JNES*, I (1942), 242 ff.

[2] George G. Cameron, *History of Early Iran* (1936).

[3] R. Ghirshman, "Une tablette proto-élamite du plateau iranien," *RA*, XXXI (1934), 115 ff.

[4] James Darmesteter, *The Zend-Avesta*, Part I: *The Vendidad* (2d ed., 1895); Fritz Wolff, *Avesta, die heiligen Bücher der Parsen, übersetzt auf der Grundlage von Chr. Bartholomae's Altiranischen Wörterbuch* (1910), pp. 317 ff.; cf. H. S. Nyberg, *Die Religionen des alten Iran* (1938), pp. 337 ff.

and laborious construction of the underground water channels. It was a world in which there was no place for the slothful.[5]

We hear of skins in use for clothing or of woven cloth, of tents made of felt such as those yet found in Central Asia, and of houses of wood like those which have left the ash mounds in the Urumia plain.[6] We might rhapsodize over the high position of the dog, elsewhere in the Orient degraded and unclean, but on the plateau treated as an honored member of the family with definite responsibilities and corresponding rewards.[7] We might prepare to rejoice with the peasants when the long snowbound winter was over and the birds began to fly, the plants to spring up, the torrents to flow down the hills, and the winds to dry the earth,[8] but we should completely misunderstand their mood.

EARLY RELIGIONS

Physically, the inhabitants belonged to their own subdivision of the Mediterranean race.[9] Culturally, they were more akin to the peoples of Central Asia, especially in their religious thinking. Greek writers tell us something of the culture of primitive peoples who still survived to their day along the southern shore of the Black Sea; in the disposal of their dead in particular, they present strange analogies to the practices of the Antidemonic Law.

For example, among the Derbices, men over seventy were killed and eaten by their kinsfolk, and old women were strangled and buried; men so unfortunate as to die before seventy were merely inhumed. Among the Caspians, who gave their name to the sea formerly called Hyrcanian,[10] those over seventy were starved. Corpses were exposed in a desert place and observed. If carried from the bier by vultures, the dead were considered most fortunate, less so if taken by wild beasts or dogs; but it was the height of misfortune if the bodies remained untouched.[11] In Bactria, farther east, equally disgusting practices continued until Alexander's invasion. The sick and aged were thrown while still alive to waiting dogs called in their language "burial details." Piles of bones within the walls testified to burial customs quite

---

[5] Vid. 3:2–6, 23–33.   [7] Vid. 13.

[6] Vid. 8:1, 25.   [8] Vid. 5:12; 8:9.

[9] Henry Field, *Contributions to the Anthropology of Iran* (1939).

[10] The Caspian Sea is mentioned in Herodotus i. 202 ff. and iv. 40; otherwise it does not occur until Hellenistic times.

[11] Strabo xi. 11.8; cf. Herod. iii. 92–93; vii. 67, 86; Plin. vi. 45.

as grim.[12] To understand the reason for these practices, set out in all their grisly minutiae by the Antidemonic Law, we must turn to read the still vaster magical literature of the Sumerians, immigrants into Babylonia from Central Asia, or the modern accounts of the Shamanism found to this day in the same regions.

To Magian thinking in its earliest form, there were no true gods, only a numberless horde of evil demons who constantly threatened the lives of the unhappy peasants and whose malign attacks could be prevented only by rites of aversion. Their home was in the north, from which more human enemies also threatened; after the Iranian conquest of Iran we are not surprised to find the Aryan storm-god Indra included among these demons.[13] As in Babylonia, the majority of the fiends were without name: "Perish, demon fiend! Perish, demon tribe! Perish, demon-created! Perish, demon-begotten! In the north shall you perish!" Others personify the various forms of illness: "Thee, Sickness, I ban; thee, Death, I ban; thee, Fever, I ban; thee, Evil Eye, I ban," and so on through a long series.[14] Many more can be driven away if the worshiper knows the demon's names;[15] of these, the most dangerous is Aeshma, "Drunkenness." One demon prohibits rain;[16] there are fiends who seize the man's incautiously trimmed hair and pared nails and from them raise lice to eat the grain and clothing.[17]

Chief of all the demons was Angra Mainyu, the "Evil Spirit" without qualification, the creator of all things evil and of noxious animals; for this reason the Magi accumulated high merit by killing the earthly representatives of these evil spirits—ants, snakes, creeping things, frogs, and birds—by stopping up their burrows and destroying their homes.[18] It is also through the incantations of the Magi, fortified by perfumes and the magic furrow,[19] that man was freed from his ailments and his uncleanness.

But powerful as was the Evil Spirit and his hordes of demons, in daily life the most feared was the Nasu Druj, the "Corpse Fiend," to whom the greater part of the Antidemonic Law refers. Burial or cremation of the dead might be practiced by neighbors or enemies, but such easy disposal was not for the followers of the Magi. Despite all precautions, it was inevitable that the Corpse Fiend should envelop

[12] Oneisicritus, Frag. 5(J); Strabo xi. 11.3.

[13] Vid. 10:9; 19:43.

[14] Vid. 8:21; 20:7.

[15] Vid. 11:9.

[16] Vid. 19:40.

[17] Vid. 17:2-3.

[18] Vid. 3:10, 22; 10:5; Herod. i. 140.

[19] Vid. 9:11; 19:24.

the living with her corruption, infection, and pollution.[20] From the very instant when breath left the body, the corpse was unclean, for the Corpse Fiend hovered over to injure the survivors. Only by the most rigid observance of the prescribed ritual was there safety: the dead must not pollute holy earth or water; corpses must be exposed, carefully tied down by feet and hair, on the highest points of land where they could be devoured by dogs and vultures. Only when the bones had been thus freed from all dead and therefore dangerous matter might they be collected in an ossuary (*astodan*) with holes to permit the dead man still to look upon the sun.[21] This taint of the charnel-house permeates the whole later Zoroastrian literature and, with the host of malignant spirits, makes it depressing reading.[22]

THE INFLUENCE OF GEOGRAPHICAL FEATURES

The majority of the Aryans left their homes in southern Russia for the plains of Central Asia; only the near-Iranian Scyths and a few genuine Aryans remained there. The Hyrcanians settled along the northern slope of Alborz and the coastal plain below, south of the sea to which they gave their name. This plain, slightly below sea-level and swept by torrential rains up to sixty inches per year, was semitropical, but dense forests on the slopes sheltered the lion and tiger for hunting. Other Iranians ascended the plateau, rimmed in by mountains on every side. To the west towered Zagros; on the north Alborz. Eastward the plateau rose steadily to the roof of the world in the Himalayas, while a lower range shut off the southern ocean. Within this rim, lesser ranges separated the subdivisions, which varied only to the degree in which the common elements in them—mountain, desert, and fertile strip—were combined.

In the center were great deserts, difficult to traverse and covered in part by salt lakes, in part by brownish-red, salt-impregnated soil. Equally barren were the mountains, generally devoid of trees or even shrubs. Between mountain and desert was good soil, needing only water—but water was a rare and precious treasure. If the mountains shut off potential enemies, they also shut off the rains; only through such passes as that between Resht and Qazvin could a few clouds pene-

---

[20] Vid. 5:27.   [21] Vid. 6:45–46, 50–51.

[22] Herodotus proves that in his day tearing by bird or dog was still confined to the Magi. A temple—possibly Magian—of the first half of the first millennium, whose floors, sills, and walls contained many small statuettes and other votive objects, has recently been excavated in Luristan by Dr. Erich Schmidt.

trate. Here the rainfall might reach eight inches; elsewhere, as at Isfahan, four inches or less. Nowhere was this rainfall sufficient to bring crops to maturity, but melting snows fortunately ran down from the barrier mountains.

During the greater portion of the year, the sun blazed with intense heat from a cloudless sky. By September the air cooled a trifle; by November the nights were uncomfortably cool. Autumn rains were followed by mists and snows and finally fierce blizzards, creeping down lower and lower from the mountains until they reached the plain. The midday sun, when seen, remained hot, and thawed out sufferers frozen by night. By January the passes were filled, and villages hidden in the snows were isolated for the winter. In spring the snows melted almost without warning. Their waters poured down the bare slopes, destroying the trails and once more isolating the villagers. The stream beds were filled with roaring waters, each precious drop utilized by the irrigation ditches, until again the beds were dry. Thereafter water was sought in the seemingly dry hills; lest the precious fluid be lost by evaporation, it had to be carried underground in *qanats*. Thus, at tremendous expenditure of time and labor, a few more square feet of former desert were won for cultivation.

This eternal search for water left a permanent impress on the Persian mind. In the sacred Avesta, hymning Anahita, goddess of a thousand rills, and in later poetry, singing the joy of flowing stream and garden, the theme is constantly repeated. To strangers from happier lands, the rivers may appear insignificant, the rows of poplars, cypresses, and plane trees scant, the garden "paradise" sickly; the contrast with desert, bare plain, and snow-capped peaks is needed to render them beautiful.

CONQUEST BY NORTHERN HORDES

Archeology shows the first trace of the northerner when the fine, painted pottery of the earliest inhabitants is supplanted by a better-made pottery of a funereal black. Judging from their skulls, Nordic tribes make their appearance. Fresh hordes continue to drift down. A great fortified structure is built at Damghan; it is assaulted and taken. The bodies of the men who defended this fortress, with those of their wives and children, have been found by the excavator on the spot where they perished.[23]

Episodes from the conquest of Iran, well mixed with good Aryan

[23] Erich Schmidt, *Excavations at Tepe Hissar, Damghan* (1937).

mythology, are found in the earliest sections of the Yashts;[24] there we read the first version of the Persian traditional history, best known to the West through the magnificent epic, the Shah Nameh or "Book of Kings," produced by the great Moslem poet Firdausi.

The story begins with Gaya Maretan (Gayomarth), "Mortal Man," who was ancestor of the Aryan people.[25] Next comes Haoshyaha (Hosheng), the first king of the Paradata (Peshdadyan) dynasty, who from a mount to the east named Hara conquered the demons of Mazana and the fiends of Varena.[26] This is generally considered a reminiscence of the subjugation of the spirit worshipers of Varkana or Hyrcania (later Mazandaran). However this may be, we do know that Zadrakarta,[27] the capital of Hyrcania in Iranian days, was probably located on a mound whose partial excavation has shown repeated settlements of Iranians over native sites of a still earlier period.[28]

Next to Haoshyaha followed Yima, the good shepherd, son of Vivahvant, who first pressed out the sacred *haoma* juice.[29] In Yima's reign there was neither cold nor heat, neither old age nor death, for he brought to man immortality. He also freed man from hunger and thirst, teaching the food animals what they should eat and preventing the plants from drying up. But although he lived on the sacred mount Hukairya near the sea Vouru-kasha, the Iranian Paradise, he sinned— Zoroaster later was to declare that his sin consisted in giving to men flesh of the cattle to eat[30]—and Yima himself was sawed asunder by his wicked brother Spityura.[31] Another brother, however, Takhma Urupa, succeeded in riding over the earth for thirty years the evil spirit, Angra Mainyu, who took the form of a horse.[32]

At this time Azi Dahaka, the three-headed, three-mouthed, six-eyed dragon, with the thousand senses, carried off Yima's two beautiful

[24] James Darmesteter, *The Zend-Avesta*, Part II: *The Sîrôzahs, Yashts, and Nyâyish* (1883); Wolff, *op. cit.*, pp. 153 ff.; H. Lommel, *Die Yäšt's des Awesta* (1927).

[25] Yasht 13:87.

[26] Yasht 5:21 ff.; 9:3 ff.; 13:137; 15:7 ff.; 17:24 ff.; 19:26 ff.

[27] Arr. *Anab.* iii. 23.6; 25.1; cf. Curt. vi. 5.22.

[28] F. R. Wulsin, "Excavations at Tureng Tepe, near Asterabad," *Supplement to the Bulletin of the American Institute of Persian Art and Archaeology*, II (1932), 2 ff.; M. I. Rostovtzeff, "The Sumerian Treasure of Astrabad," *JEA*, VI (1920), 4 ff.

[29] Yasna 9:3–4.

[30] Yasna 8:32; cf. 44:20.

[31] Yasht 5:25 ff.; 9:8 ff.; 13:130; 15:15 ff.; 17:28 ff.; 19:46; Yasna 9:5; Vid. 2:2.

[32] Yasht 15:11 ff.; 19:28 ff.

daughters and made them his wives; the dragon was killed and the ladies were rescued by Thraetaona (Feridun), son of Athwya, from Varena, now safely Aryan.[33] A second exploit of the hero Thraetaona was related, telling how he hurled into the air the wise seaman Paurva in the guise of a vulture.[34]

Keresaspa, son of Sama, was a hero who avenged the death of his brother Urvakhshaya, the judge and lawgiver, by killing the assassin Hitaspa and carrying home the corpse in his own chariot. To him also was attributed the slaughter of various enemies both human and monster, like the golden-heeled Gandareva, who lived in the sea Vouru-kasha, and the poisonous yellow sea serpent on whose broad back Keresaspa unwittingly cooked his meal.[35] Hitaspa bears a good Iranian name; perhaps he was an enemy nomad, a Turanian.

The next enemy mentioned is also a Turanian: Frangrasyan (Afrasiab), who from his cleft in the earth swam across Vouru-kasha in a vain attempt to steal the Awful Royal Glory which conferred sovereignty. Captured and bound by a loyal vassal, he was brought to be slain by the Kavi Haosravah (Kai Khosrau).[36]

Thus the Kavis, the local kinglets, enter the traditional history. Of the eight members of the dynasty listed,[37] we learn more only of the founder Kavi Kavata (Kai Kobad), of his son Kavi Usan (Kai Kaus), possesser of stallions and camels and controller of the ship-bearing sea, and of Kavi Haosravah (Kai Khosrau), who came from the salt sea Chaechasta (Lake Urumia), subdued the Aryan lands, and became a great hero.[38]

THE EARLIEST MEDES AND PERSIANS

Medes and Persians are first discovered in written annals when in 836 the Assyrian, Shalmaneser III, received tribute from kings of "Parsua," west of Lake Urumia, and reached the lands of the "Mada" southeast of its waters. Henceforth the two peoples are frequently mentioned. By 820, Shamshi-Adad V found them in what is now called Parsuash, well to the south beyond modern Kirmanshah. In 737 Tiglath-pileser III invaded the original Parsua and received tribute from Median chiefs as far east as Mount Bikni, the "mountain of

[33] Yasht 5:29 ff.; 9:13 ff.; 13:131; 14:40; 15:19 ff.; 17:33 ff.; 19:36-37.
[34] Yasht 5:61.
[35] Yasht 5:37 ff.; 13:61; 15:27; 19:38 ff.; Yasna 9:10-11; Vid. 1:9.
[36] Yasht 9:18 ff.; 19:56 ff.; Yasna 11:7.
[37] Yasht 13:132; 19:71; cf. A. Christensen, Les Kayanides (1931).
[38] Yasht 5:49 ff.; 9:21 ff.; 15:32 ff.; 17:41 ff.; 19:74 ff.

lapis lazuli," as he named majestic Demavend from the deep blue of
its snow-covered peak.

These two groups of Iranians were still on the move. Each mountain valley held its tribe, ruled from a high battlemented tower by a
"king" who now and then paid tribute to Assyria—when compelled
by an inroad. Parts of the Median country were formed into a province, though its boundaries were fluctuating and it was never effectively organized. Subject to raids, the other Medes and all the Persians
retained their full independence.

Through the whole of their earlier history the Iranians were primarily pastoral, though agriculture was not neglected. Almost contemporary Zoroastrian writings divide the people into fourfold local
units, the home (*demana*), the clan (*vis*), the district (*shoithra*), and
the land (*dahyu*).[39] Socially, there is a threefold division: *khvaetu*,
verezena, and *airyaman*.[40] Only the last represented the ruling class,
which was subdivided into priest (*athravan*), chariot-driving noble
(*rathaeshtar*), herdsman (*vastrya fshuyant*), and artisan (*huiti*). Apparently the lower classes were recognized as distinct in race, for the
name of the caste was "color" (*pishtra*).[41]

One of the local Median kinglets, Daiaukku by name, was captured
and deported to Syria in 715; he is the same Deioces whom tradition
made founder of the Median empire![42] The next traditional ruler is
Cyaxares I; he is the Uaksatar who paid Sargon tribute in 714; in the
time of Sennacherib, in 702, he himself attacked the Assyrian province of Harhar. Contingents from Parsuash and Anzan opposed
Sennacherib at Halulina in 681; presumably their leader was that
Achaemenes (Hakhamanish) whom later monarchs claimed as epony-
mous ancestor and who gave his name to the whole Achaemenid
dynasty.[43] His son Teispes (Chishpish) was "great king, king of the
city Anshan"—as the more ancient Anzan was now called, still
located northwest of Susa on the Kerkha River, but at present lost to
the Elamites. Obviously, the Persians were still on their way south.

[39] Yasna 31:18.

[40] Yasna 32:1; 33:4; cf. R. G. Kent, "Cattle-tending and Agriculture in the Avesta," *JAOS*,
XXXIX (1919), 332.

[41] Yasna 19:17; cf. J. H. Moulton, *Early Zoroastrianism* (1913), p. 117; Nyberg, *op. cit.*, pp. 56 ff.

[42] Herod. i. 96 ff.; for earlier references to the Medes and Persians see Olmstead, *History of Assyria* (1923), pp. 117, 156, 159, 178 ff., 231 ff., 243 ff.; Cameron, *op. cit.*, pp. 141 ff.

[43] Ariaramna inscription; cf. E. Herzfeld, *Archäologische Mittheilungen aus Iran*, II (1930), 118,
and *Altpersische Inschriften* (1938), No. 1; Cyrus, *Cyl.*, ll. 21 ff., in R. W. Rogers, *Cuneiform Parallels to
the Old Testament* (2d ed., 1926), pp. 380 ff.; Darius, *Beh.* § 1; Herod. iii. 75; vii. 11.

Born to Teispes were two sons—Ariaramnes (Ariyaramna) and
Cyrus (Kurash) I. A gold tablet of the former shows that Persian was
already written in cuneiform; if the suggestion came from Assyria or
Elam, there was no direct imitation in the script. For the first time in
cuneiform writing, each word was set off by a diagonal wedge. Ideograms for king, earth, land, god, and for the chief god Ahuramazda
followed the method (though not the form) of the neighbor-scripts.
The remaining signs afforded a crude alphabet. Three signs for *a*, *i*,
and *u* poorly represented the wealth of Iranian vowels. Twenty-two
were syllables in which *a* was preceded by a consonant; in four signs
an *i*-vowel followed a consonant, in seven, a *u*-vowel. When sometimes these vowels were not pronounced, the sign possessed a purely
consonantal value.

THE RELIGION OF THE IRANIANS

Iranian religion[44] had thus far remained simple Aryan nature worship of *daevas*, or true gods. At the head of the pantheon stood the
sky, whose name of Dyaosh was cognate of the Greek Zeus; more
often he was the "Lord," Ahura, or the "Wise," Mazdah. In time
these manifestations of the supreme power were united as Ahura-
Mazdah, the "Wise Lord."[45] "Says Ariyaramnes the king: This land
Parsa which I hold, which possesses good horses and men, the great
god Ahuramazda granted me. By the favor of Ahuramazda I am king
of this land. May Ahuramazda bring me help." Thus was set the
formulary for kings to come.

Second only to the all-embracing sky was Mithra, worshiped long
since by fellow-Iranians in Mitanni and by other Aryans in India. Like
all the Iranian Yazatas, he was a god of the open air. In one of his
numerous manifestations he was the Sun himself, in modern proverb
the "poor man's friend," so welcome after the cold nights of winter,
so terrible in summer when all vegetation parched. Other passages
connect him with the night sky. Again, he was first of the gods, the
Dawn, who appeared over Hara, Mount Alborz, before the undying
swift-horsed Sun; he was therefore the first to climb the beautiful
gold-adorned heights from which he looked down upon all the
mighty Aryan countries that owed to him their peace and well-being.
Over these Aryan lands ruled Mithra as lord of broad pastures. It

[44] C. Clemen, *Fontes historiae religionis Persicae* (1920).

[45] Cf. Olmstead, "Ahura Mazda in Assyrian," *Oriental Studies in Honour of Dasturji Saheb Cursetji Erachji Pavry* (1934), pp. 366 ff.

was he who protected the columns of the high-built house and made firm the doorposts. To the house with which he was pleased he granted herds of cattle and male children, beautiful women and chariots, and well-spread cushions. For his people he was the god of justice, and when his name was used as a common noun it was synonymous with "agreement," of whose execution he was protector. He could not be deceived, for his thousand ears and ten thousand eyes were spies which were ever watching the breaker of the agreement. The poor man, robbed of his rights, prayed to him with uplifted hands; whether his cry was loud or a whisper, it went over the whole earth and ascended to heaven, where it was heard by Mithra, who brought quick retribution, such as leprosy, on the offender.[46] No priest was needed for his worship; the master of the house invoked Mithra with libations and the *haoma* drink, the "Averter of Death." Part of the devotions to him consisted of nocturnal sacrifice of a bull,[47] for Mithra could be as evil for his creatures as he could be good. Similar animal sacrifices continued to be offered into Achaemenid times. At the New Year's Day, Nesaean horses were offered in his honor; they represented the sacred white horses of his solar chariot.[48] Once a year, on the Mithra festival, the Achaemenid ruler was obliged to become drunk on the intoxicating *haoma* and dance the "Persian," a survival of the war dance of more primitive days.[49]

But it was as the war-god that Mithra was most vigorously and most picturesquely invoked by the still untamed Aryans. By force they had won the plateau and by force they had to defend it against the aborigines. The hymn devoted to Mithra pictures the peaceful herdsmen attacked by flights of eagle-feathered arrows shot from well-bent bows, of sharp spears affixed to long shafts, and of slingstones, and by daggers and clubs of the Mediterranean type. Even more dangerous were the spells sent against them by the followers of the Magi. We see the bodies pierced, the bones crushed, and the villages laid waste, while the cattle are dragged beside the victor's chariot into captivity in the gorges occupied by the opponents of Mithra. The hymn continues, as the lords of the land invoke Mithra when ready to march out against the bloodthirsty foe, drawn up for battle on the border between the two contending lands. The men on horseback pray to

[46] Herod. i. 138. [47] Yasna 32:8.

[48] For misunderstood reference to Mithra see Herod. i. 131; for the sacred white horses see *ibid*. i. 189; cf. *ibid*. iii. 106; vii. 40; ix. 20; Strabo xi. 13.7–8; 14.9.

[49] Ctesias, in Duris, *Hist*. vii, Frag. 5(J); in Athen. xii. 434D.

Mithra and the drivers ask strength for their teams, for, like all early
Aryan nobles, they still fight from their chariots. In his residence on
high, shining Haraiti, the mountain with many gorges, Mithra hears
their cry for aid. As the evildoer approaches, with rapid step he
quickly yokes the four shining horses to the pole of his golden solar
chariot; these horses are all of the same white color, shod with gold
and silver, and immortal because fed with ambrosia. Against the
weapons of the demon worshipers, Mithra has affixed to the chariot
sides a thousand well-made bows, a thousand gold-tipped, horn-
shafted arrows, whose vulture feathers pollute as well as pierce the
enemy, a thousand sharp spears, a thousand two-edged battle-axes of
steel, a thousand two-edged swords, a thousand iron maces for hurling, and a huge club, cast from the yellow metal, with a hundred
bosses and a hundred cutting faces. Of their own volition all these fly
down through the air onto the skulls of the demons and their followers.
Standing up in his chariot, swinging the whip, and brandishing his
club, Mithra, protected by a silver helmet and a gold cuirass, plunges
down against the enemy, and by his superior power wards off the
weapons and the curses of the liars against his majesty.[50] He does not
go alone. To his right marches forth Sraosha, "Obedience" (to the
feudal levy), beautiful, powerful, and armed with another mighty
club.[51] On his left goes tall, strong Rashnu, the "Truest True," god of
the ordeal.[52] Around him are the waters, the plants, and the Fravashis, the souls of the dead ancestors.[53] Before him runs the god Victory, Verethraghna, in the form of a sharp-toothed, sharp-jawed boar
with limbs of iron; accompanied by the goddess of bravery, he clings
to the fleeing foe with dripping face until he has snapped the back-
bone, the column of life and the source of life's strength, until he has
cut to pieces the limbs and mingled with earth the bones, the hair,
the brains, and the blood of those who have lied to Mithra.[54]

But Verethraghna had other manifestations: he was the Wind (Vata
or Vayu), the gold-horned Bull, the gold-eared Horse, the Camel, the
Raven, the wild Ram, the Buck; or he might appear as youth or mature man. Not only did he give victory to the Aryans and protect the

[50] Yasht 10, the most ancient of these hymns; cf. Nyberg, op. cit., pp. 52 ff.; F. Cumont, Les
Mystères de Mithra (3d ed., 1913).

[51] Yasht 10:41, 52, 100; Yasht 11, Yasna 57, and Vid. 18 are all late.

[52] Yasht 10:79, 81, 100, 126; Yasht 12 is among the latest.

[53] Yasht 10:100; the later Yasht 13 gives a list of famous Fravashis.

[54] Yasht 10:70 ff., 80, 127; 14:15.

sacred Ox Soul; in addition, he granted to men virility and health.[55]
Though sometimes usurped by Mithra,[56] to Verethraghna belonged of
right the bestowal and withdrawal of the Awful Royal Glory
(Khvarenah) when he appeared in the form of the Wind or of the Bull.
It was a concept which was to dominate political thought in later
political theory.[57]

There were other gods among the nature-worshiping Aryans, of
whom we catch occasional glimpses. Among the most honored was
Tishtrya, the brilliant white Sirius, lord and overseer of all the stars,
who in the clear air of the plateau shone so brightly. As the year came
to an end, all awaited his rising, from the aged counselor among men
to the wild beasts of the hills and the tame ones of the plain, and they
wondered: "Will he bring a good year for the Aryans?" He delayed,
and in their disappointment they asked: "When will the bright
glorious Tishtrya arise for us? When will the springs of water, larger
than a horse, flow down anew?" Tishtrya himself appeared. He too
asked: "Will the Aryan lands have a good year?" for there were
difficulties to be faced. The "Seven Stars" had to remain on guard
against the magicians from the north, who attempted to prevent
Tishtrya's advance by hurling down the hostile shooting stars.
Vanant, the leader of the starry hosts of the south, had to protect
him from want and hostility.[58] For ten nights Tishtrya appeared as
a beautiful fifteen-year-old youth and gave to men their male children. Ten nights more he was like a golden-horned bull, and the cattle
increased. For the third ten nights he assumed the form of a golden-
eared white horse. He went down to the sea Vouru-kasha, where
there descended against him the black horse Apaosha, the incarnation
of Drought. Three days and three nights they fought, and Tishtrya
was worsted. Then, renewed by his worshipers' sacrifices, Tishtrya
re-entered the fray, and by noon of the first day Drought had to flee.
Then the sea began to boil and mists covered the island in its midst.
They came together to form clouds which Wind pushed south. Apam
Napat, the "son of waters" and lord of the females, the cloud-born
Lightning,[59] assigned to the various earth-regions the health-giving
waters. If the Aryan peoples duly poured libations to Tishtrya and

[55] Yasht 14.   [56] Yasht 10:16, 62, 67, 108, 141.

[57] Yasht 14:2, 7; Vid. 19:17; cf. the late Yasht 19:9 ff. (with list of those on whom the Glory
descended), the story of Cyrus quoted by Dinon *Pers.*, Frag. 7 (Athen. xiv. 633D–E), and the
Karnamak iii, for the later theory.

[58] Late Yasht 20.   [59] Yasht 5: 72; 8:34; 13:95; 19:51.

sacrificed cattle to him, all of one color, never would pestilence or disease, never would the army of the foe with his chariots and his high-raised standard, invade the lands of the Aryan people.[60]

In Achaemenid times some of these functions were usurped by an ancient nature-goddess, Anahita, who from her mountain heights brought down the waters which transformed desert into field and orchard.[61] As she was pure, so must be her rivers, which might not be polluted even by the washing of hands.[62] Other water divinities survived to become wives of Ahura.[63]

Still other nature-gods were recognized. The bright Moon (Mah) by her waxing caused the green plants to spring upon the Earth, who was herself a potent divinity.[64] Within her the Moon held the seeds of the Bull,[65] while the Cow was also honored.[66] Vayu, the Wind, sweeping down from the hills to refresh the plains in summer, but icy cold in the winter blasts, was likewise revered.[67] Atar, the Fire which carried the sacrifices to the gods, was himself a major deity,[68] and everywhere one might see fire altars for his worship; he was worthy of all honor, for he was sorely needed in winter when fuel was scarce and expensive. *Haoma*, the sacred intoxicating drink that "drives death afar," always played a large part in Aryan ritual.[69] Libations and hymns pacified the underworld gods.[70]

Except for the sacred fire, the Iranians felt no need of temples and altars. Moreover, their minds could conceive the divine beings independent of any symbols such as statues. Sacrifices were offered Ahura on the bare mountain peaks, beautiful only when covered with snow, and thus close to the generally cloudless sky. Crowned with myrtle, the sacrificer led the victim to an open place ritually pure, where he invoked by name the god, cut up the victim, and boiled the flesh. The pieces were piled upon a carpet of tenderest herbs, preferably alfalfa; a Magian then chanted a hymn which related the traditional origin of the gods.[71] Afterward the sacrificer took away the flesh to do with it what he pleased. Such is the account of the contemporary Herodotus.[72]

[60] Yasht 8; cf. Darius, *Persepolis* d: "Against this land may there enter neither enemy army nor bad year nor the Lie."

[61] Yasht 5.

[62] Herod. i. 138.

[63] Yasna 38.

[64] Late Yasht 19.

[65] Yasht 7.

[66] Yasht 9.

[67] Yasht 15.

[68] Yasna 36; Herod. iii. 16.

[69] Yasna 42; cf. 32:14; 48:10.

[70] Aeschyl. *Pers.* 219–20.

[71] Best represented in the Yashts, particularly Yasht 13.

[72] Herod. i. 131–32.

Karapan and Usij priests are named, as also the Manthra speakers,[73] but more and more the ritual practices were falling into the hands of the Magi—the usual victory of the older priestly class over the invaders. As yet, the Magi remained a separate Median tribe,[74] entirely distinct from the Aryan nobility. Their pernicious effect on the nobler Aryan paganism was far in the future.[75]

THE MEDIAN EMPIRE

New hordes from Central Asia, Gimirrai or Cimmerians and Ishguzai or Scythians, followed their Iranian cousins up the plateau and left their horse trappings, knives, and maceheads in Luristan. Assyrian cavalry in search of fresh mounts reached the land of Patusharri[76] on the edge of the central salt desert and carried off city lords named Shidirparna and Eparna, in the former we recognize the first Chithrafarna or Tissaphernes.

More important was Khshathrita, also called Fravartish or Phraortes, who, according to Herodotus, ruled Media fifty-three years —actually from about 675 to 653.[77] He began as a village chief of Kar Kashi, but after attacking various Assyrian settlements he ultimately formed an anti-Assyrian coalition of Medes and Cimmerians.

Ariyaramnes, son of Teispes, tells us that Ahuramazda gave him Parsa, good of horses and good of men; he is describing the conquest of the future Persian homeland, known to the Greeks as Persis and to us as modern Fars. To his brother Cyrus he permits only their father's title, "great king of the city Anshan"; he himself, as superior, is "great king, king of kings, king of Parsa." But his superiority was brief, for the Medes entered the country and the Persians became Median vassals. The gold tablet of Ariyaramnes was probably deposited as loot in the capital which was already Hangmatana (Ecbatana).

This city lay on the last slopes to the east of Mount Aurvant (Orontes),[78] a granite peak which towers more than twelve thousand feet above sea-level and which is part of an almost impassable range extending north and south and broken only by the high pass

[73] Yasna 41; cf. Yasna 47.

[74] Herod. i. 101.

[75] For the best account of pre-Zoroastrian Aryan religion see Herod. i. 131 ff.; cf. for further details Aeschylus, *Persae;* Xenophon, *Cyropaedia.* A few references may be found in Zoroaster's Gathas. Survivals of Aryan religion may be detected in the later Avesta, especially in the Yashts.

[76] Pateischoreis (Strabo xv. 3.1).

[77] Herod. i. 102.   [78] Ctes. *Pers.* i, Epit. 13 (Diod. ii. 13.7); Polyb. x. 27.6.

leading to the Babylonian alluvium. In summer the climate is delightful, for Ecbatana lies 6,280 feet above the sea; Aurvant hides the afternoon sun and sends down his melting snows in many little rushing streams to irrigate the lovely gardens and orchards below the city and the fertile grain fields of the wide plains beyond. Still farther out on rougher ground great herds of sheep and goats and the famous Nesaean horses could be pastured.[79] In winter the blizzards howl as the temperature sinks to twenty below zero. The snow reaches two or three feet on the level ground and fills the passes twenty feet high. Communication with the outside world is shut off on every side. But Hangmatana commanded the one tolerably easy road from the west up to the plateau and its continued importance is witnessed by the flourishing state of its successors, Ecbatana and Hamadan.

From Hangmatana, the great road continued northeast to Qazvin and then east to Raga, from which a second Media took its name. Teheran, the capital of present-day Iran, is the true successor of Raga, though the ancient site is somewhat to the south, where it was followed by the Rages of the Greeks and the Rai of medieval times.[80] Raga in turn was the successor of a prehistoric settlement under the shelter of an isolated east-west comb of rock; further protection from the chill north winds of winter was afforded by the high east-west chain of Alborz, which often reached the height of ten thousand feet and, to the east of Raga, culminated in Demavend, twenty thousand feet at the summit. Alborz shut off also the rain-bringing winds from the north but, in compensation, sent down the snows in gullies which reached the salt deserts over gravel stretches. Mounds along the edges of the plain testify to prehistoric and later occupation.

Raga, like Ecbatana, was always an important road center. From it ran the second road to the west. Through Qazvin, with side branch to the Hyrcanian Sea, the main line continued west through Tabriz to the plains about Lake Urumia or down the Rowanduz gorge into Assyria. The country traversed formed a third Media, not yet entitled Media Atropatena or Adharbaigan; here we meet toward the end of the eighth century the Medes and Persians first known to the Assyrians. Soon this territory was to be revered as the birthplace of Zoroaster. Not far east of Raga, the road turned north through the

[79] Nabu-naid Chron. (S. Smith, *Babylonian Historical Texts* [1924], pp. 98 ff.), col. II, l. 3; Darius, *Beh.* § 32; Aeschyl. *Pers.* 16; Herod. i. 98, 110, 153; iii. 64, 92; Aristoph. *Achar.* 64, 613; *Equ.* 1089; *Vesp.* 1143; Ezra 6:2; Strabo xi. 13. 7-8; 14. 9.

[80] *Beh.* §§32, 36; Yasna 19:18; Vid. 1:15; Strabo xi. 9. 1; 13. 6.

Caspian Gates and passed under Demavend; again turning eastward, it traversed other Iranian tribes and then from Bactria ran northeast into Central Asia or southeast to India.

The three Medias were inhabited by Median tribes—Busae, Paretaceni, Struchates, Arizanti, and Budii—to which was added the non-Iranian priestly tribe of the Magi.[81] These Medes were still half-nomads. On the Assyrian reliefs they are depicted with short hair confined by a red fillet and with short curled beard; over a tunic is worn the sheepskin coat, still the traveler's best friend in the bitter winter of the plateau, which also required high-laced boots to plow through the deep snows. They were armed with only the long spear and were defended by the rectangular wicker shield. With these seminomads, aided by the Persians, Phraortes dared to attack Assyria, only to meet defeat and death in battle (653).[82]

Parsa again became independent. Two years later (651), Cyrus I joined with Elam in sending aid to Shamash-shum-ukin of Babylon, who was in revolt against his brother Ashur-bani-apal of Assyria; for Parsa the Assyrian scribe uses the ancient name of Guti.[83] Then an Assyrian official at Uruk reports the return of the Elamite king Humbanigash to the land of Hidalu, together with peoples from the land of Parsuash. Another mentions the Elamite Tammaritu and quotes an enemy letter: "The men of Parsuash do not advance; quickly send them. Elam and Assyria are yours!" News of Elam forwarded to Ashur-bani-apal by his viceroy in Babylonia, Bel-ibni, includes the capture of Parsuash.[84]

Shortly after his conquest of Elam and the destruction of its capital Susa—so Ashur-bani-apal assures us—Cyrus, king of Parsuash, heard of the might the Assyrian king had established over Elam and sent his eldest son Arukku with his tribute to Nineveh to make submission and to beseech his lordship.[85] There were more weighty reasons for the embassy.

Cyaxares (Uvakhshatra) had succeeded his father Phraortes; appropriately he bore the surname of the war-god Verethragna.[86] The

[81] Herod. i. 101.

[82] Herod. i. 102; cf. Olmstead, *History of Assyria*, p. 636; Cameron, *op. cit.*, pp. 138 ff.

[83] Olmstead, *History of Assyria*, p. 442.

[84] Leroy Waterman, *Royal Correspondence of the Assyrian Empire*, II (1930), 166–67, 410 ff.

[85] E. Weidner, *Archiv für Orientforschung*, VII (1931), 1 ff.; R. C. Thompson, *Journal of the Royal Asiatic Society*, 1932, p. 239; *Annals of Archaeology and Anthropology*, XX (1932–33), 86, 95.

[86] E. Herzfeld, *Archaeological History of Iran* (1935), p. 40.

army was remodeled along modern lines and was divided into spear-men, bowmen, and cavalry. It would seem that it was Cyaxares who also changed the clothing and weapons. Two quite different forms are regularly illustrated on the sculptures at Persepolis. The Mede is at once distinguished by the wearing of the more original Iranian costume. On his head is the round, nodding felt cap with neck flap. A tight, long-sleeved leather tunic ends above the knee and is held in by a double belt with round buckle; over the tunic might be thrown on ceremonial occasions a cloak of honor. Full leather trousers and laced shoes with projecting tips indicated that their wearers spent much of their time on horseback. A short, pointed beard, a mustache, and hair bunched out on the neck were all elabo-rately curled, while earrings and necklace gave added ornament. The chief offensive weapon remained the spear of cornel wood with a flanged bronze point and the base held by a metal ferrule. To this spear many warriors added the bow, held in an extraordinarily elaborate bow case and serviced by arrows from a quiver. The Median costume is sharply contrasted with the form labeled Persian, distinguished by the fluted felt hat, the ankle-length flowing robe, and the low-laced shoes.

With the Median army reorganized, the threat to Assyria became extreme. Ashur-bani-apal died, and even weaker successors did not dare to dissipate their strength by aiding their nominal allies such as Parsa. The successors of Ariaramnes and Cyrus were again forced to become vassals of Cyaxares. Once more the Assyrians were driven back, and Nineveh was actually under siege by the Medes when news arrived that Scythians had poured through the gate between the Caucasus Mountains and the Caspian Sea. Defeated by their chief, Madys, son of Protothyes, Cyaxares had to pay tribute for twenty-eight years until he killed their drunken leaders at a banquet.[87]

Nineveh was destroyed in 612. Amid the ruins, Cyaxares, now known in Babylonia as king of the Umman Manda (from his conquest of the Scythian hordes), made peace with Nabopolassar. Two years later, by the defeat of Ashur-uballit at Harran, Cyaxares destroyed the last pretense of Assyrian rule and won all northern Mesopotamia.[88]

[87] Herod. i. 103 ff., where Herodotus makes the claim that the Scythians invaded Palestine and ruled Asia these twenty-eight years, but in iv. 1 he properly confines their rule to Upper Asia—that is, to the Iranian plateau. Some biblical scholars find in this assumed Scythian invasion the reason for Jeremiah's earliest prophecies, but there is absolutely no evidence (cf. Olmstead, History of Palestine, pp. 492–93; Cameron, op. cit., pp. 177 ff.).

[88] Olmstead, History of Assyria, p. 636.

Since the road to the south was closed by the alliance with the Chaldean, who also held Susa, Cyaxares followed the Zagros as it bends westward into the cold uplands of Armenia, where other Iranian bands had destroyed the kingdom of Haldia and introduced their own Indo-European speech.[89] The fertile valleys of Armenia led down through the Anti-Taurus into the broad plains of Cappadocia and to the river Halys, frontier of Lydia. Five years of warfare ended in a drawn battle at the time of a solar eclipse (May 28, 585) and a peace by which the Halys remained the boundary.[90] The Cadusians along the Hyrcanian Sea refused submission, but the ruler of Parthia admitted himself a vassal.[91]

Four great powers—Media, Chaldaea, Lydia, and Egypt—divided among themselves the whole of the Near East, but, of these, only Media could be called an empire. Far more significant, Media represented the first empire founded by northern warriors who spoke an Iranian language and thought in northern terms. All the more unfortunate is the sad fact that no site of Median times has been excavated. When their capital Ecbatana has received proper attention, we may venture to hope that the mound at Hamadan will grant us full details of Median culture and even permit the Medes to speak for themselves in their own Iranian tongue.[92]

[89] Cf. Jer. 51:27.

[90] Herod. i. 103.

[91] Ctes. *Pers.* iv–vi, Epit. 30–31 (Diod. ii. 33–34).

[92] For the mound at Hamadan cf. Erich Schmidt, *Flights over Ancient Cities of Iran* (1940), Pl. 91.

Chapter III

FOUNDER CYRUS

ALLIANCE WITH BABYLON

ASTYAGES now ruled Media in place of his father Cyaxares. His name in Iranian, Arshtivaiga, meant "lance-hurler,"[1] but it was quite inappropriate for the son, who in his long reign (585-550) showed only weakness. In Persian lands Ariaramnes had been succeeded by his son Arsames (Arshama); in the other line, Cyrus gave place, not to Arukku, but to a younger son, Cambyses (Kanbujiya) I, "Great King, king of Anshan." To him Astyages married his daughter Mandane, who bore to Cambyses a second Cyrus. In 559 this Cyrus II became vassal king in Anshan and ruled from his open capital Parsagarda.[2]

Shut off from the hot, unhealthy coastal plain by mountains through which wound tortuous trails, the high plateau of Parsa was well fitted to retain the old Iranian fighting spirit. Scorning a master so weakened by luxury, Cyrus plotted revolt. His own tribe of the Pasargadae could be depended upon, for his family, the Achaemenidae, provided its rulers. With it were associated two other Persian tribes, the Maraphii and the Maspii. To these were added still other Persian tribes: the agricultural Panthialaei, Derusiaei, and Germanii (the last in the oasis of Kerman), and the nomad herders—the Dai, Mardi, Dropici, and Sagartii.[3] Of these, the Mardians occupied the desert near the site of Persepolis and long retained the reputation of brigands,[4] but the Sagartians inhabited the oasis of Yazd and, while speaking the common language, were distinguished from their fellows by their lack of defensive metal armor, their only weapons being the dagger and the lasso.[5]

[1] E. Herzfeld, *Archaeological History of Iran* (1935), p. 40.

[2] Herod. i. 91, 107-8, 111; Berossus, Frag. 52(S); cf. G. G. Cameron, *History of Early Iran* (1936), pp. 219 ff.

[3] Herod. i. 125; iv. 167.

[4] Aeschyl. *Pers.* 994 ff.; a Mardian at the siege of Sardis, Herod. i. 84; Nic. Dam., Frag. 66, from Ctesias; Nearchus, in Strabo xi. 13. 6; cf. xv. 3. 1; Curt. v. 6. 12, 17.

[5] Darius, *Beh.* §§ 33, 52, Asagarta; Herod. iii. 93; vii. 85.

Now that the Persians were all united under his rule, Cyrus looked about for an ally against Media among the other great powers. The nearest as well as the most logical was Babylonia. A generation before, Babylon had been an ally of Media, but only for the moment; as soon as their common enemy, Assyria, had been destroyed and the spoils of empire had been divided, the alliance became nominal. When Nebuchadnezzar's engineers constructed the great chain of fortifications which seemed to make Babylon impregnable, the enemy he feared was his neighbor—Media.

After a long and successful reign, the great Babylonian conqueror passed away on October 7, 562.[6] After less than two years of rule, his son Amel-Marduk had by August 13, 560, been followed by Nebuchadnezzar's son-in-law, Nergal-shar-usur; he in turn lasted only until May 22, 556, when a tablet is dated by his youthful son, Labashi-Marduk.[7]

Two such brief reigns gave hope to the nationalists, who had always resented the alien rule of the Chaldaean dynasty. Three days after the tablet dated by Labashi-Marduk, there is another dated by a rival, Nabu-naid. According to him, Labashi-Marduk was a youth without understanding who, contrary to the will of the gods, had seated himself upon the throne of the kingdom. There are hints of the palace revolution to which he owed his new position, of the support by nobles and army, but in very truth it was by the command of Marduk, his lord, that Nabu-naid was raised to the lordship of the land. He also claims that he is the representative of Nebuchadnezzar and Nergal-shar-usur, his predecessors.[8] At any rate, after less than two months' rule, the young king was put to death with horrible torture, and Nabu-naid was sole ruler of the remnants of the Chaldaean Empire.[9]

Nabu-naid's claims to be the true representative of the great conqueror's policies were bolstered by the report of a convenient dream;

[6] Richard A. Parker and Waldo H. Dubberstein, *Babylonian Chronology, 626 B.C.—A.D. 45* (1942), p. 10. Henceforth dates by the Babylonian and Jewish calendars are turned into our own Julian chronology by means of their tables. As pointed out by them, "70 per cent of all the dates in our tables are astronomically correct to the day, while the remaining 30 per cent may be off by one day. Since the tables are purely for historical purposes, this uncertainty is unimportant" (p. 23).

[7] *Ibid.*, p. 10.

[8] Nabu-naid Stele (S. Langdon, *Die neubabylonischen Königsinschriften* [1912], Nabonid No. 8), col. IV, l. 34—col. V, l. 34.

[9] Parker and Dubberstein, *op. cit.;* cf. Berossus, Frag. 52(S).

by Marduk's order, Nebuchadnezzar himself appeared to interpret a celestial phenomenon as favorable, portending a long reign. Other Babylonian divinities sent equally favoring visions and were adequately rewarded. Marduk's great temple at Babylon, Esagila, was gloriously restored; the New Year's feast, beginning March 31, 555, was celebrated with all due pomp, and Nabu-naid took the part reserved for the king. He grasped the hands of Marduk and was again recognized as the lawful monarch. Rich gifts were assigned to his temple. Then Nabu-naid journeyed through all Babylonia, the cities of the south in particular, and Sin of Ur, Shamash of Larsa, and Ishtar of Uruk were recipients of the royal bounty.[10]

Although the nominee of the anti-Chaldaean party, Nabu-naid was not himself a native Babylonian. His father was a certain Nabu-balatsu-iqbi, who is called the "wise prince," though actually he seems to have been the chief priest of the once famous temple of the moon-god Sin in Mesopotamian Harran.[11] Since the last flicker of Assyrian rule from that city had been stamped out in 610, Harran had remained in the hands of the Medes, who had permitted the temple to lie in ruins. Quite literally, it was the life-dream of Nabu-naid to restore that temple, amid whose ruins his father was still living. But this required that Harran first should be taken from the Medes.

As Nabu-naid tells it, in his accession year the gods Marduk and Sin appeared to him in a dream. Marduk bade him restore the Harran temple; we wonder whether the priests of Esagila approved. When Nabu-naid fearfully protested that the Mede surrounded it and that he was exceeding strong, Marduk answered: "The Mede of whom you are speaking, he himself, his land, and the kings who march at his side are not! When the third year comes, the Gods will cause Cyrus, king of Anshan, his little slave, to advance against him with his small army. He will overthrow the wide extending Medes; he will capture Astyages, king of the Medes, and take him captive to his land."[12]

TRIUMPH OVER THE MEDES

In this hope, Nabu-naid made alliance with Cyrus, who thereupon openly rebelled against Media. To fulfil his part of the agreement,

---

[10] Stele, cols. VI–IX.

[11] Abu Habba Cylinder (Langdon, *op. cit.*, Nabonid No. 1), col. I, l. 6; cf. Harran inscription (*ibid.*, Nabonid No. 9).

[12] Abu Habba Cyl., col. I, ll. 8–32; Xen. *Cyrop.* i. 5. 2–3.

PLATE I

Salt Deposit before Caspian Gates

Traditional Caspian Gates from the Air (courtesy Aerial Survey, Oriental Institute)

THE CASPIAN GATES

PLATE II

Above the Snow Clouds

The Open Road

THE HAMADAN PASS

PLATE III

By the Caspian Sea

In the Alborz Mountains

In Shiraz

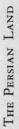

In Hamadan

THE PERSIAN LAND

PLATE IV

From below

From above

THE CHALUS PASS

PLATE V

Head of Mede (from Apadana at Persepolis) (courtesy Oriental Institute)

Hangmatana, Capital of Media (Mound at Ecbatana) (courtesy Aerial Survey, Oriental Institute)

THE MEDIAN EMPIRE

PLATE VI

Nabunaid Cylinder (from Louvre, *Encyclopédie photographique*, Vol. XII, Pl. 42*a*)

Cyrus Cylinder (from British Museum, *A Guide to the Babylonian and Assyrian Antiquities* [3d ed., 1922], Pl. XL)

CONTEMPORARY PROCLAMATIONS

PLATE VII

Amasis Worshiping the Sacred Bull (from Louvre, *Encyclopédie photographique*, Vol. V, Pl. 57)

Croesos as Pictured by the Greeks (from Furtwängler-Reichhold, *Griechische Vasenmalerei*, Pl. 113)

ALLIES IN EGYPT AND LYDIA

PLATE VIII

City of Babylon in the Alluvium Plain of the Lower Euphrates

Wall at Assur in the Hills of the Middle Tigris

CAPITALS OF CONQUERED NATIONS

Nabu-naid promptly levied an army against the "rebels" who lived in the countries once held by Nebuchadnezzar. Before he left, Nabu-naid handed over the "kingship" of Babylonia to his eldest son, Bel-shar-usur (Belshazzar as he is called in the Book of Daniel), and started off for Harran. No aid for the city was possible, since the revolt of Cyrus kept Astyages busy at home, and Harran was quickly recovered. The city was rebuilt, and the army had laid the temple foundations by 555.[13]

The next year the reconquest of Syria continued. By January of 553, Nabu-naid was in Hamath. By August he had raided the Amanus Mountains. By December he had killed the king of Edom, while his troops were in Gaza on the Egyptian frontier.[14] Disaffected Jewish captives were predicting the fall of Babylon at the hands of the war-like Medes,[15] but, as so often, they were disappointed. Astyages did send out against his rebellious vassal an army under Harpagus, but he had forgotten how he had cruelly slain that general's son; Harpagus did not forget and promptly deserted to Cyrus, bringing over with him most of his soldiers. A second army, commanded by Astyages in person, reached the capital of Parsa; here it mutinied, seized its king, and handed him over to Cyrus. Ecbatana was captured, and its wealth of gold, silver, and precious objects was carried off to Anshan (550).[16]

Media ceased to be an independent nation and became the first satrapy, Mada. Nevertheless, the close relationship between Persians and Medes was never forgotten. Plundered Ecbatana remained a favorite royal residence. Medes were honored equally with Persians; they were employed in high office and were chosen to lead Persian armies. Foreigners spoke regularly of the Medes and Persians; when they used a single term, it was "the Mede."

By his conquest of the Median Empire, Cyrus had taken over the Median claims to rule over Assyria, Mesopotamia, Syria, Armenia, and Cappadocia. In large degree, these claims were in conflict with those of Babylonia. All reason for the alliance had disappeared when each party to the agreement had attained his immediate objective. Destruction of the Median Empire upset the delicate balance of power,

---

[13] Abu Habba Cyl., col. I, l. 38—col. II, l. 8; verse account of Nabu-naid (Sidney Smith, *Babylonian Historical Texts* [1924], pp. 27 ff.), cols. I–II; Nabu-naid Chron., col. I, ll. 1–8.

[14] Chron., col. I, ll. 9–22; Abu Habba Cyl., col. I, ll. 38–40.

[15] Jeremiah, chaps. 13 and 50–51; Cameron, *op. cit.*, pp. 221 ff.

[16] Chron., col. II, ll. 1–4; cf. Abu Habba Cyl., col. I, ll. 32–33; Herod. i. 127–30; Strabo xv. 3. 8; Ctes. *Pers.* vi, Epit. 32 (Diod. ii. 34. 6); vii, Epit. 33 (Phot. lxxii).

and war between Cyrus and the three surviving powers—Lydia,
Babylonia, and Egypt—might be expected to follow.

BEGINNINGS OF BABYLONIAN DECLINE

No vision from the abandoned Babylonian divinities warned Nabu-
naid that the international situation had so dangerously shifted.
With his mind set on further conquests in the west, he left Edom on
its desert border and struck deep into the heart of the Arabian Peninsula. Tema was attacked in its central oasis and its king was slain.
For some strange reason, Nabu-naid built there a palace like that in
Babylon and took up his residence in it.[17] Business documents from the
years immediately following tell of camel caravans which carried food
to the king at Tema.[18]

Meanwhile, Belshazzar exercised in Babylonia the "kingship" with
which his father had intrusted him. Numerous letters and business
documents refer to the king's son as the chief authority.[19] From the
king's seventh year to at least the eleventh (549–545), our chronicle
regularly begins each year: "The king was in Tema. The king's son,
the nobles, and his soldiers were in Akkad. In the first month, the
king did not come to Babylon. Nabu did not come to Babylon. Bel
did not go out (from Esagila). The New Year's festival was
omitted."[20] Thus deprived of the great annual show, with its opportunities for moneymaking, the inhabitants of Babylon were naturally
angered. The influential priests of Marduk were completely alienated.
That the great lord of their city was snubbed while the alien moon-
god of Harran was extravagantly honored did not lessen the resentment.

PERSIAN CONQUEST OF LYDIA

On news that his Median ally had been dethroned, Croesus of Lydia
hastily collected his levies and crossed the former Halys boundary to
pick up remnants of the empire.[21] Cyrus, who had just revived the
title "king of Parsa," felt this a challenge to his own pretensions, and
in April, 547, he set out from looted Ecbatana to meet the invader.
After he had traversed the pass, high above the city, his road wound
steadily downward until he reached the main line of the Zagros at the
"Gate of Asia."[22] Beyond the "Gate," the descent was even more

[17] Verse account, col. II, ll. 22 ff.

[18] R. P. Dougherty, *Nabonidus and Belshazzar* (1929), pp. 114 ff.

[19] *Ibid.*, pp. 81 ff.   [20] Chron., col. II, ll. 5–25.   [21] Herod. i. 71.

[22] Cf. E. Herzfeld, *Am Tor von Asien* (1920), pp. 1–2.

rapid. The cold air suddenly became warmer, the poplars, cypresses, and plane trees of the plateau gave way to a few palms, and Cyrus was on the edge of the great Mesopotamian plains.

Cyrus might easily have turned south against Babylon, had not the skill of Nebuchadnezzar's engineers formed that city and its surroundings into the world's mightiest fortress. Wisely he postponed the assault and marched north into Assyria, already a Median dependency and therefore prepared to accept him without question. Arbela, for so many centuries overshadowed by Ashur and Nineveh, regained its prestige as the new capital of Athura. Cyrus crossed the Tigris below Arbela, and Ashur fell; the gods of Ashur and Nineveh were saved only through refuge behind the walls of Babylon.[23] Farther west on the main road lay Harran; it could be claimed as part of Athura. Nabu-naid's father had passed away at the ripe age of one hundred and four just three years earlier (550), and his successor as priest of Sin could not resist the conqueror. There is no mention of its fall in our extant sources; only the line of march and the situation which followed betrays the fact that Harran was lost and with it the temple for whose restoration Nabu-naid had sacrificed the good will of Marduk. For these losses, the only revenge possible was a Babylonian alliance with Lydia.[24]

By May, Cyrus was ready to proceed against Croesus. The Great Road was again followed through North Syria, which also was detached from Nabu-naid's recent empire, and into Cilicia; on their own initiative, the hitherto independent Cilicians accepted Persian vassalage and as reward were permitted to retain their native kings, who regularly bore the name Syennesis.[25] Through the Cilician Gates the army entered Cappadocia, which was organized as another satrapy, Katpatuka.[26] At the same time, presumably, Armenia received Cyrus as successor to Astyages and henceforth was the satrapy of Armina.[27]

After an indecisive battle in the land of Pteria, the country about the recently excavated Alaca Hüyük, Croesus retired to Sardis. His provincial levies were disbanded, while he summoned his allies, Amasis of Egypt, Nabu-naid of Babylon, and the Spartans on the Greek mainland, to meet him in the spring.[28] Cyrus had no intention

[23] Cyrus, *Cyl.*, l. 30.

[24] Chron., col. II, ll. 15–16; Herod. i. 77.

[25] Chron., col. II, l. 16; Xen. *Cyrop.* i. 1. 4; viii. 6. 8; Herod. i. 28, 74.

[26] Xen. *Cyrop.* i. 1. 4.

[27] *Ibid.* iii. 1; viii. 7. 11.   [28] Herod. i. 75 ff.; Xen. *Cyrop.* vii. 1.

of allowing the enemy time for reinforcements. Although winter, severe on the Anatolian Plateau, was nearing, he pushed rapidly west. In the small plain east of the capital, at the junction of the Hyllus with the Hermus, which hereafter was known as "Cyrus' Field," the mounted Lydian spearmen barred his road. By the advice of Harpagus, Cyrus stationed the baggage camels in front of his line; their horrid and unaccustomed odor frightened the horses and drove them off in wild flight. The dismounted Lydians re-formed and fought bravely, but at last they were forced back into the citadel. More urgent appeals were sent to the allies; there was no time to answer, for after but fourteen days of siege, the supposedly impregnable acropolis of Sardis was scaled and Croesus made prisoner (547).[29]

"In May he marched to the land of Lydia. He killed its king. He took its booty. He placed in it his own garrison. Afterward his garrison and the king were in it."[30] Such was the official report given by Cyrus. In actual fact, Croesus followed oriental custom and immolated himself to escape the usual indignities heaped upon a captured monarch before he was put to death. Within the next half-century, the Attic vase painter Myson depicted Croesus enthroned upon a pyre which a servant was about to light.[31]

Apollo of Delphi had been highly honored by Lydian kings. To Croesus he had uttered an ambiguous oracle which clearly had lured him to his death.[32] Such a blot on Apollo's prestige could not be allowed, and soon there were published "true" accounts of Croesus' fate. First the priests declared that the god himself had carried the deposed monarch to immortality in the land of the fabled Hyperboraeans, conveniently far in the north. Then came the familiar story that at the last moment, when Croesus was already on the pyre, Cyrus was seized with remorse; he attempted to save him, although the fire was already blazing fiercely. Then Apollo sent an unexpected rain which miraculously extinguished the flames, and Croesus was saved to become the king's chief adviser. Finally, the Hyperboraeans were rationalized and Croesus was settled in Barene near Ecbatana![33]

[29] Herod. i. 79 ff., 83 ff.; Xen. Cyrop. vii. 2.

[30] Nabu-naid Chron., col. II, ll. 16–18.

[31] E. Pottier, Vases antiques du Louvre (1922), pp. 201–2; cf. A. Furtwängler and K. Reichhold, Griechische Vasenmalerei (1905), Pl. 113; J. D. Beazley, Attic Red-figured Vase-Painters (1942), p. 171 (Myson 47).

[32] Herod. i. 55.

[33] Bacchylid. ii. 33 ff.; Herod. i. 86 ff.; Thuc. i. 16; Xen. Cyrop. vi. 2. 9 ff.; vii. 1–2; Ctes. Pers. vii, Epit. 30; Marmor Parium A, 42(J).

Lydia was formed into the satrapy Saparda or Sardis.[34] The satrap was the Persian Tabalus. Provincial administration was still in the experimental stage. Cyrus accordingly tried out the appointment of a native, a certain Pactyas, to have charge of the captured treasure of Croesus.[35]

SUBJUGATION OF THE GREEKS AND LYCIANS

This year 547 marks also the first contact between Persians and Greeks. Neither people recognized its fateful character. To the Greeks, Persia was simply one more barbarian monarchy, whose trade their merchants might exploit and to which, if necessary, the nearer city-states might give a nominal allegiance. They never dreamed that in a single generation the wealthiest, the most populous, and the most advanced half of the Greek world would be permanently under Persian domination and that the next generation would be compelled to resist the whole might of the Persian Empire in an attempt to subjugate the more backward Greek states which still retained their independence. They could not foresee that throughout the whole period, while these states remained free, their international relations would be dominated by the Achaemenid great king and that, even in internal affairs, political parties would succeed or fail as they were pro- or anti-Persian. To the Persians, however, during the next half-century, Greeks on the western boundary would remain only a minor frontier problem.[36]

Before the final battle with the Lydians, Cyrus had offered terms to the Greek coastal cities. For long years they had been subjects of the Lydians, but their yoke had been made easy, while the commercial classes who now controlled their governments had grown rich through the opportunities afforded by trade as part of the wealthy Lydian Empire. Quite naturally, the city states refused the generous offer, with the exception of Miletus, which was shrewd enough to divine who would be the coming power.[37] The Persians had learned their first lesson in handling the Greeks: Divide and conquer. At the same time they probably learned their second lesson.

Apollo, venal god of oracles, from his chief shrine at Delphi had

[34] Saparda proved equivalent to Sardis by Aramaic-Lydian bilingual. See E. Littmann, *Sardis*, VI, Part 1 (1916), 12; C. C. Torrey, "The Bilingual Inscription from Sardis," *AJSL*, XXXIV (1918), 185 ff.; cf. Obad. 20, Sepharad, to be read Spharda with Greek.

[35] Herod. i. 153.

[36] Cf. Olmstead, "Persia and the Greek Frontier Problem," *Classical Philology*, XXXIV (1939), 305 ff.

[37] Herod. i. 76, 141.

delivered an ambiguous saying to Croesus which contributed to his overconfidence and downfall. At Branchidae was Apollo's shrine for Miletus; he, too, might be bribed through his priests. The question inevitably arises: Did *they* have a part in the easy surrender of Miletus? However we answer the question, the fact remains that both Apollo of Miletus and Apollo of Delphi for the next half-century remained consistent friends of the Persians.

By right of conquest, title to the former Lydian subjects passed to Cyrus. Refusal of most Greeks to submit automatically made them rebels. Their position was not improved by what Cyrus must have considered an insolent demand that they should enjoy the same favored status as under Croesus. When this demand was refused as coming too late, the fortifying of their cities meant war. The rebellious Greeks appealed to Sparta, which Cyrus knew only as a summoned ally which had failed to make an appearance. To his astonishment, the victorious great king received an embassy which forbade him to injure any Greek city on pain of punishment by the Spartans![38]

On the king's departure for Ecbatana, Pactyas revolted and, with the treasure intrusted to him, hired Greek mercenaries. Tabalus was besieged on the Sardis acropolis until reinforcements under the Mede Mazares drove off the rebels and completely disarmed the Lydians. Pactyas fled to Cyme, which inquired of Apollo's oracle at Milesian Branchidae. The answer might have been expected; as consistent friend of the Persians, Apollo ordered the surrender of the suppliant.[39]

A prominent citizen of Cyme, Aristodicus, son of Heracleides, won unique reputation among the Greeks by refusing to accept so obviously prejudiced an oracle. Again an embassy visited Apollo at Branchidae. Aristodicus as spokesman repeated the inquiry and received the same answer. As he had already planned, Aristodicus then stole all the birds nesting in the temple. From the holy of holies a voice was heard: "Most wicked of men, how dare you do this? Will you steal my suppliants from the temple?" Aristodicus did not hesitate: "O Lord, how can *you* thus aid your own suppliants while you order the Cymaeans to hand over *their* suppliant?" The rebuke must have stung, for the priest furiously answered: "Yes, I do so order you, that you may the more quickly perish for your impiety and may never again come to ask my oracle about the handing-over of suppliants!"[40]

Apollo's bluff had for once been called, and, as far as we know, Aristodicus suffered no harm for his temerity. Cyme was not super-

[38] *Ibid.* 141, 152.   [39] *Ibid.* 154 ff.   [40] *Ibid.* 159.

stitious; but Pactyas was a dangerous suppliant, and so he was sent for refuge to safer Mitylene. Lesbos was an island; as yet the Persians had no fleet, and Pactyas might have remained safe had not Mazares added bribes to threats. The Mitylenians were about to sell the refugee when the Cymaeans learned of their plans and brought Pactyas by ship to Chios and to the presumed safety of the temple of Athena, guardian of the city. Chios, another island, was equally safe from threats but not from bribery, and the sorry tale was ended by the surrender of Pactyas in exchange for mainland Atarneus. The Persians had learned another lesson: Greeks could easily be bought.

Obviously, the next step should be the subjugation of those mainland Greeks who refused to submit. They resisted bravely, but each for himself, and were taken one by one. Priene was enslaved. The Maeander Plain and Magnesia were ravaged. Harpagus the Mede, rewarded for his treachery, was the new satrap. He offered peace to Phocaea if only the citizens would demolish a section of the city wall and hand over one house for royal occupancy; the Phocaeans sailed off by night from a deserted city, but soon a good half lost heart and returned.[41] Teos followed their example. The other Ionian cities on the mainland were quickly taken. The islands inhabited by Ionians, having treacherously handed over Pactyas, submitted abjectly to his executioners and were formed into a satrapy.[42] As for the Dorian cities, they showed no fight; only Cnidus attempted to insure safety by cutting through the isthmus. Apollo of Delphi followed the example of Apollo of Branchidae and forbade the project; on the approach of Harpagus, Cnidus also surrendered. Carians had fought bravely as mercenaries for Egyptian kings of the Saite dynasty; now only the Pedasians made a brief resistance to the Persians at Lide, for Ionian and Aeolian contingents were already fighting in the army led by Harpagus.[43]

But while Greeks and Carians surrendered so cravenly to the invader, their neighbors, the Trmmela (Termilae)[44] or Lycians, taught them how they should have resisted. These had not forgotten how, as Lukku, they had harried the Egypt of the Nineteenth Dynasty, how

[41] *Ibid.* 164; Strabo vi. 1. 1; Gell. x. 16. 4. Magnesia, Colophon, and Smyrna were destroyed by pride and internal faction, according to Theog. 603–4, 1103–4; for date see E. L. Highbaeger, "Theognis and the Persian Wars," *Transactions of the American Philological Association,* LXVIII (1937), 88 ff.

[42] Herod. i. 169; iii. 96: "tribute from the islands."

[43] Cf. Aeschyl. *Pers.* 773; Thuc. i. 16.   [44] Herod. i. 173.

under Glaucus and Sarpedon they had aided Trojans against the
armada collected by Agamemnon from the Mycenaean Empire. They
had retained better than other Anatolians their Caucasian language
and their unwritten ancestral customs, counting descent through the
mother. Constant warfare with the Solymi hillmen had kept them
hardy, and the colonizing Greeks had been able to effect only one
settlement—at Phaselis on their border. Even Croesus had not been
able to subdue them.[45]

Shutting themselves up in their chief city, Arnna or Xanthus, the
Lycians fought until all hope was gone, then burned their wives and
treasure in the citadel and sallied out to die.[46] In the same manner, the
Caunians perished. Now the whole seacoast could be formed into the
satrapy of Yauna or Ionia; it was not a true satrapy, for it possessed
no satrap of its own but was under the satrap of Sardis. The Greeks
along the Hellespont, on the contrary, were ruled by a satrap Mitrobates,[47] who from Dascyleium on the south shore of the Propontus
administered Hellespontine Phrygia or Tyaiy Drayaha, "Those of the
Sea."[48]

This brief episode taught the Persians much about the Greeks.
They learned that as individuals they were excellent fighters, clever
and well armed, and worthy of incorporation into their own armies.
They discovered also that Greek city-states, bitterly jealous of one
another, were incapable of united action, and that it was not difficult to find purchasable friends among them. Of such friends, Apollo,
god of oracles, was the most valuable. But the greatest discovery of
all was that there were class divisions within the city-states themselves.

Most of these city-states had long ago abandoned kingship for a
government by a hereditary nobility of landholders. Then new economic forces had brought into prominence an aristocracy of trade-
bought wealth, which often, through the tyrant, supplanted this
older aristocracy of birth. While the patriotism of the older nobility
was inevitably narrow, men of commerce could appreciate trade opportunities offered by inclusion in a wide-flung empire. Obviously, it
was to Persian advantage that Greek cities be intrusted to tyrants.

[45] Homer *Iliad* ii. 877; iv. 197; v. 478–79; vi. 78, 184–85, 204; Herod. i. 173; Heraclid. Pont., Frag. 15; Menacrates of Xanthus, Frag. 2; Nicol. Damasc., Frag. 103k(J).

[46] Herod. i. 176; Appianus. *Bell. civ.* iv. 80.   [47] Herod. iii. 126.

[48] *Ibid.* i. 160 ff.; Charon Lampscen. *Pers.*, Frag. 1; Aeschyl. *Pers.* 770 ff.; Thuc. i. 13. 6; Xenophan. *Parod.* 22; Aristox. 23.

BABYLONIA IN FERMENT

Under the rule of friendly tyrants, the conquered Greeks remained quiet while Cyrus rapidly expanded his empire. Now that Nabu-naid had made his alliance with Croesus, Cyrus might continue openly his whittling-away of the Babylonian territory. On his return from Sardis, we should expect, he would take over the remaining portions of Syria yet held by Nabu-naid's soldiers and perhaps demand some expression of loyalty from the Arabs along the border.[49] If Tema was threatened by these operations, this would be one reason why sometime after 545 Nabu-naid reappeared in Babylon.

There were other good reasons. Highly centralized in the reign of Nebuchadnezzar, Babylonia had progressively disintegrated under the weakling rule of Belshazzar. Misrule and graft were rampant, the peasants were oppressed, and their fields went out of cultivation. By 546 once fertile Babylonia faced the threat of actual starvation.[50]

In this same fateful year Nabu-naid suffered another terrible loss. From its earliest days the Chaldaean dynasty had safely held the acropolis of Susa, the most important city of Elam. One of the outstanding generals of Nebuchadnezzar, Gobryas (Gubaru) by name,[51] had been appointed governor of Gutium (as the Babylonians continued to describe Elam). Now he revolted to Cyrus, and Nabu-naid was able to save only Susa's gods by transporting them to Babylon. By June 9, 546, the troops of the Elamite had entered Akkad and were attacking the loyal governor of Uruk.[52]

CYRUS' CONQUESTS TO THE EAST

Meanwhile, Cyrus himself had turned his attention to the as yet unsubdued Iranians of the eastern half of the plateau, north and east of the great central salt desert. Varkana or Hyrcania lay south of the Hyrcanian Sea. Fertility was assured by the range to the south which blocked the path of the northerly winds and compelled them to disgorge the contents of their rain clouds in deluges which soaked the narrow coastal plain at the mountain's base. To the southeast of Hyrcania was upland Parthava or Parthia; the two were united under Hystaspes (Vishtaspa), Arsames' son, who was glad to exchange the

---

[49] Xen. *Cyrop.* vii. 4. 16; Berossus, Frag. 52(S).

[50] R. P. Dougherty, *Records from Erech* (1920), No. 154.

[51] V. Scheil, "Le Gobryas de la Cyropedie," *Revue d'Assyrologie*, XI (1914), 165 ff.

[52] Chron., col. II, ll. 21–22; verse account, col. IV, l. 2; Cyrus, *Cyl.*, ll. 13, 30–31; Xen. *Cyrop.* iv. 6; v. 5.

lesser title of *kavi*, or local kinglet, for that of satrap under his now mighty relative.[53]

East of Parthia extended Haraiva or Aria,[54] which took its name from the river Areius; on it lay the capital Artocoana,[55] which as modern Herat has resumed its ancient name. South of Aria was Zaranka or Drangiana[56] along the Etymandrus River. The Ariaspi on the Etymandrus aided Cyrus by furnishing food and henceforth were freed from tribute and were listed among the king's "Benefactors."[57] The Arachotas branch of the Etymandrus River[58] gave its name to Hauravatish or Arachosia,[59] whose capital of the same name is modern Kandahar.

From Aria, high up on the Iranian Plateau, Cyrus might follow with his eye the course of the Oxus, in its upper reaches still known as the Wakhsh Ab, as it dashed down through impassable gorges to spread out in loops over the yellow plains of central Asia. For the most part, these plains were arid, but here and there were cultivable oases along the rivers which permitted a rude irrigation to bring the fertile soil to a rich luxuriance. In the oases nearest to the plateau, Iranians had already settled, and Cyrus determined to add these to his expanding empire.

Following the trail of the Oxus, he descended into Sogdia (Su-

[53] For Parthia under the Achaemenids see N. C. Debevoise, *A Political History of Parthia* (1938), pp. 2 ff.

[54] Cf. *Beh.* § 6; Vid. 1:9; Herod. iii. 93. Areian city Susia, on Parthian border, Arr. *Anab.* iii. 25. 1; Hysia, royal city of Parthians, Artemidorus, in Steph. Byz. *s.v.;* Tesmes, Ptol. vi. 11. 8; mod. Tos, predecessor of Meshed, Herzfeld, *Arch. Mitth.*, I (1929), 106.

[55] Arr. *Anab.* iii. 25. 5; Pliny vi. 61. 93; Artacana (modern Herat), Curt. vi. 6. 33; Chortacana, Diod. xvii. 78. 1; Artacaena, Strabo xi. 10. 1; Areius River, Strabo xi. 10. 1; modern Here Rud.

[56] Zaranka, Darius, *Beh.* § 6; *Persepolis* e; Naqsh-i-Rustam A 3 (Zaranga Bab. Vers.); Sarangae, Herod. iii. 93, 117; vii. 67; Zarangea, Arr. *Anab.* iii. 25. 8; cf. 21. 1; vii. 6. 3; Zarangiana, eparchy, Isid. Char. 17; Drangiana, Strabo xi. 10. 1; Drangines, Diod. xvii. 78. 4; Drangae, Just. xii. 5. 9; Curt. vi. 6. 36; Strabo xv. 2. 8 ff.; Dardanae, Ptol. vi. 17. 3; medieval Zarang, G. Le Strange, *Lands of the Eastern Caliphate* (1905), pp. 535 ff. The capital was Phrada, Steph. Byz. *s.v.*

[57] So Arr. *Anab.* iii. 27. 4; Arimaspi, Diod. xvii. 81. 1; Just. xii. 5. 1; Curt. vii. 3. 1, by confusion with the half-fabulous one-eyed northern people of Herod. iii. 116; iv. 13–14, 27; called only "Benefactors," Strabo xv. 2. 10.

[58] Haetumant, Vid. 1:14; modern Helmand.

[59] Harauvati, Darius *Beh.* § 6; Arachoti, Strabo x. 8. 9; xi. 10. 1; Parthian eparchy Arachosia, Isid. Char. 19; Arachotus, Ptol. vi. 20. River from which named, modern Arghand-ab. City Arachosia, Plin. vi. 92; Steph. Byz. *s.v.;* modern Qalaat-i-Gilzani, W. W. Tarn, *Greeks in Bactria and India* (1938), p. 470.

gudu),[60] the territory between the Oxus and the Jaxartes rivers. Its capital was Maracanda,[61] predecessor of fabulous golden Samarcand, where, amid gardens and orchards, the great mound under which slumbered the remains of the original settlement was remembered until Moslem times.[62] By it ran the Sogdian stream, large but quickly lost in the sands.[63] The Oxus itself was at this point turbulent and impossible to bridge; no doubt Cyrus crossed it in the antiquated manner—on inflated skins.[64] Beyond the companion stream, the Orexartes[65] or Jaxartes, were half-nomad Massagetae,[66] the Chorasmians, in the Khiva Oasis along the Lower Oxus.[67] They were subdued, and Cyrus (or one of his immediate successors)[68] introduced scientific irrigation as it was known to the Persians. All the soil was declared to be royal domain; at the point where the Aces (the Lower Oxus)[69] debouched from the hills through five separate channels,[70] sluice gates were constructed; they were opened for distribution of the precious water over the fields only on personal appeal to the king and after a stiff additional tax.[71]

Perhaps Cyrus did not expect the Chorasmians to pay long the onerous tax (we shall see that by the time of Artaxerxes I the Chorasmians appear to have slipped away from all effective royal control[72] and that before the end of the empire they possessed their own

---

[60] Sugudu, Darius, *Beh.* § 6; the Sogdi, Herod. iii. 93; Soghdha, land of cattle, Vid. 1:5; Sughd in the Middle Ages, Le Strange, *op. cit.*, pp. 460 ff.; Seleucid eparchy, Strabo ii. 73; Ptol. vi. 12; cf. H. Kretchmer, "Sogdiana," *PW*, IIIA (1927), 788 ff.

[61] Strabo xi. 11. 4; Plut. *Alex. Fort.* i. 2; ii. 9–10; Arr. *Anab.* iii. 30. 6; iv. 3. 6; 5. 2; 6. 3; 16. 2; Curt. vii. 6. 10, 24; 7. 30; 9. 20; viii. 1. 7; 19. 2, 13; Ptol. vi. 11. 9; viii. 23. 10.

[62] Le Strange, *op. cit.*, pp. 463 ff.

[63] Called by the Macedonians the Polytimetes, Strabo xi. 11. 5; cf. Arr. *Anab.* iv. 5. 2; 6. 3; Curt. vii. 7. 30; 9. 20; 10. 1; modern Zarafshan, Le Strange, *op. cit.*, p. 460.

[64] Cf. Arr. *Anab.* iii. 29. 2 ff.; Curt. vii. 5. 13 ff.

[65] So Plut. *Alex.* 45. 4; Orxantes, Arr. *Anab.* iii. 30. 7.

[66] Massagetae and Sacae, Strabo xi. 8. 8.

[67] Darius, *Beh.* § 6, Chorasmii, Herod. iii. 93, 117; vii. 66; medieval Khwarizm, Le Strange, *op. cit.*, pp. 446 ff.

[68] Herodotus at first sight implies that it was at the very beginning of Persian rule, but the mention of Perse *might* indicate that Persepolis was already occupied.

[69] The earlier name of Khiva is said to have been Khivaq or Khayvak (Le Strange, *op. cit.*, p. 450), which gives the necessary connection with Aces.

[70] The passage was still notorious in the Middle Ages (*ibid.*, p. 451).

[71] Herod. iii. 117.   [72] *Ibid.* 93.

king),[73] for he determined to make the Jaxartes his northernmost permanent frontier. To protect the rich lands to the south from future raids across the river by the Turanian hordes of deeper central Asia, he constructed a line of seven guard posts along the southern bank. Gaza, the "Treasure,"[74] would be central supply depot, but the key to the defense was Cyra,[75] the "City of Cyrus";[76] and all would be based on Maracanda to the rear. Recrossing the Upper Oxus on his return journey, Cyrus probably occupied at this time the fertile oasis of Margush, so named from its chief river, at the modern Merv; it was made a subsatrapy, not of Sogdia low to the northeast, but of Bactria higher up on the north.[77]

Bactria[78] (Bakhtrish) received its name from the Bactrus River, an affluent of the Oxus.[79] Its chief city was likewise named Bactra,[80] though the older Iranian name of Zariaspa long clung to the citadel,[81] and the Magian treatment of the dead and dying was kept up until the horrified Alexander put an end to the worst of the practices.[82] Another important city was Drapsaca.[83]

From Bactria, the most eastern of the truly Iranian lands, Cyrus looked across the boundary river, the Cophen,[84] into the territory of their cousins, the Indians. At this time the Iranians still called it in their own language Paruparaesanna, the land "beyond the moun-

[73] Arr. *Anab.* iv. 15. 4–5; subjection of Chorasmi and Dahae by Alexander, Just. xii. 6. 18.

[74] Arr. *Anab.* iv. 2. 1.

[75] Strabo xi. 11. 4; Curt. vii. 6. 16.

[76] Cyropolis, Arr. *Anab.* iv. 3. 1; site at modern Chojend.

[77] Subsatrapy of Bactria, Darius, *Beh.* §§ 21, 38–39; Mouru, Vid. 1:6; Seleucid eparchy Margiana, Curt. vii. 10. 15; Margus (Murghab) River, Plin. vi. 47; later Marv, Le Strange, *op. cit.*, pp. 397 ff.

[78] Bakhtrish, Darius, *Beh.* § 6. Bactria, Herod. iv. 204; the Bactrians still unconquered by Cyrus, Herod. i. 153; Bactrians, Herod. iii. 93; vii. 64, 66, 86; viii. 113; ix. 113.

[79] Curt. vii. 4.

[80] Aeschyl. *Pers.* 306, 718, 732; Herod. vi. 9; ix. 113; Bakhdhi, Vid. 1:7.

[81] Strabo xi. 8. 9; Arr. *Anab.* iv. 7. 1.

[82] Apollodorus of Artemita, Frag. 5(M); Oneisicritus, Frag. 5(J); Strabo xi. 11. 3.

[83] So Arr. *Anab.* iii. 29. 1; Darapsa, Strabo xi. 11. 1; Adrapsa, Strabo xv. 2. 10; Drapsa, Ptol. iv. 12. 4, 6; viii. 23. 13; Amm. xxiii. 6. 59.

[84] Strabo xv. 1. 26; Plin. vi. 94; Arr. *Ind.* 1. 1; possibly the Sanskrit Kubhu.

tains,"[85] although it was known to the natives as Gandara.[86] At this date, then, this far corner of India first came under the control of the Iranians.[87] Along the lower slopes of the Hindu Kush, the "mountains" referred to by the Iranian name, stretched Thattagush or Sattagydia; north of them, in the Pamirs, were the Saka Haumavarga or Amyrgaean Sacae, "preparers of the (sacred) *haoma* drink."[88]

CONQUEST OF BABYLONIA

By these conquests Cyrus doubled the extent, though not the population or the wealth, of his empire. He was strengthened by so enormous an access of fighting men that at last he might venture to attack even Babylon. The natives were ready to welcome any deliverer, foreigner though he might be. By his archaizing reforms, Nabu-naid had alienated the priesthood of Marduk, at whose expense these reforms had been made. Other priests were dissatisfied. Jewish prophets were predicting Babylon's fall and hailing Cyrus as the Lord's Anointed who would grant return to Zion.[89] The whole land was in chaos.

The way thus paved by the dissaffected elements of the population, Cyrus made ready to invade the alluvium as soon as he had returned from his eastern campaigns. Before the snows of the winter of 540–539 could fill the passes, he was on the border. Nabu-naid brought the gods of Eshnunak, Zamban, Me Turnu, and Der to the capital before their capture.[90] He suffered a defeat on the Tigris, but the only defense he could think of was to bring to his aid Ishtar of Uruk in March.[91] Nabu-naid might try to explain the deportation as protection of the capital against the foreigner; the citizens complained loudly of temples abandoned by their divinities and lying in ruins.[92]

[85] The Iranian name is preserved in the Babylonian and Elamite versions of the official inscriptions in place of Gandara; according to Jackson, *Cambridge History of India*, I, 327, it is the Avestan Upairisaena, "higher than the eagle"; Paropamisus, Eratosthenes, in Strabo xv. 1. 11; 2. 8 ff.; Arr. *Anab.* v. 5. 3; *Ind.* 2. 3; the more usual form is Parapamisadae with numerous variants, Just. xii. 5. 9; Diod. xvii. 82. 1; Curt. vii. 3. 5; Arr. *Anab.* iii. 28. 4. Gazaca, "Treasure City," Ptol. vi. 18, among the Parapamisadae; Amm. xxiii. 6. 70; medieval Ghazni.

[86] Hecataeus, Frag. 178(M); Herod. iii. 91; cf. vii. 66; Gandaritis, Strabo xv. 1. 26.

[87] Conquest of hill tribes, Astacenians and Assacenians, Arr. *Ind.* 1. 1 ff. The name of the capital Opiae, Hecataeus, Frag. 175; cf. Seleucid eparchy Opiana; Steph. Byz. *s.v.* "Alexandreia," still identifies the site at mounds of Opian near Charikar.

[88] *Beh.* § 6; Herod. i. 153; Ctes. *Pers.* vii, Epit. 33.

[89] Isaiah, chaps. 35, 40–55.   [90] Cyrus, *Cyl.*, l. 31.   [91] Chron., col. III, ll. 1–2.

[92] Cameron, "New Light on Ancient Persia," *JAOS*, LII (1932), 304.

Marduk and his priests had to be reconciled. On New Year's Day, April 4, 539, once more "the Festival was celebrated as was right." "There was great plenty of wine among the soldiers."[93] Still relying more on the physical presence of the gods, Nabu-naid next brought in the divinities of Maradda, Zamama, the gods of Kish, Ninlil, and the gods of Hursagkalama; "until the end of August the gods of Akkad, all who are above and below the earth, were entering into Babylon." The limit of citizen patience had been reached; the gods of Kutu, Sippar, and even Borsippa did not enter.[94] Ebarra, the temple of the sun-god Shamash in Sippar, had been restored, but the priests were disgusted when Nabu-naid through one of his frequent dreams changed the form of the god's headdress.[95] Nabu had come from Borsippa to meet his father Marduk at the New Year's, but his priests also had seen the handwriting on the wall.

Near the beginning of October, Cyrus fought another battle at Opis on the Tigris[96] and burned the people of Akkad with fire. After this example of frightfulness, his opponents lost courage and on October 11 Sippar was taken without a battle. Nabu-naid fled, and on October 13, 539, Gobryas, governor of Gutium, and the troops of Cyrus entered Babylon without battle. Afterward, when Nabu-naid returned to Babylon, he was made prisoner.[97]

The last tablet dated by Nabu-naid is from October 14, the day after Gobryas had captured Babylon, but it was written at Uruk, to which the welcome news had not yet penetrated. In the capital itself business went on as usual, for contemporaries had no realization that with the fall of Babylon an era had come to an end and another had begun. By October 26 at the latest, the scribes were dating by the new ruler as "king of lands." This remained the official titulary during the remainder of the "accession year" and for a part of the first full year of reign.

Babylon was well treated by Gobryas. Until the end of October, the "shields" of Gutium surrounded the gates of Esagila. No man's weapon was set up in Esagila or in the other temples and no appointed ceremony was omitted. On October 29 Cyrus himself entered Babylon.

[93] Cf. Herod. I. 191; Xen. *Cyrop.* vii. 5. 15–21; Dan. 5:1–4.

[94] Chron., col. III, ll. 5–12.

[95] Langdon, *op. cit.*, Nabonid No. 7.

[96] Xen. *Cyrop.* vii. 5. 26–30; Herod. i. 189, near the Gyndes.

[97] Chron., col. III, ll. 12–16; for chronology see Parker and Dubberstein, *op. cit.*, p. 11; Herod. i. 178, 188 ff.; Xen. *Cyrop.* vii. 5; Berossus, Frags. 52–54(S).

Branches were spread in his path, and he proclaimed peace to everyone in the city. Gobryas was made satrap of the new province of Babirush, and he appointed subordinate officials; the administrative documents show us that, as a rule, the former officials were retained at their posts.[98]

PERSIAN PROPAGANDA

In the eyes of his Babylonian subjects, Cyrus was never an alien king of Parsa. In his proclamation to them in their own language, he heaped up the ancient titles: "I am Cyrus, king of the universe, great king, mighty king, king of Babylon, king of Sumer and Akkad, king of the world quarters, ... seed of royalty from of old, whose rule Bel and Nabu love, over whose sovereignty they rejoice in their heart."[99] During his first full year of reign, "king of Babylon" came regularly to be prefixed in the dating formula to "king of lands." The priests were rewarded for their disloyalty to Nabu-naid. From December to February of the next year, the captive gods were being conducted with all due honor back to their temples. By chance we have found the actual letter which reports the departure from Borsippa of the ship to bring back the council of Ezida, which was to escort Nana and the Lady of Uruk on their homeward journey.[100] With the gods went instructions to restore their temples. Building bricks employed at Uruk bore the inscription: "Cyrus, builder of Esagila and Ezida, son of Cambyses, great king, am I";[101] thus he praised Marduk and Nabu by use of the former title of Nebuchadnezzar. Ur had been dishonored by an unfitting ritual; new constructions repaired the damage and allowed Cyrus as "king of the universe, king of Anshan," to remind the citizens how "the great gods have delivered all the lands into my hand; the land I have made to dwell in a peaceful habitation."[102]

Large numbers of foreign captive divinities gave further opportunity for royal benevolence. The gods of Susa were returned to Elam, those of Ashur to the ancient capital; others from the old debatable

[98] Chron., col. III, ll. 16–20.

[99] Cyrus, *Cyl.*, ll. 20 ff.

[100] Chron., col. III, ll. 21–22; Cameron, "New Light on Ancient Persia," *op. cit.*, p. 304.

[101] G. Smith, *Transactions of the Society of Biblical Archaeology,* II (1873), opp. p. 146; Weissbach, *Die Keilinschriften der Achämeniden* (1911), pp. 8–9.

[102] Cyrus, *Cyl.*, l. 5; changes at Ur (Nabu-naid) in A. T. Clay, *Miscellaneous Inscriptions in the Yale Babylonian Collection* (1915), No. 45; C. J. Gadd and L. Legrain, *Ur Excavations, Texts,* Vol. I: *Royal Inscriptions* (1928), No. 194.

land between Assyria and Babylonia equally profited. The inhabitants of these cities were also collected and restored to their homes.[103] Jewish prophets had welcomed Cyrus as the monarch who would return them to Zion; since they no longer possessed divine images, it was logical that they should bring back to Jerusalem the temple utensils looted by Nebuchadnezzar.[104]

The proclamation of Cyrus to the Babylonians, issued in their own language, was a model of persuasive propaganda. After making it clear that he was the legitimate successor of their former monarchs, Cyrus made sure that the memory of Nabu-naid should be forever damned. As he tells the story, a no-account was appointed to the priesthood of the land. One like him (Belshazzar) he established over them. To Ur and the rest of the cities he gave a ritual unbefitting them. Daily he planned and made the offering to cease. The worship of Marduk, king of the gods, he overturned; he daily manifested enmity to Marduk's city; all Marduk's people he brought to ruin through servitude without rest.

Because of their complaints, the lord of the gods became furiously angry with them and abandoned their country. The gods who dwelt among them left their homes in wrath because strange gods had been brought into Babylon. But soon Marduk repented and granted mercy to all the dwelling places which had become ruinous and to the people of Sumer and Akkad who were like corpses.

Throughout all the lands—everywhere—he searched. He was seeking a righteous prince, whom he took by the hand. Cyrus, king of Anshan, he called by name; to lordship over the whole world he appointed him. The land of Gutu (Elam) and all the Medes he cast down at his feet. The black-headed people—the usual term for Babylonians —he cared for in justice and in righteousness. Marduk, the great lord, guardian of his people, looked joyously on his pious works and his upright heart.

To his city Babylon, Marduk caused him to go; he commanded him to take the road to Babylon, going as friend and companion at his side. His numerous soldiers, the number of which, like the waters of a river, cannot be known, marched armed at his side. Without skirmish or battle, he permitted him to enter Babylon. He spared his city Babylon from calamity. Nabu-naid, the king who did not fear him, he delivered into Cyrus' hand. All the people of Babylon, all Sumer and

---

[103] Cyrus, *Cyl.*, ll. 30–32.

[104] Ezra, chap. 1; Aramaic decree of Cyrus, Ezra 6:3–5.

Akkad, princes and officials, fell down before him and kissed his feet. They rejoiced in his kingdom, their faces shone. The lord, who by his power brings to life the dead, who from destruction and distress had protected them, joyously they did him homage and heeded his command.

When I made my gracious entry into Babylon, with rejoicing and pleasure I took up my lordly residence in the royal palace. Marduk, the great lord, turned the noble race of the Babylonians toward me, and I gave daily care to his worship. My numerous troops marched peacefully into Babylon. In all Sumer and Akkad I permitted no unfriendly treatment. The dishonoring yoke was removed from them. Their fallen dwellings I restored; I cleared out the ruins.

Marduk, the great lord, rejoiced in my pious deeds, and graciously blessed me, Cyrus, the king who worships him, and Cambyses, my own son, and all my soldiers, while we, in sincerity and with joy praised his exalted godhead. All the kings dwelling in palaces of all the quarters of the earth, from the Upper to the Lower Sea, and all the kings of the Amorite country who dwelt in tents (the Arabs) brought me their heavy gifts and in Babylon kissed my feet.

Then Cyrus tells how he restored all the captive gods and ends with the pious hope:

May all the gods, whom I have brought into their cities, pray daily before Bel and Nabu for long life for me, and may they speak a gracious word for me and say to Marduk my lord: "May Cyrus, the king who worships you, and Cambyses, his son, be blessed."[105]

This proclamation was for the educated; for the illiterate, scribes prepared an account of Nabu-naid's reign in good Babylonian verse which should ring in the ears of the auditors long after the proclamation was forgotten. Nabu-naid was an exceedingly wicked monarch; righteousness did not accompany him. The weak he smote by the sword. He blocked the road to the merchant. The peasant was deprived of his plow land; never did he raise the harvest shout of rejoicing. The irrigation system was allowed to fall into neglect; he did not shut off properly the field runnels. When he dug them, he left them open, and the precious waters flowed over the fields unchecked, thus destroying their property. Prominent men were imprisoned. The citizen assembly was disturbed, their countenances were changed; they did not walk in the open places, the city did not see pleasure.

A demon seized Nabu-naid, the demon who seizes the side. No one

[105] Cyrus, *Cyl.*, ll. 26–30, 34–35.

saw him in his own land. In foreign Harran he made an abomination, a no-sanctuary, and for it he made an image which he *called* Sin; it was not the familiar moon-god of Babylonia, but was like the moon at its eclipse. To himself he said: "While I am carrying on this task and am completing the period of lamentation over its destruction, I shall omit the festival and shall allow the New Year's feast to lapse."

After he had completed the work in the third year in another city, not Babylon, he intrusted the camp to his firstborn son. He took his eldest son's hands and intrusted to him the kingship, while he himself took the road to a far country. The army he took about with him throughout all the lands. The troops of Akkad advanced with him, and he set his face toward Tema of Amurru. The prince of Tema they slew with the sword; all the inhabitants of his city and land he massacred. He made that city his abode, the army of Akkad being with him. That city he adorned; they made a palace like that of Babylon.

When war broke out with Cyrus, Nabu-naid boasted of victories without justification. On his memorial stelae he wrote: "At my feet he shall bow down; his lands shall my hands seize, his possessions I shall take as spoil." His own subjects stood up in the city assembly and defied him. Their king had declared that Cyrus did not know the imprint of the stylus, cuneiform writing on a clay tablet. Perhaps, they agreed, Cyrus was in truth illiterate, but the gods themselves would send a vision, the seed of the land would spring up. In sign that *he* was king, the crescent of the gods Anu and Enlil would be passed over him.

Though Nabu-naid did finally re-establish the New Year's feast in the last year of his reign, he continued to confound the rituals and change the ordinances. He spoke a word against the divine commands and uttered impiety. By his own hands, the divine symbols were torn down from the sacred place and were set up again on his own palace. Thus he implied that to some degree he considered himself a god. Two foreigners whom he had appointed to high office, Zeria the temple administrator and Rimut the surveyor, bowed down before him; they obeyed the king's command and executed his orders. They struck together their foreheads; they uttered an oath: "According as the king has spoken, this only we know."

Cyrus entered Babylon and proclaimed peace to them. The royal officer barred the approach to the temple. Cyrus slaughtered a lamb for the offering. The incense for the god's offering he increased. Before the gods he prostrated himself, face to the ground. To do good for the gods was put into his heart; he brought his heart to build, carrying on his head the basket of bricks demanded by the ritual. He completed the city wall of Babylon, which Nebuchadnezzar had made in the grace of his heart; the moat he dug for the wall Imgur-Bel.

The gods, male and female, of Akkad, who had left their shrines, he restored to their dwelling places. Their hearts he pacified, their liver he gladdened. Their lives, already poured out, he made again to live. On the tables their food was placed. Their ruined walls he tore down, and every sanctuary was restored. The royal inscriptions and dedications of Nabu-naid were removed and burned; the winds carried off their ashes. They tore down his statue and erased his name from the sanctuaries. Everything he had left was fired; Cyrus fed it to the flames, for on Babylon his heart was set. As for the sinner himself, may they throw Nabu-naid into prison in the underworld, may mighty bonds inclose his assistants, while in joy Marduk regards kindly Cyrus' own kingdom.[106]

The results of this deliberate propaganda were curiously mixed. Cyrus' attempted "damnation of memory" did not succeed; Nabu-naid was not forgotten. When in the next generation Babylon again revolted, two pretenders in succession claimed to be Nebuchadnezzar, son of Nabu-naid.[107] Herodotus knew him as Labynetus, son of the builder queen, the famous Nitocris.[108] The Greeks forgot Belshazzar, but the Hebrews did not, though they thought him the son of Nebuchadnezzar.

But the propaganda had more subtle influences. Prophecies by a Jewish exile in Babylon so closely parallel the language of the proclamation that we wonder if he might actually have read it.[109] The picture which the Greeks present of the last king of Babylon shows the same ungodly incompetent. Even the great New Year's feast, with the quantities of wine consumed by the drunken soldiers, reappears in the account of the capture by Cyrus in Herodotus and Xenophon and in the drunken revels attributed by the author of Daniel to the last night of Belshazzar.

In the Jewish story of Daniel the character of the Nabu-naid of the verse account has been transferred to the better-known Nebuchadnezzar. He, too, is a heretic. His high officials are foreigners, who are naturally turned into Jews. Their names remind us of Zeria and Rimut. Nebuchadnezzar set up a huge statue which all the world must wor-

---

[106] Verse account; the badly mutilated text has been restored and paraphrased as above to fit the general context.

[107] Beh. §§ 16, 49, 52.   [108] Herod. i. 188.

[109] "Second Isaiah," Isaiah, chaps. 35, 40–55.

ship. For his impiety the king was driven mad and ate grass like the beast of the field. As dreams filled the life of Nabu-naid, so Nebuchadnezzar had his dream; as Nabu-naid was obliged to implore assistance in their interpretation, so was his mightier predecessor. Daniel the Jew interpreted the dream which pronounced the hoped-for doom against Babylon and foretold the future; Belshazzar, the sensual despot, was warned by the writing on the palace wall only when it was too late for repentance.

CYRUS IN BABYLON

In the eyes of men accustomed to mountain scenery, the flat monotonous alluvium must have been terribly depressing. When they suffered the blistering heat of summer, they no doubt longed for their own breezy uplands and must have dreaded the deadly fevers which sapped their strength. But the soil of Babylonia was of a fertility unimagined on the bare plateau, and the wealth of the capital was proverbial. Its peasantry was industrious and submissive. In winter the climate was pleasantly cool, though it rarely touched the freezing-point. When, therefore, the plateau suddenly turned cold and snow crept down the mountain slopes, the Persian monarchs escaped to winter in Babylon; that the luxury there enjoyed might prove insidious they never suspected.

While still residing in Babylon, Cyrus received the kings of Syria who had arrived to pay their devoirs in person and to make the adoration by kissing the royal feet.[110] Control of Phoenicia meant that Cyrus had now at his disposal a second war fleet, quite the equal in numbers and in skill to that of the combined Greek states. It was, however, far more dependable and therefore more highly favored. Henceforth, Greek traders within the empire faced the keenest of competition from merchant princes who ruled city-states much like their own and who were shrewd enough to bear constantly in mind the true source of their prosperity.

While there was a short-lived attempt to organize the Nabataean Arabs in a satrapy under the name "Arabaya," Syria, Phoenicia, and Palestine were joined to Babylonia in one huge satrapy. To the satrap Gobryas the province was officially "Babirush"; to the natives it was "Babylon and Ebir-nari," the Assyrian name for the territory "Across the River" (by which they meant the Euphrates). Over this whole vast stretch of fertile country, Gobryas ruled almost as an independent monarch.[111]

[110] Cyrus, *Cyl.*, ll. 28–30.

[111] Cf. Olmstead, "A Persian Letter in Thucydides," *AJSL*, XLIX (1933), 158 ff.

RESTORATION OF THE TEMPLE AT JERUSALEM; CYRUS IN ECBATANA

Next to Palestine lay Egypt, whose king, Amasis, had made alliance
with Croesus and might therefore soon expect to be attacked. Invasion
of the Nile Valley would be greatly facilitated by a bridgehead across
the desert in Palestine. The road into Egypt was dominated by the
ruined fortress of Jerusalem; its pro-Egyptian upper classes had been
deported to Babylon by Nebuchadnezzar, where they had remained as
exiles and had prospered. Nebuchadnezzar's son, Amel-Marduk, had
attempted to win them over; he had toyed with the idea of restoring
their former king, Jehoiachin.[112] Before the plan could be put into
execution, however, Amel-Marduk was dead, almost certainly assassinated by the nationalists. Henceforth these Jewish exiles remained bitterly hostile to the government. In their disappointment
their prophets had predicted the destruction of Babylon at the hands
of the Medes;[113] when these hopes in their turn failed, they invoked
Cyrus as the Lord's Anointed.[114]

Whatever the practical result of these prophetic effusions in the conquest of Babylon, the Jews had shown their sympathy to the new
regime. Babylon, so far from being destroyed, was actually rewarded
for submission to the conqueror. The Second Isaiah had also predicted
a glorious return to Zion; it was scarcely to be expected that Jews already rich would abandon fertile Babylonia for the barren hills of
Judah, but at least something might be done for their *amour propre*.
Besides, the majority of the former inhabitants were still in Palestine;
deprived of their leaders, they might be expected to have lost their
pro-Egyptian attitude. Cyrus had already returned the gods carried off
by Nabu-naid, not only to their native Babylonian cities, but also to
Assyria and to Elam, and had rebuilt their ruined temples; it would
only be following the same policy if he ordered the temple in Jerusalem to be restored, and, since the Jews now employed no images, to
substitute the temple utensils for the exiled divinity.

Leaving the more prosaic details of satrapal organization to
Gobryas, toward the end of his accession year Cyrus retired from
Babylon and returned to Ecbatana. Aramaic had already been adopted
as the official language of the Persian chancellery in its dealings with
the western satrapies; in it, Cyrus issued from his palace at Ecbatana
during his first regnal year (538) the following decree: "As for the
house of God which is at Jerusalem, let the house be built, the place

[112] II Kings 25:27-30; Jer. 52:31-34.

[113] Jeremiah, chaps. 51-52; Isaiah, chap. 13.   [114] Isaiah, chaps. 35, 40-55.

where they offer fire sacrifice continually; its height shall be ninety feet and its breadth ninety feet, with three courses of great stones and one of timber. And let its cost be given from the king's house. Also, let the gold and silver utensils of the house of God, which Nebuchadnezzar took from the house of God and brought to Babylon, be restored and brought again to the temple which is in Jerusalem, each to its place. And you shall put them in the house of God."[115]

The utensils were taken from the temple of Babylon, by which we naturally understand Esagila, and were handed over to the new governor of Judah, his name, Sheshbazzar, is clearly Babylonian, perhaps Shamash-apal-usur; but, in spite of his pagan name, he *might* have been, as was later claimed,[116] a Jewish prince. With the utensils, Sheshbazzar went on to Jerusalem and began the foundations of the temple.[117] The predictions of the Second Isaiah of a mass migration to a gloriously restored Zion remained as unfulfilled as similar predictions of a destroyed Babylon. Whether even any of the zealots accompanied Sheshbazzar is doubtful; a generation later the inhabitants of Jerusalem were still called "the remnant of the people" or the "people of the land."[118]

A Babylonian tablet suggests that Cyrus was still in Ecbatana a year later. In September, 537, a certain Tadannu lends a pound and a half of silver in half-shekel pieces to Itti-Marduk-balatu, son of Nabu-ahe-iddina, to be repaid in November at the ratio then prevailing at Babylon with thirty-nine talents of dried palm branches, plus one shekel of silver and twelve *qa* of dates. The same witnesses and the same scribe appear frequently on similar documents from Babylon, but this document is written in the city of the land of Agamatanu, that is, Ecbatana. Itti-Marduk-balatu is the head of Babylon's greatest banking-house, the firm of Egibi and Sons. Obviously, he and his friends have come to court, either on royal summons or to present a petition. They have spent so much on expenses, such as bribes demanded by court officials, that a loan is needed before they can undertake the homeward journey.[119] Here we must leave Cyrus, for suddenly and without warning our information comes to an end.[120]

---

[115] Ezra 6:3-5.   [116] Ezra 1:8.   [117] Ezra 5:13-16.

[118] Hag. 1:12, 14; 2:2, 4. Cf. Olmstead, *History of Palestine and Syria* (1931), pp. 541 ff., to be corrected from the present account.

[119] J. P. Strassmaier, *Inschriften von Cyrus* (1900), No. 60.

[120] Best sketch of reign, Weissbach, "Kyros," *PW*, Supplementband, Vol. IV (1924), cols. 1129-66.

Chapter IV

CAMP OF THE PERSIANS

SATRAPAL ORGANIZATION

CYRUS was now monarch of the greatest empire yet known to history. For the government of this wide-extending territory, he adopted in principle the organization first devised by the Assyrians, who replaced the states they had conquered by formal provinces. Each was ruled by a governor with a full staff of subordinates, and all kept in close touch with the central power through frequent exchange of orders and reports.[1] The chief difference between these Assyrian provinces and the twenty satrapies established by Cyrus lay in the fact that the satrapies took the place of far larger independent monarchies.

Each was ruled by a satrap whose title meant literally "protector of the Kingdom."[2] As successor to a former king, ruling a truly enormous territory, he was in point of fact himself a monarch and was surrounded by a miniature court. Not only did he carry on the civil administration but he was also commander of the satrapal levies. When his office became hereditary, the threat to the central authority could not be ignored. To meet this threat, certain checks were instituted; his secretary,[3] his chief financial official,[4] and the general in charge of the garrison stationed in the citadel of each of the satrapal capitals[5] were under the direct orders of, and reported directly to, the great king in person. Still more effective control was exercised by the "king's eye" (or "king's ear" or "king's messenger"),[6] who every year made a careful inspection of each province.[7]

[1] Cf. Olmstead, *History of Assyria* (1933), pp. 24, 146, 202, 606 ff.

[2] Khshathrapavan (cf. C. F. Lehmann-Haupt, "Satrap," *PW*, II Reihe, III [1921], 82 ff.).

[3] Herod. iii. 128; scribes, Herod. vii. 100; viii, 90; Esther 3:12; 8:9.

[4] Old Persian *ganzabara* (cf. E. Schürer, *Geschichte der jüdischen Volkes*, II [4th ed., 1907], 325–26, and G. G. Cameron, *Persepolis Treasury Tablets* [1947]).

[5] Xen. *Cyrop.* viii. 6. 3.

[6] Herod. iii. 34. 77.

[7] Aeschyl. *Pers.* 960; Herod. i. 114; Aristophan. *Achar.* 92; Xen. *Oeconom.* 4; *Cyrop.* viii. 6. 16; viii. 2. 10.

SITE OF PARSAGARDA

When the Persians entered their future homeland to which they gave their name of Parsa, they were still nomads on the march. Their royal tribe, we are told, was that of the Pasargadae.[8] When we find that the same name is assigned to their earliest capital by the majority of Greek writers, we might assume that the capital was so named from the tribe. One historian, however, calls the city Parsagada, while another interprets its name as meaning "Camp of the Persians."[9] Such an interpretation would imply that the true name was something like Parsagard. In actual fact the ruins of the settlement suggest a typical Aryan camp, for no trace of a wall can be detected.

The first capital of the Persians lay on the great north-south road of the plateau on its way from Ecbatana to the Persian Gulf. Traces of this road may still be observed in rock cuttings at the northeast and southwest corners of a small plain, nine by fifteen miles in size. To the west, southwest, and northwest it is bounded by fairly high mountains; the eastern hills are lower, and beneath them the "Median River" winds through the plain and enters at the southwest corner a still more winding gorge, through which the rock-cut road meanders. The elevation is high, over 6,300 feet above sea-level; in winter the stiff winds chill to the bone, and for as much as half the year the chill may be felt in the early morning. The winter snows fall on the plain and on the mountains, adding to the water available in the spring and summer, so necessary for the irrigation of good soil throughout the midyear droughts and until the harvest.

In the northwest corner, under the higher hills, was the primitive settlement. Today the site is marked only by masses of reddish potsherds, whose color dates them to Achaemenid times, and by small column bases of stone which archeologists assign approximately to the period of Cyrus. The latter show that the houses followed typical Iranian architectural design. We may therefore visualize them as of wood construction with wooden columns resting on stone bases and holding up the flat roofs of the porches and perhaps the beams which supported a gable roof of the main structure.

[8] Herod. i. 125; iv. 167.

[9] Curt. v. 6. 10; x. 1. 22; Anaximenes, Frag. 19(J). Cf. discussion in Olmstead, "Darius and His Behistun Inscription," *AJSL*, LV (1938), 394, n. 8.

SHRINES

A mile and a half to the southeast lay a rectangular sacred inclosure, the long side oriented southeast and northwest. It reached a short distance across a smaller stream, the Cyrus, which entered the plain from the hills to the north and formed an affluent of the Median River. Its waters, pure and cold from its source in the near-by rocky heights, would delight the heart of Anahita, who herself leaped down from similar heights. Close to its left bank, the inclosure shut in two open-air altars, built of white limestone on black limestone foundations, and with hollowed-out interiors. That to the right consisted of a single block on which was set another block cut with seven steps leading to the summit, which in turn was triply stepped and covered with cup holes. That to the left was also a single block capped by a flatter monolith. Here, then, were the original altars to the tribal divinities, Anahita and Ahuramazda.

Later, a more elaborate shrine was erected at the southwest corner of the inclosure. For the most part, the structure was built outside the inclosure itself, as were three subsidiary buildings, for the core of rock which dictated its position enforced a line slightly askew across this southwestern tip and permitted an almost exact orientation toward the east. Around this core of rock was built a sort of mound, 240 by 133 feet in size, which rose in six terraces to imitate roughly a Babylonian temple tower, but the entire height of the six was only 20 feet. The lower three terraces were protected by retaining walls of limestone set dry; behind them was the fill of debris. The upper three were constructed of mud bricks and covered by limestone. At either end of the eastern front, flights of stairs led to the next higher terrace. No remains of a superstructure have been detected. In all probability, therefore, the summit was crowned only by more altars. The "temple" of Anahita, in which the successors of Cyrus were purified by ancient ceremonies before accession and in whose recesses the younger Cyrus hid to assassinate his brother Artaxerxes, must be sought in one of the buildings north of the terraced mound and well outside the inclosure walls.[10]

CYRUS' PARK AND PALACES

Beyond low hills, and a half-mile distant by air line, lay another inclosure. It, too, was a quadrangular area, in this case oriented duly to the points of the compass; it was surrounded by a thirteen-foot wall

[10] Plut. *Artox.* 3.

of mud brick on stone foundations. Within it, the palaces and their subsidiary structures were oriented southwest and northeast. That they were placed in the midst of a regular paradise or park is shown by their isolated positions and by the water channels, a basin, and the remains of pavilions scattered over the otherwise free spaces which once must have been filled with trees.

The main entrance to the park was at the south corner, where a monumental quadrangular gateway projected from the inclosure wall. Its roof was supported by two rows of four great unfluted columns of white limestone which rested on plain black limestone disks and white foundation blocks. In the shorter sides were the passageways, guarded at entrance and exit by huge winged bulls of a lighter grayish-black limestone and resting on massive black socles. The pair at the exit into the paradise were human-headed. Very small doors led off from small rooms on either side of the exit.

Two projecting white limestone pilasters formed the north room; facing the entrance were carved two protecting genii two feet high, raising their hands in blessing; like their Assyrian predecessors, they were four-winged. From neck to ankle, a sort of toga wrapped the body. The edge down the side opening was decorated with rosettes and fringes. Bands of rosettes also showed above the elbows, while the feet were shod in the late Elamite fashion. The curled beard was slight, and the hair hung down the neck in short plaits, held in place by a circular lip with bangles hanging below the ear. From broad, flat goats' horns rose an Egyptian symbol widely employed during the centuries preceding by the peoples of western Asia: between uraeus serpents and ordinary disks were three solar disks, ostrich feathers, and balls, which surrounded tied bundles of reeds. Above, in Persian, Elamite, and Akkadian, could be read: "I am Cyrus, the king, the Achaemenid." Since he bears only this simple title, Cyrus must have erected this gateway while he was vassal king of Anshan and before his revolt against Astyages.

Exactly the same inscriptional formula dates to the same period the audience hall some two hundred yards to the northwest and across a little creek. Its mud-brick walls were ten feet thick and rested on massive white limestone foundations, heavily reinforced where the pressure from above was greater. When stone doors and niches were inserted in the mud brick, black limestone was substituted for the wood of earlier structures and afforded a pleasing contrast. Black also were the pavement slabs, large and irregularly fitted together.

The front of the audience hall, facing southwest, extended for a hundred and eighty-seven feet. A trifle more than a hundred were devoted to the central porch; the remainder, to two small corner rooms. Similar porches decorated the side walls; the back porch was longer, since here the corner rooms were missing. To either side of the black stone doorway which led from the front to the inside, two rows of four smooth white columns rose from black plinths to a height of twenty feet. The upper half of the windowed central hall towered high above the columns.

The door jambs at the front and in the rear (a survival of the carved orthostate blocks well known from Hittite and Assyrian architecture) were both flanked by the same scene: three priests, barefoot but clothed in tight, ankle-length robes, driving a bull to the sacrifice. Similar reliefs decorated the jambs of the side gateways, but now the subject was the guardian divinities, represented in Assyrian fashion either in entirely human form or with eagle's head and claws affixed to a human torso. Like their Assyrian progenitors, they bore two pairs of wings and were clad in the same abbreviated dress.

Just within the doorway at the front was the long side of the audience chamber, whose roof was supported by two rows of four columns each. The aisle thus formed led to a black stone niche at either end. The columns were slender to an extreme, for, although forty feet in height, they were but three and a half feet in circumference. The base was a flat black disk, an integral part of the foundation block. Upon the plain white shafts were set capitals, or rather, more correctly, impost blocks, which represented the forefronts of two animals crouching back to back. Among the animals might be recognized horses, bulls, lions, or composite-horned lions wearing the feathered crown of the Assyrian human-headed bull. The disproportion between the height of these excessively slim columns and the more squat pilasters, which formed the inscribed antae at the ends of the columned porches, clearly proves that the great audience chamber was lighted by high-set windows. Plates of gold covered the wooden paneling and gleamed in the sunlight.

Four hundred yards deeper into the park lay the palace, 250 by 140 feet in size. Its front was a porch of twenty wooden columns in two rows 20 feet high. The polished pilasters at either end bore the now familiar Cyrus inscription. At the rear the porch was shorter, since the palace in this respect was the reverse of the audience hall and placed the two corner rooms to the back. Deep cuttings into the side of the pilaster bonded in the mud-brick walls, while further cuttings at the top, by their irregular forms, justify the restoration of entablature beams, rafters, roof guards of mud, and battlements.

A single door to the right center, a necessary precaution against unauthorized glimpses of the interior, led into the great hall, 73 by 80 feet. The roof was upheld by six rows of columns, five to the row. The lower supporting block of the column was veined in black and white; the upper was black. Then came a high torus with horizontal channeling which was continued in the same block by the smooth white shaft. Its upper half was covered by stucco painted in vivid colors such as lapis lazuli blue, turquoise green, copper-red green, madder red, a more vivid red, and yellow. In contrast to this riot of garish color, the pavement was black set in white.

The back and front doorways presented the same scene four times: The king, in the long sweeping robe of royalty hanging in folds between the legs, shod with the royal footgear, and bearing the royal scepter, could be seen leaving the palace for an outdoor promenade in the park. Eyebrows and eyelashes, not to mention the folds and rosettes of his robe, were once filled in with gold. Behind the king, in his own proper dress, walked a smaller servant who no doubt carried over the royal head the parasol, confined in use to the king since the days of Assyrian Sargon. Over the scene of departure a trilingual inscription gave the royal titles and invoked a blessing on his house, his portrait, and his inscription. On the fold of his robe, in Elamite and Akkadian, he added: "Cyrus, great king, Achaemenian."[11]

The change from mere "king" to the Assyrian title of "great king" shows that, by the time the reliefs were engraved, Cyrus had revolted and had begun his career of conquest. By this date he had probably also erected still farther north the fire temple; though today so badly ruined, it may be described in terms of the almost completely preserved duplicate in front of the tomb of Darius, as an exact copy even to the dimensions. In its general aspect, the fire temple was simply a reproduction in more durable limestone of a typical high fort such as Assyrian reliefs show guarding a Median hill town. It was inclosed in a rectangular sacred precinct whose mud bricks represented the wall of the settlement, as the interior buildings with square stone column bases did the houses of the inhabitants. The mountain height on which the tower stood appeared as a series of three wide low platforms outside which began the narrow steep staircase climbing to the

[11] E. Herzfeld, *Altpersische Inschriften* (1938), No. 2.

small lone door high up in the face. The lowest story, half the total height, showed neither entrance nor window, only the tall narrow rectangular depressions which originally were arrow slots. In the second story was the door, the wood represented by the black limestone, under a simple molding, which in turn was below a tiny false window, once the peephole. Behind the false entrance may be seen the holes made to receive the posts on which the door valves were swung. Three rows of two false windows, each row of differing size, with double frames of dark limestone, indicated the three upper stories. The roof was held up by posts at the corners, now ordinary pilasters. A dentilated molding corresponded to the projecting heads of the ceiling beams. Huge slabs, with slight pyramidical slope, laid across the width to form the roof. Windows and arrow slots had become mere decoration, for the sacred fire burning within had to be protected from sudden drafts and would itself give sufficient light.

On a low spur of a hill at the northeast corner of the plain and overlooking the rock-cut road along which he had watched the defeated Medes streaming back to Ecbatana,[12] Cyrus began a platform for a new building to dominate this strategic passage. Above the road the frontage was 775 feet, and the platform itself rose to a height of 40 feet; where it ran back to be lost in the hill, the ground outside rose to meet it. The masonry was laid in horizontal courses, of differing heights to avoid the appearance of monotony; headers and stretchers were carefully alternated at the corners, and the blocks were held together without mortar by iron swallow-tail cramps. Behind this was another wall of carefully dressed smaller stones, and behind that was the fill. Before even the platform had been completed, Cyrus left to fight the Massagetae. He never returned, and the work was stopped. Some of the outer blocks had been dressed down in place, leaving only a narrow, chiseled border; the upper tiers retain to this day the mason's marks and the rough bosses, just as when they left the quarry.

Southwest of the palace group, Cyrus had prepared his last resting-place. Like the fire temple, it rested on a platform, 48 by 44 feet at the base, and ascending in six great steps of irregular height to a total of 17 feet. On the seventh step was placed the tomb proper, constructed of huge white limestone blocks carefully tied together by iron cramps. Its form was that of a plain house whose sharply gabled roof betrayed its northern origin. Cyme moldings on cornice and around the base were its only ornament. Presumably it bore the usual

12 Strabo xv. 3. 8.

brief royal inscription, for, according to Onesicritus, who with Alexander saw the monument, the Greek and Persian inscription read: "Here I lie, Cyrus, king of kings." Aristobulus, Alexander's general, expanded the brief but dignified epitaph to fit Greek ideas as to what would have been appropriate: "O man, I am Cyrus, who acquired the empire for the Persians and was king of Persia; grudge me not therefore my monument."[13]

DEATH AND BURIAL OF CYRUS

Cyrus' death had come suddenly. The half-nomad Massagetae, a Saka tribe across the Araxes River, were threatening the northeast frontier. A war of reprisal became inevitable, and Cyrus determined to lead it in person. Leaving the crown prince Cambyses as king of Babylon, the aging monarch started off. A bridge was built to cross the Araxes, the boundary of the empire, and Cyrus invaded the enemy country. At first, he enjoyed a certain success; then, lured into the interior by the queen Tomyris, he was defeated in a great battle and was himself wounded. Three days after, the once mighty conqueror was dead, the victim of an obscure Saka queen. Cambyses recovered his father's corpse and gave it proper burial in the tomb already prepared at the Camp of the Persians.[14]

Stooping to enter the low, imitation timber portal, only 31 by 54 inches, and pushing back the swinging stone door, the funeral attendants found themselves in total darkness, since the first door must be closed for space to draw back the second. Crowded together in the windowless tomb chamber, $10\frac{1}{2}$ by $7\frac{1}{2}$ feet, and 8 feet to the flat ceiling, they prepared the last obsequies by the light of a flickering torch. The corpse was placed in a tublike sarcophagus of gold which rested on a funeral couch whose feet also were of wrought gold. A table was set for offerings, which included short Persian swords, necklaces, and earrings of precious stones inset in gold. The candys and chiton of Babylonian manufacture, Median trousers, robes dyed blue, purple, and other colors, Babylonian tapestries and *kaunakes* clothing, all were heaped up so that the deceased monarch might enter the afterworld of his Aryan fathers with due pomp and correct circumstance. A tiny house was built near by for the Magian guardians, who were to hold their post by hereditary succession. They were granted rations, each day a sheep, with flour and wine; once a month a horse was given for the Aryan sacrifice to the hero. The tomb was surrounded by the garden paradise, whose canals watered the grass in the

13 *Ibid.* 3. 7.
14 Herod. i. 201 ff.; Ctes. *Pers.* xi, Epit. 37–39; Diod. ii. 42.2; Berossus, Frag. 55(S).

meadow and the trees of every species which were left to wave over Cyrus' last resting-place.[15]

ELEMENTS OF PERSIAN ART

Even in its terribly ruined state, the site of Cyrus' metropolis exhibits a fully developed national culture.[16] Inspiration may have come, perhaps through Susa, from Assyrian winged bulls and genii, from Hittite reliefs on black orthostates, from Babylonian or Assyrian palace platforms, from Egyptian religious symbols. The Persians were not the first to employ the column.

Nevertheless, the whole is blended into a new art whose origins must be sought in as yet unexcavated sites. This art is fully mature, though in so many respects utterly different from its immediate successor at the better-preserved Persepolis. As its special characteristic, we may cite its recollection of a direct ancestry in the wooden architecture of the north, remembered in the gabled roof, the columned porch, and the ground plan. Unique is its substitution of white limestone for the original walls of mud brick, in pleasing contrast to the black limestone which reproduced the wood of door and window frames. The few bits of sculpture which have survived prove that the artists who carved the reliefs already recognized that these reliefs must be subordinated to architectural design; they also show the Iranian feeling of rhythm, made clear by the repetition of each scene four times. Peculiar to this art is the use of the orthostate block relief, no longer necessitated by the architectural design, whose sculptures are not in relief but are sunk into the surface of the door jamb, which serves as a frame to the panel. The figures are therefore not rounded but flat, never extending beyond the line of the orthostate surface. Their drapery is undercut, a practice unknown to Greeks for at least another century.

The varied elements of this art, whether derived from native or or from foreign sources, have all been infused by the Iranian spirit. We must admire the technical adequacy of this new art; once we have reconstructed its buildings in the light of a trained imagination, its sense of restrained beauty cannot but delight us. In not a few respects, Parsagarda, although terribly ruined, is superior to the more grandiose Persepolis.

[15] Aristobulus, Frag. 37(J), in Arr. *Anab.* vi. 29. 4 ff.; Strabo xv. 3. 7.; Plut *Alex.* 69. 2; Curt. x. 1. 30. For the often-described tomb cf. especially F. Sarre and E. Herzfeld, *Iranische Felsreliefs* (1910), pp. 166 ff.

[16] Sarre-Herzfeld, *op. cit.*, pp. 174 ff.; E. Herzfeld, *Archäologische Mittheilungen aus Iran*, I (1929), 4 ff.; *Iran in the Ancient East* (1941), pp. 211–12, 221 ff., 256 ff.

Chapter V

LIFE AMONG THE SUBJECT PEOPLES

IN THE Median and Persian homelands, life was relatively simple. Cyaxares, Astyages, and Cyrus might erect palaces and collect around them a royal court, because the taxes for construction of the one and upkeep of the other were paid by freemen of their own people. The chief industry of the plateau, pasturing great flocks of sheep and goats in the mountain valleys or herding the sacred kine, was practiced by seminomads. On the plains a few had settled down to a primitive agriculture with the aid of *qanat* irrigation. Where title was held to houses or to individual plots of soil, it would be in fee simple.

ELAMITE AND BABYLONIAN RECORDS

By the conquest of Elam and Babylonia, Cyrus made contact with a far older and more complicated civilization. These countries showed their antiquity especially by their long-continued employment of written documents. For some twenty-five centuries Babylonia had known bookkeeping and had developed a wide variety of forms according to which all business transactions of the slightest importance were recorded on clay tablets. A few centuries later the Elamites modified the cuneiform signs for their own language and imitated the administrative and business formulas of their neighbors, the Babylonians. Although the Persians in turn invented an alphabet of cuneiform signs for their royal inscriptions, this alphabet seems never to have been utilized for other purposes. For the life of the subject peoples during the Achaemenid period, we must therefore find our sources in the clay tablets written in Elamite, Akkadian, or Aramaic.

Fortunately, such tablets have been recovered by the thousands. When we have copied the whole collection, something like a half-million in all, and have interpreted and analyzed the enormous amount of data thereby presented, we shall possess a complete social and economic history of an important segment of the ancient Near East reaching back almost three thousand years—more than a half of man's recorded history.[1]

[1] Olmstead, "Materials for an Economic History of the Ancient Near East," *Journal of Economic and Business History*, II (1930), 219 ff.

ARCHIVES AT SUSA

By his conquest of Elam, Cyrus fell heir to its ancient capital Susa, whose location on the edge of the Babylonian alluvium had long since resulted in the wide use of inscribed tablets. Although the great mass of Elamite tablets dates from the generation following Cyrus, we are fortunate in having over three hundred which can with little question be assigned to his reign. One refers to Cyrus himself. Another mentions a Lydian and must have been written after the conquest of Sardis in 547. A third, which speaks of the king of Egypt, obviously comes before 525.

These tablets are from the archives of the revenue officials Kuddakaka and Huban-haltash, Elamite subjects of Persia. They permit more than a glimpse of contemporary Susa. As might be expected, the late period of the Elamite language is indicated by the wide use of purely Babylonian ideograms and by not a few Babylonian and Persian loan-words. The tablets are properly authenticated by seals. Now and then the seal inscription is a dedication to a Babylonian divinity such as Marduk or Nabu. One gives our earliest example of a common Persian motif, the monarch wearing the battlemented war crown and poniarding the hostile monster. Among the names of individuals mentioned, Elamites are naturally in the majority. There is, however, a plentiful sprinkling of Babylonian and Persian names, for Susa lies between the two countries.

Business documents follow Babylonian formulas. As a typical example we may cite: "Ten shekels of silver, belonging to Ummanunu, which Rishi-kidin received in March; the tablet Huban-nugash, son of Hutrara, wrote." This is a standard formula for an individual loan by a private banker, a member of the new class which was just emerging into prominence in contemporary Babylonia. There are Babylonian parallels for such loans without mention of interest. An even closer parallel is found in another loan by this same Ummanunu: Huban-api receives six shekels of gold; if the loan is not repaid next month, interest shall increase. The tablet also proves that Elamite bankers were acquainted with the same tricks employed by their fellows in Babylonia; on the inner tablet the six gold shekels are lent at the unusually favorable rate of one pound of silver, that is, at a ratio of ten to one; but on the envelope (the only part available for inspection unless it were broken in the presence of the judge), the loan is discounted one gold shekel, the more usual twelve-to-one ratio. Other tablets deal with the sale of sheep or the assignment of sheep to shepherds.

The great majority of the archive tablets, however, are mere lists of objects received by the revenue officials. Dull as they may appear, they, too, have much to add to our picture. Easily first in quantity among the revenues collected are textiles in a bewildering variety of colors and local styles. Median tunics are manufactured in the palace gates as a royal monopoly or are turned in by North Syrian "Hittites." We hear of one hundred and twenty garments made for the trade and of two shekels' weight of the precious purple used in the dyeing.

Other tablets offer lists of army supplies. There is here mention of bows, a few of Assyrian form; there are strings for the bows, arrows and the reeds from which they are to be manufactured, spears, shields and the skins by which they are to be covered. Some of these supplies are to be furnished by the gods, Hutran and Inshushinak, the great gods of Susa; from other sources, the gods themselves are supplied. For instance, the temple tower of one god's temple receives one hundred and twenty dyed garments, an iron object weighing seven and a half pounds, together with five pounds of incense. All in all, we have a surprisingly large amount of information on the daily life of Susa during this one brief period.[2]

ADMINISTRATION OF BABYLONIA

For no portion of the three thousand years of Babylonian social and economic history are we so well supplied with documentary evidence as for the two and a quarter centuries after 625. More than ten thousand administrative and commercial documents, almost equally divided between the Chaldaean and early Achaemenid periods, have already been published and analyzed. When we add six hundred letters, to and from the highest officials, which were being sent during the very years when political control was shifting from Semites to Iranians, we find ourselves in possession of the material for an account of administrative, social, and economic changes quite unparalleled for so ancient an epoch.

Among the documents we may consult are loans of seed, food, and silver, ordinary contracts of the merchant, sales of landed property whether of houses or of fields, leases for the same and receipts for the payment of rent, slave sales in great numbers, lists of serfs on the great estates and transactions with them, other lists of officials or of free peasants at work, apprentice agreements, reports of officials high and low, and records of trials and judicial decisions. A new chapter in the

[2] V. Scheil, *Textes Elamites-Anzanites*, Vol. III (1907); *ibid.*, IV (1911), 310 ff.

history of prices may be written and may even be illustrated by elaborate graphs. The whole life of the Babylonians, nobility and commons alike, passes before our eyes in all its varied interest.[3]

In his dealings with his Babylonian subjects, Cyrus was "king of Babylon, king of lands." By thus insisting that the ancient line of monarchs remained unbroken, he flattered their vanity, won their loyalty, and masked the fact of their servitude. He secured their gratitude by returning the captive gods. But it was Gobryas the satrap who represented the royal authority after the king's departure. Ordinarily he is mentioned in our documents only as the king's substitute, by whom the contracting parties take oath and against whom a violation of the agreement is sin. In the letters he appears now and then as intervening directly in local administration. Appeals from the decision of the local judges might be carried directly to the satrapal court. In general, however, immediate control of local affairs was vested in the "king's messenger," whose approaching visit of inspection caused many an official anxious hours. Overseeing of temple finances was also placed in the hands of royal officers. Otherwise, Cyrus quieted the Babylonians by adopting the familiar administration and even at first retaining the former officials at their posts.

The letters, however, do show a definite tightening-up under the new regime. This was necessary, for the last days of Nabu-naid pictured a growing disorganization. Graft was rampant. A typical letter is the complaint of Nabu-mukin-zer to Nadinnu: "Is your act one of brotherly kindness? You have said: 'Whether you order something great or small, I shall obey.' Though you know that I need four sheep for my 'gift,' and wish to impose a tax on the Rasibtu people, nevertheless you prevent it. Is not that the way a taskmaster would act? Do not delay a single night, but send it now!" Another typical letter is that from Bel-zer-ibni to this same Nabu-mukin-zer: "Every month the king's messenger comes and inspects the posts. No one is ever at his post. The temple officials have come to see about it. Since the messenger has not yet reported it to the king, let the man in charge of the cattle who has left his post be thrown into chains and sent here."[4]

How the new regime worked in practice may be illustrated by the

[3] Waldo H. Dubberstein, "Comparative Prices in Later Babylonia (625–400 B.C.)," *AJSL*, LVI (1939), 20 ff.; cf. *JAOS*, LII (1932), 304. Publication of Dubberstein's complete study must await the conclusion of the war; meanwhile, another section is available in typescript at the library of the Oriental Institute and has been utilized in this brief survey.

[4] A. T. Clay, *Miscellaneous Inscriptions in the Yale Babylonian Collection* (1915), Nos. 26 and 139.

case of the archthief Gimillu. Taking advantage of the administrative breakdown, he had appropriated numerous animals belonging to the Lady of Uruk, though her star brand proved them Ishtar's property. Without consent of the deputies and scribes of the temple Eanna, he took sheep from the pasture lands of the temple. He induced his own shepherd to steal from Ishtar's shepherd five mother ewes already branded. Another temple steward sold him three sheep at a shekel each. His brother seized a branded goat on its way from Larsa in the very gate of the city. The governors and scribes of the temple ordered Gimillu to seize the temple shepherd who had not brought his sheep to Eanna for ten years; after extorting ten *kur* of barley, two silver shekels, and a sheep for "protection," Gimillu threw the son of the shepherd into iron fetters and left him.

Threatened reforms affected official nerves, and Ardi-Gula advises Shamash-uballit no longer to be negligent about Gimillu's misdeeds, his failure to perform the appointed task work and to pay his contributions for the New Year's gift and the impost on the fruits. The shepherd is coming to make an accounting; great is the debit, so debit the amount owed and give only the balance to Gimillu. Shamash-zer-iqisha warns Gimillu that the messenger of the administrator has come and urges the accused to go quietly with him.

In September of 538, Gimillu was brought to trial before the assembly, council, and officials of Uruk; the list of those present is a *Who's Who* of that city. No less than four temple scribes were needed to take down the testimony. Man after man witnessed to thefts. When Nidintum confessed that he had received three shekels for the sheep he had stolen, they published in the assembly the document, which read: "The silver to Gimillu was given." A second witness testified to the theft of his sheep and a goat by Gimillu's brother, while a third swore that "that goat in my presence Nadina took." Gimillu himself admitted: "I sent my brother Nadina." One theft Gimillu did not deny: "That young lamb I took," but urged as a mitigating circumstance that he "left two other sheep for the holy day!" On another occasion, while admitting a theft, he protested that he passed up the opportunity to steal two shekels and a kid. Nevertheless, the verdict imposed restitution—sixty animals for each one stolen; the total fine amounted to 92 cows, 302 sheep, and one pound and ten shekels of silver.

Not at all downcast by the adverse verdict, Gimillu appealed to the satrapal court at Babylon and meanwhile financed the appeal by continuing his thefts. The priests of Eanna and the high officials of Uruk were ordered to make their appearance at court with a witness who under severe penalties was to testify about these fresh thefts. Gimillu's appeal was disallowed. Up to April, 534, as he writes the "priest" of Uruk, he was not permitted to leave Babylon; "You, my lord, see how I limp very much." However, Nabu-taris, the butcher of the Lord Bel Marduk, and of his temple Esagila, raised five pounds of silver and gave them to three men of influence. Gimillu insists that there is no barley tax debited against him except the 1,100 *kur* of barley raised for the temple tax of Eanna. For over ten years he has requested seed barley, but the officials reply that they can do nothing for him because they are detained in Ur. "What are the temples of Eanna and Egishunugi," he demands, "that this is so? *You* are the administrator of both? What is right before my lord, that let my lord do! May the Lord God free your slave and send him home. The Lord and Nabu know that formerly I was fixed in the presence of my Lord God for five hundred *kur* of barley; see, I have sent Nabu-taris about the matter to my lord."

Whether it was due to Gimillu's outrageous flattery of his superior, comparing him to the god Marduk himself, or whether the five pounds of silver proved more effective, by December the convicted thief was back home and the balance of the oxen of the fifth year's impost was yoked and given to him! Considering his difficulty in keeping his hands from what was intrusted to him, we are surprised to find Nabu-mukin-apal ordering the staff of gold bars placed in Gimillu's boat, even though Gimillu's son was to be kept as hostage in the storehouse; let no one so much as lift his feet until Gimillu's return.

Then Gimillu and Adad-shum-usur, the chief administrator of the satrap, bring temple serfs to the goddess of Uruk and place them in charge of Nabu-mukin-apal and Nabu-ah-iddina. They request Gimillu to tell them what the satrap commanded, for, if only they know, they will perform it. Gimillu replies: "Gobryas gave no command about them. As for the people I brought and showed you, let them perform the assigned work in Eanna until you have received the command of Gobryas about them. As for the men among them whom I have freed from chains, by the tablet of Ishtar of Uruk I bear the responsibility for their not escaping."[5]

[5] A. Tremayne, *Records from Erech* (1925), Nos. 7, 31, 35, 46, 58, 82, 73, 70; Clay, *op. cit.*, Nos. 185, 8; C. A. Keiser, *Letters and Contracts from Erech* (1917), Nos. 63, 19; G. Contenau, *Contrats néobabyloniens*, Vol. II (1929), Nos. 125 and 134.

SOCIAL LIFE IN BABYLONIA

During preceding centuries the population of Babylonia had become definitely stratified, though perhaps it would be going too far to speak of castes. At the head was the king and the members of his court, whose social rank was due only to the fact that they were the "king's friends." Like the satraps and the members of their courts, they were outsiders imposed by foreign conquest upon the native Babylonian society. If Babylonian nobles might be included in this Persian official class, they owed their standing to their own position at the head of Babylonian society.

Members of this aristocracy of birth and wealth held the most important offices of the state. Their names appear frequently in every type of document. They may always be detected by their genealogical formula; while ordinary folk are given only a paternity, nobles have also an ancestor. This ancestor, of whom the individual is a "descendant," may be a definite individual or he may be indicated by a title, such as weaver, fuller, builder, fisher, smith, herdsman, or physician. One such family may be traced for seven centuries at Uruk through the late Assyrian, Chaldaean, Achaemenid, and Seleucid ages, and into the Parthian period, where cuneiform sources fail us. Further study of these genealogies will give us valuable information on the great families.

Another of the families was that of Egibi, the leading banking firm of Babylon. We shall later trace its sudden breakup after the death of its head, Itti-Marduk-balatu. A few families may be called scholars, like that of Nabu-rimanni, the famous astronomer, known to the Greeks as Naburianus, who is a witness during the reign of Darius, and who is "descendant of the priest of the moon-god." Others may be officials, as the group named the "descendant of the man of salt," otherwise the collector of the salt tax. The truly great families did not specialize; every department of business and of administration witnessed the activities of their members.

All nobles were full citizens (*mar banu*) of the Babylonian free cities, which jealously guarded their rights as guaranteed by Assyrian charters.[6] In numbers they formed the merest fraction of the population. They held their urban properties in fee simple and bought and sold by ordinary contracts. In theory their landed possessions were subject to family claims, but in practice such claims were barred through stringent penalties. Agricultural lands beyond the city walls were held

[6] Olmstead, *History of Assyria* (1923), pp. 525 ff.

by the "bow" tenure. Originally the obligation was to furnish a bow-man to the armed forces, but it was now commuted for a money payment.

These citizens met in formal assembly (*puhru*) to make important judicial decisions. Over the assembly presided the "headman of the council," assisted by a "second" and with the "king's headman" as prosecuting attorney. Ordinary routine administration was in the hands of the council (*kinishtu* or *kiniltu*), a body of some twenty-five of the leading men (*rabe bania*) who held high office in the local temple, from which the council often took its name. One might be the temple "butcher," another the "baker," etc. Undoubtedly by this time the titles had become purely honorific. After the headman of the council came in rank his "deputy" (*qipu*). Royal control was exercised by the "king's headman" and the "official who was over the king's basket," the chief fiscal agent of the temple.[7] The temple was under an "administrator" (*shatammu*), who also had his "dep-uty." Nominally the latter was subordinate to the "administrator," but the letters prove that he held the dominant authority. The "priest" (*shangu*) had likewise become an administrative official. Also important were the "officials who are over the payment," the income from fields belonging to temple or king. Royal messengers made frequent trips of inspection and kept the court informed of what was going on.

The most primitive form of taxation—forced labor—remained in use, especially for the upkeep of the canals, without which the coun-try could not live. Names of those employed on the forced labor, and those who died or escaped, were carefully registered, as were the barley and dates provided as food. Modern methods, however, per-mitted commutation in cash for those rich enough to afford it. Much of the taskwork was done by the temple itself through its serfs and dependents.

A large part of the taxes was collected in kind. That a considerable proportion of these revenues came from the temples is shown by the full title of one such finance officer, the "official who is over the king's basket in the temple Eanna." The temple received "sacrifices" (*niqu*) which still remained in theory at least "free-will offerings" of animals (*ginu*) and produce (*satukku*), though in actual practice they had be-come definitely imposed contributions which might or might not be used for sacrifices. The yearly "tithe" (*eshru*) was now paid to the

[7] Cf. the Roman use of *fiscus*, "basket."

state. The "total" tax imposed on produce was from 20 to 30 per cent of the whole. Another tax paid to the irrigation inspector (*gugallu*) and to the tax-collector (*makkesu*) was levied primarily on dates. A direct tax for the state (*telittu*) was collected from landholders in silver. Transport by canal paid "toll" (*miksu*), while octroi dues were charged at the city gate.

"Citizens," whether bankers, merchants, priests, temple or government officials, formed an upper middle class. Of a lower middle class—bakers, brewers, butchers, carpenters, laundrymen, coppersmiths, artisans—we hear much less. Those who are mentioned are generally on temple staffs, and we have seen that often the office must have been purely honorary. While a few members of this lower middle class received fairly good wages for specialized tasks, in the majority of cases it is impossible to distinguish their payment from that of the unskilled laborers.

An enormous increase in the slave population during this period brought hardships on the lower middle class. Slaves were taking the place of women in industry and were thus causing decreases in family incomes. More and more slaves were being apprenticed to trades which formerly had been carried on by freemen. Slave barbers and bakers made their appearance. Slaves were permitted to engage in business for themselves and tended to supplant the small merchant.

Threat of slave competition extended to the free laborer, though not to the same degree. Although forced labor might be used for excavation and repair of canals, strangely enough in this very period the majority of canal workers seem to have been free. Numerous tablets list their pay in silver or in produce. Hired men were especially in demand at harvest, and now and then we hear the complaint that the supply was insufficient. No wonder that there were occasions when the pay for such seasonal laborers was surprisingly high.

Theoretically, the status of the serf (*shirku*) was lower than that of the free laborer, but actually his lot must often have been happier. Although he did not receive pay, this did not much differentiate him from the hired man, whose monthly wage of a shekel of silver was, as a rule, a mere matter of bookkeeping. Like the present-day sharecropper of our own South, the Babylonian free laborer received his monthly wage as a charge account which always would be overdrawn. The serf might "rent" a farm on shares or promise a certain fixed amount of the produce to the owner. He might often rise to a position of considerable influence on the great temple estates and might execute agreements in his own name to such an extent that often we fail to realize his servile condition. The serf class was recruited from children of freemen whose parents had dedicated them to the easier life of service for the deity; men of wealth might dedicate their slaves for similar serfdom after their own deaths.

At the bottom of the social scale was the slave. Free men might be enslaved for debt or as punishment for a crime. Parents might sell their children in time of stress. Foreign names betray the captive taken in war or the slave brought from abroad. Most slaves, however, were born in the home, since marriage of slaves for breeding purposes was profitable. Unless he ran away from his master or falsely claimed free birth, the slave was, as a rule, well treated. Often he was intrusted with responsible duties, and on rare occasions he was freed. As we have seen, he competed more and more with the freeman. Slave sales form the largest single group of our documents and testify to an enormous increase in the slave population. While the serf is most often associated with the great temple estates, slaves more generally are found in possession of the upper classes.

ECONOMIC LIFE IN BABYLONIA

Persian conquest did not seriously disturb the commercial Babylonians. Not more than twelve days, at the most, elapsed after the death of Nabu-naid before commercial documents were being dated by the accession year of Cyrus. The same families dominated business and administration. Interest continued at the rate of 20 per cent per annum. The upward trend of prices noted during Chaldaean rule continued at an accelerated rate. Documents employ the same formulas and deal with the same types of loans, sales of slaves or of lands, and marriage and apprentice agreements.

1. *Monetary system.*—By the Chaldaean period, Babylonia had gone fully onto a silver basis. We do have references to gold objects and to the goldsmiths who prepared them for the temples, but there is no hint of a gold coinage. Lead, employed in early Assyria as a baser substitute for silver, had long since ceased to be accepted as a medium of exchange. For a time, copper had taken its place, but it, too, had disappeared. Where gold is mentioned in the Chaldaean period, its ratio to silver varies from ten to nearly fourteen to one.

Coinage in silver was common. Many of the documents are expressed in monetary terms, though for the most part it would seem that the terminology is for bookkeeping only and that actual money rarely passed from hand to hand. Monetary terminology was primarily according to weight. Sixty shekels (*shiqlu*) made one pound (*mana*), and sixty pounds made one talent (*biltu*). Since the talent weighed about sixty-six of our pounds, the Babylonian pound was a little heavier than our own. For actual use the shekel was the normal unit of value, though the half-shekel was the most commonly minted, and the use of the *she*, barely a grain of silver, was occasionally revived from some fifteen centuries before. In coin value the silver shekel may be estimated as worth something like a quarter of our dollar, but we must not forget that the purchasing value of the precious metals in antiquity was almost infinitely greater than today. The real value of a study of prices is that it permits us to indicate price trends; when we remember that the wage of an ordinary day laborer was one shekel per month, we may estimate what he might purchase of various commodities when we learn how much they cost.

2. *Produce*.—While some agricultural products were sold by weight, the grains which afforded the livelihood of the country were sold by measure. Thirty-six *qa*'s, about a pint and a half, made one *pi;* five *pi*'s made a *gur*, almost four and a quarter of our bushels. Since the *qa* was too small and the *gur* too large for ordinary use, they tended to be supplanted by the measure (*mashihu*). Though the most usual measure was the *pi* of thirty-six *qa*'s, others of thirty-seven or even forty-five *qa*'s were known. Thus the average measure was a trifle less than our bushel. Use of their own measure by temples or private individuals inevitably led to abuses. As early as the reign of Nebuchadnezzar, the "king's measure" of one *pi* was recognized; during the Achaemenid period it gradually superseded the private measure, which returned only in times of administrative breakdown.

Only its enormously productive soil made Babylonia habitable. Its major product was barley, raised on great estates belonging for the most part to the temples. We are especially well informed about Eanna, the temple of the goddess Ishtar of Uruk. When we hear of some fifty thousand bushels from a single farm measured at one time into Eanna, we are reminded of the great wheat fields in our own American Middle West.

At harvest the temples employed a large number of floating laborers, whose pay was a bare subsistence, and thus cost no more than their own serfs. In comparison with the nominal wage, the cost of barley was high. The price was set by its quoted price at Babylon. Naturally, barley was cheapest at harvest and increased in cost during the months succeeding, while there were also variations according as it was new or old. Wheat was little grown, and its use as food was confined to the rich.

Fortunately, throughout all these centuries, dates were always cheaper than barley. If the peasant did not too often satisfy his appetite with barley loaves, at least he could buy a handful of dates to furnish concentrated energy. The rivers and canals presented a continuous line of palm orchards and added a touch of green to an otherwise barren and monotonous landscape. Forty thousand bushels might be secured from a single plantation.

At the beginning of the Achaemenid period one shekel bought at least one *gur;* thus five or six bushels might be secured for a month's average wage. Dividing his purchases between dates and the more costly barley, a man could provide for himself and family a month's ration of something like two bushels of grain and three of dates. Soon prices began to rise, and in another century costs had doubled with no compensating increase in the peasant's wages.

Even the poorest at this time might occasionally add a relish of garlic, sold over the counter in bunches by the local grocer. Near the beginning of Cyrus' reign, we hear of a wholesale purchase of 395,000 such bunches. Oil from sesame seed was the only substitute for animal fats in a region too hot for the olive. At that, the peasant was unable to utilize the substitute to any appreciable degree, for a single bushel of the seed demanded two or three months of his pay, though a bushel measure of the oil cost but a shekel. With prices so high in terms of wages, we may be sure that only the relatively well-to-do used the oil for food and that only the rich could employ it in ointment or as a medicament for man, much less for beast. To waste the precious oil for lamps was possible only for the temples.

Next to food came drink. Wine was only for the wealthy, and the best brands were imported, as is shown by the famous "wine card" published by Nebuchadnezzar. For lesser men there was wine from the hills northwest of Assyria and from the province "Across the River," North Syria. The vine grew in Babylonia itself, whose inferior wines are frequently mentioned.

Common men must satisfy themselves with various kinds of "strong drink." The most popular was date wine, though on a lesser scale beer was also appreciated. Prices naturally varied as the "strong drink" was clear or white, new or a year old. Less than a shekel was needed for a good-sized jug of raw wine. A foreign visitor reports a wine made from the topmost shoots of a date palm, which he found sweet but headachy.[8] Those who could afford a clear grape wine paid as much as eight shekels per jar.

During the long, intensely hot summer of the Babylonian plain, the stranger from the colder north had to take refuge in an underground apartment and creep out only in the cool of the evening. But the hardened native labored all day with little or no clothing to protect him against the deadly sun, and in the brief winter, when an occasional frost might be expected, he shivered unless the sun came out to coax from his bones the chill produced by the rain and the dampness. Firewood was almost nonexistent. At best, he could hope that after a long search the women would appear with huge bundles of thorns on their heads; even these thorns burned fiercely for only a moment and then almost immediately flickered out. Heavier clothing became a necessity.

From before the dawn of written history, great flocks of sheep and goats had roamed the high desert under the protection of half-wild shepherds. From their clip of wool and goat's hair, the peasants secured clothing for the winter. During Cyrus' reign, to a greater degree than previously, the great flocks were monopolized by the temples, which kept careful statistics of births, losses by wild animals and by theft, and of animals turned in by their guardians. A single tablet listing one temple's income mentions five tons of sheep's wool and several hundred pounds of goat's hair; another temple received nearly seven thousand sheep in one lot. Temple monopoly also raised prices. Even in wholesale lots, a shekel bought only two pounds of wool. The rich paid fifteen shekels, more than a peasant's income for a whole year, for a single pound dyed by the expensive purple-blue. Under these circumstances the peasant was fortunate indeed if he bought one new garment a year.

The cultivation of flax, already an ancient practice among the Egyptians, was only now beginning. It was still confined to gardens and had not yet been transplanted to the open field. Babylonia had no protective tariff for new industries. Flax was taxed 25 per cent, and a hundred stalks cost a shekel. We may imagine the price of the finished garment produced by the linen-weaver. Obviously, the great linen industry of later Babylonia was still in the future.[9]

[8] Xen. *Anab.* ii. 3. 14 ff.; cf. i. 5. 10.

[9] Strabo xvi. 1. 7 (great linen factory at Borsippa); Herodotus is therefore mistaken when he states (i. 195) that linen was commonly worn.

In earlier centuries the health of the lower classes was kept up by the large quantity of milk drunk and by the cheese which they ate in its various forms. The small number of references to dairy products in our documents suggests that the health of the population had suffered. The large number of sheep and goats possessed by the temples may explain the change, although a single goat might afford enough of the rich milk for the children or a sheep enough for the clabbered milk familiar to every traveler as *lebben* or *yaurt*. Such an animal on the average cost two shekels in the reign of Cyrus, though continuing Achaemenid rule gradually increased the price. Mutton or lamb, goat or kid, was eaten rarely by the lower classes.

Nearly all the draft animals demanded for the tillage of the fields belonged to the great temple estates and were loaned to contractors with the necessary serfs and the iron from which the plows were to be manufactured. Ordinarily this consisted of one serf and plow to each ox. Private agriculturalists had to buy their own oxen. In the Chaldaean period the price per ox was even lower than that fixed fifteen centuries earlier by Hammurabi's "ceiling," which ranged from ten to twenty shekels for a "perfect" animal. Following the usual parallel, under the Achaemenids prices rose. To harass further the independent farmer, the temple competed, paying three or four times the normal cost for animals ritually perfect. Once we hear of the sale of a horse which cost almost four pounds of silver, equivalent to wages for almost a score of years to the ordinary workman. Even a donkey or a she-ass could rarely be bought for five or ten shekels and might reach twelve times the latter price. Like the sheep and goats, donkeys were marked, generally on the ear. The star mark of the Ishtar of Uruk is often mentioned to prove the ownership of animals and of slaves.

3. *Building and real estate.*—Temples and palaces might be constructed of baked bricks. Fuel was scarce and expensive, and we need not be surprised to find that the shekel would buy no more than fifty or a hundred baked bricks. As in Nebuchadnezzar's palace at Babylon, baked bricks would be laid in asphalt, which, though brought down by boat from Id (Hit) up the Euphrates, was cheap, costing only a shekel for six hundred pounds. Cypress or cedar wood for paneling was imported from Syria, and the price was accordingly high. A beam of cypress cost a shekel, which secured a mere ten pounds of the more precious cedar, while a large door of wood, presumably for a temple, was worth two and a half silver pounds. Ordinary houses were of

mud brick, generally formed in the brick mold by the owner or lessor. In one purchase by wholesale, 25,000 unbaked bricks are contracted to be made, counted, and delivered into the shed.

Although all the metals had to be imported, they sold for surprisingly low prices. From one importer, Iddin-ahu, who was doing business in 550, we have definite statistics. Copper in large quantities was imported from Cyprus and sold at the rate of a shekel for three and two-thirds pounds. Iron from Cyprus or the Lebanon was even cheaper, a shekel buying as much as eleven pounds. These prices are so much below those of earlier times that we may be sure improvements in mining and in smelting, as in transportation, were responsible for the remarkable drop. Other imports mentioned by Iddin-ahu include wine, honey, wood, lead, dyestuffs, dyed wool, lapis lazuli, and alum from Egypt.

Significant changes are indicated by the sales and rentals of landed property. To estimate these changes, we must first reduce Babylonian land measurements to a common factor. In this system twenty-four fingers (*ubanu*) made one cubit (*ammatu*), about eighteen inches. Seven cubits made one reed (*qanu*), ten and a half feet. Two reeds made one *gar*. Area could be computed for small lots by the square cubit or square reed; larger fields are measured by the amount of seed grain required for sowing. A *gur* is the area needing four and a quarter bushels, a *pi* requires a measure or approximately a bushel, and a *qa* is equivalent to ten *gar* of field or 675 square feet.

From eleven to twenty-four *qa* of uncultivated land could be bought for one shekel. At the beginning of the Chaldaean era, two to four *qa* of cultivated land might be secured for the shekel, but by Nabu-naid's reign only one to two, and by the time of Darius I the price had risen to two or three shekels per *qa*. Orchards and gardens cost more: one and a half shekels per *qa* in the Chaldaean period, two shekels under Cyrus, two to three under Darius, with still higher rates for especially favored lands.

In the Chaldaean period a house and lot averaged fifteen shekels per reed. By the reign of Darius, the average was forty, nearly a threefold increase. Even more significant of the drift to the cities, the number of sale contracts seriously decreased and rental contracts took their place. Under the Chaldaeans a house could be rented for ten shekels; under Cyrus the rent was fifteen. It was twenty and upward under Darius and had reached forty under Artaxerxes I. Normally the rent was paid in advance and in two instalments, at the beginning of the first and seventh months. The lessee contracted to keep the roof in repair, to renew the woodwork, and to fill up the cracks in the walls, and, if he wished a door, he was obliged to provide it himself.

4. *Banking.*—Without any doubt, the most important economic phenomenon was the emergence of the private banker and the consequent wide extension of credit. Preceding times had witnessed no such large-scale use of credit. The loan business was in the hands of the one great economic unit—the temple—and loans were made principally to temple dependents. Assyrian landlords, however, had made regular advances of grain to their peasants. These loans were made without interest, and it was regularly provided that if the loan was not repaid at harvest, increase should then accrue, generally at the rate of 25 per cent as a penalty and not as true interest. This was enlightened self-interest, for not only did it prevent the peasant from falling into the clutches of the loan shark but it also kept him in constant debt to the landlord.

Similarly in the Achaemenid period, the temple or its officials lent barley, dates, and more rarely other products to its own peasants. The loan was to be repaid at harvest in the gate of some temple storehouse and according to the measure of some local god. At times it was specifically stated that it was to be without interest, but more often the lack of interest is merely taken for granted. Even thus, the loan was not without profit, for not only did the landlord substitute old barley or dates for an equal quantity from the new crop but there might be additional perquisites such as the barley straw, good fodder for cattle, or the by-products of the palm tree, the dry branches, leaves, sprouts, or fallen unripe dates, whose value was high in a land where nothing was wasted. From the Assyrians, the Babylonian landlords had borrowed the practice of charging a penalty interest at a higher rate if the loan was not repaid at harvest. Not a few of these loans, however, did draw interest; it was regularly the standard 20 per cent, although, since the interest of a fifth was for less than a year, the interest collected was actually higher.

Private banking as a commercial proposition first made its appearance in Babylonia in the reign of Kandalanu (648–626).[10] At the very beginning we find members of the two great banking families of Babylon, that of Egibi and of the less important Iranu. Soon after their discovery, it was suggested that the former was Jewish and that the

---

[10] Cf. W. H. Dubberstein, "Assyrian-Babylonian Chronology," *JNES*, III (1944), 38–42.

name of the founder was Jacob. We shall see that there are additional reasons for believing that this is true.

Where credit was granted as a regular business transaction and the standing of the borrower was good, the document was simple in form, and amost without exception the interest was 20 per cent: "monthly on one mana one shekel of silver shall increase." Tendencies toward a lower interest rate at the beginning of the Chaldaean period were quickly checked, and throughout the first half of the Achaemenid period the rate was standardized.

Where the credit of the borrower was more dubious, a severe penalty was added if the debt were not paid at maturity. The note might be indorsed by a second individual who was responsible if payment was defaulted. In most such dubious loans, however, no interest was charged; instead, the creditor took a pledge—a house, a plot of land, or a slave. The formula ran: "When the money is repaid, the pledge will be returned; rent there shall not be for the pledge and there shall not be interest on the money."

On the face of it, remittal of the interest might appear to favor the debtor, and so we have taken the Hebrew condemnation of interest. Actually, the substitution of the pledge was all to the advantage of the creditor. If the debtor could somehow raise the money and recover the pledge, still the creditor had enjoyed the service of the slave, the use of the house, or the produce of the field—all worth considerably more than the fixed interest. At the same time, he had more than ample security for the amount lent, and if the debtor defaulted, as no doubt often he did, the creditor had bought the property at a bargain. How little the substitution of the pledge for interest protected the rights of the poor may be seen in the provision of the more "humane" Hebrew lawgiver who, as an extraordinary concession, ordered that if a man's garment was taken as pledge it should be returned to him at night in order that he might have something in which to sleep![11]

There were other loans which demanded both pledge and interest. Some, even for a small amount, add: "Whatever there is belonging to him in city and country is a pledge." On the other hand, we find an occasional loan without interest or pledge, but never from the professional bankers; these must be accommodation for brief periods to relatives or friends.

[11] Exod. 22:24 ff.

Interest often had to be paid every month, and this amounted to compound interest. Occasionally, interest might run until the principal was repaid. Payment of the debt on the instalment plan was common, and a separate receipt was given each time. When the whole debt was repaid—and now and then there were debtors so fortunate—the original tablet of indebtedness was destroyed in order that no future claim might be made. Thus we may be sure that the tablets which have survived represent those debts which were foreclosed.

The more closely we examine these documents, the more impressed we are with the wide use of credit during the period. Landed properties, houses, animals, even slaves were bought on credit. We begin to suspect that the abnormal rise in prices may be due in part to what we call credit inflation. When we discover that the final payment on a farm is made by the grandson of the original purchaser, we realize that instalment buying might have brought about the same difficulties as in our last period of depression.

One more feature of contemporary economic life is strangely modern. In earlier times the high temple officials obtained as perquisites of their offices the right to certain of the sacrifices on certain days. These prebends were now bought and sold on the open market, not only for a given day, but for a small fraction of a day. The temple had become a huge corporation, shares of which could be transferred on what almost corresponded to our modern stock exchange.

From the standpoint of the businessman, Babylonia possessed a remarkably modern system of doing business. Her credit facilities are to be especially noted. From the viewpoint of the historian interested in the social process, there is much which serves as warning. Later chapters of this book will show how, underneath the prosperity of the higher classes, there were forces at work to bring the whole impressive business structure tumbling to the ground in ruins.

Chapter VI

CAMBYSES AND THE CONQUEST OF EGYPT

CAMBYSES, eldest son of Cyrus by Cassandane, daughter of Pharnaspes, a fellow-Achaemenid,[1] was a mature man at the conquest of Babylon. Harem intrigues were not yet tormenting the Persian court, though they might be expected in the near future. To obviate any danger, Cambyses was promptly recognized as "King's Son." In the proclamation issued to the Babylonians, Cyrus informed them that their chief god, the lord Marduk, had blessed not only him but his "own son" Cambyses, "while we, before him and with sincerity, joyously praised his exalted godhead." When the gods of all Babylonia were invoked to pray daily before Bel and Nabu for long life to himself, and to speak a word of grace to the lord Marduk, Cambyses was joined with him in the prayer.[2]

Before his accession year was ended, Cyrus returned to Ecbatana, leaving Cambyses as his personal representative to carry on the ritual prescribed for the king at the approaching New Year's festival. On the fourth of Nisan, March 27, 538, Cambyses, as son of Cyrus, proceeded to the temple of Nabu within Babylon on the sacred street of Ishtar between the festival house and Esagila. There Cambyses was received by the chief priest of Nabu with his accompanying priests, and he filled them with good things, the usual New Year's presents. When he had taken the hands of Nabu, the god presented him with the scepter of righteousness. Surrounded by the spearmen and bowmen from Gutium, the King's Son marched up the sacred way to Esagila and prepared to carry out the whole ritual. Also with him marched Nabu. The barrier between the lord Marduk and his son was taken down, and the King's Son presented the scepter to Marduk, only to receive it back after he had himself seized the hands of Marduk and made his obeisance.[3] Only after Cyrus had thus received by proxy the approval of Babylon's great lord did he venture to prefix "King of Babylon" to the general title "King of Lands."

[1] Herod. i. 208; ii. 1; iii. 2.

[2] Cyrus, *Cyl.*, ll. 26–28, 34–35.

[3] Cyrus, *Chron.*, col. III, ll. 24–28.

As a rule, we know nothing about the life of an oriental crown prince before his accession to the throne; he remains hidden in the harem. Thanks to his unique position in Babylonia, Cambyses is the exception. His headquarters was not, as we should have expected, in Babylon, but farther north in Sippar. Here we find in a document of February 20, 535, reference to the house of Nabu-mar-sharri-usur, steward of the King's Son. The name is significant, for the father who called his son "May Nabu Protect the King's Son" could have had in mind only Belshazzar. In other words, Cambyses did not merely retain in office the administrators already functioning under Nabu-naid; he retained also the former palace dignitaries.[4] Bazazu, the messenger of the house of the King's Son, made his appearance at Sippar on August 10, 534. Another messenger, Pan-Ashur-lumur, was a witness in March or April, 532. Later in the same year Itti-Marduk-balatu, the great banker, lent three pounds, sixteen shekels of silver to the headman of Cambyses, the King's Son. On March 3, 530, the same Itti-Marduk-balatu apprenticed for four years his own slave to a stonecutter, a slave of the King's Son Cambyses, in order that he might learn the whole art.[5] These glimpses show us a crown prince hard at work on his routine duties.

Eight years of residence in Babylonia, during which he had acted as representative of his father at the New Year's festival, had accustomed the natives to the sight of Cambyses as their own ruler. A Persian custom decreed that the king should not leave his kingdom unprotected when he left for a foreign war but should appoint his successor. Before Cyrus took his departure for the campaign against the Massagetae, he therefore recognized Cambyses as regent by permitting him to use the formal title "King of Babylon" while retaining for himself the broader claim as "King of Lands." Immediately after Cambyses had again "seized the hands of the lord" on New Year's Day, March 26, 530, business documents were dated by the double titulary.[6] By September, 530, the news of Cyrus' death had arrived, and Cambyses assumed the full titulary of his father, "King of Babylon, King of Lands." By Elamite custom, he married his sisters Atossa and Roxana.[7] Then he prepared to invade Egypt, the last of the four great empires yet to be conquered.

[4] *VS*, Vol. V, No. 129; cf. No. 60 (second year of Darius).

[5] J. P. Strassmaier, *Inschriften von Cyrus* (1900), Nos. 199, 270, 325, 364.

[6] Waldo H. Dubberstein, "The Chronology of Cyrus and Cambyses," *AJSL*, LV (1938), 417 ff.; cf. Herod. i. 208; ii. 1; iii. 2; Xen. *Cyrop.* viii. 7. 11; Ctes. *Pers.* xi, Epit. 39.

[7] Ctes. *Pers.* xii, Epit. 43.

EGYPTIAN CAMPAIGN

Amasis had relied on Greek mercenaries to put through his anti-nationalist, anti-priestly program, and there was much dissatisfaction. Nekht-har-hebi, governor of the entrance gates by land and by sea, had already set up an inscription of very dubious loyalty.[8] The Phoenicians repeated the promise of loyalty made to his father, and their daughter-cities in Cyprus sent their formal submission.[9] Possession of their fleets meant control of the Mediterranean, and the invaders therefore concentrated at Ace.

Wary old Amasis had allied himself with the master of the Aegean, Polycrates, tyrant of Samos. Machinations of the nobles forced an about-face and Polycrates shipped off these dissatisfied citizens to serve under Cambyses. The Greek mercenary chief, Phanes of Halicarnassus, quarreled with his Egyptian paymaster and escaped to Cambyses with valuable military information. Camels to water the troops while passing through the desert were hired from the king of the Arabs, our first literary reference to the Nabataeans, who held the coast from Gaza to Ienysus.[10]

By the Serbonian bog, the hiding-place of wicked Typhon, and the Casian Mount, Cambyses reached the Pelusiac branch of the Nile, where he learned that Amasis had been succeeded by his son Psamtik (Psammenitus) III. A well-contested battle at Pelusium—there were Greeks in both armies—ended in Persian victory; two generations later Herodotus remarked the bones of the unburied dead. The naval commander Udjahorresne treacherously brought about the surrender of the strategic city of Sais. Heliopolis was taken by siege, and Psamtik fled across the river to refuge in Memphis. Early in 525 Memphis was taken; at first, Psamtik was well treated, but he was soon accused of plotting and put to death.[11]

With the "factory" at Naucratis under Persian control, the lucrative Greek trade with Egypt was at the mercy of Cambyses; fortunately, he was generous, and Greek traders flooded the country.[12] When Libyans and Greeks of Cyrene and Barca reported through Arcesilaus their submission,[13] a good half of the Greek world—certainly the wealthier and more advanced half—was ruled by Persia. A projected

[8] P. Tresson, Kémi, IV (1931), 126 ff.

[9] Herod. iii. 19.   [10] Ibid. 4 ff., 39 ff.

[11] Ibid., 11 ff.; Ctes. Pers. xii, Epit. 40, Frag. 30 (Athen, xiii. 560B); Plato Menex. 239E; Diod. x. 13–14; Just. i. 9. 3; Polyaen. vii. 9; Jamblichus Vit. Pythag. 4.

[12] Herod. iii. 139.   [13] Ibid. 13; iv. 165.

campaign against Carthage was frustrated by the refusal of the Phoenicians to attack a daughter-city.[14]

Cambyses marched up the Nile. The Kharga Oasis was occupied
from Thebes, but when the detachment attempted the Oasis of Ammon, hoping to burn the oracle, it was overwhelmed by a sandstorm.
Men from Elephantine were sent to spy on the Ethiopians, who had
built up around Napata a kingdom with a half-Egyptian culture.
Their report was full of marvels. They related that the Ethiopians
generally lived to a hundred and twenty years, some even beyond.
Their food was roast meat, and they were great drinkers of milk. In a
meadow outside the capital the city leaders placed in the night roast
meats which next day could be eaten by anyone; this was the famous
Table of the Sun. The king was said to be the tallest and straightest of
all men. Even the prisoners wore fetters of gold, but bronze was rare
and valuable. Coffins for the dead were made of glass, through which
the corpse could be seen; for a year they were kept in the house while
sacrifice was offered, then they were set up around the town. Among
other curiosities to be seen in Ethiopia were elephants and ebony.[15]
Cambyses annexed the Ethiopians on the border, but, despite "Cambyses' Storehouse" at the second cataract, supplies failed.[16] Egypt
was formed into the satrapy of Mudraya, with Memphis as the capital. Garrisons continued to guard the frontier, at Daphne in the east
Delta, at the White Wall of Memphis (said to have been founded by
Menes at the junction of the two Egypts and across the river from the
capital on the site of Old Cairo, Egyptian Babylon), and at Elephantine below the first cataract, where large numbers of Jewish mercenaries were colonized.[17]

EGYPT UNDER CAMBYSES RULE

Tales of the mad doings of Cambyses in Egypt must be discounted.[18]
The oft-repeated slander that he killed an Apis bull[19] is false. In his
sixth year (524), while Cambyses was absent on his Ethiopian expedi-

[14] *Ibid.* iii. 17, 19.

[15] *Ibid.* 18 ff., 114.

[16] *Ibid.* 25, 97; vii. 69; Diod. i. 33. 1; iii. 3. 1; Strabo xvii. 1. 5; Plin. vi. 181; Ptol. iv. 7.

[17] Letter of Aristeas 13.

[18] For Egypt under the Persians cf. G. Maspero, *Passing of the Empires* (1900), pp. 656 ff.; E. A.
W. Budge, *History of Egypt*, VII (1902), 42 ff.; W. M. F. Petrie, *History of Egypt*, III (3d ed, 1925),
360 ff.; H. Gautier, *Le Livre des rois d'Egypte*, IV, No. 1 (1915), 135 ff.; G. Posener, *La première
domination Perse en Egypte* (1936).

[19] Herod. iii. 27 ff.; Plut. *De Isid.* 44; Just. i. 9; Clem. Alex. *Protrept.* iv. 52. 6.

tion, the sacred bull died. The next Apis bull, born in the fifth year of Cambyses, survived to the fourth year of Darius.

As in other respects, Cambyses followed the precedent of Amasis, the first to place his name on the sarcophagus of an Apis and the first to fashion it from a magnificent block of gray granite. The cover was inscribed with the full royal formula to which the Egyptians were accustomed: "Horus, Samtowi, king of Upper and Lower Egypt, Mestiu-re, son of Re, Cambyses, may he live forever. He made as his monument to his father, Apis-Osiris, a great sarcophagus of granite, which the king of Upper and Lower Egypt, Mestiu-re, son of Re, Cambyses, dedicated, who is given all life, all stability and good fortune, all health, all gladness, appearing as king of Upper and Lower Egypt, forever."

On the accompanying limestone stele Cambyses was represented in the native royal costume; wearing the uraeus serpent, he knelt before the sacred beast in reverence. The inscriptions tell us how under the majesty of the king of Upper and Lower Egypt, descendant of Re, granted eternal life, the god, his father Apis-Osiris, was brought in peace to the beautiful west and was made to rest in the necropolis, in the place which his majesty had made for him, after men had carried out all the ceremonies in the hall of embalming. Others made for him the textiles, the amulets, all the ornaments, and every kind of precious object; all was done according to what his majesty had ordered.[20] In the sixth year of Cambyses the Persian Atiyawahy, son of Artames and Qanju, a "eunuch" (saris) of Persia and governor of Coptos, led a party to the desert quarries of the wadi Hammamat to secure new building material for the restoration of the temples.[21]

That the tales of savagery do not reflect contemporary opinion is proved by the account of Udjahorresne, admiral of the royal fleet under Amasis and Psamtik and priest of the goddess Neith at Sais. Writing under Darius, he was under no compulsion to speak kindly of his former master. There came into Egypt the great king of all the foreign countries, Kambujet, while the foreigners of all the foreign lands were with him. He took possession of all this land, the foreigners established their abode, and he was great ruler of Egypt, great lord of all

[20] B. Gunn, *Annales du Service*, XXVI (1926), 85–86; E. Chassinat, *Recueil de travaux*, XXI (1899), 57; XXIII (1901), 77 ff.; Poserner, *op. cit.*, pp. 3 ff.; cf. Richard A. Parker, "Persian and Egyptian Chronology," *AJSL*, LVIII (1941), 286–87.

[21] J. Couyat and P. Montet, *Les Inscriptions du Ouadi Hammamat* (1912), No. 164; Poserner, *op. cit.*, No. 28; cf. Parker, *op. cit.*, pp. 287 ff.

the foreign countries. His majesty gave the former admiral, who had come over to the invaders, the office of head physician; he was made to live with the king as a companion and was placed in charge of the palace. Udjahorresne prepared for Cambyses the official titulary, as king of Upper and Lower Egypt, descendant of Re.

Udjahorresne made Cambyses to understand the greatness of Sais, the abode of the great Neith, the mother who gave birth to Re, as well as the greatness of the abodes of Osiris, Re, and Atum. He complained to his majesty about the foreigners who were settled in the temple of Neith, and his majesty gave order that they should be driven out. The destruction of the houses of the Greek mercenaries, together with their goods, the purification of the temple and the return of all its serfs, the restoration of the revenues from the properties dedicated to Neith and the other divinities, and the renewal of their feasts and processions as before were also commanded. Cambyses himself visited Sais,[22] entered the temple, made his adoration before Neith, and offered sacrifices as had been done by every benefactor king.[23]

Not all temples were so fortunate as that at Sais. This we discover from a list of the "matters they shall consider about the temples in the house of judgment." Incomes of those at Memphis, Hermopolis Parva, and Egyptian Babylon were to be alloted as formerly; in place of the former grants, the priests of the others were to be given sites in the marshlands and southlands from which they themselves had to bring firewood and timber for boatbuilding. The number of cattle presented under Pharaoh Amasis was reduced by a half. As to fowl, Cambyses ordered: "Give them not to them! Let the priests raise geese and give them to their gods." The value of the withdrawn revenues was estimated at 60,530 deben 8 kite of silver, 170,210 measures of grain, and 6,000 loaves of bread, besides cattle, fowl, incense, papyrus, and flax.[24]

In agreement with this decree, we find no more gifts of natural products to the temples by the Persian rulers; this alone was sufficient to start the rumor that Cambyses was a harsh master to the Egyptians. A century later the Jews of Elephantine boasted how their own temple was untouched while all the temples of Egyptian gods were over-

[22] Herod. iii. 16.

[23] V. Marruchi, *Il Museo egizio Vaticano* (1899), pp. 79 ff.; Petrie, *op. cit.*, pp. 360 ff.; G. Farina, *Bilychnis*, XXXIII, Part I (1929), 449 ff.; Poisener, *op. cit.*, No. 1.

[24] W. Spiegelberg, *Die sogennante demotische Chronik* (1914), pp. 32 ff. (checked by Dr. George Hughes).

thrown when Cambyses made his invasion.[25] Ultimately, the destruction of Heliopolis and Thebes was blamed on his anger![26]

Toward the end of the eighth century, written contracts—the predecessors of the still more numerous papyri of the Hellenistic and Roman periods—had come into general use. Parallels to the cuneiform documents are close and suggest that the new system of bookkeeping had been introduced under Assyrian influence. A new and more quickly written character soon evolved; it was called by the Greeks demotic or "popular," in contrast to the more elaborate hieratic or "priestly," henceforth confined largely to copies of the sacred books. Such demotic papyri show life going on as usual after the conquest. For instance, from Siut, later Lycopolis, we learn of two cousins who in the eighth year of Cambyses agree once more as to the disposition of property already divided between their fathers in the reign of Amasis. In addition to real estate and water rights, we hear of a division of the income derived from the right to be chief priest of the Wolf nome, to be scribe, and to enjoy the prebends of the temple so many days of the year or at so many feasts. Other papyri from Siut list monthly grants of wine and oil to the head of the necropolis, to the pastophorus, to the chief priest, and to the governor of the nome.[27]

USURPATION BY BARDIYA

Leaving his relative Aryandes as satrap,[28] Cambyses started home. At Agbatana near Mount Carmel, he received news of Bardiya's usurpation, and there he died, it was said, by his own hand.[29] Bardiya, variously known to the Greeks as Mardos, Smerdis, Maruphius, Merphis, Tanaoxares, or Tanyoxarces, was a full brother of Cambyses. At his father's death he had been given charge of Media, Armenia, and Cadusia. On March 11, 522, he proclaimed himself king at a place named Pishiyauvada on Mount Arakadrish. By April 14 he was accepted in Babylonia. He had become king so late in his "accession year" that soon it was "year one." The Babylonian historians were so puzzled as to which year they should employ for dating that they have

[25] A. E. Cowley, *Aramaic Papyri of the Fifth Century B.C.* (1923), No. 30.

[26] Strabo xvii. 1. 27, 46.

[27] H. Sottas, *Annales du Service*, XXIII (1923), 34 ff.; another is from year eight (W. Spiegelberg, *Demotische Denkmäler*, III [1932], 42 ff.).

[28] Herod. iv. 166.   [29] *Ibid.* iii. 62 ff.

continued to perplex their modern successors. By July 1 Bardiya was recognized by the whole empire.[30]

The subject population welcomed Bardiya gladly, since he had suspended for three years the taxes and war levies;[31] but the feudal nobles disliked his centralization of the cult through destruction of their local sanctuaries. He was afforded little time to consolidate his reforms, for on September 29, 522, after but eight months of rule, he was slain by Darius at Sikayauvatish in Median Nisaya.[32]

[30] R. A. Parker and W. H. Dubberstein, *Babylonian Chronology, 626 B.C.—A.D. 45* (1942), p. 12; *Beh.* § 11; Aeschyl. *Pers.* 774; Herod. iii. 61 ff.; Ctes. *Pers.* xiii, Epit. 39; Xen. *Cyrop.* viii. 7. 11; Hellanicus, Frag. 180(J); cf. Olmstead, "Darius and His Behistun Inscription," *AJSL*, LV (1938), 394 ff.; chronology to be corrected by Cameron, "Darius and Xerxes in Babylonia," *AJSL*, LVIII (1941), 314 ff.; Parker, *op. cit.*, pp. 285 ff.; also W. Hinz, "Das erste Jahr des Grosskönigs Dareios," *ZDMG*, XCII (1938), 146 ff.

[31] Herod. iii. 67.

[32] *Beh.* § 13; seven-month reign, Ctes. *Pers.* xii, Epit. 45; cf. Parker and Dubberstein, *op. cit.*, p. 12.

Chapter VII

PROPHET ZOROASTER

ZARATHUSHTRA began his prophetic mission about the middle of the sixth century in the northwest corner of the plateau where, three hundred years before, Assyrians had received tribute in Parsua. His name meant "With Golden Camels"; his father was Pourushaspa, "With Gray Horses," and his mother Dughdhova, "Who Has Milked White Cows." All were taken from the simple, half-pastoral life. His race was Spitama, the "White."[1]

His god was Ahura-Mazdah, the "Wise Lord," the official head of the Persian national pantheon since the days of Ariyaramnes. In vision Ahura-Mazdah appeared to Zoroaster:

> As the Holy One then I acknowledged thee, Mazdah-Ahura,
> When at life's birth I first beheld thee,
> When thou didst make deeds and words of reward,
> Evil for Evil, a good Destiny for the good,
> Through thy wisdom at earth's last turning-point,
>
> To which turning-point thou shalt come with thy Holy Spirit,
> Mazdah, with the Kingdom, there with Good Thought,
> By whose deeds possessions increase through Righteousness,
> Their judgments shall Piety declare,
> Of thy counsel which none can deceive.
>
> As the Holy One then I acknowledged thee, Mazdah-Ahura,
> When Good Thought once came to me,
> And asked me: "Who art thou? Whose art thou?
> By what sign shall I make known the days
> For inquiry of what is thine and of thyself?"
>
> Then said I to him: First, I am Zarathushtra,
> True foe of the Liar as best I may,
> But to the Righteous would be a strong support,
> To attain the future blessings of the longed-for Kingdom,
> As I laud thee, Mazdah, and hymn thee.

[1] Cf. Olmstead, "Zoroaster," *Review of Religion*, IV (1939), 3 ff.

As the Holy One then I acknowledged thee, Mazdah-Ahura,
When Good Thought once came to me.
To his question: "For whom wilt thou decide?"
I answered: At the offering of homage to thy Fire,
I will think on Righteousness so long as I may.

Then show me Righteousness whom I invoke.
"With him associated with Piety have I come,
Ask us what should be asked by thee,
For thy asking is as of the mighty,
Since the Ruler would make thee happy and strong."

As the Holy One then I acknowledged thee, Mazdah-Ahura,
When Good Thought once came to me.
When first by thy words was I instructed;
Shall my faith bring woe to me,
In doing what ye told me was best?

And when thou didst tell me, "To Righteousness go for instruction,"
Then didst thou not give me orders unheard;
"Up, go, ere comes my Obedience,
With Destiny, rich in treasure,
Who shall portion to men the Destinies of the Twofold Award."

As the Holy One then I acknowledged thee, Mazdah-Ahura,
When Good Thought once came to me,
To learn my desire's form. Vouchsafe me this,
What none compels you to admit, to know the long duration
Of the wished-for existence that is said to be in thy Kingdom.

What a knowing man would give his friend were he able,
Grant, Mazdah, careful aid from thee,
If by thy Kingdom through Righteousness it be attained,
Let me arise to drive away the scorners of thy doctrine,
With all who bear in mind thy holy words.

As the Holy One then I acknowledged thee, Mazdah-Ahura,
When Good Thought once came to me,
Best Silent Thought bade me proclaim:
Let not man seek to please the many Liars,
For they make all the Righteous foes to thee.

Thus, Ahura, Zarathushtra chooses for himself,
Mazdah, whatever Spirit of thine is Holiest.
May Righteousness be incarnate, mighty in life's strength,
May Piety be in the Kingdom that beholds the sun,
With Good Thought may he assign Destiny to men for their deeds.[2]

[2] Yasna 43:5 ff.

ATTRIBUTES OF AHURA-MAZDAH

Whether or not this represents exactly the visions which first called Zoroaster to his ministry, it does present the chief features of his preaching. The prophet's alternate use of Ahura, Mazdah, Ahura-Mazdah, and Mazdah-Ahura recall to us days when Ahura and Mazdah were separate deities; a century before, Ariyaramnes had presented Ahuramazda as one god among many, but to Zoroaster he was sole God. Other divinities from dim Indo-European times—the sun-god Mithra, for example—might be cherished by kings and people, but to Zoroaster these daevas were no gods but demons worshiped by the followers of the Lie. Ahura-Mazdah was in no need of minor divinities over whom to rule as divine king.

Beside him are only his vaguely personified attributes. Spenta Mainyu is his own Holy Spirit. Asha is Righteousness, the universe as it should be. Vohu Manah (Good Thought) or Vahishta Manah (Best Thought) is that which reveals to the prophet the vision. Khshathra is Ahura-Mazdah's divine Kingdom, at the end of days to be supreme. Armaiti (Piety), the divine Wisdom, Haurvatat (Salvation), and Ameretat (Immortality), complete a vague group of seven attributes, to which are added Ashir (Destiny), Sraosha (Obedience), and Atar (Fire).

THE CALL

After the vision came the call:

To you the Ox Soul complained: "For what did you fashion me?
Who created me?
Frenzy and force oppress me, cruelty and brutality too.
No other herder than ye have I; procure for me good pasture."

Then the Ox Creator asked Righteousness: "Hast thou for the ox
a judge,
That those in charge care for the ox with pasture?
Who as lord at his desire can ward off Frenzy with the companions
of the Lie?"

Righteousness answered: "No helper is there for the ox without
harm.
No understanding have men how the Righteous treat the lowly.
Strongest of beings is he at whose call I come with aid.

"Mazdah remembreth the plots which indeed have already been made
Both by daevas and mortals and those to be made in future.
Ahura is the decider, it shall be as he wills.

"Then indeed with outstretched hands let us pray to Ahura,
My soul and the pregnant cow, we two pressing Mazdah with entreaties:
"Let there not be destruction for those living aright or for cattle-
breeders by the companions of the Lie."

Then himself spake Ahura-Mazdah, who knoweth the law, with
wisdom:
"No lord or judge hath been found, in accordance with justice,
But surely the Creator hath formed thee for the cattle-breeder and
peasant.

"This rule concerning the fat hath Ahura-Mazdah, of like mind
with Righteousness,
Made for the cattle, and milk for those who crave food, by his command, the Holy."
"Whom hast thou, Good Thought, to care for us two among mortals?"

"This man is known to me here, who alone hath heard our commands,
Zarathushtra Spitama; he, Mazdah, longs to make known our
thoughts and those of Righteousness,
So let us bestow on him charm of speech."

But then the Ox Soul lamented: "That for protector I must be con-
tent
With the useless word of a weak man when I long for a mighty ruler.
When shall there ever be one who can give effectual aid?"

This doubt was scarcely flattering to the newly summoned prophet,
yet Zoroaster did not hesitate:

Do ye, Ahura, grant them strength, Righteousness and that Kingdom,
Good Thought, whereby he may establish pleasant dwellings and
peace.
I at least have believed, Mazdah, that thou canst bring this to pass.

Where else are Righteousness and Good Thought and the Kingdom?
So, ye men,
Welcome me for instruction, Mazdah, for the great community.

Satisfied at last, the Ox and the Cow exclaim: "Now, Ahura, is help
ours, we are prepared to serve those like you."[3]
Suffering of poor dumb cattle at the hand of raiding nomads gave
occasion for the prophet's call. Throughout his preaching there echoes

[3] Yasna 29.

the eternal struggle between the roving men of the steppe and the peaceful tiller of the soil. Agriculture is a holy occupation. The dumb animals on whom falls the burden of the labor are sacred.

CONCEPTION OF EVIL

Ahura-Mazdah, clothed with the firmly fixed heaven, is sole God, but in eternal struggle with him is the Evil Spirit. From the beginning, there were twin spirits, the Better and the Bad. They established Life and Not-Life, the Worst Existence for the companions of the Lie, Best Dwelling for the follower of Righteousness. The daevas also took counsel together; delusion came upon them; they chose Worst Thought and together rushed to Frenzy, by whom they sicken the life of mortals. But to man came the Kingdom, Good Thought, and Righteousness; Piety gave continued existence and indestructibility of body, that at the Last Judgment he may have precedence. Man has free will; each must decide for himself before the Great Consummation.[4]

The daevas are all offspring of Bad Thought, the Lie, and Pride, long known for their deeds in the seventh region of earth, the abode of man. Men who do the worst are called pleasing to the daevas, who have defrauded man of Good Life and Immortality, taught by Evil Spirit, Bad Thought, and Bad Word to ruin mankind. It was Yima, Vivahvant's son, who gave men flesh of the ox to eat and brought evil into the world.

One convert Zoroaster made, his cousin Maidyoi-maongha,[5] but many were his opponents. The false teacher destroys the doctrines and the plan of life; he prevents the possession of Good Thought from being esteemed. He declares the Ox and the Sun are the worst to behold with the eyes—the prophet is denouncing the nocturnal sacrifice of the bull by the worshipers of Mithra. He turns the wise into Liars, he desolates the pastures, and he lifts his weapons against the Righteous. The Liars destroy life and attempt to hinder matron and master from attaining their heritage. With shouts of joy they slaughter the ox; they prefer Grehma, the Karapan priest of the daevas, and the lordship of those who seek the Lie, to Righteousness. Grehma shall attain the realms in the Dwelling of Worst Thought; so, too, the destroyers of this life shall weep in their desire for the message of Ahura-Mazdah's prophet, but he shall prevent them from beholding Righteousness. Grehma and the Kavis, the local kinglets under

[4] Yasna 30.   [5] Yasna 51:19.

Median vassalage, have long attempted to overthrow the prophet; they assist the Liar and say: "Let the ox be slain, that it may kindle the Averter of Death to help us"; Zoroaster is condemning the use of the intoxicating *haoma* drink. Thus the Karapans and the Kavis are brought to a common ruin.[6]

Bendva, the very great, perhaps the local kinglet, has always opposed him; at the judgment may he be ruined through Good Thought! The prophet has been hindered by the teacher of this Bendva, a Liar long apostate from Righteousness.[7] There are others who seek to kill the prophet, sons of the Lie's creation, of ill will to all who live. Zoroaster recalls an insult, the more bitter as it inflicted pain on his dumb friends: The Kavi's wanton displeased Zarathushtra at the Winter Gate, for he prevented him from stopping there, when his two horses came, shivering with the cold. The Karapan priests refuse to obey the decrees and laws of pasturage; "for the harm they do to the herds by their deeds and doctrines, let the doctrine bring them at last to the House of the Lie."[8]

RELIGIOUS QUESTIONS

Like all prophets, Zoroaster has his times of doubting:

> This I ask thee, tell me truly, Ahura:
> How should prayer be made to one like you?
> As to a friend, Mazdah, teach thou me.

With this same introduction, he asks all the questions which puzzle his mind. Who was created Father of Righteousness? Who fixed the path of the sun and stars? By whom does the moon now wax, now wane? Who upheld the earth from beneath and the sky from falling? Who made the waters and plants? Who yoked swiftness to the wind and to the clouds? Who created Good Thought? What artificer made light and darkness, sleep and waking, dawn, noon, and night, reminders to the understanding man of duty?

> This I ask thee, tell me truly, Ahura:
> What I proclaim, is it indeed the truth?
> Will Piety aid Righteousness by deeds?
> Will Good Thought announce thy Kingdom?
> For whom made thou the fortune-bringing
> pregnant cow?

Can he be sure of the Kingdom? Will they properly observe in word and deed his religion, the best for all men? Will Piety extend to those

[6] Yasna 32:3 ff.   [7] Yasna 49:1-4.   [8] Yasna 51:10, 12, 14.

to whom Mazdah's religion is proclaimed? For this was he set apart by Mazdah in the beginning; all others he hates. Who among those with whom he talks is Righteous and who a Liar? He doubts himself and his cause. On which side is the true enemy? Should not the Liar who opposes Mazdah's Salvation be regarded as the enemy? How shall they drive from them the Lie to those who are disobedient? Shall the Lie be put in the hands of Righteousness to destroy it by the words of Mazdah's doctrine, to work a mighty destruction among the Liars, to bring upon them torments? Has Mazdah the power to protect his prophet when the two hostile armies come together in battle? To whom will he grant the victory? Let there be signs to make known the healing judge. How shall he attain this goal, union with Mazdah himself?

And then after this incursion into mysticism comes a bit of very practical human nature:

> This I ask thee, tell me truly, Ahura:
> How, Righteousness, shall I earn that reward,
> Ten mares with a stallion and a camel,
> Which was promised me, Mazdah, with Salvation
> And Immortality, whose giving is thine?

> This I ask thee, tell me truly, Ahura:
> He who shall not give the reward to him who earned it,
> Who, true of word, fulfils it for him,
> What punishment for this shall be for him at first?
> I know what his last punishment will be.

Have the daevas ever been good rulers? This he asks of those who see how for the sake of the daevas the Karapan and Usij priests have given the cattle to Frenzy, how the Kavi has made them continually mourn, instead of increasing the pastures through Righteousness.[9]

THE AFTERLIFE

Persecution only fixed his eyes the more eagerly on the future, the awaited coming of the divine Kingdom, the Great Consumation, the Renewing of the World. This Consummation will be brought about by the Saoshyanto, the Saviors, Zoroaster and his followers; and the prophet hopes it will not be long delayed. At the Last Judgment, Righteousness will overcome the Lie. He wishes to know whether even before that the Righteous might overcome the follower of the Lie. How can he know that Mazdah and Righteousness actually have

[9] Yasna 44.

PLATE IX

Guardian Divinities in Audience Hall

Cyrus and Attendants (from *AMI*, Vol. I, Pl. III).

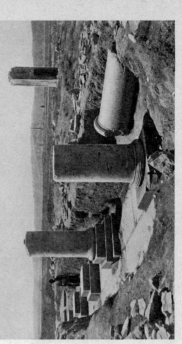

Columns from Palace (from *AMI*, Vol. I, Pl. II)

Bull Capital (from Herzfeld, *Iran in the Ancient East*, Pl. XXXIX)

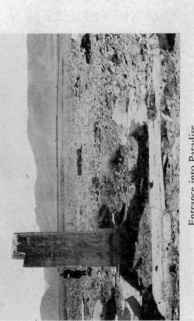

Entrance into Paradise

PARSAGARDA

PLATE X

Tomb of Cyrus (courtesy Oriental Institute)

Fortress and Plain

PARSAGARDA

PLATE XI

Fire Temple

Fire Altars

FIRE WORSHIP AT NAKSHI-RUSTEM

PLATE XII

Weaving

Basketry

Feasting

Nomadism

The Native

PLATE XIII

Building (in Egypt)

Pottery Shop (in Egypt)

Tea Shop (in Damascus)

Selling (in Jerusalem)

THE NATIVE AT WORK

PLATE XIV

The Stick Dance at Tel Tainat

The Great Feast at Seleucia

THE NATIVE AT LEISURE

PLATE XV

Wadi Hammamat

Nubian at Persepolis

Nubians in Upper Egypt

EGYPT

PLATE XVI

Inscription and Relief (courtesy George G. Cameron)

Rocks and Plains (courtesy Aerial Survey, Oriental Institute)

BEHISTUN

power over the Liars who menace him? Let there be a confirmation of his vision from Good Thought. Let the Savior know what his reward shall be. When shall the warriors learn to understand the message? When shall Mazdah smite the filthiness of the intoxicating drink, the *haoma*, through which the Karapan priests deceive the wicked rulers of the lands? Who can make peace with the bloodthirsty Liars? To whom shall the knowledge of Good Thought come? They are Saviors of the lands who strive to fulfil Mazdah's commandment.[10]

One's own Conscience, whether of Righteous or Liar, will determine his future award. With Zoroaster as associate judge, Ahura-Mazdah himself will, through his counselor Righteousness, separate the wise from the unwise. Afterward, Zoroaster will guide those he has taught to invoke Mazdah across Chinvato Peretav, the Bridge of the Separator. Those who wisely choose will proceed to the House of Song, the Abode of Good Thought, the Kingdom of Good Thought, the Glorious Heritage of Good Thought, to which one travels by the Road of Good Thought, built by Righteousness, on which the Consciences of the Saviors pass to their reward. There shall they behold the throne of mightiest Ahura and the Obedience of Mazdah, the felicity that is with the heavenly lights.[11]

But the foolish shall go to the House of the Lie, the House of Worst Thought, the home of the daevas, the Worst Existence. Their evil conscience shall bring them torment at the Judgment of the Bridge and lead them to long future ages of misery, darkness, foul food, and cries of woe.[12] He who follows his own inclination, making his thought now better, now worse, whose wrong and right deeds balance, at the last shall dwell apart in an intermediate abode.[13]

PATRONAGE OF VISHTASPA

Rejected and opposed at home, Zoroaster thought of flight, but

> To what land to flee, whither to flee shall I go?
> From nobles and priestly colleagues they separate me,
> Nor are the peasants to me pleasing,
> Nor yet the Liar princes of the land.
> How am I to please thee, Mazdah-Ahura?

He knows the reason for his lack of success: he has few cattle and so few followers. He cries to Mazdah for support as friend to friend.

[10] Yasna 48:1–2, 9–12.
[11] Yasna 31:14 ff.; 50:2, 4; 51:9, 13 ff.   [12] Yasna 46:10–11; 49:11; 53:6.
[13] Yasna 33:1; 48:4; cf. J. D. C. Pavry, *Zoroastrian Doctrine of a Future Life* (1926).

When shall the sun risings come to win Righteousness for the world, when shall the Saviors appear in accordance with prophecy? The infamous Liar has prevented the Righteous from making the cattle prosper; he who deprives the Liar of power or life shall prepare the ways of sound doctrine. He who converts a Liar, if he is sure, let him announce it to the kinsmen; may Mazdah-Ahura protect him from bloodshed.

Whom can the prophet secure as protector when the Liar attempts to injure him? Let no harm come through the man who thinks to injure Zoroaster's possessions; let his deeds recoil on himself. By their rule, the Karapans and Kavis have accustomed men to evil deeds to destroy life. Their own soul and conscience shall torment them when they come to the Bridge of the Separator; for all time they shall dwell in the House of the Lie.[14]

From his mountain home in northwest Iran, Zoroaster set forth with his Spitamid kinsmen in search of a land where his doctrines might find readier acceptance. While the prophet was laboring for the conversion of his neighbors, the face of the world was changing. The once powerful Median Empire was disintegrating, and Cyrus, of his own Persian people, was in revolt against Astyages. While Vishtaspa (Hystaspes), son of Arshama, of the rival Achaemenid line of kings, was ruling Parthia and Hyrcania, he seized the opportunity to loosen the ties binding him to his Median overlord. Here the weary prophet found a welcome, and soon Vishtaspa's wife Hutaosa (Atossa) was a convert to the faith.[15] The conversion of the husband naturally followed, and Vishtaspa became a patron of the new religion.[16]

"What reward Zarathushtra hath promised to those of his congregation, which in the House of Song Ahura-Mazdah hath first attained, with this have I promised myself through thy blessings, Good Thought, and those of Righteousness. Kavi Vishtaspa hath accepted, with the rule of the Congregation and the paths of Good Thought, the doctrine which the holy Ahura-Mazdah with Righteousness hath devised."[17] "Whoever of mortals rejoices Zarathushtra Spitama is worthy to be renowned, for him shall Mazdah-Ahura give life, for him shall he make possessions flourish through Good Thought, him

[14] Yasna 46:1–11.

[15] Yasna 15:35; cf. 9:26; 13:139; 15:35.

[16] In the traditional history Vishtaspa is a member of the Naotara Dynasty (Yasht 5:98; 15:35; 17:56).

[17] Yasna 51:15–16.

we consider a friend through Righteousness." "O Zarathushtra," asks Ahura-Mazdah, "what righteous man of thine is a friend of the great Congregation, or who desires to be renowned?" Zoroaster answers: "It is the Kavi Vishtaspa at the Judgment. Those whom thou, Mazdah-Ahura, wouldst unite in thy house will I summon with words of Good Thought."[18]

Soon after his conversion, in 550, Vishtaspa's first son was born; in witness to his new religion, the son was named Daraya-Vohumanah, "Who Sustains Good Thought," Darayavaush in the western dialect and Darius to the Greeks.[19] Some five years later Cyrus arrived in northeastern Iran, and Vishtaspa exchanged the status of a minor Kavi for that of satrap in the already mighty Persian Empire.

Under the protection of Vishtaspa, the prophet spent many happy years. He praises his cousin and first convert, Maidyoi-maongha, his clansmen, children of Haechat-aspa, descendants of Spitama—since they distinguished the wise from the unwise; by their deeds they have won Righteousness, by the first laws of Ahura. Frashaoshtra and his brother Jamaspa, of the Hvogva family, became his loyal supporters, and Frashaoshtra promised the prophet his daughter Hvovi, "Having Fine Oxen," as wife. "The fair form of a dear one hath Frashaoshtra Hvogva given me; may sovereign Mazdah-Ahura grant that she attain possession of Righteousness for her good Self."[20]

Several sons—Isatvastra, Urvatatnara, and Khvarechithra are named[21]—and several daughters were born and grew up. "The best possession known is that of Zarathushtra Spitama, for Ahura-Mazdah will give him through Righteousness forever the delights of the blessed life, and to those who practice and learn the words and deeds of the good doctrine. Then let them gladly seek by thought, words, and deeds, his pleasure, and the prayers for his worship, the Kavi Vishtaspa and Zarathushtra's son, the Spitamid, and Frashaoshtra, making straight the paths for the Doctrine of the Savior which Ahura hath ordained."

His daughter is to marry Jamaspa: "This man, Pouruchista, sprung from Haechat-aspa and Spitama, youngest of Zarathushtra's daughters, hath he given thee as thy instructor for union with Good Thought, Righteousness, and Mazdah. So take counsel with thy

[18] Yasna 46:13-14.

[19] E. Herzfeld, *Archaeological History of Iran* (1935), p. 40; cf. Yasna 31:7. Since Darius was twenty-eight at his accession in 522, he was born in 550; his Zoroastrian name proves that already in 550 his father had been converted, a very important chronological datum.

[20] Yasna 51:17 ff.; 46:15 ff.; 49:8. [21] Yasht 13:98.

understanding, wisely perform the holiest deeds of Piety." Jamaspa
promises: "Fervently will I love her, that she may piously serve
father, husband, peasants and nobles, a righteous woman for righteous
men. May Ahura-Mazdah grant her the glorious heritage of Good
Thought for her good Self."[22]

CRISIS

Gladly would we leave the prophet at this point, surrounded by his
loving family and friends. But the delightful picture was darkening
as old age drew on. The nomads were threatening, and the holy war
must be preached:

So they whose deeds are evil, let them be the deceived and forsaken, let
them all cry aloud. Through good rulers let [Ahura] bring slaughter upon them
and peace from them for the joyful villagers. Let him bring torment upon
them, he that is Greatest, with the bonds of death, and soon let it be! To
men of evil creed belongs the Place of Corruption. Despising the Law, losing
their body, they think to cast down the worthy. Where is the Righteous Lord
who shall rob them of life and freedom? Thine is the Kingdom, Mazdah,
whereby thou canst give to the right-living poor the better portion.[23]

The crisis becomes more acute:

This aid I beg in prayer with outstretched hands, Mazdah: First of all,
Righteousness, the works of the Holy Spirit, whereby I may please the counsel of Good Thought and the Ox Soul. I would serve thee, Mazdah-Ahura,
with Good Thought; grant me through Righteousness the blessings of life,
both material and of thought, by which it shall bring its supporters bliss. I
would praise thee as never before, Righteousness, Good Thought, and Mazdah-Ahura, and those for whom Piety increases the Kingdom, never to be destroyed; come ye to my support at my call.

Zoroaster feels that he is nearing life's end:

I who with Good Thought have set my heart to watch the soul, who have
known rewards from Mazdah-Ahura for my deeds, while I have power and
strength will I teach men to seek after Righteousness. When shall I, as one
who knows, see thee, Righteousness, and Good Thought, the throne of
mightiest Ahura and the Obedience of Mazdah? Through this holy word on
our tongue may we turn the robber horde to the Greatest. Come thou with
Good Thought, through Righteousness grant by thy righteous words, Mazdah, an enduring gift: strong support to Zarathushtra, and to us the means
by which to overcome the foe.

Grant, Righteousness, this reward, the blessings of Good Thought.
Grant, Piety, to Vishtaspa and to me our desire. Grant, sovereign Mazdah,
that your prophet may recite the holy word of instruction. Of thee, the Best,

of one will with Best Righteousness, I ask the best, Ahura, desiring for warrior Frashaoshtra and myself and those thou wilt give them, gifts of Good
Thought for all time. By our use of these thy bounties, Ahura, may we not
provoke thy wrath; Mazdah, Righteousness, and Best Thought, we strive to
offer hymns of praise to you, since you are best able to advance desire for the
Beneficent Kingdom. Then for those thou dost know to be worthy, through
Righteousness and as understanding Good Thought, fulfil, Mazdah-Ahura,
their longing with attainment. Then indeed I know that words of prayer,
serving a good end, are effectual with you. Therefore would I preserve Righteousness and Good Thought forevermore; do thou teach me, Mazdah-Ahura,
by thy mouth through thy Spirit to proclaim how the First Life shall be.[24]

With this last prayer, the words of Zoroaster are ended. Yashts,
which in their present form are somewhat later but contain much
early material (some of it pre-Zoroastrian), quote prayers of Vishtaspa or of the horseman Zairivari against such enemies as Tathrya-
vant, Peshana, Humayaka, Darshinika, Spinjaurushka, and Ashta-
aurvant, son of Vispa-thaurvoashti. They also refer to wars with
Arejat-aspa of Hyaona. Still later tradition informs us that Arejat-
aspa took Balkh by assault and murdered Zoroaster and his disciples
at the altar. The prophet must have died about the time of the great
series of revolts against Darius; if there is truth in the tradition, the
actual assassin may have been Frada of Margush (Margiana), who invaded Bactria, or perhaps one of his fellow-nomads.[25]

LASTING EFFECTS OF ZOROASTER'S RELIGION

But we need no late legends of a birth heralded by divine signs, of a
life filled with miracles, of a martyr death at the hands of nomads to
prove Zoroaster's greatness. From his own words we may trace his
life and the development of his thought. We may realize the loftiness
of his aspirations and the limitations which only make him more
human and more lovable. His doctrines show no trace of influence
from the more ancient Orient. They are native to his soil and his race.
They have grown from the older Aryan faiths, but they have risen
above the simple Aryan daeva-worship to heights never again
reached by unaided Aryan religious thoughts.[26]

[24] Yasna 28.

[25] Yasht 5:109, 112 ff.; 9:29 ff.; 13:101; 17:49 ff.; 19:87; A. V. Williams Jackson, *Zoroaster,
the Prophet of Ancient Iran* (1899), pp. 118 ff.; cf. Olmstead, *AJSL*, LV (1938), 404.

[26] Important works are Jackson's *Zoroaster* (1899) and *Zoroastrian Studies* (1928); J. H. Moul-
ton's *Early Zoroastrianism* (1926); C. Bartholomae's *Die Gatha's des Awesta* (1905); M. W. Smith's
Studies in the Syntax of the Gathas (1929); A. Meillet's *Trois conferences sur les Gathas* (1935); H.
Lommel's *Die Religion Zarathustras* (1930); and H. S. Nyberg's *Die Religionen des alten Iran* (1938).

Early in his career the prophet had questioned whether his followers would properly observe the doctrines of his religion. Darius the Great was the son of his patron Vishtaspa and must often have talked with the prophet at his father's satrapal court. His own inscriptions are filled with reminiscences of the great teacher's language, and the records on his tomb may actually quote one of the Gathas.[27] Despite his fine language, Darius did not live up to the prophet's teaching, and his constant use of the terms "Lie" and "Liar" only bring out the more strongly his own frequent lapses from the truth.

Scarcely was Zoroaster dead than the inevitable reaction began. While the historical Zoroaster was more and more lost in the mists of the past, while as the founder of the religion he became increasingly divine, the Gathas he composed (even those complaining of his doubts and fears, his hopes for a gift of ten mares, a stallion, and a camel, his sympathy for his shivering horses), were chanted in ritual and took on a mystic and efficacious character. To him was ascribed approval of gods and of practices revived from the ancient Aryan paganism—the very gods and practices he had so emphatically condemned. Later on, Aryan paganism was in turn submerged in part by Magism, a survival from an older and still more barbarous antiquity.

If his own people now held sacred the *haoma*, to Zoroaster the "filthy intoxicating drink," if they restored the nocturnal cults of Mithra and the sacrifices of the cattle he had so strongly protested, if they again worshiped the mother-goddess Anahita, there were others who found his own preaching more congenial. In the decay of the older national religions, the best minds found in his doctrines something so new, so fresh, so bracing that his influence may be detected in the majority of the later religious movements. It is no accident that the Gathas of Zoroaster sound so much like the first New Testament.

[27] E. Herzfeld, *Altpersische Inschriften* (1938), pp. 4 ff.

Chapter VIII

USURPER DARIUS

ACCESSION OF DARIUS

ZARATHUSHTRA, an honored guest at Vishtaspa's court, must often have conversed with the young Darayavaush—Darius, son of Hystaspes, as with the Greeks we name him. In his autobiography he boasts his descent through Vishtaspa, Arshama, Ariyaramna, and Chishpish from the founder Hakhamanish: "Therefore we are called Achaemenids. From long ago we are princely, from long ago our family was royal. Eight of my family were formerly kings, I am the ninth; nine are we in two lines."[1]

This is literally true—though not quite in the sense Darius would have us believe. His line was indeed the elder and under Ariyaramnes had enjoyed the precedence, but Median conquest had leveled both to a common vassalage. Successful revolt against Astyages the Mede had brought to power the younger line as represented by Cyrus, Cambyses, and Bardiya. While Darius' grandfather, Arsames, remained at best a petty kinglet, Hystaspes was fortunate enough to be made satrap of Parthia and Hyrcania. As such, he accompanied Cyrus on his last and fatal expedition. Cambyses took the young son into his personal service. In 522, at the age of twenty-eight, Darius was king's spearbearer in Egypt.[2] Before the year was ended, Darius was king.

How so young a man reached so exalted a position while both father and grandfather were still living[3] is explained in the autobiography in the following manner. There was a man of his family, Cambyses by name, son of Cyrus, who was king. Cambyses had a brother, Bardiya by name, of the same father and mother. Afterward Cambyses slew that brother, but it was not known to the people that Bardiya was slain. After Cambyses went to Egypt, the people became rebellious; the Lie was great in the lands. Afterward a Magian (Magush), Gaumata by name, arose and falsely claimed to be that

---

[1] *Beh.* §§ 1 ff.

[2] Herod. iii. 139; Xen. *Cyrop.* iv. 2. 46; for age, cf. Herod. i. 209.

[3] *Beh.* § 35; cf. § 13; Susa Charter 13 ff.; Xerxes, *Persepolis* h 17 ff.

Bardiya. He arose from Pishiyauvada of Mount Arakadrish on March 11, 522. All the people abandoned Cambyses and went over to the pretender. On July 1 he took for himself the kingdom. Afterward Cambyses died by his own hand.

Now that kingdom had belonged from ancient times to the family of Darius. No man, even one of his own family, was able to take the kingdom from that Gaumata. People feared exceedingly lest he slay the many who had known the true Bardiya and so could prove the falsity of Gaumata's claim. No one in fact dared say anything against him until Darius arrived. Since we last hear of him as spearbearer to Cambyses in Egypt, obviously Darius must have left the army in Palestine as soon as the death of the former monarch was known and must have hastened at once to Media to press his claim to the vacant throne.[4]

By the favor of Ahuramazda and with the aid of six other conspirators, Darius slew that Gaumata and his allies at the fort Sikayauvatish in the Median district of Nisaya on September 29, 522. By the favor of Ahuramazda, Darius became king. Later on in the autobiography Darius names the others of the "Seven," the conspirators who took part in the killing: Vindafarna (Intaphrenes), son of Vayaspara; Utana (Otanes), son of Thukhra; Gaubaruva (Gobryas), son of Marduniya (Mardonius); Vidarna (Hydarnes), son of Bagabigna; Bagabukhsha (Megabyzus), son of Datuhya; and Ardumanish, son of Vahauka. "You who shall be king hereafter, preserve well the family of these men."[5]

STRUGGLE FOR LEGITIMIZATION

Darius restored the power taken from his family. He established it on its former foundations. He rebuilt the temples Gaumata had destroyed. To the freemen he restored the pasturelands and to the nobles the cattle herds and peasants which the Magian had seized.[6] He labored until it was as if Gaumata had never taken away the family house. Such was the official version, presented in the autobiography and advertised to the world on the Behistun rock. It was accepted by the Father of History, by Ctesias, and by their Greek successors.[7]

---

[4] Cf. Herod. iii. 73.

[5] *Ibid.* 70; Ctes. *Pers.* xii, Epit. 45; *Beh.* § 68.

[6] E. Herzfeld, *Altpersische Inschriften* (1938), pp. 51–52.

[7] *Beh.* §§ 10 ff.; Herod. iii. 30–31, 61 ff.; Ctes. *Pers.* xii, Epit. 41–44; Plato *Epist.* vii. 332A; *Leg.* 695B; Just. i. 9. 4 ff.; Polyaen. vii. 11. 2.

Yet there are not lacking indications that it is far from true to the facts. Darius, we have seen, belonged to the imperial family only by a collateral branch. There is no reason to believe that he was considered next in line for the throne. Had the next of kin belonged to his line, his grandfather and his father would have had precedence over him.

Darius claims that Bardiya, younger brother of Cambyses, was put to death by that brother. Yet there is complete disagreement between our sources as to the time, place, and manner of his murder. Darius puts the episode before the Egyptian expedition of Cambyses, Herodotus during it, and Ctesias after. The official version followed by Herodotus blames a certain Prexaspes for the actual murder, but there was doubt as to whether "Smerdis" was killed while hunting near Susa or was drowned in the Erythraean Sea. After the death of Cambyses, we are expected to believe, Prexaspes publicly recanted his story, informed the people of the secret murder of the "true" Bardiya, and then in repentance committed suicide. Deathbed repentances we all know as frequent devices of the propagandist; after a suicide, the dead man can tell no tales. Furthermore, the "false" Smerdis was false only in claiming to be the son of Cyrus; his actual name *was* Smerdis! The height of absurdity is reached when we are informed that so alike were the "true" and the "false" Smerdis that even the mother and sisters of the "true" Smerdis were deceived!

Contemporary Aeschylus had no doubt that Mardos, as he calls him, was a legitimate monarch and that he was slain by the wiles, not of Darius, but of Artaphrenes, one of the "Seven," whom Hellanicus names Daphernes. Xenophon declares that immediately after the death of Cyrus, *his sons* began civil dissensions. Needful legitimization of usurped rule may be sensed in his marriages: to Atossa and Artystone,[8] daughters of Cyrus; to Phaedyme (daughter of one of the Seven, Otanes), who like Atossa had been wife to Cambyses and then to Bardiya; and to Bardiya's own daughter Parmys.[9] Last but far from least, Darius so continuously insists that all his opponents—the "false" Bardiya in particular—were liars that we are convinced "he doth protest too much."[10]

[8] For a younger Artystone cf. Cameron, "Darius' Daughter at Persepolis," *JNES*, I (1942), 214 ff.

[9] Aeschyl. *Pers.* 774; Hellanicus *Pers.*, Frag. 181(J); Xen. *Cyrop.* viii. 8. 2; Herod. iii. 68, 88; vii. 224.

[10] Cf. Olmstead, "Darius and His Behistun Inscription, "*AJSL*, LV (1938), 392 ff. It is significant that in Herod. iii. 72 Darius is made to give an elaborate defense of lying.

In his autobiography Darius, immediately after the protocol, states that Ahuramazda handed over to him the lordship: "These are the lands which obeyed me; by the favor of Ahuramazda, I was their king." He then lists the twenty-three satrapies.[11] Darius would have us believe that at his accession all these countries were loyal and only later rebelled. Further on in the narrative he admits that, when he had killed the Magian, Elam and Babylonia revolted; but he still insists that it was not until after the capture of Babylon that the other revolts occurred: of his own homeland Parsa, of Elam for a second time, of Media, Assyria, Egypt, Parthia, Margiana, Sattagydia, and the Saka.[12] Let us test the claim.

REVOLTS OF THE SUBJECT PEOPLES

Of his own immediate family, his grandfather Arsames and his father Hystaspes were alive; the one apparently possessed no authority, and the other was satrap of Parthia and Hyrcania but gave no assistance either at the accession or later. Two satraps, Dadarshish of Bactria and Vivana of Arachosia, declared for Darius; the remaining lands were either in revolt or at least indifferent. While, as Darius himself admits, the whole empire accepted Bardiya without question, his assassination brought renewed hopes of national independence which bred a perfect orgy of revolts among the subject peoples. Ambitious Persian satraps also prepared to make a bid for the vacant throne. Even in his father's satrapy of Parthia and Hyrcania there was a faction which refused to accept the son as monarch. When Dadarshish and Vivana declared for the usurper, Bactria was invaded by Margian Frada. There was also armed opposition in Arachosia. Sogdiana was cut off by rebel Margiana and was attacked by raiding Sacae.

Darius claims as loyal "Those of the Sea," Sardis, and Ionia. These three satrapies are never called rebel in the autobiography, but a Greek story gives a different picture. Oroetes had been installed satrap of Sardis in the later years of Cyrus. Toward the end of Cambyses' reign, pretending that he had incurred the royal displeasure, Oroetes invited Polycrates to come on a visit to him at Magnesia; the great tyrant of Samos, thus deceived, was taken, killed, and his body crucified. In the period of confusion which followed Bardiya, Oroetes slew Mitrobates, satrap of Dascyleium. Darius sent Oroetes a royal messenger; on the return the messenger was ambushed and killed.

<hr/>

[11] *Beh.* § 6.   [12] *Ibid.* §§ 16, 21.

Then Darius, still too weak and newly enthroned for open warfare, determined on subtlety: he sent Bagaeus, son of Artontes, to Sardis with sealed letters, by which he tested the loyalty of the scribe and then of the spearmen guards. When these obeyed, the order was given for the death of Oroetes and thus Sardis, Dascyleium, and Ionia were recovered.[13]

Although Darius had killed Bardiya in Media, he could not hold even that country. With an army which he confessed was small, he started off to recover Babylonia, only to learn that Media itself had risen under a native named Fravartish or Phraortes. The rebel assumed the name, however, of Media's great hero Khshathrita and announced that he was of the seed of Uvakhshatra or Cyaxares, despite the fact that his appearance was anything but Aryan. His round head, snub nose, deep-set eyes, and prominent cheekbones were in sharp contrast to the long beard, the hair cut straight across the forehead, the bun at the back of the neck, and the high boots, the short, straight skirt, and the narrow belt which we have come to know as the original Median costume. The palace troops in Ecbatana were won over; the second Media of Raga submitted, and Assyria and apparently Armenia and Cappadocia followed its example. An army was dispatched into Parthia and Hyrcania, and Hystaspes was unable to stem its advance; Fravartish seemed about to re-establish the former empire of Cyaxares.[14]

Parsa, the very homeland of Darius, was lost to a claimant for the name of the murdered Bardiya, a certain Vahyazdata who rose up from Tarava in Yautiya (Utii) of Carmania.[15] Naturally, he assumed the long sweeping robe, carefully draped, the laced boots, and the curled hair shown in the portrait of his pretended double. The Persians in the palace of Cyrus at Parsagarda acknowledged his legitimacy, even though his low, flat, projecting nose, his round head, and his beardless pointed chin proclaimed loudly the fact that he, too, was no Aryan. Vahyazdata sent an army against Arachosia; before he reached that country, he must have secured Aria and Drangiana.

Elam declared its independence under the leadership of Hashshina, son of Ukbatarranma. This leader is pictured as having a low, pointed nose, pronounced cheekbones, heavy moustache, and firm chin, whose contours are not concealed by a close-trimmed beard; he is clad in a

---

[13] Herod. iii. 120 ff.; Diod. x. 38; Aelian. *Var. hist.* vii. 11; Athen. xii. 522B.

[14] Median revolt against Darius, Herod. i. 130.   [15] *Ibid.* iii. 93; vii. 68.

long garment with vertical folds, quite unlike those of the other "rebels." As Darius reached the Babylonian alluvium, at the exit from the Zagros Pass, he sent to Elam a royal messenger whose appearance was enough to frighten the natives into fettering their new ruler and bringing him to Darius, who promptly put him to death.[16]

No sooner had the news of Bardiya's assassination reached Babylon, by October 3, 522, only four days after its occurrence, than that country rose against the foreigners. To his willing subjects, the new king by whom the documents were dated was Nebuchadnezzar III, son of Nabu-naid, Babylon's last independent monarch. (According to Darius, however, his true name was Nidintu-Bel, son of Aniri.) He is pictured as an old man whose deeply seamed cheeks, short upper lip, and bristly, jutting beard serve as foil to a short, bulging nose. Over his forehead his wavy hair is drawn back to a row of scallops, and under his ear falls a single lock; the back of his neck is shaven. He wears a single shirt, the lower half pulled up to expose the bare knees and twisted tight to form a girdle. His age gave credence to his claim that he was a son of Nabu-naid, dead only seventeen years before. At any rate, it is Darius who is caught lying when he inserts Babylon among the satrapies which were loyal at the beginning of his reign.[17]

Nebuchadnezzar had stationed troops in the reed thickets along the Tigris to seize all boats and to guard the crossings. Darius outflanked them by transporting his soldiers on inflated skins, quite as we see them depicted on Assyrian reliefs and as we ourselves have seen them used in recent days. This detachment was defeated on December 13. A second battle, fought five days later at Zazana on the Euphrates with Nebuchadnezzar himself, was decisive; the Babylonian forces were driven into the water, and the "rebel" fled to Babylon. He was quickly taken and slain. By December 22, 522, Babylon was dating its tablets in the "year of the beginning of the reign of Darius, king of Babylon, king of lands."[18] While there, Darius seems to have occupied the north palace of Nebuchadnezzar.[19]

Also while he was in Babylon, so declares Darius, Parsa, Elam,

[16] *Beh.* §§ 16 ff.

[17] For the documents of Nebuchadnezzar III and Nebuchadnezzar IV cf. Olmstead, *op. cit.*, pp. 399 ff., to be corrected in details by Cameron, "Darius and Xerxes in Babylonia," *AJSL*, LVIII (1941), 316 ff.; cf. R. A. Parker and W. H. Dubberstein, *Babylonian Chronology, 626 B.C.—A.D. 45* (1942), p. 13.

[18] *Beh.* §§ 18 ff.; Herod. iii. 150 ff.; cf. Cameron, "Darius and Xerxes in Babylonia" *op. cit.*, p. 318; Parker and Dubberstein, *op. cit.*, p. 13.

Cf. R. Koldewey, *Mittheilungen des deutschen Orient-Gesellschaft*, III (1899), 8.

Media, Assyria, Egypt, Parthia, Sattagydia, and Saka revolted.[20] Aryandes, left as satrap by Cambyses, had alienated the Egyptians by his harshness and was therefore expelled.[21] With him was driven out the pro-Persian Udjahorresne, who made the following defense: "I was a good man in my city. I delivered its inhabitants in the very great disturbance which came to pass in all the land, of which the like had not occurred in this land. I protected the weak against the strong"—another belated echo of Hammurabi's lawbook—"I preserved the fearful, if ill befell him, I did for them every useful thing, at the time when it ought to be done for them. I gave proper burial for him who had no burial; I supported all their children; I established firmly all their houses. I did for them every useful thing, as a father would do for his son, when the disturbance came in this nome, when the great disturbance came in the whole land."[22]

RECOVERY OF SUBJECT LANDS

But the tide had begun to turn. Already on December 9, Dadarshish of Bactria had repelled the "leader" of Margush (Margiana), the broad plains about the present Merv. (The flat-nosed Frada with long, sharply pointed beard had perhaps just murdered the prophet Zoroaster.) Sometime later, Margiana itself was recovered. On December 29, at the fort Kapishakanish, Vivana defeated the invaders dispatched by Vahyazdata from Parsa against Arachosia. On the last day of the year, Vaumisa won a victory at Izala in Assyria, the modern Tur Abdin complex of hills. Though the army of Persians and Medes with Darius remained small, he still had to deplete further his forces by dispatching an army, led by Vidarna, one of the "Seven," against Media. A skirmish took place at Marush on January 12, 521. Darius asserts that the opposing general was unable to hold his position; nevertheless, Vidarna was compelled to halt his advance until his master was able to assist him. He therefore encamped at Kanpada (Cambadene) in the great plain of Kermanshah, once occupied by the Elamite tribe of Hamban.[23]

Surrender of Hashshina only gave opportunity for a genuine Persian, Martiya, son of Chichikhrish, from Kuganaka, to descend by the direct route from Parsa to Susa and to proclaim himself Ummannish, the name of the Elamite king feared by Assyrians as Humbanigash. (On the relief his face is destroyed, but he wears a robe which hides the

[20] Beh. § 21.   [22] Cf. pp. 88–91.
[21] Polyaen. vii. 11. 7.   [23] Beh. §§ 38–39, 45, 29, 25.

arms and is pulled up to give a blouse effect and to expose the skirt.)
Darius left Babylon early in February. Before striking toward the
Zagros Gates, he made the easy detour by Susa, and the Elamites in
fear killed Martiya. Now Darius could send a force under Artavardiya
back along this same route to attack Vahyazdata, whose troops in
Arachosia were annihilated in the district Gandutava on February 20.
The general fled to the fort Arshada, where he was taken and slain
by Vivana. On March 6 Hystaspes defeated at Vishpauzatish the
Parthian rebels who had allied themselves to Fravartish of Media.[24]

With the main army of Persians, Darius himself repassed the Zagros
and joined Vidarna in Kanpada. On May 8 he defeated Fravartish at
Kundurush. This was the decisive battle. In recognition of this fact,
he soon after chose the spot to carve the inscription which commemorated his victories. Accompanied by a few horsemen, Fravartish
escaped to Raga (Rhages) in the second Media but was pursued and
brought back. His nose, ears, and tongue were cut off, his eyes were
put out, and he was exposed to the sight of all the people until Darius
was ready to impale him and to hang his allies in the fortress Ecbatana.[25] The severity of the punishment and the detail with which it is
described indicate how serious was the danger from this Mede.

On May 20 a second Dadarshish, this time an Armenian, defeated
his fellow-countrymen at Zuzu. Four days after, Artavardiya defeated, at Rakha of Parsa, the pretender Vahyazdata, who, however,
escaped and collected another army at Pishiyauvada. Six days later
the Armenian Dadarshish won his second victory at the fort Tigra. On
June 11 Vaumisa won his own second victory in the district Autiyara
in the Tiyari Mountains, where until our own day the "Assyrian"
Christians maintained a precarious independence. On June 30 Dadarshish claimed his third victory at the fort Uyama. How slight were
these alleged victories may be realized from the fact that both Vaumisa and Dadarshish had afterward to await the arrival of Darius in
person.[26]

Immediately after the execution of Fravartish and with Parsa yet in
revolt, Darius left a part of his army in garrison at Ecbatana and late
in April hurried north to Raga. Here he still further depleted his reduced forces by sending aid to his father, even now unsuccessful in reducing to obedience his own Parthian subjects. News arrived of the

[24] *Ibid.* §§ 22–23, 41, 46 ff., 35.
[25] *Ibid.* §§ 31–32; Ecbatana, the fortress, Ezra 6:2.
[26] *Beh.* §§ 41–42, 26 ff., 30.

indecisive battles in Assyria and Armenia; Darius turned west by Lake Urumia and the Rowanduz Gorge, reaching Arbela late in July.[27]

Sagartia, the eastern portion of the Median Empire restored by Fravartish, seized the opportunity to rise under the native Sagartian Chithratakhma, who, like Fravartish, claimed to be of the family of Cyaxares. The Persian and Median troops left behind to garrison Ecbatana were led against him by the Mede Takhmaspada, and the rebel was taken in battle. Brought to Darius at Arbela, he suffered the fate of Fravartish.[28]

Hystaspes, with the aid of the Persian army detached by his son from Raga, on July 11 succeeded in finally defeating the opponents of the new regime at Patigrabana, and Parthia at long last was safe.[29] Four days thereafter, Artavardiya crushed Vahyazdata and his newly raised army at Mount Parga. The news of the capture was relayed to Darius, and by royal command the claimant to Bardiya's name was impaled with his leading officials at Uvadaichaya.[30]

The last known Babylonian tablet to recognize Darius was written at Sippar on September 8. The very next day a tablet dated by Nebuchadnezzar was prepared at Uruk. The revolt had begun at the otherwise unknown village of Dubala, presumably in South Babylonia, though some time elapsed before he could rightfully claim the title "king of Babylon" by the occupation of the capital, which had been accomplished by September 21.[31] Although called by Darius an Armenian, he was not of the recent Aryan hordes who had given that land the name of Armenia. His father's name, Haldita, reverences Haldish, chief god of the older Haldian population, while Arakha's flat nose, narrow, half-closed eyes, straight hair, and spiked, outthrust beard give further indication that in fact he represented this older stratum. On November 27, 521, the false Nebuchadnezzar IV—like the third reputed to be a son of Nabu-naid—was made captive by Vindafarna (Intaphrenes), another of the "Seven." By royal order, he and the chief citizens who had supported him were impaled at Babylon.[32] The natives long remembered the plunder of the royal tombs, that of Queen Nitocris in particular.[33] In the revolts the satrap Gobryas had disappeared. By March 21, 520, we find a new satrap in Babylonia:

[27] Ibid. §§ 33, 36.
[28] Ibid. § 33.
[29] Ibid. § 36.   [30] Ibid. §§ 42–43.
[31] Parker and Dubberstein, op. cit., pp. 13–14.
[32] Beh. §§ 29–30.   [33] Herod. i. 187; Plut. Reg. imp. apophtheg. 173B.

Hystanes, as the Greeks called him, but to the natives he was known as Ushtani, governor of Babylon and of Across the River.[34]

By the end of September, 520, a ghost writer had prepared the royal autobiography. Each paragraph was to commence: "Says Darius the king." The story was to tell of Darius' ancestry, of how the Lie made the lands rebellious, and of how he fought nineteen battles and seized nine kings in his successful recovery: "This is what I did during one and the same year after I became king."[35] Actually the recovery took a little longer, from September 29, 522, to November 27, 521. Statistics of enemy killed, wounded, or taken prisoner, location of places where battles were fought, and dates exact to the day should prove its accuracy.

Let not a future reader consider the account to be a lie; Ahuramazda is the king's witness that it is true. In fact, much else was done which is not here recorded, lest in future it should seem too much. "Ahuramazda brought me help and the other gods who are"; unlike Zoroaster, Darius is not quite a strict monotheist. "According to righteousness have I walked; neither to weak nor to strong have I done wrong."

Not only did he write in cuneiform—Persian, Elamite, Akkadian: "I made inscriptions in other ways, in Aryan, which was not done before." Aramaic had already established itself as the normal language of the Achaemenid chancellery in its dealings with the western satrapies, as is amply proved by the royal decrees to the Jews, from the time of Cyrus onward, cited in Ezra; the Aramaic alphabet was now employed to write Persian. The cuneiform of Babylonia was largely written with ideograms in which a single sign might represent a whole word. A few ideograms had survived in Persian cuneiform. Now many Aramaic words were taken over, written with Aramaic signs but to be read as Persian. Thus the Pahlavi system of half-ideographic writing came into use. "It was written and read to me," is tacit recognition of the ghost writer. The autobiography was then forwarded to all the lands. A stele from Babylon has preserved one section of the Akkadian version.[36] A papyrus from Elephantine indi-

[34] Herod. vii. 77; Strassmaier, *Babylonische Texte: Darius* (1897), No. 27; cf. No. 82; Clay, *BRM*, Vol. I, No. 101.

[35] R. G. Kent, "Old Persian Texts. III. Darius' Behistan Inscription, Column V," *JNES*, II (1943), 105 ff.

[36] F. H. Weissbach, *Babylonische Miscellen* (1903), No. X.

cates that a copy of the Aramaic was prepared for the use of the Jewish mercenary colony; and, when it was worn out by frequent consultation, still another copy was later made.[37]

The full text of the autobiography, in the three official languages which employed cuneiform, Persian, Elamite, and Akkadian, was carved above the spot where the decisive Battle of Kundurush was fought. Below ran the main road from Babylon, through the Zagros Gates, and then along the plateau toward Ecbatana, sixty-five miles to the eastward and hidden behind the second high barrier range. Up a side valley from the Kirmanshah Plain, the line of mountains which shuts in the plain on the east ends abruptly in a towering spur; five hundred feet above a spring-fed pool a cleft in the rock offered a precipitous cliff for the huge incription and the accompanying panel relief, ten by eighteen feet in size.

Before his royal protégé floats Ahuramazda. On his head the bearded god wears the cylindrical hat, flaring at the top and distinguished from the king's by the horns of divinity and an eight-rayed solar disk, both of immediate Assyrian origin. His garment is the draped robe, whose full sleeve curves down to the braceleted wrists. His left hand grasps the ring which bestows sovereignty on monarchs; his right hand, palm open, is raised in blessing. He is lifted aloft on a huge ring, on either side of which are attached long, almost rectangular, wings, filled with wavy lines and divided into three sections by curls. A sort of tail, treated in the same fashion, is divided into two sections and depends from the ring; from the ring stretch down objects which have been described as two forked lightning bolts but which more probably are to be identified with the clawed legs of the Egyptian vulture-goddess of truth.

Darius, a fine Aryan type with high brow and straight nose, stands his natural height, five feet ten inches. On his head is the war crown, a battlemented gold band studded with oval jewels and rosettes. His front hair is carefully frizzed, and his drooping moustache is neatly twirled at the tip; the back hair forms on the neck a large bun which reaches almost to the prominent ear. The square beard is arranged in four rows of curls alternating with straight strands, quite in the manner of those of his Assyrian predecessors. A long robe covers the whole of his stocky body; its skimpy, sharp-pointed sleeves permit only the thick wrists and hands to emerge, and, below, it is draped at the side to allow a glimpse of the trousers and beneath them the low-

[37] A. E. Cowley, *Aramaic Papyri of the Fifth Century B.C.* (1923), pp. 248 ff.

laced shoes. The king's left hand grasps the strung bow tipped with a duck's head; his right is uplifted in worship of Ahuramazda. Behind him stand the bearers of the royal bow and quiver and of the royal spear, presumably Gobryas and Aspathines. They are dressed in much the same costume as their master but are differentiated by rounded beards and by fillets adorned with eight-pointed rosettes.

Down the road, at the Gate of Asia, earlier conquerors had ordered themselves represented in the act of proudly trampling their prostrate enemies.[38] The same attitude was adopted for Darius. Under the king's left foot, flat on his back and one foot lifted in agony, lies the robed Gaumata, stretching out his hands in vain supplication. Before their conqueror stand the other rebels, their necks roped together, their hands tied behind their backs.

So high is the relief above the road that it is completely dwarfed by its majestic surroundings. We wonder how Darius expected his autobiography, even though inscribed around the relief in the three languages of the cuneiform, to be read by the traveler from below. One's first view of this famous monument is sure to be a disappointment.[39]

Barely a century had elapsed when it was visited by a Greek physician to one of Darius' royal descendants. This Ctesias knew that the mountain was named Bagistanus and that it was sacred to the supreme Persian god whom he called Zeus. He saw the park, watered by the great spring, the cliffs whose height he estimated to be over two miles, the inscription in "Syrian letters," and the relief. But the curse of Darius was forgotten; his descendants had not preserved the memory of his deeds or even of his name. Ctesias ignorantly ascribed the monument to the half-fabulous *Assyrian* Queen Semiramis![40]

[38] Cf. N. C. Debevoise, "Rock Reliefs of Ancient Iran," *JNES*, I (1942), 80.

[39] H. C. Rawlinson, "The Persian Cuneiform Inscription at Behistun," *JRAS*, Vol. X (1847). For earlier progress in decipherment see R. W. Rogers, *History of Babylonia and Assyria* (6th ed., 1915), I, 21 ff.; definitive edition of the text, L. W. King and R. C. Thompson, *The Sculptures and Inscriptions of Darius the Great on the Rock of Behistun in Persia* (1907); for easily accessible text and translation, F. H. Weissbach, *Die Keilinschriften der Achämeniden* (1911), pp. 8 ff.; latest photograph of relief, Cameron, "A Photograph of Darius' Sculptures at Behistan, "*JNES*, II (1943), 115-16. Descriptions of the relief figures in the present volume are based on the typescript Master's thesis of Cleta Margaret Olmstead (Mrs. David O. Robbins), "Studies in the Stylistic Development of Persian Achaemenid Art" (1936), pp. 6 ff.; for general discussion see Olmstead, "Darius and His Behistun Inscription," *op. cit.*, pp. 392 ff.

[40] Ctes. *Pers.* i, Epit. 12 (Diod. ii. 13. 1-2); Isid. Char. 6.

Chapter IX

A NEW LAWGIVER

AFTER two years of hard fighting, Darius was finally recognized as king over most of western Asia. A short breathing-spell was at last afforded him to consider the state of the huge empire which had so unexpectedly fallen to his victorious arms. These years of revolt had brought virtual chaos to whole regions and had revealed hitherto unsuspected weaknesses in the imperial structure. Darius was, above all, an administrator by instinct, and throughout the remainder of his long and prosperous reign he was to devote the greater part of his energies to this imperative work of reorganization.

The first question to be decided was the location of the empire's capital. Even while Parsa was still in revolt, it would seem, he had decided to found a new imperial center in his native land. Meanwhile, as soon as Elam was reconquered, Darius settled down temporarily in Susa, where he began to erect a palace. It was already occupied by the end of the crucial year 521.[1]

Once settled, he turned his attention to his first projected reform—a new law to be enforced upon the whole empire. In his autobiography, composed sometime in 520, he announced: "By the favor of Ahuramazda, these lands walked according to my law; as was to them by me commanded, so they did."[2] This was no idle boast. Early in 519, still in this same official second year, we find the lawbook already in use among the Babylonians: "According to the king's law they shall make good" is substituted for the usual guaranty by the seller in a document recording a slave sale.[3]

The term for "law" is new. Instead of the long-familiar "judgments," we have the good Iranian *dat*, which we have long known as the Hebrew *dath* of the Book of Esther, while the *data sha sharri* of the Babylonian document is exactly identical in meaning with the

---

[1] Herod. iii. 129.

[2] *Beh.* § 8.

[3] J. P. Strassmaier, *Babylonische Texte: Darius* (1897), No. 53.

119

datha di malka, equally well known from the decree of Artaxerxes I quoted in the Book of Ezra.[4]

That the laws, which together made up the Ordinance of Good Regulations, were collected, revised, and incorporated in the new lawbook under the watchful eyes of Darius himself cannot be doubted. It is equally evident that the new book could not have been so quickly formulated had it not been based on one already in use.

BABYLONIAN SOURCES

Commercial Babylonia had, from the beginning of written history, recognized the supremacy of law. The law administered by Babylonian judges was not code law as the term is understood by continental European jurists; rather, it was akin to the common law of Anglo-Saxon nations, which is based on precedents so ancient that the "memory of man runneth not to the contrary." From these precedents, illustrated by definite cases for each of the various categories of the law, the judge formed his decisions in the specific case before him by the doctrine of logical analogy. For his assistance there was what we would call a casebook, such as is still employed in our own law schools. Though the casebook was promulgated by royal authority and was authenticated by the approval of the gods, in no proper sense should it be entitled a code.

At various times in the later third millennium before our era, casebooks in the current Sumerian were made available. The regular formula for each case was: If a man does thus and so, then certain consequences follow. The same formula was employed by the more famous Hammurabi, whose casebook we possess virtually complete.[5] He claims only that he "established justice and righteousness in the language of the land," that is, he translated the precedent cases from Sumerian into the now current Akkadian. Actually there is good evidence that there had been a progressive evolution to adapt the ancient case law to more developed legal procedures and to new social and economic conditions.

The original collection of decisions was written down in the ordi-

---

[4] Ezra 7:26; Esther 1:8, 13–15, 19; 2:8, 12, and frequently; cf. Olmstead, "A Persian Letter in Thucydides," *AJSL*, XLIX (1933), 161, n. 17; "Darius as Lawgiver," *ibid.*, LI (1935), 247 ff.

[5] For a text edition with Latin translation see A. Deimel, *Codex Hammurabi* (1930); for the latest English translation see D. D. Luckenbill and Edward Chiera, in J. M. P. Smith, *The Origin and History of Hebrew Law* (1931), pp. 181 ff. [On the use of the term "code" cf. B. Landsberger, "Die babylonischen termini für Gesetz und Recht," *Symbolae ad iura orientis antiqui pertinentes, Paulo Koschaker dedicatae* (1939), pp. 219 ff.]

nary cursive cuneiform on clay tablets to be preserved in the archives of Esagila, the great temple of Marduk, lord of Babylon. How they looked may be realized from contemporary copies made on large rectangular tablets of five or six columns which have been recovered from the ruins of Ekur, temple of a far older god of Nippur—Enlil. For more immediate use this book-hand cuneiform was "transliterated" into the older script still employed for monumental writing and was inscribed on a magnificent diorite stele set up in Esagila, where it could be read to judge and litigant alike. The laws were placed under the protection of the sun-god Shamash, the divine lawgiver, who on the stele is pictured in the act of granting the necessary authority to Hammurabi.

In time an Elamite conqueror carried off the stele to his capital at Susa, where he set it up again in the temple of his own god. This did not mean the loss of the famous casebook to Babylonia. There were duplicate stelae in other cities and copies in other temple libraries. From one of these the casebook became known to the Assyrians, who used it to supplement or perhaps to supplant their own casebook of earlier centuries. Sargon paraphrased one of the most famous statements of Hammurabi's prologue, and the same statement, "that the strong should not injure the weak," was quoted literally by his great-grandson, the scholar-king Ashur-bani-apal. Copies of the casebook, one slavishly following the Akkadian original, the other "translated" into Assyrian, bear the library mark of the great collection of ancient literature brought together by order of the same Ashur-bani-apal. They also prove that in Assyria its title was "Judgments of Hammurabi," though in Babylonia the first line of the work, "When the god Anu the exalted," remained unchanged as the title, in accordance with general usage.

Continued use of Hammurabi's collection was possible for well beyond a millennium, since it was not a detailed code demanding constant amendment but was merely a list of key decisions whose precedents might be considered eternally valid. As such, it was adopted for use by the Persian conquerors. Cyrus, in an Akkadian proclamation intended for Babylonian reading, does sincere homage to the great lawbook by imitating its very phraseology. That this was not mere lip service is proved by a document of his third regnal year which bases the decision on the "king's judgments."[6]

[6] *VS*, Vol. VI, No. 99.

COMPARISON WITH HAMMURABI'S LAWS

Darius, however, was determined that he should be ranked with Hammurabi as a great lawgiver. Fortune was not kind. While tablet after tablet has been unearthed with extracts from Hammurabi's casebook, the Ordinance of Good Regulations has been so completely lost that it is actually necessary to prove that it ever existed. The few contemporary references in the business documents do confirm its reality and witness certain legal categories it included, but there is not enough for comparison with the treatment accorded in the earlier lawbook. When, however, we compare the Akkadian texts of certain portions of Darius' inscriptions with the prologue and epilogue of Hammurabi's lawbook, we discover so many parallels in vocabulary and phraseology (as in thought and order) that we are convinced the younger statesman copied the elder, and it becomes possible to reconstitute in large degree those sections of Darius' own composition.

Hammurabi starts off his introduction with the time "when Anu, the exalted, and Enlil, lord of heaven and earth, committed to Marduk, firstborn son of Enki, lordship of all men, when they pronounced the lofty name of Babylon, made it great among the quarters of the earth, and in its midst established for him an everlasting kingdom whose foundations were firm as heaven and earth."[7]

In sharpest contrast to the Babylonian polytheist, Darius was almost—though not quite—a monotheist: "A great god is Ahuramazda, who created this earth, who created yonder sky, who created man, who created favor for man, who made Darius king, one king of many, one lord of many."[8] "A great god is Ahuramazda, who gave this beautiful work, who gave favor to man, who gave wisdom and friendliness to Darius the king."[9]

Hammurabi claims that he rules according to the will of the gods: "At that time Anu and Enlil named me, Hammurabi, the exalted prince, the worshiper of the gods, to cause righteousness to prevail in the land, to destroy the wicked and the evil, to prevent the strong from injuring the weak, to go forth like the sun over the blackheaded people, to enlighten the land, and to further the welfare of the people."[10]

"I am Darius, the great king, king of kings, king of lands of every tongue, king of this great distant territory, son of Hystaspes, an

[7] *CH*, col. I, ll. 1–26.

[8] Darius, *Persepolis g* 1; Susa Restoration of Order 1; Alvand 1; Suez c 1; Naqsh-i-Rustam A 1.

[9] Naqsh-i-Rustam B 1.   [10] *CH*, col. I, ll. 27–49.

Achaemenid, a Persian, son of a Persian, an Aryan, of Aryan seed,"
boasts his successor.[11] "Darius the king thus says: When Ahuramazda
saw that these lands were hostile, and against one another they
fought, afterward he gave it to me. And I, over it for kingship he
appointed me. I am king. In the protection of Ahuramazda, I established them in their place. And what I said to them they did according to my will."[12]

"Much which had been made ill I made for good. There were lands
which to one another were hostile, their men killed one another.
This I did, in the protection of Ahuramazda, so that these should not
kill one another. Each man in his place I established, and before my
own judgments they were fearful, so that the strong man should not
kill and should not injure the *mushkinu*." Here Darius is not only
paraphrasing a well-known passage in the preceding lawbook, repeated by Hammurabi in both introduction and conclusion;[13] he is
using the archaic term for "serf" quite unknown from late Babylonian sources though only too common in a lawbook where the social
classes were not equal before the law.[14]

Hammurabi had placed his stele under the protection of Shamash;
Darius likewise made it known that his own god was the actual lawgiver: "O man, what is the command of Ahuramazda, let this not seem
repugnant to you; do not depart from righteousness, do not revolt."[15]

Immediately after his introduction, Hammurabi had given a long
list of the cities and temples, both within and without Babylonia,
which he had restored or which had profited by his benefactions.[16]
Incidentally, the list testified to the wide extent of his rule. Darius
insists: "In the protection of Ahuramazda, these are the lands which I
seized beyond Parsa, and I am their ruler, and tribute they brought to
me. And what by *me* was said to them, that they did. And my *own*
judgments restrained them."[17] Regularly at this point a list of the sa-

[11] This is the regular formula of most inscriptions.

[12] Naqsh-i-Rustam A 4.

[13] *CH*, col. I, ll. 37 ff.; rev. col. XXIV, ll. 59-60.

[14] Restoration of Order record, V. Scheil, *Inscriptions des Achéménides à Suse* ("Mém.," Vol.
XXI [1929]), pp. 61 ff.; *Actes juridiques susiens: inscriptions des Achéménides* ("Mém.," Vol. XXIV
[1933]), pp. 116 ff.; *Mélanges épigraphiques* ("Mém." Vol. XXVIII [1939]), pp. 34 ff.; R. G. Kent,
"Old Persian Inscriptions," *JAOS*, LI (1931), 221–22; "More Old Persian Inscriptions," *ibid.*,
LIV (1934), 40 ff.; "The Restoration of Order by Darius," *ibid.*, LVIII (1938), 112 ff.; F. H.
Weissbach, *ZDMG*, XCI (1937), 80 ff.; *ZA*, XLIV (1938), 140 ff.

[15] Naqsh-i-Rustam A 6.

[16] *CH*, col. I, l. 50—col. V, l. 13.

[17] Susa Restoration 9-13.

trapies follows, always revised to be up to date. For the full list might be substituted: "Parsa, Media, and the other lands of other tongues, of the mountains and of the lands, of those this side of the sea and that side of the sea, this side of the desert and that side of the desert."[18]

From these close parallels to the prologue we turn to similar parallels with Hammurabi's epilogue:

[These are] the righteous judgments which Hammurabi the wise king established and gave the land a firm support and a gracious rule. Hammurabi the perfect king am I. I was not careless nor was I neglectful of the black heads whom Bel presented to me and whose care Marduk gave to me. Regions of peace I spied out for them, grievous difficulties I overcame; I caused light to shine forth for them. With the powerful weapons which Zamama and Innanna intrusted to me, with the breadth of vision which Ea allotted to me, with the might which Marduk gave me, I expelled the enemy north and south; I made an end to their raids. I promoted the welfare of the land. I made the peoples rest in habitations of security. I permitted no one to molest them.

The great gods have named me, and I am the guardian shepherd whose scepter is righteous; my beneficent shadow is spread over the city. In my bosom I have carried the peoples of the land of Sumer and of Akkad, under my protection I have led their brethren into security. With my wisdom I covered them. That the strong should not injure the weak, and that they should give justice to the orphan and the widow in Babylon, the city whose head Anu and Enlil raised aloft, in Esagila, the temple whose foundations stand firm as heaven and earth, to pronounce judgments for the land, to render decisions for the land, to give justice to the oppressed, my weighty words I have written upon my stele, and in the presence of the image of me, king of righteousness, I have set it up.

The king who is pre-eminent among kings am I; my words are precious, my wisdom is unrivaled. By the command of Shamash, the great judge of heaven and earth, may I make righteousness to shine forth on the land. By the word of Marduk my lord may there be none to set aside my statutes. In Esagila, which I love, may my name be remembered with favor forever.

Let any oppressed man who has a case come before the image of me, the king of righteousness. Let him have read to him the writing on my stele. Let him give heed to my weighty words. May my stele enlighten him as to his case and may he understand his case. May it set his heart at ease. Let him proclaim aloud: "Hammurabi is indeed a ruler who is like a true father to his people. He has given reverence to the word of Marduk his lord. He has obtained Marduk's victory to north and to south. He has made glad the heart of Marduk his lord. He has established prosperity for the people for all time and has led the land aright." Let him pray with his whole heart before Mar-

_____
[18] *Persepolis* g 1.

duk my lord and Zarpanit my lady. May the protecting deities, the gods who enter Esagila, the walls of Esagila, make his thoughts acceptable daily before Marduk my lord and Zarpanit my lady.[19]

Darius the king thus says: In the protection of Ahuramazda, I am of such a character: What is right I love and what is not right I hate. Never has it happened that any serf should make difficulty for a citizen and never has it happened that a citizen has made difficulty for a serf. What is right I love. The man who decides for the Lie I hate. I am not one who is angry and whoever is angry by my heart I restrain. And whoever injures, according to what he has injured I punish. And it has never happened that when he has injured he has not been punished. Of the man who speaks against the truth, never do I trust a word.[20]

As the first of the cases brought together in his lawbook, Hammurabi had cited those which deal with evidence; so Darius is here directing attention to the rules of evidence he himself has laid down. This group of precedents is ended by the case of the judge who reverses his own decision;[21] Darius proclaims that he, too, is impartial, punishing the wicked but rewarding the good. In the Persian edition this passage appears as: "What a man says against a man does not convince me until he satisfies the Ordinance of Good Regulations. What a man does or performs for others according to his ability, I am satisfied and my pleasure is great and I am well satisfied."

Like Hammurabi, Darius has no hesitation in praising himself:

Of such a character is my understanding and my command. When what has been done by me you shall see or hear, in the palace or in the camp, behold this my activity; over and above my thinking power and understanding; this is indeed my activity.

In so far as my body has strength, as a warrior I am a good warrior. Once let there be seen with understanding in the place of battle, what I see hostile, what I see not, with understanding and with command then I am first to think of friendly acts, when I see an enemy as when I see one who is not.

Trained am I both with hands and with feet. As a horseman I am a good horseman. As a bowman I am a good bowman both afoot and on horseback. As a spearman I am a good spearman both afoot and on horseback. And the skills which Ahuramazda has bestowed upon me, and I have had strength to use them, by the favor of Ahuramazda what has been done by me I have done with those skills which Ahuramazda has bestowed upon me.

This paragraph of the inscription on Darius' tomb was translated to Alexander the Great in abbreviated form: "I was a friend to my

[19] CH, rev. col. XXIV, ll. 1 ff.   [20] Naqsh-i-Rustam B.   [21] CH, secs. 1–5.

friends. As horseman and bowman I proved myself superior to all others. As huntsman I prevailed. I could do everything."[22]

Darius ends his admonitions with fresh instructions for his subjects: "Underling, vigorously make known how great I am and how great my skills, and how great my superiority. Let that not seem trifling which has been heard by your ear. Then hear what is communicated to you. Underling, let not that be made trifling to you which has been done by me. Let not the king inflict punishment."[23]

From the Babylonians, Hammurabi turned to his successors:

In days to come, for all time, let the king who arises in the land observe the words of righteousness which I have written upon my stele. Let him not alter the judgments of the land which I have pronounced, the decisions of the country which I have rendered. Let him not blot out my images. If that man have wisdom and be able to guide his land aright, let him give attention to the words which I have written upon my stele. May this stele enlighten him as to procedure and administration, the judgments of the land which I have pronounced, and the decisions of the land which I have rendered. And let him guide aright his black heads. Let him pronounce his judgments and render his decisions. Let him root out the wicked and the evil-doer from his land. Let him promote the welfare of his people.

Hammurabi, king of righteousness, to whom Shamash has given laws, am I. My words are weighty, my deeds unrivaled, too lofty for the fool, without difficulty for the intelligent, sent forth for honor. If that man gives heed to my words which I have written upon my stele, does not blot out my judgments, does not suppress my words, and does not alter my statutes, may Shamash prolong that man's reign as he has mine, who is king of righteousness. If that man does not heed my words, which I have written upon my stele, if he ignores my curses and does not fear the curses of the god, if he blots out the judgments which I have formulated, suppresses my words, alters my statutes, and blots out the writing of my name and writes his own, then may Anu [and a long list of other gods] curse him.[24]

Darius had no fear of these alien gods and did not hesitate to substitute his own name. But, with a sublime faith that a curse by the almighty Ahuramazda would be more effective than one by the numerous Babylonian divinities, he actually lifted Hammurabi's cursing

[22] Onesicritus in Strabo xv. 3. 8.

[23] For a recent edition of the two grave inscriptions see R. G. Kent, "The Nakš-i Rustam Inscriptions of Darius," *Language*, XV (1939), 160 ff. Earlier publications: F. H. Weissbach, *Die Keilinschriften am Grab des Darius Hystaspis* (1911); E. Herzfeld, *Altpersische Inschriften* (1938), No. 4. [See now Kent, *JNES*, IV (1945), 39 ff., 232.]

[24] *CH*, rev. col. XXIV, ll. 1 ff.

formulas for his own use, while in other respects closely imitating his predecessor's eloquent appeal:

Darius the king thus says: You who may be king hereafter, of lies beware. The man who lies destroy utterly, if you would speak, saying: "My land shall remain whole."

Darius the king thus says: This which I have done in the protection of Ahuramazda I have done in the same year. You who shall hereafter read what I have done—the writing which on a stele is written—believe me; for a lie do not take it.

Darius the king thus says: I call Ahuramazda to witness that it is true and not lies, all that I have done in one year.

Darius the king thus says: In the protection of Ahuramazda there is also much which I have done which is not written on this stele; for this reason it has not been written lest he who should read this writing hereafter should not believe all that I have done, but should speak, saying: "They are lies."

Darius the king thus says: Among the kings who were before me it was never done as by me in the protection of Ahuramazda in one year.

Darius the king thus says: Do you believe what I have done, and the true word speak to the people. If you do not conceal this word but tell it to the people, then may Ahuramazda be your friend, may your seed be numerous, and may your days be long. But if you should blot out these words, may Ahuramazda slay you and may your house be destroyed.

Darius the king thus says: This is what I have done in one year. In the protection of Ahuramazda have I done it. Ahuramazda was my strong help and the other gods who are.

Darius the king thus says: For this reason Ahuramazda brought me help, and the other gods who are, because I was not wicked nor was I a liar nor did I do any wrong whatever, neither I nor my seed. According to the judgments I continued, to the powerful and the serf alike no violence have I done.

When this stele you see and these images you do not destroy, but so long as is your strength you preserve them: may Ahuramazda be your friend and may your seed be made numerous; may your days be lengthened, may Ahuramazda extend them, and may whatever you do be successful.

Darius the king thus says: If you see this stele and these images and destroy them, and before this image do not offer sacrifice, and to its place do not restore it: may Ahuramazda curse you, and your seed may there not be, and what you make may Ahuramazda pull down![25]

In view of all these detailed parallels, there can no longer be any reasonable doubt that Darius and his legal advisers had before them an

---

[25] *Beh.* §§ 55–67. The Akkadian version is here followed; where broken, it is restored from parallels and from the other versions.

actual copy of Hammurabi's lawbook. Quite possibly he used the original stele, preserved in the temple of Inshushinak at Susa; or perhaps the tablets in late Babylonian writing of which fragments have been unearthed were copied for translation and adaptation. At any rate, reference to a stele is incongruous when applied to a rock-cut relief and inscription. "This image," then, refers, not to the figure of Darius overcoming his enemies on the Behistun rock, but to the royal portrait which, like that of Hammurabi, topped the stele. We may obtain some conception of the stele on which the original Ordinance of Good Regulations was presented to the Babylonians from the fragment of the Akkadian version of the autobiography on a diorite slab discovered in the northern palace at Babylon.

An explanatory passage, not required in the Akkadian, ends the inscription as prepared for the Behistun rock: "Thus says Darius the king: By the will of Ahuramazda I made stelae of other sorts, which was not done before, on baked tablets and on prepared leather. My name and my seal I ordered affixed upon them. Writing and order were read before me. Then I had these stelae carried into all distant lands to my subjects."[26] The lawbook was therefore intended for all the peoples of western Asia and not for the Babylonians alone. The parchments were, of course, in Aramaic, and thus the lawbook was made available for all who knew the language of current business and diplomacy.

ADMINISTRATION OF DARIUS' LAWS

While it is possible from the numerous inscriptions of Darius to reconstruct almost the whole of the introduction and conclusion of the lawbook, we know little of the various sections in detail. Something we may glean from incidental references in Babylonian or Aramaic documents or from stories told by Greeks or Jews. According to Herodotus, "the royal assessors are men who have been chosen from the Persians to be so until they die or until they are detected in some unjust action; they decide lawsuits for the Persians and interpret the ancestral precepts. Everything is referred to them."[27] As a Jewish writer puts it, these royal judges were "the wise men who knew the times, who knew law (*dat*) and judgment, the seven princes of Persia and Media, who saw the king's face and sat first in the kingdom."[28]

Darius, like Hammurabi, laid special weight on the rules for evi-

---

[26] Preserved fully only in the Elamite version, though present also in the Persian.
[27] Herod. iii. 31.   [28] Esther 1:13–14.

dence. Like his predecessors, he insisted on the incorruptibility of the royal judges. Herodotus has a tale in point. One judge, Sisamnes, had given an unjust judgment in return for a bribe; Cambyses slaughtered him like a sheep and flayed him. Then from the skin he caused leather strips to be tanned and with them covered the judgment seat of the son Otanes, who was appointed to the father's office with the grim admonition to remember on what he sat.[29] No wonder the Jews spoke of the "law of the Medes and Persians which alters not" and announced that "no edict or statute which the king establishes may be changed."[30]

Sandoces, son of Thamasius, was another royal judge who took a bribe. He was promptly ordered to be punished by crucifixion and was already on the cross when his life was saved by a curious whim of his royal master. In his lawbook Darius had made it clear that he was impartial, punishing the wicked but balancing up the good deeds against the evil.[31] The actual provision is given by Herodotus, who considers it most worthy of praise: "On account of one crime not even the king himself may slay anyone, nor may any of the other Persians inflict upon his own slaves a fatal punishment for a single crime. Rather, not until he has reckoned them up and has found that the unjust deeds are more numerous and greater than his services may he give rein to his wrath."[32] So Darius, after Sandoces had been actually hung on the cross, made his reckoning and discovered that the good he had done for the royal house was more than his sins against it. He was therefore released and made governor of Aeolian Cyme.[33]

Babylonian documents tell us something about the administration of the laws. One of 512 speaks of the official who is over the *dat;* his title, *iahudanu*, is not Babylonian and may be the original Iranian.[34] Another of 486 reports that two officials had imposed a new toll upon the barley, wheat, and mustard which were being cleared through the storehouse on a Babylonian canal. To the request for explanation, they answered: "It was decided, before the judges it was recorded; according to the king's law the toll for the king's house he shall give."[35] In our language, the question as to the legality of the new tax was brought before the court; the decision was given according to the prec-

[29] Herod. v. 25.
[30] Dan. 6:8, 12, 15; Esther 1:19.
[31] Cf. p. 125.
[32] Herod. i. 137.
[33] *Ibid.* vii. 194.
[34] *VS*, Vol. VI, No. 128.
[35] *Ibid.*, Vol. III, No. 159; Olmstead, "Darius as Lawgiver," *op. cit.*, p. 248.

edents in the new casebook and was, naturally, in favor of the government.

Punishments for crimes were severe. As a matter of course, offenses
against the state, against the person of the king or of his family, or
even against his property were liable to the death penalty. Of this
character is the majority of punishments described by the Greek authors; they were often horrible. There is little information on the
punishment for ordinary crimes, but mutilation of hands or feet or
blinding appear to have been common.[36]

The earliest reference to the new law shows that it contained regulations for slave sales.[37] A later reference indicates that one provision
dealt with bailments: "according to the king's *dat* which in regard to
deposits is written.[38]" For the rest, there is no suggestion in the numerous business documents from the reign or from its immediate successors that the provisions of Hammurabi's lawbook did not remain
valid.

SURVIVAL OF DARIUS' LAWS

To the end of his life Darius continued to express his pride in his
Ordinance of Good Regulations. His reputation as a lawgiver survived him. To Plato, Darius was the lawgiver whose laws had preserved the Persian Empire to the philosopher's own day.[39] As late as
218, well into the Seleucid period, the king's *dat* was still quoted as
authoritative.[40]

If this is all we learn of the contents of Darius' lawbook from cuneiform tablets, perhaps we may discover other references or even a few
fragments of the actual work incorporated in an Iranian lawbook of
the second century, which continues the use of *dat* for "law," for its
title is the Videvdat, the Antidemonic Law. Again comparison with
Hammurabi's lawbook is most instructive.

Hammurabi begins his citation of precedents with those relating to
evidence.[41] As test of the trustworthiness of a witness an ordeal is employed: throwing the accused witness into the river; the Antidemonic
Law orders rather the ordeal of boiling water, and the appeal is
to another sun-god, not Shamash but Mithra, the guarantor of agreements.[42] In a capital case the false witness is punished by Hammurabi

[36] Xen. *Anab.* i. 9. 13.
[37] Strassmaier, *op. cit.*, No. 53.
[38] Strassmaier, *ZA*, Vol. III (1888), No. 13, pp. 150 ff.
[39] Plato *Epist.* vii. 332B; cf. Xen. *Oeconom.* 14. 6.
[40] Strassmaier, *Darius*, No. 53.   [41] *CH*, secs. 1-4.   [42] Vid. 4:46.

with death. The later lawbook punishes the false witness in this world with what seems its equivalent—seven hundred stripes—and in the world to come by pains so severe that they would be worse than mutilation of limbs by knives, than nailing of bodies in crucifixion, than being hurled down cliffs, or than impalement.[43] Harsh penalties against perjury once inflicted by an Achaemenid royal judge have now been transferred to the afterlife.

Another subsection of the civil law deals with assault and battery. The antiquity of its provisions is shown by the fact that, like the precedents cited by Hammurabi, each begins "If a man," suggesting that the whole subsection is derived from Darius' lawbook. First is a definition of terms: If a man rises up with a weapon in his hand, he is a "seizer;" if he swings it, he is a "brandisher"; if he strikes the man with malice prepense, he is a "smiter"; on the fifth smiting offense, he becomes a "sinner," a habitual criminal.

The penalty for "seizing" is five stripes with the whip for the first offense, ten for the second, and so on up to ninety.[44] If he smites up to eight times without paying the appropriate penalty, he becomes a habitual criminal and receives the appropriate punishment—two hundred lashes. For "brandishing," the first penalty is ten stripes and after that the number rises in the same proportion. For smiting until the blood comes, until a bone is broken,[45] or until the man dies, the accused is given two hundred lashes.[46]

Equally clear through its relationship to Hammurabi's lawbook is the section dealing with physicians. Hammurabi announces that if a physician operates with a bronze knife on a man and the man dies or loses his eye, they shall cut off his hand;[47] thus the physician is effectually prevented from further surgical activity. According to our Iranian lawbook, no doubt adapted from that of Darius, death of three worshipers of the demons while the physician is learning his trade debars him from further practice, and if he then even dares cut one of the faithful, the punishment is that for wilful murder.[48]

Hammurabi also decreed a tariff of prices for the various operations, based as with modern surgeons on the ability of the men benefited to pay.[49] Exactly the same attitude is taken by the author of the lawbook

[43] Vid. 4:49b–55.
[44] Sixty stripes with an oxtail whip in public, CH, sec. 202.
[45] Ibid., secs. 197–99.
[46] Vid. 4:17–43. [48] Vid. 7:36–40.
[47] CH, sec. 218. [49] CH, secs. 215–17, 219–23.

quoted in this section of the Antidemonic Law. The house master is assessed merely the price of a cheap ox, the village chief one of medium
worth, the city head one of high value, but the lord of a subprovince
the value of a chariot and four. If he heals their wives, his pay is somewhat less: the price of a she-ass, a cow, a mare, or a she-camel. Cure of
the heir of a great house demands the price of an expensive ox.[50]

According to Hammurabi, the cattle doctor who saves the life of an
ox or ass must be paid by the owner a sixth of a shekel, but if the operation causes its death, he must pay the owner a quarter of its value.[51]
So, too, our lawbook: He shall heal an ox of high value for one of
low value as pay, one of low value for the cost of a sheep, and a sheep
for the price of a piece of meat.[52]

The final compilation of the canonical Antidemonic Law took place
during the reign of Mithradates the Great, king of kings, ruler of
Parthia. Naturally, he was particularly interested in Mithra, the
guardian of the plighted word, and so began his exposition of the civil
law with contracts. Yet it is significant of an earlier source that he
actually ascribes the listing of the six forms of contract to Ahuramazda, whom Darius had long since announced as the true divine
author of his own law. These six forms, then, are the word contract,
the hand contract, and the contract to the amount of a sheep, an ox, a
man, and a field; evidently our editor does not understand the exact
technical meaning which we can guess from contemporary documents
from Achaemenid Babylonia. Before he has mentioned contracts for
the delivery of goods and for the purchase of a wife,[53] in a passage
without any context he recalls the pledge of ox or garment wrongfully detained.[54] As to the six forms of contract, our editor knows only
that they rank in importance in the order of the list, that the lower is
canceled by the execution of the next higher type of contract in the
list, and that for nonexecution the damages are also those for the
higher. One question especially intrigues him: How long are the next
of kin—to the ninth degree—held responsible for breach of contract?
For from three hundred to a thousand years, while the sinner himself
suffers three hundred to a thousand stripes according to the enormity
of his offense.[55] He who does not restore the loan to the lender steals

[50] Vid. 7:41–43a.   [51] CH, secs. 224–25.

[52] Vid. 7:43b; that the section is quoted from an earlier work is shown by 7:44, where the
editor of the canonical Antidemonic Law tacitly condemns the use of operations by his vigorously
expressed preference for incantations!

[53] Vid. 4:44–45.   [54] Vid. 4:46.   [55] Vid. 4:2–16.

it; every day and every night that he retains his neighbor's property in his house as if it were his own he repeats his sin.[56] In the lawbook of Darius the crime of theft was presumably punished according to the prescriptions of Hammurabi with multiple restitution or by death.[57]

Hammurabi cites the precedent for seduction of a betrothed maid still living in her father's house; the man shall be killed and the woman be free.[58] The Iranian legist looks at the matter somewhat differently: If a man seduces a girl, whether a dependent of the family head or not, whether already contracted to a husband or not, and she conceives by him, she must not produce an abortion for shame of the people; both her father and herself shall suffer the penalty for wilful murder. If she reports the fact to her seducer and he advises resort to the old woman, and by means of her drugs an abortion is produced, all three are guilty. The seducer must support her but only until the child is born; as yet there is no hint of public acknowledgment of the child or of consequent marriage. If he will not support her and the child dies, it is wilful murder.[59]

From contemporary Babylonian documents, from the statements in the official Achaemenid records, from Greek writers, and from the later Iranian lawbooks, we have collected various indications of the contents of Darius' law. For the most part, the test has been agreement or deliberate recasting of the precedents cited by Hammurabi. Such a test has already made clear the elements in the so-called "Covenant Code" of the Hebrews which are thus dependent on Hammurabi,[60] and a similar test has here been employed for Darius. Other material may later be detected, but here is presented virtually all that can be recovered of the once famous King's Law prepared for Darius.

How the new reforms worked may be seen from Babylonian documents. Cyrus had left the internal administration unchanged, and native officials had been retained in their former posts. But his attempt to infuse new life into ancient forms had proved a failure. Darius initiated sweeping reforms. By March 21, 520, as we have seen, Gobryas had been supplanted as satrap of Babylon and Across the River by Hystanes. Soon Persians appeared in the subordinate offices

[56] Vid. 4:1.
[57] CH, secs. 6–8.
[58] Ibid., sec. 130.
[59] Vid. 15:9–16.
[60] Olmstead, History of Palestine and Syria (1931), pp. 107 ff.

and sat with natives on the bank of judges. New taxes, enforced by new officials, made their appearance.

These reforms may be illustrated by the case of our rascally old acquaintance Gimillu, son of Innina-shum-ibni, who, as we now discover, was nothing but a serf dedicated to the goddess of Uruk. During the nominal "first year" of Darius, from September 9 to November 27 of 521, Babylonia had been in revolt under the last Nebuchadnezzar. Gimillu took advantage of the consequent breakdown of governmental control. He had been given a thousand *kur* of seed barley, two hundred oxen to work the irrigating machines, and iron for making them; in return he was to furnish the Uruk temple ten thousand *kur* of barley and twelve thousand of dates. At the respective harvests he defaulted, saying that he would pay nothing unless he were given in addition four hundred peasants, six hundred oxen, and another thousand *kur* of seed barley. In that case, he would promise to give in the future the ten thousand *kur* of barley and the twelve thousand *kur* of dates. "Otherwise I will not give them. The privilege of that rental, if you wish, give me!" But times had changed. A fellow-serf who was in charge of the "basket" of Eanna made a better bid and on July 12, 520, secured the contract, which was assigned in the assembly of the citizens of Babylon and Uruk by the three high officials, Bel-iddina, administrator of Eanna, Nergal-sharusur, the deputy, and Bariki-ili, the head man of the king.[61]

In fear of arrest, Gimillu fled, but not until he had turned over the documents concerning the dates and the payment on the fields belonging to the divinities of Uruk to his brother Iddina. Andia, Iddina's wife, deposited the documents in the house of a slave who carried them off. The same high officials demanded the documents. Brought into the citizen assembly, Iddina swore by Bel, Nabu, and King Darius that no one had taken them, at least so far as he was aware. When they inquired why he had not handed over the documents, Iddina justified his action by declaring that Gimillu himself had warned him: "Do not give my documents to anyone else!" With this last defiance to constituted authority, Gimillu disappears from the scene.[62]

But the documents were recovered. On the same September 3, 520, on which the last document was written, we have another recording the dates which Gimillu had received for the last year.[63] Constituted authority had won.

[61] Louvre, Vol. XIII, No. 182.

[62] *Ibid.*, No. 181.   [63] *Ibid.*, No. 183.

Chapter X

FROM INDIA TO EUROPE

CONTACT WITH EUROPEAN GREEKS

EVEN before Egypt was recovered, Darius was thinking of new conquests to round off his frontiers. Among the captives brought to Susa from the retainers of Oroetes was his private physician, the famous Democedes of Italian Croton. Lost at first amid the crowd of slaves, he was remembered when the Egyptians, hitherto enjoying a monopoly of court practice, failed to cure a sprain of the royal foot. Although richly rewarded and given a seat at the king's own table, Democedes thought only of home; through the intercession of his patient, Queen Atossa, he persuaded the king to dispatch him from Sidon on a preliminary survey of the western coastlands. Although he himself escaped to Croton, his Persian companions ultimately returned to Darius with the first reports on the European Greeks.[1]

Fortunately for Darius, just as this time there was present at Susa another Greek, Syloson, brother of Polycrates, who as an exile from Samos in Egypt had given his red cloak to the spearbearer of Cambyses. Now that Darius was king, Syloson had identified himself as the royal benefactor; he wished no other reward than restoration to Samos. Otanes was placed in charge of the expedition, and the opponents of Syloson agreed to leave the island without fighting; a treacherous attack on the leading Persians induced Otanes to depopulate Samos, though later he aided Syloson in its resettlement.[2] The first step had been taken toward the conquest of the European Greeks.

STIRRINGS OF NATIONALISM IN JUDAH

Egypt was in revolt and must be reconquered. As preliminary to its successful invasion, the territory which controlled the desert route to the Nile had to be firmly held. Syria was part of the province Across the River, which since the conquest of Cyrus had been joined administratively to Babylonia; united, the two formed the satrapy

---

[1] Herod. iii. 129 ff.

[2] *Ibid.* 139 ff. If Herodotus is right in saying that the revolt of Babylon took place during the Samian expedition, then this occurred in 521.

Babylon and Across the River. Its loyalty must have been seriously compromised through the twice-repeated uprisings of Babylon under the two Nebuchadnezzars. Could Palestine, the one available bridgehead across the desert, be held quiet by a Jewish prince who owed his position to court favor, the invasion of Egypt should proceed as smoothly as did that of Cambyses.

At the court of Darius was the youthful Zerubbabel, son of Shealtiel, eldest son of Jehoiachin,[3] a former king of Judah whom Amel-Marduk, in reaction against his father Nebuchadnezzar's policy, had planned to restore to the throne. This Zerubbabel was chosen to be governor of Judah;[4] shortly after the New Year's celebration, April 3, 520, he set out from the royal presence and after a journey of something less than four months[5] reached Jerusalem about the beginning of August. Arrival of a Davidic prince encouraged nationalistic hopes. Soon after his appearance, on August 29, Zerubbabel and the high priest, Joshua, son of Jehozadak,[6] were met by a prophet named Haggai, who brought them a "word of the Lord." Eighteen years after the foundations were laid, the people were still excusing themselves: "The time has not yet come for God's house to be built." Fiercely Haggai reproached them: "Is it time for you yourselves to dwell in paneled houses while *this* house is in ruins?" For this reason, he announced, God had refused to bestow upon them the blessing of prosperity; let them ascend the mountain and cut wood to build the house, then God would be pleased and manifest his Glory.[7]

Of itself, such action portended revolt, which was hinted by the last phrase. Nevertheless, the work of rebuilding was begun on September 21,[8] and six days later the altar of burned offerings was set up and in use.[9] But the new structure now arising was so obviously inferior to the old that the aged men who in their youthful days had seen Solomon's temple wept.[10] To counteract this feeling of discouragement, Haggai on October 17 announced a new "word of the Lord": "Who is there among you who saw this house in its former glory, and how do you see it now? Is it not in your eyes as nothing? Nevertheless, be strong and work, for I am with you and my spirit abides among

---

[3] So Hag. 1:1, 12, 14; 2:2, 23; Ezra 3:2, 8; 5:2; Neh. 12:1. Only I Chron. 3:17–19 calls him son of Pedaiah, brother of Shealtiel.

[4] Hag. 1:1.   [5] Cf. Ezra 7:8–9.

[6] Jeshua, son of Jozadak, Ezra 3:2, which may represent contemporary pronunciation.

[7] Hag. 1:1–11.   [9] Ezra 3:1–3, 6a.

[8] Hag. 1:12–15.   [10] Ezra 3:12–13.

you. Fear not! For thus says the Lord of Hosts: Yet a little while and I will shake the heavens and the earth, the sea and the dry land, and I will shake all nations. Likewise the treasures of all nations shall come, and *this* house I shall fill with wealth. Mine is the silver and mine the gold; the future wealth of this place shall be greater than in the past, and in *this* place will I give peace."[11]

Those who opposed this wild project for declaring Jewish independence might cite the news of one victory of Darius after another over the various rebels who declared themselves native kings. Among these opponents was presumably the high priest, more in touch with current events and—after being so long recognized as the one official head of the Jewish community—scarcely prepared to welcome renewed subordination to an earthly monarch.[12]

A few days after Haggai's prediction, sometime after October 27, he was supported by Zechariah, Iddo's son, himself a priest. By this date the writings of the prophets who lived in the days of the kingdom had become virtually canonical, and to them Zechariah appealed in the Lord's name: "Be not as your fathers, to whom the former prophets preached: 'Thus says the Lord of Hosts: Turn now from your evil ways and your evil deeds,' but they did not hearken to me. Your fathers, where are they? And the prophets, do they live forever? But my words and my statutes, which I commanded my servants the prophets, did they not overtake your fathers? They repented and said: 'As the Lord of Hosts proposed to do to us, according to our ways and our doings, so he has done to us.' "[13] Their descendants should listen to Haggai, like the former prophets a speaker of the "word of God."

Meanwhile, representatives of the mixed population colonized by the Assyrians in Shechem had offered to take part in rebuilding the temple.[14] The offer was made in good faith, for since the deportation the colonists had worshiped the Hebrew local god, though retaining their former divinities.[15] Joshua apparently was inclined to accept their assistance, for throughout the Achaemenid period the high priests were regularly on good terms with their Samaritan neighbors. Haggai, on the contrary, was no cautious administrator but a fiery prophet, a strict monotheist, and an ardent nationalist. On December 18 he issued a solemn warning against the pollution which would be

---

[11] Hag. 2:1–9.

[12] Cf. Zech., chaps. 3–4, for clear indication that Joshua was no friend of Zerubbabel.

[13] Zech. 1:1–6.   [14] Ezra 4:1–2.   [15] II Kings 17:24–41.

incurred by the people if they accepted the proffered aid. That same day came a second prophecy. Once before he had declared that heaven and hearth would be shaken. To it was now added the overthrow of the thrones of the gentile kingdoms, destruction of the might of these nations, the overturn of the chariots and their riders; the horses and their riders should fall, each by the sword of his brother. To symbolize divine abandonment of Jehoiachin, Jeremiah had used the plucked-off ring; for his grandson the symbol was reversed: "In that day, says the Lord of Hosts, I will take you, O Zerubbabel, my servant, and will make you a signet."[16]

Destruction of Babylonian hopes of independence by the capture and death of the second Nebuchadnezzar only fanned higher the expectations of the Jewish nationalists. Toward the end of the year four men set out from Babylon for Jerusalem. They bore gifts of silver and gold from which, in the sequel, a crown was made for the awaited king of the Jews. Their arrival was announced by Zechariah on February 15, 519, in a long prophecy filled with apocalyptic imagery. Concealment was thrown aside; by a punning interpretation of Zerubbabel's name, "Seed of Babylon," the intended monarch was plainly indicated: "Thus says the Lord of Hosts: Behold the man whose name is the Shoot, for he shall shoot up and shall build the temple of the Lord. He shall assume majesty and rule upon his throne."[17] Other prophets whose names remain unknown issued even more poetic appeals for recognition of the "Shoot."[18]

Through his life at the royal court, Zerubbabel must have become well acquainted with the strength of the Persian army. His long journey to Jerusalem had taught him more about the empire. For him, therefore, there could be no lure in the proffered crown. But the zealots, if impractical, were insistent; by their well-circulated prophecies they had placed him in so ambiguous a position that he might justifiably be accused of high treason against his royal benefactor. That the high priest was for obviously selfish reasons cold toward the effort to elevate his natural rival indicated added necessity for caution.

Although the zealots were grooming Zerubbabel for independent

---

[16] Hag. 2:10-23.

[17] Zech. 1:7—6:15.

[18] Isa. 9:2-7; 11:1-9; 32:1-5. The story is told in fuller detail by the author's *History of Palestine and Syria* (1931), pp. 560 ff.; that account should now be revised for chronology (and therefore for the relation to external history) by the one here presented.

rule, in point of fact he was only a governor of the third rank.[19] His immediate superior was Tattenai, governor of Across the River,[20] who in turn was under the authority of Hystanes, satrap of Babylon and Across the River. Hints of the projected revolt came to royal attention; we may even suspect that the high priest himself was not without blame in the matter. While all the Jews were busily engaged in the work of restoration, suddenly Tattenai appeared and demanded: "Who gave *you* permission to build this house and to complete this foundation?" To his astonishment, the elders boldly replied: "We are servants of the God of heaven and earth. We are rebuilding the house which was built many years before this, which a great king of Israel built and completed. But after our fathers had provoked to wrath the God of heaven, he gave them into the hand of Nebuchadnezzar, king of Babylon, the Chaldaean, who destroyed this house and deported the people to Babylon. But in the first year of Cyrus, king of Babylon, Cyrus the king issued a decree to rebuild this house of God. Also the gold and silver vessels of the house of God, which Nebuchadnezzar had taken from the temple which was in Jerusalem and had brought into the temple of Babylon, these Cyrus took out from the temple of Babylon, and they were delivered to a man, Sheshbazzar by name, whom he had made governor. And he said to him: 'Take these vessels and place them in the temple which is in Jerusalem, and let the house of God be rebuilt in its place.' Then came this Sheshbazzar and laid the foundations of the house of God which is in Jerusalem. And since that time until now it has been building and is not yet completed."[21]

Evidently, Tattenai did not believe them, despite the clever reference to an early Nebuchadnezzar which was sure to recall the two rebels of the same name who had just been put down. He could not, however, reject offhand a claim that the temple rebuilding had been authorized by the empire's founder himself. He therefore prepared a report: "Tattenai, governor of Across the River, Shathraburzana (probably the Aramaic secretary with an Iranian name), and the associated officials of Across the River, to Darius the king, All peace! Be it known to the king that we went into the province of Judah, to the house of the great God, which is being built with hewn stones, and

[19] Cf. Hag. 1:1.

[20] *VS*, Vol. IV, No. 152, of 502; M. San Nicolò and A. Ungnad, *Neubabylonische Rechts- und Verwaltungsurkunden*, Vol. I (1929), No. 327; cf. Olmstead, "Tattenai, Governor of 'Across the River,'" *JNES*, III (1944), 46.

[21] Ezra 5:11*b*–16.

timbers are being set in the wall, and the work is being completed with diligence." This was an unusually strong construction; the temple mount could serve as a fortress in time of revolt, and the governor definitely implied that in his opinion the work should be halted. Already he had taken down in writing the names of the elders who were conducting the work, ready to punish them if their extraordinary claim proved to be false. In conclusion he wrote: "And now, if it seems good to the king, let a search be made in the royal archives which are there in Babylon to find out whether a decree was made by King Cyrus to build this house of God in Jerusalem, and let the king send us his pleasure regarding this matter."[22]

In the natural course of administration, Tattenai's report passed through the hands of his superior, the satrap in Babylon. Search was made in the "house of books"—in Babylon as at Persepolis an adjunct of the treasury. When no such decree was found, it was remembered —fortunately for the Jewish elders—that before his first official year Cyrus had returned to Ecbatana. Search was then extended to the fortress in that city, and their claim was proved justified. The actual decree was indeed not found, but the register roll was there. Under date of Cyrus' first year appeared the abstract of a decree restoring various temples, one paragraph of which read: "As for the house of God which is at Jerusalem, let the house be built, the place where they offer sacrifice continually; its height shall be ninety feet and its breadth ninety feet, with three courses of great stones and one of timber. And let its expenses be given out of the king's house. Furthermore, let the gold and silver utensils of the house of God, which Nebuchadnezzar took out of the temple which is in Jerusalem and brought to Babylon, be restored and brought again to the temple which is in Jerusalem, each to its place. And you shall put them in the house of God."[23]

The elders were fully vindicated. Cyrus *had* authorized the rebuilding of the temple, and a decree by the empire's founder could not be lightly disregarded, especially by a usurper whose throne was yet somewhat shaky. Furthermore, the Jewish community was small and was ruled by the king's own personal representative who should have had better judgment than to permit himself to be pushed into a hopeless rebellion by a band of wild-eyed prophets. At any rate, Darius intended to visit Judah in person before another year had

[22] Ezra 5:6-17.   [23] Cf. pp. 57-58.

passed. Once he had shown himself in all his regal glory, even the
prophets must realize that revolt was no longer possible.

FURTHER VICTORIES FOR DARIUS

This same year 519 had seen fresh victories of Darius to chronicle.
When Atamaita (Atta-hamitu) of Elam had started a revolt, Gobryas
nipped it in the bud; the rebel was brought to Darius, by whose
orders he was put to death.[24] Later in the year Darius himself had
invaded the land of the eastern Scyths, had crossed by raft the Caspian
Sea, and had inflicted a severe defeat on the Pointed-Cap Saka. The
fugitives were captured, bound, and led to their death at the royal
hands, as was Skunkha, their chief. Revenge had been taken on the
Massagetae for their slaying of Cyrus, but the time was not ripe for
the organization of a second Scythian satrapy: "There I made another chief as was my pleasure; afterward the land became mine."
The satrapy was now divided into the Saka of the marshlands and the
Saka of the plains.[25]

The space on the Behistun rock had been utilized to the full. Literature now gave way to portraiture, and a part of the side inscription
was cut away to add Skunkha as the ninth rebel. On his head is the
fool's cap, half Skunkha's own height, which gave his people their
title of Khauda-tigra-baraty, "Pointed-Hat-Bearing." His back hair
is set in a stiff upward curl ending in a knot, his beard is extraordinarily long and flowing, and he wears a short skirt and boots. An appendix
was added in a fifth column. After this last improvement, the whole
rock surface below was carefully smoothed to prevent direct access.
This precaution has saved inscription and relief from vandalism, but
it has delayed exact copy to our own day.

PEACE IN EGYPT AND PALESTINE

In the winter of 519–518, Darius was on the march to the west.[26]
Palestine lay on his road, and no doubt he paused long enough to
settle its affairs. Perhaps we have a cryptic allusion to what happened
in the prophecy which Zechariah delivered about a year later: "Be-

[24] *Beh.* § 71 ff.; cf. F. W. König, *Relief und Inschrift des Koenigs Dareios am Felsen von Bagistan* (1938), p. 78.

[25] *Beh.* §§ 74 ff.; cf. R. G. Kent, "Old Persian Texts: Darius' Behistan Inscription, Column V," *JNES*, II (1943), 105 ff.; Suez Inscription, in G. Posener, *La première domination Perse en Egypte* (1936), Nos. 8–10; Polyaen, viii. 11. 6. 12.

[26] For the date cf. Richard A. Parker, "Darius and His Egyptian Campaign," *AJSL*, LVIII (1941), 373 ff.

fore these days, there was no hire for man or beast [they were impressed for army service], and there was no safety for him who went in or came out on account of the enemy."[27] Zerubbabel presumably was summoned to account and was executed as a rebel, for his name disappears from our sources.

After the settlement of the Jewish problem, Darius took the road across the Arabian Desert and reached Memphis without incident. He found the inhabitants mourning the Apis bull who, discovered in the reign of Cambyses, had just passed away on August 31, 518. Determined to win back his recalcitrant subjects, the king ordered that a hundred gold talents be granted to the native responsible for the discovery of the new Apis; amazed by such generosity to their god, the people no longer stirred up revolt but submitted to Darius.[28] With the ceremonies of his predecessors, the dead Apis was entombed on November 8, though as usual no "Horus name" was added to that of Darius on the stele.[29] Almost immediately Darius left Egypt, for Aryandes had been reinstated as satrap.

Already Darius had prepared his lawbook for western Asia. In Egypt he found that he had also been anticipated. Not only did the natives attribute laws to Menes, the founder of a united Nile kingdom—quite as the Hebrews did to their own founder Moses—but they credited later revisions to certain later monarchs such as Sesostris, Shishak, and Bocchoris. Amasis had planned a recodification of Egyptian law but died before the project had gotten well under way. Cambyses had then taken up the plan but lost his life on the homeward journey.

Before December 30, 518, Darius wrote his satrap, the reinstated Aryandes:[30] "Let them bring to me the wise men among the warriors, priests, and scribes of Egypt, who have assembled from the temples, and let them write down the former laws of Egypt until year XLIV of Pharaoh Amasis. The law of Pharaoh, temple, and people let them bring here."[31] Unlike previous lawbooks, that of Darius was not to be confined to royal decrees; religious practices—what we might call "canon law"—and the hitherto unwritten customary procedure were also to be standardized.

After but a few months by the Nile, Darius was returning home.

[27] Zech. 8:10.

[28] Polyaen. vii. 11.7.

[29] Posener, op. cit., No. 5.

[30] Parker, op. cit., p. 373.

[31] W. Spiegelberg, Die sogennante demotische Chronik (1914), pp. 30 ff.; Diod. i. 95. 4-5.

On his way he could observe that Jerusalem was quiet. Hope of a national king had been rudely destroyed, and it would be henceforth necessary only to keep in check the high priest, the one recognized head of the Jewish people. Jewish aspirations now centered about the temple at Jerusalem, which Darius wisely permitted to reach completion. Zechariah, in his last recorded prophecy, December 6, 518, abandoned all thought of revolt and announced that the national God had returned to his former place of abode; by his presence alone he would bring to his worshipers prosperity undreamed.[32] On March 12, 515, the temple was actually completed[33]—and the people remained quiet.

In all probability the reason Darius made so short a visit to Egypt was that he had received word from home. Vindafarna, son of Vayaspara, had been chief of the conspirators who aided Darius to usurp the throne. He had put down the rebellion of the second Nebuchadnezzar, and on the Behistun rock his name had headed the roll of honor. But he had learned with what ease thrones might be won, and he determined to try for himself. He lost his life, just when we do not know; the Greek poet Aeschylus inserted Maraphis and Artaphrenes in his summary of legitimate monarchs between Mardos (Bardiya) and Darius.[34]

"While his majesty Darius was in Elam"—Udjahorresne again takes up his tale—"he was great king of all the foreign countries and great monarch of Egypt—he commanded me to return to Egypt in order to restore the department of the ruined House of Life dealing with medicine." The narrator acceded to this order, for "the foreigners brought me from land to land and made me come into Egypt, as the lord of the two lands had commanded. I did what his majesty had commanded. I furnished all their staffs, sons of prominent men, not a poor man's son among them," Udjahorresne snobbishly boasts. "I placed them in the charge of every learned man, that they might be instructed in all their crafts. His majesty commanded them to be given all good things, that they might exercise all their crafts. I gave them every useful thing and all their instruments indicated by the writings, as they had been before. His majesty did this because he knew the virtue of this art to make every sick man recover and to

[32] Zech. chaps. 7–8.

[33] Ezra 6:15.

[34] In Herod. iii. 118–19 Intaphrenes, one of the Seven, is killed immediately after the uprising against the Magian; for Artaphrenes see Aeschyl. *Pers.* 776.

make lasting the name of all the gods, their temples, their offerings, and the celebration of their feasts forever."[35]

CONQUEST OF WESTERN INDIA

Since the days of Cyrus, Gandara had formed the easternmost conquest of the Achaemenids, the only Indian territory yet under their sway.[36] Administratively, it was joined to Bactria, and it was not until shortly before 508 that it was organized as an independent satrapy, not under its ancient Iranian name of Paruparaesanna but with the native form of Gandara.[37] An important city named Gazaca, the "Treasure," hinted of the wealth that was to make Ghazni famous in the Arab Middle Ages;[38] but the capital was Pukhala, the "Lotus City."[39] After the conquest and organization of Hindush, Gandara lost much of its importance. But few of the famous gold darics have ever been found in the whole of the Indian territory.[40] Its capital Pukhala sank before the Indian capital Taxila.

To the southeast of Gandara lay the fabulous plains of India, famous for the gold dust washed from its rivers. Spies were commissioned to travel from Caspapyrus of Gandarian Pactyica, the head of navigation on the Kabul affluent of the Indus, down to the mouth where it entered the Indian Ocean. Thirty months later the spies had coasted along the whole southern shore of Iran, across the exit from the Persian Gulf, then completely around the Arabian Peninsula, and had reached the port of Suez. Their shipmaster was the Carian Scylax of Caryanda, who after his return published in the Greek of the Ionic

[35] Cf. H. Schäfer, *ÄZ*, XXXVII (1889), 72 ff.; A. H. Gardiner, "The House of Life," *JEA*, XXIV (1938), 157 ff.

[36] Darius, *Beh.* § 6.

[37] In the tenth year of Darius a Babylonian slave woman was called the Bahtarian (Bactrian) (T. G. Pinches, *Records of the Past*, IV [new ser., 1890], 105); four years later (508) she was more accurately known as the Gandarian (Strassmaier, *Darius* [1897], No. 379, l. 44; cf. F. H. Weissbach, *Die Keilinschriften der Achämeniden* [1911], p. 144, n. 1). For Gandara see Darius, *Beh.* § 6; *Persepolis* e 2; Susa 1 (Scheil) 34; Susa 15 (Scheil) 24; Naqsh-i-Rustam A 3; Xerxes, *Daiva* 25; Artaxerxes III (Davis) 12.

[38] Ptol. vi. 18; Amm. xxiii. 6. 70.

[39] The name is thus given in a local inscription (Majumdar, *JRAS Bengal*, XX [new ser., 1924], 5–6). This is the Peucela of Arr. *Ind.* 1. 8; Peucolis of Plin. vi. 94; Peucaleis of Dion. Per. 1143; as a Seleucid eparchy, Peucelaitis Arr. *Ind.* 4. 11; *Anab.* iv. 22. 6; 28. 6; Peucolatis, Strabo xv. 1. 27; Plin. vi. 62; the more usually employed Peucelaotis is found only in variants in Arrian; the equally common Sanskrit form Pushkalavati is based on the Macedonian eparchy form, but Pushkala in the epic *Ramayana* vii. 101. 11, proves the antiquity. It is the modern Charsadda, northwest of Peshawar.

[40] G. Macdonald, in E. J. Rapson (ed.), *Cambridge History of India*, I (1922), 342 ff.

dialect his *Periplus* or "Circumnavigation." The *Periplus* provided the West with its first authentic information about the more easterly peoples and, in addition, served as model for the works of later geographers and historians.[41]

The information furnished by the spies induced the king to attempt more eastern conquests. Western India was subdued and sometime before 513 had been formed into the satrapy of Hindush,[42] which before long furnished an annual tribute of three hundred and sixty talents of gold dust.[43] Trade by sea was opened up; soon after, we find a Hindu woman named Busasa keeping an inn at Kish under police supervision.[44]

But Hindush was not all India. It took its name from its greatest river, the mighty Indus (Sindhu), and included only the territories along its banks and those of its affluents. The satrapy did not extend to the east as far as the Ganges; even the Hydaspes, later the border of the Taxila kingdom, is never mentioned. In the days of Herodotus, the eastern border remained the sandy belt[45] which today separates the northern half of the peninsula into an eastern and a western India.[46] Persian Achaemenid rule never extended into the south of the great peninsula; thus the India described by contemporaries was confined to the Indus Valley.

BUILDING OF CANAL IN EGYPT

As early as the Middle Kingdom, a canal had been dug from Phacussa on the Pelusiac branch of the Nile to irrigate the fertile wadi Tumilat to the east, where later the Hebrews were to settle in Goshen. Necho vainly attempted to extend it through the Bitter Lakes to the Gulf of Suez as one phase of that policy of exploration which resulted in the Phoenician circumnavigation of Africa. After his passage

---

[41] Hecataeus, Frags. 178, 294-99(J), based on Scylax; cf. F. Gisinger, *PW*, II Reihe, Vol. III (1927), cols. 619 ff.; Herod. iv. 44; cf. iii. 102; Diod. x. 38; Strabo xiv. 2. 20; Athen. xii. 522B. Stories of India, Herod. iii. 38, 98; Chorasmia, *ibid.* 117; Arabia, *ibid.* 107 ff.

[42] Herod. iv. 44. The approximate date is secured from the first mention of the satrapy in the lists of the Egyptian version, Suez inscription.

[43] *Ibid.*, iii. 94.

[44] G. Contenau, *Contrats néo-babyloniennes*, Vol. III (Louvre XIII [1929]), No. 218.

[45] Herod. iii. 98.

[46] In the moderately early Mithra Yasht, 10:104, the god smites the foe in eastern and western India, as does Sraosha in imitation, Yasna 57:27 (cf. Jackson, *Zoroastrian Studies* [1928], p. 526). In the second century b.c., Hindush became Hapta Hindu, the Sapta Sindhavas or "Seven Rivers" of Rig Veda viii. 24. 27 (cf. *ibid.*, p. 324).

across the Arabian Desert in 518, Darius would have continued
through the wadi Tumilat and thus would have noticed this uncom-
pleted canal. His interest quickened by hopes of a cheaper and more
direct route by sea to India,[47] he resolved to complete the task.

Necho's line of excavation had been sanded up and must first be
cleared. Wells had to be dug for the workmen. When finally opened,
the canal was a hundred and fifty feet wide and deep enough for
merchantmen. This predecessor of the present-day Suez Canal could
be traversed in four days.[48]

Five huge red-granite stelae to commemorate the vast project
greeted the eyes of the traveler at intervals along the banks. On one
side the twice-repeated Darius holds within an Egyptian cartouche
his cuneiform name under the protection of the Ahuramazda symbol.
In the three cuneiform languages he decares: "I am a Persian. From
Parsa I seized Egypt. I commanded this canal to be dug from the river,
Nile by name, which flows in Egypt, to the sea which goes from
Parsa. Afterward this canal was dug as I commanded, and ships
passed from Egypt through this canal to Parsa as was my will."[49]

On the reverse is the fuller Egyptian version. Under the Egyptian
sun disk, ultimately the original of the Ahuramazda symbol depicted
on the front, stand the two Niles in the traditional ritual of "binding
the two lands." One tells Darius: "I have given you all the lands, all
the Fenkhu (Phoenicians), all the foreign lands, all the bows"; the
other: "I have given you all mankind, all the men, all the peoples of
the isles of the seas." The terms employed are those made famous by
the conquests of the Eighteenth Dynasty, but now they are employed
to fit contemporary geography. The king has been granted "all life,
fortune, and health, all joy, all offerings like Ra, all food, every good
thing, even to appear as king of Upper and Lower Egypt like Ra forever, all the lands and foreign countries in adoration before him."

Then comes the list of satrapies, the names from an Aramaic original. In good Egyptian fashion, imitating the lists from the mighty

[47] Cf. Herod. iv. 44.

[48] *Ibid.* ii. 158; iv. 39, 42; Aristot. *Meterol.* i. 14; Strabo xvii. 1. 25 ff.; Plin. vi. 165. Diodorus
(i. 33. 9), however, claims that the canal was not completed because the king was told that the
level of the Red Sea was higher than that of the Nile and therefore Egypt would be flooded if the
canal were actually opened!

[49] Weissbach, *op. cit.*, pp. 102 ff.; V. Scheil, *Revue d'Assyriologie*, XXVII (1930), 93 ff.; *Bulletin
de l'Institut Français d'Archéologie Orientale du Caire*, XXX (1931), 293 ff.; J. M. Unvala in A. U.
Pope (ed.), *A Survey of Persian Art*, I (1938), 341 ff.; R. G. Kent, "Old Persian Texts," *JNES*, I
(1942), 415 ff.

kings of the Eighteenth and Nineteenth dynasties, each name appears within a cartouche whose crenellations indicate a conquered city; captives with differing headdress kneel in adoration. Darius is indeed king of kings, son of Hystaspes, great king, but he also bears all the ancient titles of Egypt. He is born of Neith, mistress of Sais (a delicate compliment to Udjahorresne); he is also image of Ra, who placed him on his throne to complete what he had begun. While he was in the womb and had not yet come into the world, he was granted all that the sun passes in his circuit, since Neith recognized him as her son. She granted him that, bow in hand, he should overcome his enemies each day, as she had done for her son Ra. He is mighty, destroying his enemies in all the lands. As son of Neith, he extends his borders; the people with their ready tribute come before him.

After a reference to the city Parsa and to Cyrus, the stele tells how the building of the canal was discussed and how the task was accomplished. Tribute was forwarded by twenty-four boats to Parsa. Darius was complimented and order was given for the erection of the stelae; never had a like thing occurred.[50]

CAMPAIGN AGAINST EUROPEAN SCYTHIA

While Egyptian peasants were digging the canal, Darius was preparing for his first expedition into Europe. Shortly before, Ariaramnes, satrap of Cappadocia, had crossed the Black Sea and had made a reconnaissance of the northern shore in preparation for an attack on the European Scyths.[51] Darius accordingly decided to attempt to invade their lands and to lead the army in person. Setting out from Susa in 513, he crossed the Bosphorus not far south of the Black Sea entrance by a bridge of boats constructed by the Samian Mandrocles, whose fellow-townsman, Choerilus, wrote "On the Crossing of the Darius Bridge" (for by this time Samos fully recognized Persian control). Two stelae were set up on the shore, one in Greek and the other in "Assyrian" cuneiform characters, each bearing another list of the subject peoples. Six hundred ships, manned for the greater part by vassal Greeks from the mainland as well as the island city-states, were sent direct through the Black Sea to the Ister, where a second bridge

[50] J. Ménant, Recueil de travaux ..., IX (1887), 121 ff.; G. Daressey, ibid., XI (1889), 160 ff.; W. Golénischeff, ibid., XIII (1890), 99 ff.; J. Clédat, Bulletin de l'Institut Français d'Archéologie Orientale du Caire XVI (1919), 224 ff.; ibid., XXIII (1924), 61 ff.; Posener, op. cit., Nos. 8–10.

[51] Ctes. Pers. xiii, Epit. 47; Heraclid. Pont. x. 6; Strabo xiv. 1. 17; Athen. xii. 522.

was built. Within these limits the Getae were subdued and the remaining Thracians submitted.[52]

Crossing the river, the army entered Scythia, occupied by Iranian nomads who lived always on horseback and moved their families on tented, ox-drawn wagons. A century since, their coast had been colonized from Miletus, which traded objects of luxury for grain; but appreciation of Greek art had done little to change their savage customs. They delighted in fermented mare's milk, which they drank from bowls made of human skulls. The blood of the first enemy slain was also drunk; the skin was used for quivers, and the scalps for napkins and clothing. Agreements were ratified by the blood pledge. When a chief died, slain horsemen were staked upon dead horses set around the corpse on chariot wheels; his concubines, cupbearer, cook, and riding horses were killed to accompany their master to the afterworld. Spears were set up about him and roofed by planks and hides, gold cups imported from the Greeks were laid by his side, and the whole was covered by a barrow; many such *kurgans* have been excavated.

Divination was by eunuchs who employed willow wands. Many gods were reverenced, but only the war-god possessed shrines and altars; he was represented by an antique Iranian sword which was set up in a mound of faggots, and to him were sacrificed horses as well as human beings.[53]

On the approach of Darius, the Scythians ravaged their land and retired. Their mounted bowmen harassed his troops until the Great King was compelled to retreat.[54] Fortunately for him, the Ionian Greeks had guarded the bridge beyond the appointed time and Darius was able to return across Thrace to Sestos, whence he crossed the Hellespont into Asia, leaving behind eighty thousand soldiers under Megabazus, satrap of Dascyleium, to continue the war (513).[55]

FORMATION OF LIBYAN SATRAPY

At that very time,[56] Arcesilaus, who had surrendered Cyrene to Cambyses, was assassinated in Barca. His mother, Pheretime, appealed to Aryandes, satrap of neighboring Egypt. This was too good

---

[52] Herod. iv. 85, 87 ff.; Aristot. *Rhet.* iii. 16. 6; Strabo vii. 3. 9.

[53] Herod. iv. 46, 59 ff.; cf. E. H. Minns, *Greeks and Scythians* (1913); M. I. Rostovtzeff, *Iranians and Greeks in South Russia* (1922).

[54] Herod. iv. 97 ff.; Ctes. *Pers.* xiii, Epit. 48; Strabo viii. 3. 14.

[55] Herod. iv. 143–44.   [56] *Ibid.* 145.

an opportunity to be lost. Aided by her partisans, it required only
local contingents, an army under the Maraphian Amasis and a fleet
under Badres of the Pasargadae tribe, to bring the whole region to allegiance. Barca surrendered on oath after a nine-month siege, but
through a quibble Amasis foreswore himself; the leading citizens
were handed over to the enraged Pheretime, who mutilated horribly
their women and impaled them with their husbands around the wall.
The remaining inhabitants were enslaved by Amasis and forwarded to
Darius at Susa; they were later deported to a city of Bactria which
they renamed Barca.[57]

The real object of the expedition had been the conquest of the Libyans, few of whom had yet acknowledged subjection. During the nine-
month siege of Barca, Persian troops had penetrated as far west as
the Euesperides, the modern Benghazi. Although the Persians suffered greatly on their retirement, some of the natives had submitted,
and Greeks and Libyans were formed into a new satrapy to which was
given the name of Putaya (512).

On their return, it would appear, the canal stelae were being prepared. Space had been left for only twenty-four satrapies, but one
more (India) than in the list of the autobiography. "Those of the
Sea" and Gandara (although the latter was the country from which
Scylax began the long sea voyage to the planned exit from the Egyptian canal) were omitted in favor of the new satrapies, Kushiya or
Ethiopia and Putaya or Libya. Parsa was yet counted as one of the
satrapies and Saka remained single, though the division into marshlands and plains was recognized.

CONQUEST OF THE APPROACHES TO GREECE

Meanwhile, a systematic clearance of the path to European Greece
had promptly been commenced by Megabazus. Perinthus was
taken by storm after a brave resistance. One by one the peoples and
towns of Thrace were forced to terms.[58] The Paeonian settlements
were captured while their warriors were absent guarding another approach; by order of Darius, all were deported to Phrygia.[59] Envoys
were dispatched to Amyntas of Macedonia demanding the usual sign
of submission, presentation of earth and water. This was given, and,
although Amyntas' son Alexander did kill the envoys for insulting the
Macedonian women, the murder was concealed from the king by a

[57] *Ibid.* 165, 167, 200 ff.; Aeneas *Tact.* 37. 6-7.
[58] Herod. v. 1.   [59] *Ibid.* 12 ff., 23, 98.

good-sized bribe and by the marriage of Alexander's sister to the Persian general Bubares, Megabazus' son.[60]

Darius meanwhile had spent the year 512 at Sardis. Histiaeus, tyrant of Miletus, was rewarded for his guard of the Ister bridge by the gift of Myrcinus on the Strymon, while Coes was made tyrant of Mytilene on the island of Lesbos. Megabazus arrived with the Paeonian deportees and warned the king of danger from the new building by Histiaeus at Myrcinus. Darius therefore recalled the Milesian tyrant and carried him up to Susa with him on pretense that he would become royal counselor and table companion.[61]

Before leaving for Susa, Darius appointed his brother Artaphrenes satrap of Sardis with general oversight of the Ionian Greek cities. In place of Megabazus, Otanes, son of Sisamnes, became "general of the men along the sea," or satrap of Dascyleium. Byzantium, Chalcedon, Antandros, and Lamponium were taken; thereby Otanes secured a strangle hold on the grain trade through the straits. As a result, the Scythians lost their treasured objects of Greek art, the Milesian traders were finding a profitable business cut off, and Persian control of the straits was a threat to the food supply of European Greece. With ships from Lesbos furnished by Coes, Megabazus further blocked the straits by the capture of Lemnos and Imbros, islands lying off the coast (511).[62]

By 513, the circuit wall of Persepolis was ready to be dedicated. On one of the monoliths in the southern face, Darius gave a revised list of his satrapies. There is no hint that news of the formal incorporation of Ethiopia and Libya had yet arrived. Hindush is there, and Sagartia makes a temporary appearance. In addition to Ionia, here qualified as "those of the dry land," and to "those on the sea," Dascyleium, we now have also "the lands which are beyond the sea."[63] The conquest of Europe had begun.

[60] *Ibid.* 17 ff.; vii. 22.

[61] *Ibid.* v. 11, 23-24.   [62] *Ibid.* 25-26.

[63] *Persepolis* e, Weissbach, *op. cit.*, pp. 82-83; cf. Cameron, "Darius, Egypt, and 'The Lands beyond the Sea,' " *JNES*, II (1943), 307 ff.

Chapter XI

PROBLEMS OF THE GREEK FRONTIER

NEW LIGHT ON THE WARS WITH GREECE

GREECE and the Persian Wars is to us a fascinating if somewhat threadbare story. In reading this story, we naturally identify ourselves with the Greeks, since our accounts must be based almost exclusively on that of the Greek Herodotus. We quite forget that we ourselves long since passed through the town-meeting stage, when we governed ourselves much like the Athenians, and have now become a mighty world empire whose problems are those of the Persians. Not only must we re-read the delightful tales of Herodotus with eyes wide open to present-day American difficulties, but we must also forget for the moment the victories which ended for European Greece the "Great Persian War."

Needed correction to the traditional interpretation is also given in part by the huge quantity of oriental source material so recently uncovered. The rarity of sources which throw direct light on the Greeks is in itself highly significant. Every increase in our knowledge only emphasizes the overwhelming strength of the Persian Empire when pitted against the tiny and disunited independent Greek city-states which had thus far survived the earlier conquests; and it encourages the attempt to discover why these later invasions failed.[1]

With the more populous, more wealthy, and more cultured part of the Greek world already under Persian control, incorporation of the remainder must have seemed to Darius inevitable. A few more frontier expeditions by his generals, he thought, should be quite enough to bring those Greeks who still retained their independence to acknowledge the suzerainty of the Great King.

While Megabazus and then Otanes were steadily driving southwestward, Artaphrenes received in Sardis an embassy which offered direct access to the heart of continental Greece. After the expulsion of the tyrant Hippias in 510,[2] Athens, under the leadership of Cleisthenes, was experimenting with a mild democracy. As a matter of

[1] Cf. Olmstead, "Persia and the Greek Frontier Problem," *Classical Philology*, XXXIV (1939), 305 ff.

[2] Herod. v. 65.

151

course, it was threatened with war by ultraconservative Sparta. Since Sparta was the declared enemy of Persia, Persian alliance with Athens was indicated. Artaphrenes demanded the usual tokens of submission—earth and water. The envoys complied, and the first contact of Greek democracy and Persian imperialism was made memorable by the promise of the infant democracy to accept Persian vassalage![3]

During the interval public sentiment had changed; the action of the envoys was disavowed, and Cleisthenes seems to have been banished. Two years later (505) the expelled tyrant Hippias turned up at Sardis and urged Artaphrenes to attempt his restoration. To meet this threat the opponents of democracy sent their own embassy to warn the satrap not to believe Athenian exiles. As might have been expected, Athens was ordered to restore Hippias under pain of attack. The Athenians resolved to make open war against Persia.[4]

THE IONIAN REVOLT

Large numbers of Ionian Greeks had been brought together by the Scythian expedition. Conscious at last of their united strength but quite failing to realize that they had lost their chance, now that the troubles incidental to the Persian accession had been quieted, the Ionians decided to revolt. Opposition to the tyrants imposed by the Persians had grown. The commercial classes fostered by the tyrants were losing trade to the Phoenicians and to the European Greeks, and the nationalist landholding aristocracy took advantage of the shift in sentiment. Their leader was Aristagoras, son-in-law and substitute for the tyrant of Miletus—that Histiaeus now detained by the king at Susa. Aristagoras' opportunity came when Naxian exiles requested his assistance in restoring them to their island. He therefore urged Artaphrenes to send with him a hundred ships to effect the restoration and thence to extend Persian rule to the Cyclades Islands.

Thus far, Miletus had been the most loyal of vassals, but the satrap had his suspicions. The project was referred to the king, who approved the satrap's reservations; the next spring (500) the fleet set sail, but it consisted of two hundred triremes instead of the hundred requested; it was manned largely by non-Greeks, and the commander was not Aristagoras but the king's cousin Megabates. It was inevitable that Aristagoras and Megabates should quarrel, that the Naxians should be warned, and that the projected invasion should eventuate in failure.[5]

[3] *Ibid.* 73.   [4] *Ibid.* 96.   *Ibid.* 30 ff.

Urged by Histiaeus at Susa to revolt, Aristagoras next summoned the leaders to revive the Ionic League. Only Hecataeus opposed the suggestion. When preparing his *World Tour*, the historian had learned at first hand the empire's strength, and now he listed in order all the nations subject to the Great King. His protest, however, went unheeded, and it was voted to abolish tyranny. Aristagoras resigned his position at Miletus, and the other tyrants were killed, imprisoned, or expelled.[6]

Aid was sought from Sparta, which at that date was considered the strongest Greek power. Despite Sparta's previous threats to Persia, King Cleomenes held back. He must have realized that aid to the revolted Ionians might prevent a future Persian assault on continental Greece, but he was helpless. His influence both at home and abroad was at its lowest ebb, and even if he personally believed that war was advisable, he could not be sure that the chief naval members of the loose Peloponnesian alliance, Corinth and Aegina, would follow the Spartan example.[7] Once Aristagoras had displayed his bronze world map in an effort to excite the king's cupidity and had incautiously let slip that it was a three-month journey from the coast to Susa, he was expelled.[8] Argos inquired of the Delphic oracle and received the expected reply —a threat that for its wickedness Miletus would be despoiled and the god's own oracle at Branchidae would be deserted.[9] Athens, once more conservative and already irritated by the demand of Artaphrenes for the recall of Hippias, met the appeal that Miletus was a daughter-city by voting twenty ships.[10]

The Athenian fleet, aided only by five triremes from Eretria, arrived in 499. Augmented by Ionian and Milesian ships, the fleet landed at Ephesus, whence the army marched up the Caicus and across Mount Tmolus to Sardis. Artaphrenes retired to the citadel, while the allies occupied the lower city. Sardis was a collection of reed huts or of mud-brick houses roofed with reeds; when a single house was fired by a Greek, the whole town was in flames. Trapped by the fire which destroyed the famous temple of Cybebe (Cybele) on the Pactolus, the Persian garrison descended from the acropolis and, with the native Lydians, collected in the market place, through which flowed the gold-bearing river to the Hermus Plain. The allies were driven back

---

[6] *Ibid*. 35 ff.

[7] J. A. O. Larsen, "Sparta and the Ionian Revolt," *CP*, XXVII (1932), 136 ff.

[8] Herod. v. 49 ff.   [9] *Ibid*. vi. 19.

[10] *Ibid*. v. 97; Charon Lampscen., Frag. 10(J); Plut. *De malig. Herod*. 861A ff.

upon Tmolus, whence they retreated toward the sea, but just before reaching Ephesus they were crushed in a great battle by Persian levies which had been raised from the various administrative divisions west of the Halys by Darius' three sons-in-law, Daurises, Hymaees, and Otanes. Learning that war had broken out between Aegina and Athens, the European contingent abandoned the allies and sailed home. Again Persian diplomacy had done its work.[11]

Loss of Athenian support was more than compensated by accession of the Hellespontine Greeks and of Byzantium, of a majority of Carians, including Caunus, and of Cyprus under the leadership of Onesilus. Gorgus, son of Chersis, son of Siromus (Hiram), son of Evelthon, and so a Phoenician, was king of Salamis. His younger brother Onesilus, after vainly attempting to persuade Gorgus to revolt, shut the gates on him and forced him to take refuge with the Persians. Only Phoenician Amathus among the Cypriote cities remained loyal, and Onesilus was besieging this town when a great army under Artybius was reported on its way to Cyprus. Appeal was made to the Ionians, who arrived with their whole fleet; shortly thereafter Artybius landed the troops ferried over from Cilicia. The Ionians refused to send ashore their marines to aid in defense of endangered Salamis, though they did succeed in defeating the Phoenician navy. At first the land battle went in favor of the rebels, and Artybius was slain by Onesilus in person. Then Stasenor, tyrant of Curium, deserted the allies and was followed by the chariot-driving aristocrats of Salamis itself. Onesilus was killed, Salamis was recovered by Gorgus, and the Ionians returned home. Abandoned by their allies, the rebel Cypriotes were compelled to surrender, though Soli held out five months before it was taken by a mine (498).[12]

Absence of the fleet on the Cypriote adventure had offered an opportunity which the Persians were not slow to utilize. Daurises made for the Hellespont and in five days captured five important cities. Then he turned upon the Carians, whose army was defeated at the White Pillars on the Marsyas, their place of national assembly. One of their leaders, it is interesting to note, was Pixodarus of Cindya, whose father was Mausolus and whose father-in-law was Syennesis, king of Cilicia; his family hereafter was to become famous. Aided by newly arrived Greek allies, the Carians essayed a second attempt at Labraunda, in their plane-tree grove sacred to Zeus of Hosts, but were

[11] Herod. v. 99 ff., 116; Thuc. i. 14. 3; 41. 2.
[12] Herod. v. 103 ff.

crushed. Then at Pedasus they set a night ambush for the marching Persians, and Daurises met his fate (497).

Hymaees took Mysian Cius. After Daurises had left the Hellespont for Caria, Hymaees continued the work of subjugation by reducing all the Aeolians of the Troad as well as Gergithae. He died of sickness, and in 496 his place was taken by the satrap Artaphrenes and by Otanes, who secured Clazomenae and Cyme. In despair of success, Aristagoras fled Miletus and was killed fighting the Thracians.[13]

Histiaeus had persuaded Darius that he alone could put down the revolt, but Artaphrenes was not so easily hoodwinked. He made perfectly clear his suspicions, and the former tyrant fled to Chios, whence he sent letters to a number of Persians at Sardis with whom he had discussed revolt. The letters were shown to the satrap; when the would-be rebels sent their replies, they were immediately executed. Miletus refused to admit its former tyrant and wounded him when he attempted to force an entrance; Histiaeus had no other recourse but to go off to the Hellespont and there begin pirate raids (495).[14]

The revolt was approaching its end, and the Persian leaders agreed that Miletus could now be crushed. All the various armies were united, and the grand fleet—Phoenician, Cilician, Egyptian, and the newly recovered Cypriote—was brought up. Leaving the Milesians to defend themselves from the land armies, such Greeks as were still in rebellion mustered off the island of Lade in the gulf before the city. Half the Asiatic Greeks had already been subdued or had made peace, and thus the rebels could show only three hundred and fifty-three triremes to the king's six hundred. Even among them there was treachery and faintheartedness; Samians, Lesbians, and, last of all, Chians fled home, and effective sea resistance was at an end.[15]

Apollo's oracle at Branchidae, which a generation before had led the way in subservience to the Persians, received the due reward of its conduct; the shrine was burned and its treasure was carried off to Susa,[16] where the bronze statue of Apollo was used to grace the local "museum."[17] Apollo has long since disappeared, but another bit of loot has remained there to our own day—a huge knucklebone of bronze, weighing about two hundred and twelve pounds, with handles on top and at one side; in archaic Ionic characters it bears the

13 *Ibid.* 117 ff.

14 *Ibid.* vi. 1 ff.   15 *Ibid.* 6 ff.

16 *Ibid.* 19; Strabo xiv. 1. 5; xvii. 1. 43, who attributes the looting to Xerxes.

17 Paus. i. 16. 3; viii. 46. 3, though attributed to Xerxes and located at Ecbatana.

inscription: "This dedicated object from the spoil, Aristolochus and Thrason set up, a tithe; but Tsicles, son of Cydimandrus, cast it."[18]

Apollo of Delphi did not share in the disgrace of Apollo at Branchidae. Neither did another Apollo at Magnesia on the Maeander. A few years later Darius found need of writing a royal official in that city: "King of kings Darius, Hystaspes' son, thus says to Gadatas, slave: I learn that you do not obey my commands in all things. That you cultivate my land by transplanting the fruits of Across Euphrates [the Greek equivalent of the Aramaic Across the River] I commend your purpose, and because of this there shall be laid up for you great favor in the king's house. But because you ignore my policy in behalf of the gods, I will give you, if you do not change, proof of my wronged feelings, for you exacted tribute from the sacred cultivators of Apollo and commanded them to dig unhallowed ground, not knowing the mind of my ancestors toward the god, who spoke the whole truth to the Persians."[19]

Miletus was captured by mines, and the south quarter wiped out; the burning of Sardis was revenged. Most of the male inhabitants were slain and their women and children enslaved; the survivors were deported to Susa and finally settled by Darius at Ampe near the Tigris mouth. The Carians of Pedasus had already submitted and in reward were granted the hill portion of the Milesian territory. Aeaces, son of Syloson, was restored by the Phoenicians as tyrant of Samos. The Carians who had continued to hold out now likewise submitted or were subdued. Histiaeus raided Atarneus for food but was compelled to fight at Malene; defeated and captured in flight by the newly arrived Harpagus, he was taken to Sardis, where Artaphrenes impaled him.[20]

After wintering at desolate Miletus, the following spring (493) the fleet easily took exhausted Chios, Lesbos, and Tenedos. Each was "netted" by a line of soldiers with joined hands who swept the island from north to south, literally hunting down the entire population. The rebel Ionian cities on the mainland were likewise captured. The best-looking boys were made eunuchs to serve at the royal court, while the most beautiful girls were taken for the royal harem. The

[18] B. Haussoullier, in J. de Morgan, *Recherches archéologiques*, II ("Mém.," Vol. VII [1905]), 155 ff.

[19] Dittenberger, *Syl.*[3], No. 22; translation, C. J. Ogden, in G. W. Botsford and E. G. Sihler, *Hellenic Civilization* (1915), p. 162.

[20] Herod. vi. 18 ff.

cities with their temples were burned. Then the fleet meted out the same harsh punishment on the cities to the west of the Hellespont as the army already had on the right. Deserted Byzantium and Chalcedon went up in smoke, though Cyzicus had already made terms with Oebares, who was returned to his father Megabazus' satrapy of Dascyleium.[21]

Hecataeus had been justified in his prediction by the outcome; the historian was therefore the one man to make peace with the satrap. Artaphrenes professed himself quite willing to forget the wrongs suffered and the rebellion; he would restore their laws, but for a price to be set at a meeting of the Ionian deputies.[22] Hitherto the Ionians had enjoyed a considerable degree of local autonomy; now they were to be brought more effectively into the satrapal organization. Private wars between the states must be abandoned, and instead they must submit to arbitration. Persia had followed the example of Assyria in taking a census for purposes of taxation; such a census was finally enforced on the satrapy of Ionia, which was measured in parasangs—an hour's walk or about three and a half miles. Tribute was fixed at approximately the pre-war level, but punishment of the revolting cities by transfer of considerable tracts of land to non-Greek states, the ravages of army and navy, and the loss in population by death, flight, and deportation increased terribly the pressure on the comparatively few survivors. As population slowly increased again and prosperity returned, the pressure lessened, for the tribute remained unchanged to the days of Herodotus.[23]

REORGANIZATION OF SATRAPIES

The state of the empire about this time is made clear by the satrapal list affixed to an inscription from Susa. Parsa is no longer included in the list proper; Herodotus tells us that Persis was the only land which did not pay taxes.[24] Sagartia has disappeared; presumably it has been reincorporated in Media. Scythia has been divided into two satrapies, Saka Haumavarga, the Amyrgian Sacae,[25] "preparers of the sacred *haoma* drink," and the Saka Tigrakhauda or "Tall-Hat Scyths."[26] In addition to Ionia, Those of the Sea, and Those beyond the Sea, there are two entirely new satrapies. One is Skudra (Thrace and Mace-

---

[21] *Ibid.* 31 ff.; Charon Lampscen. *Pers.*, Frag. 2; Thuc. i. 16.

[22] Diod. x. 25. 2.

[23] Herod. vi. 42.

[24] *Ibid.* iii. 97.

[25] *Ibid.* vii. 64.

[26] Cf. p. 141.

donia), which takes its name from the Macedonian city of Scydra;[27] the last in the list is Karka, from the Hittite name of the Carians.[28] Also from this period comes a bronze lion weight of a Euboeic talent inscribed in Aramaic: "Exact according to the satrapy of the king"; since it was found at Abydos on the Hellespont, it must witness a similar financial reorganization also in the satrapy of Dascyleium.[29]

SUCCESSES AND FAILURES OF PERSIAN DIPLOMACY

Mardonius, youthful son of Gobryas and newly married to the king's daughter Artozostre,[30] supplanted the officers at the seat of war in the spring of 492. He announced a new policy. Darius had observed a tendency in some of the Greek cities of Asia to experiment with a primitive democracy. Adherents of democratic Cleisthenes had promised him earth and water; their Athenian opponents had disavowed the agreement and had aided Ionian rebels. When that aid had brought threats of Persian revenge, the enemies of the present conservative government, the friends of the exiled tyrant Hippias, and the members of the young democratic party had shown their teeth by imposing a heavy fine upon Phrynichus for staging a tragedy entitled *Capture of Miletus* and by prohibiting its further performance.[31] Darius had therefore instructed Mardonius to expel the tyrannies, whose usefulness was obviously past, and to reorganize the Ionian city-states as democracies. For the first time in history, democracy had conquered a large and important section of the Greek world, and the sturdy infant nestled under the protecting aegis of a "barbarian" monarchy! No wonder Herodotus quotes the policy as a very great marvel, a complete refutation of those Greeks who had refused to believe his earlier statement that Otanes had urged the Persians to adopt a democratic form of government.[32]

Darius might hope that the hint would not be lost on European Greece, where in a goodly number of states democratic factions were rising into prominence and might be expected to welcome the liberator from the hated conservatives. Furthermore, the Greek cities in Asia would remain quiet only if freed from the constant temptation

---

[27] Plin. iv. 34; Ptol. iii. 12. 36; Steph. Byz. *s.v.*

[28] Darius, Susa e.

[29] *CIS*, Vol. II, No. 108.   [30] Herod. vi. 43; cf. p. 177, n. 18.

[31] Phrynichus (ed. Nauck, p. 720); Herod. vi. 21; Diod. x. 25. 2.

[32] Herod. vi. 43; cf. iii. 80; Olmstead, "Oriental Imperialism," *American Historical Review*, XXIII (1918), 760.

offered by independent kinsmen always ready to sympathize with, if not always prepared to assist, conservative anti-Persian reaction. Once and for all to destroy the hope of outside aid, the "hot trail" of the invader must be followed back to his home.

While Mardonius accompanied by the grand fleet of six hundred ships was sailing from Cilicia to announce the new freedom to the Ionians, a huge land force was on its way to the Hellespont. When it arrived at the straits, the army was ferried over by the navy. In Europe, Mardonius publicly announced his objective—the conquest of Eretria and Athens. After his grant of democracy to Ionia, there was every reason to believe that the democrats in the threatened cities would seize the first opportunity to drive out the conservatives and to instal their own leaders under the suzerainty of their good friend, the Great King.

To allow sufficient time for the democratic leaven to work, Mardonius continued the policy of slow but safe penetration from the north under the protection of the fleet. Thasos fell to the navy without resistance, while Macedonia once more recognized Persian lordship. These successes were counterbalanced by the destruction of three hundred ships, half the grand fleet, with the loss of twenty thousand men, the result of a sudden storm off Mount Athos. Simultaneously the army suffered in Macedonia a serious defeat at the hands of the Brygi, Phrygians who had remained behind in Europe,[33] and Mardonius himself was among the wounded. Although the Brygi were ultimately subdued, at the end of the year Mardonius returned to Asia.[34]

Hitherto Persian diplomacy and strategy had been virtually without flaw, but now began that series of blunders which were to bring ultimate disaster. Because of a purely temporary setback, it was decided to abandon the safe and sure, although slow, advance from the north in favor of a sudden dash straight across the Aegean to attack Athens and Eretria.

At first there was no indication that a blunder had been committed. The heralds sent to the Greek mainland in 491 enjoyed conspicuous success. To be sure, at Sparta and at Athens they were thrown into a pit or a well and bidden to take from there the required earth and water,[35] but almost without exception the other states furnished the symbols of bondage. So did the islands; among them was Aegina, which once before had done Persia good service by starting the war

---

[33] Herod. vii. 73.   [34] *Ibid*. vi. 43 ff.   [35] *Ibid*. vii. 133.

which recalled Athens from Ionia. Athens complained to Sparta, whose King Cleomenes attempted intervention in Aegina; when his colleague Demaratus forbade the action, Cleomenes deposed his rival, and Demaratus, like Hippias, took refuge with Darius, who granted him fields and cities.[36]

Mardonius had been supplanted by Datis, the Mede, and by the king's nephew, the younger Artaphrenes. In 490 they arrived in the Aleian plain of Cilicia, where the army they had brought was placed on transports, together with its horses. Here, too, the grand fleet was mustered, raised again after the loss at Mount Athos to its normal strength of six hundred triremes. Rich gifts from the two generals decked the Rhodian shrine of Lindus to win the priests of the oracle.

From Ionia the fleet sailed by Samos to Naxos; the inhabitants fled to the hills, and the invaders burned the city with its temples. The Delians took refuge in Tenos, but the Persians begged them to return and offered three hundred talents of incense and a collar of gold to their good friend Apollo. Carystos was forced to submit.[37]

In his attitude toward the approaching threat, Theognis of Megara was typical of the average Greek on the mainland. At first he still urged revelry, not fearing the war of the Medes. Awake at long last to the danger, he could only appeal to the god—Apollo of all divinities!—for protection of his city against the insolent host of the Medes; for he was afraid when he saw the lack of sense and the folk-destroying internecine conflicts of the Greeks.[38]

As Mardonius had felt sure, Eretria was found to be divided along party lines. The conservatives finally won in the conflict, but only for a policy of defense, not of attack. After six days of resisting heavy Persian assaults, the city was betrayed by two democrats in the justifiable expectation that their party would now be given the power.

The first objective of the expedition had been attained, and there remained only Athens to submit. Datis might well hope that Athens likewise would be handed over by friends, either the partisans of Hippias, now with the army, or the democratic leaders, the Alcmaeonidae. These well-grounded hopes were dashed by a second and even

---

[36] *Ibid.* vi. 48 ff., 61, 67, 70; vii. 3; Charon Lampscen., Frag. 3(J); Xen. *Hell.* iii. 1. 6.

[37] Herod. vi. 94 ff.; Lindos Chronicle (C. Blinkenberg, *Die Lindische Tempelchronik* [1915]), C 65 ff.; D 1 ff., 54 (J. 1008).

[38] Theog. 757 ff., 773 ff.; for date cf. E. L. Highbaeger, "Theognis and the Persian Wars," *Transactions of the American Philological Association*, LXVIII (1937), 98 ff.; Hellanicus *Pers.* ii. 61(J).

more stupid blunder: destruction of the Eretrian temples and city and the enslavement of the people. It was too much to expect that any Athenian, democrat or man of trade as he might be, could behold unmoved the burning and looting and enslavement of his own beloved mother-city.

When, therefore, Datis crossed the narrow strait and, guided by Hippias, landed on the Marathon Plain, whose inhabitants were reputed to be friendly, he found the whole Athenian levy drawn up to meet him. The aid promised Athens by the Spartans did not appear, for *they* had to await the full moon, so only the Plataeans came to Athenian assistance. After a delay which spoke only too eloquently of still divided counsels, Miltiades attacked with the thought of Eretria's unjustified fate vivid in all minds. The Persians and Sacae broke through the center, but the Athenian wings united behind them and inflicted a severe defeat. The retreating Persians were pursued to the ships, seven of which were taken.

Datis, even now not realizing the full effect of his unseasonable cruelty, thought the city might surrender if the fleet arrived while the patriot army was absent. The leaders of the democrats, the Alcmaeonidae, actually did signal by shield from Cape Sunium, but the army hurried back in time. For a few days the Persian fleet hung around off Phalerum; then, convinced at last that there was no longer hope of betrayal, the disappointed invaders sailed home.

Instead of renewing democratic trust by returning the captive Eretrians, the Persians carried them off to Susa and settled them some twenty-nine miles distant in Ardericca of Cissia, home of the earlier Kashshites; five miles beyond was the well from which, by windlass and skin bucket, the liquid was drawn which (when settled in tanks) produced salt, asphalt, and petroleum. Here, in the first century of our era, Apollonius of Tyana found them, still holding in remembrance their former home and speaking their ancestral language.[39]

[39] Simonides, Frags. 89–90, 117; Herod. vi. 101 ff.; Thuc. i. 18. 1; Ctes. *Pers.* xiii, Epit. 39; Plato *Menex.* 240; *Ins.* 9. 13; Curt. iv. 12. 11; Philostrat. *Vit. Apollon.* i. 23–24.

Chapter XII

THE THREE CAPITALS: ECBATANA, BABYLON, AND SUSA

SINCE the rediscovery of Persepolis by Europeans—a gradual process beginning with the end of our fifteenth century—its magnificent ruins have stood for Persia in the thought of the Western world. It is therefore a definite shock to realize that the Greeks had no clear knowledge of that city until Alexander visited Persepolis only to complete its destruction. For contemporary Greeks, the three residences of the Achaemenid monarch were Babylon, Ecbatana, and Susa. We should not blame them for their ignorance; there is no reference to Persepolis in the extant records from Babylonia, Phoenicia, of Egypt. For the Jews, likewise, the Persian capitals were Babylon, Ecbatana the fortress, and Shushan the palace.

DARIUS' PALACE IN BABYLON

Ecbatana is yet to be excavated, and casual finds teach us little.[1] At Babylon, Darius took up his abode at first in the palace of Nebuchadnezzar at the extreme northern tip of the city, if we may judge from the discovery there of a fine diorite stele which bears the Akkadian version of his autobiography.[2] Before long, however, Darius built his own palace on the southern citadel, west of the palace of Nabopolassar and just before the massive, moated wall of Imgur-Bel. On a filling of sand were laid foundations of well-made bricks which traced an *appa danna* or hall of pillars, with porticoes to sides and front, guarded by square towers, and approached by stairways on the south, as was the palace of Nebuchadnezzar. Thus the apadana ground plan was introduced into Persian architecture. Darius also borrowed from the same palace of Nebuchadnezzar the triple pavement: a coarse layer of pebbles and lime mortar, then one which was finer, and over it a wash of excellent red coloring, already familiar to us in Greece and to become characteristic of Darius' buildings. Fragments

---

[1] References to Achaemenid buildings at Firuzabad, Qazvin, and Salmas need confirmation.

[2] F. H. Weissbach, *Babylonische Miszellen* (1903), No. X; cf. R. Koldewey, *Mittheilungen der deutschen Orient-Gessellschaft*, III (1899), 8; *Excavations at Babylon* (1914), p. 166.

of black-limestone column bases prove that the art familiar at Persepolis was already in use; other fragments of the plinth on which the columns rested bore the inscription of Darius himself.

From Nebuchadnezzar, Darius also borrowed the employment of colored bricks formed, not of clay, but of lime mixed with sand on which were placed the same brilliant glazes used by his great predecessor to adorn the Processional Road and the Ishtar Gate. As in Nebuchadnezzar's originals, figures of animals played a large part. Some were flat and others in low relief; lines of black glaze marked off the scenes. Floral designs and columns with double volute Ionic capitals, as well as members of the Ten Thousand Immortals in their rich dresses, covered the walls. Ctesias, the physician of Artaxerxes II, described the gorgeous glaze paintings, though he credited them neither to Nebuchadnezzar nor to Darius but to Semiramis, whose form he professed to see in a woman's white face which the excavators actually discovered.[3]

SITE OF THE CAPITAL AT SUSA

Darius then transferred the whole building technique to Susa. If not so central for the empire as Babylon, Susa was better located than Ecbatana, Parsagarda, or Persepolis, yet it was close to the Persian homeland. An easy road led almost due west to Babylon through the wide plain. The trail to Ecbatana ran north up the higher reaches of the Choaspes through the land of the often independent Uxii. In summer another trail to Persepolis and Parsagarda led southwest over high mountains to whose brigand inhabitants even Persian monarchs paid tribute for passage;[4] when winter filled the passes, a more roundabout road along the Persian Gulf was available, for then the coastal plain lost its unhealthy humidity.

No small portion of Susa's wealth came from trade with the Persian Gulf, much closer then than now. In the fifth and fourth centuries before Christ, the four great rivers of the region—Euphrates, Tigris, Choaspes, and Eulaeus (the last continuing in its lower courses as the Pasitigris)—flowed, not as today into the Shatt al-Arab and then into the Gulf, but into a great swampy lake much farther to the northwest along whose outer shore islands just above sea-level allowed various exits. To the trader from the Gulf, even after crossing the lake, it was at that time three hundred and seventy-five miles up the Eu-

[3] Koldewey, *Excavations at Babylon*, pp. 127 ff.; Ctesias, in Diod. ii. 8.
[4] Strabo xv. 3. 4.

phrates to Babylon. On the other hand, Susa was only sixty-two miles from Bit Iakin or Aginis at the mouth of the Tigris, and part of the distance down the Pasitigris was already navigable by boat.[5]

The plain on which stands the mound of Susa opens out from the Babylonian alluvium but is quite unlike it in physical character. Owing to its closeness to the mountains and to its slightly higher elevation, the debris brought down by its rivers is here sorted out for its gravels, leaving only the finer silt to reach the alluvium. The soil thus produced is strong and its fertility almost inexhaustible; the ancients claimed that barley and wheat regularly produced a hundred fold and sometimes reached, amazingly, two hundred fold.[6] But for nine months of the year the heat is almost intolerable. Except for the gap to the southwest which connected Susa to Babylonia, the plain was completely surrounded by mountains. To the west and northwest was the long narrow ridge of the Kabir Kuh. Directly north were the southeasterly ranges of Zagros, and east and southeast of them the still higher central mountain mass. Dim on the southern horizon might be seen low hills of gravelly conglomerate and reddish sandstone which marked the drop to the alluvium.

As the ancients recognized, the lofty mountains which almost ringed Susa intercepted the cooling northerly winds for the greater part of the year, though farther south their effects might be felt. In summer a hot dry wind from Babylonia and the Persian Gulf blew through the southwestern gap, withering all vegetation and compelling the inhabitants to find refuge in narrow rooms which, although stifling, had palm-tree roofs covered with three feet of earth and thus at least afforded protection against the blazing sun. According to one Greek author, lizards and snakes were burned to death if they attempted to cross the street in the heat of noon. Cold water exposed to the sun was at once heated for the bath. Barley spread out to dry popped like grain parched in the oven.[7]

There may be exaggeration in this account, but no Westerner can prove it from personal observation; those who dare stay until June report temperatures far above the hundred mark. By that date, the rivers are running dry. The pools which cover the sand banks are

[5] Dur Yakin, Olmstead, *History of Assyria* (1923), pp. 255–56; Aginis, Arr. *Ind.* 42. 4; cf. Strabo xv. 3. 5; Ampe, Herod. vi. 20; Aple, Plin. vi. 134; cf. Andreas, "Aginis," *PW*, Vol. I (1893), cols. 810 ff.; J. de Morgan, G. Jéquier, and G. Lampre, *Recherches archéologiques* ("Mém.," Vol. I [1900]), pp. 1 ff.

[6] Strabo xv. 3. 11.   [7] *Ibid.* 10.

PLATE XVII

The Oxen in Turkey

The Donkey in Egypt

The Camel in the Desert

The Water Buffalo in Egypt

ANIMAL POWER

PLATE XVIII

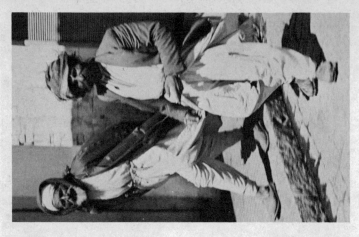

Assassins

Employees

Himation Figures

THE PAST ACCORDING TO THE PRESENT

PLATE XIX

Bosphoros

Palestine

Suez Canal

THE EASTERN MEDITERRANEAN

PLATE XX

Home of the Gods on Mount Olympos

Home of Apollo at Delphi

GREEK DEITIES

PLATE XXI

Lesbos from the Acropolis

Harbor in Thasos

The Islands

PLÅTE XXII

Marathon from the Plain

Mycale from Fortifications in Samos

GREEK AND PERSIAN BATTLEFIELDS

PLATE XXIII

Head (from Louvre, *Encyclopédie photographique*, Pl. 51)

Glazed Bricks (from Louvre, *Encyclopédie photographique*, Vol. XII, Pl. 50)

ART AT SUSA

PLATE XXIV

strongly saline, for their waters have passed through the gypsums and marls which mask the foot of the mountains. Like modern visitors from the West, in antiquity the higher classes found refuge in the near-by mountains—not in the stifling unhealthy valleys which parallel the main ranges but rather in the little elevated valleys,often up to five thousand feet high, just below the snow peaks.

By November the plain began to cool as the winds turned to the northeast, and the wheat and barley was in; by the middle of the month the first rains had fallen, as the wind veered to the southeast and south. As the winter advanced, a rare flurry of snow might reach the plain. Hailstorms were more frequent, and now and then the temperature dropped below the freezing-point at night, and at dawn a film of ice covered the ground.

During January and February, veritable tempests, stirred up in the Indian Ocean, scourged the land. Their deluges brought great destruction to soil pulverized by the intense heat of summer and to the mud-brick houses. But they brought also the welcome rain which changed the desert into beds of lovely iris. Everywhere the coarse grass sprang up. Groves of palm, acacia, tamarisk, and poplar took on fresh color. By the end of March, the rains had stopped and vegetation had begun to turn again. By the end of April, the harvest was in. In the more sheltered valleys on the edge of the plain, the pink oleander with its glossy green leaves continued for a time, otherwise only masses of yellowed grass, the thorny mimosa, and the thistle remained to represent vegetation.

The elephant, ostrich, wild bull, and wild ass have long since been hunted to extinction. Lions, so often represented in the art of Susa, are but rarely found today, and then only in the thickets along the rivers. But the bear, panther, wild boar, wolf, lynx, fox, and porcupine are still there, though in diminished numbers. At night the jackal howls his mournful cry to the wild dog. The francolin and red-legged partridge may be hunted; the eagle, falcon, vulture, and crow have proved themselves hardy. Water fowl visit the country in winter and with many a smaller song bird migrate during the long summer.[8]

By themselves the rains are not enough to bring the crops to fruition. Once more the mountains come to the rescue. From their melted snows come the *qanats* with the expensive system of irrigation. For the greater part, however, the country is irrigated by canals, drawn

[8] W. K. Loftus, *Travels and Researches in Chaldæa and Susiana* (1857), pp. 290 ff.; De Morgan *et al.*, *op. cit.*, pp. 28 ff.

from the mountain-born rivers, which bring to fruition the apricots, grapes, melons, and cucumbers. First in reputation is the Choaspes, now called the Kerkha. From its source, not far from the inscribed rock of Behistun, it runs first southwest, then southeast, and finally due south, following the parallel valleys between the ranges until it can break through in a thousand-foot gorge, and then repeating its maneuver. In the days we are studying, its clear ice-cold waters flowed close to the west of the Susa palaces; we are not surprised to learn that the Achaemenid monarch drank only from the Choaspes and that jars of its water accompanied him on his journeys.[9]

The other river of Susa was the Ulai, to the Greeks, Eulaeus,[10] which in the city's vicinity approaches the Choaspes to within two and a quarter miles, only to turn away again and enter the great lake by a separate mouth. Around Susa the two were joined by a network of canals, along whose spoil banks may be seen isolated mounds connected by building debris from the houses of the proletariat; the remains are scattered over so wide an extent of ground that we are almost prepared to accept the ancient estimate of a fifteen-mile circuit.[11]

DARIUS' CITADEL

Unlike Persepolis, Susa was no new royal foundation. From prehistoric times the site had been occupied by men whose painted pottery we admire for its beauty. On the mound which gradually piled up from their rubbish, their successors erected temples and palaces, whose records permit a genuine history of Elam to be written.[12] In turn, these structures fell into ruin, and by the reign of Darius the principal mound rose almost a hundred feet above the bed of the Choaspes, which then washed the steep western slope. Here, like the Seleucids after him, Darius placed his citadel. In the inscription which describes his own reorganization of the empire, Darius tells us: "Many fortifications which were before in ruin, I restored. The ruined citadel I rebuilt. The forts of Gurnama and Allanush I built."[13] The Greeks identified the site with the Memnonium, founded by

[9] Herod. i. 188; cf. Strabo xv. 3. 4.

[10] Olmstead, op. cit., pp. 291, 437-38, 480; Dan. 8:2, 16; Strabo xv. 3. 4; Arr. Anab. vii. 7; Ind. 42; Plin. vi. 99; Ptol. vi. 3. 2.

[11] Strabo xv. 3. 2.

[12] George G. Cameron, The History of Early Iran (1936).

[13] Weissbach, ZDMG, XC (1937), 80 ff.; ZA, XLIV (1938), 150 ff.; Herzfeld, Altpersische Inschriften (1938), No. 7; J. M. Unvala, in A. U. Pope (ed.), A Survey of Persian Art, I, 341-42.

Tithonus, father of that Memnon who came to Troy to aid its Phrygian defenders.[14] Of the fortifications of the citadel, there has been
found only a weak line of walling, apparently without even a tower,
along the very edge.[15]

During the period of Elam's greatest glory other mounds had grown
up to the north, east, and south. These, too, were utilized for building by Darius, who by the end of 521 had taken up his residence at
Susa.[16] However, they have all been so completely ruined that it is
quite impossible to present a clear picture of them. The eastern wall
of the mound to the east of the citadel was pierced at the center of its
three-thousand-foot face by a gateway with a strong tower at either
side. On the walls of these towers (if we accept the parallel with the
Ishtar Gate of Nebuchadnezzar at Babylon), the finely baked bricks
must have been placed to form the well-executed relief figures of
stalking and seated lions, winged bulls, and griffins with goat's horns,
lion's forepaws and tail, and eagle's claws instead of hind paws. Here,
too, were found smaller bricks whose glazed designs show the same
animals as well as the heraldic device of the lion killing the golden-
hoofed white bull.

The valves of the doors were made of wood but were covered with
bronze plates, tastefully decorated with sharp-pointed rosettes. They
swung on doorposts incased and shod with bronze, and these posts
were set in stone sockets five feet across. Under one such socket was a
marble vase four inches high where once were the foundation deposits. Similar fragments of hard-baked bricks forming similar animals in relief suggest other towers on the south wall, on the citadel,
and elsewhere.

Only on the artificial mound to the north of the citadel do we find a
building whose plan can be surely determined and whose date is certain. A foundation deposit shows merely a number of small sealings of
Achaemenid date, but its completion by Darius is made certain by a
unique document, preserved as a foundation-box record, and almost
the only readable example of the Persian cuneiform written on a clay
tablet. Other texts of the same document, in each of the three official
versions, are to be found everywhere throughout the settlement: in
the palace itself, on the citadel, scattered over the main part of the

[14] Herod. v. 54; vii. 151.
[15] Contrast Marcel Dieulafoy, *L'Acropole de Suse* (1893), pp. 117 ff., with J. de Morgan *et al.*,
Recherches archéologiques (1900), p. 88.
[16] Herod. iii. 129.

royal area, and even down in the so-called "donjon" projecting from the southeastern corner.

After the usual introduction, Darius goes on to tell of constructional details and of the various peoples who took part:

This is the *hadish* palace which at Susa I built. From afar its ornamentation was brought. Deep down the earth was dug, until rock bottom I reached. When the excavation was made, gravel was packed down, one part sixty feet, the other thirty feet in depth. On that gravel a palace I built. And that the earth was dug down and the gravel packed and the mud brick formed in molds, that the Babylonians did. The cedar timber was brought from a mountain named Lebanon; the Assyrians brought it to Babylon, and from Babylon the Carians and Ionians brought it to Susa. Teakwood was brought from Gandara and from Carmania. The gold which was used here was brought from Sardis and from Bactria. The stone—lapis lazuli and carnelian—was brought from Sogdiana. The turquoise was brought from Chorasmia. The silver and copper were brought from Egypt. The ornamentation with which the wall was adorned was brought from Ionia. The ivory was brought from Ethiopia, from India, and from Arachosia. The stone pillars were brought from a place named Abiradush in Elam. The artisans who dressed the stone were Ionians and Sardians. The goldsmiths who wrought the gold were Medes and Egyptians. Those who worked the inlays were Sardians and Egyptians. Those who worked the baked brick (with figures) were Babylonians. The men who adorned the wall were Medes and Egyptians. At Susa here a splendid work was ordered; very splendid did it turn out. Me may Ahuramazda protect, and Hystaspes, who is my father, and my land. [17]

Hystaspes was still living when this record was composed; the palace was therefore constructed early in the reign of his son. The numerous bricks used for the paved courts—inscribed only in Persian, although the Babylonian custom of printing from a stamp was followed—prove that most of the palace is the work of Darius, as do the building inscriptions with varying formulas. Unfortunately, there is no evidence for the spot on which they were found, and it is impossible to utilize them for a more careful chronology of the building operations. We may only notice that, while some of the brief inscrip-

[17] V. Scheil, *Inscriptions des Achéménides à Suse* ("Mém.," Vol. XXI [1929]), pp. 3 ff., 16 ff.; *Actes juridiques susiens: Inscriptions des Achéménides* ("Mém.," Vol. XXIV [1933]), pp. 105 ff.; *Mélanges épigraphiques* ("Mém.," Vol. XXVIII [1939]), pp. 33 ff.; R. G. Kent, "Old Persian Inscriptions," *JAOS*, LI (1931), 193 ff.; "The Record of Darius's Palace at Susa," *ibid.*, LIII (1933), 1 ff.; "More Old Persian Inscriptions," *ibid.*, LIV (1934), 34 ff.; E. Herzfeld, "Die Magna Charta von Susa," *Arch. Mitth.*, III (1931), 29 ff.; *Altpersische Inschriften*, pp. 13 ff.; W. Brandenstein, "Die neues Achämeniden Inschriften," *WZKM*, XXXIX (1932), 7 ff.; Unvala, *op. cit.*, p. 339.

tions carved on the column bases call the structure a *hadish* of columns or merely a *hadish*, one uses the variant term *tachara*.[18]

The palace ruins lie in terrible confusion. As Darius tells us, the palace was erected, Babylonian fashion, on a high artificial platform. The site of an older Elamite graveyard was leveled off over an extent 820 by 490 feet and the earth dug down 27 feet for the gravel support of the palace proper. In ground plan, Darius followed the principles laid down by his Assyrian and Babylonian predecessors: a series of three courts surrounded by larger halls and smaller rooms constructed of mud bricks; but in orientation the northern system was adopted with the sides facing the points of the compass. Thus, the three courts were arranged from east to west. The whole was surrounded by a mud-brick wall.

From the east, where glazed bricks repeat the spearmen of the Immortals who once guarded the gateway, we enter into the service court, 173 feet wide by 179½ feet long, paved with lime cement into which were imbedded fragments of discarded baked bricks. On the north was a portico of eight good-sized wooden columns on stone foundations; on the wall behind, winged bulls were represented in glazed bricks, in imitation of those on the great Ishtar Gate at Babylon. Here presumably was the treasury, from which the precious metals were looted by Alexander and his successors.

From the eastern gateway a broad corridor led directly through the service courtyard along the palace axis, a little north of west, to the central court, 106½ by 118 feet. As the visitor entered, he saw in the northeast corner, under the sun disk of Ahuramazda, two facing sphinxes with bodies of lions, crowned and triply horned, bearded and with their hair fluffed out on the neck; their faces are reversed so as to show the prominent eye ready to drive off the forces of evil, and their extended wings are beautifully arched. On the north are two long, narrow reception rooms, the typical architectural form of the south, joined by an opening and bounded on the west by a paved court. This court was surrounded by a portico of columns.

A series of small rooms leads into the most private court, 91 feet 10 inches by 112 feet 2 inches; this is paved with bricks just a trifle less than a foot square. Panels of winged griffins in glazed bricks surround this courtyard. Connecting vestibules are also paved with brick,

---

[18] Contrast Scheil, *Inscriptions des Achéménides à Suse*, pp. 38 ff., and Kent, "Old Persian Inscriptions," *op. cit.*, pp. 213–14, with Scheil, *op. cit.*, p. 81, and Kent, *op. cit.*, p. 225.

but the more private apartments are covered with concrete and the characteristic red-ocher wash. North of the court is the harem, where we may imagine the haughty ladies of the imperial court. Separated by two of the long rooms are the two main halls, the smaller with its entrance from the north and forerooms at both ends, and the larger, in the northwest corner, with its entrance and forerooms to the south. After traversing various small vestibules, we find three entrances leading down into the private courtyard, for the entire harem is raised 10 inches (perhaps a later restoration) by a layer of concrete, a layer of brick, and again a layer of concrete.

To the south of the private court, beyond winged bulls, guardsmen, and griffins, are two parallel adjoining long rooms, paved with brick which was topped by the red-ocher wash and set in walls so massive that the halls, while only 30 feet 3 inches deep, have a breadth of 110 feet 10 inches. To the south of them is the monarch's retiring-room.

To the northwest of the palace complex was located the throne room. This was entered by gates of wood covered with bronze plates and swung on stone sockets like the others. The base for the throne may yet be recognized in a stone with the usual building inscription. Like the *apadana* at Persepolis, which no doubt it anticipated, the column base was bell formed and the columns fluted; vertical volutes below kneeling forefronts of bulls, back to back, completed this composite type of capital on which rested the beams for the roof. Traces of red paint prove that the bull's eyes were ornamented. The great throne room was $192\frac{3}{4}$ feet square, its roof supported by six rows of six mighty columns each. To the east and west, the throne room was approached by porticoes of two rows of six more of these columns to a depth of $57\frac{1}{3}$ feet. To north and west, below the level of the platform, traces of kiosks indicate the position of the paradise or garden,[19] easily watered from the near-by river and protected by a tower at the northwestern corner.

Today, Susa is a confused heap of ruins, whose very ground plan it is difficult to restore.[20] Stone was little used in the palace proper, and of the apadana little remains. The gold was looted by Alexander, and a pinch of dust is all that is left of the cedar timbering. Only the lowly mud brick is for the most part preserved.

[19] Esther 1:5; 7:7.   [20] R. de Mecquenem, in Pope, *Survey*, I, 321 ff.

But if the multicolored hangings described in the Book of Esther have moldered, the glazed plaster bricks in all their glory may be restored from innumerable fragments. Too often we do not know where they are to be placed, but at least the designs can be put together. From them we may form some conception of the riot of color which dazzled the eyes of Greek ambassadors and drove home the realization of the wealth and power of the Great King. "Says Darius the king: What by me was done, something which never before had happened, I could not have completed had not Ahuramazda helped me. . . . . By the favor of Ahuramazda may what by me has been done seem unusually beautiful."[21]

But when all was said, Susa was an alien city in a foreign land. Behind it was a long history under ancient monarchs of another people. Darius soon tired of its atrocious heat, its mud-brick architecture, and its foreign ornamentation. He began to dream of a capital in the homeland which should be his own foundation.

[21] Susa column base, Scheil, *Inscriptions des Achéménides à Suse*, pp. 44 ff.; Herzfeld, *Altpersische Inschriften*, pp. 21-22.

Chapter XIII

PERSEPOLIS

SITE OF THE NEW CAPITAL

PARSAGARDA spoke too eloquently of the supplanted dynasty, and Darius sought a new site for his capital. Twenty-five miles down the winding gorge of the Median River that watered the Parsagarda Plain, a rock-cut road led into another and broader plain. Through it flowed a yet larger river, the Araxes,[1] to irrigate the fertile soil, until the stream disappeared in the great salt lake of southwestern Persia. Two mounds close to the eastern rock border covered prehistoric villages which testified to an earlier occupation.[2] On a cliff to the north might be seen a rock relief, dating from something like two thousand years before. Two worshipers stand before two seated snake deities with an attendant behind them, while behind the worshipers is a seated female wearing the turreted crown.[3]

Just before the Median River entered the northeast corner, the valley opened. In this secure nook, where painted sherds witness another prehistoric settlement, Darius, it would seem, founded Stakhra, the "Fort," ancestor of the famous medieval capital of Istakhr. A wall of massive stones closed the gap between hill and city fortifications and formed a "Gate." Here the traveler was compelled to pay his toll at the single gateway under its guard tower. Chariots and beasts of burden might use the central two-way passage, whose wooden roof was supported by a pillar and two piers; pedestrians employed the footpath under low stone lintels at either side.[4] Of the ancient city which preceded Istakhr, few traces have survived. Of these, the most important is a fluted column without base and still

---

[1] Strabo xv. 3. 6.

[2] Alexander Langsdorff and Donald E. McCown, *Tall-i-Bakun A, Season of 1932* (1942); cf. E. Herzfeld, *Iranische Denkmäler*, Vol. I A (1932); *Iran in the Ancient East* (1941), pp. 9 ff.

[3] Herzfeld, *Archaeological History of Iran* (1935), p. 5 and Pl. IV; for date cf. N. C. Debevoise, "Rock Reliefs of Ancient Iran," *JNES*, I (1942), 80.

[4] E. N. Flandin and P. Coste, *Voyage en Perse* (1851), pp. 70–71; *Atlas* (1843–54); C. F. M. Texier, *Déscription de l'Arménie, de la Perse, et de la Mésopotamie* (1852), Pl. 137; R. Ker Porter, *Travels* (1821–22), I, 515.

retaining the double-bull capital which was reused in the great Friday mosque. Tradition, indeed, said that the site was that of a pre-Islamic fire temple. The height of the column, 25 feet 7 inches, is much lower than any of those extant at Persepolis. Other travelers report bull capitals, bell bases, niches, door jambs, antae of huge worked blocks, and fine stone vessels, all of Archaemenid character.[5]

From this opening the hills to the left turn southward and fall back. Three miles almost due south, but hidden from the city by projecting spurs, an isolated rock tending north-northwest and south-southeast offered a natural terrace at the foot of the Mount of Mercy. Here the king determined to establish his residence. Like the land, so the new palace group was to be called Parsa. Early Greeks called it the "City of the Persians" or "Persai." Later writers followed the deliberate mistranslation of the poet Aeschylus, Perseptolis, "destroyer of cities"; and, with them, we also speak of the site as Persepolis.[6]

<h2 style="text-align:center">CONSTRUCTION OF THE CAPITAL</h2>

Once the revolts at the beginning of the reign had been suppressed, work was begun on the terrace. Along the projected line of the platform, five hundred yards of front and to a depth one-third less, the rock was scarped, with perhaps a fosse along the base. Along the line thus scarped, huge blocks of the native dark-gray limestone were laid to form the main fortification wall. Although the blocks were deliberately polygonal to afford greater coherence to the mass, they were carefully dressed, bedded, and jointed in quite regular courses and were held together without mortar by swallow-tail cramps of lead or iron. It is the same type of walling familiar throughout the eastern Aegean and western Asia Minor during this same late sixth century.[7]

To the visitor approaching from the north, the new capital presented only a high blank wall of stone, capped by yet another wall of mud brick which brought the total height to sixty feet; the same mud-

[5] Flandin and Coste, op. cit., p. 70 and Pl. 58; Herzfeld, Iran in the Ancient East (1941), p. 276; Erich F. Schmidt, The Treasury of Persepolis and Other Discoveries in the Homeland of the Achaemenians (1939), pp. 105 ff.

[6] Parsa, Xerxes Gate Ins. 3; Persai, Xen. Cyrop. viii. 7. 1 ff.; Beross., Frag. 56(S); "City of the Persians," Aeschyl. Pers. 157; Perseptolis, ibid. 65. The description which follows was written at Persepolis itself. It has since been read by Dr. Erich F. Schmidt, field director of the Iranian Expedition of the Oriental Institute of the University of Chicago, and by Dr. Donald E. McCown, assistant field director. The definitive publication is now being prepared by Dr. Schmidt.

[7] Cf. Robert Scranton, Greek Walls (1941), pp. 71, 73, 78, 167.

brick wall on the south completely hid the royal residence from profane view. The visitor from the west was more fortunate. Here, along a broad stretch the wall was unnecessary, since the scarped rock and huge wall blocks lifted the platform fifty feet above the plain; this stretch permitted a glimpse from afar of the towering palaces.

At the foot of the terrace to north, west, and south there grew up a settlement, not a true city as at Stakhra, but merely the isolated palaces of nobles, with stone column bases; they were surrounded by the mudbrick huts of their attendants and of the workmen under their supervision. Traces of thin walls hint that the settlement may not have been heavily fortified.[8]

To the east of the platform, along the foot of the Mount of Mercy, extended a second wall, this time only of mud brick. To hold back the talus from the overhanging slopes, there was, first, a thin retaining wall of brick, laid on boulders and with battered brick cover. Next came a moat which collected the water flowing down the hillside and shot it into a great tunnel cut through the living rock, four feet wide, six or seven feet high, and covered by roughly hewn slabs. The main line of fortifications was guarded by towers, sixty feet square, with a solidly packed rubble core faced by regularly formed mud bricks; they were connected by a curtain wall, thirty-three feet thick and sixty feet high.

Against the inner face of this wall, small irregularly projecting rooms housed the garrison. Large quantities of bronze and iron arrowpoints, iron spearheads and sword blades, and fragments of iron and bronze scale armor sufficiently indicate their purpose. Bronze bits show that here also were quartered cavalry. But the famous Ten Thousand Immortals enjoyed no luxury in their barracks. Sanitation was primitive, for the little brick sewers led only into the twenty-foot-wide, open street which followed the irregular barracks line. That the floors were rarely swept is suggested by the rapidity with which the floor level rose through a new paving or merely through an occasional leveling-off. There is no indication of furniture; the soldiers must have slept on the floor, and the superb armor must have been piled up or hung on pegs. That the Immortals, however, had plenty to drink is shown by the pottery—tall, slender wine jars with pointed base to be set in the clay floor, squatter jugs for more immediate use, pitchers with trefoil rim, flat canteens for the wars, and bowls whose spouts shot the liquid directly into the mouth, since cups seem not to

[8] Schmidt, *op. cit.*, p. 6.

have been needed. The fortification system was completed by a third wall, again of mud brick, which followed the crest of the Mount of Mercy.[9]

Inscriptions, carved about 513, on one enormous monolith set in the south face of the inclosure wall dedicate the fortifications:

Great Ahuramazda, who is chief of the gods, who has established Darius as king, he has given to him the kingdom. By the favor of Ahuramazda, Darius is king.

Says Darius the king: This land Parsa, which Ahuramazda has granted me, which is beautiful, possessing good horses and good men, by the favor of Ahuramazda and of me, Darius the king, it has no fear of an enemy.

Says Darius the king: May Ahuramazda bring me help with all the other gods, and may Ahuramazda protect this land from a hostile horde, from the evildoer, and from the Lie. Against this land let them not smite, neither a hostile horde, nor an evildoer, nor the Lie! With this supplication I pray to Ahuramazda, with all the gods, this to me may Ahuramazda grant with all the gods.

I am Darius, the great king, king of kings, king of the lands numerous, son of Hystaspes, the Achaemenid.

Says Darius the king: By the favor of Ahuramazda, these are the lands which I hold, together with this Persian army which fears me; to me they brought tribute. [Parsa is no longer included, Asagarta and Hindush have been added, and thus the approximate date is secured.] If you think thus: "From no enemy let me fear," then protect this Persian army; if the Persian army is protected, then for long prosperity shall not be destroyed, but it shall descend down upon this house.

Thus far, the inscription has been in Persian. Darius proceeds in Elamite:

As regards the fact that in this place this fortress has been built, formerly here a fortress has not been built. By the favor of Ahuramazda, this fortress I built, and Ahuramazda ordered that this fortress should be built . . . . , and so I built it, and I built it secure and beautiful and adequate, just as I wished to do.

The inscription ends in Akkadian. For the most part, it consists of familiar phrases, but instead of the lists of subject countries we read: "Parsa, Mada, and the other lands of other tongues, of the mountain and the plain, this side of the Bitter River (the Persian Gulf) and that side of the Bitter River, this side of the desert and that side of the desert."[10]

[9] Ibid., pp. 7 ff., 15, 85 ff.
[10] F. H. Weissbach, Keilinschriften der Achämeniden (1911), pp. 80–87.

Access to the palace inclosure was only from the west. The entrance was by a double reversing staircase, set into the platform under frowning bastions. The stairs, guarded by crenelated parapets, were twenty-three feet wide, but of so easy a tread—four inches to each of the one hundred and eleven steps—that in procession horses could be ridden to the broad landing at the top. Here the favored visitor dismounted and was conducted south to a tank cut from the solid rock, where he was directed to make his ablutions and to put on white clothing, obligatory before he could be granted audience with the Great King.[11]

A series of underground water channels joins the various structures on the terrace and proves that the whole grandiose plan was the conception of an unknown architectural genius.[12] The plan was never quite completed and in the early years of Darius was scarcely begun. Fortunately, the discovery of contemporary archives, preserved in a tower chamber of the north wall, permits more than a glimpse of building activities. The earliest tablets date from the tenth regnal year (512) and extend to the twenty-eighth (494), but the great majority come from between years nineteen and twenty-five, thus proving that 503–497 was the period of greatest construction.[13]

THE ROYAL ARCHIVES

To our amazement not a single tablet from the Persepolis archives is written in the cuneiform Persian employed for the royal inscriptions. From this strange fact we can conclude only that the Persian writing was purely artificial. Now, too, we can understand why the Persian is so regularly accompanied by Elamite and Akkadian versions.

The vast majority are written in Elamite. By good fortune, it has long since been possible to compare the Elamite version of the royal inscriptions with the earlier deciphered Persian and Akkadian and thus to discover the general character of Elamite as written in Achaemenid times. A slightly earlier archive was unearthed at Susa; these inscriptional materials, together with still older royal inscriptions, could be collected in a card-catalogue dictionary.[14] The interpretation

---

[11] Poseidon. Frag. 68(J).   [12] Herzfeld, *Iran in the Ancient East*, p. 224.

[13] George G. Cameron, "Darius' Daughter and the Persepolis Inscriptions," *JNES*, I (1942), 214 ff.; Richard T. Hallock, "Darius I, the King of the Persepolis Tablets," *JNES*, I (1942), 230 ff.

[14] Such a dictionary had been prepared by Cameron before the discovery of our Persepolis archives.

of the tablets in the Persepolis archives is further eased when we recognize the frequent appearance of Persian loan-words.

How these Elamite tablets came to be thus written is made clear by the occasional letter. Perhaps the most interesting is one referring to a daughter of Darius: "To Arriena, the chief noble, speak: Pharnaces (Parnakka) says: 'Darius the king has given me a command, saying: "One hundred sheep belonging to my estate give to Artystone (Irtashduna), my daughter." ' And now Pharnaces says: 'As Darius the king has commanded me, so I am commanding you: Now you give Artystone his daughter one hundred sheep as was commanded by the king.' Month Adukanish, sixteenth year [April, 506]. Napir-sukka inscribed (the tablet) after it had been translated."[15]

This newly discovered daughter of Darius bears the same name as his favorite wife, Artystone, daughter of Cyrus.[16] She is full sister of Arsames and Gobryas, one of whom led the Arabs and Ethiopians and the other the Cappadocians during the invasion of Greece by Xerxes.[17] At this date, she was about sixteen years old, and the grant may have been for a dowry.[18]

Even more interesting is the practice witnessed by the letter. The order is given by Darius *orally*. It is repeated *orally* by Pharnaces. Then it is translated *orally* by the interpreter, and only after this is it written down by one of the official Elamite scribes. Due authentication, however, is given by the affixing of a seal. We recall how in his autobiography Darius tells us that it was written and *read* before him.[19]

Among the other Elamite documents of this archive, a few list natural products, such as oil and sheep from the various cities, which were deposited with the caretaker of the store chamber. The majority, however, are records of disbursements to foremen of the various gangs of workmen, among them, curiously enough, the Assyrians, who are engaged on the work of the terrace structures. Generally the payment is in natural produce—so many measures of grain, so much flour, so much oil, so many jugs of wine or beer. Reckoning is by the month or its multiple; sometimes the Elamite names are preserved, but there is a tendency to substitute the Persian months; the system of intercalation is in regular use.

---

[15] Cameron, *op. cit.*, p. 216. [16] Herod. vii. 69. 72; cf. iii. 88. [17] Cf. pp. 242 ff.

[18] Cameron, *op. cit.*, p. 218. Since it is not common for mother and daughter to bear the same name we might suspect an error for Artozostre, a daughter of Darius who did marry Mardonius shortly before 492 (Herod. vi. 43).

[19] *Beh.* §70.

So far as we can check the wages, these workmen are about as well paid, if no better, than similar workmen in Babylonia, though there is a wider range of difference, especially between men and women, boys and girls. Not a few also list distributions of fodder for the numerous horses and donkeys needed on the construction work. The majority of the workmen bear Elamite names, as do the scribes, but the overseers are Persians, a few of whom are high officials. Of these, in later texts, the most important is the royal treasurer.

Although the tablets are mainly Elamite, other languages of the chancellery are represented. At least one tablet is scratched in contemporary Ionic Greek characters. Although Aramaic was employed by the chancellery for royal decrees as early as Cyrus, it was badly adapted to the clay tablet, from which the ink easily faded. Its wide use is proved by some five hundred triangular tablets. As their form suggests, they are simple labels, but they do give us the actual appearance of the Aramaic alphabet as employed by scribes contemporary with the decrees in Ezra.

Many of these tablets perform the function of scratch pads, giving the preliminary calculations of the scribes. Others bear nothing but the imprints of seals, for virtually every tablet bears a seal, generally of the higher officials, and now and then with Aramaic legends. When all this material has been collected and published, we shall have available a whole museum to present a new Achaemenid art.

INSCRIPTIONS AND RELIEFS ON DARIUS' BUILDINGS

While this particular archive throws no light on the question of the individual buildings constructed by order of Darius, it does prove that work was going on from 512 to 494 with a maximum of activity from 503 to 497. We turn, then, to the inscriptions and reliefs found in these buildings for more exact dating and find confirmation in the architectural history of the various structures.

We might conjecture that the earliest structure built on the platform was the first unit of the administration building, the "treasury";[20] it was in the same mud brick employed at Susa. Across the street which bounded the quarters of the Immortals rose its imposing façade, thirty-seven feet high and eight feet thick. To prevent monotony, the long stretch of wall was at frequent intervals broken by four-stepped niches alternating with vertical slots. Like the interior dividing walls, the façade was covered by a greenish wash.

[20] Treasuries at Parsagarda and Persepolis, Arr. *Anab.* iii. 18.

Some doorsills were of baked bricks or of well-polished stone. Above
the cemented floors was laid a red wash, characteristic, as we have
seen, of Darius' buildings. The columns were all of wood, set on a
stone discoid torus, which in turn might or might not be underlaid
by a square-topped plinth; as at Parsagarda, the wooden core was
often incased in plaster which was painted in bright blue, red, and
white lozenge designs; rosettes in the same colors bordered certain
doorways. Squared beams carried the mats or dry branches upon
which the mud roof was rolled; it would seem that the only lighting
was from tiny windows high up under the roof.[21] Here, perhaps,
Darius resided while his private palace was being erected in more
permanent stone.

From the grand entrance stairway to the platform, the visitor to be
granted audience with the Great King was conducted past the piles
of blocks ready for future construction, to another double reversing
stairway to the southeast. His eye was first of all directed to the center of the façade, where, under stout battlements and within rosette
borders, the royal building record was to be written. Like the other
inscriptions for this portion of the terrace, it remains blank to this
day, for Darius passed away before it could be inscribed, and his son
did not feel obliged to recall his father's glories. To either side of the
center of the façade, four Immortals salute the nonexistent royal
record, spear fixed in rigid attention on the toe; all wear the fluted hat
and long robe and carry the figure-eight shield on the left arm. Above
the rosetted frame and directly under the battlements, two small
winged sphinxes hold up their right paws in adoration. Behind each
is a row of conventionalized plant symbols which shut off a row of
richly dressed officials, the members of the "Seven and their families,"[22] who are about to visit the banquet hall through the monumental Triple Portal.

As the stairs ascend, we glimpse our first example of the heraldic
symbol of Persepolis, the lion tearing the hindquarters of the rearing
bull. The savage perfection of the oft-repeated scene contrasts strangely with Zoroaster's admonition of loving care for the sacred kine. In
the triangular corners of the façade are more rows of conventionalized
palms.

On the outer sides of the two staircases the scenes are in reverse
order: palms, lion and bull, a narrow space for an inscription, and
then Immortals. Here the latter alternate, either in the same costume

[21] Schmidt, *op. cit.*, pp. 16 ff.   [22] Herod. iii. 77, 84, 118.

but with quiver and bow or in high round cap, tunic, and trousers. The short Persian sword is fixed to a belt on the right thigh, a clumsy bow case swings from the left. More Immortals similarly alternated are continued around the corners on the east and west sides of the staircase.

Up the stairs in joyous anticipation of the coming banquet march the nobles by ones and twos, seventy-six on either side of each of the two staircases. To our right, as we ascend the east staircase, are nobles in the high fluted hats and long robes, shown in more detail for the Immortals; those to the left wear the high round cap, sometimes nodding slightly to the front, with neck flap to the rear. A tight-fitting tunic descends to the knees and is held at the waist by a knotted girdle, while moderately tight trousers and pointed shoes complete the costume. Over this a few have thrown an ankle-length, bordered robe, the sleeves hanging empty at the side; this is a robe of honor, for the long robes of the other group are sleeveless. A few also wear broad or narrow torques, a further sign of honor.[23] For the greater part, they are unarmed, though a few carry the bow case; to this others add or substitute the short sword.

Our artist has a keen sense of life and a perverse if somewhat robust humor; some of the courtiers definitely pose, others are caught in highly informal attitudes. Those in robes of honor march stiffly forward with only an arm upheld to bring out the rounded edging. Older officials puff up the stairs, one foot on the next step, a hand on the knee to aid the climb. Some tap the arm or shoulder of the man in front, inviting him to stop for a bit of gossip; others need no invitation. A few jerk around in irritation; some are more deliberate and pose as they turn. One places a left hand on the clumsy bow case to keep it from swaying; another performs the same service for his companion ahead. A visitor grasps the hand of a friend in the row behind. The marchers now and then self-consciously touch their beards to learn if the "permanent" still properly holds the curls; less gently another tugs his fellow's beard. All carry flowers, appropriate for the New Year's feast; while a few grasp them tightly and awkwardly, others sniff them with every sign of appreciation. A huge apple is carried by one man; his fellow around the corner turns sharply back to see the rare treat.

Bold and amusing as is the general effect, closer inspection shows how crude is the execution. In his anxiety to fill the irregular spaces,

[23] *Ibid.* 113.

the designer has resorted to a curious practice. Under the canopy which tops each block, the oversized heads of the individuals who form a group are ranged in a straight line, their caps touching the canopy; since the steps rise, the individuals are of different heights, and their bodies often appear distorted. The first three groups consist of four figures each: a tall official in long robe of honor; a second in tunic who should be the same height, but, as he lifts his foot to the next step, his left thigh appears to be shorter; a third, definitely a dwarf, turning to look back over a shoulder depicted full front, treads on the foot of a fourth, also a dwarf, almost hiding his advancing figure. In the three groups which come next, it is the second figure which wears the long robe. The last four stairway groups vary between three and four, although from the fourth group onward there are no doubled profiles, and rhythm is attained by the alternation of climbing and striding figures. From the corner of the landing a courtier decorated with a torque looks back on the ascending officials. Henceforth, there is no problem of differing heights enforced by the steps; the grouping is by fives, the third in the robe, the last two doubled figures.

Examined in detail, the boldness of conception, in sharp contrast to the lack of finish, becomes even more evident. Aside from the distortion of leg, thigh, and shoulder, we note the absence of a wrist, the arm joining the hand without transition, the failure to differentiate the thumb, the scratching-in of the knuckles, beyond which there is no attempt to indicate further details of the hand, the ugliness of beard and mustache with sketchy treatment of the curls, and the arms modeled through the drapery. Folds of the long robes fall down to either side of the hands; down the center of the skirts there are additional circular folds, and the leather boots are tied around the ankles. Stems of the flowers are never properly joined to the calyx, which is represented as a mere circle or even a square and sometimes filled with incised lines. Persian sculptors had not yet standardized design and attitude. The technical perfection of the superb "classical" art was still in the future. At least there is no hint of the stagnation into which Achaemenid sculpture was ultimately to lapse.[24]

On the landing at the top where the two staircases join, the courtiers pass before rows of Immortals, all clad in long robes and fluted hats and all at the rigid attention which bespeaks a well-disciplined

---

[24] The last two paragraphs are based on the typescript of Cleta Margaret Olmstead, "Studies in the Stylistic Development of Persian Achaemenid Art" (1936), pp. 4 ff.

army; one detachment carries shields, the other does not. The guests have now reached the monumental triple gateway building. Like the corresponding portico at the south, the one at the north is supported by two slender, imposing columns; the lower half of each is fluted, and above there are in succession a polypetaled bud, a series of four vertical volutes, and a capital formed by the forefronts of two kneeling, man-headed bulls placed back to back. Around the walls of the portico are seats for those tired by the hard climb.

Under the symbol of Ahuramazda, Darius himself steps out with scepter and lotus to welcome his guests and to review the Immortals; two smaller attendants follow to hold over his head the golden parasol[25] and fly-flapper and to carry the napkin which Assyrian practice had dedicated to royal usage. Behind him is the massive Triple portal, its roof supported by four tall columns. To the west of the south portico are rooms for attendants.

Still farther south is a tiny stairway. On its outer side stand Immortals clad in long robes, ranged step by step with spear on toe but quivers and bows on their backs. Reliefs on the inner face of the stairway make clear that its destination is the banquet hall. Ascending the stairs are servants, dressed alternately in long robes and in tunics; one group wears neck-flaps with wound headdresses brought up in a broad band around the chin, and the other the bashlyk, also coming around the chin. Under the arm of one is a lively kid, its forefeet held tightly to silence its protests; another bears a lamb under his arm. We notice a great wineskin slung over a shoulder, while rarer drinks are carefully transported in open bowls. Cooked food is kept warm under a closely pressed-down "cozy." This appetizing glimpse must have hastened the pace of even the tardiest guest.

Like the reliefs along the monumental staircases, the treatment is bold but without adequate attention to details. The eyes are enormous and are depicted in full front view. Eyelids show wide, mouths are straight, hands are large and clumsy.[26]

From contemporary literature we learn more of these royal "banquets of wine."[27] The greatest was that given on the royal birthday, when the king anointed his head and presented gifts to his fellow-Persians;[28] on such occasions, it is said, fifteen thousand might be his guests at a cost of four hundred talents.[29] Of those invited to dine with

[25] Plut. *Themistocl.* 16. 2.

[26] C. M. Olmstead, *op. cit.*, pp. 47–48.

[27] Esther 5:6.

[28] Herod. ix. 110.

[29] Deinon, Frag. 19(M); Athen. iv. 146C.

the king, the majority ate outside in the sight of all, while a more favored few were indoors in the king's company. Even then the king dined alone in a separate room with a curtain between, "white, green, and blue, fastened with cords of fine linen and purple,"[30] through which he could see while himself remaining unseen. Only on public holidays did everyone eat in the great hall with the king.

When he held a "banquet of wine,"[31] the nobles dined separately as before but were then summoned by a eunuch and were permitted to continue their drinking in the royal presence. They sat on a "pavement of blue, white, black, and red stones,"[32] while the king reclined on a couch with golden legs.[33] The royal beverage was presented in a golden cup[34] by a high court official, the eunuch cupbearer,[35] after it had been proved safe by the official taster.[36] While the nobles drank deep of the more common wines, their master enjoyed the vintage produced from the grapes of Chalybon[37] on the sunny slopes above Damascus.[38] After the banquet, the royal chamberlain was honored with the duty of putting his inebriated master to bed.[39]

In general, the king breakfasted and dined alone, though on occasion he might be joined by the queen or by his sons. Throughout the dinner he was entertained by concubines, who sang or played the lyre, one solo and the others in chorus.[40] Thousands of animals were slaughtered daily at the royal court; the list included horses, camels, oxen, asses, deer, Arabian ostriches, geese, and cocks. A rather small quantity was set before each guest, who might take home what he could not eat. This was not extravagance, for most of the food went as pay to the guard of Immortals and to the light-armed who waited in the courtyard. It was the practice for the most highly honored of the nobles to attend only the king's breakfast so that later they could entertain their own guests in the same manner. They placed all the food on the table, and after the meal the officer in charge of the table gave what remained to slaves and attendants, who were thus paid for their services.[41]

---

[30] Esther 1:6.

[31] Esther 5:6; 1:5 ff.

[34] Esther 1:7.

[35] Herod. iii. 34, 77; Xen. *Hell.* vii. 1. 38; Neh. 1:11.

[36] Phylarch., Frag. 43(J); Suid. *s.v.* "Edeatroi."

[37] Strabo xv. 3. 22.

[39] Diod. xi. 69. 1; Plut. *Reg. imp. apophtheg.* 173D.

[40] Musicians, Parnades (Athen. xiii. 608A); Suid. *s.v.* "Mousourgoi."

[41] Heracleides of Cumae, *Pers.* ii (*FHG*, II, 96).

[32] Esther 1:6.

[33] Esther 1:6; Duris, *Hist.* vii, Frag. 5(J).

[38] Poseidon., Frag. 68(J).

Meanwhile, Darius was building his permanent abode overlooking the plain from the western wall. It stands on its own individual platform and, unlike most Persepolis structures, faces south to catch the winter sun. Two rows of four stone bases still remain to make clear the position of the wooden columns which once upheld the portico, behind whose balustrade Darius might obtain a fine view over the plain to the hills on the far side. At either end is a monolithic anta whose cuttings give evidence for the setting of the roof beams. Doorways, under triple-feather cavetto and egg-and-dart moldings within a triple frame, are guarded by two enormous Immortals. Set in the mud-brick walls are monolithic stone niches, also under cavetto moldings, and adorned with tiny inscriptions. Flanked on either side by two highly polished windows, the entrance into the main hall shows Darius under the parasol, an inscription this time substituting for the Ahuramazda symbol.

Three rows of four wooden columns each upheld the roof of this square central hall. On the single door to the east the king is knifing the rampant lion; opposite, he fights the monster with lion's head, eagle's claws, and scorpion's tail. An odd door in this wall depicts the struggle with the bull. To east and west are more private rooms, small and narrow, in which the jambs of cramped passages show us the king tightly hugging the lion's cub, once captured by Babylonian Gilgamesh, and about to knife it.

Still more private are the rooms on the north, to which we are conducted by two doors bearing on their jambs the scene of the king with scepter and flower and the attendants with fly-flapper and napkin. These intimate chambers show their character by the reliefs. On one jamb is a beautifully drawn boy, whose short curly hair is confined only by a broad fillet and whose ear is ringed; in one hand he carries a tall, thin, alabaster perfume jar; a napkin is laid over the other. Facing this relief across the doorway is a man with brazier and pail. So highly polished are parts of the palace that its modern name, "Hall of Mirrors," is amply justified.

Opposite the bull doorway is one equally narrow and guarded by two more colossal Immortals. From it opens a small stairway, descending to a lower level above the western inclosure wall. Reliefs and inscriptions of the southern front come, not from Darius, but from his son. We have now visited all the constructions of Darius on the Persepolis terrace.[42]

[42] Inscriptions, Weissbach, *op. cit.*, pp. 80 ff.; J. M. Unvala, in A. U. Pope (ed.), *A Survey of Persian Art*, I, 371.

Chapter XIV

A ROYAL HUCKSTER

HERODOTUS, that great storyteller, informs us that Cyrus and Cambyses imposed no formal tribute upon their subject peoples but were content to receive gifts. Darius, however, fixed the tribute and the other dues, and for this he was called the "huckster."[1] As with so many other of the historian's apparently pointless anecdotes, only recently discovered information affords the true explanation. Not only was Darius a great lawgiver and administrator but, according to his lights, he was an outstanding financier.

STANDARDIZATION OF WEIGHTS AND MEASURES

Rarely among ancient monarchs do we find a ruler who so thoroughly understood that the successful state must rest on a sound economic foundation. The first requisite, he realized, must be a standardized system of weights and measures. As we have seen,[2] the "king's measure" (approximating our bushel) was already tending to supplant the various private measures of the landholders; it is significant that by the end of the reign the process of transference had almost reached its end. We possess an official example of the "royal cubit," a sort of ruler in black limestone exactly eighteen inches in length, and authenticated by the name and titles of Darius.[3] Three Assyrian kings—Tiglath-pileser III, Shalmaneser V, and Sennacherib—had prepared bronze weights in lion form, which were inscribed in Aramaic with their name and the number of *mana*'s (or "pounds") they weighed, and had made them legal by adding to the legend "of the king."[4] Such a lion but much heavier was found at Susa, close to the great bronze weight once dedicated to Apollo of Branchidae; it, too, has the handle by which it was placed on the scales for actual checking, but its great weight—465 pounds—shows that it must represent seven talents.[5] Another lion weight has been found at Abydos on the Hellespont; it bears the Aramaic inscription: "Exact according to the sa-

[1] Herod. iii. 89.   [2] Cf. p. 78.

[3] M. Dieulafoy, *L'Acropole de Suse* (1893), pp. 253–54.

[4] *CIS*, Vol. II, Nos. 1 ff.

[5] G. Lampre, in *Recherches archéologiques*, III ("Mém.," Vol. VIII [1905]), 175 ff.; M. C. Sontzo, in *ibid.*, IV ("Mém.," Vol. XII [1911]), 38–39.

trapy of the king," and its weight shows that its unit is the Euboeic talent.[6]

Darius also introduced a new weight, the *karsha*. Several beautifully polished and inscribed weights have been found: in the treasury of Persepolis, at Kerman, and elsewhere. The form is a pyramidion, neatly rounded off on the summit. From the example discovered in the Persepolis treasury, we learn that its weight, a little less than twenty-two pounds, represents one hundred and twenty *karsha*'s, which, the Akkadian version tells us, is equivalent to twenty *mana*'s or overheavy "pounds."[7] Earlier and later periods have given us large quantities of weights in the form of ducks; such a weight of white calcareous stone with shades of gray and pink has also been found in the treasury; it weighs about half a *karsha*.[8] It is interesting to observe that at the other extremity of the empire, at Elephantine on the southern border of Egypt, the mercenary Jews paid their debts "according to the stone (weight) of the king." The smallest weight was the *hallur* (bean), also known from contemporary Babylonia.[9] Ten *hallurin* made one "quarter," four "quarters" one shekel, and ten shekels one *karsha*.[10]

DEVELOPMENT OF COINAGE; STANDARDIZATION UNDER DARIUS

But weighing out the precious metals was already antiquated as a form of monetary exchange. In fact, coined money was no novelty in the more advanced portions of the empire, where minting had been long in use. At the very beginning of written history, Babylonia had passed beyond the age of barter and had reached a more advanced economic stage which presented all the phenomena we consider necessary for a money economy. Writing, itself, is connected with its emergence; the very tablets which give us our first examples of anything we may consider writing form a sort of tally sheet to list the most primitive pictographs and indicate our earliest bookkeeping.

The first unit of exchange was the "measure" of barley. In time, the precious metals might occasionally be substituted. They were regularly weighed out, and, when coinage began, the names were adopted

[6] *CIS*, Vol. II, No. 108; cf. p. 158.

[7] Erich F. Schmidt, *The Treasury of Persepolis and Other Discoveries in the Homeland of the Achaemenians* (1939), p. 62; earlier known weights, Weissbach, *Keilinschriften der Achämeniden* (1911), pp. xxii–xxxiii, 104–5.

[8] Schmidt, *op. cit.*

[9] J. P. Strassmaier, *Babylonische Texte: Darius* (1897), Nos. 119, 173.

[10] A. E. Cowley, *Aramaic Papyri of the Fifth Century B.C.* (1923), pp. xxx–xxxi.

from the older system of weights. One hundred and sixty *she* made a *shiqlu*, more familiar to us as the biblical shekel. Sixty *shiqlu* made a *mana* and sixty *mana*'s made a *biltu* or talent. The highest unit, the talent, weighed sixty-six pounds; the *mana*, therefore, was just a trifle heavier than our pound. As for the shekel, the weight of the silver would have had a coin value of something like a quarter-dollar in present-day currency, though, of course, we should remember that its purchasing value in antiquity would have been many times greater.[11]

At the commencement of the second millennium, accounts of the sun-god temple at Sippar were reckoned in "circles" or "Shamash heads" of silver, our first suggestion of coined money. Five centuries later, Egyptian reliefs picture the booty or tribute weighed out in silver rings. Shortly thereafter, the Assyrians, while employing silver for loans of major importance, used lead in minor transactions. Then copper supplanted lead, and afterward bronze took the place of copper. Sennacherib, in describing the ease with which he cast huge bronze bulls, declared: "I built a form of clay and poured bronze into it as in making half-shekel pieces." Bits of silver called "Ishtar heads" are mentioned in the agricultural loans made under the late Assyrian empire; how they looked may be discovered from the bits of stamped silver unearthed at Ashur.[12]

Greek poets of the classic age sang of the Pactolus, rich in gold, which laved Sardis, capital of Lydia. The gold washed down from Mount Tmolus may still be recovered, but increased labor costs make its washing no longer profitable. With a relatively large amount of the precious metal close to their very palace doors, and with much cheap slave labor at their disposal, it is no wonder that early in the seventh century the kings of Lydia should have begun minting, while Assyrian monarchs were boasting of their half-shekel pieces and nobles were lending "Ishtar heads." Proper methods of separating the gold from the less valuable silver had not been discovered, and the first Lydian coins were in electrum, a natural alloy, ranging from 40 to 60 per cent in the gold content. The obverse bore the Lydian emblem, the forefront of a snarling lion; the reverse was only the "incuse square," the mark of the die.[13]

[11] Waldo H. Dubberstein, "Comparative Prices in Later Babylonia (625–400 B.C.)," *AJSL*, LVI (1939), 23.

[12] Olmstead, *History of Assyria* (1923), pp. 321, 537–38, 563 ff.; cf. Dubberstein, *op. cit.*, p. 22.

[13] Barclay V. Head, *Catalogue of the Greek Coins of Lydia* (1901).

From the Lydians, the Greeks learned the art of coinage.[14] They must also have learned the names of the weights, for the *biltu* was turned into the *talanton*, the *mana* into the *mna*, and the *shiqlu* into the *siglos*, while the "head of Ishtar" became the *stater*. This last was made the new Lydian unit, with a weight of about 217 grains. Small change was provided in the form of thirds, sixths, twelfths, twenty-fourths, forty-eighths, and even ninety-sixths of a stater. The coinage was evidently based on the Babylonian sexagesimal system; so minute were the ninety-sixths that they weighed but a trifle more than two grains each.

The last king of Lydia, Croesus, has been immortalized by Western use of his name as a common noun, with the meaning of a millionaire. He owes that immortality to an outstanding monetary reform. The Lydians had developed new techniques for refining gold, and Croesus determined to utilize the knowledge by coining in *both* gold and silver. Since the stater was now pure gold, with only enough alloy to harden the metal against sweating, its increased value was accompanied by a decreased weight, about 164 grains. A new design for the obverse, a lion now facing the bull, announced the reform. Smaller denominations in gold could thereafter be confined to halves and thirds. Silver staters were reduced to a weight of 163 grains, though the half-staters were more popular and became the Greek *sigloi*. A twelfth of a stater was the predecessor of the *obol*, which the Greeks were to carry in their cheeks in lieu of a pocketbook.

Gold and silver coins of Croesus which accidentally escaped the looting by Alexander's soldiers have been found in the treasury at Persepolis. They occur also in the foundation deposit made by Darius under the *apadana*.[15] Thus they witness the derivation of his own coinage. The Greek states of Cyzicus, Mitylene, and Phocaea had continued to follow the older Lydian procedure of minting in electrum. Their pale "Cyzicenes" were easily distinguished from the rich yellow of the new "staters of Darius." The *daric* of 129 grains was $23\frac{1}{4}$ carats fine, 98 per cent pure gold. For the unit in silver, Darius preferred the half-stater, the shekel or *siglos*, for which he retained the old weight, 83 grains; they, too, were of refined silver, over 90 per cent fine. Subdivisions were thirds, fourths, sixths, and twelfths. Gold was on the "Euboeic" standard, while silver was reckoned by the Babylonian talent, which weighed 78 "Euboeic" minas. Twenty *sigloi* equaled the *daric*, the ratio of silver to gold being thus 13.3 to 1.[16]

[14] Herod. i. 94.   [15] Schmidt, *op. cit.*, pp. 76–77.   [16] Herod. iii. 89, 95.

Darius also fixed the coin types for his successors. On the obverse is the slim bearded king, in a half-running, half-crouching position. He wears the royal robe, and on his slightly bowed head is the war crown. His right hand grasps, point down, the butted spear over his right shoulder; a quiver is over his left shoulder, and in his left hand is the strung bow which gave the nickname "archer" to coins so often used to bribe Greek statesmen. A later type added a short, drawn dagger. As on the earlier coins of Lydia, the reverse has only the incuse square; the silver coins bear punch marks. From the enormous amount of precious metals received as tribute, only a small quantity was coined, the remainder being kept in bullion form as reserve.[17]

Monetary reform affected few of the empire's inhabitants. In the back country such trade as filtered through continued to be on terms of barter. On the great estates by the Nile and the Tigris, monetary practices were reflected in the terminology of business documents; but, for the most part, this was mere bookkeeping, and it may be doubted whether the peasants who tilled the soil ever handled real money. Even the artisans who labored on the royal edifices were normally paid in kind, though the pay was reckoned in monetary terms.

Only the merchants profited. For them, definite advantages accrued from having a fixed standard of values and from the assurance that the coins in circulation were of a uniform weight and purity. At that, the rulers of the merchant cities preferred to mint their own coins as proof of their local autonomy. Thus the *daric* and its subdivisions were of importance, not so much in themselves, as in setting the standards for this local coinage. Where we find these autonomous coins are the centers of trade, in particular the great merchant cities of Phoenicia and Greece. But these are the very cities whose history most intrigues us; for that history the autonomous coinage gives much that is new and significant.

Closely connected with Darius' monetary reform was a standardization of the values of the precious metals. A stray tablet from the treasury of Darius—as it happens, the only one preserved in Akkadian—vividly illustrates the drastic character of the revaluation and suggests the injustice which the taxpayer might suffer in the process.

During the nineteenth and twentieth years of Darius (503–502), four individuals paid into the royal treasury their tax, apparently in

[17] *Ibid.*, iv. 166; vii. 28; G. F. Hill, *Greek Coins of Arabia, Mesopotamia, and Persia* (1922), pp. cxx ff.; E. Babelon, *Traité des monnaies*, II, Part I (1907), 250 ff.; *ibid.*, II, Part II (1910), 37 ff.; cf. K. Regling, *Klio*, XIV (1914), 91 ff.; J. G. Milne, *JEA*, XXIV (1938), 245 ff.

behalf of certain groups from whom they had collected it. The money they offered was naturally that which was current in the open market, and so it was of the varying degrees of purity hitherto accepted by the merchants. We must hope that the taxpayer sometimes had tested the fineness before accepting it in trade, though it is evident that too often he had not. At any rate, the treasury did not receive it at face value, but itself refined it, and our document witnesses the discount. First there is given the nominal value of the coins presented for the tax payment, then the classes into which the various coins thus presented fell, such as white or pure silver, second-class silver, and third-class silver, next the discount for each ten-shekel piece in terms of the official *karsha*, and, finally, the total deduction from the payment on the whole tax. On the bottom margin of the tablet we may still trace the numerals by which the scribe made his calculations and may prove that his calculations were not always quite correct.

For instance, on December 30, 502, Indukka, mother of Tutu, headman of the merchants in some Elamite city such as Susa, paid the very respectable tax of fourteen and five-sixth "pounds" of silver, assuming that it was all white silver and that it was a first instalment of her tax. When it was refined, however, its value had decreased a quarter of a shekel for each ten shekels of silver, a total loss of one-half "pound" plus two shekels, and this must be made good. A second payment in second-class silver of nine "pounds" and fifty-three shekels suffered a heavier discount—a quarter-shekel plus an eighth for each ten-shekel piece; while for a payment in third-class silver of five "pounds" and three shekels, the loss was as high as a tenth. Thus on a total tax payment of twenty-nine "pounds," forty-six shekels, the lady took a loss of one "pound," twenty-four and a quarter shekels, or almost 5 per cent! Equally heavy loss was suffered by the Mede Pattemidu, "son of the shepherd," on a tax payment of forty-two "pounds," fifty shekels. No wonder the unfortunate taxpayers called Darius the "huckster"![18]

In spite of this application of heavy discounting, the inferior coinage was by no means driven from the market place. The Elephantine papyri are especially significant in this connection. Twice we have reference to the new coins, in 471 and in 411, when we hear of "refined silver."[19] Otherwise, throughout the whole period during which the papyri are preserved, we have regularly the prescription

[18] George G. Cameron, *Persepolis Treasury Tablets* (1947).

[19] Cowley, *op. cit.*, Nos. 5 and 28.

that the payment is to be made "by the king's weight," but with the deduction "two quarters (of a shekel) to the ten-shekel piece" or "two quarters to the *karsha*" to prove the survival of coins which were of the proper weight but not of sufficient purity.[20]

The archives of Darius, found in the wall tower, end with his twenty-eighth year. By his thirtieth (492), we begin to find tablets in his treasury.[21] Their changed formula gives further evidence for the financial reform: "Speak to so and so: Baradkama says: Give so many *karsha*'s, so many shekels of silver, to so and so by name . . . . at Parsa." But while the bookkeeping is in terms of coinage, the actual payments continue to be made in food and drink: "Sheep and beer are the equivalent, one sheep for three shekels, one jug for one shekel." The months for which the payments are made and the year of the reign are listed, though the name of the king is omitted. Now and then we are permitted no doubt: "Darius the king commanded it to be given to them." Since the tablets are all written in Elamite, it is natural that the scribe bears an Elamite name; most of the seals, however, are of Persian character; but one seal is in Aramaic, although the name of its owner is good Persian, beginning with the divine attribute Arta.[22] When we compare the wage paid these palace workmen with that for the ordinary day laborer in Babylonia, we discover that there was no advantage in building the Persepolis structures.

CHANGES IN POPULATION

Superficial examination of the heaps of tablets from Babylonia inscribed during the reign gives the impression of business going on quite as usual. Closer inspection proves that, under the monotonous repetition of formulas, significant developments may be sensed.

Even the dull lists of semiprofessional witnesses are worth reading, for through them we learn of changes in population. Among them we meet the sons and grandsons of the representatives of the great families with whom we have become acquainted in the time of Cyrus. Many of these, we had reason to suspect, were founded by men whose original speech was Aramaic; the occurrence of more Aramaic names in the later generations heightens the suspicion. The presence of Aramaic "dockets" on the cuneiform tablets since the end of the eighth century has been taken as evidence that even the scribes felt Aramaic

[20] E.g., *ibid.*, No. 6 (of 465) and No. 25 (of 416).

[21] Cameron, "Darius' Daughter and the Persepolis Inscriptions," *JNES*, I (1942), 218.

[22] Cameron, *Persepolis Treasury Tablets.*

easier to read than the more complicated Akkadian writing which long use in conservative Babylonia compelled them to employ; at least one such docket appears in Darius' reign.[23] One man actually was called the "Aramaean."

Naturally the question arises: "How many of these men with Aramaic names were in reality Jews of the Exile?" Was Zer-babili a relative of the contemporary Jewish prince of the same name, Zerubbabel, as he is called in our Hebrew records? Long ago it was suggested that Babylon's most prominent banking family, that of the Egibi, was Jewish in origin and that the founder's name was Jacob in his own language. At this time the head of the family was known as Marduk-nasir-apal, a good Babylonian name which reverenced the Lord of Babylon. Curiously enough, the first appearance of the "second name" so familiar in the Seleucid period is in connection with "Shirik, whose second name is Marduk-nasir-apal, son of Iddina, descendant of Egibi";[24] other documents refer to Shirik only by his Aramaic name, though there can be no doubt as to the identity. But hitherto we have known his father only as Itti-Marduk-balatu; then Iddina, which would represent the Hebrew Nathan, must be his first name.

That the descendants of Egibi bear "second names" which invoke Marduk is no proof that the interpretation is incorrect; rather, it indicates that they had apostatized. There is another influential family whose ancestor was Bel-iau; the name is a challenge to paganism and may be paraphrased: "Our God Yahweh is the true Lord (and not your alleged lord Marduk)." Yet several of his descendants bear names which reverence Nabu!

Tablets of earlier date do not refer to Iranians; the reign of Darius brings them into prominence. By 521 there is a "house of the Persians" in the vicinity of Babylon.[25] In the next year, Kakia the Mede turns up in that city.[26] By 508 Partammu the Persian owns a house there.[27] At the beginning of 505 Ummadatu, son of Udunatu, and Artabanus (Artabanush), son of Bagadatu, are actually on Babylon's bank of judges.[28] In 504 the cultivated land of Artagatum, female slave of Artashata, is rented.[29] In 501 Shishshia is majordomo of Bagasaru, who is given his proper title of *ganzabar*, or treasurer, an example of a Per-

[23] *VS*, IV, No. 143.

[24] Louvre XIII, No. 193.

[25] *VS*, Vol. IV, No. 87.

[26] Strassmaier, *op. cit.*, No. 51.

[27] *Ibid.*, Nos. 379 and 410.

[28] Louvre XIII, No. 193.

[29] Strassmaier, *op. cit.*, No. 476.

sian loan-word.[30] In 499 we hear of Ninaku the Mede;[31] in 496 of Baginu, son of Adrata;[32] by 494 Gambia, daughter of Pharnaces (Parnakka), has married the Aramaean Zerutu.[33] Comparison with the earlier tablets proves a veritable invasion of Babylonia by Iranian settlers.

There were other new ethnic strains in Babylonia. One man who appears rather frequently is called simply the "Egyptian." The persons who worship Ashur in their names must be Assyrians. Shamu, son of Ubazu, is a Kashshite. There is a town called Nabatu,[34] a Nabataean settlement; another named Gandaruitum reminds us of the land Gandara, whence came teakwood for the Susa palace.[35] There are Kardaka or Kurds, Lukshu, Inahud, and Hanana, who are mercenaries in the royal service.[36]

DRASTIC CHANGE IN ECONOMIC LIFE

Internal trading within the empire has taken a sudden spurt. For instance, Marduk-nasir-apal lends money to two men for trading "on the road." Whatever they make in silver in city or in country, half of the profit goes to him; but they bear jointly the responsibility for the capital provided, though *they* are not allowed to do any other business. It is natural that trade with Elam plays a large part in our documents. As an example, Kusurru is, at the expense of Shirik (the "first name" of this same Marduk-nasir-apal), to accompany the men of the chariot of Bel-apal-iddin, the "mayor" of Babylon, to Elam with fifty shekels of silver for trading.[37] Six men are going in 505 to Elam on a ship loaded with barley; twenty-five pounds of wool are intrusted to them.[38] In 511 a document of debt is drawn up in Shushan (Susa).[39] Frequent sales of temple prebends, even for a small part of a single day, remind us of similar transactions through our stock exchanges in the securities of secular corporations.[40]

Increased government interference with the economic life of the country is evident. In 520, dates are given to the satrap's messenger. Four years later, slave sales begin to add to the usual guaranties a further guaranty against the slave being summoned to do service for the king.[41] There is a royal storehouse for the receipt of barley in 508.[42] In the same year land is sold by the king's cubit.[43] In the sales of barley

[30] *Ibid.*, Nos. 535, 542, 527.

[31] *VS*, Vol. IV, No. 160.

[32] *Ibid.*, Vol. III, Nos. 138–39.

[33] *Ibid.*, Vol. V, No. 101.

[34] *Ibid.*, Vol. III, Nos. 170, 172.

[35] Strassmaier, *op. cit.*, No. 379.

[36] *BRM*, Vol. I, No. 71.

[37] *Ibid.*, No. 154; cf. No. 516.

[38] *Ibid.*, No. 442; cf. Nos. 569, 577.

[39] *VS*, Vol. IV, No. 134.

[40] *Ibid.*, Vol. V, No. 74.

[41] Strassmaier, *op. cit.*, No. 212.

[42] *Ibid.*, No. 285.

[43] *Ibid.*, No. 391; cf. p. 185.

or dates there is regular use of the "measure of one *pi* of the king," abbreviated as the "king's measure" or the "measure of one *pi*." By 497 the great processional street of Nabu in Borsippa is officially known as the "street of god *and* king."[44] When land is bought from Nana-zer-ibni, the king's Aramaic scribe, the purchaser must insert the stipulation that the cultivated field thus sold is not royal property but has been bought with silver; among the witnesses to this fact is Shishshiti, the Persian, son of Kammaka.[45] Here and there we find indications that the law code of Darius is in use;[46] that Persians are needed for its proper interpretation is shown by the appearance of two such foreigners on the bank of judges in Babylon itself.[47]

Our eyes, opened to the meaning of the monetary reforms, discover a new and ominous employment of the frequent "one-eighth." It is the one-eighth which the royal treasury deducts from the nominal value of the coins when presented for taxes. Regularly we hear of "white silver, depreciated, of half-shekel pieces."[48] Taken by itself, "white silver" means only that the coins have been minted at the correct weight according to the royal standard. Rarely is its fineness as well as its weight equivalent to that of coins issued by the royal mint; then it is expressly stated that the coins are both "white silver *and* legal tender"[49] or that they are "legal tender for giving and receiving."[50] More often the "white silver" is "not legal tender";[51] in such a case we may find "less a quarter-shekel."[52] Naturally, we have cases in which some of the coins were "white silver" and others "silver, legal tender."[53]

We realize the full effect of this government interference with business only when we prepare graphs of prices. They indicate that price levels were slowly rising throughout the whole of the Chaldaean and early Achaemenid periods. But so terrific and so sudden is the jump at the beginning of Darius' reign to the levels henceforth stabilized for the remainder of our period[54] that we can no longer doubt that these well-meant "reforms" contributed their share to the coming economic disintegration.

[44] *VS*, Vol. V, No. 96.

[45] *Ibid.*, Vol. VI, No. 171.

[46] Cf. pp. 119-34.

[47] Louvre XIII, No. 193.

[48] E.g., Strassmaier, *op. cit.*, No. 181.

[49] *VS*, Vol. V, No. 83.

[50] *Ibid.*, Vol. IV, No. 135.

[51] Strassmaier, *op. cit.*, No. 411.

[52] *VS*, Vol. IV, No. 138.

[53] Strassmaier, *op. cit.*, No. 516.

[54] These graphs, for the present, are to be found only in connection with the typescript dissertation of Waldo H. Dubberstein, "Prices and Interest Rates in Babylonia (625-400 b.c.)" (1934), on file in the Oriental Institute Library.

Chapter XV

PATHS OF THE GODS

DARIUS AND MONOTHEISM

ZOROASTER had been a true monotheist. For him Ahura-Mazdah was quite literally the one and only god. If he spoke of Good Thought, Piety, and the like, it was merely as a concession to man's inherent difficulty of thinking in abstract terms; in reality they were simply attributes of the unique supreme deity. The daevas reverenced by his opponents were nothing but demons, whom he hated with all the convinced monotheist's fervor.

Darius was equally monotheistic in spirit. No god but Ahuramazda is ever mentioned by name in his numerous royal inscriptions. Almost every other line hymns the praise of the great creator and lawgiver, humbly admits dependence on divine aid, or invokes divine protection for himself, his family, and all his works. He may have hated the demons worshiped by his polytheistic subjects as fiercely as did his great teacher. But while Zoroaster was a prophet whose sole purpose in life was to win adherents to the one true faith, Darius was obliged to rule a suddenly acquired empire the majority of whose inhabitants were gross polytheists. Reasons of state might be adduced for his unfriendly attitude toward their temples and their too powerful priesthoods, but his personal feelings had to be concealed; he even had to do lip service to their convictions by an occasional reference to "Ahuramazda and the other gods who are." Perhaps it is not too much of an exaggeration to imagine him, as he dictates the phrase, muttering under his breath: "But the gods of the heathen are nothing." The editor of the Elamite version of the royal autobiography knew perfectly well that Ahuramazda was the "god of the Aryans."[1]

PLACES OF WORSHIP OF AHURAMAZDA

Although Ahuramazda is so often mentioned in the royal inscriptions and although his winged human figure or its abbreviated symbol so regularly floats high in the air through the palaces at Persepolis and Susa and on the Behistun rock or the tomb of Darius, we know little of his ritual and cannot even tell for sure where he was wor-

---

[1] *Beh.* § 62 (Elamite).

195

shiped. With some plausibility, a ruined structure of two or three terraces between the Triple Portal and the private quarters of Darius has
been identified as an open-air shrine such as has been better preserved
at Parsagarda.[2] The tomb relief at Naqsh-i-Rustam shows the king sacrificing at a simple altar while Ahuramazda floats overhead, and this
implies that the ceremony took place in the open. Herodotus bluntly
states that the Persians had no temples.[3]

Yet there was a temple for Ahuramazda and the other Iranian divinities—by this time identified with their Greek cognates: Zeus, Hera,
Athena, Apollo, Helios, Artemis—on the plain northwest of the Persepolis platform, which dates from the earliest post-Achaemenid period. When we find a closely similar building, whose construction
shows that it comes from Darius or from his son, in the open fields to
the south, we may be sure that it too was dedicated to religious practice. A portico whose columns bore wooden lions led through an open
space to the main structure with porticoes to the east, north, and
west, and with rooms at the corners and at the back of the shrine.
From the north portico, looking through the door, one could see an
altar base through the third and fourth row of the sixteen columns.
To the east and at a lower level was a court, bounded on the east by a
mud-brick wall, while to the south was a low crenelated parapet with
steps; there were also steps to the north.[4]

Hidden under a mound two and a half miles northeast of Susa and
just beyond the former bed of the Eulaeus has been found another
structure. A narrow corridor ninety-five feet long but less than seven
feet wide, its walls adorned with niches, had to be traversed before the
paved court sixty feet square could be entered through openings to
the right or left. The far end of the court consisted of a broad stairway
which led up to a porch of two columns, a vestibule, and an inclosed
room with four columns. Architectural considerations would suggest
that it was built by Darius, and there is much to be said for the belief
that this is one of the *ayadana*—"house of the gods," as the Babylonian version translates—which the Magian is said to have destroyed,
but which Darius restored.[5] When we have added the exact replica of
the fire temple at Parsagarda erected by Darius near his tomb,[6] we have

[2] E. Herzfeld, *Iran in the Ancient East* (1941), p. 230.

[3] Herod. i. 131.

[4] Cf. Herzfeld, *op. cit.*, p. 231.

[5] *Beh.* § 14; M. Dieulafoy, *L'Acropole de Suse* (1893), pp. 390, 410 ff.

[6] Erich F. Schmidt, *The Treasury of Persepolis* (1939), pp. 98 ff.

reported all the architectural evidence available for the material side
of Persian religion.

THE RELIGION OF ZOROASTER'S "COMMUNITY"

Strongly as Darius was influenced by Zoroaster's thought, he was
certainly no member of the prophet's "community." While the companions of the prophet were still alive, that community might have
been satisfied by an oral transmission of their master's sayings, especially since accuracy might seem to be guaranteed by the metrical
form into which they had been cast. When, however, the companions
passed away, when the official religious practice of the empire so
clearly deviated from the true faith, and there was danger of time-
serving heresy, the only sure guaranty that the master's true doctrine
be preserved without change lay in writing. As more and more his
Gathas were chanted as ritual, the need for exactness grew more pressing. This does not mean that the Gathas ever became a "Bible," read
as a pious duty by Zoroaster's converts; rather, the few manuscripts
prepared by the priestly scribes were kept as master-scrolls through
which to check the recitation of the spoken ritual.[7]

From this early community come the Three Prayers—Ahuna Vairya,
Ashem Vohu, and Airyema Ishyo—the oldest Zoroastrian documents
after the Gathas:

As he (Ahura-Mazdah) is the best Lord, so is he (Zoroaster) the Judge according to holy Righteousness, he who brings life's deeds of Good Thought
to Mazdah and the Kingdom to Ahura, he whom they have established as
herder to the poor.

Righteousness is the best Good; according to our desire may it be, according to our desire it shall be to us, Righteousness for Best Righteousness
(salvation).

Let the beloved brotherhood come to the support of Zoroaster's men and
women, to the support of Good Thought; whatever Self deserves the precious
reward, for him I beg the longed-for prize of Righteousness which Ahura-
Mazdah will bestow.[8]

Zoroaster's faithful disciples remain poor and undistinguished. The
community might expect no reward from the secular rulers. All the
more its members look forward eagerly to the recompense which

---

[7] Compare the traditional account of the destruction by the wicked Alexander of the master-
scroll deposited in the record office ("fort of things written") in Dinkart iv. 23 (E. W. West,
Pahlavi Texts, IV [1892], xxxi, 413).

[8] Yasna 27:13–14; 54:1.

Zoroaster had promised in the blessed life beyond the grave to those who endure.

Exactly the same situation is pictured in other prayers, written in the same dialect as that used by Zoroaster for his Gathas, but the prophetic inspiration has run out, and now they are in prose.

That would we choose, Ahura-Mazdah and Righteousness the beautiful, that we may think and speak and do whatever is the best of deeds for both worlds. For the reward of the best deed we strive, that security and fodder be preserved for the Kine, whether we be instructed or uninstructed, whether rulers or subjects. Truly to the best of rulers is the Kingdom, for we ascribe the Kingdom to Ahura-Mazdah and to Best Righteousness [not to a secular Great King like Darius, is implied]. As a man or woman knows what is right, with fervor let him execute what is just, for himself and for whomsoever he can bring to understanding. For to bestow on you, Ahura-Mazdah, honor and praise, and to provide fodder for the Kine, we believe to be the best. For you would we labor and bring understanding to others as best we may. In the companionship of Righteousness, in the community of Righteousness, count every understanding person, with the best comfort for both worlds. These revealed words, Ahura-Mazdah, with better ponderings of Righteousness would we proclaim; you, however, Zoroaster, we constitute as their enjoiner and teacher. By the desire of Righteousness and of Good Thought and of the Kingdom, there shall be for you, Ahura, praises upon praises, maxims upon maxims, and prayers upon prayers.[9]

At these recompenses now, Mazdah-Ahura, remember and fulfil that which forms our solicitude through your protecting oversight, Mazdah-Ahura, what reward you have established for the community to which I belong. Provide this for us, both for this life and for the spiritual, that we should attain to companionship with you and with Righteousness forever. Make, Mazdah-Ahura, the warriors believe in Righteousness, to Righteousness may they attain; may the peasants become qualified for constant, zealous, stable companionship; may they both submit as true followers to us! In like manner may the nobles, in like manner may the peasant communities, in like manner may the (secular) associations with which we are joined, be, and in this manner may *we* be, Mazdah-Ahura, as believers in Righteousness and just. Send us what we desire![10]

Hymns and songs and praises we dedicate, devote, and consecrate to Ahura-Mazdah and Best Righteousness. In your good Kingdom, Mazdah-Ahura, may we for all time partake. May a good ruler, man or woman, bear rule over us in both worlds, O most beneficent of beings. As a god (Yazata), blessed, successful, accompanied by Righteousness, we induct you; thus may you, most beneficent of beings, be for us in both worlds life and vigor. May we serve you and procure your long-enduring support; through you may we become active and powerful. Do you continue our support, for long and as we desire, most beneficent of beings. Your panegyrists and prophets, Ahura-Mazdah, we call ourselves; such would we be, and we take our place ready, Mazdah-Ahura, for the payment which you have provided for the community. This do you provide us, both for this life and the spiritual, that we should attain to companionship with you and Righteousness forever.[11]

Zoroaster's little "church" had flourished under Hystaspes' patronage while he had remained a Kavi kinglet and perhaps even after he became a satrap. When, however, Hystaspes' son Darius was acknowledged as monarch of the entire empire, he forgot the community to which he had been born, even if he still remembered some of the prophet's teaching. During this period of neglect, the prayers cited above were composed. Even at home, the nobles, warriors, peasants, not to speak of the secular associations to which the converts belonged, remained indifferent. The discouraged leaders of the community could not understand this neglect; their great prophet had promised certain rewards in this world as well as in the next. On them had fallen the prophetic mantle, and they professed themselves eager to carry on their functions—but they did expect the promised recompense. Finally, they reached the point where they were quite willing to admit that the Great King was a Yazata, a lesser deity, to whom the ceremony of adoration was properly directed. But the times were not propitious; Zoroaster himself must become divine before the triumph of the Mazdayasnian faith.[12]

RELIGION AND THE CALENDAR

If Darius felt no personal respect for Babylonian temples and their priesthoods, he could not entirely ignore their solid contributions to practical scholarship. To them he looked for the scribes who turned his Persian dictation into Akkadian and who labored on his new law

[11] Yasna 41:1-6.

[12] The above-cited excerpts are taken from the Yasna Haptanghaiti, Yasna 35:3—41:6. Although the collection was early recognized as a unity under the title of the "Sevenfold Yasna" (Yasna 41:8 and 42:1), and although it is entirely in the dialect employed for the Gathas (if the latter were in prose), it should be obvious that it is composite. Yasnas 36–39 picture the same pagan Aryan religion familiar from Aeschylus, Herodotus, and Xenophon. Yasnas 35 and 40–41, on the contrary, show us contemporary Zoroastrianism. As a matter of fact, Yasna 35:9 definitely invokes Zoroaster as lawgiver and teacher; the oft-repeated statement that the "Sevenfold Yasna" does not mention Zoroaster is based only on the unjustified excision of the name in this passage.

code. From them also he took the scientists who made his calendar more exact.

Science was no opponent of religion in the ancient Orient; rather, it grew up in the temple's shadow. Astrology had long since acquainted Babylonian priests with the heavens and had worked out a terminology. Calendar needs brought into use an eight-year cycle and then a nineteen-year cycle to bring together at its close the lunar and solar years in almost exact agreement. In 747 this system was adopted for practical use by the Babylonian king Nabu-nasir, and thereafter the nineteen-year cycle remained standard. A trifle later, Assyrian astronomers were seeking data in a purely scientific manner, though the foundations of a truly scientific astronomy were not laid until the Chaldaean period.[13]

Chaldaean observations may be illustrated by an ephemeris prepared in 568. "On the eighteenth of the month, Dilbat (Venus) was 2°55' above the King," Regulus, brightest star of the constellation of the Lion. "Night of the eighth, evening, Sin (the moon-god) stood 6°15' under the Scales of the North." "The tenth, Mercury at evening behind the Great Twins enters," sets with the sun; "Mercury goes farther to the east." Already the course of the planets is definitely fixed in degrees and minutes with reference to the constellations and stars.[14]

More advanced knowledge is shown in a textbook, "Appearances of the Planets, behind You It Will Return," prepared by Labashi, son of Bel-shar-ibni, in 577: "Appearance of the god Sin, 27 days the time will return," that is, the moon cycle is 27 days. "Appearance of the goddess Dilbat, 8 years behind you she will return"; Venus returns to the same place in the heavens after 8 years; but "4 days you subtract, you observe," and the true cycle is 8 years minus 4 days. "Mercury 6 regular years behind you returns"; Mercury is the most difficult of planets, and Labashi knows that this is hopelessly rough, for he adds: "Its time you shall ascertain, the time of its appearance you shall ascertain and observe," in the hope that future astronomers may be more successful. Mars has a cycle of 47 years less 12 days, Saturn comes back in 59 years, but "day by day you shall observe," and the same admoni-

[13] Olmstead, *History of Assyria* (1923), pp. 588 ff., to be corrected by his "Babylonian Astronomy—Historical Sketch," *AJSL*, LV (1938), 113 ff.; for the calendar cf. also R. A. Parker and W. H. Dubberstein, *Babylonian Chronology, 626 B.C.—A.D. 45* (1942), pp. 1 ff. The fundamental study is that of F. X. Kugler, *Sternkunde und Sterndienst in Babel* (1907——).

[14] E. F. Weidner, *Babyloniaca*, VI (1912), 130 ff.; Kugler, *op. cit.*, *Ergänzungen*, p. 128.

tion is given for the 27-year cycle of the "Weapon of the Bow Star," Sirius. Not only were the cycles of all the planets but Mercury known with astonishing precision but the astronomers were not satisfied with their results and were seeking to make them more precise.[15] Further, they had already discovered the *sar* (the saros still employed by modern astronomers)—the period of 6,585 days or a little more than 18 years, after which eclipses repeat themselves in almost exactly the same order.

Not satisfied with these observations (although they were more exact than any made thereafter until the invention of the telescope), Babylonian priests anticipated their modern successors by refining their results through the complicated mathematics developed fifteen centuries earlier. Consequently, their astronomical tablets anticipate almost exactly the tables of the modern ephemeris. Take, for example, a tablet of 523. First comes the table for each month, forbidding enough, since it consists only of figures and a few ideographic signs:

Nisannu	1	DIR	30	SHI
ina	1	KAS		NA
MI	13	DIR ina	9	ME
	13	2	30	SHU
MI	14	DIR	8 20	MI
	14	7	40	NA
	27	DIR ina	16	

Resolving these abbreviations and taking the second group of numerals as counted in *ush*, 4 of our minutes, we translate: "April 1st, it is filled," that is, there is an interval of "2 hours from setting of sun to setting of moon. On the 1st, 2 hours to setting of moon. Evening of 13th, interval of 36 minutes from rising of moon to setting of sun. On the 13th, 10 minutes from setting of moon to rising of sun. Evening of 14th, interval of 33 minutes, 20 seconds, from setting of sun to rising of moon. On the 27th, interval of 1 hour, 4 minutes." Similar tables follow for the other months. For Addaru (February) we read: 13 SHU *u* NA *la ishu*, "On the 13th there is no sunrise or moonset"; the sun rises and the moon sets at the same time. At the end of the month, we find 26 23 27 12; these cryptic numbers mean that our astronomer did not know whether the last moon came on the 26th or the 27th and made calculations for both.

Then he takes up the planets: "Year VII (of Cambyses), Abu 22, the god Mulu-babbar before the face of Sherua entered"; we explain that

[15] Kugler, *op. cit.*, I, 45.

Jupiter sets with the sun, west of the constellation of the Virgin.
"Ululu 22, behind Sherua he makes his appearance"; Jupiter rises heli-
acally with the sun, east of the Virgin. "Tebetu 27, before the face of
the Scales he stands still"; he reaches his first turning-point, where to
the unaided eye he appears to be stationary 4 or more days. "Year
VIII, Airu 25, in the place of Sherua he stands still" at his second
turning-point. "Ululu 4, behind the Scales he enters" the underworld; he sets with the sun.

"Year VIII, Simanu 10, the goddess Dilbat in the evening into the
head of the Lion entered, Simanu 27, at morning, in the place of the
Crab she made her appearance"; Venus disappeared as evening star
and after 16 days reappeared as morning star. Later she moved from her
place in the Tail of the Fish as morning star to her position as evening
star in the Chariot. In similar fashion we have the movements of Kaimanu (Saturn) and Salbatanu (Mars). Next we find the moon's positions, so many cubits and fingers, behind or before, above or below,
the respective planet. Finally, we have the eclipses. "Year VII, Duzu,
night of the 12th, 1⅔ double-hours [3 hours, 20 minutes] after night
came, Sin was eclipsed, the whole was established, the going-out of
the disk went north." This very tablet may have been the ultimate
source from which Hipparchus drew his knowledge of this lunar
eclipse.[16]

About the beginning of the fifth century appeared the first great
Babylonian astronomer whose name was remembered by the Greeks:
Nabu-rimanni, son of Balatu, "descendant" of the priest of the moon-
god, who witnessed important documents at Babylon in 491 and 490.
Strabo called him Naburianus and gave him the deserved title "mathe-
matician," for, while his tables were based on observation, the details are the result of most elaborate calculation. His system is explained in a textbook, copied in early Seleucid days, which gives directions for construction of such lunar computation tables and eclipse
tables as are preserved from late Seleucid and early Parthian times.[17]

The problem set by Nabu-rimanni was determination of the true
date of new or full moon, with which was connected determination of
lunar or solar eclipses. Thus there were two sets of somewhat similar
tables, one dealing with the moon's positions, the other entitled "of

[16] J. Strassmaier, *Kambyses* (1890), No. 400; Kugler, *op. cit.*, I, 61 ff.; Ptol. v. 14.

[17] *VS*, Vol. V, Nos. 104–5; Strabo xvi 1. 6; cf. Olmstead, *JAOS*, XLVI (1926), 87; P. Schnabel, *Berossus* (1923), pp. 234 ff.; Kugler, *Die babylonische Mondrechnung* (1900), pp. 55 ff., 115 ff.

day 14" when at full moon lunar eclipses are visible. When complete, there were seventeen or eighteen columns.

The first gave the date, eclipse tablets prefixing "5 months," when, from the backward movement of the line of nodes, an eclipse would come 5 (not the usual 6) months after the last. The second column presents the changing apparent diameter of the moon's face in units corresponding to a quarter of our degree; the "fractions" often extended to six orders of the sexagesimal system.[18] Thus the minimum diameter is 1 57 47 57 46 40 or 29′26″,9 as against the modern 29′30″; the maximum 34′16″,2 as against 32′55″; the mean 31′51″,5 as against 31′12″,5. How remarkably close to the truth Nabu-rimanni came thus early may be realized from the fact that this is far more accurate than the estimates of Ptolemy, Copernicus, or even Kepler before he employed the telescope. The table is built up by adding or subtracting from the previous numeral, as the line is marked *tab* (plus), or *lal* (minus), a constant difference of 0 2 45 55 33 20 in an ascending or descending arithmetical series to or from maximum or minimum. Since the maximum is at perigee and the minimum at apogee, we may discover by calculation Nabu-rimanni's anomalistic month (the time the moon goes from perigee to apogee and return) as lasting 27 days, 13 hours, 18 minutes, 31,9 seconds. By aid of this column, apogee and perigee are secured for further calculation of the moon's movements.

A third column of Nabu-rimanni's tables gave the position of new or full moon by degrees in the constellations along the sun's path, the ecliptic, now becoming the regular signs of the zodiac. For the moment an average unchanging movement of the moon is assumed in calculating the changes in the sun's movement. From the textbook we learn that from one full moon to the next, 30° is to be added when the moon is between 13° of the Fish and 27° of the Virgin; for the remainder of the circle, only 28°7′30″; this assumes a maximum movement of the sun a few seconds too small, a minimum a few seconds too great. Rough as was the approximation, the error at any given time was slight; it brought true lunar and true solar years together at the end of the 19-year cycle when, after 12 common years of 12 months and 7 embolistic years with 13 months, sun and moon returned so exactly

[18] Just as we find calculation aided by changing fractions into decimals, though by the decimal system we can factor only 2, 5, and 10 with continuing decimals for the others, the more astute Babylonians, by the sexagesimal system, factored also 3, 4, 6, 8, 12, 15; numbers like 9, 16, 18, and the like were factored by extending the scheme one order below.

to the same position on the ecliptic that it took 236 years to bring the error to 1°.

From this column was calculated the fourth, the varying length of the day. When the sun is in the Ram 10°, the days are 3 units, 12 hours long, says the textbook; thereafter the number of minutes added or deducted are in ascending or descending series. The longest day is 14 hours, 24 minutes—nearly 15 minutes too long—and the shortest 9 hours, 36 minutes—over 13 minutes too short—but this may be forgiven when we recall that the Babylonians had no telescope or other modern instruments, that their time was computed by a water clock, that they did not realize the effects of refraction or the error due to observation from high temple towers, and that there would have been less apparent error had they not taken for observation the upper rim of the sun's disk. By use of the *ziqpu*, the upright split stick, they had discovered that the shortest shadow was cast at midday on the summer solstice, the longest at the winter; and through repeated observation and calculation they had secured an average. They learned that the seasons are of unequal length; their autumn was only half an hour too short, their spring and summer half a day too long, their winter nearly a day too short.

The fifth column of Nabu-rimanni's tables works out the setting of the moon above or below the ecliptic for the two periods of the year. The textbook gives an example: "Given 3°52'11''39''' above (the ecliptic), 1°58'45''42''' from the middle (that is, the average) subtract, and 1°53'25''57''' is secured. As much as it is made less than 2°24'—(that is), 30'34''3'''—the 30'34''3''' from 1°53'25''57''' is subtracted, and it is 1°22'51''54''' above. Further, 3°52'11''39''' above is established, 30'34''33'''' to 1°58'45''42''' add, and it is 2°29'19''45''' below established." The column is based on a dragon's month of 27,23039 days, off 26 minutes by modern reckoning.

The eclipse tablets insert another column, for the astronomers had discovered that eclipses predicted by the saros canon were not always visible in Babylon, and they were seeking to find out to what degree the rule worked in a given locality. For observable eclipses they indicated the shadow's magnitude, which rises and falls in close agreement with modern estimates. Naturally the blanks were filled only when the moon was not over 1°44'24'' from the ecliptic—otherwise, they realized, there could be no eclipse.

We must now secure the moon's motion in relation to the sun and based on the anomalistic month, for eclipses depend on this. In the second column we had the moon's apparent diameter, greatest when it nears the earth, while to the same degree the moon's apparent motion increases. "In making the change in the (daily) motion of Sin," says our textbook, "42' is added or subtracted." The limit, the ideal maximum at perigee, is established as $15°56'54''22'''30''''$; the ideal minimum at apogee is $11°4'4''41'''15''''$; from these 42' is to be subtracted or added. When the moon's diameter as taken from the second column is 2 17 4 48 53 20, $11°4'4''41'''15''''$ as the daily movement of the moon is established, and so per unit of change of diameter. The textbook gives the numerals to very minute orders; in the tables they are rounded off to seconds.

On the basis of the anomalistic month, the length of the synodic month is calculated on the tentative assumption that the sun moves backward an exact 30° per month. Here again we have an attempt to adjust the relationship with the changing moon's apparent diameter through an arithmetical progression, but the error becomes so great toward the limits that empirical correction is resorted to. The ninth column corrects this for the two halves of the zodiac, and we learn that by calculation the average month is 29 days, 14 hours, 44 minutes—about 1 hour, 49 minutes, 57 seconds too long.

A tenth column gives corrections for the changing time of sunset, since, like the common day, the astonomical day was still reckoned from the disappearance of the sun's disk. For 6 months, the tables have plus; for 6, minus, with passage through zero; the maximum and minimum and zeros are at the change of the seasons, and as in this system the seasonal changes come at 10° of the respective signs, the maximum is at 10° of the Scales, the minimum at 10° of the Ram. Thus the earliest sunset is at the winter solstice, the latest at the summer, the 6 months plus for the lengthening days, the minus for the shortening.

We are now prepared for the eleventh column, which gives the excess over the 29 days of the preceding month and so allows us to calculate the longest and shortest synodic months. Subtract from the given datum in the given line of the eighth column the datum of the ninth, plus or minus the datum of the tenth, and we have the datum for the eleventh. When the moon passes twice the perigee, we have the shortest month, 29 days, 7 hours, 17 minutes; when it twice passes apogee, the longest, 29 days, 17 hours, 13 minutes.

In the twelfth column is presented the final goal of all these calculations: the true date of new or full moon, secured by adding to the numeral in the preceding line of the preceding column the numeral in the same line of that column. On the obverse of the tablet, the series runs from Addaru to Addaru, for the new moon of the last month of the old year determines the new moon at the beginning of the new year; on the reverse it runs from Nisannu to Nisannu, for the year's first full moon is determined by its first new moon. Succeeding columns found the actual new moon, for by this, and not by the already calculated astronomical new moon, the Babylonians started their month. To obtain this, they observed the last appearance of the old moon as a thin sickle to the east in the morning sky. Until these columns and the corresponding sections in the textbook are published and explained by professional astronomers, we cannot fully appreciate Nabu-rimanni's colossal work.[19]

Nevertheless, we may note the report of a modern astronomer. In the moon-sun relation, Nabu-rimanni was 9",8 too small, in the sun-node relation 4",6 too great, in the moon-node relation, 5",2 too small; in the difficult moon perigee, the excess is only 19",9; his sun-perigee is 3",9 too small, his moon sun perigee 13",7 too small.[20] To those of us who are not astronomers, such accuracy of calculation is unbelievable; professional astronomers pay their tribute to so able a predecessor, working without their present-day advantages of highly specialized intruments and of a still more developed mathematics.

Astronomy was the one science the Orient gave the West full grown, the one science whose greatest triumphs were achieved in our later Orient. Our fragmentary sources do not permit for our period a similar picture in the other fields of knowledge, but enough has survived to prove that in pure mathematics, in botany, medicine, and grammar, the learning of the ancient past had not been forgotten, and that in important respects there had been advance.

GREEK CONTACT WITH ORIENTAL CULTURE

Greece had always been receptive to oriental influences. Minoan Crete had been in every sense a recognized member of the oriental world, and Mycenaean Greeks had been in almost as close touch. Our evidence is not confined to material remains, for the legends are even more instructive. Thebes was founded, not from Egypt, but by Phoenician Cadmus, in his native language the "Easterner," who brought to

---

[19] For a fuller description see Olmstead, "Babylonian Astronomy—Historical Sketch," *op. cit.*, pp. 122 ff.

[20] J. K. Fotheringham, *Quellen und Studien* (1933), B, II, 37–38.

Greece "Cadmean letters," the alphabet.[21] The Peloponnesus received its name from Lydian Pelops, son of Tantalus. To Argos came Egyptian Danaids. With the legendary heroes came also oriental legends: Niobe, daughter of Tantalus, weeping in stone under Mount Sipylus, Lycian Bellerophon on his winged horse Pegasus fighting the Chimera, or the monster Tryphon who fought the Olympian gods and was confined in the Corycian cave in Cilicia.[22]

The last great triumph of the Mycenaean empire was the capture of "Phrygian" Troy. Into its tale, Homer and the cyclic poets wove stories of oriental heroes such as Ethiopian Memnon or the warrior Amazons. Greeks conquered the eastern Aegean, and legend remembered how they married native women. From their wives the Greek invaders learned to worship Anatolian deities, like Ephesian Artemis of the many breasts and the Mother of the Gods with her unmanned Attis. Sidonian traders entered the Aegean and, with objects for sale, brought also the names of such objects. They brought, too, forms of decoration which modified ceramic styles, metal objects, and statues for imitation.

Rovers of the Greek dark ages brought to Homer news of a great city, hundred-gated and rich in precious metals and warriors, which they strangely called Thebes, after the Boeotian metropolis.[23] Phoenician traders carried with them the worship of their god Adonis, whom Hesiod mentions as son of Phoenix, the "Phoenician."[24] No Phoenician lady would have lamented Adonis with more zeal than does Sappho: "Woe is Adonis!" "Dying, Cythera, is the delicate Adonis! What can we do? Beat, maids, your breasts, and rend your chitons!" "Woe for Adonis of the four months' sojourn!"[25] With the Phoenician chiton, Sappho has borrowed Phoenician worship.

Conquest by Lydia brought the Ionian colonists into yet closer contact with oriental cultures. Their artists borrowed Lydian motifs, and their businessmen the art of coinage.[26] In natural reaction, Xenophanes declared that his fellow-Colophonians had been ruined by learning Lydian luxury—the use of ointment, the adornment of their hair with gold, and the purple robes.[27] Phocylides of Miletus

---

[21] Herod. v. 58.

[22] For the fragments of the logographers see F. Jacoby, *Fragmente der griechischen Historiker*, Vol. I (1923); cf. Apollodorus *Bibliotheca*.

[23] *Iliad* ix. 383.

[24] Hesiod. *Cat.* 21.

[25] Sappho, Frags. 25, 103, 136 (Edmonds).

[26] Xenophan., Frag. 9; Herod. i. 94.

[27] Xenophan., Frag. 3.

dared state that "a small city on a rock living in due order is more powerful than senseless Ninus (Nineveh)."[28]

Other Greeks traded with Egypt, like Sappho's brother Charaxus, long a resident of Naucratis;[29] they brought home from Egypt such souvenirs as statues, to be imitated by Greek sculptors in their archaic "Apollos." Yet others fought as mercenaries for Egyptian kings of the Saite dynasty. Here they revered the gods of the land, and one Greek in the Delta set up a bronze statuette of the Apis bull with the inscription: "To Panepi (Pehe-n-Hapi), Socylides dedicated me."[30] Some served under Chaldaean monarchs like Nebuchadnezzar—Antimenides, for instance, who slew a giant near Ascalon. His poet brother Alcaeus welcomed his return from the ends of the earth.[31] More than gold accompanied the wanderers back to Greece, and it is no accident that logical thinking among the Greeks began in Ionia.

INFLUENCE OF ORIENTAL SCIENCE AND RELIGION IN GREECE

Our earliest authorities insist that the first Greek philosopher, Thales of Miletus, was of Phoenician descent.[32] The statement has been doubted, but at least it is true that, as a subject of the Lydians Alyattes and Croesus, Thales was in the full current of oriental thought. The mercenary brother of Alcaeus suggests the road along which traveled the latest Chaldaean discovery, the saros, knowledge of which permitted the Ionian philosopher to predict the solar eclipse of May 28, 585.[33]

Other writers declare that Thales had studied with the priests of Egypt, from whom he learned geometry. His new knowledge was put to use when he set up his walking-stick at the edge of the great pyramid's shadow, and, from the two triangles formed by intercepting the sun's rays, showed that the height of the pyramid bore the same relation to the length of the stick as one shadow to the other. King Ama-

---

[28] Phocylid., Frag. 5.

[29] Sappho, Frags. 35 ff.; Herod. ii. 135; Strabo xvii. 1. 33; Athen. xiii. 596B.

[30] A. S. Murray, *Archäologischer Anzeiger*, XIV (1899), 205; W. Spiegelberg, "The God Panepi," *JEA*, XII (1926), pp. 34 ff.

[31] Alcaeus, Frags. 133–35; Strabo xiii. 2. 3.

[32] Herod. i. 170; Duris, Frag. 74(J); Democritus, Frag. 115a (Diels); Diog. Laert. i. 22; for Thales and his successors cf. Thomas L. Heath, *Aristarchus of Samos* (1913), pp. 12 ff.

[33] Herod. i. 74.

sis is reported to have admired immensely this new method of measuring the pyramid.[34]

Thales was the first Greek to inscribe a right-angled triangle in a circle. He also determined the sun's course from solstice to solstice and thereby fixed the seasons; in this he had been preceded by the Babylonians. His division of the year into 365 days was far more correct than the current practice of making it only 360, but for this he had been anticipated in Egypt two millenniums before. From the Chaldaeans again, he must have obtained the data which allowed him to compute the sun's size as 1/720 of the solar circle and the moon as the same fraction of the lunar circle. That he first identified the Little Bear can be true only for the Greeks, since the Phoenicians had for centuries guided their ships by it.[35]

From the time of Homer, Greek literature is filled with names of constellations and stories about them which have been familiar to us since our childhood. Only of late have we learned that these names are for the most part translations or adaptations of the Babylonian names for these same constellations. Since the time of the Third Dynasty of Ur, toward the end of the third millennium, Babylonians had arranged calendars on the basis of irregular intercalations of additional months according to a rude cycle of eight years.[36] By the seventh century, after the Babylonians had already substituted a nineteen-year cycle, the Greeks adopted this earlier cycle, which they called an *octaeteris*. Their primary objective was to regulate the fixed religious festivals. In time, it came to be realized that the system left much to be desired. Toward the end of the sixth century, we hear of a reformer, Cleostratus of Tenedos, who seems to have doubled the cycle, for his single year was counted as $365\frac{7}{16}$ days.[37]

[34] Plut. *Sept. sapient. conviv.* 147A. The most recent treatise dealing with the relationship of this branch of science to the Orient—that of Thomas L. Heath, *A History of Greek Mathematics* (1921)—requires drastic revision in the light of present-day discoveries in the sphere of Babylonian mathematical knowledge. In view of the recent date at which the priority of so much of Babylonian mathematics has been discovered, it is impossible in this general history to do more than note the various admissions by Greek authors of this priority. For some of the latest discoveries cf. especially F. Thureau-Dangin, *Textes mathématiques babyloniens* (1938), particularly valuable because the author attempts to understand the actual process of Babylonian thought, and various articles by Otto Neugebauer, in *Quellen und Studien zur Geschichte der Mathematik, Astronomie, und Physik* (1931——), better adapted to the specialist. For bibliography and summary cf. L. C. Karpinski, "New Light on Babylonian Mathematics," *AJSL*, LII (1936), 73 ff.

[35] Diod. Laert. i. 23–24, 37–38; Plin. xxxvi. 82; Joseph. *Apion.* i. 14.

[36] Kugler, *Sturnkunde*, II, 362 ff., 422 ff.

[37] Censorin. xviii. 5; cf. J. K. Fotheringham, "Cleostratus," *JHS*, XXIX (1919), 176 ff.

Meanwhile, Pythagoras of Samos and his immediate followers had broken completely with the idea of a practical calendar. Pythagoras, the second great philosopher of Thales' generation, was also said to have visited Egypt and Babylon. Of a visit to the Nile, there can be no doubt. He learned Egyptian in the reign of Pharaoh Amasis and studied with Oenuphis of Heliopolis. He was the first of the Greeks to recognize the identity of the evening and morning star, a fact known to Babylonians fifteen centuries before. The famous theorem which bears his name was new only to the Greeks.[38]

Firmly convinced of the mystic values of numbers, Pythagoras determined to base a brand new cycle on a primary foundation of arithmetic. Fifty-nine was a "beautiful" number, since it was a prime. When to this was added the undoubted fact that, when we count the days *and* nights in every one of the moon's months, the total is always 59, it became obvious to both master and disciples that the sun's "great year," after which he returns to his exact former station, must likewise be 59 of his ordinary years. Simple multiplication then proved that these 59 years were equivalent to 729 months of 59 days and nights each, a total of 43,011 days and nights. That 729 represented the mystic combination $9 \times 9 \times 9$ appeared complete confirmation. Simple division was all that was further needed to secure the true length of the single year, $364\frac{1}{2}$ days.[39]

Niloxenus of Naucratis was the guest friend, and so the host, of Thales and of the companions of Solon in Egypt.[40] Solon himself visited Egypt, meanwhile supporting himself by trade. He studied with the learned priests Psenophis of Heliopolis and Sonchis of Sais and once made a formal call upon Amasis.[41] Hypercritics may doubt the travels of Thales and Pythagoras to Egypt; that Pythagoras ever visited Babylonia is improbable, and the story of Solon's call upon Croesus bears the mark of Greek moralizing. However, they cannot doubt the visit of Solon to Egypt, for we have a poem in which he tells how he lived "at the outpourings of the Nile near the cape of Canopus."[42]

[38] Diog. Laert. viii. 3. 12. 14; Strabo xiv. 1. 16; Plin. ii. 37; Joseph. *Apion.* i. 14; Plut. *De isid.* 354E.

[39] Aetius ii. 32. 2; Censorin. xviii. 8; xix. 2; note how in Plato's *Republic*, 588A, the number 729 is concerned with days and nights, months and years.

[40] Plut. *Sept. sapient. conviv.* 146E.

[41] Hermippus, in Plut. *Solon* 2. 4; cf. *ibid.* 26. 1; *De isid.* 10; Herod. i. 30.

[42] Solon, Frag. 28; Aristot. *Polit. Athen.* xi. 1.

Yet if Greek thinkers appropriated oriental science, as a rule without specific acknowledgment, there was a fundamental difference in their approach. The Babylonian astronomer or the Egyptian rope measurer, with his prosaic search for concrete fact, his simple but effective instruments, his subordination of individual vanity and of claims for priority of discovery in the century-long accumulation of data— above all, with his constant use of a highly developed mathematics to solve his problems—would soon have felt himself quite at home in a company of present-day scientists.

To the Greeks there was almost always something of a mystic character in numbers. Carried to absurd extremes by Pythagoras and his disciples, it was almost equally marked in the thought of Plato and the members of his Academy. Oriental science grew up in the school which lay always in the temple's shadow. If it always remained practical, to the oriental mind a "practical" need was the exposition of the stellar gods' mysterious ways to educated men.

Oriental science never doubted the gods; from its very beginnings Greek philosophy was agnostic if not positively atheistic. Oriental scholars had been content to repeat cosmologies hallowed by antiquity and which ascribed creation to their native divinities. So, too, the new Greek religion, Orphism, taught a cosmology strangely like that of the Phoenicians. Ionic thinkers, on the contrary, had to discover for themselves the constitution of the universe. Yet even in their search for the primordial substance, they could not free themselves completely from the influence of oriental thought. Thales found this substance in water, the primordial mist familiar to us in the biblical Garden of Eden story. His fellow-citizen Anaximander introduced to the Greeks useful oriental inventions—the sundial, the map of the earth, and the chart of the heavenly bodies—but when he determined on *his* primordial substance, it was the "unlimited," in direct descent from Tiamat, the Babylonian chaos monster.

Shortly after the Persian conquest, Heracleitus of Ephesus gives us our first intimation that Greeks had come in touch with Persian religion, for he brackets the Magi with Night-walkers, Bacchae, Lenae, and Mystae.[43] The conquest did not check the development of Ionic philosophy. Anaximenes of Miletus, Xenophanes of Colophon, and the Ephesian Heracleitus were famous philosophers in the first generation of Persian rule, and Anaxagoras in the second. The search for the primordial substance continued, and the whole gamut of possibilities

[43] Heracleit., Frag. 124 (Jones).

was run through for suggestions. Scientific discoveries were still made or adapted. But already Ionian philosophy was going its own way and was plunging into metaphysics.[44]

GREEK TRAVELERS IN THE EAST

There were other thoughtful travelers who penetrated deep into the Levant. Scylax of Caryanda, though a Carian, wrote in Greek his Indian travels.[45] Hecataeus of Miletus traversed the Persian Empire and, after his return, prepared geographical lists of the places he had visited or of which he had heard. Now and then he added historical or ethnographic comments, not unlike the lists which appear on earlier Babylonian tablets. Both works are lost, but much of the information provided by Herodotus obviously goes back to these two sources.

From the brief quotations assigned directly to Hecataeus by late compilers, an amazing knowledge of inner Asia is disclosed. Chna (Canaan) is the former name of Phoenicia, some of whose cities are Gabala, Sidon, Dora, Aega, Ginglymote, and Phoenicussae. Cardytis and Canytis are great cities of Syria. The Camareni are islands of the Arabs, Cyre is an island in the Persian Sea. Persian cities are Paricane, Chandanace, and Sittace, though we know that the last was actually in Babylonia. The ethnographic descriptions of Herodotus are anticipated: The Cissaeans (Kashshites) dress like the Persians; Media is the land near the Caspian Gates; the people of Hyope are clad like the Paphlagonians; near the Gordians is the city of Matiene; next to the Matienians are the Colchian people of the Moschi; the Mycians are near the Araxes River, the Catannians by the Caspian Sea; round about the Hyrcanian Sea are high forest-covered mountains on which grows the prickly artichoke; east of the Parthians live the Chorasmians, who possess both plain and mountain, the latter overgrown by forest trees, the artichoke, the willow, and the tamarisk; their capital is Chorasmia. Much of this information Hecataeus may have derived from the report of Scylax. From him he certainly obtained his data about the Indian inhabitants of Gandara and the city of Gandarica, about Caspapyrus opposite the Scyths, about the Indian city of Argante and the peoples of Calatiae and Opiae near the Indus River with their walled capital, and about the desert which thence extends to the Indus, where again artichokes grow.[46]

---

[44] Sources collected by H. Diels and W. Kranz, *Die Fragmente der Vorsokratiker* (5th ed., 1934–37). The contrast between Chaldaean science and Greek philosophy is well brought out by Diodorus ii. 29.

[45] Herod. iv. 44.   [46] Hecataeus, Frags. 271–99(J); Herod. iii. 98 ff.

In the course of his travels Hecataeus visited Egyptian Thebes, and there he had a curious experience. In typical Greek attitude, he sought to impress the barbarians by the boast of a divine ancestor in the six-teenth generation. The priests led him into the temple and pointed out the three hundred and forty-five wooden statues of the high priests, each the son of the next, and each a man, the son of a man and not of a god. Hecataeus stood mute as he began to realize the hoar antiquity of the East.[47]

[47] Hecataeus, Frag. 300(J); Herod. ii. 143.

Chapter XVI

XERXES AS CROWN PRINCE

THE SELECTION OF AN HEIR

SHORTLY after his accession, Xerxes razed a portion of Darius' treasury at Persepolis and built the harem. At the foundation ceremonies he laid on a bed of sulphur and sweet-smelling wood a foundation block of fine limestone; it properly imitated a clay tablet, for on it he inscribed his own version of how his father came to choose him as successor:

"Says Xerxes the king: My father was Darius. The father of Darius was by name Vishtaspa. The father of Vishtaspa was by name Arshama. Vishtaspa and Arshama were both living when Ahuramazda, by his will, made Darius my father king of the earth." This was a precedent: "Darius also had other sons, but by the will of Ahuramazda, Darius my father made *me* the greatest after himself. When Darius my father passed away, by the will of Ahuramazda I became king on my father's throne."[1]

This is all perfectly true, but it is not quite all the truth. According to Persian law, it was imperative that a Persian monarch appoint a successor before he dared risk his life in a foreign war. The eldest son of Darius was Artobazanes; he is already recognized as successor by 507, when a Babylonian document mentions the "king's son of Elam."[2] Against his succession, however, might be urged that he had been born while his father was still in private life with no expectation of ever reaching the throne and that his mother was a commoner, an unnamed daughter of Gobryas. A younger son, Xerxes (Khshayarsha), had been born to the purple, and his mother was Atossa, daughter of the empire's founder. In the Orient these are strong arguments, and, when a bitter harem quarrel arose between the partisans of the two

---

[1] E. Herzfeld, *A New Inscription of Xerxes from Persepolis* (1932); *Archäologische Mittheilungen aus Iran*, IV (1932), 117 ff.; *Altpersische Inschriften* (1938), No. 15; R. G. Kent, *Language*, IX (1933), 35 ff.

[2] J. P. Strassmaier, *Darius* (1897), No. 411.

candidates for the throne, there could be no reason for surprise when the younger son by the more high-born wife was finally chosen.[3]

Darius followed the example of Queen Atossa's father, who had made Cambyses, when he was "king's son," his personal representative in Babylonia. By October 23, 498, we learn that the house of the king's son was in process of erection at Babylon; no doubt this is the Darius palace in the central section that we have already described. Two years later, in a business document from near-by Borsippa, we have reference to the "new palace" as already completed.[4] At this time Xerxes could have been scarcely twenty years old.

During the years following, Xerxes made his appearance in art at Persepolis. On the facing jambs of a gateway on the east of the Triple Portal and leading down to the level of the subsequently built harem were carved two reliefs. Above the scene floats the winged Ahuramazda, holding out the ring which bestowed sovereignty upon the crown prince. Below is the canopy over the throne, upheld at each corner by slim columns. Framed by rows of twelve-petaled rosettes, the Ahuramazda symbol is repeated, but this time without the human figure. Elaborate tassels depend as further decoration.

On the throne sits Darius, clad in his robe of state and prepared to hold a public audience. Behind him stands Xerxes, as the recognized heir-apparent wearing the same rich garments and sporting the same long, square-cut beard. Since this depicts a public reception, the collars, bracelets, and cidaris are worn; on the reliefs they were once outlined in gold. Below them, the platform on which the throne is set is lifted up by representatives of the peoples who composed the empire of Darius.

About the same time that these reliefs were carved, Darius completed the first addition to his treasury.[5] Porticoes on each of the four sides, their roofs supported by four wooden columns resting on stone bases, their floors covered by the reddish wash preferred by this monarch, led into an open rectangular courtyard around which the whole addition was centered. Its only flooring was coarse white plaster. At

---

[3] Herod. vii. 2–3. Herodotus, however, dates the harem struggle after the revolt of Egypt in 486; cf. Ctes. *Pers.*, Epit. 51; Marmor Parium A, 49.

[4] *VS*, Vol. III, No. 125; *BRM*, Vol. I, No. 81; R. Koldewey, *Excavations at Babylon* (1914), pp. 127 ff.

[5] R. Carl Haines, in Erich F. Schmidt, *The Treasury of Persepolis* (1939), p. 17.

the side of the western and northeastern entrances were figures in the round; in all probability they represented leopards or similar felines, comfortably stretched out on their bellies in a posture found elsewhere below the platform, though only the depressions can now be seen.

In contrast, the porticoes to south and to east show orthostat reliefs, sunk in the frame as at Parsagarda, but of much finer execution. Our eyes are at once drawn to the two central figures, Darius and Xerxes. A low platform elevates them above the common herd, from whom they are also distinguished by slightly greater size. There is no attempt at portraiture; all the individuals present have the same over-large eyes, marked eyebrows, slightly convex nose, and generous mouth, half-concealed by a drooping mustache with neatly twirled tip. But while others wear a short beard coming to a point, Darius and Xerxes alone can show a longer beard, elaborately curled and waved in the Assyrian fashion, which reaches to the chest, where it is cut off square. Hair curled with equal elaboration is rounded out on the neck and is frizzed in front under the high flat-topped hat, the cidaris. Today the faces bear the marks of deliberate mutilation at the hands of Alexander's Macedonians.

Since this is a private audience, the gold ornaments are laid aside. Father and son are clad simply but richly in the candys robe, descending to the ankles in graceful folds which permit only a glimpse of the undertunic held tight at the right wrist. Their feet are shod with soft buttonless shoes. In the color scheme of the garments, we learn, the royal Phoenician purple plays a large part.

The throne on which Darius is seated is nothing but a high-backed chair; it is supposed to be of solid gold with silver feet imitating lions' paws, though the turned rungs prove that, like those of his Assyrian predecessors, it is gold-plated over a wooden core. On it the king sits stiffly, the evident discomfort of the position when held for so long a time slightly mitigated by a cushion and by a footstool whose feet are in the form of bulls' legs and hoofs. In his powerful right fist Darius grasps firmly the long slender scepter, also gold-plated, with jeweled knob, extending to the floor. His left hand grasps as firmly a lotus with two buds.

On the low platform supporting the throne which adds to the impression of royal majesty stands Xerxes. He wears exactly the same robe, the same cidaris, and the same spade beard, and in his left hand he carries another lotus. The sculpture thus confirms his own claim that "my father made me the greatest after himself." But, after all, he is still only the crown prince and must stand humbly behind his seated father, toward whose throne he raises his right hand, palm open, in the usual gesture of worship made by the reigning king to Ahuramazda.

Before the throne are set two metal incense burners of complicated form. Tall ribbed stands with fluted half-spherical tops support the burner proper, a stepped cone from which the smoke escapes through covers pierced like arrows. A delicate chain fixes the anvil-shaped stopper to the duck's head at the tip of the stand. The use of frankincense (of which the Arabs sent a yearly gift of 66,000 pounds)[6] before the king's presence is one more hint that in Persia the monarch was reverenced as something more than human.

Leaning over the burners, hand to mouth as indication that he is making his usual daily report, is the *hazarapat*—the Greeks called him "chiliarch"—who, as the commander of the royal bodyguard, was the most powerful official at court.[7] He has come from what may have been his headquarters immediately to the south, from which the gate in the eastern treasury wall gives direct access to the barracks where in time of peace the Immortals were quartered. Quite possibly the gold-covered iron scales unearthed in a near-by room belonged to his gold cuirass;[8] the wicked bridles with doubly perforated side bars and rings on either side to hold the reins with the linked bits perchance chafed the mouth of his horse. Under his charge were the storerooms whose thousands of objects illustrate fully Persian warfare.

During the revolts which marked the accession and first years, Takhmaspada the Mede had commanded an army in the absence of Darius. Perhaps he was by now *hazarapat;* at least, the official who bows before his master wears the Median costume, strapped shoes, and earrings. On his hip is the short Persian sword, and he carries the staff of high office as he makes the adoration.

Behind Xerxes stands the cupbearer, who in later Achaemenid times was to exercise even more influence than the commander-in-chief. He is clad in a long robe, his shoes fastened by straps and buttons; his head-dress is curious: a long scarf brought three times under the chin, then wound around the head turban fashion; one short end falls down the

---

[6] Herod. iii. 97.

[7] F. Justi, "Der Chiliarch des Dareios," *ZDMG*, L (1896), 659 ff.

[8] Cf. the gold-scale armor worn at Plataea under a purple robe by General Masistes (Herod. ix 22, 24).

back of the head, the other reaches almost to the small of the back. Despite this elaborate covering, his unbearded face is sufficiently exposed to indicate that he is a eunuch. His left hand is folded over his right arm, which grasps tightly his badge of office, the looped napkin.

From the tomb relief of Darius, carved on the rock about the same date, we learn that the officer who follows is Aspachana (Aspathines),[9] holder of the king's battle-ax and bow case. Over his left shoulder hangs the bow case, ending in a bird's head, while the strap with triangular guard is held in his left hand; a similar bronze guard whose decoration consists of the legs of two joined ibexes has been recovered in the treasury armory. In his right hand is held the *sagaris*, the double battle-ax of the Scythians, one head a fish set in a wide-open duck's bill, the other shaped like an anvil but with divided tip; the grip is of wood, roughened by triangular cuts to furnish a better hold.

On his right thigh is a short sword, the scabbard slung by a leather strap from the sagging double belt fastened by a rosette; a huge rivet holds the weapon to a projecting attachment ornamented by lotus blossoms. The handle of the sword is a flattened oval, the grip tightened by two horizontal grooves and by square and triangular incisions. The blade is hidden in the scabbard, whose Scythian ornamentation is unusually elaborate. Its upper third, in bow shape, depicts two rampant griffins, back to back but glaring at each other; the face is that of a hawk with body and forepaws of a lion; the legs are clawed. The remaining two-thirds illustrate nine male ibexes prancing within a highly decorated border. At the tip is a bull's head, the horn conventionalized to form a heart-shaped blossom with nine petals, and below it is the conventionalized lion; the scabbard is prevented from swinging by a braided leather strap which passes around the right knee.

Still farther back of Xerxes two robed Immortals stand in the usual position of attention, spear resting on toe. At the opposite end the scene is closed by one more Immortal and by a similarly robed attendant who carries a metal pail from which to refuel the burners with the precious frankincense. The baldachin which once covered the whole scene is lost, and only the poles and the tassels are left. Each of the two reliefs is essentially the same; the chief difference is that in one the more important personages face to the right, in the other, to the left.[10]

[9] Naqsh-i-Rustam D; cf. Herod. iii. 70.   [10] Schmidt, *op. cit.*, pp. 20 ff.

To the east, south, and north of the courtyard are the archives. In one room to the southeast were once to be found the papyri and parchments; they were all burned by Alexander's soldiers, who enjoyed a fine bonfire, as the walls of this room bear witness. Today, only a few charred shreds of cloth remain of the precious documents; fifteen clay bullae alone retain the impression of the seals, a few of which might be attributed to Darius or Xerxes. But the fire which destroyed papyri and parchments also unknowingly preserved more numerous if intrinsically less important documents written on unbaked tablets, baked hard by the flames. The vast majority has been found, as they were stored, in a single oversized chamber.[11] This new archive begins with 492.[12]

To the west of the courtyard is a great room, roofed by means of nine rows of eleven columns each, which can be described only as an exhibition hall. Great masses of precious or rare objects which poured in as loot from the wars soon demanded a second addition to the treasury building, a second exhibition hall which covered virtually the whole northern face. While the first was almost square, the second was long and narrow, twenty columns each in five rows. In each, the wooden columns rested on a rounded discoid torus, which in turn rested on a square plinth, both carved with the individual mark of the craftsman.[13]

For the most part it is impossible to determine which of the objects preserved were first installed in this reign. So thorough was the looting by Alexander that no large-sized work of art in a precious metal has survived. The many superb vessels of stone which bear the name of Xerxes were all deliberately smashed, though fortunately a good many can be fitted together again. Of the trophies from successful wars, some come from Egypt. A creamy alabaster bowl, banded in white and light gray, bears near the small handle the cartouches of Necho. Further names of the same monarch appear on the base of a blue paste statuette. Amasis is mentioned on an alabaster vase stand and on a composite alabaster vessel. From a dining-room of the last great Assyrian king came a drinking bowl of white-and-black speckled granite, held by four lion handles; its inscription declares that it once belonged to Ashur-bani-apal. The same name is found on votive cylinders and on one of the votive "eye stones" prepared in

[11] *Ibid.*, pp. 33 ff.

[12] G. G. Cameron, "Darius' Daughter and the Persepolis Inscriptions," *JNES*, I (1942), 215.

[13] Schmidt, *op. cit.*, pp. 51 ff.

agate, onyx, or sardonyx. Another cylinder was made centuries earlier at Suhi, well up the Middle Euphrates. Owing to their style, three joined bronze lions and two galloping bronze horses must also be considered Assyrian antiques.[14]

LEGAL REFORMS IN EGYPT

The same need for reform was felt in Egypt as in Babylonia. A huge papyrus dated from 513 amusingly takes us behind the scenes and shows the true quality of "justice" as practiced on the Nile. In that year a certain Ahmosi came from Ptores to the town of Teuzoi and made protest to the administrative head of the temple (*leshoni*) Zeubestefonkh: "My prebend used to be given me every year, from the time when the satrap became prophet of Amon." The temple head answered "As your breath prospers and as lives Amon who rests here, though it is the month of harvest there is no grain in Amon's granary and there is no silver in Amon's chest." To pay the prebends would therefore demand a loan at interest. Many of the town's rascals were already in prison. "Is it our fault if there are others beside them in town?" Whom should he ask, Ahmosi then inquired, to discover how the town had been ruined? The temple scribe Petesi, he was told, was the only man who would speak the truth.

Petesi, however, was too experienced to speak the truth without compulsion; in view of what was to come, we cannot blame him. The recalcitrant scribe was carried off by force to the ship, where Ahmosi warned him: "I have refrained from beating you, because you are an old man and would die." He had a better scheme; arrived at the nome capital Hnes, the unfortunate Petesi was exposed to the blazing sun until he cried out: "Let a papyrus sheet be given me to write out everything that happened!" Ahmosi read the deposition and swore: "As Phre lives, I have found you are right." The two of them sealed the papyrus and forwarded it to the satrap.

If Petesi had escaped the sun, he must now face the wrath of the rascally priests, who, he feared, would kill him. He may have heard of Darius' projected reforms, but experience had taught him that even the satrap's court was not free of bribery. Sure enough, no sooner had Petesi returned home than Pkoip turned up with the identical papyrus Ahmosi had forwarded to the satrap! The former temple head was displaced by Ienharou, and, together with Petesi, his son, and four brothers, Zeubestefonkh was thrown into jail.

[14] *Ibid.*, pp. 54 ff., 64 ff.

On the feast of Pshou, everyone in Teuzoi was drinking beer; the guards slept and Zeubestefonkh escaped. This only made the condition of the other prisoners worse. Ienharou brought Petesi's brothers into the temple, while the remaining prisoners were beaten with staves; apparently dead, they were thrown into an old tower near the temple gate which was then to be pulled down upon them. But Petesi's son reminded the assailants that they could not kill six priests without being reported to satrap and king; the threat worked, and all were carried home, though it was three months before Petesi recovered.

He then slipped off by night to the capital on a boat laden with wood. For seven months Pkoip contrived to stave off an audience with the satrap. Finally, Petesi was recognized by Semtutefnakhte, who led him in person to the satrap's court. Four times the culprits were summoned, but in vain; at the fifth summons they dared no longer delay. Each was given fifty lashes, and all were thrown into prison. A bribe of five temple prebends—duly attested on papyrus!—changed the heart of Semtutefnakhte, and he now interceded with the satrap to procure their release.

Undaunted by this setback, Petesi next appealed for the restoration of his own prebends, which he claimed amounted to sixteen shares of the prophets of Amon and of the other sixteen gods of Teuzoi; they had been granted to an ancestor but had been lost when that ancestor visited Syria with King Psammetichus. The satrap ordered him to write up the history of the case, but the suborned Semtutefnakhte induced Petesi to accept instead a letter from Ahmosi, prophet of Horus. On his homeward journey Petesi learned that his house had been burned. Again he appealed to the satrap, and again the culprits were ordered to court; the messenger was bribed and only Ienharou appeared. Although he denied all knowledge of the fire, he was given fifty more lashes and once more imprisoned.

Ahmosi lost patience and sarcastically demanded of Petesi: "Will you die in these matters?" To escape a suit which Ahmosi hinted would never be finished, Petesi was reconciled to Ienharou, who took oath that he would straighten out the whole matter; once he was released, naturally, Ienharou disregarded his oath. For the last time, Petesi sent in a long petition, reciting the past history of his family, citing two highly dubious inscriptions of his ancestor which he claimed the priests had erased, and bringing the case up to date.[15] Whether he ultimately won his case we do not know. How correct was

[15] F. L. Griffith, *Catalogue of Demotic Papyri in the John Rylands Library*, III (1909), 60 ff.

his presentation of that case we may doubt, for we have only his word, but we do have a glaring illustration of the graft still rampant in Egypt. There was need of the new code of laws.

By order of Darius the scribes had brought the law and were writing it down in a papyrus roll until 503; why it took so much longer in Egypt than in Babylonia becomes evident when we realize that here there was no such lawbook to serve as model for the whole as that of Hammurabi. Even then it would seem that only the royal ordinances were compiled at that time, for the entire work was not finally brought to completion until eight years later in 495. One copy was written on a payprus roll in Ashur writing (by which was now meant the official Aramaic of the Achaemenid chancellery), another in letter-writing, what the Greeks called "demotic."[16] Henceforth Darius was counted as the last of the six great Egyptian lawgivers.[17]

To illustrate these laws, our reign affords a good collection of business documents. One interesting group deals with the private affairs of the water-pourers of the Valley, the Theban necropolis. For instance, Pshenesi writes a marriage contract with Tsenenhor, who gives him three silver pieces of Ptah's treasury, current money, as dowry; if he hates her and leaves her as wife, he must return the silver with a third of everything he may make, together with a third of his revenues as water-carrier of the necropolis. He makes Rouru, his daughter by Tsenenhor, copartner of other children who may yet be born. Then Tsenenhor acknowledges the rights of her own son by a previous marriage.

Pshenesi gives his wife half a vacant house site on the west of Thebes, near a king's tomb, on which he intends to build; two years later, we discover, he has yet to buy it! Another member of the community writes his wife: "I have abandoned you as wife, I have removed from you, I have no claim on earth to you; I have said to you: Take for yourself a husband in any place you may go. I shall not be able to stand before you forever." Other documents from this archive deal with loans of grain, interest to accrue if the loan is not paid before harvest, sales of cattle and of slaves with guaranties against future claims, sales of temple prebends, or exchange of private lands for the first fruits of lands in the possession of the Amon temple at Thebes.[18]

---

[16] W. Spiegelberg, *Die sogennante demotische Chronik* (1914), pp. 30 ff.

[17] Diod. i. 95. 4-5.

[18] Griffith, *op. cit.*, pp. 25 ff.; for other papyri from this reign cf. W. Spiegelberg, *Die demotischen Papyri Loeb* (1931).

Our first document from the Aramaic-speaking Jewish mercenary colony at Elephantine,[19] dated in 495, bears witness to the legal reforms. Two women exchange lands with a third, who, like them, was assigned a grant by the king's judges and by the commander of the garrison. The guaranty formula, supported by witnesses, runs as follows: "Hereafter, on a future day, we shall not be able to sue you in the matter of this your share and say: We did not give it to you. Nor shall a brother or sister, son or daughter, relative or alien, be able to sue you. And whoever shall sue you in the matter of your share which we have given to you shall pay you the sum of five *karash* and the share is yours." Here, too, the financial reforms of Darius may be detected.[20]

This Jewish colony possessed a papyrus bearing the Aramaic version of Darius' autobiography. Doubtless it was an official copy sent them by order of the king himself. It was evidently treasured and received hard usage, for, when it wore out, a second copy was prepared, though with blanks where the original papyrus had become illegible.[21]

CONSTRUCTIONS IN EGYPT

Darius followed the example of his predecessors in cherishing Egyptian gods and their temples. The great quarries of the wadi Hammamat, the black gorge on the desert road between Coptos and the Red Sea, had been exploited through expeditions sent out by all the great rulers of the past in search of the finest building material; they had added their reliefs and inscriptions to the animal figures cut on the rocks by prehistoric visitors. By order of Darius, these quarries were repeatedly visited by the director of works in the whole land, the architect Khnumibre. With his father Ahmose sa Neith, he had already worked the quarries in the forty-fourth year of Amasis; his position under a native king was not to his disadvantage, for during the years 496–492 he was repeatedly in the wadi. His titles likewise grew and finally included the prophethood of various gods, general of the soldiers, and director of every work of art. References to Min, Horus, and Isis of Coptos, and to Amon, Mut, Khonsu, and Harpocrates of near-by Thebes suggest some of the native divinities whose temples may have been restored by the architect.[22]

---

[19] Cf. p. 89.

[20] A. E. Cowley, *Aramaic Papyri of the Fifth Century B.C.* (1923), No. 1.

[21] *Ibid.*, pp. 248 ff.

[22] J. Couyat and P. Montet, *Les Inscriptions du Ouadi Hammamat* (1912), Nos. 14, 18, 90–93, 134–35, 137, 186, 190, 193; G. Posener, *La première domination Perse en Égypte* (1936), Nos. 11–23.

The Oasis of the South was beginning to prosper as the center of the desert trade through the recent introduction of the camel, as also by the introduction of the *qanat* system of irrigation, long since in use on the Iranian plateau and so well adapted to an arid region. At its capital Hebt there was already a small temple to Amon; about 490 Darius substituted a much superior structure of sandstone, in which he was honored as the beloved of Amon, the lord of Hebt. In its construction Darius naturally followed native ground plans, but instead of the usual triple sanctuary there was but one holy of holies. From the older simple papyrus capital a more composite type had already blossomed forth in rudimentary form. On the walls in sunken relief the king was depicted offering gifts to groups of the gods or, accompanied by the goddess Hathor and his own "double," making oblation to Amon, Mut, and Khonsu. Also on the walls was a hymn in which, with epithets borrowed from the Book of the Dead, all the gods were treated as simple manifestations of Amon, a good illustration of developing syncretism.[23]

Darius also worked at Busiris,[24] and left his cartouche on a portico at el-Kab.[25] He is listed as one of Edfu's benefactors for the years 507 and 504.[26] On a stele, a private individual kneels before the Horus hawk and uraeus and through them invokes the king to grant life.[27]

THE REBEL SATRAP ARYANDES

Although Darius had shown himself unusually anxious to conciliate the priesthood, the tale of Petesi is enough to show that the satrapial court was not free of corruption. The satrap himself almost certainly was implicated. Herodotus tells us that Aryandes was put to death as a rebel, though the true reason was that he had imitated Darius in coining; as the king's mintage in gold was famous for its purity, so the reputation of the Aryandic silver coins long remained. As a matter of fact, no such coins exist; indeed, all the evidence clearly proves that native Egyptians under Achaemenid rule carried on their business only through the use of weighed-out bullion. But while, according to

[23] H. E. Winlock, *The Temple of Hibis in el Khargeh Oasis*, Vol. I: *The Excavations* (1941); H. Brugsch, *Reise nach den grossen Oase el Khargeh* (1876); S. Birch, *Transactions of the Society of Biblical Archaeology*, V (1887), 293 ff.

[24] E. Naville, *Mound of the Jew* (1890), pp. 27–28.

[25] Somers Clarke, "El-Kab and Its Temples," *JEA*, VIII (1922), 27.

[26] H. Brugsch, *Thesaurus inscriptionum Aegyptiacarum*, III (1884), 538, 548 ff., 590; E. Chassinat, *Le Temple d'Edfou*, VII (1932), 219, 248.

[27] L. Borchardt, *ÄZ*, XLIX (1911), 71.

the official standard in coinage, silver was considered as acceptable at the rate of thirteen to one, its bullion value in Egypt was far higher; it has therefore been suggested that the true crime of Aryandes lay in melting down the precious royal coinage bearing the figure of the king and in selling it at a huge profit as bullion, for this would be high treason.[28]

Aryandes was executed sometime between 511 and 492, at which date Pherendates was satrap. To him, the priests of Khnum, lord of Yeb (Elephantine), submitted a list of fellow-priests to be chosen as administrative heads of the various temples according to the decree of King Darius. The majority Pherendates refused to approve; some had fled after they were appointed, while others claimed that they were already serving in similar positions.[29]

ROYAL INSCRIPTIONS

A magnificent apadana had been completed at Susa. Darius now proposed to build in his new capital another apadana which this time should be in more permanent stone; by this use of stone, it would also be possible to develop an art more truly Persian. At the foundation ceremonies for the new structure, Darius placed in a stone corner-box two pairs of exquisitely written gold and silver tablets thirteen inches square. In his last previous list of satrapies, there had been no increase in number but certain changes in nomenclature: Ionia proper still followed Sardis, but "Those beyond the Sea" were explained as Sacae; "Those of the Sea" became *Yauna takabara*, which the Babylonian version interpreted as the "Second Ionia whose inhabitants bore shields upon their head"—for thus were called the floppy *petasos* hats of the Greeks.[30] Now with justifiable pride Darius boasted: "This is the kingdom which I hold: From the Sacae beyond Sogdiana to Ethiopia, from India to Sardis, which Ahuramazda, greatest of gods, presented me."[31] It is significant that Darius does not consider the Greeks worthy of special mention.

Yet it is these Greeks who tell us how often Darius visited Ecbatana. Until its ruins are properly excavated, we depend on casual finds for further information. A gold and a silver tablet, rescued at the

[28] Herod. iv. 166. For alleged coins of Aryandes cf. R. A. Parker, "Darius and His Egyptian Campaign," *AJSL*, LVIII (1941), 373, n. 5; for explanation cf. J. G. Milne, "The Silver of Aryandes," *JEA*, XXIV (1938), 245–46.

[29] W. Spiegelberg, "Drei demotische Schreiben aus den Korrespondenz des Pherendates," *SPAW*, 1928, pp. 604 ff.; *Papyri Loeb*, No. 1.

[30] Darius, Naqsh-i-Rustam A 3.   [31] Herzfeld, *Altpersische Inschriften*, No. 6.

last moment from the melting-pot, afford a parallel record to those placed by Darius in the foundation box of the Persepolis apadana.[32] Further evidence for such a building at the former Median capital is found in a reference to an apadana by his grandson in an inscription found there.[33] High above the city, on the slope of Mount Aurvant, some distance from the old road to Babylonia, Darius also ordered his inscription carved on the rock.[34]

Furthermore, he had commanded the rock to be smoothed on the great cliff overlooking Lake Van from the east, where the former Haldian kings had left numerous records beautifully inscribed in their own native form of the cuneiform writing; at his death the inscription had not been carved, so his pious son gave order that the omission should be rectified. Xerxes also mentions the many beautiful edifices which his father had built; perhaps still one more palace near the inscription is indicated.[35] Greek writers add to the list of royal palaces others at Gabae, the modern Isfahan, and at Taoce, on the coast of Persis near the boundary of Carmania,[36] but no traces of these have been found.

PREPARATIONS FOR THE WAR ON GREECE

Meanwhile, preparations for the Greek war proceeded apace. As Darius saw it, Marathon was only a temporary setback to a hitherto successful policy of steady frontier advance. All that was needed, he thought, was a larger army under proper direction, and then, when the surviving city-states had been crushed, the whole Greek world would be incorporated within the ever expanding Persian Empire. Since his generals had so miserably failed in their attempt to punish the recalcitrant Athenians, Darius made up his mind to lead the expedition of revenge in person.

In the brief time remaining to him, Darius hastened to build the sculptures along the north front of the apadana and began those on the north end (and in the center) of the east front.[37] At the same time he was completing his palace.

[32] Sidney Smith, *JRAS*, 1926, pp. 533 ff.; L. H. Gray, *JRAS*, 1927, pp. 97 ff.; Carl D. Buck, *Language*, III (1927), 1 ff.; Weissbach, *ZA*, XXXVII (1927), 291 ff.; Kent, *JAOS*, LI, (1931), 229 ff.; Herzfeld, *Archäologische Mittheilungen aus Iran*, II (1930), 115; *Altpersische Inschriften*, No. 6.

[33] Herzfeld, *Altorientalische Studien Bruno Meissner . . . . gewidmet* (1928), pp. 85 ff.; Kent, *JAOS*, LI (1931), 231–32.

[34] F. H. Weissbach, *Keilinschriften der Achämeniden* (1911), pp. 100–101.

[35] *Ibid.*, pp. 116 ff.

[36] Strabo xv. 3. 3; Arr. *Ind.* 39. 3; Ptrol. vi. 4. 2–3; viii. 21. 15; Dionys. Per. 1069.

[37] So Cleta Olmstead Robbins.

There was no question of the succession, for Xerxes had been recognized as the crown prince since 498 and had been represented—without being named—on the Persepolis reliefs; now the time had come for fuller recognition, and on the jamb of the middle palace door, opposite his father's portrait, Xerxes was presented with the same royal dress, differentiated only by the brief inscription on his robe: "Xerxes, Darius the king's son, the Achaemenid."[38]

Preparations for the Greek war, of course, demanded fresh taxes. In June of 486 a certain Babylonian reported home that Shatamaksu and the majordomo Nabugaza had informed him that, according to the king's law, he must pay a new toll on the cargo of barley, wheat, and mustard he was clearing through the storehouse on a Babylonian canal.[39]

REVOLT OF EGYPT AND DEATH OF DARIUS

At the burial of the Apis bull, presumably that of 488, the general Ahmose (Amasis)[40] conducted the divinity to the hall of embalming and then, accompanied by archers and chosen soldiers, to his place in the necropolis. Ahmose passed all the nights watching and without sleeping, seeking to do every good thing. He placed respect for the god in the hearts of the people as well as of the foreigners of all the foreign lands who were in Egypt. He also sent messengers to the governors of the cities and nomes of Upper and Lower Egypt, and they brought their gifts to the hall of embalming.[41]

Notwithstanding these benefits, the Egyptians claimed that Persepolis, Susa, and Ecbatana had been erected from Egyptian wealth.[42] As late as 486, the *saris* (eunuch) of Pars, Atiyawahy, was again working the Hammamat quarries.[43] But on October 5 of this year Khnumemakhet wrote Pherendates from Elephantine a disconcerting letter. Osorwer, a prominent native, had in the presence of the satrap given him orders to take Artabanus, the Persian commander of the Jewish garrison, and to go with a ship to Nubia to secure grain. Artabanus then ordered the boatmen to unlade the grain on the shore. Khnumemakhet protests: Let the satrap order Artabanus to set a guard in the

---

[38] Herzfeld, *Altpersische Inschriften*, No. 18; for inscription on the Darius figure cf. Weissbach, *op. cit.*, pp. 80 ff.

[39] Cf. p. 76.   [40] Cf. Herod. iv. 167, 201 ff.

[41] E. Chassinat, *Recueil de travaux*, XXIII (1901), 78; Posener, *op. cit.*, Nos. 6–7.

[42] Diod. i. 46. 4.

[43] Couyat and Montet, *op. cit.*, No. 146; Posener, *op. cit.*, No. 24.

ship over the grain and to unload on the bank only so much as can be ferried by a boat of Syene. If precautions are not taken, the rebels will come by night and carry off the grain; already they are encamped opposite and have become so bold that they show themselves at midday.[44]

With this ominous warning, Egyptian documents come to an end. Within the next month, Egypt revolted, for the new taxes had proved too much for the natives' temper. Before he could put down the revolt Darius himself passed away—in November of 486. He was sixty-four years of age, but of these he had ruled thirty-six.[45] Once more Fortune had smiled on the European Greeks and had granted them an unexpected respite.

Sometime before, Darius had prepared his tomb.[46] The north end of the plain, on the east of which he had built his new capital, was shut in by a low range which descended southwestward and presented a straight sheer cliff, already utilized for a relief by an Elamite king.[47] Underneath this cliff Darius had already prepared a rectangular sacred precinct of mud brick, within which the most important structure was a fire temple which exactly imitated that of Cyrus at Parsagarda.[48]

For some reason, Darius abandoned the form of grave used by Cyrus and returned to the rock tomb. A little east of the fire temple his tomb was excavated into the cliff, its front in the form of a Greek cross sixty feet wide and seventy feet high. The horizontal arms were filled by a representation of the palace portico. At the ends were pilasters between which were placed four slender unfluted columns, on a plinth and a high torus with astragal; above, kneeling bulls held the projecting beams, then came the four beams of the architrave, the third bearing the toothed ornament. The door, three beams at side and at top, was capped by a feathered cornice; but the rough opening which actually gave access to the interior, about two-fifths the height of the pretended entrance, gives so unpleasant an effect that originally, we may suspect, it was masked.

In the upper arm was an elaborately carved throne, upheld by the

[44] Spiegelberg, *SPAW*, 1928, pp. 604 ff.

[45] For date cf. Cameron, *AJSL*, LXVIII (1941), 319; R. A. Parker and W. H. Dubberstein, *Babylonian Chronology, 626 B.C.—A.D. 45* (1942), p. 14.

[46] Ctes. *Pers.* xiii, Epit. 46, says that his parents were killed while inspecting the tomb.

[47] Herzfeld, *Archaeological History of Iran* (1935), p. 6; cf. N. C. Debevoise, "Rock Reliefs of Ancient Iran," *JNES*, I (1942), 80.

[48] Cf. p. 64; Schmidt, *op. cit.*, pp. 98 ff.

PLATE XXV

PLATE XXVI

Human-headed Bull (courtesy Oriental Institute)

General View (courtesy Oriental Institute)

TRIPYLON AT PERSEPOLIS

PLATE XXVII

Nobles Marching up the Stairs (courtesy Oriental Institute)

Attendants Carrying Food up Small Stairway (courtesy Oriental Institute)

A FEAST AT PERSEPOLIS (TRIPYLON)

PLATE XXVIII

King and Attendants (courtesy Oriental Institute)

Palace (courtesy Oriental Institute)

Shaven Youth (courtesy Oriental Institute)

PALACE OF DARIUS AT PERSEPOLIS

PLATE XXIX

Elamite Tablet from Persepolis Archives (from George G. Cameron, *The Persepolis Treasury Tablets*)

One Hundred and Twenty Karsha Weight Found at Persepolis (courtesy Oriental Institute)

Lion Weight from Susa (from Louvre, *Encyclopédie photographique*, Vol. XII, Pl. 59c)

Lydian Coins Found at Persepolis (courtesy Oriental Institute)

THE TOOLS OF BUSINESS

PLATE XXX

King Darius and Crown Prince Xerxes from the Persepolis Treasury (courtesy Oriental Institute)

Tomb of Darius with Scaffolding at Nakshi-Rustem (courtesy Oriental Institute)

THE END OF THE REIGN OF DARIUS

PLATE XXXI

THE PERSIAN IMMORTALS

Relief from Apadana at Persepolis (courtesy Oriental Institute)

PLATE XXXII

Kashshites (courtesy Oriental Institute)

Bactrians (courtesy Oriental Institute)

Saka (courtesy Oriental Institute)

TRIBUTE-BEARERS (FROM APADANA AT PERSEPOLIS)

thirty representatives of the empire. "If now you shall think," he tells us in his tomb inscription, " 'How many are those lands which Darius the king seized?' then look at the representations of those who bear the throne. Then you shall know, then shall it be known to you: The spear of a Persian man has gone forth afar; then shall it be known to you: A Persian man has smitten a foe far from Parsa."[49] Once each representative was properly labeled; today the names of only a limited number have been preserved, but we can still identify the Persian, the Mede, the Elamite, and the Parthian, as well as the Pointed-Cap Scythian, the Babylonian, the Assyrian, and the man of Maka.[50]

Over the throne was placed the offering scene. To the left, on the uppermost of three steps, stood Darius, clad in full regalia including the cidaris; his left hand grasped the bow, his right hand was raised, palm open in adoration. To the right, also on three steps, was the sacred fire on the fire altar. Above floated Ahuramazda; to his side, over the fire altar, was the old moon in the new moon's arms.

Twelve high officials, represented one above the other in rows of threes, aided the ceremony. All but one wore the same robe as the king. On one side, six unarmed officials extended the right arm in adoration, the left flat at the side; on the other, army officers grasped the spear firmly in both hands. The leader of one group of three is named "Gaubaruva (Gobryas) the Patischorian, spearbearer of King Darius"; the other leader is "Aspachana (Aspathines), the bearer of the battle-ax, who holds the bow cover of King Darius."[51]

The low door in the center leads into the now desecrated tomb chamber. Within are four niches sunk into the rock, each containing three massive sarcophagi intended for Darius and the more favored members of his family. But there is no further inscription to tell us which sarcophagus once contained the body of the Great King.[52]

[49] Naqsh-i-Rustam A 4.

[50] The list may be restored, and the other figures may be identified, by the exact copy made for the tomb of Artaxerxes III (cf. A. W. Davis, "An Achaemenian Tomb-Inscription at Persepolis," *Journal of the Royal Asiatic Society*, 1932, pp. 373 ff.).

[51] Cf. p. 218.

[52] Cf. F. Sarre and E. Herzfeld, *Iranische Felsreliefs* (1910), pp. 14 ff.

Chapter XVII

THE GREAT KING AND HIS ARMIES

XERXES (486–465) is in tradition the weakling monarch, dominated by his eunuchs and remembered chiefly for his insane attack on European Greece. Oriental sources picture a very different character. At his accession Xerxes was in the prime of life, about thirty-five years of age, and had been trained as successor to the throne by a dozen years of strenuous administration as viceroy of Babylon. In consequence, his reign stands out for the significance of the administrative changes; if Darius began the new Achaemenid regime through his law, Xerxes marks an even greater break with the past.

Against his one military failure in Europe, not so spectacular to his subjects as it appeared to later generations, must be placed a whole series of victories, including the previous recovery of the two wealthiest and as yet most civilized peoples of his vast empire and his retention of control over the majority of the Greeks themselves. In the field of culture the picture is the same. If the architects of his father laid out the grandiose plan of the terrace structures at the new capital of Parsa, it was Xerxes who brought the main buildings to completion and initiated most of the others. Under his direction the plan was changed in important respects. He alone was responsible for the magnificent reliefs which throw into the shade the cruder work of his father's sculptors. In a word, the Persepolis we have long admired was the work of the son and not of Darius. If he failed to understand the economic forces which already were sapping the empire's strength, he was no worse than others of the ancients.

THE ACCESSION OF XERXES

The first pious duty of the new king was to complete at Susa the palace of his father, where a few columns were still to be carved.[1] An alabaster vase bearing his inscription and a business document con-

---

[1] F. H. Weissbach, *Die Keilinschriften der Achämeniden* (1911), pp. 114–15; V. Scheil, *Inscriptions des Achéménides à Suse* ("Mém.," Vol. XXI [1929]), pp. 81 ff.; *Actes juridiques susiens; Inscriptions des Achéménides* ("Mém.," Vol. XXIV [1933]), pp. 114–15; R. G. Kent, *JAOS*, LI (1931), 193 ff.; LIII (1933), 1 ff; LIV (1934), 34 ff.; J. M. Unvala, in A. U. Pope (ed.), *A Survey of Persian Art*, I, 342; cf. J. de Morgan, *Recherches archéologiques*, I (1900), 90.

cerning a loan dated early in 483 at Susa but found in Babylonia[2] testify to his early residence in the former capital. Then he turned to his
true love, Persepolis.

Near the beginning of his reign, Xerxes prepared an inscription to
commemorate his new authority. The first paragraphs closely follow
the model of his father:

"A great god is Ahuramazda, who created this earth, who created
man, who created peace for man, who made Xerxes king, one king of
many, one lord of many.

"I am Xerxes, the great king, king of kings, king of lands containing many men, king in this great earth far and wide, son of Darius the
king, an Achaemenid, a Persian, son of a Persian, an Aryan, of Aryan
seed.

"Says Xerxes the king: By the favor of Ahuramazda, these are the
lands of which I am king outside Parsa."

Even on the tomb relief of his father, the Persian is only the first of
the empire's representatives bearing the royal throne, though the inscription definitely excludes Parsa from the list of satrapies; in this
Xerxes follows the example of Darius. "I governed them, they
brought tribute to me, they did that which was commanded them by
me; the law which was mine, that held them firm."

The list shows advances on the northeastern border. To the Amyrgaean and the Pointed-Cap Sacae has been added a third satrapy of
eastern nomads, that of the Dahae beyond the Araxes.[3] Another addition is that of the men of the Mountain Land (Akaufaka), which must
be located north of Kabul in modern Afghanistan.[4]

"Says Xerxes the king: When I became king, there was within these
lands which are written above one which was restless. Afterward
Ahuramazda brought me help. By the favor of Ahuramazda I smote
that land and put it in its place."[5]

The restless land was Bactria. At the accession of Xerxes, his brother Ariamenes had set forth from that satrapy to contest the throne.
Won over by gifts and by the promise that he would be second in the

[2] M. Dieulafoy, L'Acropole de Suse (1893), Fig. 318; VS, Vol. IV, No. 191.

[3] Strabo vii. 3. 12; xi. 7. 1; 8. 2; 9. 2–3; medieval Dahistan, east of the Caspian.

[4] Medieval Kohistan.

[5] Xerxes, Daeva Inscription, 1–4; E. Herzfeld, Archäologische Mittheilungen aus Iran, VIII
(1937), 56 ff.; Altpersische Inschriften (1938), 14; Kent, Language, XIII (1937), 292 ff.; JAOS, LVIII
(1938), 324–25; Weissbach, Symbolae Paulo Koschaker dedicatae (1939), pp. 1938 ff.; Cameron, in
Erich Schmidt, The Treasury of Persepolis (1939), pp. 12 ff.

kingdom, Ariamenes placed the crown on the new monarch's head. Henceforth he remained loyal and, as admiral of the grand fleet, met a hero's death at Salamis.[6]

Xerxes goes on to tell us that "within these lands was a place where formerly the daevas were worshiped. Afterward by the favor of Ahuramazda I destroyed that community of daevas and proclaimed: The daevas you shall not worship. Where formerly the daevas were worshiped, there I worshiped Ahuramazda and the holy Arta." Obviously, the land in question must be on the Iranian border, where the supremacy of Ahuramazda had not yet been acknowledged; in the daeva worshipers we must therefore see the hitherto unconquered Dahae.

"And there was other business which was done ill; that I made good. That which I did, all I did by the favor of Ahuramazda. Ahuramazda brought me aid until I had finished the work."

RELIGIOUS REFORM

Xerxes urges his successor to accept his own form of personal religion with its stress on holy Arta: "You who shall be hereafter, if you shall think: 'May I be happy while living and when dead may I be blest,' have respect for that law which Ahuramazda has established" —the law which Ahuramazda had revealed to his father Darius. "Worship Ahuramazda and the holy Arta. The man who has respect for that holy law which Ahuramazda has established, and for the holy Arta, shall be happy while living and blessed when dead."[7] To impress this conviction on his son and successor, Xerxes named him Artakhshathra (Artaxerxes), "Arta's Kingdom."

Thus Xerxes is describing still another reform. He is emphasizing the importance of Arta, who roughly corresponds to Righteousness in the thought of the Zoroastrian community. He is also showing us that the daevas are no longer the accredited gods of the early Aryans; the majority have sunk to the level of demons. Some, however, have been redeemed for survival in the official religion, pictured for us by the contemporary Aeschylus, by Herodotus in the generation following, and by Xenophon and Ctesias in the reign of the second Artaxerxes, who introduced, however, important changes. Presumably this reform was accompanied by a ritual; at any rate, in the "Sevenfold Yasna" are preserved certain prayers in the Gathic prose dialect which con-

[6] Plut. *Reg. imp. apophtheg.* 173B; *De amor. frat.* 488D ff.; *Themistocl.* 14. 3; the source is obviously Ctesias.

[7] Xerxes, *Daeva*, 5 ff.

trast sharply with those assigned to the Zoroastrian community and agree closely with the contemporary official religion.[8]

Both Darius and Xerxes honored Ahuramazda as the god "who made this earth, who made yonder heaven, who made man, who made welfare for man."[9] Our psalmist worships Ahura-Mazdah, who created the Kine and Righteousness, who made Water and the Good Plants, the Light and the Earth and all that is good, through his sovereign power and greatness and his beauteous deeds. He would worship with him also the holiest names, descended from Ahura and most pleasing to Mazdah, the Fravashis or Souls of the men and women, believers in Righteousness, Best Righteousness himself, and the most beauteous Spenta Amesha, Good Thought, Good Kingdom, Good Existence, Good Reward, and Good Piety.[10] In the thought of Zoroaster, these ancient divinities had become pale abstract manifestations of the one supreme deity; here, on the contrary, they retain much of their original anthropomorphic character, while the six most important are recognized as the Amesha Spentas with an actual cult of their own.

Still more of the ancient nature worship is retained in the next prayer:

We worship this Earth which bears us, and your wives, Ahura-Mazdah, who through Righteousness are excellent, through their zeal for the faith, their activity, their independence, their devotion to Piety, together with them the good Reward, the good wish, the good reputation, the good luxuriance. We worship the Waters, outspurting, running together, and off flowing, which, derived from Ahura, are themselves Ahuras, who do good deeds—you who are easy to ford, good to swim, and good to bathe,[11] a gift for both worlds. With the names which Ahura-Mazdah has given you, when as giver of good he created you, with them do we worship you, with them do we beseech your favor, with them we do homage, with them we do thank you. And you, Waters, do we call upon as the pregnant ones, as the Mothers like the milch cows, who care for the poor, the all-suckling, the best and most beautiful. Come down, you good beings, through the aid of the long-armed distributor of offerings, you who provide effective help as recompense in their misfortune, you life-giving Mothers![12]

[8] Cf. p. 106.

[9] Cf. pp. 122, 231.

[10] Yasna 37; it is significant that the same prayer is repeated in Yasna 5, *outside* the collection of the Sevenfold Yasna.

[11] Contrast Herod. i. 138: the Persians do not even wash their hands in rivers.

[12] Yasna 38.

Instead of the stern, aloof Ahura-Mazdah of Zoroaster, we detect the oriental King of Kings whose harem is full of mother-goddesses.

The Ox Soul is not a subordinate of Ahura-Mazdah. He is still a separate object of worship, and with him the souls of domestic animals (whose support of man is gratefully acknowledged) and even those of useful wild beasts—quite as important in the mind of our psalmist as the souls of righteous men and women, whose better selves have already become, or soon will be, victors in the eternal conflict between Good and Evil.[13]

Atar, the Fire, is honored by a whole Yasna devoted to him alone:

By the action of this Fire we first draw near to you, Mazdah-Ahura, by your Holiest Spirit, for him for whom you prepare torment. May *this* man draw near joyfully to the reward, Fire of Ahura-Mazdah, with the joyfulness of the most joyous and the humility of the most humble, may he draw near to the greatest of ordeals. As Fire of Ahura-Mazdah, you are delightful to us, as his Holiest Spirit you are delightful to us. What name of yours is most propitious, Fire of Ahura-Mazdah, with that would we draw near to you. With Good Thought, Beneficent Righteousness, deeds and words and doctrine, we draw near to you. We pray and confess our guilt to you, Mazdah-Ahura; with all good thoughts, with all good deeds, we draw near to you.

Throughout these Yasnas we find hints that they have been superficially revised to bring them into accord with later Zoroastrianism. But surely no true believer in the prophet's message had yet reached the point where he could pray: "And so we mention to you our desire, the most beautiful bodies of bodies, these celestial Lights, and that highest of the high, the Sun,"[14] for, despite the names of individuals who honor the manifestation in the sun-god, Mithra was not officially recognized until the reign of Artaxerxes II.

THE RECOVERY OF EGYPT

Egypt was still to be recovered. As so often, revolt on the Nile led to Jewish unrest in Jerusalem. Whether the unrest eventuated in open revolt may be doubted; the opportunity was seized by the "peoples of the land," now actively hostile to the newly arrived settlers, and in the accession year of Xerxes—from a trifle before December 1, 486, to April 5, 485—they sent him a letter of accusation against the inhabitants of Judah and especially those in Jerusalem.[15] We can conjecture

---

[13] Yasna 39.   [14] Yasna 36.

[15] Ezra 4:4, 6; R. A. Parker and W. H. Dubberstein, *Babylonian Chronology, 626 B.C.—A.D. 45* (1942), p. 14.

the details of the accusation, though not the effect on the royal mind; at any rate, before the end of another year, Xerxes was in Palestine on his way to the Nile Valley.

Egypt had been recovered by January 9, 484. Quarrying at the Hammamat gorge by the returned Atiyawahy and by Ariurta proves a certain amount of building at the royal command.[16] But the property of numerous temples was confiscated and the treatment of the natives made harsher. Apparently Pherendates had perished in the revolt, for Xerxes placed Egypt under the rule of his brother Achaemenes as satrap.[17]

Hitherto, Persian monarchs had flattered the ancient culture peoples by posing within their boundaries as native kings. Xerxes broke completely with this practice—one of the most significant changes of his reign. How the new policy worked is well illustrated in Egypt.

Thanks to the munificence of Darius, the priests of Apis had been enabled to prepare a black granite sarcophagus of unexampled magnificence for the bull discovered in 488. The exterior was polished to a glass-like surface. The cover was plain, but on either side were representations of sarcophagi having curved cornice and torus. On the sides and at one end was also paneling; the opposite end showed a house façade with a small bolted door at the lower center. But inscriptions and decoration alike were, in contrast to the splendid material, roughly scratched.

After the usual titularies, there followed extracts from the Pyramid Texts, still in use after some two thousand years:

O Apis-Osiris, someone shall stand behind you. Your brother shall stand behind you; he stands and shall not perish behind you. You shall not perish; you shall not pass away during the whole of Eternity, Apis-Osiris. O Apis-Osiris, Horus comes to succor you and has brought you the heart of the gods. Do not wail. Horus gives you his eye that by its means you may carry off the crown before the Nine Gods. O Apis-Osiris, Horus opens your eyes for you, that by them you may see. Sothis has caused Apis-Osiris to fly to heaven in company with his brethren, the gods. Apis-Osiris, Horus has caused you to encompass every god within your hands. Horus loves his father in you. He does not suffer you to go away and he does not go away from you. May you live as the *ankh* beetle lives and may you endure in Busiris. Stand up for Horus so that he may make you spiritual and dispatch you to mount up to

[16] J. Couyat and P. Montet, *Les Inscriptions du Ouadi Hammamat* (1912), Nos. 52, 74, 91, 39, 118; G. Posener, *La première domination Perse en Egypte* (1936), p. 120.

[17] Herod. vii. 7.

heaven, Apis-Osiris. O. Apis-Osiris, you return to your proper form and the gods compose your face.[18]

While the sarcophagus was being made ready, Darius was nearing the end of his long reign. In all probability he would die before the bull; a blank space, therefore, was left for the name of his successor. Then Egypt revolted and was reconquered. Xerxes refused to adopt the regular Egyptian formulary; in revenge, when the bull finally passed away and was entombed in the prepared sarcophagus, the angered priests "forgot" to fill in the name of the new monarch.

THE ECLIPSE OF BABYLON

Unlike Egypt, Babylonia had loyally accepted as their king the son of Darius whom they had so long known as his viceroy. Less than a month intervenes between the last known business document bearing the name of the father and the first dated by Xerxes, December 1, 486.[19] In the beginning, the native scribes were allowed to employ the usual titulary "king of Babylon, king of lands." Shortly after his accession, however, Xerxes revisited Babylon and entered the "tomb of Belitanes,"[20] by which we must understand Marduk's temple of Esagila. Something went wrong, for on his return to Ecbatana Xerxes gave order for a disquieting change in the titulary: "King of Parsa and Mada" was to be prefixed to "king of Babylon, king of lands." Variations in spelling and doubt as to whether Persia and Media were cities or countries betray its strangeness to the scribes. No doubt other repressive measures accompanied the changes in titulary, but that alone was quite enough to prove that a new policy had been adopted. Although "king of Babylon" was yet retained, it was now subordinated to both Persia and Media; the question might well be raised whether, in view of what had just happened in Egypt, Babylon would long be permitted to retain even this faint shadow of her former independence.

While Xerxes was still in Ecbatana, news came that Babylon had revolted and that the satrap Zopyrus had been killed.[21] The revolt was led by a certain Belshimanni in whose name—as "king of Babylon," to which "king of lands" might be added—tablets from Dilbat and Borsippa are dated from August 10 to August 29, 482. By September 22

[18] B. Gunn, *Annales du Service*, XXVI (1926), 87 ff.
[19] Parker and Dubberstein, *op. cit.*
[20] Ctes. *Pers.* xiii, Epit. 52; Aelian. *Var. hist.* xiii. 3.
[21] Ctes. *Pers.* xiii, Epit. 53.

he had been supplanted by Shamash-eriba in Borsippa and, before October 20, in Babylon, with the same title or titles.[22]

Fortunately for Xerxes, his brother-in-law and the greatest general within the empire, Megabyzus, was available. He was promptly dispatched against the rebel city and as promptly took it. Babylon was terribly punished. The splendid city fortifications constructed by order of Nebuchadnezzar were demolished and made completely useless. Esagila with its towering ziggurat was torn down, as were the other temples. The eighteen-foot statue of Bel Marduk, weighing twelve talents (nearly eight hundred pounds) of solid gold, was carried off and melted down as bullion. The priest of Esagila who protested the sacrilege was killed. With Marduk no longer in existence, no future rebel might legitimize his rule by seizing the hands of Bel at the New Year's festival.

The estates of the merchant princes and citizens were confiscated and granted to Persians. So thoroughly was Babylonia ravaged that barely a half-dozen tablets have survived from the remainder of the reign. Syria was detached from Babylon and made a fully independent satrapy. Babylonia itself lost its identity through incorporation with Assyria and was henceforth ferociously taxed.[23]

In Babylonia, as in Egypt, no official inscriptions were set up during the entire reign. The lone usage which may in any sense be considered official—on trilingual seals and on brief statements of ownership inscribed on splendid vases of Egyptian alabaster in the four culture languages—reads only: "Xerxes the great king."[24]

THE PERSIAN ARMY ROSTER

In the quelling of these rebellions the powerful army machine built up by Darius was further strengthened. From a native Persian source, perhaps through the Zopyrus who was a grandson of the general of that name,[25] Herodotus secured a copy of the official roster.[26] It is well

---

[22] For date lists of Xerxes, Bel-shimanni, and Shamash-eriba, with chronological discussion, see Cameron, "Darius and Xerxes in Babylonia," *AJSL*, LVIII (1941), 319 ff.; Parker and Dubberstein, *op. cit.*, p. 15.

[23] Of the classical sources, Ctesias (*Pers.* Epit. 52–53) correctly dates the revolt before the expedition against Greece; cf. Plut. *Reg. imp. apophtheg.* 173C; Diod. ii. 9. 4 ff.; Strabo xvi. 1. 5; Arr. *Anab.* vii. 16. 4; iii. 16. 2 (dating the destruction *after* the Persian Wars); Herod. i. 183; in iii. 150 he gives only the capture by Darius but assigns the action to Zopyrus, who must rather belong to the reign of Xerxes. For the union of Babylonia with Assyria see Herod. iii. 92; vii. 63

[24] Recently published in Posener, *op. cit.*, Nos. 43–77.

[25] Herod. iii. 160.   [26] *Ibid.* vii. 61 ff.

worth our detailed study, and not only for military affairs; when combined with the data from the Persepolis reliefs which commemorate the appearance of the subject peoples at the New Year's festival, we have an invaluable picture of the geography and ethnography of the far-flung empire.

THE IMMORTALS

The core of the army was formed by the Persians themselves, for if they no longer paid tribute,[27] they did pay the blood tax. At the head, under the immediate leadership of Hydarnes, son of Hydarnes, the *hazarapat* or commander-in-chief,[28] was the famous bodyguard, the Immortals, who received their name because their number was never permitted to fall below ten thousand, a substitute being always ready when one fell sick or was killed. Not only were they gorgeously clad in gold-decked raiment, but on the march they were permitted to take with them their concubines and servants on wagons, while special food was brought on camels and other baggage animals.[29]

The Ten Thousand Immortals included detachments of Medes and Elamites as well as of Persians. Colored glazed bricks at Susa enliven the picture of the Elamites. Some are swarthy, almost black; others have a lighter complexion; but all are armed and clothed alike. The head is bare, with the hair held down tightly by a greenish twisted-rope fillet; the short beard is curled, as is the bun at the neck; their junction is noted by a gold earring. Each soldier stands stiffly; both hands, adorned with big drooping gold bracelets, firmly grasp a spear of cornel wood whose silver blade and silver pomegranate set hard on the toe prove that they are members of the Ten Thousand. Over the left arm is the uncased bow, and over the left shoulder is the quiver. An elaborate robe covers the whole body from neck to wrists and ankles, leaving only a glimpse of bare flesh above soft leather shoes which are buttoned or laced and which have high projecting tongue.

It is in the quivers, robes, and shoes that exact symmetry is forgotten and textile design and color run riot. Bits of leather, cut out in the form of crescents, decorate the quiver; they may be pale yellow or pale blue on browns of differing shades, or brown on a white ground. The whole quiver may be of the same design and color save for a narrow strip of alternating triangles—brown and white or blue and white —at the ring from which hang down colored strings and tassels. The shoes may be yellow or blue. Sometimes the robes are a plain yellow

---

[27] *Ibid.* iii, 97.   [28] Cf. p. 217.   [29] Herod. vii. 83.

or very light purple; if so, a rich, velvety brown cape, with an edging of green decorated with rows of white circles, is draped over the breast and under the arm to cover the hip. More elaborate robes are studded with ornaments: white or yellow stars on blue or dark-brown circles, or large, closely placed squares quartered or halved by brown lines, are sewed on the yellow or white cloth.[30]

We must imagine similar colors for the Persian and Median Immortals at Persepolis. Here the soldiers who guard the inscriptions, climb up the staircases, line up for the nobles who visit their lord, or stand at attention while reviewed by the monarch all wear headgear, either the fluted hat of felt or the nodding felt cap. According to their ancestry, their dress is the Persian robe or the Median jacket and trousers. They may be armed only with the spear or the bow and quiver; both may be combined, and the bow case may be added. Among them are to be found the One Thousand who gave their name to the *hazarapat*, for these are distinguished from the remainder of the Ten Thousand by carrying pomegranates of gold.[31]

<h3 style="text-align:center">SATRAPAL CONTINGENTS</h3>

Next to the Immortals ranked the Persian infantry, wearing loose felt caps, tiaras, varicolored sleeved tunics (*kithones*), over iron-scaled armor,[32] and trousers. For defensive armor they also bore the wicker shield; a long bow whose quiver was filled with reed arrows, a short spear, and a short sword slung from a girdle on the right hip aided the offense. Their commander was Otanes, father of Queen Amestris.[33]

Contingents from the satrapies followed, each under its own satrap. Comparison with the lists of Darius indicates certain administrative changes. Each contingent was divided into squads of tens, companies of hundreds, regiments of thousands, and, if needed, brigades of ten thousands. The whole formed six army corps, under Mardonius, son of Gobryas, Tritantaechmes, son of Artabanus, Smerdomenes, son of Otanes, Masistes, son of Darius and Atossa, Gergis, son of Arizus, and Megabyzus, son of Zopyrus, who had just recovered Babylon.[34]

Tigranes the Achaemenid commanded the Medes, dressed and equipped like the Persians, who had actually borrowed from them their armor. The Cissians—the ancient name of Kashshites is here used for the Elamites—were led by Anaphes, son of Otanes. Herodotus

[30] Dieulafoy, *op. cit.*, Pls. V–VII.
[31] Herod. vii. 41.
[32] Borrowed from Egyptians (*ibid*. i. 135).
[33] *Ibid.* vii. 61.
[34] *Ibid.* 81–82.

tells us that they were dressed like the Medes save for a fillet (*mitra*) in place of the cap; at Persepolis they wear full Median dress, but the round caps are lower and are bound by a broad fillet. Two bear high-strung bows and short swords, the next Elamite urges on a lioness who turns back on her leash to see if her two cubs, held in the arms of attendants, are safe.

Eastern Iran shows the beginning of a combination of satrapies which raises a suspicion of decline on this frontier. The Hyrcanians, equipped like the Persians, had been detached from Parthia; these able fighters were led by Megapanus, who later was in charge of Babylon. In place of Hyrcania, it was Chorasmia which was now joined to Parthia under Artabazus, son of Pharnaces. The Sogdians were led by Azanes, son of Artaeus, the Gandarians and Dadicae by Artyphius, son of Artabanus, and the Bactrians and Amyrgian Sacae by the king's brother, Hystaspes, son of Darius and Atossa.

Like the majority of these Iranians, the Bactrians wore a head-dress almost exactly like that of the Medes and carried cane bows and short spears. We see them at Persepolis in almost identical groups, bare head confined by a fillet, mustache down-twisted, beard cut short before reaching the point; extremely short tunic, baggy trousers, and low boots form their costume. Some lead huge two-humped Bactrian camels which sneer above their master's heads; others bring textiles, cups, bowls, or horses. The Arians under Sisamnes, son of Hydarnes, carry Median bows.

Of the three satrapies of Saka listed by Darius, but one remains, and that is joined to Bactria. At Persepolis they appear with the tall peaked hat which gave them the name "Hat-bearing," made more strange by neck flap and by chin strap under spade beards, though short tight jackets, full trousers, low shoes, bow and bow case, dagger, and sword slung from the girdle are all typically Iranian. Even the *sagaris* battle-ax[35] has been found at Persepolis, carried by a high official as shown on a relief or recovered in actual fact from the barracks. One Sacaean guides a horse with braided hair and tail whose harness is headstall, lotus crest, and bell; the next presents two collars; three others bear peculiar robes as gifts. The Sarangians in brightly dyed clothing, with buskins to knee and Median bows and lances, were commanded by Pherendates, son of Megabazus.

The Indians added little to the martial array. Their clothing was of tree cotton, their only weapons cane bows and arrows tipped with

---

[35] Used by the Massagetae (Herod. i. 215).

iron. Their leader at Persepolis has a fillet, knotted rudely at the back to bind his long straight hair, a draped robe over a short tunic sewed at the side, and low slippers; his servants wear only the fillet and a single square cloth, wrapped about the loins and turned and tucked in at the waist. From a yoke over the shoulders of the first hang two woven baskets, filled with ointment jars; the second leads a wild ass, which the third hastens on with uplifted stick; the last holds aloft two short swords. Their satrap, Pharnazathres, son of Artabates, led also the eastern Ethiopians, equipped like the Indians, but wearing a headdress of horse's scalp and carrying a craneskin shield. Utians and Mycians were under Darius' son Arsamenes, the Paricanians under Siromitres, son of Oeobazus, and all were like the Pactyans. The islanders from the Persian Gulf and from the Exile Islands were like the Medes and were led by Mardontes, son of Bagaeus.

If there were serious losses on the northeastern frontier, there were compensating gains on the north, where better organization of the scattered tribes is evident. North and east of Armenia were the Alarodians (whose name preserves the Urartu of Assyrian times and the biblical Ararat) and the Saspeiri along the Araxes, both under Masistes, son of Siromitres; they wore wooden helmets and carried small rawhide shields, short spears, and swords. There is no mention by Herodotus of the Carduchi, or Kurds, who play a considerable part in later Achaemenid history;[36] at that time we also hear of mercenaries named Cardaces, but business records prove the Kardaka mercenaries employed as early as 515, when we learn that Lukshu the Kardaka has received silver for his sheep, flour, salt, mustard, oil, and good date brandy—all rations for the first three months of year seven.[37]

Moschi and Tibareni had been pushed back since the years when, as Mushki and Tabal, they had fought the Assyrians; now they were led by Ariomardus, son of Darius and Parmys. Like the Macrones and Mosynoeci along the south shore of the Black Sea, under Artayctes, son of Cherasmis and later to be satrap of Sestus, they all wore wooden helmets and carried small spears and shields. The Colchians at the eastern end of the sea were equipped like the Alarodians; with the Mares (wearing plaited helmets and bearing small leather shields and javelins) they were commanded by Pherendates, son of Teaspes. The Caspians under Ariomardes, son of Artabanus, wore skin coats and

[36] Xen. *Anab.* iii. 5. 15; iv. 1 ff.; v. 5. 17; Diod. xiv. 27; Strabo xvi. 1. 24; Plin. vi. 44; in post-Achaemenid times the form "Gordyene" is more common.

[37] A. T. Clay, *BRM*, Vol. I, No. 71.

carried a scimitar and a cane bow, while the Pactyans were clad in skins with native bow and dagger and were commanded by Artayntes, son of Ithamitres. Dotus, son of Megasidrus, was in charge of the Paphlagonians and Matieni, who were known for their plaited helmets, buskins, and small shields and spears or javelins and daggers. The large number of satrapies and the high birth of their satraps indicate the military character of their contingents.

Armenians and Phrygians were commanded by the king's son-in-law Artochmes. Armenians led the second division at Persepolis; their dress was the typical Iranian, except for a strange cap of three nodding projections with broad neck flap and streamers. One brought a horse for which Armenia has always been famous, the other a beautiful vase whose two handles were carved as winged griffins. Gobryas, son of Darius and Artystone, led the Cappadocians, Caballians—called also Maeonians and Lasonians—and Milyans; their skullcaps were leather, and their clothing was fastened with buckles; their bows were Lycian and their spears were short. At this point we may place the Pisidians; their crested bronze helmets with horns and ears of an ox, their little rawhide-covered shields, their pairs of wolf-hunter's spears, and their purple leggings gave them an extraordinary appearance. No satrap is mentioned for these untamed mountaineers, who probably fought solely for booty under their native chieftains.

Sardis included Lydia, whose soldiers were almost Greek in armament, and Mysia, where the equipment was helmet, buckler, and wooden javelin, the tip hardened in fire. The former "Second Ionia" is represented in the list only by the "Asiatic Thracians" (the Bithynians), under Bassaces, son of Artabanus, in their foxskin headdress, tunics under varicolored cloaks, and fawnskin buskins; they carried small shields, javelins, and daggers. From other sources we find that the satrapy of Dascylium continued in existence.

The satrap of Sardis also had general oversight of First Ionia, which included Aeolian as well as Ionian Greeks; Dorians—with Lycians and Pamphylians—seem to have been bracketed with the Carians as one portion of this Ionia, which would imply that Karka was no longer administered as a separate satrapy. The majority of the peoples in this expanded Ionia were armed in Greek fashion, but the Carians (under the immediate direction of their princes, Histiaeus, son of Tymnes, Pigres, son of Hysseldomus, and Damasithymus, son of Candaules) and the Lycians (under Cybernis, son of Cossicas) added falchions and daggers to their goatskins, plumed hats, greaves, breastplates, and cornel-wood bows shooting unfeathered arrows. After their conquest, the Lycians had been left under their local dynasts, some of whom, liked Cybernis, coined money on the reduced Lydian standard.[38]

Cilicia was still ruled by a native king bearing the hereditary title of Syennesis, now a son of Oromedon.[39] Cilicians in woolen tunics, armed with two javelins and an Egyptian sword and defended by helmets and a small rawhide shield, manned an important naval squadron. Cilicians at Persepolis wear short beards and bunched-out hair elaborately curled; a narrow band is wound four times around the head. The plain short-sleeved robe, girt by a four-banded girdle tucked in at the right, reaches the knee, and low boots are buttoned on the side. While the leader of the delegation bears a woolen robe, two others escort fine examples of rams bred on the fertile Cilician plain.

The satrapy Across the River, detached from Babylon after the revolt of 482, was now once more truly west of the Euphrates. By far the most important subdivision was Phoenicia; its chief cities were Sidon under Tetramnestus, son of Anysus; Tyre under Metten, son of Hiram III; and Arvad under Marbaal, son of Agbaal.[40] Phoenician merchant kings recognized the value of membership in a world empire and willingly sent their representatives to the great annual festival. On their heads are curious high turbans, wound in broad bands and leaning backward; a ribbon behind the ear draws attention to the bunched-out curls and to the short beard. Over a knee-length tunic rippled vertically is worn a mantle, draped diagonally to show the edge of the tunic; the shoes have slightly pointed toes. One of the Phoenicians carries two beautiful vases, their two handles shaped as griffin heads, their bodies channeled horizontally; the next has two low bowls; the third, two large bracelets. A groom, his turban lower and flatter, his mantle straight above the tunic, leads two horses drawing a chariot. Phoenician ships formed the core of the fleet, three hundred triremes out of the twelve hundred; on them rested Persian sea power. The men were armed with javelins and were defended by Greek-like helmets, linen breastplates, and rimless shields, but their chief offense and defense alike rested in their ability to maneuver their ships. More trustworthy than the Greeks, the Phoenicians flourished as never before.

Cyprus and Syrian Palestine were also included in the satrapy. Ef-

[38] G. F. Hill, *Coins of Lycia* (1897); E. Babelon, *Traité des monnaies*, II, Part II (1910), 173 ff.
[39] Herod. iii. 90; v. 118; vii. 98; Aeschyl. *Pers.* 326–27.
[40] Cf. Herod. viii. 67; leadership of Sidon first, then Tyre.

fort to develop a separate satrapy of Arabia was abandoned, but Arab camel-riders were enrolled among the cavalry for frontier duty and armed with long backward-bending bows. Turning to Persepolis, we find the Arabs wearing long draped and girdled robes with ornamented hem; they present textiles, and a youth leads a dromedary. In the army organization they were bracketed with the Ethiopians under Arsames, son of Darius and Artystone. These savages went into battle with painted bodies, one-half chalk and one-half vermillion; for clothing they wore lion and leopard skins and they were armed with six-foot bows made from palm ribs, stone-tipped arrows, spears tipped with sharpened antelope horn, or knobbed clubs. Leather-clad Libyans, whose sole weapon was a javelin hardened in the fire, were under Massages, son of Oarizus. Kinky-haired, beardless Negroes at Persepolis, in long robes and long shoes, offer a curiously foreshortened giraffe, but there is no probability that Punt on the Somali coast was ever organized as a regular satrapy.

Next to the Phoenicians, the Egyptians, contributing two hundred triremes, were considered by the Persians the most important naval power at their disposal. Most of their sailors wore the cuirass (from whom the Persians had borrowed it)[41] and were armed with long swords; to this equipment was added a plaited helmet, hollow shields with broad rims, spears adapted to fighting at sea, and huge poleaxes. The satrap Achaemenes functioned as admiral.[42]

A MERCENARY COLONY IN EGYPT

From this list we should assume that Egypt furnished only sailors. Fortunately, Herodotus elsewhere mentions a land army.[43] In all probability, this army was largely if not entirely mercenary, for native Egyptians neither form good military material nor can be trusted to fight for their masters. It is therefore a lucky chance that we actually possess the archives of such a mercenary settlement, strangely enough of Jews, at Elephantine near the first cataract.

At first sight these Jews form a normal, rather commonplace community. With them are their wives and children; they are married and divorced as might be expected. They buy and sell houses and estates, which they seem to hold in fee simple. Their houses cluster around the temple of the national God. Regular formulas are employed in their contracts, and there is a considerable amount of litigation.

But while Egyptians still wrote in their native demotic, these Jews

---

[41] Ibid. i. 135.   [42] Ibid. vii. 236.   [43] Ibid. iv. 167.

use, not Hebrew, but the current Aramaic, the official language of their Persian masters. The formulas of their documents, including the dates by the kings, are closer to Assyrian than to Egyptian. They are not citizens; they are regularly entitled "Aramaean(s) of Sin (Syene) the fortress" or "Aramaean(s) of Yeb (Elephantine) the fortress." The individual soldier is a "lord of a standard," equivalent to the Ptolomaic cleruch or military colonist. Their organization is military, divided into "hundreds" and these into "standards" (*degel*), which are always commanded by officers with Persian or Babylonian names. The entire garrison is under the charge of the "chief of the force" (*rab haila*), and this under the governor of the nome, the *fratarak*. In disputed cases, final appeal is to "our lord" the satrap, who occasionally sends his orders direct. Disputes may be brought before regular judges, though normally they are settled by their own higher officers. We hear of a subgovernor (*sagan*) associated with a judge, of scribes of the nome, recorders, accountants of the treasury, "ears" or examiners, "those who execute orders," and simple police.

Their food comes from the government. In 484 two Jews of Yeb acknowledge the receipt from an Egyptian boatman of fifty-five ardabs of barley and beans, rations for the soldiers of two "hundreds," each to obtain a little over two measures. Their hearts are content; they will convey the grain and render the account before the chief of the "hundred," the chiefs of the king's house, and the scribes of the treasury, under penalty of a hundred *karash*, pure silver, as sworn by their God.[44] Perhaps the most striking evidence of their loyalty to their Persian master is the gift, careful preservation, and recopying of Darius' autobiography.

OTHER ARMY AND NAVY UNITS

While Egyptians were still trusted, at least as sailors, there were no soldiers identifiable as Babylonians. After the last revolt, Babylon disappeared as an independent satrapy and was annexed to Assyria. Her troops were intermingled with those from Assyria to prevent further uprising and were now known as Chaldaeans, for since 482 the very name of Babylonia was officially under ban. From the enlarged province, governed by Otaspes, son of Artachaees, was recruited an important infantry contingent. Herodotus found their bronze helmets strange. They wore linen breastplates and carried shields; to their

[44] A. E. Cowley, *Aramaic Papyri of the Fifth Century B.C.* (1923); cf. Olmstead, *History of Palestine and Syria* (1931), pp. 598 ff.

spears and Egyptian-like daggers they added wooden clubs studded with iron spikes.[45]

Cyprus furnished a hundred and fifty ships to the navy. Its local kings, such as Gorgus, son of Chersis, and Timonax, son of Timagoras, wore turbans and tunics; otherwise the Cypriotes were Greek in dress and equipment. Cilicians and Pamphylians contributed a hundred ships each, Lycians fifty, and Carians seventy. Of the Greeks, the Dorians sent fifty, the Aeolians sixty, the islanders only seventeen, though the Ionians and the Greeks from Hellespont and Pontus furnished each another hundred ships.

Phoenicians, Egyptians, Anatolians, and Greeks thus furnished the triremes and brought the grand fleet to its war strength of twelve hundred ships. In addition, there were ships of fifty, thirty, and fewer oars, as well as transports for men and horses—a total of three thousand more boats. It was estimated that each trireme had a complement of two hundred sailors, while ships of fifty oars carried eighty. To guard the triremes and to prevent defection, each ship also had on board thirty marines—Persians, Medes, and Sacae.[46] Four admirals are named: Achaemenes for the Egyptians, Ariabignes, son of Darius and a daughter of Gobryas, for the Ionians and Carians, and, for the remainder, Prexaspes, son of Aspathines, and Megabazus, son of Megabates. Over the grand fleet as a whole was the king's own brother, his former rival Ariamenes.[47]

Most of these peoples also furnished cavalry. First came the Persians, Medes, and Cissians, with the same equipment as the foot-soldiers except that some wore helmets of hammered bronze and iron. The Sagartian nomads carried only daggers and plaited leather lassoes. While the Indians usually formed cavalry, their nobles had not abandoned the old Aryan custom of fighting from chariots drawn by horses or wild asses. Chariots were also used by the Libyans. Cavalry commanders were Harmamithras and Tithaeus, sons of Datis; a third leader, Pharnuches, did not take part in the Greek expedition, since he had been injured and so must remain behind in Sardis.

Long as is this army roster, it is not all dull. Not only does it contain valued data on the military organization, but it presents an equally valuable supplement to the lists of provinces given by Darius and Xerxes. Strange peoples and strange customs and costumes appear on every page. To the casual reader the names of individuals may seem

[45] Herod. vii. 63.   [46] Ibid. 184.   [47] Plut. Themistocl. 14. 3.

tiresome, but they requite the specialist with an almost complete *Who's Who* of Persian officialdom, with many of whom we shall be better acquainted in the course of our narrative. Finally, there are many familiar names, descendants of heroes from the earlier culture peoples, friends or enemies of the Greeks, and individuals known from the Bible.

When, under these leaders, the vast host took its march through peaceful countries, the baggage train went first, followed by half of the infantry divisions. After an interval came the thousand picked horsemen and then the thousand picked infantry, their reversed spears marked out by gold pomegranates. Next there followed ten stallions bred on the Nesaean plain in Media. Eight white steeds drew the sacred chariot of Ahuramazda; the charioteer was on foot, since no mortal dared mount the seat. Behind that was the chariot of his vicegerent on earth, Xerxes, also drawn by Nesaean horses; his charioteer, Patiramphes, son of Otanes, stood beside his lord. When wearied, Xerxes would change for a time into a wagon. The royal entourage was guarded by another regiment of a thousand picked infantry (their spears not reversed) with pomegranates of gold, another thousand of chosen horsemen, and, finally, the Ten Thousand Immortals. Nine thousand of these Immortals bore spears with the silver pomegranates and were surrounded by the other thousand with pomegranates of gold. After ten thousand more cavalry, the other half of the army closed the martial parade.[48]

On a regular expedition into enemy country, the king took along his own food supplies and flocks. Boiled water from Susa's river, the Choaspes, for the royal use alone was carried in silver vessels on mule-drawn wagons.[49] The higher officials and the Immortals also brought with them their own food and their servants, even their concubines. But, despite all this appearance of luxury, the host which the great king led into battle was a formidable military array.

---

[48] Herod. vii. 40-41, 55.   [49] *Ibid.* i. 188.

Chapter XVIII

FAILURE IN EUROPE

XERXES was more interested in completing the magnificent structures begun by his father on the Persepolis terrace than he was in testing by further adventure the formidable military machine that his father had built up, but the fates did not permit. His cousin Mardonius, ambitious to become satrap of newly won territories, urged him on. The exiles from Athens fell so low as to hire an already discredited oraclemonger. The petty kings of Thessaly sent their invitation. At last Xerxes reluctantly prepared to follow his father's policy of expansion on the northwestern frontier.[1]

PREPARATIONS FOR INVASION

Direct attack across the Aegean had failed, and Xerxes showed his wisdom by returning to the former policy of gradual advance, the army supported by the fleet. The entire navy—Phoenician, Egyptian, and Greek—was to be utilized, as well as half the regular troops—three of the six army corps, each about sixty thousand strong.[2]

To avoid another shipwreck at Athos, Bubares, son of Megabazus, and Artachaees, son of Artaeus, were ordered to dig a canal behind the promontory. Three years were spent on the task, with natives being impressed for the forced labor under the lash. In a near-by meadow was held a market to which grain already ground was transported from Asia, and provisions were stored at strategic points along the Thracian coast. Across the neck of land at the end of the peninsula a line a mile and a half long was drawn, and each nation was assigned a section; only the Phoenicians were experienced enough to broaden the trench at the top and so prevent the earth from sliding. The canal, wide enough to allow passage for two triremes while rowing, is today traced by a few shallow ponds.[3]

[1] Herod. vii. 5–6.

[2] Cf. Olmstead, "Persia and the Greek Frontier Problem," *Classical Philology*, XXXIV (1939), 314 ff.; bibliography, *Cambridge Ancient History*, IV (1926), 613 ff.; of special importance, G. Rawlinson, *Herodotus* (1861–64); H. Delbrück, *Die Perserkriege und die Burgunderkriege* (1887), for military data; G. B. Grundy, *The Great Persian War* (1901), for relation of parties in Greece to Persia.

[3] Herod. vii. 22 ff.; Thuc. iv. 109; Hellanicus *Pers.* ii. 61(J); T. Spratt, "Remarks on the Isthmus of Mount Athos," *Journal of the Royal Geographical Society*, XVII (1847), 145 ff.

From the rendezvous, Critalla in Cappadocia, the armies crossed the Halys and through Phrygia reached Celaenae, where was the source of the Maeander and its affluent, the Catarrectes, which rose in the market place. There also might be seen the skin of the Silenus Marsyas, who had been flayed by Apollo. Next they passed Anava and the lake from which salt was extracted, the great city of Colossae, where the Lycus ran five-eighths of a mile underground, and Cydrara with the inscribed stele of Croesus to mark the boundary of Lydia. The armies then crossed the Maeander, and by Callatebus, where honey was manufactured from wheat and tamarisk, reached Sardis.[4]

The threatened Greeks vainly attempted to form an effective anti-Persian alliance. Naturally, they all appealed for advice to Delphi, and Apollo outdid himself. Sparta, first warned by Demaratus, was told of the coming foe, powerful as Zeus, whom no bulls or lions could defeat and who would either tear the city or one of their kings.[5] The oracle to Athens was still more appalling: They were asked why they were delaying; they must flee from houses and city to the ends of the earth. Their city is destroyed by fire, their forts and temples shall be burned, the black blood flows, they must go at once. As suppliants the envoys demanded a more favorable answer; again they were told to retire from the enemy and to abandon their land, though there would be hope in the wooden walls, and divine Salamis should destroy the children of women; Themistocles persuaded the Athenians that by the wooden walls Apollo meant their fleet.[6] Argos, already suspected of inviting Persian intervention after a staggering defeat by Sparta, was advised to adopt armed neutrality.[7] The Cretans asked whether they would gain by aiding the mainland Greeks; bluntly the oracle told them not to be such fools as they had shown themselves when they aided Menelaus in the Trojan War.[8] Corcyra's ships were "detained" by hostile winds.[9] Gelo of Syracuse promised much—if he were made supreme commander—and sent three small boats to watch the outcome.[10]

Discouraged by this apathy or worse manifested by the few Greeks of the west who still retained their independence, the allies were still more affrighted by the confidence of Xerxes, who, when three allied spies were caught at Sardis (481), ordered them to be shown the

[4] Herod. vii. 26 ff.
[5] Ibid. 220, 239.   [8] Ibid. 169.
[6] Ibid. 139 ff.   [9] Ibid. 168.
[7] Ibid. 148 ff.   [10] Ibid. 153, 157-58.

whole vast array and then released to report home.[11] In the spring of 480 the army broke camp and from Sardis traveled down the Caicus Valley into Mysia, then by Atarneus with Mount Cane on the left to Carene, through the Plain of Thebe, by Adramytteium and Antandrus, and finally reached Ilium. The once famous Scamander proved too little to water the host. Xerxes climbed the pergamum of Priam and sacrificed a thousand cattle to Trojan Athena, while the Magi poured libations to the spirits of those who had died in defense of Troy. Thus Xerxes announced himself the protagonist of the Orient in the new Trojan war[12]

THE INVASION OF GREECE

Between Rhoetium, Ophryneium, and Dardanus on the left and Gergithae on the right, the army reached Abydos. Between Abydos and Sestos the Phoenicians and Egyptians had constructed two bridges, held by cables of flax and papyrus; when they were destroyed in a storm, those in charge were beheaded. The Greek Harpalus built new bridges of ships anchored stem to stern by huge cables, with gaps for the passage of boats. On them were laid planks, then twigs, then earth; later, a parapet was added.[13]

Assembled at the Isthmus of Corinth, which the Peloponnesian members of the alliance had already decided was the sole tenable line of defense, the allies received the Thessalian request for aid in guarding the Olympus Pass. Ten thousand hoplites, supported by a naval contingent and reinforced by Thessalian cavalry, the representatives of the conservatives, occupied the vale of Tempe. As might have been suspected, they found the Thessalian commons pro-Persian. Alexander of Macedon did good service for his Persian master by urging the allies not to stay and be trampled by the king's host. Although Xerxes was still at Abydos, after a few days the allies returned to the Isthmus.[14]

Seated upon a white stone throne on a hill near Abydos, Xerxes reviewed his troops. Incense was burned on the myrtle-strewn bridges, and at dawn the king poured libations from a golden cup, prayed with his face toward the rising sun, and cast into the sea the cup, a bowl, and a sword.[15]

Seven days and nights the soldiers were continuously crossing one

[11] *Ibid.* 146 ff.

[12] *Ibid.* 42-43; for the Persian explanation of the Trojan War see *ibid.* i. 4-5.

[13] *Ibid.* vii. 25, 33 ff.; Ctes. *Pers.* xiii, Epit. 54.

[14] Herod. vii. 172 ff.   [15] *Ibid.* 44, 54.

bridge under the lash, the baggage being transferred by the other. Supported by the fleet, they followed the coast road in three divisions. Food must be provided by the cities along the road at the cost of 400 talents for a single meal per day. Months before, heralds had been sent ahead to prepare grain, cattle, and poultry for the royal table. Only Xerxes enjoyed a tent; the remainder slept in the open.

A second review was held at Doriscus—occupied, since the Scythian expedition, by a garrison and now placed under the control of Mascames, son of Megadostes. From Doriscus the three divisions followed parallel lines, one under Mardonius and Masistes along the coast keeping in touch with the fleet, a second under Smerdomenes and Megabyzus guarding Xerxes farther inland, and a third under Tritantaechmes and Gergis marching well in the interior. The Strymon was crossed by bridges, while Magi sacrificed white horses to the stream for good omen; at the Nine Ways nine children were sacrificed to the underworld gods. Artachaees, who had built the canal, died while the army was at Acanthus, and the army poured libations at his tomb; to be associated with his death is probably the hoard of three hundred gold darics, minted by Darius and his son.[16] At Therma, Xerxes was met by heralds bringing earth and water from abandoned Thessaly, Locri, and all Boeotia except Plataea and Thespiae, for already it was only too obvious that the Peloponnesians had no intention of offering serious resistance north of the Isthmus.[17]

Victory appeared certain to the Persians. Not only did they control all the Greeks of Asia and Africa, whose ships were included in their navy, but already half the European Greeks had submitted. There remained to be subdued only a few recalcitrant states of the Peloponnese, since it was now clear that all north of the Isthmus was to be abandoned. Apollo of Delphi was their loyal friend. Athens, ruled by the democracy under Themistocles, would certainly go over to democracy's patron once the Peloponnesians retired behind the Isthmus. With the Athenian fleet safely Persian, the Isthmus wall could be turned, Argos would declare itself openly, a wedge would be driven between Sparta and Corinth, and each would be defeated when fighting alone.[18]

[16] H. P. Borrell, *The Numismatic Chronicle*, VI (1843), 153; G. F. Hill, *Coins of Arabia, Mesopotamia, and Persia* (1922), p. cxxix.

[17] Aeschyl. *Pers.* 65 ff., 722 ff.; Herod. vii. 55 ff., 100 ff., 174.

[18] Herod. vii. 139 proves that the "Father of History" realized the exact situation; cf. vii. 235; Thucydides (i. 69. 5 and 73. 4) shows a similar understanding.

THE STAND AT THERMOPYLAE

Nor was the situation changed as the march southward was resumed. Loss of Thessaly did bring Leonidas north as far as Thermopylae with three hundred Spartans and a few allied contingents, but the small number loudly proclaimed that rear-guard skirmishes were intended only to delay, not to stop, the advance until the Isthmus wall was complete.[19] Apollo of Delphi was at last frightened into patriotism and gave an oracle that the Greeks should pray to the winds who would show themselves powerful allies.[20]

The allied fleet took its position near Artemesium but retired to the still narrower Euripus once fire signals announced the approach of the advance Persian squadron. The grand fleet rode at anchor off Cape Sepias; at dawn the Hellespontine wind from the east began to blow and continued three days, wrecking hundreds of warships, transports, and grain boats. The allied ships returned to Artemesium, but even the sign of divine favor manifested in the destruction of so large a part of the enemy fleet did not encourage Leonidas; the Peloponnesians demanded immediate return to the Isthmus, and only the indignant protests of the Phocians and Locrians induced the king to remain to win posthumous fame.[21] Xerxes arrived and ordered the Medes and Cissians of Artapanus to attack the little force at Thermopylae, but they suffered heavy loss, and the Immortals under Hydarnes fared no better. Then a path over the hills to the rear was reported, and the Immortals surprised the Phocian guard at daybreak. Realizing that they were doomed, the Spartans defended themselves with fury; many of the assailants, driven under the lash, were trodden to death or forced into the sea, among them two sons of Darius by Phratagune, daughter of his brother Artanes, Abrocomes and Hyperanthes by name. At last Leonidas was killed, Hydarnes gained the Spartan rear, the Thebans surrendered and were branded, and the pass was opened.[22]

Meanwhile two hundred ships had been ordered around Euboea to take the allies in the rear. The secret was betrayed, and the Euboeans suborned Themistocles to bribe the captains to abandon their plan of withdrawal. As the flanking squadron did not appear, the fleet resolved to attack the Persians again at Artemesium. Thirty ships were lost to the allies, and the disabled hulks were driven ashore by an evening thunderstorm which also destroyed the flanking squadron. Next

---

[19] Herod. vii. 175, 202 ff.   [20] Ibid. 178.   [21] Ibid. 207.

[22] Simonides 21 (Edmonds); Herod. vii. 175 ff., 201 ff.; Ctes. Pers. xiii, Epit. 54–55.

day the Cilician ships were sunk. Xerxes determined that the straits must be forced at all costs. At noon, the whole Persian fleet advanced in a semicircle; the Egyptians had taken five ships and half the Athenian ships had been disabled, when, at the close of the day, news arrived that Thermopylae was open; the allies, therefore, retired.

Phocis was thoroughly ravaged by Thessalian urging, and the Persians entered friendly Boeotia, held safely by Macedonian Alexander. A flying column took the road to Delphi, to reward Apollo for his pro-Persian oracles and to support his further efforts—or to loot the treasures, as the priests later explained with considerable plausibility. As he had promised, the god protected his own; he thundered and hurled down cliffs on the barbarians who fled with great slaughter—such at least was the Delphic version, after the Persian defeat.[23]

Denounced by the Thebans, deserted Plataea and Thespiae were burned by Xerxes, who, four months after crossing the Hellespont, entered Attica. He found it also deserted, for the allied fleet had come to Salamis merely to evacuate the civilian population. The men of military age were already on board ship, and only a few zealots had barricaded the Acropolis with wooden planks in obedience to Apollo's ambiguous oracle. The barricades were fired from the Areopagus by arrows carrying lighted tow, and when terms offered by the partisans of Hippias were refused, the precipitous rock was climbed and the defenders met their death as suppliants in Athena's temple. The whole Acropolis was burned before the exiles with the army were permitted to offer sacrifice.[24]

THE CHECK AT SALAMIS

The grand fleet anchored off Phalerum, and panic seized the allies. Salamis was a veritable trap, and all but the interested Athenians, Aeginetans, and Megarians were determined to escape before that trap was sprung. Only the threat of Themistocles to sail off with the whole Athenian fleet and the knowledge that the democratic leader was quite capable of carrying out his threat drove the Spartan admiral Eurybiades to command preparation for the battle.

At the Persian council, Artemesia, lady tyrant of Halicarnassus, alone opposed immediate attack. There was every prospect of success. Sparta had abandoned one ally after another, and the alacrity with

[23] Simonides 12 ff.; Herod. viii. 1 ff.; Ctes. *Pers.* xiii, Epit. 58.

[24] Herod. viii. 40 ff.; Thuc. i. 18. 2; image of Artemis taken from Brauron, Paus. viii. 46. 3; Antenor's statue of the tyrannicides, Harmodius and Aristogeiton, carried off by Xerxes, Paus. i. 8. 5.

which each had made terms indicated the strong pro-Persian sentiment hitherto repressed. Athenian ships were manned by the commons and captained by the leader of the democratic faction; flouted at every turn by the Peloponnesians, Themistocles should be prepared for return to the normal attitude of his party, now that it was amply clear that the Peloponnesians had determined to leave the Athenians in the lurch. Immediately after Thermopylae, they had begun a wall across the Isthmus, and so sure were the Persians that the last effective resistance would be made at this spot that the very night of the council the land forces were started toward Corinth.

The awaited message was quickly received from the pedagogue of Themistocles' children: He was the king's friend who desired his success. The Greeks were discouraged and prepared to flee, let the king prevent their escape! Dissensions had broken out, and soon the pro-Persians would fall upon the king's enemies. There was no reason for Xerxes to doubt these protestations of loyalty.

Yet both letter and decision of immediate attack were mistakes. Had Xerxes taken no action at all, the few remaining allies would have retired to the Isthmus. The Athenians, Megarians, and Aeginetans would have been compelled to accept terms. With their aid, the Isthmus wall would have been outflanked, and there would have remained only the mopping-up.

Quite as effective was the actual procedure of Xerxes. The eastern exit from the strait was blocked by a triple line of ships; the Egyptians, "marsh dwellers, skilful rowers of galleys," with two hundred ships sailed to block the western exit and to attack the allied rear. Now the whole allied naval force was bottled up and could be left for exhaustion of supplies and for mutual recriminations to do their work; it would either be compelled to surrender or, if it attempted to break the encirclement, there would be ample opportunity to pick off the ships as they emerged. On the basis of the actual situation, the Persians were entirely justified in dispatching their infantry and cavalry to fight the decisive battle at the Isthmus.

Unfortunately for Persia, Xerxes was not content to leave well enough alone; he must win a spectacular victory, and he therefore ordered a direct attack on men entrapped and fighting desperately for escape. Infantry were landed on Psyttaleia, the island in the midst of the strait, to kill those who might escape from the sinking boats. Aristides broke through to report complete encirclement, and the allied sailors prepared sullenly to fight.

It was September 22, and Xerxes prepared to watch the battle from a silver-footed throne at the base of a hill by the strait. The allies moved out but at the first sight of the enemy backed water until an Athenian started the battle. The first assault was a success for the Persians, since the Ionian Greeks badly worsted the Spartans. Later the Athenians broke through the line and in turn attacked the invaders. Two hundred ships were lost, a third of the grand fleet; the allies lost but forty. Multitudes of the Persian sailors were drowned, for only a few could swim; among the dead was the naval commander Ariabignes, the king's brother. Aristides crossed with the hoplites to Psyttaleia and slew all the Persians, among them three nephews of the king.

BLUNDERS IN DIPLOMACY

Taken by itself, Salamis was a check to the Persian frontier advance and nothing more. None of the recently acquired territory was lost, the army was intact, the fleet was still powerful and needed only reorganization. The allies, to be sure, had been encouraged by an unexpected victory, but they were reduced in numbers and the next year should see them also conquered.

What made Salamis important was not the victory itself but its effect on the mind of Xerxes. Although he and no one else was responsible for the defeat by ordering an offensive when a simple blockade would have been effective, he completely lost his head and executed the Phoenician captains for alleged cowardice; incensed by their maltreatment, the Phoenicians returned home and were followed by the Egyptians. It was this justified desertion and not the defeat at Salamis which left the Aegean wide open to the allied fleet and permitted the truly decisive operations of the next year.

In a very real sense, Salamis was actually a Persian blessing. Discouraged by his fiasco, Xerxes hurried off by land to Sardis, where he spent the next year keeping watch over Ionia. Direct conduct of the war was transferred from the unwarlike king to the seasoned campaigner Mardonius, who retained for himself only one army corps, composed of Immortals, Persians, Medes, Bactrians, and Indians—a force almost exclusively Iranian and so of the best fighting material. Even thus reduced, it was superior in number to the allies; it was also supported by half the troops of continental Greece. A second army under Artabazus, son of Pharnaces, guarded the long seaboard route by which alone supplies could now be forwarded; a third under Tigranes held Ionia quiet.[25]

Potidaea revolted and Olynthus threatened to follow its example. Artabazus took Olynthus and handed over the ruins to the Chalcidians. A friend of Persia led a detachment under the walls of Potidaea at ebb tide, but the tide returned too soon, and those who were not drowned were slaughtered from boats.[26]

From his winter camp in Thessaly, Mardonius sent the Athenian proxenos, Alexander of Macedon, to offer complete forgiveness, rebuilding of the burned temples, restoration of territory with any additional lands that might be desired, and equal alliance as an autonomous free city. Such generous terms must have appealed strongly to the poorer classes for whom a new invasion could mean only fresh miseries and loss of their few remaining possessions.

But the democracy had lost control. Themistocles had admittedly written a letter to the great king urging him to attack at Salamis; though now he maintained that he had done it in subtlety, he was not believed. After his exile, he once more claimed that he had acted as Persia's friend; this time he *was* believed and was richly rewarded by Artaxerxes, Xerxes' son! The reaction had therefore given power to the conservatives, who delayed a reply to Alexander until the Spartans were present. Oracles had been circulated to the effect that the Medes and the Athenians would drive all Dorians from the Peloponnese; frightened by such oracles, the Spartans sent an embassy which blamed the Athenians for starting the war by their ill-starred expedition in aid of the Ionian rebels and which promised to support their noncombatants for the duration of the war. The Athenians rejected the proposal brought by Alexander but once more warned the Spartans to send an army for an invasion of Boeotia before Attica was again attacked.[27]

Mardonius was advised by the Thebans to remain in Boeotia and win over the recalcitrant Greeks through bribes to their leaders. It was sound advice, based on intimate knowledge of their own ethnic character, and Mardonius' refusal was another in the chain of Persian blunders. Ten months after the first inroad, in July, Athens again fell into his hands and once more the failure of the Peloponnesians to give

[25] Simonides 91, 163 ff.; Aeschyl. *Pers.* 302 ff.; Herod. viii. 66 ff., 113, 117, 126; Thuc. i. 14. 3; 73–74; Ctes. *Pers.* xiii, Epit. 57; Timotheus, *Persae* (Edmonds, No. 19); Ephor. 188(J); Diod. xi. 17 ff.; Plut. *Themistocl.* 12 ff; Aristodemus 1(J).

[26] Herod. viii. 126 ff.   [27] *Ibid.* 136, 140 ff.; ix. 8.

adequate support drove the citizens to take refuge on the ships or on Salamis. Mardonius repeated his proposals in hope that his presence with an army might enable his friends to enforce compliance, but the democrat who merely urged consideration was stoned to death with his wife and children. Yet there was still hope for Mardonius. As usual, the Spartans were "celebrating a feast"; the Isthmus wall was completed and could be held, they fatuously imagined, against the Athenian fleet. Even after the victory of Salamis, it appeared, the inability of Sparta to understand the most elementary factors of the situation would drive Athens, despite the conservatives, into the Persian alliance. Finally, after still more delay, the disillusioned Athenian ambassadors told Sparta this was exactly what they would do. To their amazement, the envoys learned that at long last a Tegean had convinced the Spartans of their utter folly and that troops were already on the way. At the very last second, fortune had again snatched victory from the Persians.

Friendly Argives relayed the information to Mardonius, who had hitherto refrained from plundering Attica in the well-grounded hope that Spartan procrastination, if not actual disloyalty to an ally, would force Athens to come to terms. Once more disappointed, he again burned Athens and withdrew to Boeotia, where, with Thebes as a base, he could secure adequate supplies. Trees were cut down to construct a stockade over a mile square, and Mardonius awaited the allied moves.

DEFEAT AT PLATAEA

The allied forces advanced through Attica and timidly encamped on the north slopes of Cithaeron opposite the Persians on the Asopus. Immediately squadron after squadron of cavalry under Masistius charged the Megarians on the low ground which constituted the weakest part of the allied line in the hope of breaking through to the pass and thus cutting off supplies. Athenian reinforcements came up, and Masistius was thrown from his horse and slain; the golden bit and his purple robe over gold cuirass were made spoil.[28] Encouraged by this first success, the allies descended to the lower slopes where encampment was easier and where there was water. The Persians moved up to meet them. Both armies had been promised victory by their soothsayers if they remained on the defensive.

Again Mardonius was advised, this time by Artabazus, to retire and

---

[28] Cf. Plut. *Aristid.* 14; Paus. i. 27. 1.

employ bribery; again the general mistakenly refused the advice. The position of the allies was already desperate. They suffered incessant cavalry raids, one of which closed the passes and the road home from the Peloponnesus and captured a much-needed provision train. Food was scant; the fountain of Gargaphia was choked, and the men suffered from thirst. The generals decided to retire at nightfall, and retirement was made in disorder. The main body lost their way; a stubborn captain delayed the Spartans, who at dawn were drawn up in a thoroughly untenable position. Had the allies been permitted to withdraw unmolested, the coalition would undoubtedly have broken up, for the Athenians would have made terms, the Peloponnesians would have retreated to the Isthmus, and the individual states could have been subjugated in turn.

Once more the end of the war was in sight. Once more a Persian commander underestimated the fighting ability of the individual Greek, backed against a mountain wall. Once more the general was lured by hope of an immediate and spectacular victory and threw away the advantages of a dilatory policy.

Assuming that the retreat was a rout, Mardonius led out his troops on the run, not even stopping to form a regular line of battle. When they came into contact with the Spartans, the Persians set up their wall of wicker shields and from behind it poured flights of arrows upon their opponents. Pausanius requested aid from the Athenians, who started to the rescue but were assailed by the Medizing Greeks. Even when the Tegeans, followed by the Spartans, broke through the wicker wall, the Persians fought on, snapping off the enemy spears with their bare hands. Their lack of defensive armor did not prevent them from constant attacks on the mailed Greeks. Then Mardonius made his last and fatal mistake; he entered the battle in person and, with his guard of a thousand picked Persians, was slain.

Deprived of their leader, the Persians fled to the stockaded camp. Learning of their flight, the Greeks at the Heraeum rushed pell-mell to share the victory; the Corinthians reached the Spartans in safety, but the Megarians and Phliasians were routed by Theban cavalry and fled to the passes. From their towers on the stockaded camp, the Persians long held off the Spartans; the tide turned when the Athenians came up, though the Tegeans were the first to breach the walls, and the spoils of Mardonius were their reward. The Persians were slaughtered without mercy.[29] Pausanias was a national hero; no one dreamed

[29] Simonides 92; Aeschyl. *Pers.* 800 ff.; Herod. ix. 1 ff.; Ctes. *Pers.* xiii, Epit. 56.

that, before another year had passed, he would be plotting to betray his fellow-Greeks for the empty honor of being a son-in-law to the Persian king.

Immediately after the battle, the commanders as representatives of their respective states assembled at Plataea and drew up a new form of organization. Naturally, Pausanias, as a Spartan and as victor in the recent battle, presided, but the mover of the enabling motion was the Athenian Aristeides. The former war alliance was to be continued and expanded as the "symmachy of the Hellenes." The representatives of the contracting states were to assemble each year on the anniversary of the glorious triumph, and the war against the barbarian was to be brought to a conclusion through the levy of a force (consisting of ten thousand hoplites, a thousand cavalry, and a hundred ships) contributed by all the associated Greeks. Sparta was to retain the leadership.[30]

Like the earlier battles, Plataea also by itself was not decisive. Only one of the Persian armies had been engaged, and the second had not even entered the battle. Yet instead of throwing fresh troops upon the battle-weary allies and sweeping them rapidly to the southernmost tip of the Peloponnese, Artabazus retired, and the war in Europe was lost. The reason was that he had heard news from Asia.[31]

DISASTER AT MYCALE

In the spring of 479 a new allied fleet had been made ready. The Athenian contingent was under Xanthippus, for his fame as the victor of Salamis had not saved Themistocles from the suspicion of planned betrayal, and this had aided the conservative reaction. At first, the captains feared to sail beyond Delos, even when offered the opportunity of deposing the Samian tyrant. Half the grand fleet was available to Xerxes, but it was composed chiefly of Ionians, whose loyalty had been badly shaken by Salamis. It had wintered at Cyme, but now under Mardontes, son of Bagaeus, Artayntes, son of Artachaees, and his nephew Ithamitres, it ventured to Samos.[32]

The allies plucked up courage to visit the island, and the Persians retired. The still dissatisfied Phoenicians were permitted to sail home;

---

[30] Plut. *Aristid.* 10. 6; 19. 8; 21. 1–2; Thuc. ii. 71. 2; iii. 68. 1; Dittenberger, *Syl³*, No. 835A; cf. J. A. O. Larsen, "The Constitution of the Peloponnesian League," *CP*, XXVIII (1933), 262 ff.; "The Constitution and Original Purpose of the Delian League," *Harvard Studies in Classical Philology*, LI (1940), 176 ff.

[31] Herod. ix. 66, 89.   [32] *Ibid.* viii. 130 ff.

the others beached their craft on Cape Mycale, where they formed a stockade of stones and tree trunks surrounded by a deep trench and under the near protection of the Third Army, commanded by Tigranes. The allies pursued. A herald summoned the Ionians to revolt. The Samians were disarmed by the suspicious Persians; the Milesians, deeply incensed by the betrayal of the treasures of Didymaean Apollo to Xerxes, were sent off on pretense of guarding the trails. Then on August 27, 479, the allies attacked; after a desperate resistance, the Athenians broke down the wicker wall and followed their flying opponents into the stockade. While their other subjects fled and the Ionians turned against them, the native Persians died almost to the last man, and with them Mardontes and Tigranes. Stockade and ships were burned.[33] By their own request, the Milesians who had betrayed Didymaean Apollo were settled in Sogdiana, where they built a new Branchidae, and the oracle of Apollo became silent.[34]

The allies returned to Samos and held council. The proposal of the Peloponnesians was that the Ionians be transferred to European Greece and settled on the lands of the Medizers. To this the Athenians objected, and, instead, the Samians, Chians, Lesbians, and other loyal islanders were received into the war alliance.[35]

Still failing to realize that Mycale was the decisive battle, the allied fleet sailed to the Hellespont to learn whether there was danger of fresh invasion and to cut the bridges. Finding them destroyed, the Peloponnesians returned home, but the Athenians determined to invest Sestos, held by the satrap Artayctes, son of Cherasmis, and the general Oeobazus. The siege lasted into the winter, when famine drove the leaders to slip off in hope of joining Artabazus; his army passed on without stopping, for Ionia was now denuded of troops, and crossed the Bosphorus near Byzantium. Oeobazus was caught by the Thracians and sacrificed to their god; Artayctes was captured at Aegospotami and crucified because he had confiscated the dedicated wealth and lands of the precinct about the tomb of Protesilaus at Elaeus. Then the Athenians sailed home, carrying the bridge cables as trophies (479).[36]

Mycale and not Plataea was in truth the decisive battle. Two of the

[33] Ibid. ix. 90 ff.

[34] Strabo xi. 11. 4; xiv. 1. 5; xvii. 1. 43; Curt. vii, 5. 28.

[35] Herod. ix. 106.

[36] Ibid. vii. 33, 78; ix, 89, 106, 114 ff.; Thuc. i. 89. 2; viii. 72. 3; Diod. xi. 34 ff.; Paus. iii. 4. 6.

six Persian armies had been completely destroyed. A third must abandon Europe to guard disaffected western Asia. Truly the Allies might say that the gods had fought for them;[37] the war had been lost by the Persians through repeated military and diplomatic blunders and not won by timid, incompetent, or disloyal allied commanders. "You know," the great historian Thucydides reminded his contemporaries of the next generation, "that it was chiefly his own fault that the Barbarian failed."[38] But, however won, victory it was, and a new phase of Perso-Greek relations was initiated.

[37] Herod. viii. 109.   [38] Thuc. i. 69. 5.

Chapter XIX

DELIAN LEAGUE AGAINST PERSIA

THE TREACHERY OF PAUSANIAS

MYCALE offered hope that the Persian power was crumbling and that the empire would disintegrate as rapidly as it had been formed. Of the six army corps, the three best had ceased to function; from the others, more distant and inferior in quality, serious resistance could scarcely be expected. If the war was now carried into enemy country, the next phase of the operations would be naval; the Persian grand fleet had been defeated and dispersed to a sullen hiding, while the navy of the Hellenic League had never been so strong. The future looked as rosy to the allied Greeks as it was alarming to the Persians.[1]

Destruction of the Hellespont bridges by the Persians themselves had at last convinced Leotychides, the commander-in-chief of the naval forces of the League, that the war had actually come to an end. Before the close of 479, he returned to Sparta, taking with him all the Peloponnesian contingents. Spartan authorities at home took a different and more farsighted view of the situation. Greeks of Asia had been promised liberation, and to fulfil their solemn pledge the members of the League must be prepared to continue the war. Furthermore, the League offered Sparta an exceptional opportunity to increase her strength beyond that allowed by the former Peloponnesian League, while the leadership of the naval operations, now so necessary to follow up the recent victories, should not be permitted to lapse by default to the rival Athenians, who by their investment of Sestos had shown more than willingness to undertake the new task.

Accordingly, in the spring of 478 a new commander-in-chief of the Hellenic League forces was sent out. At first sight, the choice was excellent. No other Spartan could vie in prestige with Pausanias. Not only was he the honored victor of Plataea, but he had been recognized as such by the equal honor of presiding officer of the constituent as-

[1] For the period following cf. M. L. W. Laistner, *History of the Greek World from 479 to 323 B.C.* (1936); *Cambridge Ancient History*, Vol. V (1927); E. Meyer, *Geschichte des Altertums*, Vol. IV (3d ed., 1939); K. J. Beloch, *Griechische Geschichte*, Vol. II (2d ed., 1914–16).

sembly of the new Hellenic League; and as leader of all its forces in the new operations he was only completing the work of liberation. His success was quite as great as at Plataea. The Greek cities of Cyprus were freed from their Persian garrisons, and Pausanias was equally fortunate at Byzantium.

Yet, despite these solid achievements, events were quickly to prove that the choice of Pausanias was a terrible mistake on the part of the home authorities. Not content with all his previous honors, Pausanias aspired to the rule of the whole of Greece. This could be attained only by the support, financial more than military, of the Persian Empire, and, accordingly, Pausanias prepared to betray the Greeks whom he had just liberated at Plataea! In hope of a generous dowry, useful for bribes, he was betrothed to a daughter of Megabates, satrap of Dascyleium.[2] Soon his hopes soared higher. A number of the king's relatives who had been made prisoner at Byzantium were secretly returned, and the Spartan traitor promised to force all the Greeks to become Persian vassals if he were given the king's daughter in marriage.

As reward for his successful retreat, Artabazus was granted the satrapy of Dascyleium in place of Megabates, and there he founded a hereditary line of satraps. With him he carried this letter: "Thus says King Xerxes to Pausanias: Because of the men whom you have saved for me across the sea, from Byzantium, there shall be laid up for you favor in our house, forever recorded, and with your words I am well pleased. And let neither night nor day hinder you from taking care to accomplish anything of what you have promised me, neither for expense of gold and silver let them be hindered nor for size of army, wherever they should be at hand, but with Artabazus, a good man, whom I have sent you, boldly execute both my affairs and yours, whatever is finest and best for both."[3]

Whether the fulfilment of Pausanias' ambitious designs appeared as impossible to Xerxes as it does to us in the light of the later development may be doubted. From the very first contact with the Greeks, Persian monarchs had been well aware of the outstanding weakness of Greek statesmen—their susceptibility to bribes—and now that Xerxes had suffered a crushing series of military defeats Persian diplomacy backed by the empire's gold must be brought into play. That the Greek hero should utilize his opportunity to make himself king seemed perfectly natural, and that he should buy his way to the throne

[2] Herod. v. 32.

[3] Thuc. i. 129. 3; cf. Olmstead, "A Persian Letter in Thucydides," *AJSL*, XLIX (1933), 154.

by the purchase of an army and navy justified the promise of heavy subventions. If he wished in return a daughter of the Great King in marriage, how could a member of Xerxes' expanded harem be more usefully employed?

As prospective son-in-law of the Great King, Pausanias followed the royal advice to act boldly. He wore the Median dress, adopted Persian table manners, and from his captives formed a bodyguard of Medes and Egyptians. But Xerxes had failed to understand another Greek characteristic—intense loyalty to the individual city-state and equal devotion to "liberty." Furthermore, he had failed to recognize the growing breach between Athens and Sparta.

THE LEADERSHIP OF ATHENS

It had become clear that Pausanias was about to sacrifice to his ambition the newly admitted members of his own League. The Athenians had been responsible for their denouncement of allegiance to the empire and for their acceptance of the authority of the Hellenic League. Accordingly, the Ionians called upon the Athenians to redeem their promises of liberation by assuming the leadership of the projected crusade.

The Athenians cautiously replied that they would protect the Ionians, but for the moment they ignored the suggestion of leadership; instead, Aristeides and Cimon demanded the recall and trial of Pausanias by Sparta. By the time Sparta acted, the damage had been done. Before the end of 478 the Delian League had been formed, not as a substitute for the Hellenic League, which long continued a more or less nominal existence, but as an entirely new organization within its framework.

The new league organized under the presidency of Aristeides was to consist only of those states around the Aegean whose interests were predominantly maritime and whose intentions were to revenge the attacks of the Persians and to carry the war into enemy territory until all the Greek cities in Asia had been liberated from barbarian rule. Aside from Athens, now raised to the position of "leader" or executive of the new organization, and Samos, Chios, and Lesbos, whose independence from Persia had so recently been acknowledged, there were included other islands off the Asiatic coast—Miletus on the mainland to the south, and Abydos, Cyzicus, and Chalcedon on the north— but the great majority of the cities on the mainland continued under Persian sway.

Although Athens held uncontested "leadership," each city remained "autonomous." No action could be taken by Athens as executive without formal approval by an assembly of the representatives of the constituent states which met regularly in Apollo's temple on the already sacred island of Delos. For the expenses of the proposed wars of liberation, "contributions" were to be made by the states, either in ships or in money, and the assessment was settled by Aristeides the "Just." The sums thus collected (for the smaller states did not contribute ships) were to be deposited on the same sacred island under the supervision of "Hellenic treasurers," who, however, from the beginning seem to have been exclusively Athenian citizens. The members swore to have the same enemies and friends. That the offensive and defensive alliance was from the start intended to be permanent was indicated by a solemn ceremony: from altars on the ships by which the oaths of the commanders had just been sworn, iron ingots were cast into the sea in token that the alliance would last until the iron rose from the waves. Sparta made no protest but, in the spring of 477, did send Dorcis as successor of the disgraced Pausanias; when the new allies refused to accept him as their commander-in-chief, the Spartans raised no objection, willingly turning over the thankless task of conducting fresh naval operations to their good friends the Athenians![4]

RENEWAL OF THE WAR

Apparently the Athenians at home took the same attitude toward the responsibilities they had so recently assumed. Propaganda for continuing the war was required, and in 476, under the auspices of Cimon, Phrynichus brought out his tragedy called the *Phoenician Women*. The story of Salamis was retold; among the surviving fragments we note: "This is the watery abode of the Persians," "Leaving the Sidonian city and watery Aradus"; "Abandoning the Sidonian ship."[5] Enough interest was stirred up so that in the year following, 475, Cimon was enabled to lead the League fleet to Eion, from whence he drove off the Thracians who were provisioning the town. Its walls were undermined by damming the Strymon, but so long as food held out Boges

---

[4] Simonides, Frag. 131 (Edmonds); Herod. viii. 3; Thuc. i. 18. 2; 75. 2; 77. 6; 94 ff., 128 ff.; iii. 10. 4; 11. 3 ff.; v. 18. 5; vi. 82; Aristot. *Polit. Athen.* 23. 4–5; Duris *Hist.* xxii, Frag. 14(J); Diod. xi. 44; 47. 1; Just. ii. 15. 13 ff.; Nepos *Paus.* 2–3; Plut. *Aristeid.* 23; *Cimon* 6. 2; Polyaen. i. 34. 2; Chrysermus Corinth. *Pers.* ii (*FHG*, IV, 361). Cf. the convincing study of J. A. O. Larsen, "The Constitution and Original Purpose of the Delian League," *Harvard Studies in Classical Philology*, LI (1940), 175 ff.

[5] Phrynichus, Frags. 8 ff. (Nauck).

continued a vigorous resistance; then he killed his family and burned their corpses on the funeral pile, threw his gold and silver into the river, and immolated himself, leaving the inhabitants to be enslaved.[6] Mascames, however, retained Doriscus as the last Persian stronghold in Europe.[7]

Athenian interests then shifted to the building-up of the Delian League as an instrument of the rising power of Athens or to the renewed struggle between conservative and liberal. Even the performance in 472 of Aeschylus' *Persians*, glorifying the victory at Salamis in which so many of his auditors had participated, could not reawaken the war spirit. In the partisan debates the letter sent by Themistocles to Xerxes was not forgotten; Aeschylus might lavish his praises on the great democratic leader,[8] but the charge of Medism persisted.[9] Pausanias, who, on his first recall to Sparta, had been tried and acquitted and afterward had returned to Byzantium, was driven from the city in 471. When his treason was exposed, his relations with Themistocles came to light; in the following year, Themistocles himself was ostracized.

After this victory over his democratic rival, Cimon was all-powerful at Athens. Under his leadership war was resumed in 466 by the Delian League. Once more, there seemed every reason for success.

HAREM INTRIGUES

The fine promise of Xerxes' younger years had not been fulfilled. Failure of the European adventure opened the way to harem intrigues, with all their deadly consequences. On the retreat from Mycale, the king's brother Masistes had laid the blame for the defeat upon the admiral Artayntes and had called him worse than a woman—to a Persian, the most deadly of insults. Artayntes started to wipe out the insult in blood but was prevented by Xenagoras of Halicarnassus, who, as reward for saving the royal kinsman, was granted the rule of all Cilicia.

Masistes was soon to find himself in yet greater danger. While dallying at Sardis, Xerxes had fallen in love with his brother's wife. As a virtuous woman, she repulsed his attentions, whereupon the king married her daughter Artaynte to his eldest son Darius in hope that the mother would now be more amenable.

---

[6] Herod. vii. 107, 113; Thuc. i. 98. 1; Ephor., Frag. 191(J); Aeschin. *Ctes.* 183 ff.; Diod. xi. 60. 1–2; Nepos *Cimon* ii. 2; Plut. *Cimon* 7; Paus. viii. 8. 9; Polyaen. vii. 24.

[7] Herod. vii. 106.   [8] Aeschyl. *Pers.* 355 ff.   [9] Plut. *Themistocl.* 21. 5.

After the court returned to Susa, the fickle affections of Xerxes veered from mother to daughter, and Artaynte proved more compliant. Xerxes was tricked into giving the ill-fated girl the robe of state which Amestris had woven with her own royal hand. The queen was outraged and, blaming the mother for the trick, demanded the wife of Masistes at the New Year's feast when the king must grant every requested gift. The unfortunate woman was horribly mutilated; Masistes with his whole family fled toward Bactria, intending to raise a revolt, but, before he could reach his satrapy, he was overtaken and all were put to death.[10]

The royal example proved contagious. Sataspes, son of Teaspes, a member of the Achaemenid family, wronged the virgin daughter of Zopyrus, son of Megabyzus. Xerxes ordered the criminal impaled, but the mother of Sataspes, a sister of Darius, persuaded her nephew to substitute as punishment the command to repeat the Phoenician circumnavigation of Africa. Taking ship from Egypt, Sataspes traveled west through the Pillars of Heracles and then south along the coast of West Africa to the land of the pygmies. Many months elapsed, Sataspes became frightened, and he returned to court. Xerxes did not believe his tale that the ship had been forcibly prevented from sailing on; by his return, the king had lost the opportunity to pose as the patron of a spectacular geographical discovery. The royal order had been disobeyed, and the original penalty was therefore carried out.[11]

More and more the character of Xerxes disintegrated. The enlarged but still crowded harem at Persepolis tells its own story. For a time he continued his interest in the completion of the Persepolis buildings. Toward the end of his reign, he was under the influence of the commander of the guard, the Hyrcanian Artabanus, and of the eunuch chamberlain Aspamitres.[12]

DISASTER AT THE EURYMEDON

This degeneration in character could not have remained unknown to the European Greeks. With Themistocles out of the way, Cimon sailed with two hundred ships to Caria in 466. The Greek cities were easily induced to revolt and to accept garrisons, but those which were bilingual in speech remained loyal to Persia and must be reduced by force. For instance, Cimon had begun the siege of Phaselis when the Chians, old friends of the Phasaeliotes, shot in letters affixed to arrows

[10] Herod. ix. 107 ff.; contrast Ctes. *Pers.* xiii, Epit. 59.
[11] Herod. iv. 43.   [12] Ctes. *Pers.* xiii, Epit. 60.

which persuaded the inhabitants to pay ten talents and to take part in the wars of liberation.

Roused from his lethargy, Xerxes dispatched against Cimon a large force under Ariomandes, son of Gobryas; Pherendates commanded the land troops, while the fleet of two hundred Phoenician, Cypriote, and Cilician vessels was under Tithraustes, a natural son of Xerxes himself. Since eighty more Phoenician ships were expected from Cyprus, Ariomandes refused battle and retired to the mouth of the Eurymedon; when the Greeks prepared to follow, he again came out. After a mere show of fighting, the Persians beached their ships, and most of the sailors escaped. The infantry sallied out to their aid, and Cimon landed the hoplites, who after a long struggle took the Persian camp. He then sailed off in search of the missing eighty ships, which he found still delaying at Hybrus in Cyprus; the city was surprised and the boats were captured with their crews (466). Next year, with only four ships, Cimon drove off thirteen Persian ships from the Chersonese, even though they were aided by the Thracians.[13]

Eurymedon was decisive. With the exception of Doriscus, which was still Persian when Herodotus composed his *History*,[14] Europe had been lost to the empire; and now large numbers of the Asiatic Greeks, together with many Carians and Lycians, were enrolled in the rapidly expanding Delian League. When, for example, Athens granted a new constitution to Erythrae, the councilors were forced to swear that they would not receive back those who had fled to the Medes without the permission of the Athenian people.[15]

GREEK INFLUENCE IN ASIA

After Cybernis, the isolated initials or monograms do not permit us to identify the Lycian dynasts who issued coins with symbols of true or mythological animals like the sphinx, the chimera, the winged horse of the Lycian hero Bellerophon, or of the curious triskeles, the joined three legs. For contemporary dynasts, however, we have their names fully spelled out, and of them some fifteen are known. Once in the Delian League, the pride of the Lycians was flattered by the der-

---

[13] *IG* (ed. minor), Vol. I, Nos. 16 and 928; Thuc. i. 100. 1; [Simonides] *Anthol. Palat.* vii. 258; Plato *Menex.* 241E; Lycurg. *Leocrat.* 72; Ephor., Frag. 191(J); Callisthen., Frag. 15(J); Diod. xi. 60–61; Nepos *Cimon* ii. 2; Plut. *Cimon* 12 ff.; Bell. Pacat. (Athen. vii. 349D); Paus. i. 29. 14; x. 15. 4; Front, *Strat.* ii. 9. 10; iii. 2. 5; Polyaen. i. 34. 1; Aristid. *Panathen.* 246, 276; Aristod. xi. 2. Cf. W. Peek in *Athenian Studies Presented to William Scott Ferguson* (1940), pp. 97 ff.

[14] Herod. vii. 106.

[15] *IG* (ed. minor), Vol. I, No. 10= Dittenberger, *Syl.*³, No. 41.

ivation of their name from the Athenian hero Lycus, son of Pandion.[16] Athenian influence often appears, for example, on the coins of Kharega, minting at Xanthus and at Antiphellus; on the obverse, Athena is seated with her owl, or we have the helmeted Ares or the bearded and horned Ammon of Egypt.[17]

Greek influence is even more evident in the tomb of Kharega's general Marahe. The main scene shows four plumed and plunging horses drawing a chariot. Marahe in full panoply is about to spear a lion; his driver wears a Phrygian cap. Above we see Marahe again, with his long hair visible around a bald spot. He reclines on a couch, his shoes at the side, and holds up a bowl, while a servant at the foot of the couch introduces a visitor. Marahe's wife, her feet on a stool, is seated on a backless chair behind him and holds her robe to her chin; before him is their young child. An elder, clad in a himation caught around the waist, crowns a nude beardless athlete; this nudity is in itself a sign of Hellenization, for Thucydides tells us that even to his day the barbarians of Asia wear a loincloth when contesting for the prize in boxing and wrestling.[18] A youth with short hair and beard holds out his hand to an older man, who responds halfway; two elderly men, one bent with age, clasp hands; another bent elder extends his hand to the master, who is here seated with dog and scepter.[19]

Hellenization was making equally rapid progress in Caria. The local alphabet employed for the native Carian by the mercenaries in Saite Egypt had virtually disappeared, and so had the language for polite society. Scylax of Caryanda had written the first description of India in Greek.[20] Pigres, brother of Artemisia, the lady tyrant of Halicarnassus, though a native Carian, exhibited his Greek culture by turning out a curious production in which each hexameter line of Homer's original *Iliad* was followed by an elegiac pentameter. There were scholars who even thought him worthy of the authorship of the *Margites* and of the *Battle of the Frogs and Mice* popularly attributed to Homer.[21]

---

[16] Herod. i. 173.

[17] F. Babelon, *Traité des Monnaies*, II, Part II (1910), 273 ff.

[18] Thuc. i. 6. 5.

[19] Otto Benndorf and George Niemann, *Das Heroon von Gjölbaschi-Trysa* (1889), Fig. 41; *TAM*, Vol. I, No. 43.

[20] Cf. p. 212.

[21] Suid. s.v., "Pigres"; cf. Plut. *De malig. Herod.* 43.

ORIENTAL INFLUENCES IN GREECE

The Orient likewise was coming to be better known to the Greeks of Europe. Phrynichus had already exhibited his tragedy of the *Egyptians*. Aeschylus re-worked the old legends and brought up to date the stories of oriental worthies. In his *Suppliant Maidens*, the maidens flee to Argos from the fine sands at the seven mouths of the Nile—from the distant pastures so close to Syria. They wear linen veils from Sidon and resemble Nile women or camel-riding nomads near the Ethiopians. Io wanders through Asia—sheep-pasturing Phrygia, Teuthras of the Mysians, and the hollows of Lydia, across the Cilician mounts and Pamphylia. She visits the one-eyed Arimaspi who guard the gold, the dark race dwelling by the sun's waters at the river Aethiops, the cataract where from Bibline Mountains the Nile sends forth his sacred stream, whose waters no disease may touch, and comes to Canobus and Memphis. There the sacred calf Epaphus, whom the Greeks also call Apis, is born to her. Aeschylus, furthermore, knows of the papyrus plant, of the crocodile, and of Egyptian beer. He has heard that the Phasis is boundary between Europe and Asia, that incense comes from Syria, and that there is a sea called the Erythraean.[22]

Aeschuylus' *Persians*, the story of contemporary Salamis, gives more opportunity to display new information. He mentions the "city of the Persae," though he is not quite sure whether it is different from the "Wall of the Susians," of the Ecbatanians, or of the Cissians. Golden Sardis and Babylon have greatly impressed him. He can give correctly the Persian line of kings. Queen-Mother Atossa is wife of the Persian god and also mother of a god; on earth her son Xerxes was like to a god, the Susa-born god of the Persians. When dead, her husband rules the underworld gods;[23] no clearer proof could be found that the Persians had adopted king worship from their predecessors.

He tells also of libations to Earth and to the dead—milk from an unblemished cow, water from a virgin spring, old wine, honey, olive oil—and of the ritual use of garlands. Atossa presents her offerings to the lower gods and pours libations to the chambers beneath the earth. Meanwhile the elders chant hymns, beseeching the conductors of the dead to hearken graciously to their prayers, and beg the holy underground demons—Earth, Hermes, and the king of the dead—to permit

---

[22] Phrynichus, Frags. 720–21 (Nauck); Aeschyl. *Suppl.* 3 ff., 120 ff., 278 ff., 311, 315, 547 ff., 760, 953; *Prometh vinct.* 804 ff.; *Agamem.* 1312; Frags. 105–6, 161, 206.

[23] Aeschyl. *Pers.* 157, 634, 644, 691 ff., 711, 857.

the spirit of Darius to behold the light.[24] Pindar is acquainted with the Phasis and the Nile of mysterious sources, Babylon and the shrine of Zeus Ammon, and the many cities founded by Epaphus in Egypt; his song goes over the sea like Phoenician merchandise.[25]

Aeschylus declared that Persians were lamenting: "Those dwelling through all Asia will not long be governed by Persians or pay their tribute by the compulsion of their lord or bow to earth and do reverence, for the royal power is utterly destroyed."[26] Only for Greek lands was this boast in any sense true. The conservative anti-Persian element was all-powerful at Athens. The Delian League was in full activity. Persian influence in the West was apparently at an end. Simonides wrote poems on the "Kingdoms of Cambyses and Darius," on the "Sea Fight with Xerxes," and on the "Naval Battles of Artemesium and Salamis," not to speak of many epitaphs for the slain heroes of the Great Persian War. Charon of Lampsacus composed a *Persian History*, and Dionysius of Miletus an account of the *Events after Darius*, as if Persian history had come to a close. The fact was that soon Persia would change the whole political aspect of the Greek world.

[24] *Ibid.* 219–20, 623 ff.

[25] Pindar, *Isth.* ii. 41 ff.; vi. 23; *Paen.* iv. 13 ff.; *Nem.* x. 5; *Pyth.* ii. 68; iv. 16.

[26] Aeschyl. *Pers.* 584 ff.

Chapter XX

NEW YEAR'S DAY AT PERSEPOLIS

DARIUS laid down the general plan of the Persepolis buildings, but the Persepolis we know is the work of Xerxes. The first eight years of his reign were indeed devoted primarily to war and administration, in which he took a personal part. But already in 485 work was resumed on the palace terrace, and without completely neglecting the empire during the remaining thirteen years his real interest obviously lay in building up the new capital.

THE ARCHIVES OF XERXES

To the evidence obtained from the architectural history and from the rare inscriptions Xerxes ordered to be inscribed, we may now add about two hundred clay tablets inscribed in Elamite which have been found in the archives building, together with a smaller collection of stone vessels written in Aramaic. A few similar documents had come from the reign of Darius, but the period of greatest activity is the last three years of the reign of Xerxes.

These documents are requisitions drawn by higher officials on the treasurer (*ganzabara*) for the pay of the workmen on the terrace. The payment is by the month or by several months and is regularly stated in terms of shekels of silver and their fractions; actually, as sometimes we are expressly informed, this is only bookkeeping, for the payment is in wine or a sheep according to a given rate. We may, therefore, contrast the wages in Babylonia with those paid at Parsa to discover the standard of living. Equally interesting are the names of the officials, the nationalities represented by the workmen, the tasks assigned them, and even a suggestion as to the buildings on which they are engaged.[1]

As in the last days of Darius, the chief figure is Baradkama, now given the full title of treasurer. To him, in 483, Aspathines reports the wages needed to pay 313 workmen for six months and, again, 470 for one month; of the latter, 66 are paid one shekel, 112 three-quarters of

---

[1] Professor George G. Cameron has permitted me to examine the preliminary transcriptions and translations of the texts to be published in his *Persepolis Treasury Tablets*.

a shekel, and 292 one-half. Evidently, as contrasted with payments in Babylonia, the workers at Parsa are underpaid, especially if we bear in mind the enormous increase in the price of food which had followed the Persian conquest and had not yet leveled off.

We hear of a man, evidently an expert artisan, who comes from Susa to Parsa. That same year there are 201 workmen who are laboring on one of the structures and who come from the Hittite land, from Egypt, and from Ionia; if among them were Greek sculptors, there is no indication that they were unduly paid. Next year Shakka is in charge of 34 workmen, wood beautifiers, who are making sculptures of the same material; in this case a trilingual seal of Darius is employed. In 480 Shakka draws a year's pay for two makers of iron doors at Parsa, each of whom earns a salary of a shekel and a half per month. Workmen from the Hittite land are again employed on a structure. In 479 Shakka reports 28 workmen who are making stone sculptures—perhaps the reliefs on the apadana—and are also ornamenting the wooden sculptures at Parsa.

By this year, the "man of Parsa" has succeeded Baradkama as treasurer. He is asked to pay 11 men who are ornamenting wood; the payment stipulated (two-thirds, one-half, and one-third of a shekel) represents only one-third of their total wages. In 476 Shakka has under him 18 men carving stone sculptures and ornamenting wood. Near the beginning of 473, Vahush, a subordinate in 480, has been promoted to the office of treasurer, and we now hear of the "king's treasury." Artatakhma has 20 men who are ornamenting bronze. Chithravahu in 471 is in charge of 238 men, workmen of the treasury. Two of them are overseers and receive the high wages of two shekels; 22 receive one shekel, others two-thirds, one-half, and one-third; but 159 receive only a fourth. These last are children—who today perform the actual labor for the oriental silversmith's art. Women appear who earn a shekel, the average wage of a male artisan. By now the seal of Darius is no longer used for authentication; the new seal is inscribed: "I am Xerxes the great king."

In two of the last years of the reign (467–466) the tablets pile up. Buildings are still in process of erection, and one gang of workmen from the treasury at Parsa has now reached almost 1,350 in number. Vahush the treasurer is at the "Fortress," an alternate term for Parsa, and there he receives from Megabyzus a requisition for payment of 12 men at two and a quarter shekels, 9 boys at one and two-thirds, 9 more at two and a quarter, 17 women at one, and 17 girls at two-thirds.

Artatakhma needs money for his Carian goldsmiths. The overseer receives four and one-sixteenth shekels. Twenty-six receive two and a half. As in the modern Orient, not only do boys and women do the greater part of the work but they are unusually well paid. While 4 boys receive five-sixths and a fifth receives five-twelfths, 27 women are given a wage far above that of the average man, one and two-thirds; 5 of the more skilful girls, one and a quarter; 4 draw four-fifths, and 4 more five-twelfths.

Artatakhma is the superior of Megabyzus, whose 12 boys receive for one month forty-five and a half shekels (almost four shekels for each boy), but this is nothing compared to the overseer, who receives for one month seven and a half shekels! There are artisans under Pherendates and those who carve the stone sculptures or ornament the iron and wooden doors. But while goldsmiths receive such exorbitant amounts and silversmiths are paid more than the average, the artists who prepare the magnificent reliefs are not paid even the bare subsistence wages given in trade to the average Babylonian peasant, unless we assume (as sometimes we must) that the payments stipulated are but a portion of the total wages.

THE APADANA RELIEFS

Darius had begun the Persepolis apadana but had died soon after the sculptures along the north front had been completed. It was left for Xerxes to carry on the magnificent structure upon which he lavished all his interest and thus produced the most impressive building on the terrace.

To reach its higher level, there were monumental staircases on the north and east. On either side, two facing stairways met in the center, while two more were set deeper near the corners. To a length of 292 feet along the north and east face the terrace was covered by sculptures which show Persian art at its very best. Those to the north were first seen by the visitor but are now sadly weathered; those to the east repeated the scenes but in reverse order. Thanks to the soil which has protected the latter since Alexander's wanton destruction, their recent excavation has made them live again in all their pristine beauty.

Below the central landing hovers Ahuramazda's symbol, here minus the divine figure; a winged griffin with paw uplifted in adoration crouches before palm trunks on either side. Directly before the divine symbol should have been the building record of Xerxes; two Immortals at present arms guard the bare slabs, but elsewhere on the eastern and northern fronts were the inscriptions praising Ahuramazda and the king.[2] Among palm trunks set in the triangles formed by the stairs, lions sink their teeth into the hindquarters of rearing bulls. Trees in the form of cypresses, but with the needles, cones, and bark of pines, grow on the outside parapets between rows of rosettes and below crenelations.

All this is but preparation for the main theme, the procession of soldiers, courtiers, and subject peoples advancing to greet their lord at the New Year's feast. To one side and framed by rosettes are three divisions in three rows. First place in each is held by a squad of Immortals in full dress, the ankle-length flowing robe, caught up at the side and falling over the arm and below the waist in deep folds, and laced shoes. The spear is held on the toe—in the same rigid attitude of attention which bespeaks a well-disciplined force—by every one of the ninety-two Immortals in the detachment.

In pleasing contrast appear the nobles and attendants. All must be introduced by ushers or mace-bearers,[3] who as sign of their office hold a knobbed staff and wear a metal torque or collar.[4] One leads three attendants who bear whips in their right hands to keep off the crowds and who carry canopies tucked under their left arms; such were the hangings of white, green, and blue which were fastened by cords of fine linen and purple to silver rings and pillars of marble.[5] A fourth carries on his back the royal footstool of gold[6] on which the king would rest his feet when seated on the throne or upon which he would step when, on the march, he abandoned the chariot for the more comfortable wagon;[7] it was necessary because of the rule that the monarch should never pass on foot outside the palace.[8]

The next usher, his right hand laid over his left wrist, bears only a staff. He leads three grooms who throw an arm lovingly over the backs of the tiny Nesaean stallions,[9] their only harness a headstall of round and flat beads and a small bell. A third usher precedes two empty chariots: one for the invisible Ahuramazda,[10] the other for the

---

[2] Xerxes, *Persepolis* b; F. H. Weissbach, *Die Keilinschriften der Achämeniden* (1911), pp. 108 ff.; E. Herzfeld, *Altpersische Inschriften* (1938), No. 13; Unvala, in A. U. Pope (ed.), *A Survey of Persian Art*, I, 342.

[3] Herod. iii. 84; Xen. *Cyrop.* viii. 4. 2; cf. F. Justi, *ZDMG*, L (1896), 660 ff.

[4] Herod. viii. 113.

[5] Esther 1:6.

[6] Herod. vii. 41.

[7] *Ibid.* iii. 146.

[8] Athen. xii. 514C.

[9] Cf. pp. 25 and 30.

[10] Sacred chariot of Zeus (Herod. viii. 115).

king. The harness for the sacred white horses[11] remains simple, a head-stall and a cruel gold bit;[12] the bridles are gold mounted and are sometimes covered with embroidered housings.[13] The reigns are kept from tangling by a comblike metal disk; the remainder of the harness consists of a band around the chest and another, ornamented by a tassel, behind the forelegs. For additional decoration, a forelock is tufted as a lotus blossom and the hair along the neck is trimmed to a crest. The chariot pole is set directly into the axle, which is held to the wheel by a pin in the form of a nude dwarf. Twelve spokes swelling at the middle form an unusual number when contrasted with Assyrian examples, while the tire is studded with huge spikes to afford a tighter hold on the ground. Lions parade around the edge of the body, on which is hung the royal quiver. At the rear, a thong assists the upward climb of the monarch and a metal handgrip permits a firmer stance, for, since the body is placed directly over the axle, the jolting must have been horrible.

Courtiers, alternately Median and Persian, complete the two lower rows of these reliefs. A few stride pompously forward, fully conscious of their high dignity as also of their robes of scarlet, crimson, and purple (mingled, on occasion, with a more sober gray)[14] and set off by gold earrings and collars.[15] Now and then one walks half-turned in order to hold the hand of a friend. Another deliberately poses, his left hand resting with casual grace on the handle of a stout sword thrust into his girdle; thus he brings out to best advantage the elaborate fall of the robe over his arm, while in his left hand he lifts up for inspection a rare object he intends to present to his king. His successor bears only a flower, an appropriate gift for the spring festival, and lays his hand approvingly on the fop's shoulder. A courtier in front turns back abruptly, his bow case swinging from his girdle, to learn the cause of all the excitement.

On the opposite side of the central staircase, each scene set off by a stylized cypress, are twenty-three groups of representatives from the different subject peoples marching along to present their annual "king's gift." Each group is introduced by an usher, who with his right hand holds the knobbed staff and with his left firmly grasps the hand of the leader of the delegation. Each delegation wears its national dress, already described from Herodotus,[16] and brings its most re-

[11] Ibid. i. 189.
[12] Ibid. ix. 20.
[13] Xen. Cyrop. viii. 3. 16.
[14] Ibid. 3.
[15] Herod. ix. 80; Xen. Anab. i. 2. 27.
[16] Cf. pp. 239–46.

nowned products, textiles, metalwork, vases, but, above all, its animals, the largest and most perfect, and every one on its best behavior.

ARTISTIC CONVENTIONS

In these reliefs Persian art reaches its climax. They illustrate both its strength and its weakness. It would be grossly unfair to censure its defects, for we must realize that the men who produced it, underpaid and treated as mere artisans, were nevertheless men of true artistic genius. To give them belatedly their due, we must examine their work in some detail.

Compared to the reliefs on the staircases of Darius' triple gateway, there is definite artistic advance, even on the earlier and cruder north front of the apadana. The robust humor has almost completely disappeared, and with it the strange alternation of tall, medium, and squat figures. The attempt to represent climbing figures has been abandoned; the thighs are no longer of different lengths, figures do not overlap, nor does one seem to step on the toes of another. Grouping is more systematic and more subtle, details of anatomy are more accurate, the drapery is more skilfully handled, and the general effect is more pleasing.

North and east sides alike were planned by master-designers, who presumably scratched in the outlines of the whole composition before assigning individual figures to the various sculptors; that their names have been ignored by the monarch who claimed the whole credit for himself is only one more illustration of the difficulties under which the ancient artist did his magnificent work. Since he thought primarily in terms of architectural decoration, it was inevitable that this decoration should be sculptured in bands and that within these bands rhythm should be attained by mathematical proportions, though not so mechanically applied that flexibility was lost.

Along the less well-preserved north front, the figures are earlier and the composition, therefore, less subtle. In the lower row the groups are by fives and sixes, in the middle by threes except for one group of five. There is no relationship between the figures in the same position on different bands, and those in the same band are not often brought into connection, even by the joining of hands. The figures are thin and separated by wide empty spaces. Lines of the arms are all in horizontal planes, even when bent at the elbows or placed on a companion's shoulder. The headdress is square cut, sometimes without rifling; the drapery most often falls naturally in a fold to either side of the arm, though the more developed treatment —sleeves smooth over the arm, four folds swinging from the elbow, and a lining visible below and marked off by one incised line—already makes its appearance. Hair and beard are irregularly treated, while the common view is the profile with the line of the arm drawn almost to the necklace. The bracelets are large and unadorned; the hands are tiny when clenched and huge when open.

Much more elaborate, and prepared by a somewhat later master, was the design for a similar procession of nobles on the east staircase. In the first band, the horses and chariots of the god and the king are by the usual convention made overlarge and therefore fill the space apportioned to five men in the lower bands. With the smaller chariots, the horse is assigned the width of four men, but the scheme of five is completed by an attendant in front. In the middle band, the sixth figure from the right faces backward and thus closes the gap between the two larger chariots above, but in the lower it is the seventh. The first and last of four small figures in the middle of the first band indicate the position for the first and sixth of the next, while the figure carrying the footstool stands between the figures in the next. In the two lower rows the two ethnic types are regularly repeated, hands joined at the same intervals, quiver cases with the same figures, the broad shoulder indicating the same connections. Straight lines are contrasted with slanting lines: a noble sniffing a flower or touching a comrade's shoulder.

Five different sculptors have left the marks of their varying styles on this one scene. The master-artist loved curves. His figures have long beautiful fingers, daintily crooked. A curved line distinguishes the palm of the hand from the arm, another curve indicates the fall of the sleeve. The drapery is rounded and smoothed, and the streamer of the hat is given depth. Between the profile head and the full front shoulders, the cord of the neck is taut. The breast is modeled through the drapery. While the long narrow tip of the beard is left rough, the ends of the mustache are waxed and twisted; many small curls surround the ears.

Our next artist is all for flat surfaces and straight lines. His angles are sharp, long, and deep, his long-fingered hands are clumsy, and his short beards heavy and divided both horizontally and vertically. The meeting of beard with hair is irregular; the streamer is flat. A third artist depicts thin figures, whose shoulders, heads, and skirts are excessively narrow; the whole is outlined by numerous little curves. His flowers are linear, as are the folds of his skirts; his fingers are as short and stubby as his feet are small; the vertical lines of his beards are emphasized. A fourth has short, heavy streamers, plain bracelets, powerful arms, and small feet; while his drapery is linear, he does model his breasts, and his fingers are elegantly crooked. Last of all comes a poor copyist, whose oversize heads, squat figures, stubby flowers, and double bracelets show not a trace of originality.

From the viewpoint of decorative art, the tribute groups on the east front are much less successful than those on the north. On the latter there is considerable experimentation in detail, though the figures are slighter and less realistic. The tendency of the master-artist to add one more figure to each group, however, is a boon to the student of costume. This designer is a master in the effective use of broad plain surfaces and in the exact co-ordination of perpendicular lines to tie the whole scene into a flowing whole. His scheme demanded the use of ten figure spaces to each of the groups, separated by the conventionalized cypress trees.

The designer of the similar groups on the eastern front employed the nine-figure space in which three or four spaces were devoted to an animal. No effort was made to secure exact spacing, in which each figure would be beneath the one above. As a result, all sense of rhythm is lost through irregular crowding and then bare surfaces. Since the order of procession is reversed from that on the north, the figures are seen from the right side; they hold their staffs vertically, the others diagonally. On the north, garments are shorter and necklaces hang across the shoulders, not down. The leader of each delegation, on the east front, is often represented with left shoulder in front view and right in profile to suggest the strain of the arm on the shoulder; on the north, the garments only are thus treated, though the shoulders they drape are straight.

In the treatment of animals, two main schools may be distinguished. One produced the royal horses of the facing panel, the horses from Armenia and Punt, the Arab camel, the giraffe, the antelope, the horned bulls; the other is represented by the Scythian and Cappadocian horses and the Indian donkey, though many of the animals represent a combination of both. In its characteristic features, the first school shows the tuft of the forelock striated with lines radiating from the bottom and with long ties falling together just beyond the forehead. Eyes are hollowed out to produce a small round eyeball, the upper eyelid overlaps the lower, the top of the tear duct is larger than the bottom, and a deep hollow is around the eye; from the tear duct a line runs down toward the nose. Ears are squarely attached to the head, curved lines run under the chin, and deep lines separate the neck from the head. Lips are firmly modeled, the mouth is slightly open, and the nostrils have a sharp point.

Double lines mark off the musculature of the inside of the leg, a small single line the outside. The bodies are long and narrow, and their feet seem about to prance. Manes are carefully trimmed. The feet of the attendants are distinctly visible.

Animals following the other school show almost complete contrasts. In the Scythian horses, the lines of the forelock branch from a center, the ties divide—to front and onto the forehead. Eyeballs are large and the eyes merely incised. A simple point is opposite the tear duct, then a stubby disconnected line takes the place of the hollowed line from the tear duct to the nose. Ears are less squarely attached to the head; a straight line separates chin from neck and is continued across the snout. Lips have no modeling, the mouth is forced open or tightly clamped, and the nostril is a mere curve. The leg musculature is modeled without lines; bodies are large, and feet heavy. These are work horses, as is also indicated by the untrimmed manes. Another characteristic feature of the school is that the heels of the attendants are hidden by the hoofs of the beasts. Subject to the modifications due to physical differences, treatment of the other animals falls into one or the other schools.

Careful analysis of this greatest monument of Achaemenid art has proved that the appearance of monotony is a deliberately fostered illusion. By this analysis, we have discovered the individual workman, have learned his individual characteristics, and have seen the varying methods by which he solved his artistic problems. When the whole of Iranian art has been subjected to the same patient analysis, we shall be prepared for the first time to do justice to the high quality of the classic Achaemenid sculpture and to assign it to its proper place in the history of ancient art.[17]

THE APADANA AUDIENCE CHAMBER

Reluctantly turning our eyes from the finest example of Achaemenid art we shall ever behold, we follow the escort of the bowmen

[17] As with the other analyses of Achaemenid sculpture, this section is based on the work of Cleta Margaret Olmstead, "Studies in the Stylistic Development of Persian Achaemenid Art" (1936), pp. 20 ff.

up the northern stairway to observe what lies behind the high crenelated parapet. Before us we see a portico, flanked by corner towers of mud brick; the mud is concealed by colored glazed bricks forming scenes or inscriptions.[18] Thirty feet apart rise two rows of six columns; although seven feet in diameter, they soar up to a height of sixty-five feet, the most impressive and yet the most slender and airy columns ever produced by the hand of man. Similar porticoes are on the east and the west. All possess a highly ornamented bell base, a simple torus, a tapering fluted shaft, and a capital of two kneeling animals back to back. On the side porticoes this order is seen in all its light simplicity, with bull capitals on the west and horned felines on the east; on the front portico the upper half of the shaft is ornamented with brackets and double vertical volutes of more doubtful appeal. The kneeling beasts of the capitals have horns of bronze, with gold leaf on their eyeballs; between them, two long beams hold the entablature, two or three beams high. Next above may be recognized the curved ends of the rafters; above them, the cornice of three or four beams to hold in place the beaten clay roofs which keep cool the rooms below. Battlements hide the gold and silver tiles which cover the roof.

Two doorways approach the interior from the northern portico, and one each from its eastern and western porches. Six rows of six columns, resting on a square base and a plinth cut from the same stone but otherwise like those of the front portico, uphold the paneled roof of sweet-scented cedar from Lebanon and give a forest-like appearance to the audience chamber, a hundred and forty-five feet square.

So much we may safely reconstruct from preserved remains. But today the apadana is a ruin. Of the forest of columns, but a few remain to lift high their strange capitals against the open sky. The gold plating which once hid the bare mud walls[19] has long since been looted, and a few bits of gold leaf are all that are left to suggest the wealth here lavished. The wood carving[20] on which so many workmen toiled (as we learn from the archive tablets which register the pittance doled out to them) became charred beams and ashes as a result of the holocaust instituted by the Macedonian conqueror. The gorgeous hangings have moldered and may be restored only from Hebrew or Greek descriptions. Crowds which once filled these courts are temporarily replaced by the few hundred workmen needed for the modern excava-

[18] Herzfeld, *op. cit.*, No. 16.

[19] Aeschyl. *Pers.* 159; Philostrat. *Imag.* ii. 32.   [20] Aelian. *Var. hist.* xiv. 12.

tions; soon the terrace will resume its century-long silence. But we re-read the ancient sources, examine the reliefs, and then ascend to the apadana; as we view the lone columns against the sunset and look out over the plain, little effort of the imagination is required to dream that we are ancient visitors privileged to await the ceremonial entrance of Xerxes into the great audience chamber.

ROYAL SPLENDOR

From the palace to the south, where for the most part he lives in godlike seclusion,[21] a private passage brings him into the apadana. On his head is the high cidaris,[22] to whose rim the frizzed hair is combed up over the forehead and fluffed out to the neck; on occasion he might wear the upright tiara[23] around which is wound the diadem, a fillet of blue spotted with white.[24] Gold are his earrings with inset jewels.[25]

If we stand close enough to the royal presence, we discover that his eye is bulging and his eyebrows marked, his nose slightly curved, and his mouth firm; the mustache droops but is twirled at the tips. His beard is cut square at the waist and imitates the Assyrian fashion with its horizontal rows of curls. His outer robe, the candys,[26] is dyed with the costly Phoenician purple,[27] and is heavy with gold embroidery, representing fighting hawks or monsters;[28] according to rumor, it cost twelve thousand talents.[29] It is worn over the purple chiton with white spots reserved for the king alone.[30] Purple-edged are his white or crimson[31] trousers just showing under his robe. The plain heeled, pointed shoes are blue[32] or saffron.[33] Gold bracelets and a gold collar add to the effect,[34] while a golden girdle supports the short Persian sword, whose sheath is reported to be a single precious stone.[35] In his right hand he carries a gold scepter,[36] slender and knobbed; his left holds a lotus with two buds.

[21] Just. i. 1. 9.

[22] Persian *khshatram;* Hebrew *kether,* Esther 6:8, cf. 1:11; 2:17, of the queen; Greek *kitaris,* Plut. *Artox.* 2; *kidaris,* Arr. *Anab.* iv. 7. 4; Curt. iii. 3. 19; both forms, Pollux vii. 58.

[23] Aeschyl. *Pers.* 668; ordinarily confined to the slightly lower hat of the nobles, Xen. *Cyrop.* viii. 3. 13; *Anab.* ii. 5. 23; Aristophan. *Aves* 461–62.

[24] Xen. *Cyrop.* viii. 3. 13; Curt. iii. 3; Dio xxxvi. 35.   [25] Arr. *Anab.* vi. 29.

[26] Xen. *Cyrop.* i. 3. 2; viii. 3. 13; *Anab.* i. 5. 8; Diod. xvii. 77. 5; Strabo xv. 3. 19; Plut. *Alex.* 51.

[27] Xen *Cyrop.* viii. 3. 13; Just. xii. 3. 9.

[28] Curt. iii. 3. 8 ff.; Philostrat. *Imag.* ii. 32.   [29] Plut. *Artox.* 24. 6.

[30] Xen. *Cyrop.* i. 3. 2; royal apparel of blue and white, Esther 8:15.

[31] Xen. *Cyrop.* i. 3. 2.   [34] Xen. *Cyrop.* i. 3. 2; Arr. *Anab.* vi. 29.

[32] *Ibid.* viii. 3. 11.   [35] Curt. iii. 3.

[33] Aeschyl. *Pers.* 661.   [36] Xen. *Cyrop.* viii. 7. 13; Esther 4:11; 5:2; 8:4.

When at last we avert our sight from this glittering vision which persuades us that in very truth we are looking upon the lord of all the earth, we notice two attendants. They wear robes and purple shoes, but their hats are lower and their beards are rounded, not square. One holds over his master's head the royal parasol with curving ribs and pomegranate top, a loan from the Assyrians, which must accompany the king even on a military expedition;[37] the other, the chamberlain,[38] bears napkin and fly-flapper.

The king takes his seat under the canopy, inlaid with jewels and supported by golden pillars; rosettes border two bands where the divine symbol is saluted by roaring lions, the whole edged by netting weighted down by heavy tassels.[39] Turned rungs on the throne prove that a wood core is plated with gold, though the Greeks insist that the whole is of the precious metal; the feet are lion's paws resting on turned balls of silver.[40] Its back is straight, and there are no arms, though a cushion affords some comfort. The king's feet rest on a footstool ending in the hoofs of bulls. When the king raises his right arm to extend the scepter and thus to indicate a favorable reception, his undertunic shows on his right waist; its long full sleeves droop down, and the candys descends in graceful folds to the ankles.

At the royal entrance all must prostrate themselves in adoration,[41] for by ancient oriental custom the king is in a very real sense a divinity.[42] During the whole audience, hands must be kept in the sleeves to prevent the threat of assassination.[43] After the king has retired, we may inspect the throne, though we are warned that it is death to sit upon it,[44] and even to step on the Sardis rug upon which he walks is forbidden.[45]

THE RESIDENCE OF THE GREAT KING

During the earlier years of his reign, when all his energies were devoted to the completion of his father's enormous apadana, Xerxes resided close by in the palace of Darius to the southwest. Since the pal-

[37] Plut. *Themistocl.* 16. 2.

[38] Diod. xi. 69. 1; Plut. *Reg. imp. apophtheg.* 173E.

[39] Chares of Mitylene, in Athen. xii. 514C; Plut. *Alex.* 37.

[40] Xen. *Hell.* i. 5. 3; Demosthen. *Adv. Timocr.* 741; Chares of Mitylene, *loc. cit.;* Philostrat. *Imag.* ii. 32.

[41] Herod. vii. 136; Just. vi. 2; Plut. *Artox.* 22; Aelian. *Var. hist.* i. 21.

[42] Calvin W. McEwan, *The Oriental Origin of Hellenistic Kingship* (1934), pp. 17 ff.

[43] Xen. *Cyrop.* viii. 3. 10.

[44] Herod. vii. 16; Curt. viii. 4. 17; Valer. Max. v. 1; Front. *Strat.* iv. 6. 3.

[45] Chares of Mitylene, *loc. cit.*

ace was not quite finished, the son must add stairways along the southern face, which his own artists decorated with their characteristic reliefs. On the huge inscribed antae which closed both ends of the portico, Xerxes even remembered that the palace had been commenced by his father Darius.[46]

After the completion of the apadana, Xerxes changed his base of operations. A new palace was erected farther east between his father's triple portal and banquet hall and his treasury; their respective northern fronts were so arranged that they appeared to be deliberately stepped back from west to east. From the great triple gateway of Darius, a side entrance led to steps which gave access to the main hall of the new building. On the east and west sides were long, narrow rooms. To the north an open portico with a single row of four columns seemed to offer access to the service quarters but actually led only to a single corridor-like room. The above-mentioned steps connecting the triple gateway with this area led to a long, narrow corridor, from which the visitor returned to a small court east of the corridor, and then to the main room still farther east, which was roofed by two columns and decorated by receding niches quite similar to those on the exterior walls of the treasury.[47]

On the south of the courtyard was the entrance to the palace proper, two rows of four wooden columns each, between antae; beyond were guardrooms, on the jambs of whose doors were to be seen, appropriately, two Immortals. Passing the familiar scene of the king under a parasol, the visitor entered the great hall, forest-like because of its three rows of four columns. Ten stone niches surrounded the hall, while to right and left long, narrow rooms were reached through doorways on which were pictured the fight of the king with a lion or a demon monster with scorpion tail. Set irregularly on the right side, a single door, on which one might behold the king and his attendant bearing fly-flap and napkin, opened into a narrow room which completed the semipublic part of the palace. None of the reliefs is inscribed, though in style and content they show close likeness to similar reliefs in the palace of Darius, which this building also resembles in ground plan. From it Xerxes had brought a doorknob of artificial lapis whose inscription explained that it was made for the "house

<hr>

[46] Xerxes, *Persepolis* c, Weissbach, *op. cit.*, pp. 110 ff.; Unvala, *op. cit.*, I, 342.

[47] Erich F. Schmidt, *The Treasury of Persepolis and Other Discoveries in the Homeland of the Achaemenians* (1939), pp. 89 ff.

of Darius," and his son prepared a duplicate which bore his own name.[48]

To the west of the final treasury building, and separated from it by a street, was the harem which Xerxes completed for his imperious queen, Amestris. Surrounded by the guardrooms of the watchful eunuchs was a tier of six apartments to house the royal ladies. Each tier consisted of a tiny hall whose roof was upheld by only four columns, and a bedroom so minute that even with a single occupant the atmosphere must have been stifling. More apartments of similar size and character continued the harem toward the west, where at one point the original height of the building is indicated by cuttings in a wall of bedrock.

THE GATEWAY OF "ALL LANDS"

When we examine the general plan of the Persepolis structures, the reason for the change of base becomes obvious: Xerxes was developing a building project even more ambitious than his father's apadana. In the original plan of Darius, the visitor who had climbed the platform staircase would at once turn right and then ascend the north stairway to the apadana. Xerxes had completed this plan, but so superior was the work of his artists that only the reliefs on the eastern stairway became worthy of attention.

Thus far, the northern and northwestern sections of the platform had remained unutilized; Xerxes filled in most of this gap. Directly in the axis of the platform stairway he placed a monumental portal, eighty-two feet on the side and forty feet high, with only a side gate toward the apadana. To either side of the entrance the visitor passed between enormous bulls, twenty feet high and half-free from the stone. Above their bodies might be read: "I am Xerxes, the great king, king of kings, king of the lands of many peoples, king of this great earth far and wide. By Ahuramazda's favor I made this gate 'All Lands.' Much else that is beautiful has been built in this Parsa which I and my father have built. What now has been built and appears beautiful, all that we have built by the favor of Ahuramazda."[49]

Under the four tall columns with vertical volutes and bull capitals, the visitor of rank might await his summons on a bench along the wall; in the middle of the north side a step and a pedestal perhaps bore the royal symbol for his adoration. Then he would be conducted

[48] Herzfeld, *op. cit.*, Nos. 10–11.

[49] Xerxes, *Persepolis a*, Weissbach, *op. cit.*, pp. 106 ff.; Unvala, *op. cit.*, I, 342–43.

due east between two human-headed bulls. Like their slightly smaller
Assyrian predecessors, these bulls wore the three horns of the highest
divinity, high feather crowns starred with rosettes, and long, curled,
square-cut beards; their bodies were also feathered, with their wings
curving high upward. Again the visitor passed almost due east to a
smaller gate, now sadly ruined.

THE "HALL OF A HUNDRED COLUMNS"

From here, the visitor turned sharply south to enter a massive new
structure first begun by Xerxes in his declining years and known in our
day as the "hall of a hundred columns." Before the audience hall on the
north was a porch, with two rows of eight columns topped by double
human-headed bulls. The anta at either end was composed of the fore-
part of a colossal bull; each body was treated in a purely architectural
manner, but the head proves to our amazement that the Persian artist
understood a refinement of sculptural composition which hitherto we
had assumed had just been invented by the Greeks. As a result of the
use of this refinement, each head is turned slightly toward the spec-
tator, who, as he passes between them, sees at every step a different
but still rhythmic outline of the parts. Closer examination shows that
the refinement is deliberate; if a plumb line is dropped from the top of
the head, it will be observed that the right side is not quite the same as
the left, for the head is slightly tilted to one side and the details on the
outside are not so carefully worked out as on the inside, which is more
likely to be observed by the casual passer-by.[50]

Doorways to the guard chambers at either corner beyond the antae
were protected more adequately than by the bulls, at least to modern
thought, by two colossal Immortals. We may enter the great hall
through either of two gateways, for two is the number of entrances
on each of the four sides. Only short stretches of crude brick walling
were left to be pressed into the scooped-out edges of the forty-four
doors, windows, and storage niches of stone set closely together. The
columns from which the structure takes its modern name were in ten
rows of ten each; they were similar to those of the apadana, though
much smaller and set more closely together. Gateways to north and
south represent the audience scene, the king enthroned under a canopy
and winged disk, the two attendants behind, and the nobles before;
on the north, five tiers of guards, alternately Persians and Medes, face a

[50] The refinement was observed by Cleta Margaret Olmstead only after the head had been set
up in the Oriental Institute's Iranian gallery.

narrow path which leads upward to their master, but on the south they are replaced by the twenty-eight supporting peoples. On the jambs of the side gates, the king, his skirt girded high, is represented with his gold dagger[51] knifing the rampant beasts of evil—the bull, the lion, the winged lion with eagle claws, and the demon with lion's head and scorpion tail. All these sculptures are the work of artists trained in the school of Xerxes and represent the very finest of classical Achaemenid art. Their careful attention to minute detail and their smooth finish cannot but delight us. Perhaps it is a little too smooth, for strength has been lost, and we can foresee rapidly approaching decay.

In the development of Persian art, the sculptures of Xerxes' harem-palace form the transition between the "hall of a hundred columns" and the apadana of Darius and of Xerxes in his younger days. In turn they explain why the southwest corner of the new audience chamber is physically joined by steps to the northwest corner of the harem-palace: to permit easy access by the king. Another significant fact emerges when we contrast the audience chamber with the apadana in respect to its ground plan. Although the general plans are much alike, there are essential differences. There is only one approach to the chamber, that to the north, and the whole treatment of anta, capital, and column is not the same. In place of porches on the other sides, there are only narrow corridor rooms. The columns of the great hall are much smaller and more closely crowded together. New also is the large use of stone niches to minimize the employment of crude mud. Most startling of all is the use for an audience hall of reliefs hitherto considered appropriate only for a residential palace.[52]

XERXES' LAST PALACE

The characteristic ground plan and the style of the reliefs prove that the last residence which Xerxes constructed for himself on the highest point of the platform is to be dated to these same last years of his reign. Almost due west of the harem-palace courtyard, a flight of steps leads up to a small gatehouse of four columns which gives access to a long but rather narrow elevated court ended on the west by a descending staircase into the court south of the palace of Darius, the stairway is prolonged to join the northwest corner of the new palace. Inscriptions

[51] Herod. ix. 80.

[52] That Xerxes laid the foundations of this house while his son built and completed it is stated in the newly discovered inscription of Artaxerxes I (Herzfeld, *op. cit.*, No. 22); the style of the reliefs indicates that Xerxes played a larger part in the construction.

on these stairways announce that it was Xerxes who built this residence,[53] while the style of the reliefs, portraying banquet-hall attendants, as clearly indicate their relatively late date. To water this residence a tunnel, which tapped that leading to Darius' palace, was cut south through the court and along the palace axis.

South of this court is a lone portico, twelve columns in two rows between antae which bear inscriptions similar to those on the stairways. From the north, two doors, whose jambs represent the king under his parasol, lead into the square main hall, its pavement the living rock, its roof upheld by six rows of six wooden columns. Stone windows frame attendants bearing food; those to the rear bring ibexes. To east and west of the hall, a door gives entrance to a bedroom with four columns; as in the palace of Darius, the purpose of these rooms is indicated by the door-jamb reliefs of youths with censer, pail, napkin, and perfume bottle. On north and south of the bedchambers are rooms, twelve in all, which are nothing but cubbyholes. On the majority of the palace reliefs, even on the royal drapery, we find repeated the same inscription.[54] A narrow passage along the south wall, once protected by a balustrade of stone, offers a fine view over the plain. At either end, a narrow flight of steps descends sharply to the lower level, namely, to the western rooms of the harem.

Darius may claim all credit for the choice of the site, the construction of the massive inclosure walls, and the general plan. The major buildings were begun, but he must leave their completion to his son. Xerxes is the great builder at Persepolis, and to him must be assigned significant changes in the plan. During his reign Achaemenid art reached its classic development. But his plans were too ambitious. The work slowed down in his later years, and he died before either the "hall of a hundred columns" or his palace was quite complete.[55]

---

[53] Xerxes, *Persepolis* db; Weissbach, *op. cit.*, pp. 112 ff.

[54] Xerxes, *Persepolis* e; Weissbach, *op. cit.*, pp. 114–15.

[55] Artaxerxes I, Persepolis inscriptions, Herzfeld, *op. cit.*, Nos. 20–22; Weissbach, *op. cit.*, pp. 120–21.

Chapter XXI

OVERTAXATION AND ITS RESULTS

THE ESCAPE OF THEMISTOCLES

EURYMEDON was the high-water mark of Athenian success against Persia and the triumph of conservative rule in Athens. After Cimon's victory over his mighty rival in 470, Themistocles had retired to Argos, whence he continued his anti-Spartan policy. Pursued by Sparta as by the pro-Spartan party now all-powerful at Athens, he must flee for his life. Rightly or wrongly, he had been accused of Medism by his political enemies, and he determined to take advantage of the accusation to find a safe refuge at the only place where it seemed possible—under the protection of the great king.

After a series of thrilling adventures, he finally escaped to Ephesus. Still fearing assassination, he was carried to Susa hidden in a tent under pretense that a Persian lady was being escorted. Here he made friends with the all-powerful Artabanus, the *hazarapat* or commander of the palace guard. But while he was devoting the year to a study of the Persian language and customs, a palace revolution took place.

ACCESSION OF ARTAXERXES I

Near the end of 465,[1] Xerxes was assassinated in his bedchamber. At the head of the conspirators was Artabanus, aided by another favorite, the eunuch chamberlain Aspamitres, and by Megabyzus, son of Zopyrus, the king's son-in-law, who resented the refusal of Xerxes to take action on his charge that his wife Amytis was an adulteress. Xerxes was buried in a rock-cut tomb he had excavated in the cliff to the east of his father's; though without inscription, the execution is even finer.

His successor should have been his eldest son Darius. But Darius had good reason to hate his father, who had seduced his wife Artaynte,[2] and Artabanus found no difficulty in persuading the eighteen-year-old Artaxerxes to slay his brother as a parricide. Soon after, Artabanus fell out with the new monarch and attempted to put him also out of

---

[1] R. A. Parker and W. H. Dubberstein, *Babylonian Chronology, 626 B.C.—A.D. 45* (1942), p. 15.

[2] Herod. ix. 108.

289

the way. Artabanus was now looking forward to seizure of the throne for himself, but he was betrayed by his fellow-conspirator Megabyzus, who had no wish to see the dynasty supplanted.

Although he managed to wound Artaxerxes, Artabanus lost his life in the ensuing scuffle. Aspamitres died by an inhuman type of punishment called the "boat." In a later battle the three surviving sons of Artabanus perished and Megabyzus was dangerously wounded. Forgetting that he had once accused his wife of unchastity, Megabyzus had made his peace with Amytis, and, through the intercession of her brother Artaxerxes, her sister Rhodogune, and their mother Amestris, he was cured by the skill of Apollonides, the court physician from Cos. Another son of Xerxes, Hystaspis, revolted in Bactria; the first battle was a draw, but, in the second, Artaxerxes, aided by a strong wind blowing directly in his enemies' faces, won the victory.[3]

THEMISTOCLES' ARRIVAL

Roxanes, the new chief of the guard, was a bitter personal enemy of Themistocles. Despite his opposition, Themistocles used his newly acquired knowledge of Persian to win over the king in a personal interview. Artaxerxes believed his claim that he had sent the message to Xerxes in good faith and trusted his many promises for the future. He was given the honorary title of "King's Friend," together with the rule of certain subject Greek cities; in lieu of support at the court, he was assigned the revenues from these cities: Magnesia paid him fifty talents for his bread, Myus supplied his fish, Lampsacus its noted wines, Percote and old Scepsis his bed and clothing. Epixyes, satrap of Phrygia, attempted to assassinate him at the Lion's Head, but Themistocles reached Scepsis in safety. He settled down at Magnesia, where he married a Persian lady whose daughter he dedicated as priestess of the Didymene Mother of the Gods. Feasts were instituted in various cities, as the inhabitants long remembered, and at Magnesia he minted coins in his own name and with the figure of the nude standing Apollo, the god already honored by Darius.[4]

---

[3] Ctes. *Pers.*, Epit. 59–62; Aristot. *Polit.* v. 8. 14; Deinon, Frag. 21(M); Duris, Frag. 8(J); Diod. xi. 69; Just. iii. 1; Nepos *De reg.* i. 4–5; Aelian. *Var. hist.* xiii. 3.

[4] *IG*, Vol. I, No. 432; Charon Lampscen., *Hell.*, Frag. 11(J); Herod. viii. 109–10; Thuc. i. 135 ff.; Isocr. *Panegyr.* 154; Ephor., Frags. 189 ff.(J); Theopomp., Frags. 86–87(J); Aristot. *Polit. Athen.* 10. 5; 25. 3; Neanthes, Frag. 17(J); Diod. xi. 54 ff.; Nepos *Themistocl.* 8 ff.; Strabo xiii. 1. 12; xiv. 1. 10, 40; Plut. *Themistocl.* 16. 27 ff.; *Fort. Alex.* 328F; Athen. i. 29F; xii. 533D; Paus. i. 26. 4; Possis *Hist. magnes.* (*FHG*, IV, 483); Amm. xxii. 8. 4; F. Babelon, *Traité des monnaies*, II, Part II (1910), 74 ff.

THE TRIBUTE LIST OF HERODOTUS

In general, Artaxerxes followed the administrative policies of his father. In Babylonia, he was only "king of lands" though Ishtar of Babylon was honored with a stele, and by 462 it would seem that the priests of Bel Marduk had been reinstated and some of their lands restored.[5] His rare Egyptian inscriptions employ a single cartouche for his name, but on vases inscribed in the four languages he added "Pharaoh the Great."[6]

When compared with the six satrapal lists published by Darius, the list of Xerxes, and his army roster, the official tribute list incorporated by Herodotus[7] shows decided administrative changes. As under Cyrus, there were again twenty satrapies, but the larger number of Darius had been reduced by the union of some hitherto separate. This process, already to be detected in the army list of Xerxes, but accelerated in the tribute list of Artaxerxes, again suggests actual loss of territory.

THE EASTERN SATRAPIES

Persia had long since ceased to pay taxes. The huge satrapy of Media, including now the Paricani (the Hyrcanians) and the "Straight-Cap Men," the Saka Tigrakhauda, was assessed a tribute of 450 talents, to which was added 100,000 sheep and the pasturage of 50,000 Nesaean horses for the king. Susa and the Cissaean land paid 300 talents. Armenia with Pactyica and the country as far as the Black Sea paid 400; the satrapy sent 20,000 Nesaean foals yearly to the king for the Mithra feast.[8] The Matieni, Saspeires,[9] and Alarodians were assessed at 200 talents, the Moschians, Tibarenians, Macrones, Mosynoeci, and Mares 300. Every five years the Colchians presented a "gift" of a hundred boys and a hundred girls, predecessors of the Circassian beauties of Turkish days.

If in this region the strengthening of Persian rule already manifest in the army list of Xerxes has been carried still further, the union of satrapies in eastern Iran begun by the father and continued by the son points in the opposite direction. The Caspians, Pausicae, Pantimathi, and Daritae paid 200 talents, the Sacae and Caspii 250, the Parthians, Chorasmians, Sogdians, and Arians 300; that four satrapies of Darius

---

[5] *MDOG*, XXXII (1906), 5; J. N. Strassmaier, *Actes du huitième congrès international des orientalistes* (1889), II, Sec. I B (1893), 279 ff., No. 24.

[6] J. Couyat and P. Montet, *Les Inscriptions du Ouadi Hammamat* (1912), pp. 61, 89; M. Borchardt, *ÄZ*, XLIX (1911), 74 ff.

[7] iii. 89 ff.   [8] Strabo xi. 13. 7-8; 14. 9.   [9] Cf. Herod. iv. 37.

should thus be merged into one reveals serious difficulties in tax collection if not actual losses on this frontier. Again, three former satrapies are joined into one comprising the Sagartians, Sarangians, Thamaneans, Utians, Mycians, and the exile islands in the Persian Gulf, this vast territory paying 600 talents; the absence of Arachosia from the list is one more reason for suspicion. Two satrapies are united in the case of the Sattagydians, Gandarians, Dadicae, and Aparytae, whose tribute was 170 talents. Bactria as far as the Aegli paid 360, the Paricanians, worshipers of the unclean desert spirits, the Pairika, and the Asiatic Ethiopians are listed for the impossible sum of 400 talents.

The Gandarians thus make their last appearance as Persian tribute-paying subjects in the lists of Artaxerxes,[10] though the land continued to be known under the name of Gandhara down to classic Indian times. The Indians of Hindush nevertheless remained loyal to the reign of the last Darius, who recognized their loyalty and their fighting ability by placing them next to the Thousand Immortals who guarded his person.[11] There was enough contact with the West almost to the end of the fifth century for Herodotus to be able to declare that in number the Indians were far greater than all the other peoples known to the Greeks,[12] that they paid their Persian lords the heaviest tribute (360 talents of gold dust),[13] that Indian dogs were used in the Persian army,[14] and that in his day four Babylonian villages were set aside for their support.[15] He noticed the change in war practices from the chariot-driving Aryans glorified in the Indian epics to the cavalry intermingled with them, while by 480 the Indian contingent was composed of cavalry and infantry.[16] Herodotus does tell of amazingly large ants who dug out the gold in the desert and compelled the natives who attempted to steal it to flee for their lives,[17] but he has some slight knowledge of Indian tribes who live beyond the Persian frontier, he has heard of Indians who will not kill any living being[18] and of the marvelous tree cotton from which others weave their clothing.[19] There is, however, no mention of the chief city of Hindush, Taxila, which was rapidly taking the place of Peucela, the former capital of Gandhara.

[10] Ibid. iii. 91.

[11] Arr. Anab. iii. 11. 5.

[12] Herod. iii. 94; v. 3.

[13] Ibid. iii. 94.

[14] Ibid. i. 192.

[15] Ibid. vii. 187.

[16] Ibid. 86; viii. 113.

[17] Ibid. vii. 98, 102, 104–5.

[18] Ibid. 100.

[19] Ibid. 106.

PLATE XXXIII

Indians (courtesy Oriental Institute)

Armenians (courtesy Oriental Institute)

Cilicians (courtesy Oriental Institute)

THE SUBJECT PEOPLES (FROM APADANA AT PERSEPOLIS)

PLATE XXXIV

Portrait (courtesy Oriental Institute)

Bracelet (courtesy Oriental Institute)   Vase (courtesy Oriental Institute)

A PHOENICIAN AND HIS TRIBUTE

PLATE XXXV

West from Syrian Coast

Acropolis from Agora at Athens

THE MEDITERRANEAN, EAST AND WEST

PLATE XXXVI

The Euripus and Euboea

The Canal and Corinth

APPROACHES TO MAINLAND GREECE

PLATE XXXVII

Apadana (courtesy Oriental Institute)

Delos

CENTERS IN GREECE AND PERSIA

PLATE XXXVIII

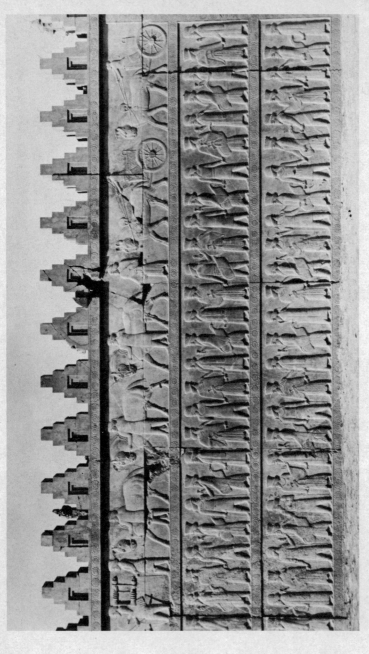

The King's Chariots, Horses, and Footstool, with Attendant Nobles

From Apadana (courtesy Oriental Institute)

PLATE XXXIX

King Fighting Beast (courtesy Oriental Institute)

General View (courtesy Oriental Institute)

HUNDRED-COLUMN HALL, PERSEPOLIS

PLATE XL

Bull from Hundred-Column Hall (courtesy Oriental Institute)

"Xerxes Harem Palace" (courtesy Oriental Institute)

RECONSTRUCTIONS OF ACHAEMENID ART

BABYLONIA

After its last revolt, Babylonia had been joined to Assyria and its identity had been lost. Its silver payment was the highest in the empire (1,000 talents), while its humiliating "gift" consisted of five hundred boys to be made eunuchs. The fertility of its soil and its proximity to Susa in times when land transport of food over long distances was almost impossible laid upon it also the crushing burden of providing supplies for the court four months in the year. Herodotus tells us that in his day, when Tritantaechmes, son of Artabazus, held the satrapy, it gave him daily an *artaba* of silver. The peasants must also support his war horses, his eight hundred stallions and sixteen thousand mares; four large villages were freed from other payments to feed his Indian dogs.

Herodotus has a story that formerly the Babylonians auctioned off their young women, providing dowries for the ugly from the sums received for the beauties; the story may be apocryphal, but not his statement that now, to prevent their daughters from suffering violence and being dragged off to foreign towns, the natives dedicated them to be courtesans, for since the Persian conquest the common people had been so mistreated by their masters that their families had been ruined.[20]

ACROSS THE RIVER AND EGYPT

Across the River, detached from Babylonia a generation back and now including Cyprus in addition to Palestine-Syria, paid a tribute fixed at 350 talents.[21] Libya, including Cyrene and Barca, had once more been incorporated with Egypt, and the enlarged satrapy was assessed 700 talents, to which must be added profits from the leased fisheries of Lake Moeris and 120,000 measures of grain furnished a Persian garrison at the White Castle of Memphis and such mercenaries as the Jews at Elephantine. Every three years the Ethiopians on the border brought their "gift": two choenices of virgin gold, two hundred ebony logs, five boys, and twenty elephant-tusks.

ARABIA

Long ago abandoned as a tribute-paying satrapy, Arabia brought a yearly "gift" of a thousand talents of frankincense. Herodotus tells us that the trees are defended by winged snakes and vipers which can be driven off only by burning storax. Myrrh is easy to secure, but cas-

[20] *Ibid.* i. 192, 196.

[21] In 462 we hear of Bel-shunu, governor of Across the River (Strassmaier, *op. cit.*, No. 25).

sia grows in shallow lakes guarded by batlike animals which are avoided by covering body and eyes with skins. Cinnamon (a Phoenician word) consists of stalks carried by huge birds—the rocs of later story—to nests of mud on the cliffs; the Arabs lay out great chunks of meat for the birds to carry off, but the weight of these breaks the nests and the fallen cinnamon may then be picked up. Labdanum comes from the beards of he-goats. There are two breeds of sheep, one of which has a tail eighteen inches broad, the other fifty-four inches long; the shepherds place carts under these tails to bear them along.[22]

From these travelers' yarns, including a modicum of truth but deliberately fashioned by the Nabataean traders to frighten away foreigners who might envy their control of the lucrative spice trade with southwestern Arabia, we may turn to the native records. Alphabetic writing had begun in the Sinaitic peninsula during the eighteenth century when some native utilized the incomplete consonantal alphabet, already formed in Egypt for foreign names and words, for his own language; native names were given to the pictographic signs, and their consonantal values were assigned on the acrophonic principle.[23] While the form from which our own alphabet was evolved developed in Phoenicia, another appears in the eighth century at Solomon's port on the Red Sea, Ezion Geber. By the middle of the sixth century the inhabitants of Dedan, well into the North Arabian Desert, were using for their North Arabic dialect this developed Sinaitic form of writing for rude graffiti. One such graffito gives us the name of a Dedanite king.[24] A cylinder seal found at Ana on the middle Euphrates just before it enters Babylonia proves trade in this direction and Babylonian influence in Arab culture.[25] A scarab with a Dedanite legend, "Great Is Adad," shows similar relationships with Egypt.[26] There are several other graffiti, mostly from Dedan, the modern el Ula.[27]

Even closer to the original Sinaitic character and presumably of about

[22] Herod. iii. 107 ff.

[23] Cf. Olmstead, History of Palestine and Syria (1931), pp. 90 ff.

[24] A. J. Janssen and R. Savignac, Mission archéologique en Arabie (hereinafter cited as JS) (1902–22), No. 138.

[25] W. H. Ward, Seal Cylinders of Western Asia (1910), Figs. 768, 1207, 1211; D. H. Müller, Epigraphische Denkmäler aus Arabien ("Denkschriften der Kaiserlichen Akademie der Wissenschaften," Phil.-hist. Klasse, Vol. XXXVII [Wien, 1889]), Pl. V.

[26] M. S. R. Cohen, Documents sudarabiques (1934), Nos. 34–35; a gem, Müller, op. cit., Pl. V, No. 20.

[27] H. Grimme, OLZ, XXXV (1932), 753 ff.; F. V. Winnett, A Study of the Lihyanite and Thammudic Inscriptions (1937), pp. 10–11, 49–50.

the same date is the earliest form of what is called the Thammudic, whose brief records are found near Tema. We have family groups, such as "His name is Ibn Fagiꜣ"; "His mark, Ibn Fagiꜣ"; "By Samrafa, he has given his name"; "Yakfuril has given his mark." "By Biathar, son of Gilf, he is lovesick" is unexpected. "By Samda, he camped here," "Rahimil, son of Busrat, camped in Dedan," and "the caravan" witness the desert trade.[28]

Other graffiti throw light on religion. "Naamil, son of Hafraz. Allah is exalted" introduces us to the god of the Moslems a millennium before Mohammed. Samda honors in his name Sam, the Salm introduced by the famous stone from Tema; he is answered: "Salm is a mean god," "A foul god is Salm." Perhaps this rivalry between the tribal divinities is the reason Naamil insists that Allah is exalted.[29]

According to Herodotus, the only Arab gods are Orotalt, who corresponds to Dionysus, and Alilat, who is Aphrodite. The worshipers cut their hair and shave their temples like the god. They make pledges which are binding on their friends and fellow-tribesmen; a third man, the go-between, cuts with a sharp stone the second finger; with a scrap from the himation of each he smears the blood on seven stones placed between them, invoking these two gods.[30]

Before the end of this century, so it would seem, the kings of Dedan had been supplanted at Dedan itself by the kings of Lihyan; a few of their inscriptions, written in an earlier form of script, are found also at near-by Hegra. Typical inscriptions are "Abdmanat the trustworthy; grant him long life, O God, and good luck"; "Prosper the workmen"; "Baalsamin has consecrated the rock so that no woman can ascend it—by Bahiani the priestess";[31] "Niran, son of Hadiru, inscribed his name in the days of Gashm, son of Shahar, and Abd, governor of Dedan"; the date is closely fixed, for this is the Arab Geshm, opponent of Nehemiah.[32]

THE SATRAPIES OF ASIA MINOR

The peculiar status of Cilicia, ruled again by a native Syennesis, is reflected by its tribute. Of the 500 talents collected, 140 were retained at home for payment of the native cavalry guard; a white horse for each of the 360 days of the year was a further "gift." On the border

[28] *JS*, Nos. 557, 573, 376, 495, 561, 517, 513, 580.

[29] *Ibid.*, Nos. 450, 519, 546, 548; cf. Winnett, *op. cit.*, pp. 18 ff., 50.

[30] Herod. iii. 8.

[31] *JS*, Nos. 8, 264, 319, 64; Winnett, *op. cit.*, pp. 11 ff.   [32] *JS*, No. 349; Neh. 2:19.

between Cilicia and Syria lay Poseidium, said to have been founded by Amphilochus, son of Amphiaraus, an early identification of a local Cilician divinity with those of the Greeks.[33]

Cappacodia and its "Syrians" had been merged—as had also the Mariandynians, Paphlagonians, and Asiatic Thracians or Bithynians —with the Hellespontine Greeks; the former Second Ionia was generally known to the Greeks as Dascyleium, and the huge satrapy paid a tribute of 360 talents. Ionia proper included also the Magnesian and Aeolian Greeks, as well as the Carians, Lycians, Milyans, and Pamphylians, which no longer constituted the satrapy of Karka. The enlarged administrative unit could afford to pay 400 talents, while 500 talents were not too much for the satrapy of Sardis, now comprising, in addition to the Lydians, the Mysians, Lasonians, Cabalians, and Hygenians.

According to Herodotus, the Lydians, Carians, Caunians, and Mysians all spoke the same language,[34] but they did not use quite the same characters. Not long after the Greeks had borrowed their alphabet from the Phoenicians, by the middle of the eighth century at least, the Phrygians in turn had borrowed the alphabet from eastern Greeks; "Golden" Midas, opponent of Assyrian Sargon,[35] had left his record at Tyana in Cappadocia and on his tomb at the Midas City. Since his language was Indo-European, similar sounds were easily represented by similar characters. Somewhat later, the Pamphylians borrowed a Western form of the alphabet for their Caucasian language.[36]

Three other Caucasian-speaking peoples followed a different principle; they borrowed such characters as fitted approximately their sounds, but they adapted or invented new characters for the more numerous vowels and for the additional nasals or nasalized vowels in which their languages were so rich. Of these, the first to be employed was Carian, known to us mostly through the scratched names of mercenaries serving the Twenty-sixth Dynasty in Egypt and through a few coins and more formal inscriptions from the earliest Achaemenid times.[37]

The Lydians borrowed or adapted their alphabet of twenty-six

[33] Herod. iii. 91; Myriandic Gulf, Herod. iv. 38.   [34] *Ibid*. i. 171-72.

[35] Olmstead, *History of Assyria* (1923), pp. 221 ff., 422.

[36] V. E. Gardthausen, "Kleinasiatische Alphabete," *PW*, XI (1921), 601-12; W. Brandenstein, "Kleinasiatische Ursprachen," *PW*, Supplementband, VI, (1935), 165-81.

[37] A. H. Sayce, *Transactions of the Society of Biblical Archaeology*, IX (1893), 112 ff.; *Proceedings of the Society of Biblical Archaeology*, XVII (1895), 39 ff.; F. Bork, *Archiv für Orientforschung*, VII (1931), 14 ff.; J. Friedrich, *Kleinasiatische Sprachdenkmäler* (1932), pp. 90 ff.; W. Brandenstein, "Karische Sprache," *PW*, Supplementband VI (1935), 140-46.

characters from Rhodes; brief inscriptions from vases or from buildings date from the native kings, but all the longer inscriptions are from the Achaemenid period. One from Sardis, written under Artaxerxes II, is a bilingual, Aramaic and Lydian, and assists our decipherment; but it cannot yet be asserted that these inscriptions are freely read.[38] The twenty-nine Lycian characters have much in common with the Lydian, but only the initial characters or monograms of royal names on coins indicate their use thus early; true inscriptions, of which a hundred and fifty are now known, must be assigned to the last half of the fifth or to the fourth century.[39]

All these inscriptions are still in process of decipherment. The value of their signs may be learned from brief bilinguals, Greek and Lydian, Greek and Lycian, Greek and Aramaic, or from transliterations of Greek or Iranian names. These fix the meaning of a few words and afford a glimpse into the structure of the language. Despite tantalizing likenesses to Indo-European, it seems virtually certain that we are dealing with Caucasian languages, perhaps distant kin to the Haldian and true Hittite. This is evident from the large use of nasals and nasalized vowels and from the intermediate value of certain sounds leading to difficulty in deciding when foreign names should be transliterated b or p, d or t, g or k. It is still more clear in the grammar, if grammar it can be called, in which inflection in our sense is absent, in which there is no gender but distinction between animate and inanimate, and in which quite different distinctions from our familiar mood and tense are indicated by the verb.[40]

Herodotus cites some of the peculiarities of the Caunians, who belonged to this group of peoples. They were reputed to find their chief entertainment in drinking bouts, the men, women, and children in their separate groups. A curious ceremony was observable when, in full panoply, they drove out the foreign religions, smiting the air with their swords, and forcing the stranger gods beyond their boundaries.[41]

RUINOUS TAXATION

From the satrapies a constant stream of silver flowed in, reckoned by Herodotus as amounting to 9,880[42] Euboeic talents, presumably re-

[38] Now collected by W. H. Buckler, *Sardis*, Vol. VI, Part 2 (1916–24).

[39] Collected by E. Kalinka, *Tituli Asiae Minoris*, Vol. I: *Tituli Lyciae lingua Lycia conscripti* (1901).

[40] A. Torp, *Lykische Beiträge* (1898–1901); T. Kluge, *Die Lykische Inschriften* (1910); F. Bork, *Skizze des Lükischen* (1926); G. Deeters, "Lykia," *PW*, XXVI, 2282 ff.

[41] Herod. i. 172.   [42] *Ibid.* iii. 95; the manuscripts read 9,540.

duced from 7,600 Babylonian talents. Reckoning with him the relation of gold to silver as thirteen to one, the gold dust from India
would be 4,680 Euboic talents, a grand total of 14,560. Our own recent shifting of gold values adds to the difficulty of ancient shifts and
makes it quite impossible to compute the sum in modern terms, but if
we say something like twenty millions of dollars with purchasing
value several times greater, we may form some conception of the Persian monarch's wealth.

Little of this vast sum was ever returned to the satrapies. It was the
custom to melt down the gold and silver and to pour it into jars
which were then broken and the bullion stored. Only a small portion
was ever coined, and then usually for the purchase of foreign soldiers
or of foreign statesmen. Thus, despite the precious metals newly
mined, the empire was rapidly drained of its gold and silver; our Babylonian documents clearly witness a lessened use of the precious metals.
For a time, credit made possible a continuance of business, but the in-
sensate demand for actual silver in the payment of taxes drove the landlords in increasing numbers to the loan sharks, who gave money in exchange for the pledge—the actual use of the field or the slave, whose
services were thus lost until the improbable redemption. As coined
money became a rarity, hoarded by the loan sharks, credit increased
the inflation, and rapidly rising prices made the situation still more intolerable.

The drastic changes enforced by Xerxes and dimly seen in the few
documents from Babylonia which survived the destruction of Babylon, appear in their full rigor in the somewhat more numerous ones
from the reign of Artaxerxes. For the first time, a large proportion of
the land held by the citizen bow tenure is in the hands of Persians,
though now and then we hear of the "share" still possessed by the
former owner. The panel of judges tends to be composed of a majority
of Persians. New officials appear in numbers (generally with Persian
titles), and the staffs have Persian names (though the fathers may
have good Babylonian ones), but quite as often the subordinates are
slaves. Babylonia has become truly polyglot, for Iranian, Egyptian,
Aramaic, and Hebrew names are common. Naturally, our first interest
is in the large Jewish colony, but other ethnic groups are settled in
the "House of the Tyrians," the "House of the Cimmerians," and the
like. But the most significant change is the levy of new taxes by the
new officials. At Persepolis we saw the glittering parade of the subject
peoples, bringing their gifts to Darius and Xerxes at the New Year's fes-

tival. Babylonian documents present the reverse of the picture, the "gift for the king's house" added as a matter of course to the other burdensome taxes and included without comment in the total. We may observe holders of bow land borrowing money for taxes and "gift" at 40 per cent per annum (double the 20 per cent standard since the days of Hammurabi) from such loan sharks as the Murashu family of Nippur, whose archives we happen to possess. Their pledged lands, meanwhile, were worked by the loan sharks for their own advantage until title was completely lost to the original owners. When additional fields reverted to the state because of failure to pay taxes, they were actually leased by corrupt officials to these same loan sharks! No more than the natives were the Persian landholders exempt from this ruinous taxation. The inevitable result was that the whole period is filled by the story of revolts by oppressed subjects.

For a time the disaffected satrapies were held down by a still efficient administration and army. One of the most effective elements in this system of repression was the intelligence division—the *angareion*, as the Persians called it—by which news was rushed across the empire. Each messenger rode a day; at the evening halt another horse was ready with his successor. Day and night, without regard to weather, the posts kept the capital in touch with the most distant parts of the empire.[43]

They followed well-traveled routes—roads we can scarcely call them, for while the Assyrians had paved roads and milestones, at least near the cities,[44] there is no indication that in this the Persians followed their example as they did in their correspondence between provincial official and court. From still another official document, Herodotus describes for us the Royal Road, free from brigandage, with its fine stopping places for the night (*katalyseis*) and the posting stations for fresh horses. Like the similar itinerary along the more southern route to the east, utilized by Xenophon for his *anabasis* and so unfortunately missing for his *katabasis*, like the "Parthian Stations" of Isidore of Charax and the still later Roman *itineraria*, it gave the distance in *stathmoi*, "stages," and also in parasangs, from one posting station to the next. Herodotus estimates the parasang as 30 stades, $2\frac{1}{2}$ miles; actually, like the modern *farsakh*, it is the distance

[43] *Ibid.* viii. 98; Xen. *Cyrop.* viii. 6. 17–18.
[44] Olmstead, *History of Assyria*, pp. 271, 334, 556.

traversed on foot in an hour's time. His estimate of the average day's journey, 150 stades or a little less than 19 miles, is probably not too much exaggerated.

From Sardis, with its connection to the Aegean coast, the road ran through Lydia and Phrygia to the Halys River, 20 stages, 94½ parasangs (236 miles), which is remarkably close to the actual distance. Before the river was crossed, there was a gorge, guarded by a strong fort; apparently the earlier bridge[45] had been permitted to fall into disuse.

From the Halys the road traversed Cappadocia by a great loop, which testified to the historic fact that once the road center was the Hittite capital, and reached the Cilician frontier, where two gorges were held by two forts. This clearly describes the Cilician Gates, but the distance traversed—28 stades, 104 parasangs, 260 miles—is quite impossible. There are no more difficulties of terrain than in the preceding section, yet the actual distance is only about a half. According to Herodotus, the road then ran through Cilicia only 3 stades, 15½ parasangs, 38 miles—not quite the distance through the easily traversed plain from the Cilician to the Amanus Gates.

We should then expect to continue through North Syria and Mesopotamia, but instead we cross the border of Cilicia and Armenia at the Euphrates. This is impossible, since Cilicia never extended to the Euphrates, from which it is separated by the whole mass of the Anti-Taurus. But we now realize what has happened. Herodotus has followed, from about the site of Mazaca, later Caesarea of Cappadocia, the cross-road to the southern route taken by the younger Cyrus and continued along this to the Amanus Gates. Then he turned back to the main road which crossed the Euphrates beyond Melitene; it is the combination of the two routes which gives the long distance of 260 miles.[46]

The royal road passed through the southwestern corner of Armenia only 15 stages, 56½ parasangs, to Elaziz-Harput, and then south across two high passes through the barrier range, with fine views of snow-encircled Lake Göljik. The fort is probably that at the main pass.

Next is the long stretch through Matiene, 34 stages, 137 parasangs. Four rivers must be ferried, the first three named "Tigris." One

---

[45] Herod. i. 75.

[46] Such incorporation of two alternate routes into one is by no means unknown in the later itineraries.

comes from Armenia, the West Tigris, which emerges from a rock tunnel and passes the barrier range through wild scenery to Amida-Diyarbekir, where the road crossed the stream. From here it followed the north bank to the junction of the West Tigris with the east branch, whose source is in Matiene southwest of Lake Van. The third "Tigris" is the Upper Zab, whose abundant waters might well be mistaken by the hasty traveler as an additional branch; this would be crossed at Arbela, for some time the capital of Assyria. The next river crossed was the Gyndes (Diyala); then a journey through the Cissian land (11 stages, 42½ parasangs) brought the traveler to the Choaspes and Susa with the Memnonian palace.[47]

At this point Herodotus ends his account of the road. Later, Ctesias gave the whole east-west route from Ephesus to Bactria and India,[48] but that has been lost. Xenophon gives the important southern branch which passed southeast through Asia Minor, dipped into Cilicia and cut across North Syria, then passed down the Euphrates to Babylon and across the plain to Susa.[49] When to the last we add the southward extension through Syria and Palestine into Egypt of the great road of the older orient,[50] we have traced the main arteries of the Persian Empire, as important for trade as for government.

[47] Herod. v. 52–53.

[48] Ctes. *Pers.*, Epit. 94.

[49] Xen. *Anab.* i.

[50] Olmstead, *History of Palestine and Syria*, pp. 43 ff.

Chapter XXII

TRIUMPHS THROUGH DIPLOMACY

SINCE the crowning victory at the Eurymedon, Cimon had been the acknowledged guide of Athenian policy. When Sparta's helots revolted, he had persuaded the Athenians to dispatch to her assistance a body of troops in accordance with the terms of the war alliance formed at Plataea, for to his thinking the Hellenic League was still in existence despite the Delian League, which he himself had helped to organize. But there were others in Sparta who thought differently; the proffered aid was insultingly rejected, and the Athenian troops were sent home. Under such circumstances it was inevitable that the growing distrust between Sparta and Athens should come to a head. Sparta herself, it could be argued, had denounced the former war alliance; new alliances were made by 462 with Thessaly and with Argos, both notoriously pro-Persian during the wars against the "barbarian."

The influence of Cimon, still clinging to his policy of friendship with Sparta, declined, and the conservatives under his leadership lost their dominance. Ephialtes brought the democrats into power. Their triumph was marked by the ostracism of Cimon in the spring of 461. But this did not mean that Athens was yet prepared to return to the traditional democratic attitude of friendship with the "barbarian" empire.

Democrat enough in home policy, Pericles was at heart both an aristocrat and an imperialist. In fact, if not in theory, the Delian League had already evolved into the Athenian Empire, and Athens had harshly put down the first attempt of an "ally" to secede. Pericles could not but fear lest Artaxerxes try to recover the Greek cities in Asia now paying tribute to Athens, for their loss had never been officially admitted.

During the brief period of leadership exercised by Ephialtes, an Athenian fleet captained by himself had sailed eastward in vain search of the Persian grand fleet, and Pericles followed his example. The war against the "barbarian" was accordingly renewed, and the original purpose of the Delian League was thereby justified. Nevertheless, it was a serious mistake for the great democratic leader to continue his reversal of the traditional policy of the democrats. To be sure, had there actually been a "Greek cause," it might have been pointed out that the Delian League, whatever its demerits, was the only effective makeweight possible against Persian imperialism. But, while over-taxation was bringing in its train a new impulse toward nationalism which was to provoke fresh revolts throughout the empire, Greek nationalism remained confined to the individual city-state. Even here, loyalty was felt to the party rather than to the city, especially when the opposition was in control. By now the subjects of Athens all felt dissatisfied; her enemies could always raise the specious war cry of "freedom," which in practice meant only freedom of the individual city-state under antidemocratic, anti-Athenian leadership. Such a situation was made to order for Persian diplomacy, backed as ever by Persian gold.

REVOLT IN EGYPT

Now that negotiations at Susa had failed, Pericles brought together a fleet of two hundred ships, intending to renew the war by the invasion of Cyprus. Before they sailed, a better opportunity to harass Persia was offered. Ienheru or Inarus, son of Psammetichus and so presumably of the old Saite line, had held a precarious kingship over the Libyans from Mareia above Pharos. Soon after an inscription at the Hamammat quarries had been dated by Artaxerxes,[1] news came of the Bactrian revolt. With the assistance of another pretender named Amyrtaeus, also from Sais,[2] Inarus drove out the hated tax-collectors, collected mercenaries, and soon all Egypt was in revolt. Inarus next requested aid from Athens (460).

Alliance with Egypt offered a grain supply not endangered by the long journey from South Russia through the dangerous Hellespont. The ships destined for the operations in Cyprus were therefore transferred to Egypt in aid of the rebels. The satrap Achaemenes perished in a desperate struggle at Papremis, and his corpse was forwarded in bitter mockery to his royal nephew. Memphis was taken without difficulty—all but the White Wall, which remained in the hands of the Persians and the loyal natives (459).[3]

---

[1] J. Couyat and P. Montet, *Les Inscription du Ouadi Hammamat* (1912), No. 89.

[2] Amyrtaeus II of Sais was presumably his grandson.

[3] Herod. iii. 12, 15; vii. 7; Thuc. i. 104; Ctes. *Pers.*, Epit. 63; Plato *Menex.* 241E; Diod. xi. 71. 3 ff.; 74. 1 ff.; Plut. *Themistocl.* 31. 3.

During the revolt one of the Jewish mercenaries at Elephantine found it necessary to negotiate a loan. Since these Jews were not popular with the natives, the terms were harsh. Every month the abnormally high interest must be assigned from the borrower's salary direct from the treasury; if not paid on time, the interest must be added to the loan. The only concession was that a receipt should be written for all interest and for all repayments on the principal. As a symbol of the new Egyptian freedom, the money was given, not by the king's stone, but by the weight of Ptah; the depreciation of the currency—one shekel in ten or double the normal amount of base metal allowed in the coinage—afforded unpleasant evidence of the unsound financial basis of the new rebel state.[4]

THE WORK OF EZRA IN JUDAH

To the revolt of Egypt was added an Athenian raid on Phoenicia.[5] In Judah an anonymous prophet whom we call Malachi was preaching the coming "day of the Lord," with its summons to open rebellion.[6] Attention was thus focused on the critical situation in Judah. Just at this time, Ezra presented to the court a scheme of Jewish reorganization which made strong appeal to Artaxerxes.

In the official hierarchy, Ezra held a double office. He was the priest, the acknowledged religious leader of his own people, the Jews of Babylonia, the ancestor of the "head of the exile" in later times; he was also the scribe of the law of the God of heaven, or, as we might say, the secretary of state for Jewish affairs, responsible to the king for his community.[7] Though he was interested in a genuine colonization of the weak Jerusalem, his chief desire was to introduce to the Jews of Palestine the still unknown Law (Torah) of Moses as set forth in a new lawbook.

Jews of Babylonia were often substantial citizens. As against the natives, they could be trusted to be loyal. Some of them were already in minor administrative positions. Persia was tolerant of the various ethnic religions but insisted that their cults should be well organized under responsible leadership and that religion should never mask plans for rebellion. The head of the Jewish community in Babylonia was charged with the administration of its own new lawbook, sig-

---

[4] A. E. Cowley, *Aramaic Papyri of the Fifth Century B.C.* (1923), No. 11.

[5] *IG*, I, 433 (929).

[6] Cf. Olmstead, *History of Palestine and Syria* (1931), pp. 581 ff.

[7] Ezra 7:12; H. H. Schaeder, *Esra der Schreiber* (1930), pp. 39 ff.

TRIUMPHS THROUGH DIPLOMACY 305

nificantly entitled *data* like the king's law; he might be expected to remain as loyal to the royal lawbook to which he owed his authority as to that which laid down the procedure for Jewish religion.

As an officer of state, Ezra was granted unusual privileges:

> Artaxerxes, king of kings, to Ezra the priest, scribe of the law of the God of heaven, complete peace. [And now to the point:] I make a decree that all who, in my kingdom, from among the people of Israel and their priests and the Levites, wish to go with you to Jerusalem, shall go, since you have been sent by the king and his seven counselors to make an investigation about Judah and Jerusalem in accordance with the law of your God which is in your hand, and to bring the silver and gold which the king and his counselors have offered to the God of Israel whose house is in Jerusalem, and all the silver and gold which you shall find in the province of Babylon, together with the freewill offering of the people and of the priests, offered for the house of their God which is at Jerusalem. With this money you shall carefully buy bullocks, rams, and lambs (ritually pure), with their accompanying meal offerings and their drink offerings, and shall offer them upon the altar of the house of your God which is at Jerusalem. And with the rest of the silver and the gold do whatever shall seem right to you and to your brethren according to the prescription of your God. Also the utensils which have been given you for the ritual of the house of your God, hand over before the God of Jerusalem. And whatever more is needed for the house of your God, which you shall have reason to bestow, bestow it from the royal treasury. And I, Artaxerxes the king, make a decree to all the treasurers of Across the River that whatever Ezra the priest, scribe of the law of the God of heaven, shall request of you, it shall be done with all care up to a hundred talents of silver and to a hundred *kors* of wheat and a hundred *baths* of wine and a hundred *baths* of oil, and salt without prescribing how much. Whatever is ordered by the God of heaven, let it be done exactly for the house of the God of heaven; for why should there be wrath against the kingdom of the king and his sons?
>
> Also we direct you that as regards the priests, the Levites, and the servants of this house of God, it shall not be lawful to impose upon them tribute in money, tax in kind, and toll [the new imposts so constantly mentioned in contemporary documents from Babylonia]. And you Ezra, according to the wisdom of your God [the lawbook], which is in your hand, appoint magistrates and judges who may judge the people of Across the River, that is, all those who recognize the laws of your God, and instruct him who knows it not. But whoever will not carry out the law of your God, as well as the law of the king, let judgment be executed upon him with all care, whether to death or exile or confiscation of goods or to imprisonment.[8]

[8] Ezra 7:12–26.

After citing the decree in its original Aramaic, Ezra turns to the sacred Hebrew to express his feelings: "Blessed be the Lord, the God of our fathers, who has put this into the heart of the king to glorify the house of the Lord which is in Jerusalem and has granted me favor before the king and his counselors and all the king's mighty princes." Thus strengthened by the hand of his God, he goes on to say, he collected from the Jewish community leading men to accompany him on his expedition. They gathered at the river Ahava, where they encamped three days; there were no Levites, and representatives must be summoned from Casiphia (our first mention of the later capital Ctesiphon). A fast was proclaimed to pray for a successful journey; naïvely, Ezra explains: "I was ashamed to ask the king for a body of soldiers and cavalry to aid us against the enemy on the road, because we had told the king: 'The hand of our God is over all those who seek him for good, but his power and wrath is against all those who forsake him.' "[9]

On April 19, 458, the augmented company left the Ahava. The hand of their God was indeed over them, and he saved them from the enemy and the bandit on the road. The weary journey was ended August 4,[10] and four days later Ezra, like the careful administrator that he was, weighed out the gold, silver, and utensils into the hands of a local priest.[11]

By October 2, Ezra was ready to present the new lawbook. Naturally, it was written in the ancient Hebrew, for all the sacred prescriptions were now assigned to the great lawgiver Moses; as naturally, the majority of Ezra's hearers did not fully understand it, for they spoke the current Aramaic. Accordingly, with the very first introduction of the new lawbook to the Palestinian Jews came the practice of giving a translation into the vernacular. The "original" words of Moses were, of course, *read* in the sacred language, but the translation was *spoken*, and we may be sure that from the beginning a written Aramaic copy had been prepared to serve as aid for the translators and to guarantee the accuracy of the translation.[12]

Day after day the reading and translation continued until the task was completed. The great work of Ezra was done, and the lawbook of Moses was henceforth accepted as authoritative. Its influence cannot

---

[9] Ezra 7:27–28; 8:15, 17, 21–23.   [11] Ezra 8:31–34.

[10] Ezra 7:9; 8:31–32.   [12] Nehemiah, chap. 8; cf. esp. vs. 8.

possibly be exaggerated. Whoever may be conjectured as the author of the lawbook, to which in fact many hands through the centuries had contributed, Ezra was rightly considered the second founder of Judaism, inferior only to Moses himself. He did not succeed in stopping permanently the activities of the prophets, whose dreams of a coming national kingdom returned again and again, but he did point the way to the only safe policy for the salvation of Judaism— abandonment of nationalistic hopes, reconciliation to the political rule of foreigners, loyalty to the powers that be, and full acceptance of the unique position of the Jew as the guardian of God's moral law. Fortunately for the world, succeeding generations have generally followed his guiding principle; the reactionary minority which has time and again raised the standard of separate nationality has only increased the woe of their fellow-Jews.

The great work of Ezra, the introduction of the law, was completed. There remained only enforcement in detail. Of the needed reforms, the most pressing was the abolition of mixed marriages, through all centuries the most dangerous threat to Judaism. "Mingling of the holy seed with the daughters of the peoples of the lands" might be condoned in a community in which males were in the majority, but that the higher classes should be the chief offenders was unforgivable. A proclamation was issued to the effect that the people should assemble in Jerusalem; absence was to be punished by "devotion" of property and exclusion from the congregation. The assembly was held in the rain on December 19, 458, and divorce of the alien women was accepted in principle; detailed examination of each individual case was begun on December 30 and ended March 27, 457.[13]

Ezra then returned to Babylonia, where tradition said he died and where his alleged tomb may still be visited. The lawbook had been accepted, but the problem of mixed marriages remained. Eliashib, the high priest at Jerusalem, openly flouted the reform,[14] though his son Jehohanan had come over to Ezra's position.[15] For their acceptance of foreign marriages, Ezra's opponents could appeal to the evidence of the historical sections of the lawbook itself; one of these opponents, in a tale whose beauty should not blind us to its deliberate propaganda, recited the episode through which Ruth the Moabitess became the ancestress of that great Hebrew monarch David.[16]

[13] Ezra, chaps. 9–10; Olmstead, *op. cit.*, pp. 583 ff.

[14] Neh. 13:4.

[15] Ezra 10:6.

[16] Olmstead, *op. cit.*, p. 636.

PERSIAN SUCCESSES IN EGYPT

Meanwhile, Artaxerxes had countered the Athenian operations by sending a certain Megabazus to Sparta (458). His money was accepted and used to defeat Athens at Tanagra (457) two or three months after the conclusion of Ezra's reforms, though two months later Oenophyta restored Athenian prestige. Ezra's success in quieting Judah permitted the safe passage across the border of the huge army collected by Artabazus and by Megabyzus, now appointed satrap of Syria; in 456 Inarus was wounded in a great battle, and the Athenians were driven from Memphis to Prosopitis, a large island in the Delta near Papremis. Here they were blockaded for a year and a half. When the canal which joined two arms of the Nile to form the island was drained, the Athenians burned their ships. A few of their men escaped to Cyrene; the remaining survivors were promised safe return home by Megabyzus and surrendered—as did Inarus, trusting in the Persian's word of honor. Elbo, a tiny island barely a mile square, was left as the sole base from which Amyrtaeus could raid the Delta marshlands. Thannyras, son of Inarus, and Pausiris, son of Amyrtaeus, were formally appointed to their fathers' places as petty vassal princes.

Arsames, the new satrap, arrived with a great force of Phoenician ships and land troops. Athens had sent out a relieving squadron of fifty triremes under Charitimides; not knowing that Athenian resistance had collapsed, this incompetent commander put in at the Mendesian mouth of the Nile. Arsames attacked with his united strength, and few escaped destruction. Megabyzus returned to Susa in triumph, carrying with him Inarus and the Greek generals. Savage Queen-Mother Amestris demanded their execution, but her son-in-law Megabyzus pointed out that he was bound by his plighted word, and for a time the captives were reprieved (454).[17]

THE ATHENIAN EMPIRE

At the height of its triumph, Athens had received a crushing blow. The Athenians were as depressed as they had been joyful. By Persia's latest victory, the eastern Mediterranean had once more become a Phoenician lake; at the mere rumor of an approaching Phoenician navy, the Athenians in a spasm of fright hastily removed the league treasury from exposed Delos to the safety of the Acropolis at Athens. This transfer marked the disappearance of a last pretense to a Delian

[17] Herod. ii. 41, 140, 165; iii. 15, 160; Thuc. i. 109–10; Ctes. *Pers.*, Epit. 64 ff.; Isoc. *De pace* 86; Diod. xi. 74. 5–6; 75; 77.

League composed of equals, and the transformation into the Athenian Empire was indicated by tribute lists, that invaluable aid to the historian, which were begun in the summer of 454.[18]

Athens was too exhausted to fight. When it gave a constitution to Erythrae, the councilors must swear that they would never take back those who fled to the Medes. Miletus returned to its Persian alliance. Evanthes lost Salamis to a Phoenician who alternated on his coins his native language with the Cypriote dialect and Greek characters. Lapethus was ruled by the Phoenician Sidqimilk. Baalmilk I had become king of Citium shortly after the end of the great war. He introduced on his coins the nude Melqart of Tyre with his lionskin and bow, placing on the reverse a seated growling lion and his own name. With Persian aid, Baalmilk attacked Idalium but was beaten off; its king, Stasicyprus, honored the physician, Onasilus, son of Onasicyprus, and his brothers who tended the wounded in the wars with the Medes.[19]

Cimon returned from his ten years' ostracism early in 451. Under his influence the treaty with Argos was denounced and a truce made with Sparta. Athens was turning conservative, and a more active anti-Persian policy might be expected. Arthmius, son of Pythonax, was a proxenos, an official guest friend of Athens from Cappadocian Zeleia. He was sent to Greece with ample funds to counteract this tendency. The infuriated Athenians voted that he should be considered "dishonored and a foe of the Athenian people and of their allies, himself and his family, because he brought the gold from the Medes to the Peloponnese." A bronze plate inscribed with the decree was set up on the Acropolis, where it was often consulted and cited by orators of the next century.[20]

After such a conservative triumph, it was a matter of course that at the beginning of 450 a renewal of the war should be voted and that the command should be assigned to Cimon. Sixty ships were sent to Amyrtaeus, who still held out in the swamps of Egypt. The remainder of the two hundred triremes voted accompanied Cimon to Cyprus, where he found the island held loyal by Artabazus with three

[18] B. D. Meritt, H. T. Wade-Gery, and M. F. McGregor, *The Athenian Tribute Lists*, Vol. I (1939).

[19] Plut. *Pericl.* 12; Aristid. 25. 2; *IG*, I, 9(10); 22*a*(22); E. Babelon, *Traité des monnaies*, II, Part II (1910), 695 ff., 822–23, 731 ff., 766 ff.; H. Collitz, *Sammlung der griechischen Dialektinschriften*, Vol. I (1884), No. 60.

[20] Demosthen. *Philip.* iii. 41 ff.; *De fals. leg.* 271; Aeschin. *Ctes.* 258; Deinarch. *Aristogeiton* 24–25; Plut. *Themistocl.* 6. 3.

hundred ships from Phoenicia, supported by the Cilician troops of Megabyzus. Despite his definite inferiority in numbers, Cimon did not hesitate to attack. Marium was captured, and Citium was under siege when provisions failed, Cimon died, and the siege was abandoned (449). Athenian pride was salved when a combined land and sea assault was beaten off, but the expedition then returned home, picking up on the way the squadron sent to the aid of Amyrtaeus. After the Athenian withdrawal, Baalmilk's son, Azbaal, finally subdued Idalium; as symbol of Citium's victory, he substituted for the defiant lion of his father's coins the triumphant Phoenician lion devouring the Greek stag.[21]

THE "PEACE OF CALLIAS"

Now that Cimon, consistently anti-Persian, was out of the way, there could be no serious opposition to a proposal for peace. The hard logic of events had at last convinced Pericles that Athens, supported by a Delian League which already was showing indications of threatened dissolution, was no match for the vast resources of the "barbarian" empire. Both empires had come to realize that border clashes were of minor importance when compared with the undoubted fact that Sparta with her Peloponnesian League was their common enemy. To avoid her intervention, it was to their mutual advantage to formulate an enduring peace which should reduce to a minimum the possibility of boundary disputes.

Early in 449 an embassy headed by Callias was dispatched to Susa. By designed "accident," no doubt, there appeared at the same time an embassy from Argos, the ally of Athens. The Argives reminded Artaxerxes of their former friendship with the king's father and inquired whether that friendship still held or whether he now considered them his enemies; they were reassured: "Certainly it remains! No city do I consider a better friend than Argos!"[22]

Aided, we may be sure, by the Argives, Callias and his associated ambassadors then negotiated with Artaxerxes the treaty which thereafter was known to the Greeks by his name. Both parties made concessions to attain this masterpiece of wise statesmanship. The peace itself was made on the basis of the *status quo ante bellum*. Persia for the first time acknowledged the loss of the Greek cities in Asia which

[21] Thuc. i. 112; Isocr._De pace_ 86; Plato *Menex.* 241E; Aristodem., Frag. 13(J); *Diod.* xi. 62; xii. 3-4; Nepos *Cimon* 3.4; Plut. *Cimon* 18; *Pericl.* 10. 4; 7; [Simonides] *Anthol. palat.* vii. 296; Babelon, *op. cit.*, pp. 739-40.

[22] Herod. vii. 151.

had been admitted into the Athenian Empire, while Athens in its turn abandoned the pretense of "liberation" for those cities which of right belonged to the Great King.

This did not at all imply that these Greek cities had been callously left to their fate. Those under Athenian rule of course possessed "autonomy," which was guaranteed by the constitution of the Delian League and which never had been formally disavowed; although naturally Athens preferred that this "autonomy" should be exercised through a democratic home government, there were still conservative exceptions. Athens was therefore in excellent position to demand that Persia likewise should permit a similar "autonomy" to her Greek vassal states, and, to make sure that it would not be endangered by ambitious satraps, Artaxerxes added the further proviso that even the satrapial levies should not be permitted within three days' journey from the seacoast. In the Delian League the "contributions" made by the individual contracting states had been assessed by the power which had been voted the "leadership," and, as the League evolved into the Empire, the "contributions" had been changed into "tribute" and the individual assessments had been increased. The cities which remained under Persian overlordship were more fortunate; Artaxerxes promised that *their* tribute would remain what had been imposed two generations before after the almost forgotten Ionic Revolt, and this was now merely nominal in view of the increased prosperity of the Greek states under Persian rule.

To obviate future disputes, the contracting parties adopted the statesman-like plan of a demilitarized zone through the territory on the border of the two empires. Recent excavations of contemporary ruins show how thoroughly the order prohibiting fortifications was observed and how the cities prospered in consequence. Regular troops were not to march westward beyond the Halys, while, as we have seen, even the satrapal levies were to be held well away from the sea. The grand fleet had been permitted to disintegrate, and it meant little that its activities were henceforth limited to the Mediterranean east of Phaselis, the Nessus River, the Cyanaean Rocks, and the Chaledonian islands. We may be sure that the treaty also limited the Athenian navy in the same manner. Even more important, Athens specifically renounced future support of rebels in Egypt or in Libya.[23]

[23] *Ibid.* vi. 42; i. 155 ff.; vii. 151; Thuc. iii. 33. 2; viii. 5. 5; Craterus, Frags. 75–76(J); Aristodem., Frag. 13. 2(J); Diod. xii. 4. 5; Plut. *Cimon* 13. 4 ff.; *Pericl.* 17. 1; Paus. i. 8. 2; Suid. *s.v.* "Kimon." This treaty, so often cited by fourth-century Athenian orators (Isocr. *Panegyr.* 118, 120; *Areop.* 80; *Panathen.* 59; Demosthen. *De fals. leg.* 273; Lycurg. *Leocr.* 73), was declared un-

DIPLOMACY IN EGYPT AND ACROSS THE RIVER

Protected by this treaty, Artaxerxes took up the problem of Egypt. Building stones from the Hammamat quarries were ordered in 449 and again in 448. Arsames was recalled to court and returned, carrying with him Inarus and the captive Greek generals. Queen-Mother Amestris continually demanded their punishment, but for five years Artaxerxes resisted her importunities. Then Inarus was impaled and fifty Greeks were beheaded; a cylinder seal of Artaxerxes pictures the slaying of the rebel, still wearing the double Egyptian crown, while the roped Greeks await their punishment. Later Thannyras was granted his father's domain.[24]

His pledged word violated through the intrigues of the queen-mother, Megabyzus retired to his satrapy of Across the River and himself revolted.[25] His sons Zopyrus and Artyphius valiantly aided their father, but the Egyptian Usiris was sent with a huge army against him. The two commanders fought a duel in which Usiris drove a spear into his opponent's thigh but was himself wounded in thigh and shoulder. Both fell out of their saddles, but Megabyzus protected his enemy and ordered his life to be spared. Captor and captive became such good friends that, when the king sought to regain his general, Usiris was returned.

A second force was dispatched under Menostanes, son of Artarius, the king's brother and satrap of Babylon. Menostanes was even less fortunate, for in the inevitable duel he alone was wounded, shot in shoulder and head, and barely escaped with his army. Since the honor of Megabyzus had been satisfied by two resounding victories, Artarius thought the time had come to suggest a return to loyalty; Megabyzus professed himself quite willing, but only on condition that he remain in his satrapy. Queen Amestris and the all-powerful twenty-year-old eunuch Paphlagonian favorite, Artoxares, added their entreaties. At her suggestion, Artarius himself, the satrap's wife Amytis, Artoxares, and Usiris' son Petisis descended in mass on Megabyzus, who after

---

authentic by contemporary Theopompus, Frags. 153-54(J), and his judgment has been almost universally accepted by recent scholars. The reality of the treaty, its terms, and its future vicissitudes have been convincingly set forth by H. T. Wade-Gery, "The Peace of Kallias," in *Athenian Studies Presented to William Scott Ferguson* (1940), pp. 121 ff.

[24] Couyat-Montet, *op. cit.*, Nos. 61 and 89; Herod. iii. 15; Thuc. i. 110. 3; Ctes. *Pers.*, Epit. 66-67; C. Lenormant, *Gazette archéologique*, 1877, p. 185.

[25] Ctes. *Pers.*, Epit. 68.

much persuasion and many promises went up to the king and was ultimately pardoned. But the tragicomedy was by no means ended.[26]

THE WORK OF NEHEMIAH

All the efforts of Ezra had not convinced a fanatical minority that obedience to the newly introduced law was an adequate substitute for national independence. Stirred by the successful defiance of royal authority by Megabyzus, the hotheads had restored the Jerusalem walls in preparation for another attempt at revolt. Judah was directly under the administration of Samaria; its governor, Rehum, through his secretary, Shimshai, sent a warning to the king. First they reminded Artaxerxes by their salutation that the inhabitants of Across the River were loyal former Babylonians and Elamites, deported from Uruk, Babylon, and Susa by the Assyrian King Ashur-bani-apal, and by him settled in Samaria and the other cities of the province. Then they came to the point: "Be it known to the king that the Jews who came up from you [the comrades of Ezra] have arrived in Jerusalem, a rebellious and wicked city. They are rebuilding it and are repairing the walls. Let the king realize that if it is rebuilt and the walls completed, they will pay neither tribute in money nor tax in kind nor toll, and in the end it will be harmful to the kings. Now because we eat the salt of the palace and because it is not right to see the king being stripped, we have therefore sent and reported to the king, so that search may be made in the record book of your fathers; thus you will discover in the record book that this city is rebellious, injurious to kings and provinces, and that they have revolted in it from of olden times; on account of this the city was devastated. If this city is rebuilt, we advise the king, and if the walls are completed, because of it you will have no possession in Across the River."

Artaxerxes replied: "The letter which you sent us has been translated before me. I gave order and search has been made. It was discovered that this city from of olden times has raised insurrections against kings and that revolts and rebellions have been made in it. Also, mighty kings have been in Jerusalem, who have reigned over all Across the River, and to them tribute of money, tax in kind, and toll was paid. Give order now to make these men stop and let this city not be rebuilt until a decree is made by me. Do not be negligent, lest damage to kings should increase." On receipt of the royal orders, the building was stopped by force.[27]

26 *Ibid.*, Epit. 68–70.   27 Ezra 4:8–23.

The Jews were not without their local friends. Through the assistance of a Persian official named Mithredath, a certain Tabeel secured from the local archives copies of the two letters just quoted and with them copies of the earlier rescripts of Cyrus and Darius. Thus he proved that the city had been resettled and the temple rebuilt by order of the empire's founder and of his greatest successor. He also proved that the question of Jewish rights had already been raised and that it had been settled in favor of the Jews by Darius on the basis of the earlier decree of Cyrus. The documents, written in the ancient sacred Hebrew letters, were transcribed into the newer Aramaic characters (still little employed in Judah) and incorporated into a formal appeal to Artaxerxes; the appeal itself was written in the official Aramaic language of the royal chancellery.[28]

Since Rehum controlled the official post, the letter could be forwarded to Susa only through a private delegation; it was headed by Hanani, son of Hacaliah, a brother of Nehemiah, the cupbearer of Artaxerxes, whose influence should be decisive. The delegation arrived sometime between December 17, 446, and January 14, 445. Nehemiah must have had a suspicion as to what his compatriots had been planning, for immediately he demanded news of Jerusalem and of the Jews there, both the descendants of those who had escaped Nebuchadnezzar's deportation and the recently returned exiles. To his horror, he was told that the exiles in the province were in terrible affliction, while the wall of Jerusalem had been broken down and its gates had been burned with fire!

Apparently the king was out of town, for Nehemiah's services would not be demanded until the New Year's feast, April 13, 445. Three months of grace were available in which he might weep and wail, might fast and pray. His memoirs give us the very words of the prayer; they also show us that Nehemiah employed prayer only as a prelude to action, and we are not surprised to find that his prayer ends in the hope that his Lord would prosper what was clearly an already formed plan and grant him favor in the eyes of his master.

From his position as royal cupbearer, permitted to wait on the royal women, we may be sure than Nehemiah was a eunuch. Despite his well-advertised forthrightness of speech, his memoirs indicate much of the eunuch's subtlety. At the first glance, it was obvious that Tabeel's letter would never do, for it required a flat reversal of a royal decree, a thing unheard of at court. More underhand means were re-

[28] Ezra 4:7–23; 5:3–6:15; cf. H. H. Schaeder, *Iranische Beiträge*, I (1930), 212 ff.

quired; in fear and trembling (for his plan was dangerous) he appeared with a sad countenance before the king at the feast. Artaxerxes solicitously inquired the reason from his favorite. "May the king live forever" was the courtly answer. Then, plucking up his courage, Nehemiah went on: "Why should not my countenance be sad when the city, the place of my fathers' sepulchers, lies waste and its gates have been consumed with fire?"

"What are you asking for?" sharply retorted the king.

Still more frightened, Nehemiah breathed a hasty prayer to the God of Heaven, and answered: "If it please the king and if your slave has found favor in your sight, send me back to Judah, to the city of my fathers' sepulchers, that I may build it."

Nehemiah's prayer was answered because he had carefully planned his line of approach. By this time the wine with which the cupbearer had been so liberally plying his master must have been taking effect. Also, the queen—no doubt by previous arrangement—was sitting by the side of her husband. Fortunately, the tipsy monarch did not identify Nehemiah's paternal city in Judah with the Jerusalem whose walls he had just ordered destroyed. The only question he raised was how long his favorite wished to be absent; the time was set and permission was given. Nehemiah wasted no time: "If it please the king, may letters be given me to the governors of Across the River to allow me to pass through until I come to Judah; also a letter to Asaph, keeper of the royal paradise, to give me timber to make beams for the gates of the castle belonging to the temple [on the site of the later Tower of Antonia] and for the city wall, and for the house I am to occupy." Put in this fashion, the request seemed innocuous enough, and again permission was granted.

No time was lost in departing. His faith was not equal to Ezra's, and Nehemiah preferred an escort of royal cavalry. Since Megabyzus had left Syria to make his peace with the king, Nehemiah experienced no difficulty in reaching the new governors of Across the River, to whom he presented the royal authorization. Two of them, Sanballat the Horonite, his immediate superior in Samaria, and Tobiah, his colleague in Ammon, at once manifested their hostility. "They were grieved," Nehemiah tells us, "to learn that a man had come to seek the welfare of the children of Israel." They might have argued that the reasons adduced by Rehum were still valid, but the surrender of the rebel satrap had deprived the argument of its immediate force, and the direct order of their king must be obeyed; they might mutter

among themselves that their loyal warning had been disregarded
through a harem intrigue, but there was left to them nothing but a
policy of obstruction. To the opponents of Nehemiah was soon added
Gashm the Arab, the son of Sahar, whom we have already met as
the governor of Dedan.[29] The threat of a revived Jerusalem to the
trade of his subjects with the seacoast was a real danger; for the same
reason, the inhabitants of seaport Ashdod were found ranged with
the anti-Jewish opposition.

Within Jerusalem itself there were divided opinions as to the feasi-
bility of the proposed rebuilding. Eliashib the high priest did place
himself at the head of the project, and Nehemiah lists an imposing
number of prominent Jews who followed his example. Many of the
leading citizens, however, kept Tobiah well informed as to what was
going on. The prophets, of course, were enthusiastic, for they naturally took Nehemiah's activities as a prelude to revolt. Some were already proclaiming: "A king is in Judah." Others would put Nehemiah on guard against the officials, among them the prophetess
Noadiah and the prophet Shemaiah, who urged him to fortify the
temple against siege. But the former cupbearer had no illusions about
the possibility of revolt; angrily he declared that the alleged preparations for rebellion were barefaced inventions of Sanballat. As for the
proposal to retire into the temple, "Should such a man as I run away
and enter the temple to save his life?" He professed to have discovered
that Sanballat and Tobiah had suborned Shemaiah. When his superior
invited him to a conference, Nehemiah brusquely replied that he was
too busy. He also professed to fear attack from Sanballat and kept his
workmen under arms while they labored. By October 2, 445, the wall
was completed and the gates in place. There followed a ceremonial
procession by which the wall was dedicated, and Nehemiah's great
task was done.[30]

The work of rebuilding had taken but fifty-two days. Evidently
the walls had not been so thoroughly destroyed as we might think,
and repairs had been made with the utmost haste. No regard could
have been paid to beauty or even to good workmanship. The winning
enthusiasm and amusingly naïve self-appreciation of Nehemiah's
memoirs cannot blind us to the fact that Sanballat and his colleagues
had a good prima facie case. But built the walls were, and the Jews
now had a safe refuge. Hasty as was the repair, Nehemiah preserved

[29] Cf. p. 295.

[30] Neh. 1:1–7:5; 12:31–43; Olmstead, *op. cit.*, pp. 588 ff.

the ground plan of the pre-Exilic city, and this continued without essential change until a few years after the death of Jesus. One thing more we owe him: his careful description of the city's topography; by its aid, we better understand the Holy City as it was in Jesus' day.[31]

THE "FATHER OF HISTORY" IN ATHENS

That same year (445) Herodotus appeared in Athens. His original "Tour of the World" had grown into a full-length history of the great war in which the European Greeks had fought successfully the Persian invaders. After his travels throughout the Persian Empire, he had visited the battlefields in Europe and ultimately reached Athens, rapidly becoming the center of enlightenment as the cities of Asia declined under foreign Athenian or Persian rule. His story of how Athens, almost unaided, had repulsed the mighty hordes of Darius and Xerxes was most welcome, for, despite the informal peace negotiated by Callias, Persia and Athens were drifting once again toward war. Herodotus publicly recited his history in 445 and was rewarded by a public grant.[32]

[31] Olmstead, *Jesus in the Light of History* (1942), pp. 56 ff.

[32] Diyllus, Frag. 3(J).

Chapter XXIII

ORIENTAL TALES AND ROMANCES

HERODOTUS is the "Father of History." His native city, Halicarnassus, was half-Carian; among the higher classes Carian names were common, and it would have been strange had not he himself had at least a few drops of Carian blood. Certainly he was sympathetic to the Anatolian peoples.

With his poet uncle, Panyasis, he was expelled by the tyrant Lygdamis and took refuge in Samos. Although Lygdamis was recognized by Athens,[1] Herodotus later assisted in driving him out. Taking advantage of his status as a Persian subject, he traveled widely throughout the Empire, presumably supporting himself as a merchant; ultimately, he determined to write a better "Tour of the World" than Hecataeus.

Hecataeus had visited Egypt, that land of ancient knowledge which had taught so much to Ionic philosophers, and Herodotus would follow his trail. He seems to have reached it while Athenian forces were aiding the rebel Inarus (459–456), and he came ready to be impressed; no country, he tells us, has so many marvelous sights. Naucratis, the ancient Greek colony in the Delta, was, of course, his base; a vase dedicated with his name still exists to give evidence for his visit.[2] Everywhere he made inquiries, from Sais on the seacoast to Elephantine below the first cataract; when, for instance, the priests of Memphis told him what seemed a tall story, he traveled to Heliopolis and to Thebes to check their tales.

Egypt, he says, is the gift of the Nile. He knows how the Delta was formed; the proof is its famous black soil and the seashells along the Nile cliffs, though he ascribes their formation to historical times. No one could explain the inundation which each year turns Egypt into a sea. Only the clerk of the register of the sacred treasure of Athena (Neith) at Sais professed to describe the Nile's source; he declared that

---

[1] Dittenberger, *Sylloge inscriptionum Graecarum* (2d ed., 1898), No. 10.

[2] D. G. Hogarth, H. L. Lorimer, and C. C. Edgar, "Naukratis, 1903," *Journal of Hellenic Studies*, XXV (1905), 116.

between Syene and Elephantine were bottomless fountains from which one river flowed to Egypt and another to Ethiopia. Herodotus was not quite sure that he was not joking, but, if he had looked more closely when visiting at Thebes, he would have found a representation of this very source of the cataract-god.[3]

He carefully noted the queer dress, food, customs, and religion, so often the exact reverse of the Greek. He examined strange animals such as the hippopotamus and the crocodile, also the phoenix, though only from a painting. Physicians who specialized were a novelty. Religion especially intrigued him. All the accessible temples were visited, and all the ceremonies open to the public were observed. He saw the scandal-shouting boatmen and boatwomen of Bubastis, the Feast of Lights at Sais, and the temple fights at Papremis. Naturally, he equated the Egyptian divinities with Greek gods, but Isis, Horus, and Osiris were so outlandish that he must give them their true names. Secrets of the mysteries, he informs us, he has carefully refrained from divulging, giving us the unwarranted impression that he was one of the initiates. He learned of oracles, divination, and horoscopes. He describes in all its gruesome details the process of mummification, of animals as well as of men, and the bringing of the mummy to the feast.

Brought face to face with the overwhelming evidence of a mighty past, Herodotus could make no boast of Greek superiority over the barbarian. To his surprise, he discovered that the Egyptians actually called all foreigners who could not speak their own language "barbarians," and he could not protest! His guides found him an eager, generally credulous listener. It is to be feared that the notorious Egyptian sense of humor was not equal to the strain.

Egypt, they proved to Herodotus, was the mother of all civilization. The Egyptians first named the twelve gods who were borrowed from them by the Greeks. From the stars they first discovered the solar year, divided it into twelve months of thirty days each, and added five more days to return the seasons uniformly. Herodotus admits that this is much superior to the Greek custom of adding a full intercalary month each alternate year. To their visitor's satisfaction, the Egyptians proved that they themselves had first set up altars, images, temples, and sculptures. Religious ceremonies, festivals, mysteries, the belief in immortality—all found their origin in Egypt. To cap the climax, the priests of Thebes repeated for their humbler disciple the lesson

[3] Harold H. Nelson, *Reliefs and Inscriptions at Karnak*, Vol. II (1936), Pl. 80c; cf. *ibid.*, I, ix.

taught the boastful Hecataeus and showed him the three hundred and forty-five wooden statues of their direct ancestors.

Herodotus was now prepared to accept the truth of Egyptian history as related by the priests at Heliopolis. In the beginning, the gods ruled Egypt, the last of whom was Horus, son of Osiris, who deposed the wicked Typhon. Men, the first human monarch, diverted the Nile to found Memphis, with its temple of Hephaestus (Ptah). From a papyrus roll, something like the extant Turin papyrus, the priests next read a list of the three hundred and fifty kings who left no monuments until the last, who constructed Lake Moeris and its pyramids.

Sesostris conquered all Asia, also Scythia and Thrace, and left monuments in Palestine and Ionia which Herodotus piously visited. Some of his soldiers formed colonies in Colchis, as the Colchians and Egyptians both recalled. On his return Sesostris employed the captives to dig canals, and henceforth no one was permitted to use horse or chariot. He also divided the land into equal estates and from them collected rent; as a result, the art of geometry was developed. No Babylonians were present to controvert these preposterous claims, but at least, Herodotus insisted, the sundial, the gnomon, and the twelve-hour day came from Babylonia.

He asked about the Trojan War, and the answer was at hand. Proteus, grandson of Sesostris, expelled Paris when he arrived with the stolen Helen but retained the fair lady. The Trojans were therefore in the right when they told the invading Greeks that they did not hold Helen captive. Sure enough, when the city was captured, Helen was not found, and so Menelaus sailed on to Egypt and there recovered his wife; Euripides was to expand this story into his play named *Helen*.

In the days of Rhampsinitus (Ramses) occurred the episode of the clever thief. Good government and prosperity changed to oppression when Cheops forced his subjects to build one great pyramid, and Chephren a second; the builder of the third, Mycerinus, was more kindly. Then Egypt was invaded by the Ethiopian Sabacus (Shabaka). Sethos (Seti) was delivered from Sennacharibus (Sennacherib), king of the Arabs and Assyrians, by mice who ate the invaders' bowstrings.[4]

Extraordinary chronological mixture of true and false as was this account, it set the style for future Greek historians of the Orient. Especially marked was its effect on various later attempts to correlate Greek and oriental legends. Herodotus' friend Sophocles quoted the

4 Herodotus, Book ii.

historian almost literally in his statement that the work of women
and men was reversed in Egypt. He also knew about Egyptian mum-
mies.[5]

Then Herodotus sailed off to Tyre, where he marveled at the temple
of Heracles (Baalmelqart), with its "emerald" pillars of glass. He
learned that the Phoenicians had invented the alphabet, and heard of
the queer rite of circumcision practiced by certain peoples of Palestine-
Syria. Babylonia did not so much impress him, though in Babylon he
visited the imposing ruins of the temple of Bel and was told of Bel's
golden image carried off by Xerxes. He listened to stories about the
famous queens Semiramis and Nitocris. The religious prostitution in
honor of Mylitta (a byname of Ishtar) profoundly shocked him, and
his eyes were open to the terrible decline of the once rich land under
the severe taxation.

HERODOTUS AS TRANSMITTER OF ORIENTAL TALES

Herodotus, the Father of History, was also the greatest storyteller
of antiquity. Critics, ancient and modern, have too often ignored his
frequent "So they say, but I don't believe them." They have asserted
that his "garrulity"—to his readers, his most delightful characteristic
—weakens his credibility as a historian. Year by year new discoveries
from the older Orient have proved that the critics and not the historian were in error. Furthermore, Herodotus knew what his successors
have learned but slowly—that one good story about an individual,
even though the man never existed in actual life, may better illumi-
nate for us an alien psychology than many a dull collection of routine
facts.

If recent years have witnessed a certain realization of this important
principle, there is still failure to recognize that in these "unauthentic"
tales we have the evidence for one of the most outstanding facts in
world literary history. Greek legendary history had many a tale of
Orientals. Poets and dramatists followed the example. Taken as a
whole, they are stories *about* the East by westerners rather than true
oriental tales. It is Herodotus who first gives on a large scale genuine
Eastern stories and thus plays a major part in the transmission of oriental tales and romances to the West and to ourselves.

Before the Persian conquest, the Ionian Greeks had been brought
within the Lydian Empire, and Anatolian stories became familiar. To
be sure, the Croesus stories best known to us do not belong to this cy-

[5] Sophocl. *Oedipus Col.* 337 ff.; Frag. 646 (Nauck).

cle; they represent the well-known Greek invention to prove that oriental despots are always wicked and stupid. But the story of how Gyges was compelled to found a new dynasty could never have been thought up by a Greek. The anger of Candaules' wife on discovery that her husband had exposed her naked to his favorite, her insistence that but one man who had seen her nude should remain alive, fits exactly the oriental sensitiveness about indecent exposure.[6]

From the grim Anatolian cycle comes the episode of the death of Croesus' son Atys. Warned by a dream that Atys was destined to be slain by an iron spear, the king took every precaution. Finally, Atys persuaded his father to allow him to hunt the boar from Mysian Olympus. By accident he was killed by his best friend, Adrastus, son of the Phrygian monarch Gordias, whom Croesus had received as a fugitive and himself had ritually cleansed from the guilt of fratricide. The Lydian king did not blame Adrastus; he recognized at last how the gods taught that man cannot avoid his destined fate.[7]

Another cycle was Iranian. One good example is the story of Deioces, who in actual history was a petty village chief, captured and deported to Syria by Sargon, king of Assyria.[8] According to the native tale, however, he was a very wise man who for a time did justice among the neighbors. When they had become accustomed to accepting his judgments, he discontinued the practice on the ground that he was wasting his time without reward. In natural consequence, they made him king of Media to retain his justice, whereupon he retired to the solitude of a palace he built at Ecbatana and became inaccessible.[9] A second typical story is that of Mandane, the mother of Cyrus, who dreamed that from her womb grew a vine which overshadowed all Asia.[10] The dream of Cyrus, just before his death at the hands of the Massagetae queen, when he saw Darius with wings on his shoulders, the one overshadowing Asia and the other Europe, is our earliest indication of belief in the "awful royal glory" which to later Iranian monarchs so regularly portended that the man on whom it descended would soon become king.[11] A variant tale explained Darius' unexpected accession to the throne by the story of the clever manner in which his groom Oebarus caused his stallion to neigh first.[12]

Babylonian stories are of queens, Semiramis and Nitocris,[13] the for-

[6] Herod. i. 8 ff.

[7] Ibid. 34 ff.

[8] Olmstead, History of Assyria (1923), pp. 20, 9, 243 ff., 636.

[9] Herod. i. 96 ff.

[10] Ibid. 107 ff.

[11] Ibid. 209.

[12] Ibid. iii. 85.

[13] Ibid. i. 184 ff.

mer much elaborated by later authors. Another universal favorite, that about Sardanapalus the luxurious despot, makes its first appearance in Herodotus;[14] this is of Assyrian origin, for Sardanapalus is a combination of two of their kings, Ashur-nasir-apal (885–860) and Ashur-bani-apal (669–633).

Genuine Egyptian folklore is preserved in the story of the clever thief who succeeded in marrying the daughter of King Rhampsinitus;[15] twenty-three and a half centuries later, far out in the desert one could hear a modern variant from the lips of an illiterate and stupid camel-driver whose home was on the borders of Egypt. From the priests of Hephaestus at Memphis, Herodotus tells us, he learned how King Psammetichus discovered what was the earliest language by depositing two children with shepherds and leaving them to speak without coaching; the language turned out to be Phrygian![16] From the priests also he probably heard a more typical story. When Egypt was divided among twelve kings—the petty local rulers before the Saite Dynasty—an oracle declared that he who poured a libation in the Hephaestus temple from a bronze cup would become king of all Egypt. On the last day of the feast the officiating priest-issued only eleven gold cups, and Psammetichus must use his bronze helmet. His eleven fellow-kinglets recognized that the oracle had unwittingly been fulfilled, but nevertheless drove him out into the marshes. To his inquiry at the oracle of Leto in Buto, Psammetichus was informed that the first oracle would be fulfilled when he saw men of bronze arising from the sea. Bronze-clad Ionians and Carians arrived to plunder; they were taken into his army as mercenaries, and by their aid Psammetichus made himself ruler of all Egypt, the founder of the Saite Dynasty.[17] Native stories deal with the same period of disorder. Not the least of the many virtues of Herodotus is this passing-on of the oriental tales to the West.

THE WISDOM OF AHIQAR

About this time a story which was to enjoy even wider popularity was being copied in the mercenary colony at Elephantine. For it, there is a solid basis of fact. In the year 698 a certain Ahiaqar was second officer of the Assyrian city Barhalza and also an official of the city Bit Sin-ibni mentioned in a letter.[18] Doubtless he is the original of the

[14] Ibid. ii. 150.   [16] Ibid. 2.
[15] Ibid. 121 ff.   [17] Ibid. 147, 151–52.

[18] C. H. W. Johns, Assyrian Deeds and Documents, Vol. I (1898), Nos. 468, 251; Leroy Waterman, Royal Correspondence of the Assyrian Empire, II (1930), 258–59.

storied Ahiqar, a "wise and ready scribe," whose words in an Aramaic version were treasured by these Jewish colonists. He was counselor of all Assyria and sealbearer of King Sennacherib, who relied on his advice. Sennacherib died and was succeeded by his son Esarhaddon; Ahiqar had no son and therefore took his sister's son Nadin and educated him to be his own successor. Sure enough, the scribe Nadin appears in a business document dated 671 and also writes letters to Esarhaddon and Ashur-bani-apal.[19] Nadin was made wise and was shown great kindness. Before the king and his courtiers he sat in the gate of the palace with Ahiqar. Ahiqar made Nadin approach before the king and instructed him how to answer every royal inquiry. Esarhaddon loved him and said: "Long live Ahiqar!" When he spoke thus, Ahiqar bowed down and made obeisance; since he was old, Ahiqar requested that Nadin should be his successor.

But Nadin said to the king: "This old man has corrupted the land against you," and Esarhaddon was filled with rage. He summoned Nabu-sum-iskun, one of his father's chiefs who ate his bread; he, too, is well known as the "rein-holder" of Sennacherib and the writer of several letters to the king.[20] Esarhaddon bade Nabu-sum-iskun to seek out Ahiqar and kill him. So Nabu-sum-iskun mounted his swift horse and found Ahiqar walking in the vineyards. At the sight, the official rent his garments in lamentation.

Ahiqar admitted that he was afraid but reminded Nabu-sum-iskun how he himself had been saved from an undeserved death when Sennacherib was angry and sought to kill him; then Ahiqar had concealed the fugitive in his own house after declaring that the criminal had been slain. Many days later he brought Nabu-sum-iskun before Sennacherib and caused his sins to pass away from before the king, who did him no evil but rather was pleased because he had been kept alive. Let Nabu-sum-iskun now do the same for him. Esarhaddon the king is merciful; more than any other will he remember Ahiqar and desire his counsel. Let a eunuch slave be killed in his place; afterward Esarhaddon will remember Ahiqar and desire his counsel; he will grieve and say to his chieftains and courtiers: "I will give you riches as the number of the sands if you will find Ahiqar."

The narrative in the papyrus breaks off at this point, but from later versions we learn that everything came out as expected. Esarhaddon

[19] Johns, *op. cit.*, Nos. 60, 368; Waterman, *op. cit.*, I (1930), 274–75; II, 36 ff., 274.

[20] Johns, *op. cit.*, No. 253; Waterman, *op. cit.*, I, 296–97; II, 44 ff.; cf. Olmstead, "Intertestamental Studies," *JAOS*, LVI (1936), 243.

expressed his wish for Ahiqar's counsel. Nabu-sum-iskun brought forward the supposedly dead official, who now told the true story. Nadin was disgraced and handed over to his uncle for punishment. The punishment of the wicked Nadin was severe: every day he must listen to his uncle's interminable aphorisms.

These aphorisms varied with every edition, until the "Wisdom of Ahiqar" became a regular compendium of the world's best literature in Aramaic, Syriac, Arabic, Armenian, and Ethiopic. Democritus cites it, Aesop uses it, it was imitated in our present edition of Tobit, the New Testament is filled with its wise sayings, and Jesus of Nazareth condescended to employ it.[21]

In the Elephantine papyrus only a small proportion of the aphorisms is preserved, and no doubt many more from the "original" can be detected elsewhere. But those found in this papyrus, at least, must for the most part be translations of still earlier Babylonian wisdom, for, as the story is Assyrian, so must be the aphorisms:

> What is stronger than wine foaming in the press? The son who is trained and taught, and on whose feet the fetter is put, shall prosper. Withhold not thy son from beating, if thou canst not keep him from wickedness. If I smite thee, my son, thou wilt not die, and if I leave thee to thine own heart, thou wilt not live. A blow for a slave, rebuke for a maid, and for all thy slaves discipline.
>
> From fear of the lion, the ass left his burden and will not carry it. He shall bear shame before his fellow and shall bear a burden that is not his and shall be laden with a camel's load.
>
> Two things are a merit, and a third is pleasure to Shamash: the man who drinks wine and gives, the one who hears a word and does not reveal it.
>
> Even to the gods wisdom is precious. To it forever belongs the kingdom; in heaven it is treasured up, for the Lord of Holiness has exalted it.
>
> As to thy mouth, keep watch, let it not be thy destruction. More than all watchfulness guard thy mouth, and concerning that which thou hast heard harden thy heart, for a word is like a bird, and when he has sent it forth a man does not recapture it. Count the secrets of thy mouth; afterward bring forth advice to thy brother for his help, for stronger than the ambush of the mouth is the ambush of fighting.
>
> Suppress not the word of a king, let it be a healing to thy brother. Soft is the speech of a king, but sharper and stronger than a two-edged knife. Behold, before you is something hard; in the presence of the king do not delay, swifter is his anger than lightning, take thou heed to thyself. Let him not show it at thy words, that thou goest not away in thy day. In the king's

21 Olmstead, *Jesus in the Light of History* (1942), pp. 11, 16–17, 103, 150, 166.

presence, if a thing is commanded thee, it is a burning fire; hasten, do it; put not sackcloth upon thee, and hide thy hands, for also the word of the king is with wrath of heart.

The Bramble sent to the Pomegranate, saying: "Bramble to Pomegranate: What is the good of thy many thorns to him who toucheth thy fruit?" The Pomegranate answered and said to the Bramble: "Thou art all thorns to him who toucheth thee." The righteous among men, all who meet him are for his help. The house of wicked men in the day of storm shall be degraded, and in moments of calm its gates shall be cast down, for the plunder of the righteous are they.

My eyes which I lifted up to thee and my heart which I gave thee, in its wisdom thou hast despised. If the wicked takes hold of the skirts of thy garment, leave it in his hand. Then approach Shamash; he will take his and give it to thee.

One said to the wild ass: "Let me ride upon thee and I will feed thee." He replied: "Keep to thyself thy feeding and thy saddle, but I will not see thy riding." Between flesh and shoe let not a pebble make a sore place in thy foot; let not the rich man say: "In my riches I am glorious."

Show not an Arab the sea or a Sidonian the desert, for their work is different. He who treads out the wine is he who should taste it, and he who bottles it should guard it.

Do thou, my son, borrow brain and wheat, that thou mayest eat and give to thy children with thee. A heavy loan and from a wicked man borrow not, and if thou borrow, take no rest to thy soul until thou pay back the loan. A loan is pleasant when there is need, but the paying of it is the filling of a house.

All that thou hearest thou mayest try by thy ears, for the beauty of a man is his faithfulness, but his hatefulness is the lying of his lips. At first the throne is set up for the liar, but at last his lies shall overtake him, and they shall spit in his face. A liar has his neck cut like a maid of the south who hides her face, like a man who makes a curse.

Despise not that which is thy lot, and covet not some great thing which is withheld from thee. Increase not riches and magnify not thy heart. He who is not proud of the name of his father and mother, let not the sun shine upon him, for he is an evil man.

The son of my body has spied out my house, and what can I say to strangers? There was a malicious witness against me, and who then has justified me? From my own house went forth wrath; with whom shall I strive and toil? Thy secrets reveal not before friends, that thy name be not lightly esteemed before them.

With one that is higher than thou, lose not thy temper in a quarrel. With one who is a noble and stronger than thou, contend not, for he will take of thy portion and add it to his own. Behold, so is a little man who contends with a great man.

Be not overcrafty and let not thy wisdom be extinguished. Be not sweet lest they swallow thee up, be not bitter lest they spit thee out. If thou, my son, wouldst be exalted, humble thyself before God, who humbleth the lofty and exalteth the humble.

A man excellent in character, whose heart is good, is like a strong bow which is bent by a strong man. If a man stand not with the gods, how then will he be saved by his own strength?[22]

22 F. C. Conybeare, J. R. Harris, and A. S. Lewis, *The Story of Ahikar* (1898); also in R. H. Charles, *The Apocrypha and Pseudepigrapha of the Old Testament* (1913), pp. 715 ff.

Chapter XXIV

SCIENCE WITHOUT THEOLOGY

OPPOSITION TO NEW SCIENCE IN ATHENS

NEW science from the Orient received in Athens a more qualified welcome than the city was soon to extend to the Ionian charmer Thargelia and her sister-courtesans. The Babylonian sundial, with its 12-hour day, was practical and even conservative; Sparta permitted Anaximenes to set up one in her capital.[1] At the same time, his pupil Anaxagoras left Persian Clazomenae to visit Athens, just rising to fame under Pericles.

There Anaxagoras taught that it was Reason which placed in order what was hitherto all commingled and that the universe was composed of minute homogeneous particles. When, however, he turned to the celestial bodies, declaring that the stars move in a revolving dome where originally the celestial Pole was directly overhead, and began to explain the Milky Way, the comets and meteors, along with meteorology, the winds, thunder, and lightning, he was treading on more dangerous ground. He went on to announce that the moon received its light from the sun and had hills, gullies, and even dwellings, and that the sun was a mass of red-hot metal, larger than the Peloponnese. This was too much for the superstitious Athenians. At the very time when Herodotus was being welcomed by Athens and given a public grant, Anaxagoras was summoned to trial for impiety in teaching astronomy—and for being pro-Persian—and he fled for his life.[2]

REVISION OF BABYLONIAN CALENDAR

While Athens was declaring the very study of astronomy illegal, the Orient continued to refine its scientific results. In the field of practical calendar formulation, Babylonia had since the "era of Nabu-nasir" (747) enjoyed the advantage of a 19-year cycle. At first its scientists had been content with a rough alternation of "hollow" and "full" months of 29 and 30 days, respectively, and had adjusted their calen-

[1] Plin. ii. 187; cf. Herod. ii. 109.

[2] Diog. Laert. ii. 6 ff.; Plut. *De superstit.* 169F; *Pericl.* 32.

328

dar to the "sun's year" by adding 7 intercalated months within the cycle. Repeated experimentation had shown (by 443 at the very latest) that the most practical arrangement of these 7 extra months was to insert 6 at the end of the third, sixth, eighth, eleventh, fourteenth, and nineteenth years of the cycle as a second Addaru, which began with the new moon in March and thus ended in April; only in the seventeenth year did the traditional second Ululu, beginning with the new moon of September, break the year into two equal divisions.[3]

From the Third Dynasty onward, the Egyptians had known that the year contained 365 days. As early as the First Dynasty, astronomers seem to have begun to check their civil year against heliacal risings of Sirius, who is "opener of the (lunar) year"; by this date they were sure that a few hours and minutes must be added to secure the true length of the solar year. By this time, also, they had estimated the excess as a third of a day. Although the 19-year cycle worked clumsily in practice, it definitely gave more precise results.

Nabu-rimanni's calculations had been so exact that we have no reason for expecting any significant advance for a generation or two. As a matter of fact, there are few astonomical texts which appear to come from the immediately succeeding period. One, dated through modern calculation to 425, is merely an example of Nabu-rimanni's system in practical use. It is a thoroughly modern "almanac," with the data calculated in advance and presented in tabular form.

Horizontal lines divide each month. These lines are crossed by vertical lines which form two columns. Of these two, the column at the left indicates the length of the preceding month—29 or 30 days—and so fixes the appearance of the following new moon. Next we learn the day when the moon is full, either the fourteenth or the fifteenth; and then the last appearance of the old moon in the sky is indicated. The column at the right gives the day when the five true planets and Sirius "shine forth" in heliacal rising or "enter" the underworld at their last setting at the end of their period.

Every one of these calculations is correct to the day, proof that even at this early date Babylonian astronomers possessed accurate tables of the planet periods. Equally correct is the placing of the autumnal equinox at September 27. However, the summer solstice, set for June

[3] The table given by R. A. Parker and W. H. Dubberstein, *Babylonian Chronology, 626 B.C.—A.D. 45* (1942), Pl. I, shows only one exception: second Addaru in 385 is the second and not the third year of the cycle. The change took place after the cycle 481–463 but might have been made in 462.

29, is too late by a day. A solar eclipse on October 23 was not visible at Babylon because it occurred after sunset; this the astronomer knew, but for the sake of completeness he included it, though he did not trouble to repeat his calculation. On the other hand, a lunar eclipse was total and visible at Babylon; according to modern calculations, it began at 18 hours, 36 minutes (true Babylonian time), while the Babylonian datum, reduced to our figures, places it only 4 minutes earlier![4]

Even after the accuracy of these calculations of the rising and setting of the planets in this commonplace "calendar," we are not prepared for the advanced textbook which gives us the short and long "light days," the periods of the planet-gods. The moon's period is 684 years, a relatively easy calculation. Jupiter has a long period of 344 years; actually, Jupiter makes 29 circuits plus $4°33'$ in 344 years, while the sun's 344 circuits lack $19'$. This is an amazingly good showing, though the 12-year period is better and the 83 still more accurate; his shorter period is 63 months, 10 days. Various periods are assigned to Venus: 7 days; about 14 days; about 21 days; 63 months, 20 days; while by more elaborate calculations an enormous period of 6,400 years is attained. Mars is assigned a smaller period of 65 months and a longer one of 284 years. Our astronomer realized the variability of this planet, but his great period is more exact than the usual one of 79 years, for, if we subtract 2 days from 284 Julian years, the sun makes 284 circuits plus $11'$ and Mars 141 circuits plus $1°22'$. To secure the great period of Saturn, our astronomer multiplied by 10 the 59-year period, then deducted the excess, $1°13'$; his apparent error—$38'$—may not all be to the discredit of the ancient scientist, for modern astronomers calculate that, under the perturbing influence of Jupiter, the planet during 930 years may vary from his average $49' 10''$ plus or minus.[5]

ATHENS RE-ESTABLISHES CONTACT WITH EGYPTIAN ASTRONOMY

The Ionic Revolt, its continuation in the Great Persian Wars, and the counterattacks of the Delian League had broken the contact with Persian-controlled lands. Athenian support of rebellious Egypt opened the way once more to the Nile. Soon after 459, the Pythagorean Oenopides of Chios,[6] a younger contemporary of Anaxagoras, was among those who visited Egypt. He chanced to witness an inundation and on

[4] F. X. Kugler, *Sternkunde und Sterndienst in Babel, Ergänzungen*, II (1914), 233 ff.

[5] Kugler, *Sternkunde und Sterndienst in Babel*, I (1907) 48 ff. Whether the tablets dated 387–345 and 379 are copied from originals this early is doubtful.

[6] H. Diels and W. Kranz, *Die Fragmente der Vorsokratiker* (5th ed., 1934–37), I, 393 ff.; cf. Plato *Amator*. 132A.

the authority of this firsthand knowledge evolved a queer theory as to its cause.[7] There, too, he studied with the geometers and solved certain problems which he considered would be of use to astronomy. Anaximander had first drawn Greek attention to the strange fact that the ecliptic is inclined;[8] Oenopides carried on the demonstration, though his suggestion that the Milky Way represented the burned-out remains of the sun's former path was never accepted.[9]

CALENDAR REFORM OF OENOPIDES

Oenopides, however, was best known for his calendar reform. He had accepted without question his master's calendar, so beautiful and logical. His visit among the Egyptians made him realize that their astronomers knew better. According to them, the year was not $364\frac{1}{2}$ days long but $365\frac{1}{3}$. As a loyal Pythagorean, Oenopides was faced with the necessity of proving that the faith of his sect was in full agreement with the latest results of science.

The foundation of the now sacred cycle was the logic of the number 59. This beautiful number might be retained if Oenopides accepted the true length of the year as $365\frac{22}{59}$ days—an excess of almost exactly one-third of a day, that is, 8 hours and 57 minutes. Thus the 59-year cycle was salvaged, though at the expense of the still more beautiful $9 \times 9 \times 9$ (months), which resulted in 729; the number of months in the cycle then became 730, each increased to $59\frac{44}{730}$ nights and days, and the total of days plus nights was 43,114.[10]

The compromise was not a success. Scholars ignored the attempt to rehabilitate the Pythagorean "great year," though philosophers like Plato might still hold it in reverence. In the revised form it might have been forgotten even more quickly had not Oenopides in 456 inscribed his "great year" on a bronze tablet and set it up for the examination of such Greeks as might read when they assembled from all corners of the earth to witness the much more exciting Olympic Games.[11]

DEMOCRITUS OF ABDERA

The same causes which opened Egypt to Oenopides opened it also to a far greater scientist, Democritus of Abdera,[12] whose long years of

[7] Diod. i. 41. 1 ff.; 98. 3.   [8] Plin. ii. 31; Aetius ii. 25. 1.

[9] Oenopid., Frag. 10 (Diels and Kranz); Aristot. *Meteorol.* i. 8; Diod. i. 98. 2; Macrob. i. 17. 31; Theon Smyrn. p. 198. 14 (Hiller); Aetius ii. 12. 2.

[10] Censorin. xix. 2; cf. H. Y. Wade-Gery, *Cambridge Ancient History*, III (1925), 762 ff.

[11] Aelian. *Var. hist.* x. 7; cf. K. von Fritz, "Oinopides," *PW*, XVIII (1937), 2258 ff.

[12] T. L. Heath, *Aristarchus of Samos* (1913), p. 121, completely misunderstands and strangely minimizes the scientific importance of Democritus.

wandering were to bring him into all the more civilized countries of the Levant. At a later date he summed up his travels in a *Circumnavigation of the Ocean*. Like the others, this book is lost, but we may trace the course of his journeys from the titles of his treatises (a list of which has been preserved),[13] for what Democritus learned on his travels was to form the basis of many of his publications.

A "Phrygian Treatise" proves knowledge of the interior of Asia Minor. Five years of study, possibly after 459, with Egyptian priests[14] who were geometers and astronomers, left their imprint in a series of mathematical and astronomical studies. "On Those in Meroe," at this time the capital of Ethiopia, showed an interest in, if not a visit to, this far-off land up the Nile.

For a few years after the so-called "Peace of Callias" (449), it was possible for a citizen of Abdera, a member of the Athenian Empire, to travel freely through the rival empire of the Persians. Democritus seized the opportunity and from Egypt passed on to Babylonia. By this time, the originally ethnic term "Chaldaean" had been specialized to mean a wise man, and in this century an astronomer in particular;[15] Democritus therefore summed up the results of his investigations in a "Chaldaean Treatise." Another tractate was entitled "On the Sacred Writings of Those in Babylon";[16] by this, of course, he meant not the Egyptian "hieroglyphics" but the Babylonian cuneiform.

Was Democritus actually capable of reading the clay tablets in the original? Could he make out the numerals and the few ideograms of technical character necessary to understand the tables which eminent modern scientists have considered all that was needed, or did he depend on translations?

Such questions take us far beyond the limits of a history of science. Democritus saw on a stele—which in this case should mean a cuneiform tablet—the sayings of the wise Ahiqar. Among the famous sententious sayings attributed to both Ahiqar and Democritus may be quoted: "The dog's tail brings him food, his jaw gives him stones. Don't let your neighbor step on your heel, lest tomorrow he tread on your neck. Be not oversweet, lest you be swallowed down; be not overbitter, lest you be spit out. Better stumble with the foot than with the tongue. The pig went to the bath with the gentleman; when it came out, it saw a mud hole and wallowed in it."[17] Were these not too

[13] Diog. Laert. ix. 46 ff.

[14] Diod. i. 98. 3; Clem. Alex. *Strom*. i. 69.

[15] Herod. i. 181.

[16] Clem. Alex. *Strom*. i. 69; ii. 130.

[17] Cf. R. H. Charles, *The Apocrypha and Pseudographa of the Old Testament* (1913), II, 716–17.

difficult wisdom sayings read in the original cuneiform, was he rather acquainted with the Aramaic translation copied by the Jews of Elephantine, or did all he know come from incorporation of some of Ahiqar's proverbs in the fables of the Phrygian slave Aesop? Finally, we ask: Are the extant quotations to be assigned to the "Phrygian Treatise"?[18]

From Babylonia, Democritus went on to Persia, where he learned enough of religious practices to write a "Mageia." There he also inquired about India (some even said that he traveled there, though this is highly improbable), but, unlike Ctesias half a century later, Democritus was not taken in by the tall stories he was told.[19]

Democritus is the first Greek scientist known to have visited Babylonia in person. How great was the scientific harvest brought back from this virgin field may be learned from his extant fragments and from the list of his writings when examined in the light of contemporary scientific literature in the cuneiform. We shall not expect to find traces of Babylonian influence in his ethical, philosophical, or musical works. When we see that the group of treatises headed *Physics* begins with the *Great Diacosmus* of his teacher Leucippus, we shall look for no more there.

The group headed *Mathematics* seems more promising. If we knew the content of the sections entitled "Geometrics," "Arithmetic," "On Geometry," "On Incommensurable Magnitudes and Solids," and "On Contacts of Circles and Spheres with a Tangent," we might be able to distinguish between Egyptian and Babylonian contributions. All we can state with certainty is that he first announced to the Greeks the theorem that the volume of a cone is one-third the volume of a cylinder of the same base and height, that this also holds good with prisms, and that he knew the size relationship of two closely adjacent horizontal sections of a cone.[20]

His astronomical treatises, on the contrary, can be explained only in terms of Babylonian tablets. He began with a tetrology—"Uranography," "Geography," "Polography," and "Actinography"—descriptions of heaven, earth, pole, and light rays or meteorology. The first described the starry heavens, the fixed stars in their various constellations, with a few of the brightest stars included by name. Babylonian astronomers had already divided the concave celestial sphere

[18] Cf. pp. 323 ff.   [19] Megasthenes, in Strabo xv. 1. 38.

[20] Archimedes, fragment published by J. L. Heiberg, "Eine neue Archimedes-Handschrift," *Hermes*, XLII (1907), 425 ff.

into three concentric zones: "The Way of Anu," god of the sky above the Pole where revolved the "stars which see the Pole and never set"; "The Way of Enlil," god of the atmosphere, which the Greeks were to call the ecliptic and still later the Zodiac; and "The Way of Ea," god of the deep, far down in the celestial ocean. With the "Uranography," which we can restore almost completely from Vitruvius, went a number of "planispheres," on which were pictured, in imitation of the Babylonian terms, the human and animal figures which have come to represent the constellations.

Naturally, Democritus begins his description with the Way of Anu:

The Chariot has set, behind it its Driver. Not far distant is the Virgin, on whose right shoulder is a very bright star, Protrugetes; a still more brilliant star is Spica. Opposite is another star, Arcturus, between the knees of the Driver. From the part of the head of the Chariot opposite the feet of the Twins, the Chariot stands on the tip of the horns of the Bull. Likewise on the tip of the left horn the Charioteer holds at his feet the Kids of the Charioteer. Capra is on his left shoulder. Above the Bull and the Ram is Perseus, his right foot supporting the Pleiades, and to his left is the head of the Ram. With his right hand he rests upon Cassiopeia, with his left he holds Medusa's head over the Bull, laying it down at the feet of Andromeda.

The Fish are beyond Andromeda and are level with her abdomen and with the back of the Horse, whose belly a very bright star cuts off from the head of Andromeda. The right hand of Andromeda is placed over Cassiopeia and the left upon the Fish of the North. The Water Carrier is above the head of the Horse. The hoofs of the Horse touch the knees of the Water Carrier. Cassiopeia is pictured between. High up above Capricorn are Eagle and Dolphin. Next to them is the Arrow. Next to it, however, is the Swan, whose right wing touches the right hand and scepter of Cepheus and whose left rests upon Cassiopeia. Under the tail of the bird the feet of the Horse are concealed.

Next above the Archer, Scorpion, and Scales, the Serpent touches the Crown with the tip of his tongue. At his middle, the Serpent Holder grasps in his hands the Serpent, with his left foot treading down the forehead of the Scorpion. By the side of the Serpent Holder's head, not far away, is the head of the Kneeling Man. The tops of their heads are more easily recognized because they are marked out by not inconspicuous stars.

The foot of the Kneeling Man rests on the temple of the Serpent in whose folds the Chariot is caught. Dimly among them the Dolphin swims. Opposite the beak of the Swan is placed the Lyre. Between the shoulders of the Driver and the Kneeling Man the Crown is set.

Democritus has traversed the sky from near the celestial Pole to the Way of Enlil and now is back again to the Way of Anu.

In the Northern zone is the Chariot and the Dog's Tail, the two pictured head to tail. Between their tails is said to be the highest spot (in the celestial sphere). Here the Serpent is stretched out and from it the star which is called the Pole shines around the top of the Chariot, for what lies next to the Dragon (the alternate and more original name of the Serpent), is entangled around its head. Actually around the head of the Dog's Tail is thrown its folds which reach to the bottom. These are also twisted and wind back from the head of the Dog's Tail to the Chariot. Furthermore, above the Dog's Tail are the feet of Cepheus, and there at the highest point are stars forming a Triangle with equal sides above the Ram. However, many of the stars belonging to the Little Chariot and Cassiopeia are intermixed.

Having described the positions of the constellations between the ecliptic and the Chariot (as we would say, the northern celestial hemisphere, but, as he puts it, "to the right of the east"), Democritus turns to those "to the left of east toward the south."

Extended under Capricorn is the Fish of the South, looking toward the tail of the Sea Monster. Above this to the Archer, the space is vacant. The Altar is under the Scorpion's sting. The foreparts of the Centaur are next to the Balance and the Scorpion; in his hands he holds the Beast. The Virgin, the Lion, and the Crab are girdled by the Hydra, which in its squirmings extends through a procession of stars; in the region of the Crab, it raises up its beak, against the Lion it supports by its middle the Crater, and toward the hand of the Virgin it lifts up its tail which is in the Crow. The stars which are above its shoulder are all equally brilliant.

At the lower portion of its belly, under the tail, is placed the Centaur. Next the Cup and the Lion is the ship Argo, whose prow is obscured, but the mast and what is around the rudder are seen projecting. The boat and its stern are joined to the tip of the Dog's Tail. The Twins are followed by the Lesser Dog opposite the head of the Hydra, for the Greater follows the Lesser. Orion lies stretched across, pressed down by the hoof of the Bull, grasping it in his left hand and with his other lifting his club toward the Twins.

At his foot is the Dog following at a short interval the Hare. Under Ram and Fish is stretched out the Sea Monster, from whose mane is a thin mixture of stars, arranged in what are called Bands, toward both Fish; at a great interval a twisting mass of snakes touches the top of the mane of the Sea Monster. A River flows forth, taking its beginning from a Fountain at the left foot of Orion. The water poured out by the Water Carrier flows between the head of the Fish of the South and the tail of the Sea Monster.[21]

[21] Vitruv. ix. 4. 1—5. 3; this section is specifically ascribed to Democritus, otherwise from content and treatment we should have assigned it to the scheme of Eudoxus and Aratus.

In this case, Democritus has abandoned the Babylonian division into three zones and has himself divided it into northern and southern hemispheres. To him also an appendix is probably to be attributed. He has already explained those constellations whose risings and settings can be observed by Greek eyes. They have been divided into two groups, situated and figured with stars on the right and the left of the ecliptic, to the south and to the north.[22] They have been divided, then, into northern and southern hemispheres; this implies northern and southern poles. Just as the Chariot revolves around the North Pole, and neither sets nor goes beneath the earth—to enter the underworld for a season, as the Babylonians would have explained—so around the hypothetical South Pole other constellations must revolve. But, on account of the oblique inclination of the earth, they must always remain concealed from us, neither shining forth above the horizon nor rising above the earth. The reason for this is that the earth intervenes and prevents our observation of their figures. A proof that this hypothesis is correct is the fact that Canopus, a star quite unknown to the Greeks at home, shines brilliantly in the Egyptian Delta, as Democritus himself can witness, and still brighter farther south, as merchants have reported.[23]

This booklet, apparently translated virtually complete, was simply a manual to accompany the figures pictured in the "Planispheres." If we wish to know what they looked like in their original Babylonian form, we need only examine such tablets from Seleucid days as one which depicts "The Virgin Standing before the Face of Mercury," a somewhat stout lady with ears of grain in her hand, before the star symbol of the god.[24] We have no such evidence for the contents of the "Geography" and the "Actinography." "Causes," whether "celestial," "atmospheric," or "terrestrial," may have been Greek in point of view, but the Babylonian principle that meteorology and geography were integral parts of astronomy was even more clearly enunciated. Democritus' successors, Euctemon and Eudoxus, wrote largely on meteorology, and the system of the latter is still preserved in the poem written by Aratus; we have already discovered that in the major portion of the poem, the description of the heavens, Aratus versified Eudoxus and had as the ultimate source Democritus, and the same is presumably true of the meteorological appendix.

Most of what we definitely know about the contents of his "Polog-

22 *Ibid*. 3. 3.   23 *Ibid*. 5. 4.

24 F. Thureau-Dangin, *Tablettes d'Uruk* (1922), No. 12.

raphy" must be gleaned from the above translation. Elsewhere we hear of the celestial sphere revolving about the earth on the hinges of its axis. The North Pole is at a huge distance from the earth and is placed at the very top of this sphere behind the stars of the Chariot; the hypothetical South Pole is under the earth and in the regions of the south. We read also of the gnomon by whose shadow the seasons are determined.[25] This is the split stick employed originally as a rude transit to determine north-south orientation of buildings and later to secure altitudes of stars. Still later the term *ziqpu*, literally a "pole" in contrast to a "beam," became the appellation for that theoretical point in the heavens, then close to *alpha* of the Dragon, around which the celestial system had been discovered to revolve.

"Water-clock contests" must have dealt with the various methods of reckoning time by the *clepsydra;* in Egypt the quantity of water was *measured* from the rising or falling levels marked on the inside, while in Babylonia the amount of water escaping was *weighed* to the shekel, the talent representing a full day of 12 double-hours. This led to the question of chronology. A treatise called "The Great Year" or, more simply, "Astronomy," is described as a *parapegma*, such a table as the bronze tablet set up by Oenopides at Olympia; a later example which fortunately has been preserved shows us that, like our own almanacs, it also predicted movements of sun, moon, and other planets and contained predictions of the weather. A similar "calendar" in cuneiform was calculated long before for 425. The late author who reports the data has misunderstood them, but there can be no doubt that Democritus was the first to introduce the 19-year cycle to the Greeks.[26]

To check this cycle for himself, Democritus had to understand the movements of sun, moon, and other planets in time relation. This information was presented in an advanced textbook "On the Planets." Just before the description of the constellations, as we have seen ascribed specifically to Democritus, Vitruvius tells how the sun, wandering through the constellations, augments and diminishes month by month the length of the days and hours.

When he enters the constellation of the Ram and wanders through an eighth part, he brings about the vernal equinox. When he goes on to the tail of the Bull and the constellation of the Pleiades from which the foreparts of

---

[25] Vitruv. ix. 1. 1–2.

[26] Censorin. xviii. 8; the number of years in the cycle—82—is certainly wrong, but the number of intercalated months—28—is the 4×7 of Callippus' adaptation of the 19-year cycle to which that of Democritus is paralleled.

the Bull stand out, the space through which he runs is more than half of the celestial sphere, as he moves on to the north. When from the Bull he enters into the Twins at the time of the rising of the Pleiades, he rises higher above the earth and increases the length of the day. Then from the Twins, when he enters into the Crab, which holds the shortest space of the sky [full proof that he is speaking of constellations and not of the equally spaced signs of the Zodiac], when he comes into the eighth part, he completes the time of the (summer) solstice. Going on, he passes through to the head and breast of the Lion, which parts are then attributed to the Crab. Going forth from the breast of the Lion and the limits of the Crab, the Sun, running through the remaining parts of the Lion, diminishes the length of the day and of his orbit and returns to the same course (rate of movement) he had in the Twins. Then crossing from the Lion into the Virgin and proceeding to the lap of her robe, he contracts his circuit and makes equal this stretch of his course to that which the Bull holds. Proceeding from the Virgin through her lap, which occupies the foreparts of the Scales, in the eighth part of the Scales he completes the autumnal equinox. This part of the course equals the circuit which he made in the constellation of the Ram.

When, however, the Sun enters the Scorpion, at the setting of the Pleiades, proceeding south he diminishes the length of the days. When proceeding from the Scorpion, he enters the Archer at his thighs, and he flys through a shorter daily course. When he begins from the thighs of the Archer, the part which is assigned to the Capricorn, at the eighth part he runs through the shortest region of the sky. Crossing from the Capricorn into the Water Carrier, he increases the length of the day and equals the circuit of the Archer. From the Water Carrier he enters into the Fish as the west wind blows, and completes a circuit equal to that of the Scorpion. Thus the Sun, in his wandering around the constellations, at fixed times augments or diminishes the length of the days and hours.[27]

There is here nothing which was not known to contemporary Babylonian astronomers, and therefore we are justified in taking Vitruvius to mean that this, too, came from Democritus.

"Causes of Celestial Phainomena"[28] do not refer to phenomena as we use the term; we must translate literally, the "shining-forth" of the planets, that is, their heliacal risings.[29] From this or from the work "On Planets" must be taken the last section in Vitruvius which we may assume to have been translated from Democritus.

Excising certain sections where the thought is undoubtedly later, we read first of the twelve constellations, figured along the transverse

[27] Vitruv. ix. 2. 4–3. 3.   [28] Ptol. Syntax. 93D.
[29] Cf. Olmstead, "The Chronology of Jesus' Life," Anglican Theological Review, XXIV (1942), 24–25.

circle in the middle of the celestial sphere and inclined toward the south, our ecliptic. Six of these constellations are always above the earth. While the constellations revolve continuously from east to west, the planets—Moon, Mercury, Venus, Sun, Mars, Jupiter, and Saturn—each with an orbit of its own, "wander" in an opposite direction in the celestial sphere from west to east.

Lastly comes the determination of periods, the "great years" of the seven planets. The Moon, after running through the circuit of the sky, returns to the constellation from which she started in 28 days and about an hour more and thus completes the lunar month. The Sun passes through the space of a constellation in a month, and when he returns to the constellation from which he started, he completes the length of a year. From this it is evident that the Moon runs through her orbit thirteen times in 12 months, while the Sun measures in the same months just one.

The planets Mercury and Venus, circling around the Sun's rays as through a center, on their journeys return backward and make a delay. Also because of their orbit they delay at the stations (nodes) in the regions of the constellations.

This is particularly well recognized in the case of Venus, for, when following the Sun, it shines forth in the sky after the Sun's setting and, shining most brightly, is called the "Evening Star"; at other times, however, it runs before him and, rising before daylight, is called "Dawn Bringer." For this reason, sometimes they delay several days in a constellation (the Babylonians called this a planet's "standing place"); at other times they enter more quickly into another constellation. Therefore, because they do not wander an equal number of days in the individual constellations, they now make up by accelerated movements the amount of time they formerly delayed.

The planet Mercury so flits along its path in the celestial sphere that, running through the regions, on the 360th day through the constellations it arrives at that constellation from which, on its previous revolution, it began to follow its course, and its path is so averaged that it has about 30 days in each constellation.

Venus traverses the space of some constellations in 30 days. To the degree that it suffers delay for 40 days in certain constellations, when it has made a station (at the nodes), it restores that exact amount lost while delaying. Therefore, it completes the whole circuit of the celestial sphere again on the 485th day, in that constellation from which it began its first journey.

In much the same language we are told that the period of Mars is
683 days, Jupiter 11 years and 313 days, Saturn 29 years and about 160
days. Those planets which traverse their orbit above the path of the
Sun, especially when they are in the Triangle which he has entered,
do not advance but return and delay until that same Sun has made the
transfer to another constellation.

Jupiter, traversing an orbit between Mars and Saturn, follows a
course greater than Mars and less than Saturn. The other planets, by
as much as they are distant from the topmost spot of the celestial
sphere, have an orbit nearest the earth; they seem to move more quickly because each of them, traversing a lesser orbit, more often passes
under and crosses the planet above it.[30]

Everything we have read can be found in the works of Nabu-rimanni and of his immediate successors. There is no reason, then, to deny
that the words of Democritus were something like this. From Democritus this knowledge was transmitted to Euctemon, Meton, and Eudoxus, from whom it was in turn passed on to authors whose works
have been preserved—Aratus, Geminus, Cicero, Vitruvius, Pliny, and
many another of later date. When, therefore, in these later writers we
find data which correspond with those in the textbook of Nabu-rimanni and his disciples, and omit the still more advanced studies of the
Hellenistic age, we have ample reason to assign them in their original
form to Democritus, the first Greek scientist to present the Babylonian
discoveries to his fellow-countrymen.

In his *Great Diacosmus* Leucippus had laid down the principles of the
atomic theory; his still greater pupil developed and corrected it. "Man
is that which we all know," argued Democritus. "Only the atoms and
the void exist in reality. They form the substrate, not merely of animals but of all compound substances." Atoms are conceived as bodies,
solid, indivisible, unalterable, and impassive. Unlimited in size and
number, they are borne about through the whole universe in a vortex,
a vacuum of indefinite extent, having neither top nor bottom nor middle, neither center nor circumference. The motion of these atoms is
such that they collide and thus cohere; from this process there result all things which exist. For this process there is no beginning,
since it goes on through all eternity.

Thus are generated fire, water, air, and earth, which must therefore be considered compounds and not original elements. Nothing can
come into existence from what is not, nor can it pass into nothingness;

[30] Vitruv. ix. 1. 1–11. 14; cf. ix. *praef.* 2.

this is the first statement of the modern law of the conservation of energy. There is no limit to the number of possible worlds which come into being and then perish. The sun, the moon, the soul—by Democritus identified with reason—are all nothing but combinations of atoms. Necessity is only another name for the creative vortex, and the practical end of the philosopher's search is simple tranquillity.[31]

No one but a Greek philosopher could have worked out a theory so beautifully plausible; no Greek philosopher, we should hasten to add, could have worked out the theory without the preliminary labors of the Babylonians, who afforded the theorist not only a firm basis of sound knowledge but also much of the necessary terminology. Greek and Oriental first worked together on Babylonian soil; the result of the co-operation was a theory in large part still accepted by the modern scientist.

Democritus had been welcomed in the Orient as a fellow-student, and Babylonian treasures of knowledge had been freely opened. At home he had made an outstanding reputation, which would not be lost in future generations. In an eloquent funeral oration (439), Pericles had expressed his just pride in Athens' past history, when she alone stopped the Persian invader, in her democracy and her empire, her economic prosperity, her literature and her art crowned by the immortal Parthenon. He had boasted that Athens was the school of Hellas, for the city was open to the world, and there foreigners were allowed every facility for learning; Democritus heard of the invitation and decided to visit the new school. He found that the prejudice against science was yet strong. In fact, Pericles evidently felt that Athens herself had nothing to learn. Says Democritus: "I came to Athens and no one knew me!"[32]

LATER ATHENIAN ASTRONOMERS

Yet the next important astronomer, who, like Democritus, combined meteorology and geography in his astronomy, was an Athenian, Euctemon by name. He made his own observations on the changing positions of the planets and calculations on the lengths of the seasons. But Athens was such unfertile soil for the scientist that in 436 Euctemon abandoned Athens to become a colonist in Amphipolis.[33]

[31] Sext. Empir. *Pyr.* ii. 23–24; Cic. *De fin.* i. 17; Diod. Laert. ix. 44–45.

[32] Thuc. ii. 39, 41; Democritus, Frag. 116.

[33] Callippus, in Simplic. *De coelo*, p. 497, 20 (Heib.); [Theophrast.] *De sign.* Geminus viii. 50; Vitruv. ix. 6; Column. ix. 12; Ptol. *Syntax.* iii. 1; Amm. xxvi. 1. 8; Pap. Eudem. p. 301W.; Avien. 47 ff.

Of course, Democritus' almanac tables were quite unknown at Athens. A metic named Phaeinus first drew Meton's attention to the superior merits of the 19-year cycle.[34] Euctemon placed at his fellow-citizen's disposal his own calculations as to planet changes and lengths of the seasons, the latter of which presumably were responsible for Meton's beginning his year at the summer solstice, and not with New Year's Day in the spring, as in Babylonia. Nor did he start with the seventeenth cycle of the 19-year system—the twenty-second year of Artaxerxes I (April 22, 443)—but at the summer solstice of the twelfth year, observed by Meton, through use of a sundial, to occur on what was then the thirteenth of the Athenian month Scirophorion in the archonship of Apseudes, June 28, 432. Meton's cycle consisted of 235 months, 110 "hollow" or of 29 days each, and 125 "full" of 30. The length of the single year, $365\frac{5}{19}$ days, was then obtained by division; the excess is slightly more than a quarter of a day, $0.2632+$ to be exact. This is a better approximation than that learned by Oenopides from his Egyptian teachers, but it is still 30' 11" too long; it does not compare with the calculations of Nabu-rimanni, who in 492 was only 6' 2" off.

Meton never saw his calendar put into actual operation. In the comedy of *The Clouds* (423) and in the lighter persiflage of *The Birds* (414), the clever but shallow Aristophanes poked fun at Meton. In the latter year Meton also was ridiculed by Phrynichus in his *Solitary*. This was the popular attitude of the Athenians, and their calendar was not reformed.[35]

[34] Diels and Kranz, *op. cit.*, I, 41.

[35] Aristophan. *Nub.* 616; *Av.* 992 ff.; Phrynich., Frag. 21 (Kock); [Theophrast.] *De sign.* 4; Philochor., Frag. 99 (*FHG*, I, 100); Geminus viii. 50; Diod. ii. 47. 6; xii. 36. 2; xx. 36. 2–3;Vitruv. ix. 6. 3; Plut. *Alcibiad.* ii. 4; Ptol. *Syntax.* iii. 2; Aelian. *Var. hist.* x. 7; Censorin. xviii. 8; Schol. Aristophan. *Av.* 997; Schol. Arat. 752; H. Diels, *Abhandlungen der Preussischen Akademie der Wissenshaften* (Berlin,) 1904, p. 93; Dessau, *ibid.*, p. 267; Heath, *op. cit.*, p. 294; W. Kubitschek, "Meton," *PW*, VIII (1932), 1458 ff.

Chapter XXV

DIVIDE AND CONQUER

RENEWAL OF THE PERSIAN-ATHENIAN WAR

THE flattering reception accorded Herodotus at Athens was public evidence that by 445 Pericles was once again veering toward an anti-Persian attitude. That same year he concluded a thirty years' peace with Sparta by which he surrendered the land possessions of Athens in return for protection in his rear. Thus prepared for a renewal of the war against Persia, he could resume the Egyptian adventure by the acceptance of a present of gold and of 45,000 bushels of grain from the Libyan rebel Psammetichus.[1] Still more provocative was the formation of Athenian tribute districts among the remaining states which continued loyal along the lines of the former Persian satrapies—Caria, Ionia, Hellespont, and the Islands—for this was clear indication that Pericles intended to hold his own.[2] Persia met the threat by the detachment of Lycia.

A quarrel between still oligarchic Samos and democratic Miletus led to the defeat of the latter. Miletus appealed to Athens, and Pericles, late in 441, made an expedition which reorganized the island as a democracy. The ousted oligarchs appealed in their turn to Pissuthnes, son of Hystaspes and satrap of Sardis; with the seven hundred mercenaries he permitted them to hire, the island was recovered and the Athenian garrison handed over to the satrap. Pericles, however, regained Samos in the spring of 439, when the promised Phoenician aid by sea failed to arrive. The peace had been openly broken, and by the end of 440 Persia had won back Gargara, Scepsis, Cebren, the western Zeleia, and Astacus. Next, the whole Carian interior was secured with so much of the coast that the forty-nine cities in the tribute list of 440 had dropped by twelve in the list of two years later, and the Carian district was united to the Ionian.[3]

---

[1] Philochorus, Frag. 90; Cratinus, Frag. 73; Plut. *Pericl.* 37. 3.

[2] B. D. Meritt, "Studies in the Athenian Tribute Lists," *AJA*, XXIX (1925), 292 ff.; M. N. Tod, *Greek Historical Inscriptions* (1933), p. 54; *Cambridge Ancient History*, Vol. V (1927), Map 2 opp. p. 33. The districts first appear fully formed in 443–42.

[3] Thuc. i. 115 ff.; Isocr. *De permut.* 111; Ephor. 194–95(J); Duris 66–67(J); Diod. xii. 27–28; Nepos. *Timoth.* 1; Plut. *Pericl.* 25 ff.; Aelian. *Var. hist.* ii. 9; cf. A. B. West, *Classical Philology*, XX (1925), 224–25.

Pericles sought compensation in the Black Sea. Amisus was colonized as a second Piraeus. The tyrant Timesileus was expelled from Sinope, which also became a colony (438). A garrison was placed in Astacus to protect the Greeks from Doedalsus, the first-known semi-independent king of Bithynia (435).[4]

MEGABYZUS

Megabyzus faced another crisis of his interesting if sometimes dangerous existence when at a hunt he saved Artaxerxes from a charging lion. So far from expressing gratitude, the king only remembered the proscription that no subject on pain of death might kill an animal before his master.[5] Orders were given that the offender should be beheaded, but the ladies again came to his assistance and the sentence was commuted to exile at Cyrtae on the Persian Gulf.[6] Artoxares was banished to Armenia for daring to advocate Megabyzus' cause, while Zopyrus followed his father's example by open revolt against the king. In 441 Zopyrus visited Athens,[7] where he probably met Herodotus and to whom he may have contributed some of the Persian tales and official documents with which the historian decked his pages. He was well received at Athens because of his parents' efforts in behalf of the Athenians captured at the surrender of Egypt. Aided by an Athenian contingent, though this meant an act of open war, Zopyrus fell upon Caunus. Significantly enough, the inhabitants professed themselves quite willing to submit, though they would not receive his Athenian allies. Zopyrus refused their terms and began an assault; while climbing the wall, he was struck on the head by a stone and killed. Alcides, the Caunian who slew him, was rewarded by Amestris with crucifixion for the death of her grandson.[8]

Five years of the terrifically hot retreat at Cyrtae proved too much for Megabyzus. Pretending that he had become that fearful, unapproachable thing, a leper, he went back unmolested to Susa and his wife. For the last time the royal ladies pleaded his cause. For the last time Artaxerxes forgave him and restored him to table companionship. The tragicomedy ended when Megabyzus died at the age of seventy-six, sincerely regretted by his lord! Amytis lived on to be-

---

[4] *IG* (ed. minor), I, No. 944; Theopomp., Frag. 389(J); Strabo xii. 3. 14; Diod. xii. 34. 5; Memnon xx. 1; App. *Mithr.* 8. 83; Arr. *Peripl.* 15. 3; Plut. *Pericl.* 20; *Cimon* 13. 4.

[5] Ctes. *Pers.* xvii, Epit. 71.

[6] Islands of the exiles (Herod. iii. 93; vii. 80; Ctes. *Pers.*, Frag. 31).

[7] Herod. iii. 160.   [8] Ctes. *Pers.* xvii, Epit. 71, 74.

come the mistress of the Greek physician Apollonides. In a fit of conscience she confessed her sin to her mother. The scandalized Amestris passed on to her regal son the information that his sister had polluted the royal blood. Artaxerxes left the penalty of the culprit to Amestris, who held Apollonides chained for two months and then ordered him buried alive. Amytis died on that very same day.[9]

CRISIS IN JUDAH

For twelve years Nehemiah had remained governor of Judah, apparently forgotten by the king. A crisis arose in 433. Overtaxation was producing in Judah the same evil results we have already observed in Babylonia. The bitter cry of these Jews and their wives might have been the outcry of all the peoples of the Persian Empire.

The city proletariat shouted: "We, our sons, and our daughters are numerous; give us grain that we may eat and live!" The peasants declared: "We are mortgaging our fields, our vineyards, and our houses to obtain grain on account of the famine!" Landholders of the supposedly better-off class were actually in worse case: "We have borrowed silver to pay the king's tribute in money; our flesh is like the flesh of our brothers, our children like their children, and yet we must make *our* children slaves! Some of our daughters have been enslaved, and we cannot redeem them, for other men possess our fields and our vineyards."

Totally ignorant of the underlying causes for their misery, all laid the blame on their rich fellow-Jews, who, in fact, had only taken advantage of the opportunity offered. So did Nehemiah, for he had not the slightest suspicion that the real villain was the bureaucracy by whose exactions he was himself supported. So he summoned the businessmen and poured out his wrath upon them. In a speech filled with a most unprepossessing self-righteousness, he told them how to the best of his ability he had redeemed fellow-Jews sold to foreigners. He had loaned both money and grain without the wicked interest charged by the bankers. This very day, he insisted, they must return to the original owners the pledged fields, vineyards, olive groves, and houses they had wrongfully occupied, along with the one per cent carrying charge they had exacted on the silver, grain, new wine, and oil. Placed squarely on the spot by the peppery governor, they could only promise to accede, though they fully realized that legitimate business must cease if all contracts were voided in accordance with his

[9] Ctes. *Pers.*, Epit. 72–73.

demands. Evidently, Nehemiah did not take a mere promise too seriously, for he immediately called in the priests and forced the businessmen to take oath, to which he added for good measure his own mighty curse. Unthinkingly, the people who were listening glorified their Lord.

While the former governors, Nehemiah goes on, had laid heavy burdens upon the people, taking from them bread and wine at the rate of forty shekels, and even their slaves acted as masters, he and his colleagues during the twelve years of his administration had never once eaten the bread of the governor. Instead, he himself supported daily at his own table a hundred and fifty Jews, commoners and nobles alike, in addition to visitors from foreign parts. To prove his point, he gives statistics: Every day one ox and six choice sheep were butchered, fowl also, and every ten days all sorts of wines were doled out. "Yet for all this I demanded not the governor's bread, because the bondage was heavy on the people." Nehemiah was one of those bureaucrats who naïvely assume that in some mysterious fashion the expenses of the state are obtained from the air and not from the pockets of the people.[10]

If the merchants dared not publicly talk back to the governor, they could bring their complaints to higher officials who understood that both state and bureaucracy were paid for out of taxes. The hatred displayed by Nehemiah against certain individuals of the higher class, including one former supporter, the high priest Eliashib,[11] suggests the route by which the complaint reached the court. At any rate, before the end of the year 433 in which he attempted his reforms, Nehemiah was recalled by Artaxerxes.[12]

CIVIL WAR IN GREECE

As the breach between Athens and Sparta rapidly widened, despite the Thirty Years' Peace, the Persian government sent to the democratic capital Thargelia (reputed to be a great beauty) and her fellow-courtesans; they were eagerly welcomed by the leading statesmen, and the innermost secrets of Athens were soon at the king's disposal.[13] Suddenly, though not without warning, the Peloponnesian War broke out in 431. The whole situation on Persia's northwestern boundary was thereby completely changed, for the fratricidal struggle which convulsed the whole Greek world—with its Spartan war cry of

---

[10] Nehemiah, chap. 5.

[11] Neh. 13:4 ff.

[12] Neh. 13:6.

[13] Plut. *Pericl.* 24. 2; Athen. xiii. 608–9.

"freedom" for the subjects of Athens—was a not unexpected boon to the great king.

That same year Euripides staged his *Medea*. In it Jason coolly informed his wife that by her temporary marriage to him she had received more than she had given! She was living in Hellas, not a barbarous land. Her life was passed under the rule of law and not of force. She was known to all the Greeks, a glory she could not have experienced while dwelling on earth's outskirts.[14] This was scarcely good propaganda to win the assistance of Persia. From Ethiopia the plague descended upon Egypt and thence upon Athens and large parts of the Persian Empire. Multitudes died, and the economic life, already thrown out of joint by overtaxation, was still further dislocated.[15]

Pharnaces, son of the first Pharnabazus, was now hereditary satrap of Hellespontine Phrygia. From its capital, Dascyleium, near the Rhyndacus, have come reliefs of an interesting monument which dates from the time of his father. Apparently the seven-foot-high slabs of Proconessian marble were to face an open-air altar; half the height is mere smooth border, capped by egg-and-dart molding, and the whole scene forms a low, narrow, slightly sunk panel from which the figures stand out in low, flat relief.

A file of captive women is mounted on mules whose manes are cut short and braided and whose only housing consists of an embroidered saddlecloth on which the ladies sit uncomfortably sidesaddle. A *sakkos* covers their hair, which is waved around the face, and an embroidered himation is drawn as a veil over their heads. The short-sleeved chiton-like undergarment is belted at the waist with an overfall. Before each alternate woman walks a groom, his head covered by the bashlyk, his body by a knee-length robe, while in his hand he carries upright some large object. Behind the women ride the escorts, mounted on horses whose manes are clipped and tails bobbed with the ends tied in a knot; they ride on saddle blankets, their feet stiffly thrust out. Under a mantle of skin with open sleeves, the pelt turned inside out to expose the hair, may be seen the tunic, trousers, free-hanging dagger, and shoes. Traces of an inscription are too faint to afford evidence for its dedication. The style and treatment are predominantly Iranian based on Greek antecedents; only the egg-and-dart molding and the seemingly Ionic epigraph defiantly prove that Greek lands are close.[16]

[14] Eurip. *Medea* 534 ff.   [15] Thuc. ii. 48. 1.

[16] E. Herzfeld, *Am Tor von Asien* (1920), pp. 24 ff., Pls. XII–XIII.

The Peloponnesians appealed to Pharnaces. He promised aid to their envoys, Nicolas and Aneristus, on their proposed journey to the king. Before they could reach his protection, they were captured on the Hellespont by the Thracian king Sitalces, who handed them over to the Athenians for slaughter.

Spartan efforts were continued, but Artaxerxes was more than content to watch the Greeks destroy one another. He closed his eyes to the privateers from southwest Asia Minor who prayed on the merchant ships sailing from Phoenicia and Phasaelis to the Piraeus. Once Sophocles had noted a Sidonian huckster at Athens, Ion the mantle of Egyptian flax, Achaeus the Egyptian unguents and the drink from Byblus, Cratinus the wine from Mendes; the latter also told of travelers to the Sacae and of Sidonians who brought back robes from Syria. Now the rigged sails and the papyri imported from Egypt, the frankincense of Syria, the Phrygian salves, the Paphlagonian acorns for tanning, the almonds, dates, and fine wheat flour of Phoenicia, so proudly sung by Hermippus, were no longer safely transported. Pherecrates expresses his fear that a risk is run by his friend even in traveling to Egypt. It was definitely to the king's advantage that Carians and Lycians scornfully refused tribute to Athens.[17]

LYCIAN DYNASTS

Lycia was by now in the full current of world affairs. Its cities, each in a little valley or perched on a rock, made some pretense to Greek culture and were ruled by a dynast and a local senate. Their tombs, while still retaining in stone the evidence of their timber origin, were decorated with Greek architectural details. Tomb inscriptions in the native writing were beginning to be abundant, rarely with a Greek translation. One bilingual has fortunately survived from one of Limyra's dynasts, Sedareia, whose stater, bearing goat and griffin, we also possess. It shows the tomb formula in its simplest form: "This memorial made Sedareia, Parmena's son, for himself and his wife and his son Pobealaia."[18] Usually the inscription is longer, though the exact interpretation is not always certain; with varied formulas the stranger is forbidden to bury his own dead within the tomb under penalty, so many *ada* or so many shekels, to be paid to the city council, the treasury, the priesthood, or the grave association.

[17] Herod. vii. 137; Thuc. i. 82; ii. 7. 1; 67; 69; Sophocles, Frag. 823 (Nauck²); Ion, Frag. 40 (Nauck²); Achaeus, Frags. 5, 41 (Nauck²); Cratinus, Frags. 183, 207–8 (Kock); Hermippus, Frags. 63, 82 (Kock); Pherecrates, Frag. 11 (Kock).

[18] *TAM*, Vol. I, No. 117; E. Babelon, *Traité des monnaies*, II, Part II (1910), 227–28.

Coin legends become longer and more frequent. Koprlle has left us an enormous number to prove his importance. His legends show that he coined at Xanthus and Marra-Myra, while types indicate other mint cities such as Telmessus and Limyra. Complete absence of Athenian motifs prove that he was no longer an Athenian vassal. Regularly the Lycian "coat-of-arms," the trisceles, is on the reverse. The obverse has a perfect medley of symbols: the Egyptian eye of Horus, the dolphin, goat, flying eagle, or plunging boar, the horse standing or reclining, the mule, the cow suckling her calf, or the native winged horse, Pegasus. Oriental reaction is indicated by the sphinx, the lion (often winged or even horned), and the nude winged genius. Persian influence may be seen in the imitation of the "coat of arms" at Persepolis, the lion devouring the bull, the human-headed bull with wings and horns, and, above all, the bull or bull-and-horse capitals. Nevertheless, the round shield with winged lion, the helmeted Ares, the Hermes carrying the ram over his shoulders, the nude Heracles, Apollo, and Zeus Ammon, suggest that Greek influence was not negligible.[19]

Kharee was son of Arppakho or Harpagus, a good Median name which may indicate that he was, in part, of Iranian blood. Harpagus seems not to have reigned, for Kharee apparently owed his throne to his descent from his maternal grandfather Kharega and to his father-in-law Koprlle. He minted at Xanthus and at Tlawa-Tlos. Regularly the obverse bears the helmeted Athena; once her helmet is crowned with olive, and she is accompanied by her attribute the owl; as regularly, the reverse carries the bust of the dynast himself, with long ringleted beard, ribboned tiara, and olive crown of victory. Rarer types depict Athena riding the dolphin, the bull (at times winged or even human-headed), the eagle, or the shield with two fighting cocks.[20]

This honor of Athena did not imply that Kharee was pro-Athenian. He has left us at Xanthus an inscription of some two hundred and fifty lines; here and there we may conjecture the meaning of the Lycian, especially when he tells of his allies. His brother is Trbbeneme, perhaps the colleague of Zemo, for on their coins they employ alone or together the lion mask and trisceles. Later, Trbbeneme is associated with Wadb, and his son Krostte built a tomb at Limyra. Arbbene coins at Talaba-Telmessus with the regular device of the helmeted Athena or of Heracles wearing the lionskin; once his name

[19] Babelon, *op. cit.*, pp. 233 ff.   [20] *Ibid.*, pp. 265 ff.

is abbreviated "Er" in Carian letters. Methrapta is a Persian Mitrobates whose coins have the lion mask and trisceles, more rarely the
murex purple shell and Apollo. Arowateiase shows also lion mask and
trisceles, now and then the helmeted Athena; Kharee entitles him
sttratakha, the Greek *strategos*, or "general." Like Eta, whose coins
from Telmessus bear dolphin and trisceles, Arowateiase was a relative
of Kharee. The last ally, also seemingly from Telmessus, was Tath-
rhewaebe; his symbols are the boar's head (sometimes on a shield),
a fighting cock or two as a shield device, or the head of Athena,
though the reverse is always the trisceles. In presenting this long list
of dynasts with their strangely spelled names and the types on their
coins, we are adding new and interesting pages to both narrative and
cultural history.[21]

Zagaba and his men, Etretomena and his men, Pttara-Patara and its
senate came together, and Trbbeneme smote the army and Mela-
santra. Kharee, as prince of Xanthus and chief of the Lycians, commanded the men of Tlawa-Tlos and the men of Tarbeda, and he smote
the army and Wakhssapddeme. Like Harakla (Heracles) and Hakhlaza (Achilles), he distinguished himself, a prince of the general-in-
chief. We are reading the native account of the slaying of the Athenian
Melesander when he came to collect tribute by force from the Lycians
(430). Two years later the Carians slew Lysicles on a similar errand.
In connection with the same events, the general of the Lycians,
Izraza, erected his pyramid at Tlos. On the base, Izraza is shown in
cavalry cloak fighting another horseman similarly clad. Next he
fights on foot, his garment shielding his left arm as he thrusts a spear
into a falling horseman. A third relief depicts the conflict of two
hoplites protected by round shields, while a fourth is an assault upon
a hill fort.[22]

NEHEMIAH'S REFORMS

Nehemiah had been recalled from Jerusalem near the end of 433.
During the twelve years he had held the strenuous post of governor
in Judah, the youthful beauty which had won the susceptible heart of
Artaxerxes had dimmed, but he still retained his ability to intrigue.
After certain days—the exact date cannot be fixed—he again asked
permission of the king to return to Jerusalem. Eliashib the high priest
was no longer his friend; he had made his peace with Tobiah and had

---

[21] *Ibid.*, pp. 3, 7 ff., 325 ff., 283 ff., 315 ff., 307 ff., 213 ff., 257 ff.; *TAM*, Vol. I, Nos. 128, 135.

[22] *TAM*, Vol. I, Nos. 44 and 24; Thuc. ii. 69; iii. 19; Paus. i. 29. 7.

assigned him an abode in the very court of the temple. Never averse to direct action, Nehemiah promptly threw out Tobiah's household goods, ordered the rooms to be cleansed, and restored the temple utensils, meal offerings, and frankincense to their former place of storage.

He found that the Levites and singers had fled to their own fields because their portions had not been given them from the temple revenues. The responsible officials were sharply rebuked: "Why is the house of God forsaken?" Levites and singers were restored to their former offices, the tithe of grain, new wine, and oil was brought into the temple treasuries—by this time Nehemiah had forgotten his care for the peasants—and honest treasurers were appointed to supervise their distribution.

In those days Nehemiah saw the Sabbath being violated by treading of the wine press, the gathering of the sheaves, and the lading with them of asses; wine, grapes, and figs were being brought into the city. Resident Tyrians were selling their wares, fish in particular. Nehemiah ordered the gates to be shut at twilight before the Sabbath and not opened until the holy day had ended. When the hucksters camped outside the gates, Nehemiah in person warned them off by threat of arrest, and they came no more.

His attention was drawn to the problem of mixed marriages, which had already baffled Ezra. Jews had taken to themselves women of Ashdod, Ammon, and Moab, and their children spoke, not Jewish, but the language of their mothers. With characteristic vigor, Nehemiah scolded the fathers, cursed them, beat them up, pulled out their hair, and made them swear to reform.

The friendship of Eliashib with Tobiah had been sealed by a marriage alliance. Manasseh, son of Jehoiada, Eliashib's son, had married Sanballat's daughter Nicaso, and Nehemiah chased him out. He fled to Sanballat, who, on Mount Gerizim, built for him a new temple which long remained in close touch with the older shrine at Jerusalem.[23]

Nehemiah finally tells how he purified the people of everything foreign and appointed the charges for the priests and Levites, each to his task, and for the wood offering in its proper season and for the first-fruits.[24] All this and much more was ratified by the priests, Levites, and chiefs of the people, eighty-four in number, in a solemn

[23] Neh. 13:4-29; Joseph. *Ant.* xi. 302 ff.   [24] Neh. 13:30-31.

covenant. The name of the governor, of course, heads the list of signatories, but that of Eliashib is naturally missing.[25] In the hope that the ecclesiastical organization was now as well grounded as were his walls, Nehemiah could return to Susa, for the death of Artaxerxes was obviously approaching. Properly he concludes his narrative: "Remember me, O my God, for good."[26]

NEW ARTISTIC DEVELOPMENTS

If we may trust the evidence of the coins assigned him, Artaxerxes was no true Achaemenid. In contrast to the fine straight nose of his father and grandfather, his was short and curved; his features were coarse, his beard rough.[27] Early in his reign he completed his father's Hall of a Hundred Columns at Persepolis.[28] The well-trained workers of his father were still available, and the execution of the sculptures remaining to be finished represents the very best of the developed classic art.[29] A significant modification in style is, however, to be noted. Xerxes had introduced the monumental classic form of sculpture limited by and dependent upon monumental architecture, comparable to the art in the temple of Zeus at Olympia. In the reign of Artaxerxes, Pheidias and his colleagues directed the decoration of the Parthenon at Athens, and the sculptors at Persepolis completed the Hall of a Hundred Columns. In this new style the figures are becoming less grand and more human in proportion and three-dimensionally independent of their architectural background; their unified integrity is finished by perfection of detail and technique.[30]

By 461 Artaxerxes had removed to Susa,[31] and most of the remaining years of his long reign he remained there but did no building. Near the close, the palace in which Xerxes and his son had received so many Greek embassies burned to the ground and was not restored.[32] After this catastrophe Artaxerxes retired to Persepolis and took up his abode in the former palace of Darius, which seems to have required

[25] Neh. 9:38—10:39.

[26] Neh. 13:31b; for Nehemiah cf. Olmstead, History of Palestine and Syria (1931), pp. 588 ff.

[27] Babelon, op. cit., pp. 43 ff.; G. F. Hill, Greek Coins of Arabia, Mesopotamia, and Persia (1922), pp. 153 ff.

[28] George G. Cameron, Persepolis Treasury Tablets (1947).

[29] An inscription of Artaxerxes I (Herzfeld, Altpersische Inschriften [1938], No. 22) proves the location of his own sculptures in the southeast corner of the Hall of a Hundred Columns.

[30] So Cleta Margaret Olmstead.   [31] Herod. vii. 151.

[32] Susa inscription of Artaxerxes II (F. H. Weissbach, Die Keilinschriften der Achämeniden [1911], pp. 122–23).

little repair after its completion by his father Xerxes. Fragmentary reliefs, prepared to illustrate an inscription of Artaxerxes I,[33] are today found scattered along the walls of the court south of the palace. They show that the artist had replaced the earlier styles of monumentality with a new art of delicacy and refinement. To date the reliefs, there remains but one group, copied from the tribute procession of Xerxes' apadana but framed by lines of rosettes, since there was no room for the conifers which, on the model, divide each series. Here the figures are smaller in size and importance and are more widely spaced—a tendency developed in the Erechtheum on the Athenian acropolis.

To this inscription, and to the text found in the Hall of a Hundred Columns, we may add a few epigraphs on alabaster vases and others on silver libation bowls "made for the palace" at Ecbatana;[34] this done, we have collected all the extant inscriptional evidence for the reign.

Before his reign was quite at an end, Artaxerxes seems to have returned home to Susa to die. He was buried, however, at Naqsh-i-Rustam, where his tomb had been excavated to the west of the last resting-places of his father and his grandfather. Like that of his father Xerxes, his tomb bore no inscription.

GREEK POLITICS AND COMEDY

Even before his death, Artaxerxes had lost interest in the Greek civil war. He raised no objection when Pissuthnes supplied mercenaries to free Colophon's port of Notium from Athenian control in 430, and he took no action when Athens re-established her supremacy there in 427, for it soon returned to Persian allegiance. He might have smiled if he had heard that Pherecrates had caricatured the Persians in his play and had given unheard-of luxuries to their poor or that Aristophanes in 426 had named his *Babylonians* from a chorus of slaves taken from the empire and detained at Samos, or had brought on the stage ambassadors returning from the king. The loss of Cerasus and Trapezus on the north shore of Asia Minor in 425 was a more serious danger to Persia. Euripides that year triumphantly announced that Asia was serving Europe as a slave.[35]

[33] *Ibid.*, pp. 120–21; Herzfeld, *op. cit.*, Nos. 20–21; J. M. Unvala, in A. U. Pope (ed.), *A Survey of Persian Art*, I, 343.

[34] Weissbach, *op. cit.*, pp. 120–21; Herzfeld, *op. cit.*, No. 23; *Archäologische Mittheilungen aus Iran*, VII (1935), 1 ff.; VIII (1937), 8 ff.

[35] Thuc. iii. 31, 34; Aristot. *Rhet.* iii. 2. 15; Pherecrat., Frags. 126 ff. (Kock); Aristophan., Frags. 64 ff. (Kock); Eurip. *Hecuba* 481–82.

In the autumn the dying monarch sent Artaphernes to the Spartans with the peevish complaint that he could not make out what they wished; of the many ambassadors who had reached the court, no two said the same thing. If they would only speak plainly, they might send back envoys with Artaphernes. The messenger was intercepted at Eion and the dispatches written in "Assyrian letters"—Aramaic— were translated into Greek; Artaphernes was sent back, but this time he was accompanied by Athenian ambassadors. Aristophanes in his *Acharnians* again brought on the stage the king's ambassador and parodied Herodotus. Athenian hopes ran high, but at Ephesus the envoys learned that Artaxerxes was dead, and dejectedly they returned home.[36]

[36] Thuc. iv. 50; Damastes, Frag. 8(J); Aristophan. *Achar.* 61 ff., 647 ff.

Chapter XXVI

DECISION FOR SPARTA

ACCESSION OF DARIUS II OCHUS

SOON after the death of the aged Queen-Mother Amestris, Artaxerxes and Damaspia passed away on the same day, about the end of 424.[1] His one son by Queen Damaspia, Xerxes II, was recognized as his successor, at least in Susa. Xerxes II lasted but forty-five days, when he was killed while sleeping off the effects of the drinking which followed a festival. His assassin was Secydianus, Artaxerxes' son by the Babylonian concubine Alogune, who was aided by the eunuch Pharnacyas, a favorite of his father. Bagorazus, the most influential courtier of the former monarch, brought the corpses of father, mother, and son in a mule-drawn wagon to Parsa, where they were buried in the tomb prepared for Artaxerxes, to the west of Xerxes' sepulcher in the Naqsh-i-Rustam cliff. On his return, the new king ordered Bagorazus stoned to death because, he claimed, the royal corpse had been interred without his own consent. Menostanes, a former rival of Bagorazus, became the new *hazarapat*.

Another son by a Babylonian concubine was Ochus; his mother's name was good Akkadian, Cosmartidene, though it meant that the Edomite god "Kos has given a daughter." Artaxerxes had married him to Parysatis, his half-sister by a third Babylonian concubine, Andria, and had made him satrap of Hyrcania. Later he had gone to Babylonia.

Secydianus repeatedly demanded that he come to Susa. As repeatedly Ochus promised that he would obey, but he was only seeking delay until he could raise an army and declare himself king. He succeeded in winning over the commander of cavalry Arbarius, the satrap of Egypt Arsames, and the eunuch Artoxares, banished some time ago to Armenia. By February 13, 423, he was recognized under his new name of Darius in Babylonia.[2]

Although both Darius and Parysatis were half-Babylonian by

---

[1] Ctes. *Pers.* xvii, Epit. 74; R. A. Parker and W. H. Dubberstein, *Babylonian Chronology, 626 B.C.—A.D. 45* (1942), pp. 15–16.

[2] Ctes. *Pers.* xviii, Epit. 75–79; Parker and Dubberstein, *op. cit.*, p. 16.

355

birth, there is no indication that the satrapy profited thereby. Instead, the notorious Enlil-nadin-shum, head of the Murashu firm of loan sharks, hurried off to Babylon to greet his new master and to see that the privileged position of Murashu Sons be maintained. That he might be housed in a manner befitting that position, on February 13 he rented a dwelling on the ramparts of Bel close to the ruins of Esagila; his landlord bore the good Babylonian name of Apla, but his father was the Egyptian Harmachis. For this house, "until the going-forth of the king," he paid the enormous rental of a pound and a half of silver; evidently the temporary capital was crowded. Unfortunately for Enlil-nadin-shum, he had not realized that the crowds portended the immediate departure of Darius for Susa, and eleven days afterward we find him back in Nippur recouping his losses by charging two poor women more than double the normal rate of interest.[3]

If Enlil-nadin-shum had not paid homage to the king, he had certainly "seen" some of his higher officials, for in the first year of Darius II (423–404) Murashu Sons continued to gather in "bow lands" on a scale utterly without precedent. In the years immediately following, the firm kept on picking up the remnants of crown lands still in possession of the original grantees.

Arrived at Susa, Darius found the soldiery—despite the lavish donations of the usurper—completely alienated by the assassination of the legitimate ruler Xerxes and of their favorite Bagorazus. Menostanes warned his master against the new pretender, but on the advice of Parysatis her husband was able to induce Secydianus to accept the promise of a divided kingdom. Darius promptly ignored his solemn assurances and seized Secydianus, who had reigned but six and a half months. The punishment inflicted was cruel; after Secydianus had been stuffed with food and drink, he was placed on a beam overhanging a bin of ashes into which he dropped when at last he fell asleep.[4]

Artoxares reached Susa from Armenia and, against Darius' hypocritical protestations, set the citaris on the pretender's head. Another pretender, his full brother Arsites, was aided by Artyphius, the remaining son of Megabyzus. Artasyras, general of Darius, after two defeats, bribed the Greek mercenaries of Artyphius, and, since Arsites did not support him, the rebel was compelled to surrender on terms. Parysatis made it clear to her husband that it would be unwise to break the oaths until Arsites also was in his hands; when he, too, was

3 A. T. Clay, BE, Vol. IX, No. 108; Vol. X, Nos. 1 ff.
[3] A. T. Clay, *BE*, Vol. IX, No. 108; Vol. X, Nos. 1 ff.
[4] Ctes. *Pers.* xviii, Epit. 77, 79; Valer. Max. ix. 2. 6.

PLATE XLI

Indian (courtesy Oriental Institute)

Babylonian (courtesy Oriental Institute)

Arabian (courtesy Oriental Institute)

Lydian (courtesy Oriental Institute)

THE TRIBUTE LIST ACCORDING TO HERODOTUS

PLATE XLII

Amanus Gates

Upper Zab River

THE ROYAL ROAD

PLATE XLIII

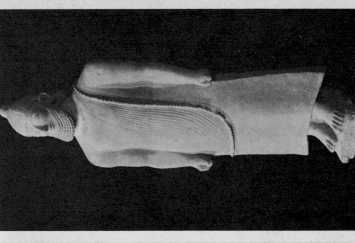

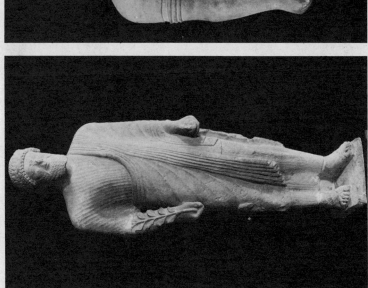

Greek Type

Egyptian Type

Assyrian Type

CYPRIOTE ART (FROM CESNOLA COLLECTION, COURTESY NEW YORK METROPOLITAN MUSEUM)

PLATE XLIV

Statuette for Healing (from Louvre, *Encyclopédie photographique*, Vol. V, Pl. 139)

Saite Horus (from Louvre, *Encyclopédie photographique*, Vol. IV, Pl. 120)

EGYPTIAN INFLUENCES ON HERODOTUS

PLATE XLV

Xanthos Relief

Cypriote Sarcophagus (courtesy New York Metropolitan Museum)

THE ART OF ACHAEMENID DEPENDENCIES

PLATE XLVI

Relief from Southern End of Hall of Hundred Columns
(courtesy Oriental Institute)

Metope from Northwest Corner of Parthenon

THE CLASSICAL ART OF GREECE AND PERSIA

PLATE XLVII

Tribute-bearers on Relief of Artaxerxes I (courtesy Oriental Institute)

Odysseus and Penelope on Attic Vase (from Furtwängler-Reichhold, *Griechischer Vasenmalerei*)

LATE CLASSICAL ART

PLATE XLVIII

Cedars of Lebanon

Pines of Cyprus

THE FORESTS OF THE EMPIRE

Palms of Iraq

seized, all followed Secydianus into the ashes. For his part in the murder of Xerxes, Pharnacyas was punished by stoning. Death was also
the penalty of Menostanes, but, before execution in more savage
fashion could be carried out, he saved himself by committing suicide.[5]

Darius might now claim to be the legitimate avenger of Xerxes.
His coins represented him with eye in profile, bulging Armenoid nose,
full cheek, and long beard. Eunuch influence was strongly exerted by
the reinstated Artoxares, as by Artibarzanes and Athous, but the real
master was his sister-wife Parysatis. Before his accession, she had
borne him a daughter named Amestris and a son Arsaces; afterward,
the sons were Cyrus, Artostes, and Oxendras, the only children of an
original thirteen who survived infancy. As so often happened, the
mother's favorite was not Arsaces, actually the oldest son, but Cyrus
—the eldest born to the purple, to whom she gave the name of the
empire's founder.[6]

PEACE AMONG THE GREEKS

An attempt on Pontic Heracleia by the Athenian Lamachus in the
summer of 424, during the period of civil disturbance, had failed when
the anchored ships of the blockading fleet were destroyed by an unexpected gale.[7] In one of his comedies Aristophanes spoke of a Greek
plot with the Medes and the king. By 423 the maternal uncle of the
orator Andocides, Epilychus, had led an Athenian embassy to Darius
and had made a treaty of friendship, by which the understanding with
Callias was renewed; Aristophanes thereby learned of the very expensive *kaunakes* garment woven at Ecbatana.[8] Pharnaces, the satrap of
Dascyleium, in 422 granted Atramytteium on the Aegean to the
Delians ungratefully expelled by the Athenians.[9] In 421 Aristophanes
indicted Zeus for surrendering Greece to the Medes and declared that
the sun and the moon had plotted to betray Greece to the barbarians
because they sacrificed only to these divinities.[10] In March, however,
the great civil war between the Greeks was ended by the Peace of
Nicias.

[5] Ctes. *Pers.* xviii, Epit. 78, 80–82; Diod. xii. 64. 1; 71. 1; Paus. vi. 5. 7.

[6] Ctes. *Pers.* xviii, Epit. 80, Frag. 32 (Plut. *Artox.* 1).

[7] Thuc. iv. 75. 2; Diod. xii. 72. 4; Just. xvi. 3. 9 ff.

[8] *IG* (ed. minor), II, No. 8; Dittenberger, *Syl.*, No. 118; Andoc. *De pace* 29; Aristophan. *Equites*
478; *Vesp.* 1137 ff.; Leucon *Presbeis*, in T. Kock (ed.), *Comicorum Atticorum fragmenta*, I (1880), 703.

[9] Thuc. v, 1; Diod. xii. 73.

[10] Aristophan. *Pax* 107 ff.

Darius followed the example of his predecessors by interfering with Jewish religious practices. Through the satrap Arsames, as announced to the mercenaries at Elephantine by a certain Hananiah, the king sent in 419 a rescript enforcing the Passover celebration according to the lawbook recently introduced into Judah by Ezra. This induced a new interest in religion and made possible a great collection of funds for the local temple of Yahu.[11]

Two years later (417) the firm of Murashu Sons at Nippur suddenly disappears. Since the slave who acted as their chief agent is later named in the service of a Persian official, we may conjecture that royal commissioners had made a visit, had recovered the lost crown lands, and had punished the usurers. Thereafter a few scant documents, dealing only with grazing lands, are mute witnesses to the fields which had gone out of cultivation through the rapacity of the loan sharks and the ruinous taxation of the bureaucracy.

The equally ruinous fratricidal struggle of the Greeks had apparently been quieted by the Peace of Nicias. As late as 415, Euripides could recall how Pallas Athena had tempted Paris with the leadership of the Phrygian army to defeat Hellas, and Hera had promised the tyranny of Asia and Europe, but in vain.[12] Athens herself broke the uneasy peace by an insane expedition to Sicily, which so weakened her power that the war was renewed in 413. Nevertheless, Athens still ruled the Aegean, and only Persian aid could bring victory to Sparta and her confederates. Thanks to the shortsighted politicians of Greece, at the very moment when the already shattered empire was to suffer a new outbreak of revolts, the skilled diplomacy of Persian leaders, backed by gold wrung from impoverished subjects, was to make Persia dictator to Greece.

The first of the new revolts was begun by Pissuthnes, satrap of Sardis (413). Against him were sent Tissaphernes, Spithradates, and Parmises. The revolt was of more than local importance for the Greeks, since it brought on the scene Tissaphernes, son of Hydarnes, the ablest and most unscrupulous diplomat that Persia ever produced. Given oversight of the whole peninsula, he quickly justified his ap-

[11] A. E. Cowley, *Aramaic Papyri of the Fifth Century B.C.* (1923), Nos. 21–22; Olmstead, *History of Palestine and Syria* (1931), pp. 604–5.

[12] Eurip. *Troad.* 925 ff.

pointment; the mercenaries led by Athenian Lycon were bribed by the gift of a few towns, and Pissuthnes was compelled to surrender. Trusting to the promise that he would not be killed, he went with his captor to Susa; ignoring the terms agreed, Darius ordered the rebel's fate for Pissuthnes, and he followed his predecessors into the cinders. Amorges, his natural son, held out on the Carian coast with Athenian aid; this last insult determined the king to assist the Spartans against the Athenians.[13]

The time seemed propitious to demand the tribute once paid by the Greek cities which Athens had caused to revolt, and the loss of which had never been admitted by Persia. Tissaphernes, now governor of Sardis, was given orders to send in the arrears. With the envoys to Sparta from the revolting Lesbians, Chians, and Erythraeans, he sent his own representative and promised to maintain such forces as the Spartans might dispatch to Asia. His steady rival Pharnabazus, who had just succeeded his father Pharnaces[14] as hereditary satrap of Dascyleium, sought through the good offices of a Megarian and a Cyzicene exile at his court to persuade the Spartans rather to order their fleet to the Hellespont, where also Athenian subjects might be induced to rebel. In reply, the Spartans promised Pharnabazus that later they would make the expedition, but first their ships must visit Chios, the leader in the revolt against Athens (413).[15]

In return for this aid, Tissaphernes assisted the attack on Teos with troops under his lieutenant Stages. Miletus revolted while Euripides was declaring that, of the barbarians, all were slaves but one, and so they could have no relations with the Greeks. Clazomenae, Teos, Lebedos, Ephesus, Phocaea, and Cyrene admitted Persian garrisons and paid up their back taxes. Chalcideus the Spartan signed a treaty between the Lacedemonians and their allies and the king and Tissaphernes; had there been a "Greek cause," it would have been complete betrayal: "Whatever land and cities the king has or the king's fathers had shall belong to the king. Whatever came to the Athenians as tribute money or as any other thing, the king, the Lacedemonians, and the allies shall jointly prevent the Athenians from taking. Furthermore, the king, the Lacedemonians, and the allies shall jointly wage war against the Athenians, and the war shall not end until it is agreed by both. If any revolt from the king, they also shall be enemies

[13] Thuc. viii. 5. 5; 19. 2; 54. 3; Andoc. De pace 29; Ctes. Pers. xviii, Epit. 83.
[14] Still alive in 414 (Aristophan. Aves 1028).
[15] Thuc. viii. 5. 4–5; 6. 1 ff.; 8. 1–2; Diod. xiii. 36. 5; Plut. Alcibiad. 24. 1.

to the Lacedemonians and their allies, and the contrary in the same manner."[16]

In pursuance of this agreement, Tissaphernes destroyed the wall of Teos but was defeated before Miletus. In the autumn, Iasus was captured in sudden assault by the Peloponnesians, and the city with the rebel Amorges was handed over to Tissaphernes, who welcomed his mercenaries into the satrapal service.[17] Kharee of Xanthus tells his part in the smiting of the Ionians (Eiana) in the Chersonessus (Krzzanasa), of the men of Iasus (Eiaaos); of how he helped the people of the god Tarqu (Torakhss) to conquer the army and Amorges (Homrkhkha). Tissaphernes (Kezzaprnna), son of Hydarnes (Wedrnna), Otanes (Otana), and Ariaramnes (Areiamana) gave orders that the dead should be properly buried, after the Persian (Parzza) prince and the Spartans (Sppartazi) had conquered the Athenians (Atanazi)—those who had conquered the army of the foreigners. In an uncertain context, we hear of Darius (Ntareiaosa) and Artaxerxes (Artakhsseraza), of two mercenary generals Sbareda and Sogenes (Sokhenaia), and of the Spartans.

A full account of the victory and of the burial honors to the dead was placed on a column erected at Xanthus in a sacred inclosure near the theater; once it was crowned by reliefs depicting the warlike deeds of the prince who made the dedication. For the most part the record is in Lycian, but at the end is a curse by the gods in an older dialect, the metrical scheme clearly marked.

Set in the midst is a poem in Attic Greek. The letters are transitional between Old Attic and Ionic (another indication of date). It is a hodgepodge of quotations and reminiscences; the first line is lifted from a poem, supposedly written by Simonides to commemorate the great victory of Eurymedon, in reality praising the last exploit of Cimon in Cyprus, and eked out from Hesiod and from Sophocles' *Trachinians*. Our translation is at least as good as the original:

From the time when Europe and Asia asunder the sea divided,
  None as yet of the Lycians such a stone has erected,
Unto twelve gods of the market in a pure inclosure;
  'Tis of conquest and war an ever-living remembrance.

Krois, Harpagus' son, who was the most skilled in all things,
  With his hands, in contest with those of his age of the Lycians,
Many the city forts, with Athena, destroyer of cities,
  He sacked, and to his relations he gave a monarch's portion.

[16] Eurip. *Helen* 276, 440; Thuc. viii. 16. 3; 17–18; Plato *Menex.* 243B.
[17] Thuc. viii. 20. 2; 25 ff.; 36. 1; 54. 3.

Wherefore the immortal gods, who gratitude remember for his justice,
  Seven the hoplites he killed in one day, Arcadian warriors,
To Zeus he set up trophies, the most of all mortals,
  With the most beauteous works, he crowned the Carican people.[18]

Alcibiades, expelled from Sparta and hoping for recall to Athens, had become adviser to Tissaphernes; his advice coincided with the satrap's own conviction that one party should be played off against the other to the king's ultimate advantage. Sparta had proceeded calmly to collect the tribute formerly paid by the Greek cities of Asia to Athens; this was in flat contradiction to the Treaty of Miletus and set a precedent dangerous to Persia. As substitute, Tissaphernes took upon himself the support of the Spartan fleet and advanced a month's pay.[19]

The Treaty of Miletus thus nullified, the dissatisfied Spartans negotiated a second with King Darius, the king's sons, and the satrap: "Neither the Lacedemonians nor the allies shall war against or harm or exact tribute from the country or cities which belonged to the king or to his father or to his ancestors. King Darius and those over whom he rules shall not fight or harm the Lacedemonians or their allies. If they need anything from the king or he needs anything from them, whatever they persuade one another, that shall be right to do. War and peace shall be made jointly. Whatever army is in the king's land to which it has been summoned by the king, the king shall bear the cost. If any of the cities in this agreement shall go against the king's land, the others shall prevent them and aid the king to the best of their power," and the king makes the same promise.[20]

Once he had brought about surrender of Spartan claims to tribute by this ancient anticipation of "lend-lease," Tissaphernes immediately lost his enthusiasm for the fleet payments. With even the three obols per day for the common seaman in arrears, discipline suffered.[21] A special commission reached Cnidus, which Tissaphernes had recently induced to become a willing subject.[22] Lichas, its head, denounced the two treaties and proposed a substitute; his government would never ratify a shameful agreement which recognized Persian claims to the islands and to European Greece north of the Corinthian Isthmus. Such a treaty would stultify the Spartan claim that they had come as liberators by handing over Greek cities to the empire; personally, he did not wish financial support at so heavy a price. Tissaphernes,

[18] TAM, Vol. I, No. 44; S. Bugge, Festschrift für O. Benndorf (1898), pp. 231 ff.
[19] Thuc. viii. 29. 1; 45 ff.; cf. 54. 3; Plut. Alcibiad. 24. 3.
[20] Thuc. viii. 37.   [21] Ibid. 45. 2; cf. 29.   [22] Ibid. 35. 1.

naturally concluding that Alcibiades told only the truth when he declared that Sparta intended to free the Greek cities in Asia, left the
conference in a huff.[23]

Representatives of the Athenian conservatives approached Tissaphernes and were encouraged to plot a revolution at home. They had
hoped that Alcibiades would act as go-between; when, however, the
formal embassy visited the satrap, Alcibiades as his representative
made such impossible demands—surrender of Ionia and the islands—
that negotiations were broken off.[24]

Sparta had been taught her lesson. In the spring of 411 the third
treaty within a year was signed. It began: "In the thirteenth year of
the reign of Darius," with the Lacedemonian ephor mentioned in
second place; the change in the dating formula by itself showed that
Sparta admitted her inferiority to the empire. The agreement was
made in the Maeander Plain, not only with Tissaphernes and the royal
secretary Hieramenes, but also with the sons of Pharnaces, Pharnabazus and his brothers. The affairs of the king are given precedence
over those of the Lacedemonians and their allies. The country of the
king, whatever is in Asia, shall belong to the king, and regarding his
own land the king may do as he pleases. (This met the objection of
Lichas by excluding European Greece and the islands, but all the more
definitely it abandoned all Asiatic Greece to the king.) Tissaphernes
agreed to pay for all Peloponnesian ships now present and to continue
to do so until the royal fleet arrived; after that, at their option, they
could maintain their ships at their own expense or borrow what they
needed from the satrap as a war debt to be paid at the end of the conflict.[25]

The Phoenician fleet, for the first time in years at something like
war strength—a hundred and forty-seven vessels—held back, but payment to the allies continued irregular. Pharnabazus sent word that he
would be a more satisfactory paymaster, and ships were dispatched
to his coast. Miletus became thoroughly disgusted with the situation and captured the fort erected by Tissaphernes to guard its land,
while Cnidus also expelled the Persian garrison. A Milesian embassy
to Sparta protested against Tissaphernes' friendship with Alcibiades,
temporarily recalled by Athens; in his defense the satrap dispatched
Gaulites, a Carian who also spoke Greek.

[23] *Ibid.* 39. 1; 43. 3–4; Diod. xiii. 37. 4–5; Plut. *Alcibiad.* 25. 1.
[24] Thuc. viii. 47 ff.; 56; Nepos *Alcibiad.* 5. 2–3; Plut. *Alcibiad.* 25. 3 ff.
[25] Thuc. viii. 57–58.

While the Milesian embassy was in Sparta, the melic poet Timotheus of Miletus was in Athens. There he exhibited *The Persians*, almost certainly at the greater Panathenaea of 410.[26] He took as his theme the naval victory of Salamis, already utilized by Aeschylus for propaganda on the stage; there were sly digs against his personal opponents, the Spartans, to whom his fellow-citizens were protesting, while in the mouth of Themistocles he placed the proud boast: "Ares is master! Hellas, at least, does not fear gold!"—a barbed reference to the subsidy promised the Lacedemonians by treaty but already falling into arrears.[27] The account of the battle ended with the setting-up of the trophy, the shouting of the victorious "Paean," and the joyful chorus of dancers. Swept off their feet by the encouraging picture, no wonder the Athenians gave their votes for the poet's own triumph in the contest of poets.[28] Salamis was also glorified by the Samian Choerilus in his epic, *The Persians;* the Athenians decreed that the poem should be publicly recited at the Panathenaea along with Homer.[29]

By now the Phoenicians had reached Aspendus; their arrival allowed Tissaphernes to dispense with further payments of subsidies. Thoroughly alienated by his action, the few remaining Peloponnesian vessels had by summer followed their companions and joined his rival. Arsaces, his cavalry general, had not bettered the situation by the treacherous slaughter of the leaders of the Delian exiles settled at Atramytteium; irritated by the heavy taxation and fearing a similar fate as a result of a quarrel, the Antandrians expelled the Persian garrison from their acropolis. Their suppression provided a welcome excuse for Tissaphernes to keep in sight that rival, and he started for the Hellespont.[30]

HAREM INTRIGUES

Tissaphernes explained the refusal of the fleet to advance westward as due to its smallness in number. The actual reason was that Darius had his troubles much nearer home. First there was a Median revolt, though it was quickly suppressed.[31] Next Artoxares, puffed up by his

---

[26] S. E. Bassett, "The Place and Date of the First Performance of the *Persians* of Timotheus," *Classical Philology*, XXVI (1931), 153 ff.

[27] Timotheus, Frag. 17 (Edmonds); Thuc. viii. 37; 45. 2.   [28] See Bassett, *op. cit.*, p. 158.

[29] Suid., *s.v.* "Choirilos"; cf. Bethe, "Choirilos," *PW*, III (1899), 2359 ff.

[30] Thuc. viii. 78; 80. 1; 81. 3; 84. 4; 85; 87; 99; 108; Isocr. *De bigis* 18; Theopomp., Frag. 9(J); Plut. *Alcibiad.* 26. 6–7.

[31] Xen. Hell. i. 2. 19.

record as kingmaker, decided to make himself king. Although a eunuch, he had taken to himself a wife; childishly believing that he would be accepted as a man if he wore beard and mustache, he gave her instructions to manufacture some. This was too much for his wife, who promptly betrayed the plot; Parysatis ordered him seized, and the would-be kingmaker died.[32]

Much more serious in its consequences was a conspiracy of Teri-teuchmes, who had been assigned his father Hydarnes' satrapy of Hyrcania on his marriage to the king's daughter Amestris. But Teriteuchmes still loved his beautiful though masculine half-sister Roxana; as a wife of so high degree could not be divorced, he agreed with three hundred companions to share the guilt of rebellion by placing Amestris in a sack which each should pierce with a sword. Letters from Darius to Udiastes, armor-bearer of the satrap, persuaded him to kill his lord, and Amestris was saved. Terrible was the revenge of Parysatis for the attempted murder of her daughter. Roxana was hacked to pieces. Arsaces pleaded for the life of his wife Stateira, also a sister of the rebel, and finally won over his mother, though his father prophetically warned Parysatis that she would live to regret her leniency. The mother of the rebel, his brothers Mitrostes and Helicus, and all his remaining sisters were savagely put to death. For his great services as a diplomat, the other brother Tissaphernes was spared for a time, although Parysatis did not conceal her hatred. A son of the rebel also survived; to him Mitradates, son of Udiastes, turned over a city named Zaris.[33]

COMPLAINTS OF JEWISH MERCENARIES IN EGYPT

Another Hydarnes—Vidarnag in Aramaic—had in 420 been "chief of the army" in Syene. Between 416 and 411 he was promoted to the rank of *fratarak* or governor of the district in place of Damadin. When the satrap Arsames returned to the king in July, 410, Hydarnes seized the opportunity to revolt, with the support of the priests of Khnub and of the Egyptian standards, now commanded by his son and successor Nephayan.

Egyptian support had evidently been secured by a promise to destroy the Jewish temple, so offensive to popular sentiment because of its animal sacrifices. Nephayan led out his Egyptian and other standards. The temple was razed to the ground, its stone pillars were broken, its five gateways of cut stone were torn down, its doors

---

[32] Ctes. *Pers.* xviii, Epit. 84.   [33] Ctes. *Pers.* xviii, Epit. 85–87; Plut. *Artox.* 2.

(whose hinges were shod with bronze) and its roof of cedar were burned, and its gold and silver utensils were looted.

Joyfully the Jewish elders tell how quickly the revolt was put down. They, their wives, and their children put on sackcloth and fasted and prayed to the Lord of Heaven, who permitted them to see their desire on that Hydarnes; the dogs tore the anklet from his legs, all the riches he had acquired were destroyed, and all those who had wrecked their temple were put to death.

But this did not result in the restoration of the temple. Even before the revolt had been subdued, Jedoniah and his fellow-priests had appealed to the authorities in Palestine for assistance. Nehemiah had been succeeded as governor of Judah by Bagoses (Bagohi), while Nehemiah's enemy Eliashib had been followed by Joiada his son, and after a short occupancy of the high priestly office he by his own son Johanan.[34] A letter, addressed to the governor, the high priest, and his colleagues (the priests who were in Jerusalem), for double assurance named also Ostanes, the brother of Anani, and the Judaean nobles; quite naturally no answer was returned, for the destruction of a rival shrine could win only their applause.

So, on November 25, 407, a second letter was dispatched, this time to Bagoses alone. There were the usual fulsome good wishes: "The health of your Lordship may the God of Heaven seek exceedingly at all times, and give you favor before Darius the king and the princes of the palace more than now a thousand times, and may he grant you long life, and may you be happy and prosperous at all times." Next, Jedoniah and the associated priests tell the story of the attack. They recall how their fathers had built that temple in Yeb the fortress before the Persian invasion and how, when Cambyses entered Egypt and destroyed all the temples of the native gods, no one did any harm to their own.

But for the more than three years since the destruction of their temple, they have worn sackcloth and fasted, have not anointed themselves with oil, and have drunk no wine; their wives have become as widows. Since the natives will not permit temple restoration, they appeal to Bagoses: "Look on your well-wishers and friends who are here in Egypt. Let a letter be sent from you to them concerning the temple of the God Yahu to build it in the fortress of Yeb as it was built before, and they shall offer the meal offering and incense and sacrifice upon the altar of the God Yahu on your behalf. And we will

[34] Neh. 12:22-23, called wrongly "Jonathan" in 12:11; cf. also Joseph. *Ant.* xi. 297.

pray for you at all times, we, our wives, our children, and the Jews, all who are here, if the temple is rebuilt, and it shall be a merit for you before Yahu the God of Heaven, more than a man who offers him sacrifice and burnt offerings worth as much as the sum of a thousand talents."

They did not rely solely on the promise of effective prayers, however, for "as to gold, we have sent and given instructions." They have also sent another letter to Delaiah and Shelemiah, the sons of Sanballat, still governor of Samaria.[35]

No formal reply was sent. The messenger returned with oral instructions which he reported to his anxiously waiting fellow-Jews as follows: "Memorandum from Bagoses and Delaiah: They said to me: 'Let it be an instruction to you in Egypt to speak to Arsames about the altar house of the God of Heaven . . . . to rebuild it in its place as it was before and they may offer the meal offering and incense upon that altar as formerly was done.'"[36]

Arsames had returned to cope with the growing disaffection. A policy of conciliation was demanded. The messenger's claim that Bagoses and Delaiah, minor officials under another satrap, had urged the rebuilding of the Jewish temple, was unsupported by a scrap of writing; moreover, it was none of their business, and in the excited state of the country such a restoration would be positively dangerous. As a matter of course, Arsames did nothing.

Unmindful of the gathering storm, the Jews persisted in their letter-writing. Jedoniah and four other leaders of the community sent another letter to a high official, probably the local governor of Thebes. Their tone is humble: If their temple is rebuilt as it was before, they will promise not to offer sheep, oxen, or goats but only incense, meal offerings, and drink offerings. Even under these limitations, they will pay his lordship's house a sum of money and a thousand *ardabs* of barley.[37] As they took their place in the gate of Thebes to present their petition, they were seized and imprisoned until a ransom of a hundred and twenty *kerashin* was paid the subgovernor; they were also deprived of their rule at Yeb. Yet they still hope on: "Peace to your house and your children until God permits us to see our desire."[38]

[35] Cowley, *op. cit.*, No. 30 (No. 31 is another copy).
[36] *Ibid.*, No. 32.
[37] *Ibid.*, No. 33; cf. Olmstead, *op. cit.*, pp. 605-6.
[38] Cowley, *op. cit.*, No. 34.

There were Egyptian and Arab threats against Phoenicia. Even more serious was the situation in Cyprus. About 425, Baalmilk II, son of Azbaal, son of Baalmilk I, was king of Citium and Idalium. Then Abdemon, an exile from Phoenicia, from Citium as base captured Salamis and murdered the reigning tyrant. He failed in his attempt to seize Evagoras, a member of the former royal family, who escaped to Soli, which he took with fifty men. After a time, Evagoras won back Salamis (411). Beset by troubles nearer home, Darius made no effort to eject him, even when Evagoras sent grain to hostile Athens and was rewarded with a grant of Athenian citizenship (410).[39]

PERSIAN SUCCESS IN THE GREEK WAR; THE YOUNGER CYRUS

All these revolts seriously hampered the conduct of the Greek war. The Peloponnesian sailors were defeated off Abydos in the autumn of 411, and Pharnabazus must himself come to their rescue. They were employed as coast guards and given a garment and two months' pay; money and wood from Mount Ida were also granted to construct new ships at Antandrus. For these expenses, new "staters" were minted, adorned by the satrap's head and the ship's prow, symbol of Cyzicus; the head of Pharnabazus in full satrapial regalia was engraved by local Greek artists of such ability that his portrait and those of the satraps who followed—Tissaphernes, Spithridates, Autophradates, and Datames—are so superb as to rank as the equals if not as the superiors of the better-known coin portraits of early Hellenistic days which they introduced.[40]

Tissaphernes reached the Hellespont, and Alcibiades visited his former friend but was seized and carried off to Sardis. After a month's imprisonment, he escaped, broke up the Peloponnesian fleet, and compelled Pharnabazus to evacuate Cyzicus.[41]

When the oligarchic generals of the Syracusan fleet were deposed by a change of government at home, Pharnabazus provided funds for mercenaries and ships to effect their restoration. Tissaphernes was accused of supporting an anti-Spartan revolution in Thasos (410). In the spring

[39] Diod. xiii. 46. 6; xiv. 98. 1; Andocid. *De reditu* 20–21; Isocr. *Evagoras* 19. 26 ff.; *Nicocl.* 28; [Lys.] *Andoc.* 27–28; Theopomp., Frag. 103. 2(J); *IG*, Vol. I, No. 64 (113).

[40] E. Babelon, *Traité des monnaies*, II, Part II (1910), 390–91; cf. F. Imhoof-Blumer, *Porträtköpfe auf antiken Münzen* (1885), Taf. III, Nos. 1–5.

[41] Xen. *Hell.* i. 1. 6, 9 ff.; 19. 24–25; Plut. *Alcibiad.* 27 ff.

of 409 the Athenians began a vigorous offensive. Thrasyllus defeated the Milesians, took Colophon, and burned the ripened grain in Lydia. No longer able to depend on the Spartans, Tissaphernes mustered his own provincial levies. A detachment under Stages attacked the cavalry protecting a foraging party and drove them back to the coast. By this time sufficient reinforcements had arrived for the satrap to aid the Ephesians in beating off the Athenians, who, however, again defeated Pharnabazus near Abydus.[42]

Andocides the orator had been forced into exile in 415. Oligarch as he was, he had provided equipment to his country's democratic fleet and thus had given valuable assistance toward the victory off Cyzicus in 410. In a period of famine, between January of 409 and September of 408, he appeared before the Athenian assembly with a plea for reinstatement; he told how he had foiled a plot to prevent the sending of grain from Cyprus and announced that fourteen grain ships were about to sail into the Piraeus, with more to follow.[43] For his recall, however, the Athenians were not yet prepared.

Already by 416 the Bithynians had grown so powerful that the citizens of Byzantium and Chalcedon must check their inroads by a savage devastation of their lands, and now Alcibiades enforced upon them a treaty by which they surrendered the property intrusted by the Chalcedonians, after which he invested Chalcedon itself. Pharnabazus attempted to raise the siege; failing, he accepted an armistice which was to continue until he could escort Athenian ambassadors to the king.[44] Gorgias delivered a powerful oration at Olympia before crowds assembled from the entire Greek world in protest against an alliance with the ancient foe, but the times were not propitious (408).[45]

Athenian and Argive envoys met rivals from Sparta and Syracuse at Cyzicus. They all wintered at Gordium and in the spring of 407 started again, only to meet a second Spartan embassy with fresh complaints against Tissaphernes. The Athenians and their colleagues might look forward to a favorable reception, for it was felt at court that the satraps had failed in their Greek policy. Furthermore, Tissaphernes, as the brother of the rebel Teriteuchmes, was hated by Parysatis, who had also her own game to play.

---

[42] Xen. *Hell.* i. 1. 31 ff.; 2. 4 ff., 16; Diod. xiii. 64. 1; Plut. *Alcibiad.* 29. 1.

[43] Andocid. *De reditu* 10. 21–22.

[44] Xen. *Hell.* i. 3; Diod. xiii. 66; Plut. *Alcibiad.* 29.2 ff.

[45] Gorgias, Frags. 7–8 (Diels); Aristot. *Rhet.* iii. 14. 2; Plut. *Coni. praec.* 43 (144B–C); Clem. Alex. *Stromat.* i. 51; Philostrat. *Vit. sophist.* i. 9. 2; 17. 4.

From the beginning of Darius' reign, Arsaces, eldest son of the king and Parysatis, had been acknowledged as crown prince and as such had his residence in Babylonia. When, however, Arsaces saved his wife Stateira from her family's fate, his mother turned against him and made Cyrus her favorite.[46]

At this time the bulk of the Persian forces was operating in the west. If Cyrus was made their commander, he would be in a position to win the war for Sparta and thus secure the gratitude and, consequently, the support of the best professional soldiers in the world when he made his bid for the throne. Thus, for the advancement of her favorite son, Parysatis unpatriotically abandoned the policy of "divide and conquer" so wisely followed by Tissaphernes and Pharnabazus.

The youth—at the most, barely sixteen years of age—was assigned the satrapies of Lydia, Greater Phrygia, and Cappadocia, while Tissaphernes was restricted hereafter to Caria. Even more significant, he bore a sealed commission: "I send down Cyrus as *karanos* of those who muster at Castolus." In other words, Cyrus became commander-in-chief of all the Persian armies operating in Asia Minor.

Lysander, the new Spartan commander, hurried to Sardis and complained of Tissaphernes' actions. He was reassured: Cyrus had been given specific instructions to assist Sparta, and five hundred talents had been granted for this purpose; when these were exhausted, Cyrus continued, he would open his privy purse and at need would even sell his gold and silver throne. Each ship was to have thirty minas a month, each sailor four obols a day, and one month's pay was provided in advance. Tissaphernes was snubbed when he urged return to the former policy of division and was no more successful in his attempt to introduce Athenian envoys. But the Athenians continued their victories; Clazomenae was lost to Alcibiades, and Thrasybulus was besieging Phocaea and Cyme (407).[47]

Lysander's successor, Callicratidas, visited Sardis and demanded more pay. Kept waiting two days for an audience while Cyrus engaged in heavy drinking, he departed for Ephesus, cursing those responsible for teaching the power of wealth to the enemy and making them insolent. On his return, he swore, he would do his best to reconcile the

[46] Ctes. *Pers.* xviii, Epit. 80; Xen. *Anab.* i. 1; Plut. *Artox.* 2.

[47] Thuc. ii. 55. 12; Xen. *Hell.* i. 4. 1 ff.; 5. 1 ff.; *Anab.* i. 1. 2; 9. 7; Diod. xiii. 70. 3; Plut. *Lysand.* 4.

warring Greeks, stop them from asking aid against one another, and cause them once more to be feared by the barbarian.

After Callicratidas had defeated Conon at Mitylene, Cyrus did advance him funds, but the Spartan admiral refused all private gifts, declaring that he was quite satisfied with the official friendship. Callicratidas lost his life at Arginusae, and Cyrus, yet longing for his friend, utilized this disaster to secure through his ambassadors the return of Lysander at the end of 406. The allowance of his father was already exceeded, but Lysander was greeted by still more presents.[48]

Trouble was brewing for the young prince. He had executed two sons of the king's sister, Autoboesaces and Mitraeus, because they had not hidden their hands in their sleeves in his presence; such action claimed royal honors, and the king's secretary Hieramenes reported to Darius that this portended revolt. His father was seriously ill, and on this pretext Cyrus was recalled. Before leaving, the young prince gave Lysander all his ready money as well as the tribute from the cities in his personal possession. So great was Lysander in the estimation of the Greek cities of Asia that Ephesus set up his statue in the precinct of Artemis.[49]

Euripides was exhibiting his *Bacchants* to Macedonians. In the play he was telling how Dionysus, with his mixed crowd of Hellenes and barbarians, had celebrated the rites of the great mother Cybele to the music of Phrygian flutes and in the smoke of frankincense from Syria. He also told how the god left Tmolus, the fortress of Lydia, the very golden fields of Lydia and Phrygia, the sun-burned regions of the Persians, the dangerous lands of the Medes, Happy Arabia, and Asia for his new home in Greek Thebes. In his *Iphigenia at Aulis*, he asserted that it was proper for Greeks to rule barbarians but not for barbarians to rule Greeks;[50] nevertheless, that very year (405) the Spartans, financed by Cyrus, won the Battle of Aegospotami and closed the straits to Russian grain. Next year (404) Athens was starved into submission.[51] Through her diplomacy and her money, Persia had won the second Greek war.

[48] Xen. *Hell*. i. 6. 6 ff., 18; ii. 1. 7, 11; Diod. xiii. 104. 3, 6; Plut. *Lysand*. 6 ff.; *Apophtheg. Lac.* 222C ff.

[49] Xen. *Hell*. ii. 1. 8–9, 13–14; 3. 8; Diod. xiii. 104. 4; Plut. *Lysand*. 9; Paus. vi. 3. 15.

[50] Eurip. *Bacchae* 13 ff.; 55; 78 ff.; 127–28; 144; *Iphig. Aul*. 1400–1401.

[51] Xen. *Hell*. ii. 1. 21 ff.; 2.

Chapter XXVII

DICTATOR TO GREECE

ACCESSION OF ARTAXERXES II MEMNON

PERSIA had won the second great war with the European Greeks. Through her financial aid to Sparta, she had in effect dictated the peace. Theopompus, in his comedy *The Mede*, fully realized the opportunity given the Persians after the Peloponnesian War.[1] But that assistance had been granted despite the warnings of the wisest diplomats she possessed, and events were to prove immediately that Tissaphernes and Pharnabazus were right. Sparta felt no loyalty to the empire and only a mild gratitude to the young Cyrus, but even the small amount of assistance she voted the pretender was to expose the empire's vitals to Greek attack, was to permit revolts which almost tore the empire to pieces, and was to make public those weaknesses which, if always ignored by Greek politicians, were obvious to Greek publicists and were ultimately to bring destruction at the hands of Philip and Alexander.

Cyrus reached his father at Thamneria of Media, whither he had gone to put down yet another revolt, that of the Cadusians, most vigorous of Iranians. Before it could be suppressed, the illness of Darius became dangerous, and he retired to his mother's home in Babylon, where he died in March of 404.[2] He was the last of the four kings to be buried at Naqsh-i-Rustam.

On his accession, Arsaces took his grandfather's name of Artaxerxes, to which the Greeks added Memnon, the "Mindful." His first public action was to order the execution of Udiastes, the treacherous squire who had assassinated his liege lord Teriteuchmes; the punishment was cruel, for his tongue was pulled out by the roots. His son Mitradates had publicly cursed his father Udiastes and had saved the city

---

[1] T. Kock (ed.), *Comicorum Atticorum fragmenta*, I (1880), 740–41.

[2] Xen. *Anab.* i. 1. 2; *Hell.* i. 2. 19; Ctes. *Pers.* xix, Epit. 88; Plut. *Artox.* 2. 2; Aelian. *Var. hist.* iii. 20; xiii. 8. 9; for the date (before April, 404) cf. R. A. Parker and W. H. Dubberstein, *Babylonian Chronology, 626 B.C.—A.D. 45* (1942), p. 16. R. G. Kent, "An Inscription of Darius II," *JNES*, I (1942), 421 ff., ascribes to him the Susa records in V. Scheil, *Inscriptions des Achéménides à Suse* ("Mem.," Vol. XXI [1929]), pp. 40–41, 82–83.

Zaris for Teriteuchmes' son, though the latter was quickly poisoned by the still-enraged queen-mother; for his loyalty Mitradates was rewarded with his father's satrapy.

The punishment of Udiastes had been urged by Queen Stateira, and the queen-mother was furious. An opportunity for revenge was quickly available. According to custom, the coronation ceremonies were to be held in the temple of Anahita at the ancient capital of Parsagarda. Her priests were to clothe the new monarch in the robe of the elder Cyrus, after which he was to be fed with fig cakes, to chew turpentine wood, and to drink a cup of sour milk. As the ceremonies were about to begin, Tissaphernes brought to Artaxerxes a Magus, a recent tutor of the young Cyrus, who declared that this brother intended to assassinate the new king while he was changing his garments to assume the robe of the empire's founder. Caught lurking in the temple recesses, Cyrus was obviously guilty of the charge, and the justly enraged Artaxerxes was about to execute his would-be murderer. Although it must have been perfectly obvious that hers was the subtle mind behind the plot, the unnatural mother took advantage of the normal respect felt by a son for the woman who bore him and not only secured her favorite's pardon but induced Artaxerxes to permit his return to his satrapy.[3]

THE REVOLT OF CYRUS

Gratitude was not to be expected. Immediately after his return in the summer of 403, Cyrus began preparations to contest the throne. Sparta had disclaimed control of the Ionian cities which had originally belonged to the satrapy of Tissaphernes, and Cyrus was able to win them all over with the exception of Miletus, which Tissaphernes held by banishing the aristocrats. They were received by Pharnabazus, who gave to each a gold stater and settled them at Clauda; to restore the exiles was a welcome excuse for collecting an army, and Cyrus besieged Miletus.

Alcibiades, after the fall of Athens, had learned Persian and had adopted Persian dress to ingratiate himself with Pharnabazus. In this he succeeded and was given the Phrygian fort of Grynium with a yearly allowance of fifty talents. Discovering that Sparta was about to meet her treaty engagements, not with the king but with the pretender, he demanded safe-conduct to Artaxerxes, intending to lay before him the information. Lysander threatened to denounce the

---

[3] Xen. *Anab.* i. 1. 3; Ctes. *Pers.* xix, Epit. 88; Just. v. 11. 3–4; Plut. *Artox.* 3; *Reg. imp. apophtheg.* 173E–174A.

treaty if Alcibiades were not killed, and so the tricky Athenian met his fate (402) and was buried at Melissa between Synnada and Metropolis.[4] Artaxerxes was not warned, and Pharnabazus might be counted a rebel.

To the Persian troops under his command, Cyrus added thirteen thousand mercenaries collected from adventurous Greeks who had lost their pay by the ending of the Peloponnesian War. In the spring of 401 he started east. Not daring to inform the Greeks of the true objective, he pretended at first that the expedition was directed against the wild Pisidians, always a menace to peace and security. Next it was against the rebel tyrants of Cilicia; color was given to the second objective by a mobilization off the coast of the united Persian and Peloponnesian fleets, which also brought a contingent of Spartan infantry. Syennesis of Cilicia sent his queen and one son with some troops to Cyrus, while another son proceeded to the great king and assured him that his father was truly loyal and would revolt behind the pretender's back. Each advance inland meant new demands from the suspicious mercenaries, which were met by an issue of darics. On these a half-Greek Cyrus was represented without beard; his nose was straight but slightly upturned, and he wore the unpointed diadem and Median robe of rough material; on the reverse, the incuse bore a purely Greek mask of the bearded and horned god Pan.[5]

Naturally, the Greeks have only praise for the character of Cyrus, most extraordinary in the case of the Athenian Xenophon, whose ancestral empire the young prince had helped to destroy. From the standpoint of Persia, Cyrus was worse than a traitor. He was attacking the empire with hostile Greeks and was making the attack when that empire was in serious difficulties. Close at hand, the Cadusians were still in revolt. Even more serious than this threat was the fact that the Egyptians had followed their example.

THE REVOLT OF EGYPT

In 405 the Delta rebelled under a second Amyrtaeus (presumably a grandson of the first), whose six years of reign were counted by the chronologers as the Twenty-eighth Dynasty coming from Sais; "the Law was in his time" says the native chronicler. The revolt spread

[4] Xen. *Anab.* i. 4. 2, 6 ff.; 9. 9; Isocr. *De bigis* 40; Ephor. 70(J); Diod. xiv. 11. 1 ff.; Nepos *Alcibiad.* 9 ff.; Just. v. 8. 13–14; Plut. *Alcibiad.* 37, 39; Polyaen. vii. 18. 2; Ovid. *Ibis* 633–34; Athen. xii. 535D; xiii. 574E–F.

[5] E. Babelon, *Traité des monnaies*, II, Part II (1910), 52–53; G. F. Hill, *Greek Coins of Arabia, Mesopotamia, and Persia* (1922), p. 156.

rapidly up the Nile; at Karnak a gate was built for the southern extension of the Montu temple. Despite their protestations of loyalty to Persia and their sufferings at the hands of Egyptian priests during the last abortive revolt, the Jewish mercenaries at Elephantine were forced to change their allegiance. According to the last-dated papyrus from their archives, written Phamenoth 25, fifth year of Amurtis, Menahem, son of Shallom, an Aramaean of Yeb the fortress, of the standard of Nabu-kudurri, promises to pay the claim of his wife Sallua, daughter of Samuah, two shekels—that is, silver, one stater; if he does not pay it in five days, the sum will be doubled. Use of the stater as the unit of exchange proves the Greek influence which was steadily to increase during the coming period of Egyptian independence; the fate of the colony under the rule of strongly nationalistic monarchs can scarcely have been happy.[6]

CUNAXA AND THE MARCH OF THE TEN THOUSAND

Abrocomas, the satrap of Syria, had prepared a great army which might have reconquered Egypt. When Cyrus appeared, Abrocomas fell back, and the Nile Valley obtained a long respite. Without serious opposition, the invaders marched down the Euphrates to Cunaxa, only sixty miles from Babylon. Crowds of deserters flocked out, hoping for reward as the first to greet the coming victor. Artabarius intended to follow their example but was detected and thrown into the ashes. Encouraged by these defections, Cyrus prepared to meet the huge army collected by his brother, with whom Abrocomas was now united. The decisive battle was fought on September 3, 401. By the skilful maneuvers of Clearchus, the mercenaries defeated their opponents on the right flank. Cyrus had been advised by the Greek commander not to expose himself needlessly, but, when he saw his brother opposite, he forgot the caution and rushed furiously upon him. He wounded Artaxerxes but was himself killed.

Artaxerxes personally mutilated the body but commanded the head and the hand which dealt the blow to be severed so that he might parade them about to prove his victory. Parysatis was in disgrace. While Cyrus was back in his satrapy, collecting his army for invasion, Orontes was charged by Satibarzanes with taking the queen-mother as mistress. Ctesias, the royal physician, insists that the charge was

[6] R. Lepsius, *ÄZ*, XII (1874), 78; Demotic Chronicle, III, 18–19; IV, 1; A. E. Cowley, *Aramaic Papyri of the Fifth Century B.C.* (1923), No. 35; Xen. *Anab.* i. 8. 9; ii. 1. 14; 5. 13; Isocr. *Philip.* 101; Diod. xiii. 46; cf. P. Cloché, "La Grèce et l'Egypte de 405 à 342/1 avant J.-C.," *Revue égyptologique*, I (new ser., 1919), 210 ff.

groundless; Artaxerxes evidently thought otherwise, for Orontes was executed.

On the news that the invasion had failed and that her beloved son was dead, Parysatis hurried to Babylon. After much argumentation, she persuaded her reluctant son to hand over what was left of the body, and a part, at least, of Cyrus was given honorable burial at Susa. Nothing was left but revenge, and this the lamenting queen-mother quickly accomplished. Bagapates had sliced off the head; although he had acted at the royal order, he was weakly surrendered when Parysatis won him at dice and ordered him flayed alive and crucified. She tortured to death the Carian reputed to have wounded Cyrus, while the satrap Mitradates, who in his cups rashly boasted that he had inflicted the death blow, likewise received cruel punishment.[7]

Tissaphernes was at court. His warnings had all proved true, and his master needed his aid to settle the most immediate problem—the large body of well-trained Greeks in the heart of the empire. Menon, already disgruntled by the open preference of the young prince for Clearchus, was easily won over. On the insistence of the common soldiers, the generals, including the suspicious Clearchus, were induced to visit Tissaphernes. Immediately they were thrown into chains and forwarded to Babylon, where Artaxerxes was recuperating from his wounds. Ctesias did his best for Clearchus, whom Parysatis tried to free, but she had less success with her friends than with her enemies; Stateira's urgings prevailed, and all but the traitor Menon were slain. Parysatis could honor only a memory by ordering her eunuchs to plant palms in secret about Clearchus' grave.

Greek lack of discipline had sent the generals to their deaths; the self-discipline of free men was never better exhibited than in the reaction of the army to this disaster. New leaders were chosen by vote, and their orders were obeyed as the lost mercenaries pushed north through the rigors of an Armenian winter. In the spring of 400 the Ten Thousand reached the longed-for sea at Trapezus.

It was an extraordinary achievement. Later orators never ceased their praise and again and again cited the march of the Ten Thousand to prove how easily the imposing Persian Empire could be destroyed. But for the cities along the north shore of the Black Sea, there was nothing romantic in these tattered, quarrelsome, swashbuckling merce-

[7] Xen. *Anab.* i; *Hell.* iii. 1–2; Themistogenes and Sophaenetus in F. Jacoby (ed.), *Die Fragmente der griechischen Historiker*, IIB, 522–23, Nos. 108–9; Ctes. *Pers.* xx, Epit. 88–90, Frags. 33–35; Isocr. *Panegyr.* 146; Hellanicus, Frag. 184(J); Marmor Parium A, 66; Diod. xiv. 12. 7–8; Just. v. 11. 5 ff.; Plut. *Artox.* 4 ff.

naries, rogues from every corner of the Greek world, with their constant demands for supplies of food. Instead of the expected recognition for a deed of remarkable valor, with the consequent reward, they were hastily shipped on from one trembling city to the next.[8]

Ariaeus had followed Cyrus in his invasion and had taken part in Cunaxa. After Cyrus' death, he had been offered the vacant "throne" but refused. He played his part in the seizure of the Greek generals and as reward was given the satrapy of Greater Phrygia.[9]

The following year (400) the queen-mother brought to an end the struggle for dominance over the weak king by poisoning the queen at a common meal in Susa. Artaxerxes was horrified and banished Parysatis to her native Babylon. But with Stateira gone, he must have someone stronger on whom to lean, and soon Parysatis was back at court.[10]

WAR BETWEEN PERSIA AND SPARTA

Although Darius II had given more than five thousand talents to Sparta and thus had won for her the war against Athens,[11] she had repaid his legitimate successor with the basest ingratitude. The Spartan navy had forced a reluctant Syennesis into open disloyalty, and Artaxerxes had found it necessary to transform the Cilician kingdom into an ordinary satrapy. Her troops had accompanied the pretender on his invasion and had participated in the Battle of Cunaxa. It was no fault of the leader of the Greek mercenaries, the Spartan Clearchus, that the battle did not turn in favor of the pretender or that Cyrus lost his life. Her government could not justly complain when Clearchus suffered capital punishment and when Artaxerxes treated her treacherous conduct as a declaration of open war.

In the spring of 400 the fully vindicated Tissaphernes reappeared on the western frontier. He was now successor of Cyrus as margrave of Anatolia. Naturally, his first act was to demand that the Ionian cities acknowledge his overlordship. Fearing punishment for their support of Cyrus, they refused and appealed to Sparta, which ordered the cities left alone. In so acting, Sparta was admittedly betraying the worst ingratitude, but already the news of the Ten Thousand and of their defiance of the great king was known, and the Spartans could not resist the temptation to equal their exploits.

---

[8] Xen. *Anab.* ii–vii; Ctes. *Pers.* xxi, Epit. 91–93, Frags. 36–40; Plut. *Artox.* 18 ff.

[9] Xen. *Anab.* i. 8. 5; 9. 31; ii. 1. 3 ff.; 2. 1 ff.; 4. 1 ff.; 5. 27 ff.; *Oecon.* 4. 19; Diod. xiv. 22. 5; 24. 1; 26. 3, 5 ff.; 80. 8; Plut. *Artox.* 11. 1; 18. 1.

[10] Ctes. *Pers.* xxi, Epit. 92; Plut. *Artox.* 19.   [11] Andoc. *De pace* 29; Isocr. *De pace* 97.

Tissaphernes replied by the siege of Cyme. In the autumn Thibron arrived with the expressed intention to liberate Asia. Hitherto the Ten Thousand had led a precarious existence, obtaining food by threats from the reluctant cities through which they were hurried, fighting on their own with the Bithynians and the subjects of Pharnabazus for what loot they could win, or aiding for pay the tyrants of Pergamum. It is significant of the changed attitude that now, in the spring of 399, they were incorporated into Thibron's army as well-paid mercenaries.

With this addition of war-seasoned troops, Thibron could face the satrap as an equal. Former Persian subjects could be won over. Alexander, garrison commander of Aeolia, surrendered the region under his control. Certain Greeks, expatriates from Europe because their ancestors had favored the Persians, also came over. Eurysthenes, grandson of the Spartan Demaratus, ruled Pergamum, assigned to his grandfather after the failure of Xerxes' expedition. From thence he issued coins bearing the figures of Athena, Apollo, and himself, bearded and wearing the Persian tiara. His younger brother Procles had accompanied Cyrus on his unfortunate attack and had thus become a rebel; he had escaped, aided Xenophon, and now held Teuthrania and Halisarna, where he minted coins with figures of Apollo and his own youthful head rivaling the tiara of his brother. Gongylus of Eretria had been go-between for Pausanias in his attempted betrayal of the Greeks after Plataea. When this failed, he had come to Asia and there had received Old and New Gambreium, Myrina, and Grynium. Now his descendant Gorgion ruled the Old and New Gambreiums, while his brother held the others; the coins of both showed Apollo or Artemis. So-called Egyptian Larisa, where the earlier Cyrus was believed to have settled captured Egyptians, resisted a siege. Dercylidas in the autumn supplanted Thibron, who was fined and exiled on the charge of the allies that he had allowed the troops to plunder them. That year (399) his enemies urged the Athenian orator, the conservative Andocides, to return to his exile in Cyprus, where he could be sure that he would be given plenty of good land.[12]

The new commander made a truce with Tissaphernes and marched against Pharnabazus, with whom he had a personal quarrel. Parts of Aeolis had belonged to a Dardanian named Zenis. After his death, his

---

[12] Xen. *Anab.* ii. 1. 3; 5. 11; vi. 4. 24; vii. 6. 1; 8. 17, 24; *Hell.* iii. 1. 3 ff.; *Cyrop.* vii. 1. 45; Andoc. *De myster.* 4; Isocr. *Panegyr.* 144; Ephor. 71(J); Diod. xiv. 35 ff.; Polyaen. ii. 19; vi. 10; Athen. xi. 500C.

widow Mania had through magnificent gifts won the "satrapy" from Pharnabazus and become noted for the promptness with which she paid the tribute. With the aid of Greek mercenaries, she captured Larisa, Hamaxitus, and Colonae, watching the fighting from her war chariot. She accompanied Pharnabazus on his expeditions against the Mysians and Pisidians, who were constantly raiding the royal lands, and was even honored as an occasional counselor. When she reached the age of forty, this remarkable woman was killed by her son-in-law Meidias, who also killed her seventeen-year-old son and seized her treasure cities Scepsis and Gergis. The other cities refused to accept the usurper, and, when Meidias presented gifts to the satrap, they were rejected and he was warned that vengeance would be taken for a murdered friend.

Most opportunely Dercylidas arrived and in one day was welcomed by Larisa, Hamaxitus, and Colonae. Neandria, Ilium, and Cocylium followed, for after Mania's assassination their Greek garrisons had been badly treated. Cebrene was garrisoned. Meidias proposed terms of alliance to Dercylidas, who agreed on condition that the Greeks be permitted autonomy. The usurper's troops were driven from Scepsis, where the Spartan commander sacrificed to the local Athena on the acropolis and handed back control of the city to its citizens. At Gergis he compelled Meidias to open the gates. The mercenaries were taken into his own service, and with the treasure of Mania he could pay eight thousand soldiers for a year.[13]

As winter drew on, Dercylidas offered Pharnabazus his choice of war or peace. The satrap, alarmed at the threat to his Phrygian estates, made a hasty truce. Thereupon the army marched into Bithynia, always hostile to Persians and Greeks alike, and without protest from Pharnabazus plundered it to their hearts' content. In the spring another truce was agreed, and at once Pharnabazus went up to the king and urged a renewal of the war by sea.[14]

In his policy of Hellenizing the island, Evagoras had already received Greek fugitives in Cyprus, and after Aegospotami he had welcomed the defeated Athenian admiral Conon.[15] He had already begun to correspond with the Greek physician Ctesias in 399. Letters had been received from Abuletes, and Ctesias replied urging reconcilia-

---

[13] Xen. *Hell*. iii. 1. 10 ff.; Isocr. *Panegyr*. 144; Diod. xiv. 38. 2–3; Polyaen. ii. 6; viii. 54.

[14] Xen. *Hell*. iii. 2. 1 ff.; Diod. xiv. 38. 3.

[15] Andocid. *De myster*. 4; *De redit*. 21; [Lysias] *Contra Andoc*. 28, 44; Isocr. *Evag*. 51 ff.; [Plut.] Andocid. 834E.

tion with a Cypriote prince named Anaxagoras. More letters went
back and forth, and Conon suggested to Evagoras that he would like
to visit the king. Then Conon wrote to Ctesias, while, to support his
friend, Evagoras agreed to pay up the tribute long in arrears. Through
the mediation of Ctesias, of his physician-colleague Polycritus of
Egyptian Mendes, and of Zeno, the Cretan dancing master—note how
many Greeks held positions at court—Conon next forwarded letters to
Artaxerxes himself, requesting command of the Persian fleet. Bribes
from Evagoras to Satibarzanes were no doubt for the same purpose.
Ctesias read Conon's letter to the king and made a speech in his
favor.

Pharnabazus appeared at court in 398 and urged the same policy. He
was granted five hundred talents to build new ships, though he was instructed to build them in Cyprus, and after their completion they were
to operate under the joint command of Conon and the satrap. Joyfully
the Athenians sent Conon seamen to man them and the requisite weapons.[16]

Meanwhile Ionian envoys urged the Spartans to attack Caria, the
headquarters of Tissaphernes; if the war were brought home to him,
he might be induced to grant their cities independence. Dercylidas
was accordingly given instructions to march into Caria, and the fleet
was to assist. To meet this threat, Pharnabazus, returned from court,
visited Tissaphernes, who had just been given the supreme command,
and promised to work loyally with him as his subordinate.

To pay his mercenaries, Tissaphernes struck coins in his satrapy on
the Rhodian standard. The artist depicts a strong face with markedly
aquiline nose, firm lips and chin, mustache, and short beard; he wears
the tiara and diadem, the head covering, with bands to the neck and
over the cheek to under the chin. On the reverse is the king as a bowman, the Sidonian trireme, and "Of the King" in Greek.

After the Carian strongholds had been garrisoned against sudden
attack, the two satraps fell upon unprotected Ionia. Dercylidas hastened to its defense. Under the impression that the satraps were on
their way toward Ephesus, he was marching along carelessly when
suddenly the grave tumuli ahead showed Persian scouts. The satraps
had drawn up their armies—Carians bearing white shields, Persians,
Greek mercenaries, and a huge body of cavalry—in battle array direct-

16 *Hell. Oxyrhync.* ii. 1; Xen. *Hell.* ii. 1. 28; Ctes. *Pers.* xxii, Epit. 94, Frag. 44; Isocr. *Evag.* 56 ff.;
Aristot. *Rhet.* ii. 23. 12; Diod. xiii. 106. 6; xiv. 39. 1 ff.; Nepos *Conon* 2 ff.; Just. vi. 1. 4 ff.; 2. 11 ff.;
Plut. *Lysand.* 11. 5; *Artox.* 21; Paus. i. 3. 2; iii. 9. 2.

ly across the road near Tralleis. Dercylidas' Ionian and islander contingents were thoroughly frightened; some abandoned their arms in the high grain which filled the Maeander Valley, while others were poised for flight. Pharnabazus urged immediate attack, but his superior, impressed by the fighting quality of the Ten Thousand, proposed a conference. The Spartans demanded "freedom" for the Greek cities; the satraps countered with a demand for the withdrawal of the army and of the Spartan harmosts or garrison commanders from the cities of Asia. On pretense that the leaders on both sides must consult their principals, it was agreed that there should be truce for a year.

CTESIAS, PHYSICIAN-HISTORIAN

While the Spartan ambassadors were still detained at Susa (thus preventing knowledge of the shipbuilding project from filtering back), Ctesias visited Cyprus to present the king's rescript in person to Evagoras (398). In the spring of 397 he proceeded to Sparta with another royal letter which still further obscured the true situation.[17]

Ctesias did not return to his post as court physician. Instead, he retired to his native Cnidus and wrote up what he had learned during his seventeen years at court. He claimed that his *Persian History* was based on royal parchments;[18] actually it gives the court gossip he had gleaned from Parysatis and his other Persian friends. For the events of the last century, Ctesias gives us much information which we should otherwise seriously miss, though we must regret that he did not make better use of his opportunities. For Persian origins, he utilizes native legends, though not as Herodotus, whom he constantly tries to better. His *Assyrian History*, on the contrary, is a wild romance whose heroine is Queen Semiramis. Despite hesitations of the judicious, his storytelling ability imposed on his successors, and what passed for ancient oriental history among the Greeks owed more to Ctesias than to Herodotus.[19]

Likewise, Ctesias wrote *On the Tribute throughout Asia*,[20] a contribution to economic history whose loss is irreparable. He prepared his own *Tour of the World*. He was remembered best, however, for a published work on India, a queer combination of genuine information de-

[17] Xen. *Hell*. iii. 2. 12 ff.; Ctes. *Pers*. xxiii, Epit. 94–95, Frag. 45; Isocr. *Panegyr*. 144; Diod. ii. 32. 4; xiv. 39. 3 ff.; 46. 6.

[18] Ctes. *Pers*., Epit. 30; Diod. ii. 32. 4.

[19] The best edition of the scattered remains is John Gilmore's *The Fragments of the Persika of Ktesias* (1888).

[20] Athen. x. 442B.

rived from Indian visitors and of stories he had picked up at court, plus the results of a vivid imagination which attracted, though it could never entirely convince, those who craved more knowledge of this far-off mysterious land.[21]

Perhaps it is not strange that later compilers who excerpted what they considered the best of Ctesias' tall stories have not preserved a reference to Taxila,[22] the great city of Hindush, which in later Achaemenid days was taking the place of the former capital of Gandara, Peucela (Pukhala). When Alexander visited it, Taxila was already the richest and most prosperous city in the fertile region between the Indus and the Hydaspes,[23] that is, of Hindush. Ctesias can scarcely have failed to mention it, however, for he has a full account of the Indus and knew the Hydaspes.[24]

The mound which covers the ruins of the pre-Greek settlement at Taxila has been identified and excavated.[25] Few objects of the Achaemenid period have been recovered, but much indirect light has come. For instance, an inscription from the reign of the Buddhist Asoka, who almost immediately followed the last Darius, is written in beautifully engraved Aramaic characters of the later fourth century and shows the same combination of Aramaic and Persian formulas which must have been employed in the royal chancellery of the time; it is proof of the Aramaic origin of the familiar Kharoshthi writing of the immediately succeeding period.[26]

In the second stratum, representing the later Achaemenid and early Macedonian periods, was found a great hoard of coins. A single well-worn daric alone proves continuing relations with the Persian homeland, but more than a thousand punch-marked coins in silver illustrate the earliest native coinage, ranging from tiny bits averaging little over two grains (which might have been imitated from those of the

[21] J. W. McCrindle, *Ancient India as Described by Ktesias* (1882).

[22] Local Indian Takkasila or Takhsila, Sanskrit Takhssila; for native references see V. S. Sukthankar, *Archaeological Survey of India, Reports, 1914–15*, II, 36 ff.

[23] Arr. *Anab.* v. 3; fertility, Strabo xv. 1. 28; cf. Plut. *Alex.* 59; Plin. vi. 23.

[24] Ctes. *Ind.*

[25] John Marshall, *A Guide to Taxila* (3d ed., 1936).

[26] L. D. Barnett, "An Aramaic Inscription from Taxila," *JRAS*, 1915, pp. 340–41; A. E. Cowley, "The First Aramaic Inscription from India," *JRAS*, 1915, pp. 342 ff.; F. C. Andreas, "Erklärung der aramäischen Inschrift von Taxila," *Nachrichten* . . . . *Göttingen*, 1932, pp. 6 ff.; E. Herzfeld, *Epigraphia Indica*, XIX (1928), 350 ff.

Lydians), to oblong bent bars cut from imported silver sheets or to polygonal, square, and round true coins; their weight alone proves relation to Persia, for they represent quarter, half, and double silver shekels.[27] Of such a character was the silver offered by the ruler of Taxila to Alexander.[28]

The excavations afford no support to the belief that Iranian elements influenced native art during the Achaemenid period.[29] But in that period, in parts of India beyond Hindush, great religious movements were taking place which were profoundly to influence the whole country. The triumph of Buddhism was to be delayed a few years after the fall of Persia, but, at Taxila, Alexander met Brachmanes, who practiced asceticism quite in the Jain fashion.[30]

SPARTA'S SECOND TROJAN WAR

A Syracusan newly come from Phoenicia arrived at Sparta during the winter of 397–96 He reported that he had seen a fleet of three hundred ships assembling—Conon's dream had become a reality. So great was the scare that Lysander could persuade the ephors to send King Agesilaus himself to succor Asia.

His hopes were high. As a second Agamemnon, he would wage a second Trojan War against the Orientals. But if Persian soldiers had degenerated since the conquests of Cyrus, Persian diplomats had not, and they were backed by the empire's gold; when Agesilaus would begin his crusade in style by a second sacrifice at Aulis, the Boeotians stopped the ceremonies by force.

The appearance of Agesilaus in Asia during the early summer of 396 was no more glorious. Arrived at Ephesus, he was met by a request from Tissaphernes for a three-month truce; on oath, the satrap promised to negotiate a peace by which the Greek cities in Asia should be independent, and the innocent Spartan believed him. Lysander had greater success, for on the Hellespont he won over a subordinate of Pharnabazus named Spithridates, whose daughter, already betrothed to the king's young son, his superior was planning to seize by force.

Tissaphernes' "consultation" with his master, however, was only a

---

[27] E. H. C. Walsh, *Punch-marked Coins from Taxila* ("Mem. Arch. Survey of India," No. 59 [1939]).

[28] Arr. *Anab*. v. 3. 5.   [29] Marshall, *op. cit.*, pp. 26–27.

[30] Aristobulus, in Strabo xv. 1. 61; Onesicritus, in Strabo xv. 1. 63 ff.; Megasthenes, in Arr. *Anab*. vii. 2. 2 ff.; Plut. *Alex*. 8.

request for more troops. Early in the year, with the first contingent of
forty triremes prepared by Evagoras, Conon had sailed by Cilicia to
Caunus, where he was blockaded until relieved by Artaphrenes and
Pharnabazus. By now Conon's fleet was increased to eighty ships, and
it was possible to detach Rhodes from the Spartans.

Encouraged by these successes and by the arrival of the new reinforcements, Tissaphernes changed his tone and ordered Agesilaus to
leave Asia at once. The Spartan commanded the cities on the road to
Caria to provide markets; assuming that a second invasion of Caria
was in the offing, Tissaphernes prepared his defense there, but suddenly Agesilaus swung off into Phrygia, where he captured several towns
belonging to Pharnabazus. A cavalry skirmish near Dascyleium forced
a retirement to the coast; attacks from the troops of Pharnabazus were
prevented only through the ultramodern device of screening the marching soldiers by captives to either side.[31]

Thanks to the invasion of the Persian homeland by Cyrus and to the
Spartan war which developed from it, Egypt had remained independent. Amyrtaeus, the sole representative of the Twenty-eighth Dynasty, had been supplanted by a pretender from Mendes, Naifaaiurut
(Nepherites), who began the Twenty-ninth. He, too, was acknowledged throughout all Egypt, while a stone slab and a scaraboid bearing his name found at Gezer suggests that he had extended Egyptian
control into Palestine. When Tamos, the Egyptian admiral of Cyrus'
fleet, escaped home after the catastrophe, he was killed for his treasure by Psammetichus of Mendes, as the Greeks called Nepherites.

An offering scene from Thmouis shows remarkably delicate carving, an anticipation of the beautiful art of the Thirtieth Dynasty. In
his second year Nepherites buried an Apis bull. He dedicated a huge
granite shrine at Athribis, and at Thebes restored a small temple of the
famous Thutmose III. All this testifies to the renewed prosperity of
Egypt when the inhabitants collected their own taxes, and justifies
the king's boast that he was the beloved of Ptah and Osiris. Since
Artaxerxes had built ships for Athenian Conon, it was to the advantage of Nepherites to make alliance with the enemies of Persia, the
Spartans; he sent them gear for a hundred ships and half a million

[31] Hell. Oxyrhync. ii. 1; iv; Xen. Anab. vi. 5. 7; Hell. iii. 4, 1 ff.; vii. 1. 34; Ages. i. 6 ff.; Isocr.
Panegyr. 142; Philip. 64, 86-87; Epist. ix. 11 ff.; Isaeus Hagn. 8; Philochor., in Didymus On Demosthen. (ed. H. Diels and W. Schubart [1904]), vii. 35 ff.; Diod. xiv. 39. 4; 79. 4 ff.; Nepos Ages.
2-3; Front. Strat. i. 4. 2; Plut. Ages. 6; Lysand. 23-24, 27; Apophtheg. Lac. 209A; Paus. iii. 9. 1 ff.;
vi. 7. 6; Polyaen. ii. 1. 8-9, 16.

measures of grain, but he did not know that Rhodes had been taken by Conon, who intercepted the whole consignment.[32]

During the winter of 396–95, Conon had persuaded Pharnabazus to dispatch the Rhodian Timocrates with fifty talents to work up an alliance against the Spartans in Europe. Thebans, Argives, and Corinthians accepted his gifts, for the Athenians required no fresh subsidies.[33] Agesilaus passed the winter in Ephesus and in the spring threatened Lydia. Suspecting another ruse, Tissaphernes again prepared to defend Caria while the king marched through a land denuded of troops and affording much spoil. In the Hermus plain close to Sardis the Persian cavalry was badly defeated, since the infantry had not yet caught up; the camp with the satrap's funds, and the camels which Agesilaus was later to exhibit to a marveling Greece, fell into the victor's hands. Tissaphernes retired to the city and then cautiously followed the enemy, as, with all ranks broken, the soldiers on their return journey to Priene plundered the country at will.[34]

All this time Parysatis, firmly re-established in her son's affections, had been plotting the death of the last survivor in her hated rival's family. Thus far, Tissaphernes had retained the confidence of his master, deeply conscious of how he had saved both throne and life, but the last year's fiasco had obliterated all memory of gratitude, and Parysatis persuaded her son to condemn the satrap as a rebel. Tithraustes, commander of the royal bodyguard, was assigned personal charge of the border war. Headquarters for Asia Minor were established at Colossae, and Ariaeus, satrap of Greater Phrygia, was instructed to summon the revolted favorite. At Celaenae, Tisssaphernes was decapitated, and his head was then forwarded to the king. Parysatis had her revenge and could die well satisfied, but Persia had lost her ablest diplomat.[35]

---

[32] R. A. S. Macalister, *Excavations of Gezer*, II (1912), 313; Alan Rowe, *Catalogue of Egyptian Scarabs* (1936), pp. 230–41; C. C. Edgar, *AS*, XIII (1914), 278; R. Lepsius, *Denkmäler* (1849–1913), III, 284*b, c;* E. Revillout, *Notice des papyrus démotiques* (1896), pp. 469–70; G. Maspero, *Recueil de travaux*, VI (1885), 20; A. Wiedemann, *Proceedings of the Society of Biblical Archaeology*, VII (1885), 111; Diod. xiv. 35. 3 ff.; 79. 4; Just. vi. 2. 1–2.

[33] *Hell. Oxyrhync.* ii. 2. 5; xiii. 1; Polyaen. i. 48. 3; incorrectly ascribed to Tithraustes, Xen. *Hell.* iii. 5. 1–2; v. 2. 35; Plut. *Ages.* 15; *Lysand.* 27; *Artox.* 20; *Apophtheg. Lac.* 40; Paus. iii. 9. 8; iv. 17. 5.

[34] Xen. *Hell.* iii. 4, 21 ff.; *Hell. Oxyrhync.* vi ff.; Diod. xiv. 80; Nepos *Ages.* 3. 4 ff.; Plut. *Ages.* 10; *Apophtheg. Lac.* 209C; Paus. iii. 9. 6.

[35] Xen. *Hell.* iii. 4. 25; Diod. xiv. 80; Nepos *Conon* 3; Plut. *Ages.* 10; *Artox.* 23; Polyaen. vii. 16. 1.

COUNTERTHRUSTS IN PHRYGIA

Tithraustes brusquely ordered Agesilaus home. Their mutual enemy Tissaphernes had been punished, and the king had agreed to permit the Greek cities autonomy provided they paid the ancient dues. Agesilaus replied that compliance was impossible unless he received instructions from home. While awaiting instructions, Tithraustes countered, the Spartan might ravage the lands of Pharnabazus, and he backed the suggestion by a gift of thirty talents. An eight-month truce was arranged during which Agesilaus promised not to mistreat the Lydians, and his army entered Hellespontine Phrygia.

But two could play at this game. Recently Pharnabazus had ignored Conon's pressing demands for financial support; now, from confiscated properties of Tissaphernes, he gave Conon two hundred and twenty talents. Both Greek alliances were for the moment in Persian pay! Tithraustes, his assigned task completed, returned to his former post near the end of the year, leaving behind Ariaeus and Pasiphernes as generals with seven hundred talents for further diplomatic purchases. As a result, the Greek cities of Asia were again garrisoned. Conon was in great danger from rebelling mercenaries in Cyprus but finally succeeded in suppressing them. To obviate further difficulties through lack of funds, Conon determined to appeal to Artaxerxes; from Caunus he sailed to Cilicia, crossed the Euphrates at Thapsacus, and then proceeded down the river to the winter palace in Babylon where the returned Tithraustes took him in charge. He was highly honored by the king, who granted all the money Conon wished and gave him the deciding vote in the conduct of the naval operations (395).[36]

Meanwhile, in the autumn of 395, Agesilaus crossed the Caiacus, the border of Pharnabazus' satrapy, and invited the Mysians to make common cause with the invaders; those who refused found their lands devastated. But while he was taking the difficult road over Mount Olympus, the natives fell upon his rear guard, and a new agreement had to be negotiated even to secure guides into Greater Phrygia. At the Sangarius he was met by Spithridates, now his ally. The Lion's Head, the strongest village in Phrygia, resisted capture; we do not wonder when we see its modern successor, Afyon Kara Hissar, "Black Opium Castle," on its isolated volcanic rock rising sheer from the plain. The old Phrygian capital Gordium, protected by the fortifications pre-

---

[36] *Hell. Oxyrhync.* viii; xiv ff.; Xen. *Hell.* iii. 4. 25 ff.; iv. 1. 27; 3. 11; Isocr. *Panegyr.* 127, 153–54; Theopomp., Frag. 321(J); Diod. xiv. 81–4 ff.; Nepos *Conon* 2 ff.; Just. vi. 2. 11 ff.; Plut. *Ages.* 10; *Artox.* 23; Paus. iii. 9. 2, 7; Polyaen. i. 38. 3.

pared under Rathames, defied a six-day siege. Spithridates then led the army into Paphlagonia, where alliance was made with King Otys, the successor of Corylas, who had disobeyed the royal order to present himself at Susa and since 400 had been virtually independent. From Otys, Agesilaus obtained a thousand cavalry and two thousand light armed; he also presided over the idyllic marriage of the young king to a daughter of Spithridates.

Winter was coming on, and Agesilaus decided to retire. Ten days were spent at Cius in plundering the Mysians as punishment, after which he passed through Hellespontine Phrygia, by the "Wall of Miletus," and down the Rhyndacus Valley to winter quarters along the Lake of Dascyleium. On the shore was a fort protecting the satrap's palace, from which has come an interesting contemporary relief.

Before a window or niche with triple frame and projecting ornament stand two priests, a bearded elder and his youthful colleague. Both wear over a tunic a skin mantle and conspicuously full trousers. Not only is each head covered by the bashlyk, but a corner is drawn over the mouth so that the holy fire be not polluted by human breath. In the left hand is held the barsom bundle of sacred twigs, while the right is lifted in prayer. The animals soon to be sacrificed, a ram and a bull, raise their heads above the pen to which they have been conducted. A scene like this could not have been found at Persepolis; it illustrates fourth-century religion as found in contemporary Yashts, in the "Sevenfold Yasna," and in other Yasnas of the prose Avesta. It also betrays contacts with the Greeks, apparent in the molded window frames, in the drawing of eyes in profile, in the rendering of the irregular drapery folds, and in the converging lines of the pen, which disappear into the background in a sort of perspective.[37]

Here, too, were parks filled with wild beasts for hunting. Near by flowed the Odryses, swarming with all sorts of fish. Game birds abounded, while villages with plentiful supplies of grain lay round about.

The only defect in this quite literal "paradise" was that foraging parties were often cut off by cavalry and scythed chariots. Once, for example, Spithridates found the enemy at the large village of Caue. Herippidas took the camp at dawn with much loot, and Pharnabazus,

[37] E. Herzfeld, *Am Tor von Asien* (1920), pp. 24 ff. and Pl. XIV; cf. Th. Macridy, "Reliefs gréco-perses de la région de Dascylion," *Bulletin de correspondance hellénique*, XXXVII (1913), 340 ff.; R. W. Rogers, *A History of Ancient Persia* (1929), Fig. 38.

in fear lest he be surrounded, fled from spot to spot like a nomad, hiding his camping places. Then Herippidas made the mistake of depriving Spithridates and his Paphlagonians of their share of the booty; the whole army decamped to Sardis, where they felt safe with Ariaeus, who had himself rebelled against the great king. The loss of the Paphlagonians changed the situation; through a mutual friend, Apollophanes of Cyzicus, king and satrap met, and Agesilaus agreed to withdraw from Pharnabazus' satrapy.[38]

THE END OF SPARTAN LEADERSHIP

In the spring of 394 the truce made with Tithraustes came to an end. Agesilaus therefore retired as he had promised and encamped at the shrine of Athena Astyrene in the Plain of Thebe, to which he was collecting fresh troops. He was dreaming of an invasion still deeper into the peninsula, as far as Cappadocia, when he was suddenly recalled.

Agesilaus had discovered for himself the slackness of Persian rule, the disloyal satraps, and the natives regaining their independence. He could not take advantage of his knowledge, for, long since, the Persians had discovered a yet more fatal Greek weakness. In his blunt Spartan epigram, Agesilaus rightly announced that he had been driven from Asia by the king's ten thousand archers; he meant not the Ten Thousand Immortals but the coins bearing the image of the bowman king!

All that was left to show for the great expenditure of lives and money in the war of liberation was a brief acquaintance with strange lands and peoples. A student of Greek affairs is perfectly justified in passing hastily over this unedifying chapter. For the historian of the Persian Empire, the chapter is almost as unedifying, but virtually every paragraph of the pertinent Greek sources makes its contribution to our knowledge of the contemporary Orient. Business documents in cuneiform are no longer available; by their stories of broad fields wasted and property looted during the interminable wars and the frequent revolts, the Greek sources explain why business documents had ceased to be written.

Sparta's European enemies had gladly accepted the fifty talents brought by Timocrates and had used them for war. The would-be Agamemnon must return to the barren victory of Coronea and then await the decay of the Spartan Empire. Conon reached the seacoast backed by unlimited supplies of Persian gold and joined with

[38] Xen. *Anab*. v. 6. 8; vi. 1. 2; *Hell*. iv. 1. 1 ff.; *Hell. Oxyrhync*. xvi-xvii; Isocr. *Panegyr*. 144; Theopomp., Frag. 21(J); Plut. *Ages*. 11-12.

Pharnabazus. In August of 394, their Phoenician- and Greek-manned ships crushed the Spartan navy off Cnidus and thus won back the sea for Persia; the famous "Lion Grave at Cnidus" marks the victory. The garrisons left behind by Agesilaus were of no avail; Conon and Pharnabazus sailed about "freeing" the whole list of cities in Asia from their Spartan "liberators." Democratic forms of government were installed, and thus, after a long interval, Athens and Persia resumed their natural friendship. Only the resistance of Abydus and Sestus marred the end of the year.[39]

From Asia, Pharnabazus and Conon turned to Europe. On the darkest night before the dawn of Salamis, when Persian troops had reached the Corinthian Isthmus, it was the Athenian fleet which turned back the Persian navy. Eighty-seven years later a Persian fleet for the first time ravaged Laconia under Athenian guidance. A Persian garrison threatened the Peloponnese from the near-by island of Cythera. Pharnabazus gave money to the allies gathered at Corinth and returned home, while Conon rebuilt the walls at Athens with the fifty talents and the labor of the sailors furnished by the satrap. Greek cities in Asia joined Athens, whose dreams of empire began to revive (393).[40]

SHIFT IN PERSIAN POLICY

During the retreat of the Ten Thousand, Tiribazus had been satrap of western Armenia and had made a treacherous agreement with them. His honorable duty had been the mounting of his royal master. In the year 392 he was advanced to the difficult position of satrap of Sardis, in command of the frontier war. Before him appeared two delegations, one headed by the Spartan Antalcidas and the other by Athenian Conon, while envoys were also present from Thebes, Corinth, and Argos. Tiribazus announced the peace which the king was willing to grant, the important item of which was the surrender of Asia by the Greeks. Antalcidas professed that the Spartans would gladly surrender Asia if the islanders and European Greeks were left independent. Met

---

[39] Xen. *Hell*. iv. 1. 41; 2. 2 ff.; 3. 1, 10 ff.; 8. 1 ff.; Andoc. *De pace* 22; Lys. *Aristophan*. 28; Isocr. *Panegyr*. 119, 142, 154; *Philip*. 56 ff.; *Epist*. viii. 8; Philochor., in Didym. vii. 39 ff.; Diod. xiv. 83–84; 97. 3–4; Nepos *Conon* 4. 1 ff.; Just. vi. 2. 16; 3; Plut. *Ages*. 15. 6; 17; *Artox*. 20. 3–4; 21; Dio Chrys. xiii. 26; Paus. iv. 17. 5; vi. 3. 16; viii. 52. 4; Polyaen. i. 48. 3 ff.; ii. 1. 24.

[40] *IG*, Vol. II, Nos. 5 (7), 10b (20); 830 ff. (1656 ff.); Dittenberger, *Syl.³*, Nos. 124 ff.; Xen. *Hell*. iv. 8. 7 ff.; Andoc. *De pace*; Lys. *Aristophan*. 39 ff.; Isocr. *Panegyr*. 119, 142; *Evag*. 57; *Philip*. 62 ff.; *Epist*. viii. 8; Plato *Menex*. 245AB; Demosthen. *Lept*. 68; Philochor., in Didym. vii. 51 ff.; Nepos *Conon* 1. 1; 4. 5; Diod. xiv. 84. 3 ff.; 85. 2; Just. vi. 5. 6 ff.; Plut. *Ages*. 23; *Apophtheg. Lac*. 213B; Paus. i. 2. 2; 3. 2.

by this complete about-face on the part of the Spartans, which clearly betrayed the hypocrisy of former claims to "liberation," the Athenians stoutly answered that they would not accept a peace in which it was written that the Greeks living in Asia should be all in the king's house. Tiribazus quite realized that this answer implied a renewed claim to a rival Athenian empire and imprisoned Conon as a sinner against Persia. In secret he gave Antalcidas money for the construction of a Spartan navy to act as a counterweight.[41]

Sparta summoned a congress of representatives from Athens, Thebes, Corinth, and Argos to meet during the winter of 392–91. The Spartan proposals were set forth, and the Athenian orator Andocides favored their acceptance. As a conservative, he naturally passed over in silence the surrender of the Asiatic Greeks. At Sardis his fellow-Athenians had loudly objected when Lemnos, Imbros, and Scyros were included among the islands to be made independent. In the draft now presented, the three islands were specifically exempted by name from the general rule of autonomy and assigned to Athens, which should therefore be satisfied. Athens, Andocides argued, is not strong enough to win back her former empire with her own resources; she can do so only through Persian aid. Even if Athens should defeat Sparta—but "we have no strength for that"—"assuming that we did, what then do we think we would suffer from the barbarians?" Athens had caused the king to fight the Spartans, the Persians had assisted Conon to defeat them on the sea and to destroy their naval supremacy, yet Sparta is still willing to make concessions in order to further the peace. The ambassadors were persuaded and ratified the proposed draft, but on their return the Athenian delegates were denounced and exiled, Andocides among the rest.[42]

Tiribazus' policy, however, did not appeal to Artaxerxes; when this winter the satrap went to report at court, he was not sent back. Struthas, a bitter personal foe of Agesilaus, took his place as satrap of Ionia, now definitely separated from Sardis. As such, Struthas acted as arbitrator in a boundary dispute between Miletus and Myus. He proved himself a good friend of Athens, and the Spartans quickly renewed the war. Thibron returned and from Ephesus, Priene, Leucophrys, and Achilleium ravaged the territories still loyal to the king. The raids were carried on without due protection; Struthas caught

---

[41] Xen. *Hell.* iv. 8. 12 ff.; v. 1. 28; Lys. *Aristophan.* 39 ff.; Isocr. *Panegyr.* 154; Philochor., in Didym. vii. 19 ff.; Diod. xiv. 85. 4; xv. 43. 5; Nepos *Conon* 5. 3–4; Plut. *Apophtheg. Lac.* 213B.

[42] Andoc. *De pace;* Philochor., in Didym. vii. 23 ff.

Thibron offguard while indulging in an after-breakfast discus game and slew him. His army was practically destroyed by the Persian cavalry, but Thibron's successor Diphridas held safe the cities which had accepted Sparta's offer of "liberation" and secured funds for the hire of fresh mercenaries by the ransom of Tigranes and his wife, the daughter of Struthas (391).[43]

Upon the arrival of Struthas, Conon was permitted to escape to Cyprus, where he soon died. His fall from grace changed the status of his protector Evagoras, who thereupon declared himself an open rebel by issuing gold coins with "King Euwagoro" in the ancient Cypriote syllabary; in addition, they bore the bearded Heracles, his head covered by the lion's skin, and the goat which punned on his own name. The greater part of the island was now in his power, and the surviving cities—Amathus, Soli, and Citium—appealed to Artaxerxes.

Although still nominally a friend of Persia (through Struthas), Athens directed her ships to aid the rebel; Sparta, fighting the empire, stopped the fleet on the way (390). Xenophon rightly observes that both acted contrary to their best interests; it is only one more example of the queer contradictions which marked this phase of the war. Milkyaton, son of the prince Baalram and perhaps an uncle of the Baalram, son of Baalmilk, who was our last known king of Citium, imitated Evagoras by coining in gold and thus tacitly announcing his independence also. That this independence was not secured without battle is proved by gold plating he gave in Idalium to his god Reshup-Mekal "because he had heard his voice" and by a statue "because with his aid he conquered those who came out and their helpers."[44]

About the same time that Struthas arrived, there was further reorganization in the administration. While Struthas was made satrap of independent Ionia, Caria became autonomous under a native prince whose family had long held the first place in Cindya. Pixodarus, son of Maussollus, had married a daughter of the Cilician monarch Syennesis. Idrieus had been a friend of Agesilaus. About 391 his son Hecatomnos, now settled at Mylasa, was appointed satrap of Caria, once more detached, like Ionia, from Sardis. The coins of Hecatomnos show the native Zeus of Labraunda, bearded and laureled, in a long robe and with a mantle over his left shoulder; in his left hand is a long scepter, while over his right shoulder is the *labrys* or double battle-ax which

---

[43] Dittenberger, *Syl.*[3], No. 134; Xen. *Hell.* iv. 8. 17 ff.; Diod. xiv. 99; Polyaen. vi. 10.

[44] Xen. *Hell.* iv. 8. 24; Lys. *Aristophan.* 21 ff.; Ephor., Frag. 76(J); Theopomp., Frag. 103. 4(J); Diod. xiv. 98. 2–3; Babelon, *op. cit.*, pp. 706 ff.; W. Landau, *Mittheilungen der Vorderasiatischen Gesellschaft*, 1904, Part 5, pp. 64 ff.; *CIS*, Vol. I, Nos. 90–91; cf. *ibid.*, Nos. 13, 17–18, 39, 77, 83–84.

afforded his surname. The god and his attributes are Carian, but the
representation is Greek; so too is the legend which identifies the satrap, for the Carian alphabet and language would seem to have fallen
into disuse. Other coins, with a lion and the conventionalized Milesian
rose, suggest that Hecatomnos ruled also Miletus.[45]

<h2 style="text-align:center">AUTOPHRADATES IN LYCIA</h2>

Autophradates became satrap of the diminished Sardis. Coins with
his abbreviated name prove that Lampsacus and Cyme belonged to his
satrapy. Ephesus was seized while its magistrates were in consultation
by his summons.[46] But the strangest fact is that Lycia appears in his
sphere of influence.

Lycian dynasts continued their coinage. About 400, Sppntaza em-
ploys a device of the cow suckling her calf, the head of Athena, or
Heracles in the lionskin. At Telmessus is the record of his stepson
Tawenazee. Ddanawala first uses helmeted Athena and lionskin Heracles, then demotes olive-crowned Athena to the reverse, while assuming the obverse for himself with tiara and long beard. Heroma
shows Athena and Hermes wearing the winged cap; as Hmprama, he
left tombs of himself and of his nephew Ahqqade at Xanthus. At
Phelles is that of Sbekazeree, son of Mrakesa, general of Wataprddata,
in whom with some difficulty we recognize Autophradates, the satrap
of Sardis![47]

Easily the most interesting contemporary monument from Lycia is
the magnificent sarcophagus which Autophradates ordered prepared
at Xanthus for Paiawa, "chief of the army of the Trmmilian people."
Scenes on its base, identified by inscriptions in the Lycian character,
present a "life of Paiawa" in immortal stone.

On the base appears Paiawa, long shield on thigh, riding over a
fallen enemy and attacking three Greek hoplites; all of the latter wear
crested helmets, but one is nude and the others are in chitons. A nude
fourth hastens to their rescue, while three horsemen follow the general. After the battle comes the triumph, pictured on the front of the
sarcophagus. Paiawa rests on his spear, while the satrap raises high
his right hand to crown his friend with the emblem of victory. Watching the scene with interest are two long-haired bearded attendants in
knee-length chitons, with mail over their thighs and greaves on their

[45] Herod. v. 118; Isocr. *Panegyr.* 162; Diod. xiv. 98. 3; Strabo xiv. 2. 17, 23; Vitruv. ii. 8. 11;
Plut. *Ages.* 13; Babelon, *op. cit.*, pp. 141 ff.

[46] Babelon, *op. cit.*, pp. 120 ff.; Polyaen. vii. 27. 2.

[47] *TAM*, Vol. I, Nos. 3, 36–37, 61; Babelon, *op. cit.*, pp. 291 ff., 299 ff.

legs; their cloaks swing back from their shoulders. Next we are shown
two crowned and seated sphinxes (which we must envisage in the colors of the Susa glazed bricks), two seated men, a seated woman—
Paiawa's wife, wearing a chiton and with a himation over her knee
—and his son, a naked youth. The group is ended by a seated, beardless, long-haired man, whose left shoulder, arm, and lower body are
covered by a himation, though the remainder is bare; his feet on the
footstool and his upheld scepter indicate that he is Paiawa's royal
father.

Autophradates himself is seated on the other side of the base. He
wears the tiara of office and the girdled chiton, but the cloak leaves the
arms free; on his right hip is a sword; his right hand touches the beard,
as at Persepolis, while his left is on the hip. Before him marches the
funeral procession, represented by a man who carries a libation bowl
for ceremonies at the tomb. The dead Paiawa is shown as yet living,
and his young son, supported by a staff, closes the group. On the reverse we see the hunt. A servant looses a hound, and others on horseback pursue the stag, the charging boar, and the bear rising up on his
hind legs.

The composition reaches its artistic climax on the rounded roof of
the sarcophagus, where, behind two outbounding lions with lolling
tongues, a chariot of four-spoked wheels is borne along by a quartet
of wildly rearing steeds; the driver leans far out to spur on the horses,
but Paiawa in full panoply is falling from the chariot. Splendid as is
the representation, the monument could not end on a note of defeat,
and so on the "hog's mane" at the very top we see the final revenge
—one horseman smiting a foe who is sinking to his knee, and another
pursuing the flying enemy, the nearest of whom raises his hand in
token of surrender.

Autophradates intrusted the decoration to a superb artist, who may
have been a Greek; if not, he surely must have been under Greek inspiration. For us the chief interest is in the picture of a Lycian noble
whose life had already been more than half-Hellenized.[48]

ATHENIAN INTRIGUES

Autophradates was ordered to put down the rebel Evagoras, with
Hecatomnos, the Carian satrap, to assist him as admiral of the fleet.
Neither enjoyed any success, and soon the Carian was secretly financ-

[48] *TAM*, Vol. I, No. 40; Charles Fellows, *A Journal Written during an Excursion in Asia Minor*
(1839), pp. 228 ff.; *An Account of Discoveries in Lycia* (1841), pp. 165 ff., 490 ff.; O. Benndorf and
G. Niemann, *Das Heroon von Gjölbaschi-Trysa* (1889), Fig. 40.

ing the rebel. Athenian intrigues became more open. Thrasybulus sailed along the southwest coast of Asia Minor, collecting money from "friends" and plundering those who refused to "contribute." Finally, he anchored in the mouth of the Eurymedon. After compelling the inhabitants of Aspendus to pay up, he permitted his soldiers to plunder them; he met a well-deserved death when the enraged Aspendians slew him by night in his tent. Meanwhile, although Diphridas remained in charge of an inactive army, Sparta appointed Anaxibius to be governor of Abydus and permitted him to raise a foreign legion; with it he recovered the Aeolian cities from Pharnabazus, but he himself fell in an ambush set by Iphicrates, the well-known leader of light-armed troops (389).

Next year Athens sent out Chabrias, another professional soldier, to assist Evagoras openly. Amathus and Soli were captured, and Athenian Demonicus took Milkyaton's place as king of Citium. He issued coins with his own Greek name in Phoenician characters and replaced the local Melqart with the fighting Athena of his native city. To fill up its cup of iniquity, Athens made alliance with Egypt.[49]

"The second ruler after the Medes was Pharaoh Nepherites; since what he did was done wisely, his son was permitted to follow him" is the explanation of the apocalypse editor. After a six-year reign (399–393), he was buried at Memphis in a beautiful black-granite sarcophagus which was filled with his named ushabtiu. "After a short time"—in the year 393–92—his son Muthes "was deposed because of the many sins which were committed in his days; because he forsook the Law, they gave him a successor in his lifetime. The fourth ruler who was after the Medes, Psemut, was not; he was not on the way of God, he was not long permitted to be a ruler." In his year's reign (392–91), Psemut began a small shrine just south of the Avenue of Rams, which runs from the river to the Karnak inclosure; on the walls to right and to left, though ignored by the hasty tourist, may be seen the incense offered to Amon's boat.[50]

But "the fifth ruler who came after the Medes, Hacoris, lord of the diadem, was permitted to complete the time of his lordship because he was generous to the temples." His generosity is proved by the excava-

[49] Xen. *Hell.* iv. 8. 30, 33 ff.; v. 1. 10; Aristophan. *Plut.* 178; Lys. *Aristophan.* 21 ff.; Isocr. *Panegyr.* 161–62 ff; *Evagor.* 60 ff.; Demosthen. *Lept.* 76; Diod. xiv. 98. 3; 110. 5; xv. 2–3; Nepos *Chabr.* 2. 2; *Thrasybul.* 4. 3; Front. *Strat.* i. 4. 7; ii. 5. 42; Polyaen. iii. 9. 33, 44; Babelon, *op. cit.*, pp. 745 ff.

[50] Demotic Chronicle, III, 20 ff.; IV, 3–4, 6–7; Mariette, *RT*, IX (1887), 19; Loret, *RT*, IV (1883), 110; Daressy, *AS*, XVIII (1919), 37 ff.

tions. Records at Turra and Nasara show how much he used the quarries for building. The temple at Karnak was completed, though Hacoris chiseled out Psemut's name and wrote his own in red paint. A chamber was added to the Thutmose temple at Medinet Habu, and the hypostyle hall of the first temple was turned into a court. The hypostyle hall in the great temple of Sebek at el Kab was rebuilt. A great basalt shrine and a stele commemorated a grant of lands to the god of Heracleopolis Magna. Bubastis, Heliopolis, and Medinet Habu were graced by his statues, and an extraordinarily fine basalt sphinx honored Memphis.[51]

There is evidence to suggest that, despite all this honor to the temples, Hacoris (391–378) by descent was not an Egyptian but a Libyan. Perhaps this explains why Setekh-irdis, son of Redet-neb, chief of the foreign lands, repaired the desert oracle of Amon, which had supplanted Thebes in the minds of the Libyan Greeks.[52]

Following the example of Amasis, Hacoris properly considered Syria and Cyprus as the most important outposts of Egypt. His influence in Phoenicia was publicly witnessed by his inscription in the Eshmun temple just north of Sidon. Now his position was strengthened by alliances with Evagoras and with Athens.

THE "PEACE OF ANTALCIDAS"—THE "KING'S PEACE"

Athenian alliances with such dangerous rebels as Hacoris and Evagoras proved too much for even the easygoing Artaxerxes, and he determined to change sides. To remove possible opposition, Pharnabazus was summoned to court and rewarded for his victories by marriage to the king's daughter Apame (387). Ariobarzanes took his place as satrap of Dascyleium, and Tiribazus supplanted both Autophradates and Struthas.

Sparta took the hint suggested by the return of Tiribazus and, as admiral, appointed Antalcidas, well known to be the friend of the *hazarapat*. From Ephesus, Antalcidas was escorted by his friend in person to Susa to meet the king. An Athenian embassy was also in the *hazarapat*'s train, but its members could not have been competent. Plato, the comic poet, in his *Ambassadors* roundly accused Epicrates and Phormisius of accepting many bribes from the king and then of stealing even the royal ladies. Whatever the cause, the Athenian embassy failed, and Artaxerxes promised to assist Antalcidas if the

[51] Demotic Chronicle, IV, 9–10; to the lists of W. M. F. Petrie, *History of Egypt* (3d ed., 1925), III, 374–75, add Capart, *AS*, XXXVII (1937), 8.

[52] E. Revillout, *Revue égyptologique*, XIII (1910), 32; G. Steindorff, *ÄZ*, LXIX (1933), 21.

Athenians held out against the terms proposed. To enforce the threat, naval contingents from the newly appointed satraps accompanied the Spartan and Syracusan fleets when Tiribazus and Antalcidas destroyed the Athenians guarding the Hellespont. Athens was thus exposed to the danger of such a famine as had brought the imperial city to her knees and ended the Peloponnesian War.[53]

Tiribazus announced that he was ready to make public the king's decision to all who wished. Early in 386 the delegates from the Greek states hurriedly assembled at Sardis. The commander of the guard exhibited the royal seal and read the curt decree:

"King Artaxerxes holds it right that the cities in Asia should be his own, also the islands of Clazomenae and Cyprus. The other Greek cities, small and great, shall be autonomous, except Lemnos, Imbros, and Scyrus, which shall belong as of old to the Athenians. Whoever shall not accept this peace, with them will I fight and those who agree with me, on foot and by sea, with ships and with money."[54]

Modern historians grant Antalcidas the dubious honor of naming the peace. With more insight, the ancients regularly called it the "King's Peace." No contemporary could deny that the peace was dictated; "King Ahasuerus [writes the Jewish author of the Esther roll] laid tribute on the lands and the isles of the sea."[55]

Without a word of protest, the populous and wealthy Greek cities of Asia were surrendered to a monarch whom poets and orators never wearied of defaming as "the barbarian." All pretense of "liberation" was abandoned. Athens enjoyed the unpleasant distinction of being the only European state mentioned by name, and that because the principle of universal autonomy was broken in her favor alone—as had already been agreed at the otherwise abortive conference at Sparta. Evagoras, Athens' sincere friend, was basely abandoned to his enemies. Greek victories of the last few years lost all meaning. Worst of all, European Greeks had admitted the right of Persian intervention in purely European affairs—a most dangerous precedent for the near future. Artaxerxes might well boast that *he* had succeeded where Darius and Xerxes had failed!

[53] Xen. *Hell.* v. 1. 6, 25 ff.; *Ages.* 3. 3; Lys. *Adv. frumentar.* 14; Plato Comicus, *Presbeis* (Kock, pp. 119–20); Diod. xiv. 110; Hegesander Delphus, *FHG*, IV, 414; Plut. *Pelop.* 30; *Artox.* 21; Polyaen. ii. 24; Aelian. *Var. hist.* xiv. 39; Athen. ii. 48E.

[54] Xen. *Hell.* v. 1. 31; vi. 1. 30 ff.; Plato *Menex.* 245B–C; Isocr. *Evag.* 60–61; *Panegyr.* 123, 137, 141, 179–80; *Plat.* 10; Theopomp., Frag. 103, 5 (J); Demosthen. *Aristocrat.* 140; Polyb. i. 6. 2; vi. 49. 5; Diod. xiv. 10. 3–4; Just. vi. 6. 1 ff.; Plut. *Ages.* 23. 3; *Artox.* 21. 4–5; *Apophtheg. Lac.* 213B; Aristid. ii. 370.

[55] Esther 10:1; Olmstead, *History of Palestine and Syria* (1931), pp. 611 ff.

Chapter XXVIII

THE LAST EGYPTIAN EMPIRE

THE BEGINNINGS OF HELLENIZATION

STRANGELY enough, the "King's Peace" held decided advantages for the abandoned Greeks of Asia. European Greece had enjoyed a brief flash of glory, but the terms of the peace completely disintegrated the Spartan and Athenian empires. The golden days of Pericles were gone, never to return. Democracy of a sort lingered on at Athens, but it was more and more discredited. Constant wars had ravaged soils already exhausted by overcultivation and were completing the destruction of the free agriculturalist, brought low by the same factor we have seen at work in the Persian Empire. When Pericles ruled the Athenian Empire, the wine and oil of continental Greece were exported in beautiful painted vases to the barbarians across the frontiers, and with them many an article of luxury—cups and jewelry in gold, textiles, and even manufactured objects of everyday use. Now the barbarians were themselves growing the vine and the olive, were manufacturing their own vases, their own jewelry, and other objects of luxury. The trade of the Greeks languished, and there was little to exchange for the grain and raw material so necessary for their very existence.[1] To add to the confusion, the practice of banking had been imported from Babylonia; as in Babylon, the great bankers were aliens —for the most part Phoenicians from the homeland or from Cyprus. Athens was flooded with resident aliens; in 355 Xenophon could speak of Lydians, Phrygians, Syrians, and all sorts of other barbarians.[2] By the end of our period there was a regular Phoenician colony in the Piraeus which set up inscriptions in both Phoenician and Greek. With the destruction of the free farmer, the cities became crowded with a disorderly, poorly fed proletariat; the states were bankrupt, and the most successful administrator was he who balanced the budget.

Greek cities in Asia found at least partial compensation for Persian taxation. The ravages inflicted by the incessant wars of "liberation" were brought to a close. Membership in the wide-flung Persian Em-

[1] Cf. M. Rostovtzeff, *Social and Economic History of the Hellenistic World* (1941), I, 90 ff.

[2] Cf. Demosthen. *Meid.* 165, 175; (Demosthen). *Adv. Phorm.* 6; *Lacrit.* 1, 18, 20, 32; Xen. *De vectigal.* ii. 3.

pire once more restored trade opportunities. The unsettled elements of the Greek population were drawn off to serve as mercenaries in "barbarian" armies, Persians and their Egyptian opponents in equal numbers; the pay and loot they carried home contributed to an invisible balance of trade.

It would be wrong to draw too rosy a picture of the situation. Overtaxation still crushed the natives and continued to drive them to revolt. Egypt, parts of Cyprus, and at times Phoenicia and Syria retained their independence. Rebel satraps ravaged the empire and witnessed the decline of Persian administration. Class war arose from a half-starved proletariat and was put down savagely, too often by a tyrant.

But evidence of new prosperity for the Greek cities of Asia may be sensed in the numerous issues of beautifully minted coins. Economic welfare, though so often confined to the higher classes, permitted a new cultural development. A fresh outburst of Ionic literature with a quite different content is dimly envisaged in fragments preserved from contemporary authors. Ruins of imposing buildings marked by increasing quantities of inscriptions show how prosperity was translated into architecture and art. The germs of what we call Hellenistic civilization become evident, and the way is paved for the Hellenization of the Orient, continued on a larger scale by Macedonian rulers.

Nowhere can this tendency toward fusion of East and West and the oriental counterresistance be studied better than in the last Egyptian empire. Perhaps the strangest of all strange facts to be chronicled during this highly unusual period is that the diplomatic triumph of Artaxerxes over the Greeks was won at the very moment when Persian dominion was being successfully challenged within the empire itself. It was an open secret that peace had been made in order to settle the Egyptian problem, while by the terms Cyprus was legally surrendered to Persia. For Artaxerxes to regain the rebel lands by force of arms was to be quite another matter.

TROUBLES IN JUDAH; FAILURE IN EGYPT

According to the treaty, Athens could no longer assist Evagoras, even by the loan of Chabrias. There was no such provision regarding Egypt, and so Chabrias was summoned by Achoris. Greek mercenaries for him to command were hired in large numbers. Alliances were made with disaffected Hecatomnos of Caria, with the Greeks of Barca, and with the perennially rebellious Pisidians.[3]

[3] Isocr. *Panegyr.* 162; Theopomp., Frag. 103. 1 and 13(J); Demosthen. *Lept.* 76; Diod. xv. 29. 2; Nepos *Chabr.* 3; Just. vi. 6. 3.

A great host was brought together in Syria by Pharnabazus, Tith-raustes, and the satrap Abrocomas, able at last to continue the attempt at reconquest frustrated by Cyrus in 401. Sometime after the accession of Artaxerxes, the governor of Judah, Bagoses, had quarreled with the high priest Johanan and as a result had promised to transfer the office to Johanan's brother, Jeshua. Open warfare between the partisans of the rivals was ended when Johanan slew Jeshua in the temple, but Bagoses then determined to enter the sacred courts and carry on an investigation. Attacked by the Jews defending their holy site, he bluntly demanded: "Am I not then more pure than the corpse of the man who was killed in the Temple?" and went on in. In his reply to the letter of the Elephantine Jews begging him to assist them in the restoration of their temple, Bagoses had suggested that the task might be easier if they would abandon the practice of animal sacrifice; he dared not go quite so far with the more important temple at Jerusalem, but at least he could salve what conscience he possessed by imposing an almost prohibitive tax of fifty drachmas for every lamb offered in the daily sacrifices.

In all probability, Johanan was punished for his brother's murder, for, soon after, we find his son Jaddua occupying the high priestly office. Manasseh, the son-in-law of Sanballat and now head of the rival shrine on Mount Gerizim, was a dangerous threat to Jewish unity, since those who contracted mixed marriages—priests and commoners alike—went over to Sanballat, who gave them money and lands in compensation for what they had lost. The elders in Jerusalem ordered Manasseh to divorce his foreign wife or to abandon active exercise of his priestly duties, and in this they were supported by Jaddua. The priestly excommunication had no practical effect, since Manasseh was outside Jaddua's jurisdiction; Jaddua himself enjoyed a long and uneventful reign, since he continued as high priest up to the time of Darius III.[4]

In Egypt, Chabrias was busily engaged in reorganizing the native army and navy; Egyptian sailors, directed by interpreters, were trained in Greek tactics on rowing machines. Fortifications, thrown up between the Pelusiac branch of the Nile and the Serbonian bog, were still known in Roman days as the "Palisade of Chabrias," while a "Village of Chabrias" was remembered in the Delta.

Achoris called upon Sopd, lord of the East, the divinity of the Arabian nome which guarded the road from Asia. For three years

4 Joseph. *Ant.* xi. 297 ff.; Neh. 12:11, 22.

(385–383) the war continued, but in the end the invaders were driven back from Egypt. To prove his control of Palestine and southern Phoenicia, Achoris left inscriptions at the Eshmun temple north of Sidon and an altar stand of polished gray granite carried from far-distant Syene to Ascalon. Meanwhile Evagoras had captured Tyre by assault and won a large part of northern Phoenicia and Cilicia.[5]

REBEL EVAGORAS

Although abandoned by the European Greeks, the position of Evagoras was still good. Aside from his alliance with Achoris and a king of the Arabs whom we cannot identify, Tyre furnished twenty triremes and the Cypriotes seventy, he could muster six thousand mercenaries and many auxiliaries, and Hecatomnos was secretly giving him money for more. Tiribazus had collected three hundred ships. From two thousand talents granted him for the war, he struck numerous coins at Tarsus, Soli, Marlus, and Issus; on those bearing his legend in Greek, he placed his own bust and the head of Heracles. On those with "Tiribazu" in Aramaic, he depicts "Baal Tarz," the "Lord of Tarsus"; here an old Anatolian divinity originally known as Sandon appears fully Hellenized, bearded and half-nude, leaning on a scepter and extending his right hand to an eagle; on the reverse, however, is Ahuramazda, though he, too, has been Hellenized: bearded and nude, he holds in his hand a lotus and places a wreath on the satrap's head. The army was under Aroandas, often called Orontes, a Bactrian, the son of the "king's eye" Artasyras, who had married Artaxerxes' daughter Rodogune and for this reason had been given the satrapy of Armenia.[6]

From Phocaea and Cyme—Ephesus was for the moment independent —Aroandas descended upon Cilicia, which was soon completely recovered. His army was then ferried over to Cyprus, where it took Citium. Milkyaton was restored as king of Citium and Idalium. Through friendly pirates, Evagoras saw to it that the Persians were cut off from food. A mutiny of the Ionian mercenaries was thereby precipitated, but Glos, son of Cyrus' admiral Tamos, supplied the camp from Cilicia, and the mutiny was suppressed. With a navy raised to two hundred ships (fifty from Achoris), Evagoras fell upon the ene-

---

[5] Isocr. *Panegyr.* 140; *Evagor.* 62; Diod. xv. 2. 4; Strabo xvi. 2. 33; xvii. 1. 22; Plin. v. 68; Polyaen. iii. 11. 7; Alan Rowe, *Catalogue of Egyptian Scarabs* (1936), pp. 295–96.

[6] Plut. *Artox.* 12. 1; 27. 4; cf. Xen. *Anab.* ii. 4. 8; iii. 4. 13; 5. 17; iv. 3. 4; Trog. x; Ins. of Antiochus of Commagene, W. Dittenberger, *Orientis Graeci inscriptiones selectae* (1905), Nos. 311–12; E. Babelon, *Traité des monnaies*, II, Part II (1910), 379 ff.

my off Salamis, and only the tactical ability of Glos turned defeat into victory (381).

Salamis was besieged on land and sea. With ten vessels, Evagoras slipped out by night and secured additional funds in Egypt; they were not enough, and finally Evagoras must sue for peace. Tiribazus, who meanwhile had visited Susa, offered to retain him as king of Salamis on condition that he surrender his other cities, pay his tribute, and as a slave obey the orders of his master. Evagoras promised to submit as king to king, but he would not admit himself a slave, and Tiribazus rescinded his offer (380).[7]

While the war dragged on, Isocrates delivered his *Panegyric* at Olympia (380). He summoned the assembled Greeks to a crusade against Persia, recalling the triumphant march of the Ten Thousand and predicting an easy victory. He deplored the scandal of the Hellenizer Evagoras in danger from an army filled with Greek mercenaries and a fleet almost exclusively Ionian. Once peace was made, he insisted, Athens could forget her hatred for Greek enemies, but she could feel no gratitude to Persia, even when receiving benefits from the empire. Throughout his long life consistently opposed to the "barbarian"— whom he could not recognize as human but considered so low that even common honesty was unnecessary—Isocrates was no exponent of a narrow particularism; with prophetic vision, he praised the Athenians as the teachers of others, for it was Athens which had brought it about that the name Hellene no longer connoted race but intelligence, and those are called Hellenes who partake of Greek culture, not merely those of common descent.[8]

He spoke too soon, for no one listened. Athens, which Isocrates had just praised, abjectly ordered Chabrias under penalty of death to return home, once Pharnabazus had complained that his presence in Egypt was a violation of the "King's Peace" (379). Evagoras owed his salvation not to Greek aid but to Persian dissensions. Jealous of Tiribazus' popularity with the soldiers, Aroandas charged him with plotting revolt; when he might have captured Salamis by assault, he contented himself with a private alliance with the Spartans. Also he had sent to the Delphic oracle to inquire the success of a projected uprising, and he was winning over the mercenaries by gifts. The accusations sounded like a duplicate of those vainly made against Cyrus, and

[7] Isocr. *Panegyr.* 134–35; Theopomp., Frag. 103. 6, 9(J); Diod. xv. 2 ff.; 8; xii. 20; Polyaen. vii. 20; *CIS*, Vol. I, Nos. 10–11.

[8] Isocr. *Panegyr.* 50, 141, 157.

Artaxerxes was deceived; he ordered Tiribazus thrown into chains and forwarded to court. Autophradates was restored to Sardis and Aroandas became commander of the army in Cyprus. He was no more successful than his predecessor in the fighting and before long was compelled to accept the surrender of Evagoras on exactly the same terms rejected by Tiribazus (379). Glos had been compromised by the disgrace of his father-in-law Tiribazus; he therefore retired to Ionia, which he occupied, made alliance with Achoris, and attempted to win over the Spartans.[9]

REVOLT OF CADUSIA

Meanwhile the Cadusians were in open revolt, and so dangerous became their inroads that Artaxerxes must take the field in person. His presence only increased the straits of the invaders in the foggy mountains. Lack of food in the desolate country forced the soldiers to kill their animals, and the army was saved only through the diplomacy of the accused Tiribazus, who persuaded the two Cadusian kings encamped separately to make separate peace. After great suffering and loss, the Persians returned, even the king on foot; fearing the effect of this disaster on the public mind, Artaxerxes put to death many nobles who were suspected of disaffection. Tiribazus, however, was exonerated, while Aroandas was stricken from the list of the king's friends. Glos met his death by treachery, apparently while fighting with Autophradates, and although his army was held together for a time at Leucae by a certain Tachos, he, too, was later slain (378).[10]

On the retreat from the Cadusian lands, the Carian Camisares had lost his life. His son Datames succeeded to his satrapy, that part of Cilicia which lay next to Cappadocia and was then inhabited by the White Syrians, as the Greeks called them. His first exploit was to drive out from the captured camp of Autophradates certain rebels, presumably Glos and Tachos. Thyus, his cousin on his mother's side, had long been independent in Paphlagonia; Datames attempted to win him back to his allegiance and barely escaped with his life. Ariobarzanes refused further aid from Dascyleium, but ultimately Datames captured Thyus and forwarded him and his family to the king.[11]

[9] Plato Comicus, Frag. 184 (Kock); Aeneas Tact. xxxi. 35; Theopomp., Frag. 103: 9 ff. (J); Nepos *Chabr.* 3. 1; Diod. xv. 8 ff; 29. 3; Trogus ix–x; Polyaen. vii. 14. 1; Plut. *De superstit.* 168E.

[10] Diod. xv. 3; 8. 4; 10–11; 18. 1–2; 19. 1; Nepos *Datam.* 1. 2; 2. 1; Trog. x; Plut. *Artox.* 24–25; *Reg. imp. apophtheg.* 174A; Aristid. xvi. 257.

[11] Theopomp., Frag. 179(J); Diod. xv. 91. 2; Nepos *Datam.* 1 ff.; Athen. iv. 144F; x. 415D; Aelian. *Var. hist.* i. 27.

RISE OF THE THIRTIETH EGYPTIAN DYNASTY

According to the Egyptian record, Achoris was "deposed because he forsook the Law and did not regard his brethren; the sixth ruler who came after the Medes, Nepherites II, was not"; "it came to pass that they forsook the Law in the days of his father and the sin was visited upon his son." After four months, Nepherites II was killed by Nekhtenebef, who to the Greeks was the first Nectanebo; it was claimed that he was son of Nepherites I, though actually he was son of a general named Djedhor. Thus began the last independent Egyptian dynasty, the Thirtieth from Thebnute or Sebennytus, and by far the mightiest for many a long century.[12]

Nekhtenebef (378–360)[13] at once announced his program: He would be the strong king who would protect Egypt like a wall of bronze about her, active with his arms, lord of the scimitar, who cuts out the heart of the miserable and does good to those who are loyal to him, so that they sleep in the day, since their hearts are full of his wonderful deeds. He seeks good for the temples and inquires of the priests in every matter of the temples; he covers their altars with incense and makes numerous their utensils; he prepares increase in all things. The mountains tell him what is in them, the sea gives its produce, the deserts bring him their incense. For once the bombastic ancient formulas are reused with exact propriety.

His Majesty was crowned in the palace at Sais and betook himself to the temple of Neith. He appeared before his divine mother wearing the red crown and brought his libation to his father Osiris, the lord of eternity. He announced a decree: "Let them give a tithe of gold, silver, wood, and carpenters' wood, and of everything else which comes from the Sea of the Ionians, everything which they tax, to the treasury of the city called Hent, as well as a tithe of gold, silver, and all that is produced in Naucratis, on the bank of the Anu stream, which they have taxed for the treasury, for the offering of my mother Neith, forever, in addition to what has formerly been, and let them make from them one ox, one goose, five jars of wine, as an eternal daily offering. The remainder is for the treasury of my mother Neith, since she is the Lady of the sea and she it is who gives them their support. Let

---

[12] Demotic Chronicle, IV, 4–5, 10 ff.; K. Sethe in *Urkunden des aegyptischen Altertums*, ed. G. Steindorff, II (1904), 26; Theopomp., Frag. 103. 10(J).

[13] Nineteen years of reign (Demotic Chronicle, IV, 14), but sixteen in the previous line; Manetho gives eighteen.

them establish these matters upon this stele, which they shall set up at Naucratis."

In other words, this rescript imposes a new 10 per cent tax on all goods—imported or domestic, manufactured or raw material. The inscription is beautifully engraved on black granite. To the right the king, wearing the white crown, is standing and offering vases to the seated goddess Neith, also wearing the white crown; on the left, Nekhtenebef, with horns, ball, and feathers, presents a hawk-headed neckpiece to a replica Neith.[14]

Under the beneficent rule of Nekhtenebef and his vizier Horsiese, son of Onnophre, priest of Bahbit,[15] Egypt saw a new prosperity. From one end of the Nile Valley to the other, a long line of buildings once carried his cartouches; in Upper Egypt impressive ruins exist to our own day, but the far more richly adorned Delta may be glimpsed only from numerous but widely scattered fragments—all that have survived the ravages of time and man.

In his first year he was rebuilding for Horus the temple at Edfu. In his third he was quarrying at Hammamat, where he honored Min, Ptah, Horus, and Isis. In the same and the following year his workmen quarried at Tura; in the sixth and ninth they were at the quarry near Amarna.

In his sixteenth year he constructed a wall at Coptos, with a fine gateway. Another, equally fine, was built for the south temple. For Min of Coptos he prepared a shrine in green breccia transported from Hammamat; its beauty we may enjoy, though its two doors of sweet-smelling wood, incrusted with gold, have disappeared.

One of the first buildings on the island of Philae, now usually covered by the waters backed up by the Assuan dam, was a small but exquisitely beautiful temple, whose columns bore floral capitals or a sistrum. The sacrificing Nekhtenebef is pictured on the screens, and the first pylon bore his reliefs. The porch was indicated as belonging to his mother Isis, revered at Abaton, mistress of Philae; it was also for the Hathor of Senmet.

He enlarged the temple at Nekhab (el Kab) and ornamented the east gate with reliefs of the king worshiping its patron goddess Nekhbet. At Medinet Habu he built a small gate in the court of the first temple,

[14] G. Maspero, in E. Grébaut, *Le Musée égyptien*, L (1900), 44 ff.; A. Erman and E. Wilcken, *ÄZ*, XXXVIII (1900), 127 ff.; K. Sethe, *ÄZ*, XXXIX (1901), 121 ff.; G. Posener, *AS*, XXXIV (1934), 141 ff.; parallel from Mit Rahina stele, B. Gunn, *AS*, XXVII (1927), 222 ff.

[15] W. Spiegelberg, *ÄZ*, LXIV (1929), 88 ff.

and in the temple itself he set up clustered columns with bud capitals and stone screens. There, too, he made a Nilometer to determine the height of the Nile during each season. On the grand pylon at Karnak might be remarked an offering scene where he sacrificed to Amon and Mut, and there he restored the temple of Thutmose and Khonsu. At Dendera he started a birthhouse for the local god. Abydos had a temple and a gray-granite shrine, Hermopolis a limestone altar, Letopolis an unusually fine green-breccia sarcophagus, Damanhur a black-granite shrine, and Maskhuta a sistrum.[16]

From these and other sites the architecture of Nekhtenebef comes alive. Statues and reliefs demand adequate study before their superb art will be properly appreciated. While the artists of the Saite period had gone back to the days of the Empire for their inspiration, those of the Thirtieth Dynasty found a purer source in the art of the Middle Kingdom. If in contrast to the older sculpture their statues lack something of anatomical correctness, there is a greater naturalism and a delicacy and vigor which proves a very live art. Fragmentary reliefs show the same delicate touch.[17] This art reaches its climax in the magnificent red-granite lion bearing his name.[18] While the art of western Asia is even thus early largely affected by Greece, that of Egypt remains entirely free of foreign influences.[19] This last bloom of a purely native art is among the greatest in the long career of Egypt.

THE SECOND ATHENIAN CONFEDERACY

With Evagoras out of the way, Pharnabazus began preparations for a second invasion of Egypt. As a first step, Athenian Iphicrates was hired to act as leader of the Greek mercenaries (379). This was all to the advantage of Athens, which had scrupulously kept to the letter of the "King's Peace," even when violating its spirit; for instance, by the treaty contracted with Chios in 383, Athens specifically recognized the agreements which king, Athenians, Lacedaemonians, and other Hellenes had sworn.[20]

Athens specifically excluded the king's subjects as acceptable mem-

---

[16] To the impressive list given by W. M. F. Petrie, *History of Egypt* (3d ed., 1925), III, 378 ff., may be added Legrain, *AS*, VI (1905), 122–23; R. Weill, *AS*, XI (1911), 110 ff.; G. Daressy, *AS*, XIX (1919), 136 ff.; H. Gauthier, *AS*, XXIII (1923), 171 ff.; J. Capart, *AS*, XXXVII (1937), 6.

[17] W. Spiegelberg, *ÄZ*, LXV (1930), 102 ff.

[18] F. W. von Bissing, *Denkmäler*, Pl. 74.

[19] Cf. Margaret Murray, *Ancient Egypt*, XIII (1928), 105 ff.; H. Schäfer, *Von aegyptische Kunst* (2d ed., 1922).

[20] Dittenberger, *Sylloge inscriptionum Graecarum* (3d ed., 1915), No. 142.

bers when next year she organized the Second Athenian Confederacy (378). Since the war alliance was in the first instance directed against Sparta, stress was laid upon "liberty" and "autonomy." The sins which had made odious the memory of the former Athenian empire were carefully avoided. The members, who for the moment included Thebes, were full allies, never subjects. The term "tribute" was never employed; all paid a not too great "contribution," which they retained in their own hands. Allied affairs were determined by their own "common council of allies" in which Athens had no vote. The state which was officially the "leader" solemnly promised that there would be no more cleruchies for destitute Athenians, no more Athenian "overseers," and no more garrisons, while judicial appeal to the "leader" was rejected; under threat of death any attempt to amend this constitution to the contrary was banned.

Yet the new league was far from perfect. Athens still held executive powers, with all the control thereby implied. The "common council of the allies" met at Athens and therefore was susceptible to local pressure. Every vote must be taken by the Athenian assembly as well as by the "common council." Worst of all, each state, whatever its wealth or its population, possessed only one vote, and as the membership grew, it was more and more easy for Athens as the executive to dominate the common council through its control of the smaller but ultimately more numerous states.[21]

DISINTEGRATION IN ASIA

Under such conditions it was inevitable that Athens should encroach gradually upon the sovereign rights of such members as continued in the alliance. It was also inevitable that the new confederacy should in the end follow the example of the older Delian League and become hostile to Persia. For the time, however, Athens remained on good terms with the Great King, while the process of disintegration continued so obviously in Asia. Bithynia retained its independence when Doedalsus was succeeded by Boteiras and he by Bas (377–327). Hecatomnos was monarch of Caria in all but name and transmitted his office without question to his eldest son Mausollus (377–353).[22]

At Telmessus, Artompara (Artembares) the Mede coined with the heads of Athena or Heracles or substituted his own portrait wearing

[21] IG, Vol. II, No. 17 (43); Dittenberger, Syl.², No. 47; Diod. xv. 28. 3; F. H. Marshall, The Second Athenian Confederacy (1905).

[22] Memnon xx. 1–2; Isocr. Panegyr. 161–62.

Persian beard, tiara, and headdress. Opposed to him was the dynast of Limyra, whose Greek leanings were indicated by his Athenian name of Parekla or Pericles, and whose coins bore the lion and trisceles, Hermes, the radiate Apollo, or Pan with the goat's horns; in a war with the Telmessians, he shut them up in their city and forced them to come to terms.[23]

From Lycian inscriptions we may read both sides of the narrative. At Pinara is the elaborate free-standing tomb made by Dapssmma, who commanded the army of the Lycians with Artembares, though the tomb of his father Padrama is at Xanthus. At Limyra is a two-story rock tomb of Taborssale, descendant of Zzaiaa, to bury his adopted son Losantra (Lysander) and Khntabora, a general of Pericles. On a near-by rock ten soldiers are fighting; beneath is the statement that Taborssale made the relief when, with Pericles, he defeated Artembares and his troops. Three other men, whose names appear in the weird Lycian spelling, claim also to be Pericles' generals, while a fourth is his chancellor. Pericles, furthermore, caught the mercenary general Charimenes of Miletus as he was escaping to Phasaelis and not only defeated him but apparently took the city. Proclean games at Telmessus celebrated his victories.[24]

THE SECOND INVASION OF EGYPT

Artaxerxes enforced another peace on the Greeks in 374. The younger Dionysius of Syracuse made a treaty with him.[25] After his surrender, Evagoras remained quiet, but, in 374, he and his son Pnytagoras were murdered by a eunuch. Although another son, Nicocles, next held the throne, not only was his state in disorder and his treasury empty but he must contend against the dislike of Artaxerxes. Nevertheless, he was able to pay a huge number of his coins, graced by Athena and Aphrodite—twenty talents, it was later said—to Isocrates for composing a eulogy of his father.[26]

Since 379, Pharnabazus had been collecting Greek mercenaries for the Egyptian expedition. To pay them, he minted frequent issues of

[23] TAM, Vol. I, No. 29; Babelon, op. cit., pp. 285 ff., 329 ff.; Theopomp., Frag. 103. 17(J).

[24] TAM, Vol. I, Nos. 11, 48–49, 103–4, 67, 83, 132 ff.; CIG, Vol. III, No. 4198; Polyaen. v. 42.

[25] Isocr. Plat. 5, 10,˜14, 17; De permut. 110; cf. Xen. Hell. vi. 2. 1; Philochor., in Didym. Halon. 64; Ephor., Frag. 211(J); Diod. xv. 38. 1-2; Nepos Timoth. 2; Plut. Artox. 22.

[26] Isocr. Evagoras 71; Nicocles 31, 34; Theopomp., Frag. 103. 12(J); Aristot. Polit. v. 8. 10; Diod. xv. 47. 7-8; Plut. Vit. Isocr. 838A; Aelian. Var. hist. vii. 2; Babelon, op. cit., pp. 711 ff.

coins, made by Greek artists who often copied types from famous Sicilian originals with some degree of success; so blundered, however, are the Aramaic legends "Pharnabazu," "Kilik," "Hilik," and "Baal Tarz" that it is difficult to make out that they are intended to mean "Pharnabazus," "Cilicia," and "Lord of Tarsus." The god is represented in the form that was to become standard: half-nude, seated on a backless throne with elaborately carved feet, and holding a scepter ending in trident or eagle. At times the Greek engraver inappropriately substitutes Arethusa, nymph of Syracuse, for the Lord of Tarsus. With more reason, the head of a warrior in crested helmet acknowledges the Greek mercenaries to be paid with these coins. Those struck at Nagidus are localized by the city name in Greek and by the local Aphrodite, who, long-haired and fully clad, is seated on a throne adorned by a sphinx and smells a lotus, while she holds out a small saucer; the reverse gives an Aramaic legend near the Greek head.[27]

There were difficulties about supplies. Men died in camp—Isaeus mentions an Athenian mercenary who lost his life at Ace. Iphicrates must put down two traitors among the generals. The Phoenicians were unfriendly. But at last by the summer of 373 Pharnabazus had brought together three hundred triremes, twelve thousand Greeks, and a huge force of Orientals.

The land forces discovered that the seven outlets of the Nile had been blocked up and were guarded with forts surrounded by canals. Unable to force the Pelusiac mouth from the Suez Isthmus, the navy landed three thousand infantry at the Mendesian mouth and captured the fort. Iphicrates learned from captives that Memphis was poorly garrisoned and urged that the ships force their way up the Nile and fall upon the capital before the natives were able to concentrate their troops. This was too risky for the aging Pharnabazus, and he decided to await the coming of his whole vast array. Iphicrates countered with an offer to lead the attack with such troops as were already present, but by this time Pharnabazus had come to suspect his good faith and again refused.

Through the delay, the Egyptians recovered their courage. Memphis was adequately garrisoned, and the invaders were harassed and lost heavily. Summer arrived, and with it the inundation; Pharnabazus found he could not resist the rising waters and retired into Asia. Each commander blamed the other for the fiasco; remembering Co-

[27] Babelon, *op. cit.*, pp. 390 ff.

non's imprisonment, Iphicrates bribed a ship's captain to steal him by night from the camp, and had returned to Athens by November.[28]

Nekhtenebef attributed his victory to the god of the Arabian nome, Sopd, hawk of the east, who smites the Mentu and the Fenkhu (ancient names for the Asiatic). In Sopd's temple the king placed a superb black-granite shrine whose inscription presents an Egyptian account of the war. Naturally, it is somewhat vague as to details, but there we read that Nekhtenebef came and killed the monster Apopis; the gods and goddesses rejoice in his sanctuary because he chained the enemy with his wings. The land of the east rejoices because he has killed his enemies. He is the good god, very brave, who drives back the foe; the wise and intelligent, who fights for Egypt against the rebels of the provinces, who treads underfoot the Asiatic. The barbarians are struck down under his feet, and his hand is brave among the chiefs of the Haunebu (a term once applied to the feared men of the sea but now disdainfully assigned to their former allies, the Greeks!)[29]

ANOTHER "KING'S PEACE"

Pharnabazus offered the position left vacant by the flight of Iphicrates to a younger professional soldier, Conon's son Timotheus. Since he had just lost the command of the Athenian armies to the returned Iphicrates, Timotheus gladly accepted and within six months was on his way to the east (May, 372). There he remained until 367, though we have no hint of any special activity.[30]

Artaxerxes imposed another "King's Peace" upon European Greece in 371; years later, Demosthenes could appeal to the recognition of Athenian ownership of the Thracian Chersonese and of Amphipolis by the king and by all the Greeks. This time it was Thebes which refused to accept the terms; that same year Epaminondas by the victory of Leuctra forever crushed the Spartan power and elevated Thebes to supremacy in European Greece. Jason of Pherae had united Thessaly and was dreaming of the conquest of Persia, which the march of the Ten Thousand seemed to prove so easy; in his calculations, however,

[28] Isaeus Nicostrat. 7; Polyb. xxxviii. 6. 2; Diod. xv. 29. 1 ff.; 38. 1; 41 ff.; Trog. x; Nepos Iphicrat. 2. 4; Plut. Artox. 24. 1; Polyaen. iii. 9, 25, 38, 56, 59, 63.

[29] E. Naville, The Shrine of Saft el Henneh and the Land of Goshen (1887), pp. 6 ff.

[30] [Demosthen.] Timoth. 25 ff., 60; Diod. xv. 47. 3; Nepos Timoth. 4. 2 ff.; Chabr. 12. 3–4; Athen. xii. 532B; cf. Xen. Hell. vi. 2. 13.

he had ignored the might of the king's "ten thousand archers," and before the end of 370 he was dead by the hand of assassins.[31]

Pharnabazus died in old age, and Timotheus returned to Athens. As reward for his capture of Thyus, Datames was made his successor in charge of the impending expedition against Egypt. Fresh mercenaries were collected and fresh coins for their pay minted.

Tadanmu, as he is called by Aramaic legends probably closer to the original Carian pronunciation than the more familiar Greek, employed largely the types of Pharnabazus, especially the crested Greek soldier. Baal Tarz was placed within the battlemented circle of a fortification, a lotus under his throne; a grain stalk and a grape cluster in his left hand commemorated the provisioning of the army. Datames was seated on a throne with ornamented feet; his bow was in front, while with both hands he grasped an arrow. On his head was a ribboned tiara; he wore tunic and trousers, but both arms were protected by brassards, and, for still greater protection, the winged Ahuramazda floated above. Another scene was staged in a flat-roofed temple crowned with semicircular acroteria; in front of a censer stood the god Anu, bearded and nude, extending his index finger in command; before him the half-nude Datames raised his hand, palm to face, in token of reverence.

About to start for the Nile, Datames must return home to fight another rebel. Aspis held the forest land of Cataonia through strong forts whose occupants ravaged the surrounding lands and held up convoys destined for the king. Taking a small force, Datames sailed to Cilicia, crossed the Taurus by day-and-night marches, and persuaded Aspis to surrender and permit himself to be handed over to the king's son Mithridates.[32]

Following a visit to Susa by the Spartan Euthycles, Artaxerxes made one more attempt in 368 to enforce a general peace on Greece. For the necessary diplomatic purchases, the satrap Ariobarzanes dispatched his subordinate Philiscus of Abydos to Delphi with large sums of money. Through the returned Timotheus, Athens granted citizenship to Ariobarzanes and Philiscus and praised Dionysius of Syracuse because he aided the "King's Peace." All the remaining European states agreed to the terms, but Diomedes of Cyzicus failed in

[31] Xen. *Hell*. vi. 3. 12 ff.; 4. 31; 5. 2–3; cf. 1. 12; Isocr. *Philip*. 119–20; Demosthen. *Philip*. iii. 16; Dionys. Halicarnas. *De Lys*. 12; Plut. *Ages*. 28.

[32] Babelon, *op. cit.*, pp. 405 ff.; Nepos *Datam*. 3. 5; 4 ff.; Polyaen. vii. 21. 2, 5.

his attempt to bribe Epaminondas, and again Thebes held out. On his return to Asia, Philiscus left behind him the two thousand mercenaries he had bought to aid—of all peoples—the once invincible Spartans! Astyanax of Miletus, thrice victor at Olympia in the pancratium, was invited to visit Ariobarzanes; to meet a boast, he ate all the food prepared for guests at a great banquet.[33]

To protest the action of Ariobarzanes, Pelopidas led a Theban embassy to Susa in 367. Other embassies assembled from Argos, Arcadia, and Elis, but Antalcidas (and with him Sparta and its present ally, Athens) was now in disgrace. Artaxerxes was reminded how, after all the aid given them by his father, the Spartans had assisted his rebel brother and had followed this by the invasion of Asia; here was a broad hint that, like Cyrus, Ariobarzanes was playing for his own hand. Thebes, on the contrary, had always been pro-Persian and had actually fought on the Persian side at Plataea. This was confirmed by one of the Athenian envoys, Timagoras. Asked what he desired, Pelopidas declared that Messene should be independent from Sparta and that the Athenians should be forced to dock their warships. At this point, another ambassador called out: "By Zeus, Athenians, it seems time for you to hunt out some other friend than the king!" The royal secretary interpreted, and Artaxerxes added: "If the Athenians know anything more just than this, let them come to the king and show it." The negotiations ended in failure; Antalcidas committed suicide on the homeward way, while Timagoras, accused of making adoration to the king and of having accepted from him a bribe of forty talents, was condemned to death.[34]

Artaxerxes had decided a boundary dispute for Elis against Arcadia. The Arcadians were less disturbed after their envoy Antiochus had reported to their Ten Thousand that the king had indeed more than a plenty of breadmakers, cooks, cupbearers, and porters, but of men capable of fighting he had looked them over and had found none; as for the famous golden plane tree, it could not shade a locust.

When Artaxerxes at last broke with Athens, the prestige of the empire was at its lowest. It was now the turn of Thebes to attempt en-

[33] *IG*, Vol. II, No. 52 (103) Dittenberger, *Syl.*³, No. 163; Xen. *Hell*. vii. 1. 27, 33; Demosthen. *Aristocrat*. 141, 202; Diod. xv. 70. 2; Nepos *Epaminond*. 4; Plut. *Reg. imp. apophtheg*. 193C; Theodorus, in Athen. x. 413A ff. (*FHG*, IV, 513).

[34] Xen. *Hell*. vii. 1. 33 ff.; Isocr. *Archidam*. 27; Demosthen. *De fals. leg*. 31, 137, 191; Diod. xv. 81. 3; Nepos *Pelopid*. 4; Plut. *Pelopid*. 30; *Artox*. 22. 3–4; Athen. ii. 48D–E, 251B.

forcement of the latest "King's Peace." At the meeting called for ratification, the Persian representative showed the king's seal and read the decision of Artaxerxes; in spite of Theban pressure, their own allies professed themselves quite satisfied with the former terms and refused to take new oaths (367).[35]

Strato, king of Sidon from 370 to 358, had forwarded the Athenian ambassadors to the best of his ability and had given the city the sum of ten talents. He was rewarded by the official grant of the honor of proxenos; of more advantage for his subjects, the Sidonians were granted exemption from the tax imposed on resident aliens. Abdashtart, as Strato was known at home, considered himself quite a Greek. He contended for the reputation of luxury with Evagoras' son Nicocles, imported courtesans from the Peloponnese and musicians from Ionia, and celebrated Greek games. A sacred embassy brought from Tyre and Sidon statues to Delian Apollo which bore inscriptions in Phoenician and Greek.

The local coins were less Hellenized. About 475 an unknown king had introduced a type showing a Sidonian galley with one or four sails and the Persian great king in a chariot. Toward the end of the fifth century, other kings, whose abbreviated Phoenician names cannot be identified, abandoned the sails, though the mast remained, for the galley was now propelled by oars; it was moored at the base of the crenelated walls and towers which surrounded the city. On the coins of Bodashtart the walls disappeared and the galley rode conspicuously high waves. On the reverse the royal chariot was followed on foot by an Egyptian king, posed half-sidewise and wearing the short Egyptian dress and the high white crown; in his left hand was an oenochoe, and his right upheld a scepter ending in the head of a horned animal with open mouth. Exactly the same types were followed by Abdashtart, though later the Egyptian was omitted after Nekhtenebef unkindly refused to be captured![36]

THE DEFECTION OF PERSIAN LEADERS

While still continuing to mobilize troops for the renewed offensive against Nekhtenebef, Datames learned that his enemies at Susa were intriguing against him. Once more court intrigues burdened the un-

[35] Xen. *Hell*. vii. 1. 38 ff.; 4. 2 ff.; Diod. xv. 76. 3; *IG*, Vol. IV, No. 556.

[36] *IG*, Vol. II, No. 86; *CIS*, Vol. II, No. 114; Theopomp., Frag. 114(J); Aelian. *Var. hist*. vii. 2; Athen. xii. 531A; Babelon, *op. cit*., pp. 547 ff., 595 ff.

fortunate Artaxerxes with another rebel. Leaving the army in charge of the Magnesian Mandrocles, Datames hurried to Cappadocia and occupied Paphlagonia.

Persian weakness and revolts against the central authority had given welcome opportunities to the native peoples. When Datames sent a detachment against marauding Pisidians, his own son Arsidaeus was slain. His father-in-law, the Paphlagonian Mithrobarzanes, deserted to these same Pisidians; the detachment was attacked suddenly and its camp was taken with great slaughter.

Another son, Sesamus or Sissynas, was ordered to attack Sinope on the coast near by. The citizens begged assistance from his father, who assured them that all he really needed was the loan of some artisans. With their aid, he then constructed ships but used them to besiege their own city. The inhabitants armed their women and paraded them upon the walls to prove that they were well defended. When a royal order arrived forbidding the siege, Datames made adoration before the letter as if to the king in person and sacrificed as if for good news and for a great gift. For the moment, the siege was lifted, but soon the satrap returned, occupied Sinope, and made it his capital. Now his coins showed the nymph Sinope and the eagle seizing the dolphin. Later Amisus also was secured.

When the mercenaries of Datames demanded their pay in arrears, he visited a rich native shrine close by (probably the Pontic Comana) and carried off on the backs of camels and donkeys utensils worth thirty talents. The spoil was shown to the mercenaries; however, the satrap announced, the metal must be taken to Amisus for minting. Inasmuch as Amisus was far distant and access was over rough paths, he was able to keep his unruly force quiet throughout the whole winter before they learned how they had been misled. Another of his shrewd practices was to keep as a private monopoly the hire of artisans; the gains of sutlers were also his own.

Sissynas deserted to the king and afforded him the first certain evidence that his father was in actual revolt. His fellow-satrap Autophradates was ordered to put down the rebellion. Unable to collect his troops in time to seize the forests in which lay the Cilician Gates, Datames took up a position from which he could block the defile without exposing himself to danger. There were numerous skirmishes; once he escaped across a river only by leaving his camp standing. Finally, Autophradates was compelled to offer a truce on condition that envoys be sent to the king. Datames retired in the direction of

Phrygia, but Pisidians had occupied the intervening passes, and only by a pretended retreat could he seize these passes by night.[37]

Autophradates had been compelled to offer Datames a truce because he was faced by another revolt. Ariobarzanes was already suspect at court because of doubtful activities with Athens and Sparta during the preparations for the proposed "King's Peace" of 368. Pharnabazus' son by the Princess Apame, Artabazus, was at last full grown, and Ariobarzanes was ordered by Artaxerxes to hand over to the proper heir the hereditary satrapy of Dascyleium. Like Datames, Ariobarzanes revolted (367).

Through Agesilaus, Sparta had made friends with the Egyptian Crown Prince Tachos. Prepared thus for still more opposition to Artaxerxes, Sparta dispatched Agesilaus to Ariobarzanes, nominally as ambassador but in fact as leader of his mercenaries. Athens gave thirty ships and eight thousand mercenaries to Timotheus for Ariobarzanes, though with specific instructions not to violate the treaty with the king. They found that Autophradates had expelled Ariobarzanes from the greater part of his satrapy and was besieging him by land and by sea in Adrammyttium. Ariobarzanes ordered his garrison commander Pteleon to pretend betrayal of a near-by island; while the loyal fleet was awaiting its surrender, Ariobarzanes brought into the city the supplies and mercenaries needed for its defense. Then Maussollus, the "satrap" of Caria (377–353), was induced by Autophradates to besiege Assos by land, while the Thracian Cotys did the same at Sestos. On the arrival of Agesilaus, Cotys and Autophradates withdrew, while Maussollus not only took off his ships but gave the Spartan money. Agesilaus by-passed Lampsacus and after a long investment took Phocaea by first cutting off the allies.[38]

When Timotheus discovered that Ariobarzanes was in open revolt, he turned to Samos, which, after a ten-month siege demanding most of the year, he freed from Cyprothemis, a garrison commander sent by the satrap Tigranes; and there Athens founded a colony. Timotheus was rewarded for the slight services he had rendered Ariobarzanes with the gift of Sestos and Crithote for Athens, but Agesilaus received his pay in hard cash. Meanwhile Artabazus held the Troad through

[37] Aeneas *Tact.* xl. 4–5; [Aristot.] *Oeconom.* ii. 2. 24; Diod. xv. 91. 2–3; xxxi. 19. 2; Trog. x, Nepos *Datam.* 4 ff.; Front. *Strat.* i. 4. 5; ii. 7. 9; Polyaen. vii. 21. 1–2, 4 ff.; 27. 1; 28. 2; Babelon, *op. cit.*, p. 415.

[38] Xen. *Ages.* ii. 26–27; Demosthen. *Rhod.* 9; Diod. xv. 90. 3; Nepos *Ages.* 6; Trog. x; Polyaen. ii. 1. 16, 26; vii. 21. 6; 26.

mercenaries led by the Rhodians Mentor and Memnon, whose sister he had married. Carians sent envoys to complain of Maussollus at court, but the king, trusting still to the loyalty of his "satrap," punished his accusers (366).[39]

Heracleia, boasting a population of six thousand inhabitants possessing citizen rights and a navy of forty ships, was coming into prominence as the most important Greek city on the Black Sea coast. The villagers and peasants of native stock did not have citizen rights, and rich and poor were therefore at variance. During the ensuing disturbances, Mithridates, son of Ariobarzanes, occupied Heracleia, thereby following the normal Persian practice of supporting the democracy (364). The senate appealed to Timotheus and then to Epaminondas for assistance against the populace.

Their appeals went unanswered, and in desperation the senate called in Clearchus, an exiled citizen who had collected about him a band of mercenaries. At first, he pretended to rule as a garrison commander of Mithridates, but when the Persian arrived, expecting the city to be handed over, he was imprisoned and compelled to pay an exorbitant ransom. Clearchus thereupon announced that *he* was the true protector of democracy; actually he ruled as tyrant (363–352). Sixty of the senate died under torture, the slaves were granted citizenship, and aristocratic women were compelled to accept them in marriage. So many of the citizens, we are told, were poisoned by aconite, that the remainder ate rue as antidote.

Tieium and Cierus were quickly forced to recognize him as tyrant, while much of Paphlagonia accepted his rule. His attitude toward the Persian court was correct, and both Artaxerxes II and Artaxerxes III received his ambassadors. Clearchus founded a library and patronized literature, for he was a pupil of Plato and Isocrates, and the latter corresponded with his son Timotheus. But despite these pretensions to culture, the rule of Clearchus was savage. Under the influence of the oriental concept of king-godship, he declared himself a son of Zeus and named his own son the "Thunderbolt." Clearchus was a sign and a portent, the first of a group of adventurers who took advantage

[39] Dittenberger, *Syl.*[3], Nos. 167 ff.; Isocr. *De permut.* 108, 111–12; Demosthen. *Rhod.*; 9; *Aristocrat.* 154, 157; Hermippus [Demosthen.] *Halon.* 29; Demosthen. *De fals. leg.* 137, 253; Aeschin. i. 53; [Aristot.] *Oeconom.* ii. 2. 23; Diod. xv. 90. 3; Nepos *Timoth.* 1. 2–3; *Ages.* 7. 2; Trog. x; Polyaen. iii. 10. 5, 9–10.

of the growing economic difficulties (which in turn produced social discontent) to make themselves city tyrants.[40]

Revolt of one satrap after the other in Asia Minor was a serious threat to the integrity of the empire and even to the safety of the sovereign himself. With the accession to the rebel cause of Aroandas, dissatisfied at his demotion from satrap of Armenia to subsatrap of Mysia, the situation became extremely dangerous (353). Accepted as the head of the satraps' coalition, he issued staters in gold (a right belonging only to a legitimate monarch) and thereby challenged the rule of Artaxerxes. Coins from Lampsacus depicted Pegasus, Athena, or Zeus; from Mysian Cisthenes the galloping horseman; from Colophon the lyre and the Greek word for "king"! On those from Clazomenae, he frankly recognized his mercenary support: the hoplite, protected by his shield, sunk to one knee, with his spear at rest to receive the enemy charge as Chabrias had taught his men. With their aid he captured Pergamum.

Among the rebel satraps was Maussollus. Ordered by the great king to send in his tribute, he used the opportunity only to collect more money. Confiding to a favored few —the richest—of his subjects that he was quite unable to pay, he suggested that they promise more than they expected actually to give and thus, by playing on the very human desire of emulation, others were induced to offer more than they had intended.

Mylasa was an unwalled city. One day Maussollus summoned the inhabitants and announced that the great king was advancing against him; they must give him money to build a wall if they would save their possessions from looting. Once the money was safe in his treasury, they were informed that the god would not permit the construction just then. Maussollus was playing his own hand; the rebel satraps could expect no real assistance.

The appearance of their leader Aroandas in Syria (362) was greeted by a native revolt, and Lycians, Pisidians, Pamphylians, and Cilicians followed the example. Autophradates found himself driven to join the rebels, and Artabazus was imprisoned. Egypt retained its independence, even with its king meekly following on foot the great king's chariot—on Phoenician coins! Half his revenues had been lost by Artaxerxes. The next step would be junction of the armies of

---

[40] Isocr. *Epist.* vii. 12; Theopomp., Frags. 28, 181(J); Polyb. xxxviii. 6. 2; Diod. xv. 81. 4–5; Memnon i; xx. 1; Plut. *Alex. fort.* 338B; Polyaen. ii. 30.

Nekhtenebef and Aroandas, a joint invasion of Mesopotamia, and then on to Susa for the kill.[41]

Near the beginning of his reign, Artaxerxes had won Persia's greatest diplomatic victory. He had repeatedly imposed a "King's Peace" upon European Greece, which no longer challenged his right to Greek cities in Asia. A quarter of a century later, his throne and his very life were in danger. The Achaemenid empire seemed about to disintegrate through lack of internal cohesion.

[41] W. Dittenberger, *Orientis Graeci inscriptiones selectae* (1905), No. 264; Hermippus [Demosthen.] *Halon.* 31; [Aristot.] *Oeconom.* ii. 2. 13–14; Diod. xv. 90. 3; 91. 1; Trog. x; Polyaen. vii. 14. 2–3.

Chapter XXIX

BRIEF RECOVERY

COLLAPSE OF THE THREAT FROM EGYPT

PERSIA seemed about to disintegrate into its component parts. That the empire enjoyed a brief return to unity was not to the credit of its weak and aging monarch but was the result of a whole series of quite unexpected accidents.

First came the death of Nekhtenebef (360), who was buried at Memphis in a green-breccia sarcophagus, one of the finest works of art produced under the dynasty.[1] As a result of his death, there ascended the throne his son Djedhor (361–359), Tachos or Taos to the Greeks. That he was already on good terms with both Athenians and Spartans was to be a significant factor in the changing situation.[2]

Meanwhile, in the summer of 362, Sparta had been crushingly defeated at Mantinea by pro-Persian Thebes. Fresh ambassadors from the king arranged another general peace;[3] Sparta assumed her accustomed place as objector, but disgusted Athens was bribed by the king's recognition of Athenian right to Amphipolis.[4] Anxious to lead one more attack on the Persians, Agesilaus made his appearance in the Delta near the end of the year 360 and professed himself ready to aid his friend Tachos.

Chabrias had completed his year as general at Athens; unfortunately, as it turned out, he was then recalled to his former sphere of activities. Athens was not sufficiently reconciled by the advantageous new "King's Peace" to prohibit his departure, and Chabrias was able to collect ten thousand more mercenaries. Tachos brought together a large native force and a regular navy of a hundred and twenty triremes. Reomithres, the representative of the disloyal satraps, added fifty more ships, together with a gift of five hundred talents.[5]

---

[1] G. Daressy, *Receuil de travaux*, X (1888), 142; *Annales du Service*, IV (1903), 105 ff.

[2] Plut. *Ages.* 37.

[3] Diod. xv. 90. 3, where the reference to Tachos dates the peace to 360; cf. J. A. O. Larsen, *Classical Philology*, XXXIV (1939), 377.

[4] Demosthen. *De fals. leg.* 137, 253; Hegesippus [Demosthen.] *Halon* 29.

[5] Xen. *Ages.* ii. 28–29; *Cyrop.* viii. 8. 4; Theopomp., Frags. 106 ff., 263(J); Diod. xv. 91. 1; 92. 2; Nepos *Ages.* 8; *Chabr.* 2. 1. 3; Plut. *Ages.* 36. 3; 37; Paus. iii. 10. 2; Athen. ix. 384A; xv. 676D; xiv. 616D–E.

It was an imposing force which collected in the spring of 359, but there were elements of weakness which could not be ignored. From their first contacts under the Saite dynasty, there had been constant clashes between natives and mercenaries. Contemporary writers of comedy show how the Greeks despised the Egyptians. For instance, Eubulus makes his hero swear by the Zeus of Mendes—that he is drunk! The younger Cratinus pokes fun at the Egyptiades, Sochares, and Paamyles. Timocles in his *Egyptians* scornfully asks: "What help can an ibis or a dog give? If those who sin against them are not immediately punished, who is likely to be smitten by the altar of a mere cat?" Anaxandrides tells the natives: "I couldn't bear to be your ally; our manners and customs are so utterly different. You worship a cow; I sacrifice it to the gods. For you, the eel is a mighty divinity; for us a mighty—dainty. You don't eat pork; I love it. You worship a bitch; I beat her when she eats my choicest food. Our priests are whole; you castrate them. If you see a cat in trouble, you mourn; I'd be glad to kill and skin it. The field mouse is strong by you, by me not!" Contempt for native religion so openly manifested could not but incite resentment.[6]

Worse still, all Greek mercenaries demanded their pay in hard cash. Egypt had made little progress toward a money economy since the kings of the Saite dynasty had hired Greek and Carian mercenaries. Since that time, the constant drain of the precious metals by Persian administration had checked whatever momentum the movement might have had.

The clever but unscrupulous Chabrias was ready with a new plan. By his advice, Tachos informed the priests that most of them must be discharged, since the expense of the war enforced the closing of certain temples. Naturally, each temple gave a bribe to remain open. After collecting large sums of money from each, Tachos issued fresh orders: Each temple was permitted to retain as an act of grace one-tenth of its revenues, while the remaining nine-tenths was to be a forced loan which, it was promised on the faith of the government, would be repaid at the end of the war. Tachos also added to the former imposts a house and poll tax and the payment of an obol by both seller and buyer on each artaba of grain. The tithe on imports by sea and on manufactures and general industry, granted by his father to Neith of Sais, was transferred to the crown.

[6] Eubulus, Frag. 126 (Kock); Cratinus, Frag. 2 (Kock); Timocles, Frag. 1 (Kock); Alexandrides, Frag. 39 (Kock).

All gold and silver in private possession was called in. From the precious metals were struck coins to pay the mercenaries; a gold daric bearing the name Tao in Greek letters and the helmeted Athena and her owl has survived. Those who thoughtlessly surrendered their hoards were "commended" to the monarchs who were supposed to repay them from the local taxes. Another brilliant scheme of Chabrias was to draft crews for a hundred and twenty ships when but sixty were needed. The crews of the remaining sixty were ordered to provide the first draft with supplies for two months; if they did not, they would no longer be exempted from active service. Even before the Macedonian conquest, the natives were given a foretaste of what it would mean for the state finances to be administered by a group of bright young Greeks.[7]

Tachos publicly declared that he had been summoned to the throne by Onuris of Sebennytus. But Egypt enjoyed little of the money collected, even through his buildings. His father had added a few scenes to the Khonsu temple at Karnak, and Tachos claimed its embellishment; there are traces of his building operations, of his statues, and of his reliefs at Gizah, Lake Menzalah, Athribis, and Matariya.[8] But this was small compensation for the "reforms," which alienated priests, traders, and commoners alike. As if this were not enough, there were dissensions among the leaders. The Egyptians despised the simple Agesilaus, who as the elder and a Spartan demanded for himself command of the entire host and even went so far as to insist that the king should remain in Egypt. Tachos had other plans. He announced that he would lead the expedition into Asia in person. Agesilaus was to command the mercenaries and Chabrias the fleet, but the native levies were to be under the king's nephew Nekht-har-hebi. Many gifts were required to mollify the angered Spartan.[9]

An elaborate plan of campaign was worked out in co-operation with the revolted satraps. Tachos advanced across the isthmus and secured all but a few forts in Palestine and Phoenicia; then he was to join Aroandas in Syria for a common invasion of Mesopotamia. Datames crossed the Euphrates leading the advance guard. So great was the emergency that the aged Artaxerxes must take charge of the de-

[7] [Aristot.] *Oeconom.* ii. 2. 25, 37; Polyaen. iii. 11. 5; cf. W. Schur, *Klio*, XX (1926), 281 ff.

[8] U. Bouriant, *RT*, XI (1889), 153 ff.; G. Daressy, *RT*, XVI (1894), 127; *AS*, XVII (1917), 42; C. C. Edgar, *AS*, XIII (1913), 277; W. Spiegelberg, *ÄZ*, LXV (1930), 102 ff.

[9] Xen. *Ages.* ii. 30; Theopomp., Frags. 106–7(J); Diod. xv. 92. 2–3; Nepos *Ages.* 8. 2 ff.; *Chabr.* 2. 3; Plut. *Ages.* 34 ff.; *Apophtheg. Lac.* 214D.

fense in person. Ochus, a younger son of the king, attempted to hold Phoenicia but was quite unable to meet the assault of Greek mercenaries. The empire seemed doomed.

Persia owed her salvation to an unnamed Egyptian, a brother of Tachos. Left as regent in Egypt, he took advantage of the universal hatred for the tax "reforms" by declaring his son Nekht-har-hebi king. On his father's urging, Nekht-har-hebi (359–340) himself revolted in Syria. Chabrias, the author of the detested "reforms," could expect no mercy and escaped to Athens, where he was made general for 357. Tachos, equally incriminated by his support of the alien "financier," surrendered to Ochus at Sidon after but a single year of reign and was forwarded through Arabia to Susa, where Artaxerxes gave him a warm reception. Agesilaus, rejoicing in the fall of his rival, Chabrias, referred the question of his future allegiance to the ephors at home; granted full powers, he declared for the rebel.[10]

Revolt broke out in new quarters, once the example of rebellion had been given. Absolutely opposed to the Greeks and their oppressive domination, the feudal chiefs refused to obey Nekht-har-hebi and chose as their king a prince of Mendes. Nekht-har-hebi must abandon his Asiatic conquests—and with them the allied satraps—to return to Egypt. There he was quickly shut up in Tanis by regular siege works, but Agesilaus drove off the besiegers by a night sortie, and the rebellion collapsed. His task completed, the Spartan sailed off toward home but died on the journey at the beginning of 358. Artaxerxes sent Tachos back as a vassal king, but he, too, died from dysentery on the way.[11]

COLLAPSE OF THE SATRAPAL REVOLT

Thanks to these two fatal revolts, Artaxerxes was enabled to advance without fear against Datames. Only the slow march of the king's huge army and the difficulties of obtaining supplies permitted the rebel to recross the Euphrates by the expedient of yoking chariots together to break the force of the stream. Abandoned by his Egyptian allies, Aroandas made his peace by surrendering the other rebels in

[10] Demotic Chronicle, IV, 16; Xen. *Ages.* ii. 30; Isocr. *Philip.* 118, 160; Theopomp., Frag. 108(J); Diod. xv. 92. 3 ff.; xiv. 48; Trog. x; Plut. *Ages.* 37; Lyceas of Naucratis, *Aegyptica* (*FHG*, IV, 441); Syncell. 486. The reign of Nekht-har-hebi was officially counted as beginning November 21, 359; actually it might have begun a little later.

[11] Demotic Chronicle IV, 16 ff.; Satrap Stele of Ptolemy I, K. Sethe in *Urkunden des aegyptischen Altertums*, ed. G. Steindorff, II (1904), 17; Xen. *Ages.* ii. 30–31; Diod. xv. 93. 2 ff.; Nepos. *Ages.* 8. 6–7; Plut. *Ages.* 38 f.; *Reg. imp. apophtheg.* 191C–D; *Apophtheg. Lac.* 214–15; Paus. xxx. 10. 2; Polyaen. ii. 1; 22. 31; iii. 11. 7; 13. 14; Lyceas of Naucratis, *Aegyptica* (*FHG*, IV, 441).

PLATE XLIX

Pharnabazus (from K. Lange, *Herrscherköpfe der Altertums*, Pl. 33)

Pericles (from Brunn-Bruckmann, *Denkmäler*, Pl. 156)

Tissaphernes (from K. Lange, *Herrscherköpfe des Altertums*, Pl. 34)

GREEK AND PERSIAN PORTRAITS

PLATE L

March of Cyrus down the Euphrates (Ana)

March of Ten Thousand to the Sea (south of Samsun)

EXPEDITION OF CYRUS

PLATE LI

Amazon Rhyton by Athenian Sotades Found in Meroe (courtesy Boston Museum of Fine Arts)

Satrap Sarcophagus from Sidon (courtesy Istanbul Museum)

CULTURAL DIFFUSIONS

PLATE LII

Dascyleium Ram Relief (from Arthus U. Pope, *Survey*, Pl. 103B)

Nereid Relief from Xanthos (from Brunn-Bruckmann, *Denkmäler*, Pl. 215)

PROVINCIAL ACHAEMENID ART

PLATE LIII

Relief Portrait (from *The Art of Egypt through the Ages*, Pl. 232)

East Gate to Temple Area at Karnak

King under Horus Falcon (courtesy New York Metropolitan Museum)

THE ART OF NEKHTANEBEF (NECTANEBO)

PLATE LIV

Lycian tombs (courtesy Turkish Press Department)

Across from Rhodes (courtesy Turkish Press Department)

TELMESSUS

PLATE LV

Apollo of Phillip of Macedon (from Hill, *Select Greek Coins*, Pl. VIII, 3)

Artemis of Achaean League (from Hill, *Select Greek Coins*, Pl. XXXIII, 3)

Zeus of Arcadian Federation (from Hill, *Select Greek Coins*, Pl. VIII, 2)

Tadanmu (Datames) (courtesy Numismatic Society)

Bel of Tarsus under Mazaeus (courtesy Numismatic Society)

Lion and Stag from Tarsus (courtesy Numismatic Society)

Zeus of Mausollos (from Hill, *Select Greek Coins*, Pl. XLIII, 3)

Aphrodite from Aphrodisias in Cilicia (from Hill, *Select Greek Coins*, Pl. XLII, 2)

FOURTH-CENTURY COINAGE

PLATE LVI

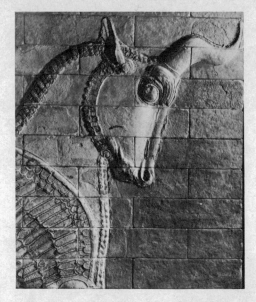

Head (from Louvre, *Encyclopédie photographique*, Vol. XII, Pl. 55)

Winged Bull (from *Encyclopédie photographique*, Vol. XII, Pl. 54)

Glazed Bricks from Susa

his company; he was rewarded by the retention of his satrapy, to which was added the general oversight of the Aegean coast. Although his wife and children had been left as hostages in Egypt, Reomithres sailed for Leucae at the Hermus with the ships and money given him by Tachos, captured numerous rebels, and sent them bound to the king. The danger to the empire disappeared as suddenly as it had arisen.[12]

Autophradates freed the captive Artabazus and thus made his own peace. The mercenaries collected by Mentor and Memnon had fallen into the hands of the adventurer Charidemus, who with them took Scepsis and Cebren and fought with the restored Aroandas. A bribed slave led thirty mercenaries disguised as captives into Ilium; Athenodorus of Imbrus, another adventurer, but fighting in the service of the great king, was informed of the plot. He, too, pushed his way in during the confusion, but his men did not know the password and so were detected and expelled. Athenodorus himself was defeated before Atarneus by the famous Athenian Phocion, but, when he compelled his mercenaries to swear that they would conquer or die, he won a second battle.

Artabazus marched against Charidemus, who was making a practice of demanding pay for his soldiers from the cities he was "protecting." After the first "contribution," they declared that no money was left; Charidemus resorted to a highly approved trick: since he was moving his own property under guard, he pretended that he would be glad to offer the same protection if they wished to transfer their money and valuables to a safer place; once the convoy was outside, he took what he needed and returned what was left. Another trick much admired was the announcement of a fine for the possession of arms by the citizens; after they had come to the conclusion that he did not mean to enforce it, by a sudden house-to-house search he made a goodly sum. He was finally besieged by Artabazus, but when the latter's sons-in-law pleaded on his behalf, he was permitted to escape under armistice before the year was over.[13]

Similar tyrannies sprang up elsewhere. Philiscus, aided by the troops of Ariobarzanes, took Lampsacus and other Greek cities, castrating the free boys and mistreating the women, but was promptly

[12] Xen. *Ages.* ii. 30–31; *Cyrop.* viii. 8. 4; Theopomp., Frag. 47(J); Diod. xv. 91. 1; 92. 1; Nepos *Datam.* 9; Polyaen. vii. 21. 3.

[13] Aeneas *Tact.* xxiv, 3 ff.; Demosthen. *Aristocrat.* 154 ff. (cf. 202); [Aristot.] *Oeconom.* ii. 2. 30;ꞌ Diod. xv. 91; Plut. *Sertor.* i. 3; Polyaen. iii. 14; v. 21.

murdered. His successor Astyanax was also killed because he neglected to open a letter which revealed the plot. Pytho, aided by confederates within, captured his native city of Clazomenae by blocking its gates with wagons loaded with wine jars. Struggles between rich and poor in Abydus made Iphiades tyrant; Parium was added when brush-laden carts fired the gates and distracted the citizens. Eubulus the banker made himself tyrant in Atarneus and Assos and successfully resisted a siege of the former city by Autophradates.[14]

Ariobarzanes was betrayed by his own son Mithridates and was crucified. Artabazus secured Paphlagonia and invaded Cappadocia. Once Datames was treacherously attacked by one of his soldiers at Aspendus and escaped only by dressing a subordinate in his own garments and callously abandoning him to his fate. After many other such attempts, he was at last slain by Mithridates at a conference which was called to continue the satraps' revolt. His son Sysinas was given his father's satrapy and under the Aramaic name of Abd Susin minted at Sinope with his father's types of nymph and eagle; a few of these coins have been excavated at Persepolis.[15]

CONSTRUCTIONS OF ARTAXERXES

Artaxerxes was reaching the end of his long and, despite numerous revolts, moderately successful reign. Much of his wealth was employed in building. Early in his reign he had restored the palace of Darius I at Susa, destroyed in a conflagration during the last days of the first Artaxerxes. Even now it is possible to identify his restorations. In the apadana they are detected by his trilingual inscriptions on the supporting bases of the immense gray-limestone columns whose huge bull capitals afford some idea of contemporary sculpture. Other inscriptions, full of grammatical mistakes which betray degeneration in literary style, are found everywhere throughout the palace inclosure.

In the palace proper to the southwest of the apadana, our reliance for dating must rest on bricks. In sharpest contrast to the magnificent glazed bricks manufactured for the first Darius, those of the second Artaxerxes are in softer glaze and of less delicate color. Yet the effect

---

[14] Aeneas *Tact.* xxviii. 5 ff.; xxxi. 33; Demosthen. *Aristocrat.* 141–42; Aristot. *Polit.* ii. 4. 10; v. 5. 5, 9; Callisthen., Frag. 4(J); Strabo xiii. 1. 57.

[15] Xen. *Cyrop.* viii. 8. 4; Demosthen. *Aristocrat.* 155; Aristot. *Polit.* v. 8. 15; Diod. xv. 91. 2, 7; xvii. 17; Nepos *Datam.* 10–11; Polyaen. vii. 29. 1; Valer. Max. iv. 11. 2; E. Babelon, *Traité des monnaies*, II, Part II (1910), 423 ff.; Erich Schmidt, *The Treasury of Persepolis and Other Discoveries in the Homeland of the Achaemenians* (1939), pp. 75–77.

is still gorgeous, and the contrast of the bright colors of the glaze with the soft rose or gray tones of the crude mud or well-baked bricks is appealing.

This art is best seen in a small throneroom in the western section. As entablature around its walls (and in a gate leading to the west), there was once a frieze of lions, some eighty feet above the mud bricks of which the lower walls were composed. The lions have been reconstructed from fragments; again they stalk along with open jaws and spiked tail high in the air. All the bricks are made from the same mold, but variety is obtained by the alternation of colors. The huge outstanding muscles may be green or blue, the mane brown or green, but most of the body is white; the ornaments are pale green, dull brown, straw, or white, and all are placed on a deep turquoise blue background. In the gate, the frieze is topped by a line of open battlements, below which is a rosette border framed to either side by triangles, linked lotus buds, and projecting frame.

Artaxerxes also restored the fortifications, including a strong redoubt at the southeast corner of the inclosure, as likewise the pavements and the whole system of roads about the advanced wall for the whole circuit. "Says Artaxerxes the king: By the favor of Ahuramazda, this is the hadish palace which I built in my lifetime as a pleasant retreat; may Ahuramazda, Anahita, and Mithra protect me and my hadish from all harm." The addition of goddess and god to the divinity who in the eyes of Darius was without colleague hints of significant religious changes. This is the palace described by the Jewish author of the Esther roll; it is also the home of the Great King from which Artaxerxes dictated his royal peace to the Greeks.[16]

By the aid of this same trinity of gods, Artaxerxes gave Ecbatana a new apadana and sculptures.[17] During the major part of his life he seems not to have built at Persepolis, but just before his death he started one innovation. His four greater predecessors had taken for themselves the best tomb sites at Naqsh-i-Rustam; it was apparently his tomb that was cut in the mountain cliff high up above the southeastern part of the Persepolis platform. The lower quarter of the normal cross on the face was omitted, while the upper beam of the en-

[16] W. K. Loftus, *Travels and Researches in Chaldaea and Susiana* (1857), pp. 343 ff., 352 ff., 364 ff., M. Dieulafoy, *L'Acropole de Suse* (1893), pp. 87, 137, 326, 429; V. Scheil, *Inscriptions des Achéménides à Suse* ("Mém.," Vol. XXI [1929]), pp. 91 ff.; *Actes juridiques susiens* ("Mém.," Vol. XXIV [1933]), pp. 126–27; W. Brandenstein, *WZKM*, XXXIX (1932), 88 ff.; R. G. Kent, *JAOS*, LI (1931), 228–29; J. M. Unvala, in A. U. Pope (ed.), *A Survey of Persian Art*, I, 344.

[17] F. H. Weissbach, *Die Keilinschriften der Achämeniden* (1911), pp. 122 ff.

tablature became a procession of lions whose treatment is still artistic
enough to possess a certain appeal. The tombs of Xerxes, Artaxerxes I,
and Darius II at Naqsh-i-Rustam were without inscriptions; Artaxerxes II returned to the practice of Darius I, but only to copy untruthfully the names and reliefs of the subject peoples who supported the
throne of his more powerful predecessor.[18]

ACCESSION OF ARTAXERXES III OCHUS

From the three hundred and sixty concubines assigned him (one for
each day of the civil year), there were born to Artaxerxes a hundred
and fifteen sons. Only three, however—Darius, Ariarathes or Ariaspes,
and Ochus—were children of Queen Stateira. Following ancient custom, the eldest son Darius was associated in the kingship when his
father departed for the Cadusian war. Artaxerxes lived too long after
he returned, and Darius was persuaded by Tiribazus to enter into a
conspiracy which was joined also by fifty of the king's other sons. The
conspiracy was betrayed by a eunuch, and Darius was caught in the
royal bedchamber; tried by royal judges who gave written decision in
the king's absence, he was condemned to death. Ariaspes was kindly
and beloved by the masses; working through eunuchs and favorites,
Ochus led him to believe that his father was angered against him, and
so Ariaspes poisoned himself. Arsames, a natural son but celebrated for
his wisdom, was now favored by his father; at the instigation of
Ochus, he was murdered by Tiribazus' son Artapates, and the aged
Artaxerxes died of grief (358).[19]

Ochus had already shown his savage character; as Artaxerxes III he
was reputed the most bloodthirsty of all Achaemenid monarchs. His
coin portrait—short straight nose, short hair, long pointed beard, and
dour expression—does not bely the reputation.[20] No sooner was he
seated on the throne than he killed off all his relatives without distinction of age or sex.

His first official act would seem to have been another attempt to put
down the still rebellious Cadusians; the attempt was successful, and
henceforth bodies of their troops are found in the Achaemenid
armies.[21] Soon after, he ordered the satraps in Asia Minor to disband

[18] A. W. Davis, "An Achaemenian Tomb-Inscription at Persepolis," *Journal of the Royal Asiatic Society*, 1932, pp. 373 ff.; E. Herzfeld, *Altpersische Inschriften* (1938), No. 24.

[19] Diod. xv. 93. 1; Just. x. 1-2; Plut. *Artox.* 26 ff.; *De frat. amor.* 480D; Aelian. *Var. hist.* ix. 42; xii. 1; Marmor Parium A, 77.

[20] Babelon, *op. cit.*, pp. 55 ff.

[21] Diod. xvii. 6. 1; Just. x. 3. 2 ff.; Arr. *Anab.* iii. 8. 5; 11. 3; 19. 3; Curt. iv. 12. 12; 14. 3.

their Greek mercenaries. Artabazus thereupon revolted, and Ochus ordered an army of twenty thousand to be collected in Phrygia. The rebel appealed to Athens, where the government seriously considered using their own mercenaries to grant the requested aid. Isocrates had preached the crusade against the barbarian Persian under the leadership of Athens in 380;[22] since that year, his ardor had cooled. Now he observed with alarm that the barbarians were becoming hostile; "as for what the king has against us, he made clear by the letters he sent."[23]

A HELLENIZED ORIENTAL RULER: MAUSSOLLUS OF CARIA

Maussollus of Caria had been forgiven, for he had committed no overt act of treason. Immediately after the collapse of the great satrapial revolt, he began to expand his "satrapy" into what was virtually an independent kingdom. Halicarnassus, Iassus, and Cnidus were already in his possession. Cos, however, dominated the entrance to the Halicarnassus harbor, and, though Maussollus attempted to seize the island, he failed. Miletus remained free despite an effort by Aegyptus to effect its betrayal. Ephesus also resisted successfully, but even the resistance could be utilized; pretending that the Ephesian Herophytes was about to attack, Maussollus enrolled three hundred citizens of Heracleia on Latmus to go to Pygela as guards, then seized the deserted city as the inhabitants poured out to view his approach. A large part of Lydia fell into his hands. After the satraps' revolt, Pericles of Lycia had disappeared, and Maussollus occupied his country.[24]

Meanwhile, Demosthenes protested against Athenian mistreatment of the allies: "When anyone buys the office of trierarch, he sails off to plunder and pillage everybody; the profits he reaps himself, but you citizens pay the damages. You are the only people who can travel nowhere without a herald's staff because these men seize hostages and thus provoke reprisals; if one faces the situation truthfully, he will discover that such triremes have sailed out, not in your behalf, but against you."[25]

His warnings were unheeded, and in the autumn of 356 the allies revolted. Maussollus took advantage of the Social War to detach

---

[22] Cf. p. 400.

[23] Isocrat. *Areop.* 10. 81 (for date see Werner Jaeger, *Athenian Studies Presented to William Scott Ferguson* [1940], pp. 409 ff.); Diod. xvi. 22. 1; 34. 1–2; Just. x. 3. 1; Curt. x. 5. 23; Polyaen. vii. 17.

[24] Dittenberger, *Syl.*, Nos. 167 ff.; *TAM*, Vol. I, No. 45; Aristot. *Polit.* v. 2. 5; Polyaen. vi. 8; vii. 23. 2; Lucian. *Dial. mort.* 24.

[25] Demosthen. *Steph. trierarch.* 13–14.

Rhodes, Chios, Cos, Erythrae, and Byzantium and to form them into a new confederacy headed by himself. The coins of Chios showed Maussollus as Heracles and thus mark the beginning of his divinization.[26]

Maussollus, who set more than one precedent for the future, is our best example of a thoroughly Hellenized oriental ruler. He was married to his sister Artemesia[27]—an anticipation of the brother-sister unions of the Ptolemies. All his official inscriptions were in Greek, and even in Lycia he added Greek to the native language. Equally Greek were his coin types and legends. He posed as a patron of Greek culture; for instance, the well-known Athenian orator Aeschines and the famous mathematician-astronomer Eudoxus were for a time guests at his court. The comedian Theopompus described his deeds. On his coins, as a further proof of his Hellenic attitude, the ancient Zeus of Labraunda was removed from his place of honor on the obverse and relegated to the reverse in favor of Apollo.[28]

One of the most characteristic features of the Hellenistic age was to be the union of small towns into one great city; Maussollus removed his capital from Mylasa to the twelve-hour-distant Halicarnassus. Of eight Pedasian cities, only Mylasa and Myndus retained their separate identity; Pedasus itself, the famous abode of diviners, Telmessus, Euralion, Medamsa, Sibde, and Theangela-Syangela were depopulated to increase the inhabitants of the enlarged capital (362).

Halicarnassus was well fortified by nature and already possessed a fine harbor and an excellent market. Viewed from the sea, the city sloped upward on terraces like a great theater; its stage was the harbor, beyond which was the market place. In the middle of the curve was a broad street; after her husband's death, Artemesia was to build at its center the famous mausoleum. On the highest point of the city was a temple of Ares and a colossal marble herm of the god, generally attributed to Leochares, though some ascribed it to Timotheus. To the right was a temple of Aphrodite and Hermes, near the font Salmacis in the native quarter, which was supposed to give a disease of Aphrodite. To the left was the palace, drawn according to the satrap's own plan, and built of burned brick so finished with stucco that it seemed to later generations to have the translucency of glass; the facing was of

---

[26] Dittenberger, *Syl.*³, No. 168; Demosthen. *Rhod.* 3, 27; *De pace* 25; Diod. xvi. 7. 3; G. F. Hill, in *Anatolian Studies Presented to William Mitchell Ramsay* (1923), pp. 207 ff.

[27] Theopomp., Frags. 297, 299(J); Diod. xvi. 36. 2; Strabo xiv. 2. 17.

[28] Theopomp., Frag. 48 (Kock); Diog. Laert. viii. 87; Philostrat. *Vit. sophist.* i. 482; Babelon, *op. cit.*, pp. 146 ff.

marble from Proconnesus. From the palace alone could be seen the secret harbor under a high cliff.[29]

All this building required money, and Maussollus was often in financial difficulties, which he resolved in the manner of his time. His governor Condalus would make a journey throughout the land. When he received as a gift a sheep, a pig, or a calf, he would note the name of the donor and the date, then return the animal with the request that it be kept for him until his return; later he would ask for it and also demand the produce tax! Trees that fell into the royal roads or even projected over them would be sold for timber. When a mercenary died, Maussollus would charge a drachma fee for permitting the corpse to pass the gates; incidentally, this was an excellent check to prevent officers from claiming pay for soldiers already dead. The Lycians wore their hair long; Maussollus published orders as if from the king demanding hair for false fringes, and thus enforced a poll tax through which to purchase hair from Greece![30]

GREEK ALLIANCE WITH REBEL ARTABAZUS

In his intrigues with their allies, the Athenians naturally assumed that Maussolus was acting as the agent of Ochus. When their attempt to win back the islands by force proved a failure and peace negotiations must begin, Isocrates could only suggest acceptance of the terms of the King's Peace which he himself in 380 had so emphatically condemned.[31] The government thought otherwise; taking advantage of the growing resentment against Persia, its leaders proposed to accept the generous pay offered by the rebel Artabazus for Athenian aid. Rumors filled the air: Artaxerxes would be a second Xerxes who planned that again the Greeks would enslave their fellow-Greeks; the rumormongers even knew that twelve thousand camels were on their way bringing gold to purchase Greek mercenaries. But, as in the days of Xerxes, the barbarian would again be easily defeated, and Persia would be destroyed, this time for good.

Demosthenes answered this proposal in 354 by his maiden speech before the assembly. Certain of the orators had been preaching a crusade against the barbarian. Demosthenes is quite ready to admit that "the king is the common foe of the Greeks," but Athens cannot wage war against him by herself, especially when some of the Greeks are

---

[29] Vitruv. ii. 8. 10 ff.; Callisthen., Frag. 25(J); Diod. xv. 90. 3; Strabo xiii. 1. 59; Plin. v. 107; xxxvi. 77; Gell. x. 18. 2; Lucian. *Dial. mort.* 24.

[30] [Aristot.] *Oeconom.* ii. 2. 13 ff.; Polyaen. vii. 23. 1.   [31] Isocr. *De pace* 10.

still his friends. Were they sure that he is actively hostile—Demosthenes implies that he doubts whether Maussollus is actually an agent of Ochus—other states might join, but if Athens begins a war against him before this is clearly evident, the king will bribe them and they will accept the bribe. War with the king will be difficult, for, though Athens has the better men, the king has more money. Many Greeks will fight against Egyptians or against Aroandas, but they will not fight against fellow-Greeks. Let not Athens afford an opportunity for the king to pose as the protector of the Greeks.[32]

Pro-Persian sympathies were not required to demonstrate the plain common sense of the argument, but nevertheless the speech was a failure. Athens made alliance with the rebel, to whose support Chares was sent toward the end of the year. Phrygia was invaded, a great victory over the king's forces was won, and the territories of the loyal satrap, the younger Tithraustes, were ravaged; Chares wrote home that the battle was a sister of Marathon!

Aroandas, however, lost his first battle with the royal army and retired to Mount Tmolus, where he established a fortified camp. Slipping out by night with picked horsemen, he destroyed enemy supplies on the Sardis road. Then, sending advance notice to the besieged, he so arranged the disposition of his separated forces that both detachments fell simultaneously upon the besiegers who were utterly destroyed. In Cyme, with ten thousand Greeks, he beat off ten thousand cavalry led by Autophradates, and followed this up by an attack on Ephesus. By arming natives with Greek weapons and by giving Greek commands through interpreters, he frightened off Autophradates, who by this time had developed a healthy respect for Greek mercenaries.[33]

Ochus countered by ordering a fleet of three hundred ships to be brought together for the use of the enemies of Athens; he also commanded the Athenians to recall Chares under threat of open war. Demosthenes' protest was justified, and Chares was bidden to fight no more for the rebel satraps. Before leaving, he arranged terms between Artabazus and Tithraustes, then retired to the coast and to his reward—the gift of Sigeium and Lampsacus for Athens. Athens must sign a peace with her former allies which admitted the loss of the last

[32] Demosthen. Symmor. 31; cf. Paul Cloché, Démosthenès et la fin de la démocratie athénienne (1937); Werner Jaeger, Demosthenes (1938); A. Schaefer, Demosthenes und seine Zeit (2d ed., 1885).

[33] Demosthen. Philip. i. 24; Diod. xvi. 22. 1; 34. 1; Plut. Arat. 16. 3; Polyaen. vii. 14. 2 ff.; 27; Pap. Rainer, F. Jacoby, Die Fragmente der griechischen Historiker, IIA (1926), p. 505.

vestiges of her former island empire (353). Demosthenes enjoyed the pleasure of winning a private case in court through Athens' enforced change of attitude. On an embassy to Maussollus, Androtion and two companions captured an Egyptian ship hailing from Naucratis; brought into the Athenian courts, the ship was condemned as a proper prize because Egypt was in revolt against the great king, and Athens was now the friend of Persia![34]

After the fiasco of 355, Thebes assumed the place of Athens as the ally of Artabazus, to whose aid she sent her best general, Pammenes, with five thousand soldiers. The royal satraps were defeated in two great battles. In one, he saw that the Persian right was strongest, and therefore placed opposite a relatively weak force which was ordered to retire at the first onslaught to rough wooded ground; with the best of his own cavalry and infantry, Pammenes then enveloped the enemy's right and thus defeated the whole body (354). Artabazus, however, suspected the Theban of secretly treating with the loyalists, for his countrymen had been consistently pro-Persian; Pammenes, accused of winning over the soldiers by gifts and grain, left for home after turning over the command to the satrap's brother Oxythras (353).

Aroandas remained in successful revolt, but loss of Theban support so weakened Artabazus that soon he must take refuge with Philip (355–336) in Macedonia; other exiles with Philip—now rapidly coming to the fore as the expected leader of the crusade against Persia—were Sissenes, agent of the satrap of Egypt, and the Egyptian Minapis. In this same year 353, Maussollus died and was succeeded as ruler of Caria by his sister-wife Artemesia, though his brother Idrieus became satrap. Next year Clearchus of Pontic Heracleia was murdered; since his son Timotheus was a minor, the regency was held for the next seven years (352–345) by his uncle Satyrus.[35] Through these and similar changes, the ground was being cleared for a last assault on Egypt.

[34] Demosthen. *Timocrat.* 11; Theopomp. *Philip.* xiii, Frag. 105(J), xlv; Athen. xii. 532B ff.; Diod. xvi. 22. 2; 34. 1; Nepos. *Chabr.* 3. 4; Arr. *Anab.* i. 12. 1; Schol. Demosthen. *Olymp.* iii. 31; *Philip.* i. 19.

[35] Dittenberger, *Syl.*², No. 573; Diod. xv. 81. 4; xvi. 34. 1–2; 36. 2–3; xx. 77. 1; Just. xvi. 5. 12 ff.; Memnon ii; Front. *Strat.* ii. 3. 3; Polyaen. v. 16. 2; vii. 33. 2; Curt. iii. 7. 11; vi. 4. 25.

Chapter XXX

THE NILE REGAINED

THE LAST FLOWERING OF EGYPTIAN ART

NEKHT-HAR-HEBI won back the regard of the priests by much building. Inscriptions from Tura prove almost constant quarrying. So much stone was taken from the sacred mountain back of Abydos that by his fifth year the king must issue a decree prohibiting any more cutting. Beautiful red granite from below the first cataract was transported the whole length of the valley to the Delta, which was specially favored in this work of reconstruction. Today the whole region is covered with fragments of red and black limestone, beautifully polished and filled with reliefs and inscriptions. Building remains prove the erection of huge temples vying with those of the Eighteenth Dynasty.

Of this wealth of structures, only fragments remain, but even these are too many for description in minute detail. Sebennytus, the capital, could boast a shrine of schist. Bubastis could show a great hall of quartzite, shrines of red and black granite, and a statue of black schist with magical texts and figures of the gods. Bahbit, probably the king's birthplace, owned a huge Isis temple. Enormous ceiling blocks at Pharbaethus indicate the size of an otherwise destroyed temple. Bast was honored at Bilbeis with a temple and a black granite shrine, and Thoth with two obelisks at Heliopolis. At Tell Maskhuta was found a blue limestone column with offering scenes to Atum, one side of which is plated with thin gold.

Memphis, the ancient capital, had two new obelisks. In his second year the king erected a temple for the living Apis; he tells how much gold, incense, and beer was granted to the god. In year two and again in year eight the Apis bull was entombed with all due pomp. Tuna was given a shrine of rose granite, Mit Rahina another building, Ehnasya a red granite shrine, Coptos a brown granite obelisk. Abydos has preserved statues of artistic ability almost equal to the best produced by the Eighteenth Dynasty sculptors.

At Karnak his cartouche untruthfully claimed the gate added by Amyrtaeus II to the Montu temple, though the temples of Khonsu

430

and Mut were repaired. Edfu rejoiced in a granite shrine so beautiful that it continued in use under the Ptolemies. The temple at El Kab was given a cornice. Khnum had a temple at Elephantine. One must travel the valley from end to end to learn how this last outburst of native Egyptian building adorned the whole land.

Out in the western desert the story is the same. In the great oasis there was a new pylon entrance.[1] In the more famous shrine of Amon, soon to be visited by Alexander, the oasis prince Wen Amon built the valley temple Ummabeda for Nekht-har-hebi, "who sets the hearts of the gods at rest and establishes the native laws."[2]

We hear nothing of the cost of all this building, but at least Egypt had the look of prosperity, and it was far better for taxes to go into local constructions than into the treasury of a distant foreign king. Nekht-har-hebi deserved the sarcophagus of green breccia, showing the twelve divisions of the Duat and figuring thirty-seven of the seventy forms of Ra, even though it was destined never to be used as his resting-place.[3]

There is other evidence for a renewed interest in the ancient literature. From his reign comes a copy of the famous Book of the Dead. A contemporary stele is well known for its magical texts and illustrative scenes.[4]

Contemporary funerary customs are illustrated by the tomb of Djedhor and his family at Abydos. Djedhor—who died while Ochus was beginning his last invasion—was a new man, for his parents are assigned no title, but he himself heaps up the honors: he is hereditary prince, sole beloved friend, overseer of Lower Egypt, land inspector, overseer of the land, whom the king made great for his wisdom, who made the Lord of Both Lands rich, whom the king made head scribe, who reckoned all things in officialdom, while he filled both ears of the Horus with truth. When he died in the fifteenth year, the royal scribe of the West (the Necropolis) through the garrison commander of Selle—good proof that the king was campaigning on the Asiatic frontier in 344—provided that the head scribe should be made divine in the afterworld and that they should make every preparation that

[1] H. E. Winlock, *The Temple of Hibis in el Khargeh Oasis*, Vol. I: *The Excavations* (1941), pp. 26 ff.

[2] W. F. M. Petrie, *History of Egypt* (3d ed., 1925), III, 378 ff.; H. Junker, *Mitteilungen des deutschen Instituts für Ägyptische Altertumskunde*, I (1930), 30 ff.

[3] E. A. W. Budge, *Egyptian Sculptures* (1914), Pl. xliv.

[4] V. S. Golenishchev, *Metternich Stele* (1877).

he might wish for all eternity. With him was buried his dwarf, also named Djedhor, who danced on the day of the feast of eternity, on the feast of the dead of Apis in the Memphis Serapeum and by the holy lake of Hieropolis.[5]

THE MAUSOLEUM OF HALICARNASSUS

While the line of temples along the whole lower course of the Nile reflects the last superb bloom of a purely native art, the massive structure erected at Halicarnassus by Artemesia to honor her brother-husband looks forward to other phases of the approaching Hellenistic civilization. Its architects were Satyrus and, later, Pytheas, who wrote a book on its construction. In form, it was the old-fashioned free-standing tomb of southwestern Asia Minor, on a square base and rising in three stages to the triumphal chariot of Maussollus drawn by four horses at the summit. It was the second stage which made the Mausoleum at Halicarnassus one of the seven wonders of the ancient world and its name a common noun for later generations, for among its columned porches were to be recognized statues by the most famous sculptors of the day. To Scopas were assigned those on the east front, to Bryaxis those on the north, to Leochares those on the west, and to Timotheus those on the south.

Equally all-Hellenic were the athletic games celebrated at the dedication. Theodectes of Phasaelis exhibited a tragedy under the dead monarch's name. A contest was held for the honor of writing the funeral oration to be delivered for the mighty dead; some say that the prize was won by the historian Theopompus; others, by Naucrates of Erythrae.[6]

FAILURE OF THE FIRST EGYPTIAN CAMPAIGN

Ochus meanwhile was building up a huge army in a determined effort to conquer Egypt. In hope of future mercenaries, a subsidy was granted the Thebans to finish their Sacred War against the Phocians. Nekht-har-hebi also obtained fresh mercenaries led by the Athenian Diophantus and the Spartans Lamius and Gastron. At first Ochus was successful and Phoenicia was occupied. Strato of Sidon was compro-

---

[5] W. Spiegelberg, *ÄZ*, LXIV (1929), 76 ff.

[6] Theopomp., Frags. 297, 299(J); Cic.*Tuscul*. iii. 75; Vitruv. *praef*. 12–13; ii. 8. 10; Strabo xiv. 2. 16–17; Mart. i. 1; Plut. *Vit. X Orat*. 838B; Valer. Max. iv. 16. 1; Gell. x. 18. 3; Quintill. iii. 6. 3; Plin. xxxvi. 30; Paus. viii. 16. 4; Polyaen. vii. 23; Lucian. *Dial. mort*. 24; *Necyon*. 17; Porphyr. in Euseb. *Praep. Evangel*. x. 3; Hieron. *Adv. Jovin*. i. 44; Suidas, *s.vv*. "Theodectes," "Isocrates"; C. T. Newton, *A History of Discovery at Halicarnassus* (1862); reconstruction, M. Rostovtzeff, *A History of the Ancient World*, Vol. I: *The Orient and Greece* (1926), Pl. LXXXVI, 1.

mised by his alliance with Egypt; on the Persian approach he determined to commit suicide, but Greek luxury had sapped his courage,
and it was his wife who anticipated the more dreadful fate he faced.
Tennes was appointed to his place and on his coins showed himself
meekly following on foot his master's chariot.

The conquest of Egypt was not so simple. We hear of one episode—
of how Gastron exchanged the arms of Greeks and natives so that the
Persians fought well against Greeks but fled before Greek-armed natives. Finally, after a year's campaigning (351–350), Ochus must retire. At his capital Nekht-har-hebi set up a figure of himself, standing
between the legs of a gigantic hawk to represent the god Horus; the
inscription to accompany it makes the proud boast that he is the protector of Egypt, who drives back the foreign lands and strikes the nine
bows.[7]

ARTEMESIA OF HALICARNASSUS

Although Idrieus as satrap of Caria monopolized coinage, Artemesia
herself was actually sovereign and was so recognized by contemporaries. Her rule was vigorous. Heracleia on Latmus was again captured,
this time by troops hidden while the whole body of citizens poured
out to watch the queen, accompanied by her eunuchs, women, pipers,
and cymbalists, march in procession to a grove of the mother of the
gods a mile beyond the city.[8]

Accession of a woman seemed to offer the Rhodians an opportunity
not merely to win back their own freedom but to capture Halicarnassus itself. They appealed for aid to their recent enemy Athens, and
Demosthenes took up their cause. Shortly after the retirement of
Ochus, the orator appeared before the assembly to express his wonder
at the strange sight of men anxious to fight Persia in behalf of Egyptians but afraid to assist Rhodes. Since the king has failed to take
Egypt, he predicts, Artemesia will make no foray on Rhodes.

Demosthenes might sneer at the men who were so anxious to fight the
Persians in Egypt, but Aristotle thought differently. As a typical example of sound logic, he cites the argument: "One must prepare
against the great king and not allow him to take Egypt; for Darius
and Xerxes did not attack Greece until they had taken Egypt; there-

---

[7] Isocr. *Philip.* 101; *Epist.* viii. 8; Diod. xvi. 40. 1 ff.; 46. 4; 48. 1 ff.; Trog. x; Front. *Strat.* ii.
3. 13; Polyaen. ii. 16; Hieron. *Adv. Jovin.* i. 45; Oros. iii. 7. 8; P. Tresson, "Sur deux monuments
égyptiens inédit," *Kêmi*, IV (1931), 126 ff.; E. Babelon, *Traité des monnaies*, II, Part II (1910),
575 ff.

[8] Polyaen. viii. 53. 4.

fore, if the great king takes Egypt, he will also attack Greece." The argument fully exposes the *non sequitur* lurking in the oration.

More fatally, Demosthenes did not know Artemesia. When the overconfident Rhodians arrived before Halicarnassus, she ordered the inhabitants to pretend surrender. The Rhodians had already landed and were busily engaged plundering the market, when from an artificial channel leading into the secret harbor there emerged the hidden Carian fleet. The empty Rhodian ships were seized, while from the walls along the sea front the invaders in the market place were shot down. Then, with Carian-manned vessels wreathed in laurel as for a victory, Artemesia sailed for the island and was admitted into its harbor before the trick was discovered. The leading citizens were executed, and Artemesia set up two statues: one of herself, the other of Rhodes, branded with the slave mark.[9]

THE SIDONIAN REVOLT

The setback delivered to Ochus led to widespread revolts. Sidon, headquarters for the invasion, had in consequence suffered from the insolent soldiery. Tennes now punished the offenders, drove out the garrison, and burned the cavalry supplies heaped up for a new attempt; he also cut down the trees of the "paradise" on the eastern slopes around a palace whose locally carved bull capitals have survived to our own day.[10]

As capital of their federal league, the Arcadians had recently founded the new city of Megalopolis with a surprisingly modern federal district where their representatives met. Much earlier, the Phoenician cities of Arvad, Sidon, and Tyre had united three small villages (known to the Assyrians as Mahalata, Maisa, and Kaisa) to form Athar, Tripolis to the Greeks. Here, too, met the delegates—a hundred each from the three chief cities—who formed the common council or *synedrion* of the Phoenicians; apparently the Greek term had already been adapted to Phoenician as *sanhedrin*, for so it was later employed by the Jews.

The deputies now met at Tripolis and voted that all Phoenicia should revolt. From their enormous wealth, the Sidonians collected a large number of triremes and hired a considerable force of mercenaries. Nicocles had been murdered in neighboring Salamis, presumably by his brother Evagoras II, who became his successor. For four years

[9] Demosthen. *Rhod.* 3–4, 11; Aristot. *Rhet.* ii. 20. 3–4; Vitruv. ii. 8. 14–15.

[10] G. Contenau, "Deuxième mission archéologique à Sidon," *Syria*, IV (1923), 276 ff.

Evagoras minted coins with his name abbreviated in Phoenician; their designs included the galley and star, or the Great King fighting a lion or riding in his chariot in front of the bareheaded Evagoras. Then another member of the family, Pnytagoras, chased him out to a refuge in Caria, and the nine kings of the island followed the Phoenician example and proclaimed their independence. Parts of Cilicia also joined the revolt.[11]

PHILIP OF MACEDONIA

Aroandas remained in rebellion; as late as 349 he was honored at Athens by citizenship and by a golden crown, for the city made a favorable commercial treaty with him. Eubulus of Assos had owned a eunuch named Hermeias who had been sent to Athens, where he was trained in philosophy by Plato and Aristotle; on his return he repaid his master's philanthropy by slaying him and reigning in his stead. Aristotle, tutor of Philip's son Alexander, thought it no disgrace to seek hospitality at his court and ended by marrying the eunuch tyrant's niece. Another philosopher, Xenocrates, also arrived to share the tyrant's bounty.[12]

Early in 346 a truce to the war in continental Greece was made through the Peace of Philocrates. Philip was recognized as the outstanding figure among the Greeks, and Isocrates hastened to publish his *Philippus*, in which he summoned the Macedonian king to follow up his mainland conquests by leading a long-awaited crusade against the barbarian. The time, he declared, was opportune. Egypt was still unconquered. Cyprus, Phoenicia, and Cilicia were in revolt. Now that Artemesia was dead, Idrieus (350–344) might be detached from his dubious loyalty, and he was the most prosperous of the continentals. This leads the publicist to remark with some bitterness that it was a shame to observe how Asia was doing better in a material way than Europe and how the barbarians were more flourishing than the Greeks.[13]

For the moment, Idrieus was indeed friendly to the European Greeks. That very year—the first since Delphi had been free of Pho-

---

[11] Theopomp., Frag. 114(J), Athen. xii. 531D–E; Isocr. *Philip.* 102; Diod. xvi. 40. 5; 41–42; 46. 1; Babelon, *op. cit.*, pp. 715 ff., 589 ff.

[12] *IG*, Vol. II (ed. minor), No. 207; Isocr. *Philip.* 102–3, 132; Demosthen. *Philip.* iv. 32; *Cherson.* 30; Plato *Epist.* vi; Anaximenes [Demosthen.] *Epist. Philip.* 6; Strabo xiii. 1. 57; Diog. Laert. v. 3 ff.; Didym. vi. 6. 1; Suid. *s.v.* "Aristoteles." Pergamum returned to king by Aroandas, Dittenberger, *Orientis Graecae inscriptiones selectae*, No. 264.

[13] Isocr. *Philip.*

cian looting and was once more open to gifts from the outside world—
the Milesians dedicated to Pythian Apollo bronze statues of their
overlord Idrieus and of his sister-wife Ada which had been made for
them by the Parian sculptor Satyrus.[14] Their figures and names accompanied a relief of the Zeus of Armies from Labraunda set up at Tegea.[15]

Philip was actually thinking in all seriousness of a union of the
European Greeks against the common enemy, but he was too shrewd
to preach the crusade before closer unity at home had been achieved.
Nevertheless, he gave a clear indication of what he had in mind when
at Olympia he built a Philippeium in his own honor and for its adornment recalled all the famous artists who had found lucrative employment in Caria. The loss could not have been pleasing to Idrieus.

Unlike Isocrates, Androtion did not trust the Carian. As a subject of
Persia, he was like a dog freed from chains; as it falls upon a man
and bites, so Idrieus when freed from chains was dangerous. Androtion
was right; before the year was ended, Idrieus had answered, not the
lure of Philip—as Isocrates had expected—but the orders of his master.
With him he brought to Ochus forty Carian triremes and eight thousand mercenaries led by the Athenian Phocian, for now there were
Athenian generals on either side! For some time rebel Cyprus had enjoyed peace, and rich loot might be expected; soon the number of
mercenaries had doubled. Typical is the hero of Antiphanes' *Soldier:*
he boasts how he was in Cyprus during the whole war and how he
lived at Paphos in luxury.[16]

RECONQUEST OF PHOENICIA

At the beginning of 345 Ochus collected a huge army in Babylon
and marched against Sidon. Tke citizens sent abroad their funds for
safety, dug around the city a triple ditch, and raised the walls. More
than a hundred ships were brought together, not triremes only but
also the newly invented quinquiremes with their five banks of oars.
Mentor and Tennes, however, conspired to betray the city. As one
group of the leading citizens after another was sent out, all were slain
by the waiting Persians, but when Tennes himself escaped to receive
his expected reward he found only the punishment of a discarded
traitor.

[14] Th. Homolle, "Inscriptions de Delphes," *BCH*, XXIII (1899), 385 ff.; *IG*, Vol. V, Part 2,
No. 89; cf. Vitruv. vii *praef.* 12.

[15] P. Foucart, *Monuments Piot*, XVIII (1910), 145 ff.

[16] Aristot. *Rhet.* iii. 4. 3; Antiphan., Frag. 202 (Kock); Diod. xvi. 42; 46. 1 ff.; Polyaen. viii.
53. 4.

The betrayed citizens fired their ships, shut up their families in their homes, and burned to death the whole mass. Ochus had only the ruins to sell to speculators who paid him many talents for the right to search for melted gold and silver. From Babylonia comes a tablet whose docket reads: "In the fourteenth year of Ochus, whose name is called Artaxerxes, in October, the prisoners whom the king made captive in the land of Sidon entered Babylon and Susa. That month, day 13 [October 24, 345] a few soldiers among them entered Babylon. Day 16, the numerous women whom the king sent to Babylon, on that day entered into the king's palace."[17] The tablet affords a vivid glimpse of the suffering endured by women under the ancient system of deportation; the women entered the palace, not for honor, but as slaves.

Phoenicia was then handed over to Mazaeus and combined with Cilicia. For his earlier Cilician types of coins Mazaeus thereafter substituted the Greek stag devoured by the Asiatic lion or bull. Two battlemented walls, each showing four towers, have been explained as the Cilician Gates, though more probably they represent Tarsus itself; the legend reads: "Mazdai Who Is over Abar Nahara and Hilik." Coins bearing Aramaic legends were issued from Tarsus, Issus, and Mallus, but Greek was added on those from Mallus; on his Sidonian coins, Mazaeus employed the galley of the former native kings from the sixteenth year (343) to the close of the reign.[18]

THE END OF THE LAST EGYPTIAN EMPIRE

Envoys of Ochus appeared in the principal Greek states and requested mercenaries. Athens and Sparta, whose generals were already in Egypt, refused to assist, though Athens qualified her refusal by declaring that she wished to remain at peace with the king—provided he did not attack Greek cities. Thebes, however, sent a thousand soldiers under Lacrates, and the Argives three thousand under Nicostratus, while six thousand more came from the Greek cities of Asia and were to be led by the traitor Mentor (344).[19] The Persians were commanded by Rosaces, a descendant of one of the Seven and at present satrap of Ionia and Lydia, and by Aristazanes. Bagoas, the chief eunuch, served as commander-in-chief, while the whole vast array was personally directed by Ochus himself.

[17] S. Smith, *Babylonian Historical Texts* (1924), pp. 148 ff.

[18] Diod. xvi. 43 ff.; Trog. x; Joseph. *Ant.* xi. 297; Babelon, *op cit.*, pp. 443 ff. and 581 ff.

[19] *IG*, Vol. IV, No. 556; Isocr. *Panathen.* 159; Anaximen. [Demosthen.] *Epist. Philip.* 6; Diod. xvi. 44. 1 ff.; Didym. viii. 5 ff., 18 ff.

After losing a considerable portion of his army in the Barathra swamp, the king reached Pelusium, which he found defended by Philophon at the head of fifteen thousand Greeks. Unable to force the stronghold in the first day's fighting, Ochus divided the invading forces: one division, commanded by Lacrates and Rosaces, was left to besiege the border fortress; Nicostratus and Aristazanes were placed in charge of the second, while the main body continued to be under Mentor and Bagoas. To oppose them, Nekht-har-hebi had mustered twenty thousand Greeks, almost the same number of Libyans, and sixty thousand natives; there was also a large fleet of boats on the Nile, whose Arabian bank was held by a string of fortresses.

The defense was strong and, as in the past, should have held the invaders. But all was of no avail because the commanders of the mercenaries—Athenian Diophantus and Spartan Lamius—were unable to force compliance with their proposed tactics. Contrary to their advice that he attack at once, Nekht-har-hebi determined to await the coming inundation, confident that once more the rising waters would compel the enemy to retire from a flooded Delta.

The reason for this confidence, a promise from the war-god Onuris that he would himself save threatened Egypt, is hinted by a popular folk tale which has survived only in Greek translation on a papyrus of somewhat later date. Here we are told that on the night of the twenty-first to the twenty-second of the month Pharmouthi, the night of the full moon, in the sixteenth year of the reign, Nectanebo the king residing in Memphis performed a sacrifice and besought the gods to make clear to him the future. Modern astonomical tables prove that in this year of Nekht-har-hebi's reign full moon in the month Pharmouthi might be observed on July 5, 343; thus we have obtained not only the date of this particular series of events but actually the key to the whole chronology of independent Egypt during the fourth century.[20]

In the answering dream vouchsafed him, the folk tale goes on, Nectanebo saw a papyrus float—which in Egyptian is called Romps, the translator glosses—and it anchored at Memphis. On it was a great throne, and seated thereon was Isis, the worthy benefactress of fruits and mistress of the gods; all the gods stood about her, on her right hand and on her left. One, twenty cubits in stature, advanced to the

---

[20] J. G. Smyly, *Archiv für Papyrusforschung*, V (1909–13), 417; S. Witkowski, *ibid.*, p. 573; E. Bickermann, *La Chronologie de la XXXe Dynastie* ("Institut Français d'Archeologie Orientale du Caire, Mém.," Vol. LXVI [1935–38]), pp. 77 ff.

midst; his name is given as Onuris in Egyptian, but in Greek Mars is another gloss. Falling on his stomach, he spoke as follows:

"Come to me, goddess of gods, thou who hast the greatest power and ruleth those in the universe and maketh to live all the gods. Have mercy on me, Isis, and hearken to me! As thou hast commanded have I blamelessly watched over the land and have done everything needful for Nectanebo, the King Samaus, who hath been established by you to rule. But he neglecteth my temple and hath fallen away from my commandments. Without my temple am I, and the works in the holy of holies called Pherso [Pershu, "Shu's house"] are half-finished because of the chief's wickedness." The goddess made no reply.

Nectanebo awoke and hurriedly summoned the high priest and the prophet of Onuris from inland Sebennytus—still in Egyptian possession on this July 6, 343. They reported that the situation was by no means so desperate as the dream had intimated; everything had been completed with the exception of carving on the stone walls the sacred characters, the hieroglyphics.

Thus far we have apparently the recollection of an actual dream or oracle through which Onuris had promised his aid for Egypt, though in the present version the coming disaster already is foreseen. We now enter the realm of pure folk tale: In haste the king wrote to summon those who were skilled in carving the sacred writings; arrived at court, they were asked who of them could most quickly finish the task. Petesius, Ergaeus' son from Aphroditopolis, arose and modestly announced that *he* was able to complete the task in a few days, and his companions unanimously agreed that he told the truth, for not a man in the land approached him in skill. So Nectanebo gave Petesius much money, and off he went to Sebennytus.

Being by nature a winebibber, Petesius decided that he ought to enjoy a little fun before settling down to work. And so it happened that, as he was sauntering about the southern parts of the temple, he met the daughter of a perfume-maker, the most beautiful of those he had seen at that—and here the student copyist assigned the task grew weary and instead of satisfying our awakened curiosity as to the further progress of the sculptor's romance contented himself with drawing a caricature of our hero.[21]

Did the folk tale ascribe the dislike of the native war-god and his consequent refusal to protect Egypt solely to the unfortunate love affair of the sculptor and his failure to complete the hieroglyphics on

[21] U. Wilken, *Mélange Nicole* (1905), pp. 579 ff.; G. Maspero, *Popular Stories* (1915), pp. 285 ff.

time? That we cannot tell, but there can be no doubt that Nekht-har-hebi's delay for the arrival of the inundation was fatal. Before its saving floods had reached the Delta, Nicostratus with eighty triremes had found his way to the Egyptian rear. Cleinias attacked this flanking force but was killed, and with him five thousand Greeks. Abandoning the Delta, Nekht-har-hebi retired to Memphis. Mentor promised the deserted garrison of Pelusium an honorable surrender if they gave up the fight but threatened the fate of Sidon if they continued to resist. The Egyptians came to blows with the Greeks over the question of surrender, but the mercenaries recognized no obligation to a retreating paymaster and promptly accepted the generous terms.

Persians and Greeks fought over the spoils. At the sack of Bubastis the mercenaries went so far as to imprison Bagoas himself, who was rescued only by the personal intervention of Mentor. But, one by one, the individual cities made terms; loading himself with all the movable wealth he could carry, Nekht-har-hebi fled up the Nile to seek refuge in Ethiopia. The last Egyptian empire had come to a close, and the lower Nile was no longer ruled by a master of its own race.

Greek mercenaries in Egyptian pay were forgiven and sent home, while those in Persian employ were generously rewarded. Bagoas was made vizier, and Mentor was intrusted with oversight of the Aegean seacoast. Egypt received harsh punishment for its rebellion of almost a century. The walls of the cities were destroyed and their temples plundered. With his own hand Ochus stabbed the sacred Apis bull and in his place set up in bitter mockery an ass which he bade the natives to worship. The equally holy ram of Mendes was slain. In the loot from the temples were included the sacred rolls which Bagoas later sold back to the priests at an exorbitant price. At the close of 343, Ochus returned to Persia, where he settled as exiles the leading Egyptians whom he had carried off with him, and Pherendates was left behind as satrap.[22]

Still the natives refused to accept Ochus as legitimate king. From his safe refuge in Ethiopia, Nekht-har-hebi retained control of Upper Egypt. In his eighteenth year, 341, he was yet recognized at Edfu, where he made to the local Horus a grant of lands, the validity of which was later recognized by the Ptolemies.[23] Under these same Ptol-

[22] IG (ed. minor), No. 356; Theopomp., Frag. 368(J); Diod. xvi. 46 ff.; Trog. x; Front. Strat. ii. 5. 6; Aelian. Var. hist. iv. 8; vi. 8. Down to his own day, according to Plutarch, the Egyptians still called Ochus the "Sword" (De isid. 355C).

[23] H. K. Brugsch, Thesaurus, III, 549; date corrected by Bickermann, op. cit., p. 82.

emies was likewise written the so-called Demotic Chronicle, which also ascribes to Nekht-har-hebi a reign of eighteen years.[24]

There were, however, some members of the local aristocracy who were not ashamed to serve under the generally hated foreigners. Semtu-tefnakht, of Heracleopolis Magna, for example, had been permitted by his local divinity Heryshef to enter the palace. There he served Nekht-har-hebi, and the heart of the good god—the king—was satisfied by his words. But when Heryshef took back his protection over Egypt—as shown through Ochus' victory over Nekht-har-hebi—Semtu-tefnakht made his peace with the new monarch. Heryshef elevated him before the multitude, making love of him spring up in the heart of the ruler of Setet—an ancient name for Asia—whose royal friends offered fulsome compliments to the renegade. He was raised to the place of his paternal uncle Nekht-heneb, to the dignity of chief of the priests of Sekhmet throughout Upper and Lower Egypt.[25]

Petosiris became head of the most important family at Hermopolis in 339, less than four years after the Persian reconquest. He, too, made his peace with the powers that were, but writing during the reign of the Macedonian Philip Arrhidaeus he has much to say of Persian misrule: "I passed seven years as administrator of this god Thoth, administering his goods without any fault being found, although a king of a foreign land was in power over Egypt. And there was no one who was in his former place, because of the struggles which occurred in the midst of Egypt; the south was in disorder and the north was in revolt. Men traveled in fear, there was nothing in the temple which was at the disposal of those who deserved it. The priests were far distant and were ignorant of what took place. I exercised the function of administrator of Thoth, lord of Khmunu, during seven years; men of a foreign land ruled Egypt. I did everything well in his temple while men of a foreign land governed Egypt. No work was done (in the temple) since the foreigners had come and had invaded Egypt."[26]

THE PLACE OF THE MINAEANS IN HISTORY

This war between the Medes and Egypt is mentioned in an inscription from southwestern Arabia and settles at last the long-debated

---

[24] Demotic Chronicle, IV, 18.

[25] Naples (Pompeii) Stele; latest discussion, P. Tresson, *Bulletin de l'Institut Français du Caire*, XXX (1931), 361 ff.; cf. A. Erman, *ÄZ*, XXXI (1893), 91 ff.

[26] G. Lefebvre, *Le Tombeau de Petosiris* (1924), I, 3 ff.

question as to the antiquity of the Minaean records.[27] About the beginning of the fourth century, when the Jewish author of Chronicles substitutes in his revised history Meinim for earlier tribal names from North Arabia,[28] the North Arabic alphabet derived from Sinai makes its first appearance in southwestern Arabia. As early as the beginning of the eighth century, cuneiform documents told of kings of Saba who presented "tribute" to Assyrian monarchs;[29] but, when local monuments speak for themselves, this corner of the peninsula is dominated by the Minaeans. In their native tongue the land is called Main and the people Mainum. Their capital is Qarnawu, but Yathil is a secondary capital. By their position north of Saba, they controlled the great northern trade route to the Mediterranean. Farther east along the coast lay Hadhramaut, which already employed a different dialect and a slightly different written character. So beautifully formed are the characters that some time must have elapsed since the crude North Arabic graffiti had been adapted to the language of southwestern Arabia, which differs so much from the northern that it must be considered rather a separate language than merely another dialect.

Equally great is the different level of culture, for the Minaeans are no mere nomads but a highly civilized people. The basis of their life is agriculture. There are highly fertile spots in southwestern Arabia, but there would be scant population were it not for the most elaborate system of irrigation. There are already good-sized cities with imposing buildings, defended by strong walls, whose architecture we may elaborately describe. We know something of the temples, and more of their gods and ritual practices. There is also an elaborate system of land tenure, servile and not free as in the desert oases.

Their nomad origins are clear in their careful attention to genealogy, parentage, family, and tribal relation. Through their genealogical statements and through a certain number of synchronisms, it is possible to relate in surprising detail the intricacies of political relationships from the fourth century downward.[30]

About 400 or perhaps a little before, we become acquainted with the

[27] The Minaean mirage, which would place them in the second millennium, has finally been dissipated by F. V. Winnett, *Bulletin of the American Schools of Oriental Research*, LXXIII (1939), 3 ff.

[28] I Chron. 4:41; II Chron. 26:7; Ezra 2:50; Neh. 7:52.

[29] Olmstead, *History of Assyria* (1923), pp. 189, 200, 211, 310, 379.

[30] The definitive collection of South Arabian inscriptions is *CIS*, Vol. IV; they are, however, cited as *RES* from *Répertoire d'épigraphie sémitique* (1900–1938), a more complete series with revised text, translation, and commentary.

first known king of Main, Ilyafa Yathi,[31] who, in the custom which was to be usual, next appears associated with his son Abiyada Yathi. Under their joint rule, Yadhkaril built his town Yafush, its superstructure, its light court, and its terrace in wood and in hewn stone, and made dedications to the gods. Maadkarib and his son Hamathat offered a similar dedication at Yathil. An incense altar was dedicated to Matabnatyan through the lord Maadkarib Raidan and Hawtarathat, king of Harimun.[32]

When Abiyada reigned alone, he made brotherhood with Maadkarib, who now appears as king of Hadhramaut; that this brotherhood was in reality a subject alliance is proved by the fact that Maadkarib set up the inscription in the Minaean capital, though he retains the script and dialect peculiar to his own Hadhramaut. In it he also told how he had consecrated for the oracle of Athtar dhu Qabdim a tower built by his uncle Shahharum Allan, son of Sadiqil, king of Hadhramaut, in whom we may see an independent older contemporary of Ilyafa Yathi.

Another of Abiyada's inscriptions gives insight into Minaean administration. Alman, son of Ammikarib, of the Hadhar family and the tribe of Gabsan, was the "friend" of Abiyada Yathi, king of Main. He had vowed, built, and dedicated to Athtar dhu Qabdim and Wadd and Nikarhum the whole construction and the pillar support for six towers and the six connecting curtains on the city wall of Qarnawu. Their location is given precisely: by the canal of the Ramsawu quarter, from the tower erected by the "sons of the interrogators of souls" (some sort of council) to the "three ways' junction" within the city. Alman built the work and roofed it with wood and hewn stone and finished the covering wall of the scarp. This was done from the proceeds of the imposts which Athtar dhu Qabdim had fixed, and also from what Alman had added of his own.

Incense offerings were burned to Wadd, and offerings were slaughtered to Wadd and to Athtar dhu Qabdim in the temple forecourt. The reason was that Abiyada Yathi had granted to Alman through the great council of Main the administration and control of what was prescribed both in war and in peace for his god, his tribal patron, his king, and his tribe. Furthermore, the king had handed over to him for administration the land secured from the income of the royal spinning factories, forty-seven cubits by fourteen in extent, and rations according to the law of Main.

---

[31] *RES*, Nos. 3012 and 3022.   [32] *RES*, Nos. 2789, 2942, and 3459.

Boundaries are then carefully described, both according to the compass points and by the water channels which provided for its irrigation, and all is inscribed on the basis of an earlier written document. Oath is taken by the rising Athtar, by a sort of trinity consisting of Athtar dhu Qabdim, Wadd, and Nakarhum, by all the gods of Main and Yathil, by the king, and by their tribes Main and Yathil. Against any who would alter the construction and the corroborating inscriptions, during all the days of the earth, the whole is placed under the protection of the gods.[33]

By far the most important inscription of the reign, however, is that of Ammisadiq, son of Hamathat and of the Yafan family, and of Saad, son of Walig, of the Dhafgan family. Both were *kabir* officials of Musran and Maan Musran—the "Egyptian" region about Dedan and the northern town named for the Minaeans, whose influence, steadily advancing northward, had already been shown at Dedan, where some of the later Lihyanian graffiti showed traces of Minaean characters;[34] soon after, Minaean was to dominate the oasis.

The purpose of Ammisadiq and Saad was the dedication to Athtar dhu Qabdim of a corridor named Tanum connecting two towers on the city wall; the façade was ornamented with wood and cut stone, the counterscarp in rough stone. More interesting for us, our authors give the reason: When on a journey to Misr, Ashur, and Ibr Naharan—in which we recognize without difficulty Egypt, Assyria, and Across the River—their gods Athtar dhu Qabdim, Wadd, and Nakarhum, saved their gods and guided them in an assault which Saba and Khawlan made against them, their goods, and their camels. It took place on the journey between Main and Ragmatum, during the war between the Medes (Madhay) and Egypt. This is one of the attacks made by Artaxerxes II or Artaxerxes III. The date could not be later than 343, though it might be considerably earlier; but at least we now have fixed within half a century this earliest dynasty of Main.[35]

Their gods returned them in peace and well-being to the land of the city of Qarnawu. Athtar indicated that he was satisfied with their offering, and the two *kabir* officials and Maan Musran placed their goods and their business documents under the protection of the gods and the king. Once again Ammisadiq took a similar trip and returned

[33] *RES*, Nos. 2775, 3012, 3022, and 2774; other inscriptions, *RES*, Nos. 2808, 2944, 2959, 2971*bis*, and 3006.

[34] Winnett, *op. cit.*, p. 6.

[35] Cf. Olmstead, *History of Palestine and Syria* (1931), p. 619.

in safety. Again the two *kabirs* assisted in the building of the city wall; they also reported the construction of their own houses and towns and the digging of wells and of their own private reservoir.[36]

Following the regular custom, Abiyada Yathi near the close of his reign associated with himself his son Waqahil Riyam. Saad, the fellow-traveler of Ammisadiq, had twice held the office of *kabir* of Maan Musran. When the kings and council of Main had in the great council confided to him the administration of the contributions prescribed for the gods, the tribal patrons, and the kings, he and his son Hawfathat dedicated from his imposts a corridor to Athtar dhu Qabdim. The two kings themselves dedicated a corridor when they built their palace Yagur in the city of Yathil.[37]

If the famous adventure took place in the very last year of Egyptian independence, then by now Alexander was invading Persia. More probably we must assign before his date the remaining monarchs whose place in the dynasty is fixed by an exact genealogy. In due time Waqahil reigned alone,[38] then in association with his son Hufnsadiq;[39] Hufnsadiq also reigned alone[40] and next with Ilyafa Yafush,[41] whose sole reign[42] brings our connected history to an end. Later kings of the dynasty can be identified, but the Egypt visited by their merchants was ruled by the Ptolemies.

[36] *RES*, Nos. 3022 and 3012.

[37] *RES*, Nos. 3535 and 2962; other dedications from the double reign, *RES*, Nos. 2929, 2952, and 3013.

[38] *RES*, No. 3055; perhaps alone, *RES*, Nos. 3005 and 3033.

[39] *RES*, Nos. 3039, 3049-50, and 3052.

[40] *RES*, No. 2886.

[41] *RES*, No. 2762.

[42] *RES*, No. 2982.

Chapter XXXI

SCIENCE TRUE AND FALSE

SOCRATES, PLATO, AND THE ORIENTAL SCIENCES

SOCRATES had been a student of Archelaus, a pupil of Anaxagoras,[1] and in his earlier years he had shown keen interest in astronomy and physics. It was this Socrates who was parodied in 423 by Aristophanes in the well-known scene which opens the *Clouds*. Even after his recantation, the great philosopher could be accused by Meletus on his death trial of disbelief in the ancestral gods. He studied, Meletus declared, what is in the air and beneath the earth—Democritus had written *On Those in Hades*—and he says that the sun is a stone and the moon an earth. In so talking, he is just like the books of Anaxagoras, which are full of the same sort of stuff.[2]

We should be the last to regret that Socrates changed utterly his attitude when he neared old age, for otherwise European thought would have been immeasurably poorer. As regards science, however, the result was catastrophic. Until now, Ionic philosophers and their successors had been definitely scientific in their interests if not always in their methods. Now Socrates flatly challenged the whole scientific point of view and inaugurated a period of conflict, this time not between science and theology but between science and philosophy.

No longer could he see any use in studying astronomy, in learning the course of the heavenly bodies, planets, and comets, their distances from the earth, and their periods of revolution. Indeed, Socrates unexpectedly went so far in defense of orthodoxy as to declare that it was impiety to investigate what the god had not intended man to know and that Anaxagoras was crazy to try to explain the mechanism of the gods.[3]

In such an antiscientific atmosphere Plato became the pupil of the aging Socrates. As a philosopher, Plato was truly among the greatest. He was also the master of a superb style, but such a genius rarely condescends to the pedestrian labors demanded by science. Yet, unlike his

[1] Aristoxenes, in Diog. Laert. ii. 19.

[2] Aristophan. *Aves* 94 ff.; Plato *Apol*. 18B-C; 26D-E.

[3] Xen. *Memorabil*. iv. 7. 5-6; cf. Plato *Phaedo* 97B.

master, he was profoundly impressed by the Pythagorean doctrines, and it had become a tradition in that school that numbers possessed a mystic but also a quasiscientific value which was evident particularly in the heavens and in the divisions of time which the heavenly bodies taught.

Of course, we look in vain for traces of serious oriental science in Plato; at best, now and then, we sense the technical astronomical terminology. If a contemporary Babylonian priest-astronomer, himself an expert in the most complicated celestial mathematics, could have read Plato's latest exposition, the *Timaeus*, he would sometimes have approved but, more often, have been disagreeably surprised. He would have ratified the belief of Socrates and Plato against the atheists that the celestial bodies were gods, worthy of ritual worship for and by themselves. He would have insisted against Socrates that it was his pious duty to explain the mechanism of these gods. Like all scholars of his day, he would have accepted as axiomatic fact the central position of his own earth in the universe, though he would probably not have accepted the further statement that the earth was a perfect sphere. He knew better than to believe that the planet orbits formed a perfect circle, since his own observations and calculations proved that at least the sun (and presumably the moon and the other planets) moved in a slightly flattened ellipse.

The celestial bodies did furnish portents; numerous tablets provided (for those who could read the deliberately cryptographic writing) proofs that astrology was a science which formed a proper division of astronomy. They also gave our "time-measurers." But the Oriental would have been shocked to discover that at this late date the Greek philosopher was so behind the times as to think that the year was only 360 days in length. Plato seemed not yet to realize that Dawn-bringer was only another manifestation of Venus as Evening Star. Neither did he know that his order of the planets from the central earth—moon, sun, Dawn-bringer, Hermes, Mars, Jupiter, and Saturn—could not be fitted into the evidence provided by his observed ephemerides, checked as they were by other ephemerides calculated in advance.

After some difficulty our oriental scholar would have discovered that by the unintelligible "Circle of the Same and Circle of the Other" intersecting diagonally, Plato meant only the familiar circles of the ecliptic and of the celestial equator. Just what did he mean by orbits of the planets equal to the sun but opposite in direction, so that sun and moon and star of Hermes and Morning Star regularly overtake and are overtaken by one another? He would shake his head when he read: "But the circlings of these same gods and their coming alongside one another, and the manner of the returnings of their orbits upon themselves and their approachings, which of the deities meet one another in their conjunctions and which are in opposition—here at last were terms he could understand—in what order they pass before one another, and at what times they are hidden from us and again reappearing send, to those who cannot calculate their movements—and equally to those who can, he would add—terrors and portents of things to come—to declare all this without visible models of these same movements is wasted time." Our scientist could explain many of these difficulties, for *he* could refer to easily available textbooks and tables. But, as he puzzled over the alleged expositions, he would have asked himself, as has many a commentator ancient and modern since Plato's day, whether the great philosopher was not beyond his depth when he ventured into the difficult field of astronomy.[4]

Fortunately, there are better reasons why the Orientalist should scan the many pages of Plato's writings. After his master's condemnation, a blot on Athens' reputation never to be erased, Plato departed for Egypt, where he paid his expenses by selling oil and took the opportunity of visiting those who interpreted the will of the gods— among others, no doubt, the astrologers.[5] He may have been thinking of his own experience when he tells of Solon's formal call on King Amasis at his home in Sais, founded by the goddess Neith (whom the Greeks call Athena) in the Egyptian Delta where the Nile divides. Solon, as cocky as Hecataeus was soon to show himself at Thebes, proudly expounded the Greek cosmogony. One of the priests, however, was as capable at taking this barbarian down as his Theban colleagues of the next generation; his only comment was: "O Solon, Solon! You Greeks are always children; there is no old Greek!" Then he chided Solon: "You have not one ancient belief or old science."[6]

In the face of such claims to high antiquity for other cultures, Plato, like Hecataeus and Herodotus before him, is surprisingly humble. He repeats the words of his teachers: Theuth, the ancient native god of Naucratis, whose bird is the ibis, invented arithmetic, geometry, and astronomy, as well as the games of draughts and dice, not to speak of

---

[4] The fullest exposition in the *Timaeus;* cf. also *Leg.* vi. 756B; vii. 821C ff.; *Rep.* x. 616. For a more laudatory estimate cf. T. L. Heath, *Aristarchus of Samos* (1913), pp. 134 ff.

[5] Strabo xvii. 1. 29; Plut. *Solon* 2. 4; Diod. Laert. iii. 6.

[6] Plato *Tim.* 21E–22B; cf. above, pp. 210, 318 ff.

letters. At that time Thamus was king of all Egypt, ruling at the great city in the upper country which the Greeks call Egyptian Thebes. To him came Theuth, showing off his inventions and demanding that they be made known to the other Egyptians. Each invention was praised or condemned until the king reached letters, which he announced to Theuth would ruin their memories.[7]

From the beginning of things, on the testimony of the Egyptians themselves, they have made a study of first principles. They first used divination and medicine and first adopted shields and helmets.[8] All Egyptian tunes—Plato was very much interested in music—are said to have been composed by Isis herself; since her time the postures and tunes have been prescribed and posted in the temples. Painters and sculptors are prohibited from making any changes; sculptures ten thousand years old—and Plato insists that he means this to the letter—are exactly the same as those today.[9]

He knows of Egyptian embalming and of the separation of castes, of the preserves of fish in the Nile and the royal swamps, that natives drive out strangers by food and sacrifices, and that Egyptian children learn mathematics with their letters. After the recital of all these wonders, we are not surprised to find Plato making Phaedrus accuse Socrates of faking stories about the Egyptians. Yet his final estimate shows Plato still a Greek consciously writing about barbarians; education, he says, has only made scamps instead of wise men out of Egyptians and Phoenicians.[10]

Herodotus had given the Egyptian version of the Trojan War and its causes. Plato knows a different reason: the Trojans began the war in reliance on the Assyrian power as manifested under their ruler Ninus, for Troy was part of the Assyrian Empire, feared then as Greeks of Plato's day feared the Persian king.[11]

In his early travel days Plato had intended to visit the Magi, but he was prevented by the Spartan wars of liberation in Asia.[12] At least he could talk with Persian visitors in Athens, or he might even have read a treatise of Democritus on the subject of Magian practice. His earliest book, the *First Alcibiades*, is set in the age of Artaxerxes I (to whose reign he properly dates Queen-Mother Amestris, widow of Xerxes) and shows a fair knowledge of Persian customs and religion.

[7] Plato *Phaedr.* 274D ff.; cf. *Phileb.* 18B.

[8] Plato *Tim.* 24.   [9] Plato *Leg.* 656D–E, 657B.

[10] Plato *Phaedo* 80C; *Tim.* 24; *Politic.* 264C; *Leg.* vii. 819A; xii. 953E; v. 747C; *Phaedr.* 275B.

[11] Plato *Leg.* iii. 685C.   [12] Diog. Laert. iii. 6–7.

Persian monarchs, he tells us, are descendants of Achaemenes, whom Plato, as a Greek, makes the son of Perseus, son of Zeus. He knows something of Persian administration and speaks of one fertile tract of land a day's journey wide which is called the "girdle of the king's wife," another which is named her "veil," and still more with similar appellations.

Quite as much as Herodotus and his contemporary Xenophon,[13] Plato was interested in Persian education. At seven the crown prince is given horses and trained in riding and the chase. At fourteen he is assigned four royal pedagogues. The wisest teaches him the *mageia* of Zoroaster, son of Oromasdes, which is the worship of the gods, and also matters of royalty. The most just pedagogue teaches the crown prince to speak the truth all his life, the most temperate to obtain self-mastery, while the bravest trains him to be fearless.[14]

His interest in oriental religions other than Egyptian and Persian is scant. Theodorus of Cyrene swears by his *own* god Ammon. For founding or reorganizing a city, Ammon's oracle is considered inferior only to Delphi and Dodona. Plato has heard of planting seed in the middle of summer in a garden of Adonis and how the plants appear after only eight days. He knows that the Greeks, particularly those living under the barbarians, have taken from them many words.[15] Plato was indeed not interested in oriental science, but he did visit the Orient and he learned not a little. Did the influence go deeper? There are some who argue that Plato's latent dualism has come from the eternal conflict of good and evil preached by Zoroaster.

MEDICAL ADVANCES

Homer had known of Egyptian medicine.[16] Herodotus had marveled at Egyptian specialists. In this period Hippocrates began scientific medicine among the Greeks. His native city Cos had long been the headquarters of the Asclepiadae, a professional association of physicians under the patronage of Asclepius, the god of healing. Hippocrates was a contemporary of Plato and soon came to be recognized as the greatest physician of antiquity.[17] Some of the writings collected under his name certainly did not come from the master's hand,

---

13 Xen. *Cyropaedia.*

14 Plato *I Alcibiades* 120E, 121C, 121E–122A ff.

15 Plato *Politic.* 257B; *Leg.* v. 738C; *Phaedr.* 276B; *Crat.* 409D.

16 *Odys.* iv. 229 ff.

17 Plato *Protag.* 311B–C; *Phaedr.* 270C–D; Aristot. *Polit.* vii. 4. 3.

but they did come from his school and his century.[18] Contrast with the earlier oriental medical literature is instructive.

An Egyptian surgical treatise at least fifteen centuries previous amazes us by its cold-blooded analysis of cases which are undoubtedly curable, possible of cure, or hopeless;[19] the same cold-blooded analysis is found in the Hippocratic *Epidemics*, while another treatise, *In the Surgery*, both in form and in content reminds us of the Egyptian predecessor. For the most part, however, the difference between the oriental and Greek treatments is more apparent than the likeness.

Hygiene was not unknown in the Orient,[20] but the chief reliance was on drugs and instruments. Many of these instruments were rude precursors of those still employed, while the Babylonian names for the drugs appear in the literature of later centuries until the modern pharmacopoeia was supplanted by the coal-tar derivatives. What strikes us as peculiar in the fourth-century tractates is the almost complete absence of drugs and instruments and the insistence on regimen.

Babylonian medical treatises were in their own way logical, describing the various diseases in the order of the body from head to foot; this practical method was scorned by the Hippocratics, who preferred their own Greek logic. To the end, oriental physicians resorted to magic, though now and then they permit us to realize that it was employed for its psychological effect much as their modern successors may use bread pills for the young. Greek medicine, even if under the aegis of the god Asclepius, so far as the Hippocratic pamphlets are concerned, has broken with the supernatural.

Perhaps the most curious of these early Greek medical works is the one *On Airs, Waters, and Places*. The author, whether Hippocrates or not, repeats the differences between Asiatics and Europeans. The differences he explains as due to differences in climate. He is, however, honest; he admits that institutions are contributing causes, for, though men are tamed by despotism, the free Asiatics who labor for themselves are the most warlike of all men.[21]

ASTRONOMICAL DISCOVERIES

As we come down to the fourth century in our study of Babylonian astronomy, more detailed ephemerides of the individual planets become common. As an illustration, we may take: "Appearances of

[18] W. S. H. Jones, *Hippocrates* (1923-31).

[19] J. H. Breasted, *The Edwin Smith Surgical Papyrus* (1930).

[20] Cf., e.g., Olmstead, *History of Assyria* (1923), p. 413.   [21] Hippocrat. *De aere* 16.

Mulu-babbar (Jupiter), which from year XVIII (387) of Arshu, who is called by name Artakshatsu (Artaxerxes II) the king, to the end of year XIII (345) of Umasu, who is called by name Artakshatsu (Artaxerxes III) the king. Copy of the clay tablets and wooden tablets, observations of the feasts, which a son of Gimil- . . . . wrote. Clay tablet for the son of Marduk-paqid-zer."

A typical paragraph reads: "Year XX (385), May 14, in the head of the constellation Mulmullu he made his appearance. June, night of the 2d, at dawn he was above the Tablet 2 cubits, 6 fingers. About the time of September 10th, standing point; $1\frac{2}{3}$ cubits behind the face of the Bull of the Chariot of the North he stood still. November 8th, last appearance. Night of the 15th at evening, in his return he was above the Tablet 1 cubit 20 fingers. January 1st (384), to the west he stood still; 1 cubit 8 fingers before the face of the Tablet he stood still. On the 10th, beginning of the return. February 10th, at evening, in his return he was above the Tablet $1\frac{2}{3}$ cubits. April, night of the 17th, at evening, he was below the Bull of the Chariot 2 cubits. Year XXI, May 14th, behind the Chariot he entered."[22] In similar fashion the planet tables trace each luminary through one cycle of his travels along the path of the ecliptic from his "shining-forth" at his heliacal rising to the points where he "stands still" at conjunction and opposition and then on to setting, his "entrance" into the underworld. Each spot on his travels along the ecliptic is marked by cubits and fingers in reference to the constellations which still remain groups of stars and have not yet been degraded into mere signs of the zodiac.

A tablet from the year 379 gives still more data for determining the planet's progress along the ecliptic: "November 25, the moon made his appearance; 58 minutes before sunset was the appearance of the new moon. Night of the 26th, Anu (Mars) turned to the west on his return below the first star of the constellation Ku. The moon god Sin was below the last star of the head of Ku 2 cubits 10 fingers. Night of the 5th, beginning of the night, Sin was before the star Mat-sha-rikis (in the Fish). Night of the 7th, the midst of Sin was surrounded by a sheepfold; Anu stood in the midst." Here we begin our first example of intermixture with meteorological observations, for, as we have seen, meteorology to the Babylonian was merely a subdivision of astronomy. An astrological element is also present: the appearance within the halo of the red planet (red being the color of mourning and

[22] F. X. Kugler, *Sternkunde und Sterndienst in Babel*, I (1907), 80 ff.

of death) presaged danger to "the king and the king's son of the government house," especially as "the land was covered by a mist."

"On the night of the 9th, 38 minutes before sunset, in the evening, Sin was behind the Tablet ⅔ of a cubit. Also on the 9th, 18 minutes after dawn the moon set. On the 11th, Mulu-babbar in the Scorpion made his appearance, in the east he was visible 46 minutes. Night of the 12th, at dawn, Sin was below the Twins and behind them 1 cubit. Night of the 13th, at dawn, he was behind the head of the Lion ⅔ cubit. Cirrus clouds. Night of the 15th, at dawn, Sin was behind the King [Regulus, as we still call the brightest star of Leo] 1½ cubits. Cirrus clouds. Night of the 17th, at dawn, Sin was above Kaimanu (Saturn) 2½ cubits. To the east he stood still. On the 17th also the Shining Bull (Mercury) at morning made his appearance in the Archer. Toward the 17th, Anu is in his western standing place. Night of the 19th, at dawn, Sin is behind the Spring of the Virgin 1⅔ cubits. Night of the 21st, at dawn, Sin is before the Qablu star which is in the head of the Scorpion 2 cubits; before the face of Dilbat (Venus), 3 cubits for entrance he goes."

This is not calculation but observation, as is proved by the meteorological conditions used for practical astrology. Reference to the king's son indicates that the science is still confined to predictions about royalty and that horoscopes for private individuals are yet in the future. So close are the descriptions to those translated by Democritus that tablets in a simpler form but otherwise exactly alike must have been available. There is one innovation; in October, notes our astronomer, 15 *qa* of sesame sold for a shekel, and in November 52½ *qa* of barley brought the same price.[23]

KIDINNU (CIDENAS), ASTRONOMER EXTRAORDINARY

Such observations and calculations paved the way for the greatest of Babylonian astronomers, Kidinnu, well known to the Greeks as Cidenas.[24] On astronomical grounds his system has been dated to 379 or 373;[25] there is good reason to believe that he was responsible for the very slight change in the nineteen-year cycle which was made in

[23] *Ibid.*, pp. 75 ff.

[24] Strabo xvi. 1. 6; Plin. ii. 39; Vettius Valens ix. 11 (ed. Kroll, pp. 353–54); Schol. *Ad Ptol. Syntax.* (*Catalogus codicum astrologorum Graecorum*, Vol. VIII, Part 2 [1911], pp. 125 ff.).

[25] P. Schnabel, "Kidenas, Hipparch und die Entdeckung der Präzession," *ZA*, III (new ser., 1926), 1 ff.; J. K. Fotheringham, *Quellen und Studien*, B, II (1939), 39; cf. Olmstead, *JAOS*, XLVI (1926), 87.

367 and was repeated to the day, cycle by cycle, until A.D. 45![26] A "New Moon Tablet of Kidinnu," copied in 145 at Sippar, in all probability his home, permits us a view of his system.[27]

Kidinnu began with a column which gave the changing position of the sun from one new or full moon to the next. By addition or subtraction of 18', the numbers follow an arithmetical progression to a maximum of 30°1'59" and a minimum of 28°10'39"40'''. From this we build up the next columns to determine the moon's location among the zodiacal signs. For example, Shabatu begins 21°17'58"20''' of the Fish. Add from the first column the value for the next month, Addaru, 28°57'17"58''', and the result is 50°15'16"18'''; the moon is now in the next sign, so subtract 30°, and the moon stands 20°15'16"18''' in the Ram.

Nabu-rimanni had placed the turning-points of the seasons at 10° of the respective signs. Kidinnu set them at 8°15; this is far from the proper 3°14' resulting from the movement backward to the west of the ecliptic itself. Yet the change was made, and somewhat later the 8°15' was again corrected to 8°0'30". Inadequate as was the correction, it is difficult to resist the conviction that the corrections were made through a dim recognition of the phenomenon we call the precession of the equinoxes; needless to remark, Kidinnu no more than Hipparchus (to whom the discovery is always credited) had the slightest suspicion as to the actual cause of the phenomenon.

Other tablets show the apogee with the slowest apparent movement placed at 20° of the Archer, the perigee with the most rapid motion at 20° of the Twins, a position incorrect by about 10°. To Kidinnu, the moon's path was an exact circle, along which his movement was uniformly accelerated to a maximum and then retarded to a minimum. The average of this column, 29°6'19"20''', divided by 29°,53059413 (Kidinnu's mean synodic month), gives the daily recession of the sun as 59'8"9'''36''''47''''', more accurate than Nabu-rimanni by 1'''18'''' and smaller by 1'''57''''9''''' than the present-day calculation; an error of less than one-thirtieth of a second of arc would seem accurate enough to most nonastronomers!

This in turn gives the sidereal year, 365 days 6 hours 13 minutes 43,4 seconds—1,5 minutes closer than Nabu-rimanni, but still 4 minutes 32,65 seconds too long. The anomalistic year, from perigee or apogee

---

[26] Cf. R. A. Parker and W. H. Dubberstein, *Babylonian Chronology, 626 B.C.—A.D. 45* (1942), Table I.

[27] F. X. Kugler, *Die babylonische Mondrechnung* (1900).

and back, was 365 days 6 hours 25 minutes 46 seconds, exactly correct according to modern astronomers. His greatest daily movement of the sun is 1°1'19",56, only .34 of a second too small, his least daily movement 56'56",7, or 14",8 too small, his mean sidereal month of 27 days 7 hours 43 minutes 14 seconds is 3 seconds too much, his sidereal movement of the moon, 13°10'34"51'''3''''',6, is 1'''6, too little. This last is an error of one in about ten million. Only by the presentation of these figures can we appreciate the extraordinary mathematical ability of this outstanding genius.

The third column gives the length of the day in units representing 4 hours, 4 minutes, and 4 seconds. It is assumed that the spring equinox comes at 8°15 of the Ram, when the days are three units, or 12 hours long. For each succeeding degree we add 36, or 2 minutes 24 seconds. On New Year's Day, Nisannu 1, the moon is at 0°52'45"38''' of the Bull, and the day is 3 14 or 12 hours 56 minutes long. We continue to multiply the number of the degrees by 36 until we reach 10°15, and thereafter by 24; adding the result to 3 14, we have 3 26. For the twelve periods beginning 8°15' of each sign, the series is 36,24,12 plus, 12,24,36 minus, 36,24,12 minus, and 12,24,36 plus; Nabu-rimanni's system ran 8,24,40.

A fourth column, the length of the half-night, was now demanded, for Kidinnu had abandoned the shifting sunset beginning of the common day and began his astronomical day at midnight; the numeral in the third column was subtracted from 6 (the Babylonian equivalent of 24 hours), and the result halved. For example, Addaru 1, the day is 2 56 long; 6 minus 2 56 equals 3 4, which, halved, is 1 32 or 6 hours 8 minutes, which is the time from sunset to midnight.

The fifth column gives the position of new and full moon, for Kidinnu had discovered that, the closer the moon's path to the ecliptic, the greater the probability of an eclipse. He must learn the period after which the moon returns to the same node, the so-called dragon's month. In the table the figures move from *bar*, zero, where the moon at the node crossed the ecliptic, upward or downward as "above" or "below" is suffixed to the numeral, to a maximum of 9 52 15, 4°56' 7",5, either positive or negative. The regular difference is 3 52 40, of course divided unequally when the ascending or descending series passes through zero. After the zero point, there is a regular correction: 0 52 30 instead of 3 52 30. Calculation shows that 5,458 synodic months equal 5,923 dragon's months, so Kidinnu's dragon's month is 27 days 5 hours 5 minutes 35,81 seconds—exactly the same as ours.

In the sixth column was given the daily movement of the sun. The regular difference is 0 36 to a maximum at perigee of 15° 16′35″ and a minimum at apogee of 11°5′5″; this would indicate a mean value of 13°10′35″, but a Greek who evidently used a lost textbook[28] gives the "Chaldaean" value more exactly as 13°10′34″51‴3⁗,6, which is only 1‴38⁗,4 too small. From study of maxima and minima we find that 251 synodic months equaled 269 anomalistic months.

The seventh column gives the sum we must add to 29 days in order that we may determine the longest and shortest synodic months, the difference being 22 30, the maximum 4 29 27 5, and the minimum 1 52 34 35. This makes Kidinnu's synodic month 29 days 12 hours 44 minutes 3⅓ seconds, the anomalistic month 27 days 13 hours 18 minutes 34,7 seconds—1,9 seconds less than the modern.

This column assumes that the movement of the sun is constant, but the next corrects the length of the synodic month for the anomalistic movement of the sun. The maximum, 21, or 1 hour 24 minutes, is at perigee, when the sun's movement is faster and the moon takes a longer time to come into conjunction with it, so for 6 months the signs are positive; the minimum of the same amount is at apogee when the converse is true. As the signs go, plus or minus, we add or subtract what is in this column from the preceding line in the next column to secure in that column the correction to the length of the synodic month as given in the seventh column on the assumption of an unchanging movement of the sun. The maximum is now plus or minus 32 28, or 2 hours 9 minutes 52 seconds, which allows a possible variation of the synodic month through the sun's changing motion of 4 hours 19 minutes 44 seconds.

True intervals between two conjunctions or oppositions are shown in the tenth column, which is secured from the seventh by adding or subtracting the datum in the ninth. By adding to its last line the datum of the next line in the preceding column, the eleventh secures the date of the astronomical new moon. Since the seventh column gives the correct synodic month but not the anomalistic path of the moon or the length of the month, and, since the ninth column does not follow exactly enough the irregular path of the sun, the calculated date varies from our reckoning from ½ to 2½ hours; this also explains the variations in the time of calculated eclipses.

Six more columns, never yet properly studied by any astronomer, calculate the actual new moon, since in practice the month was still

[28] Geminus xv. 2.

determined by its appearance.[29] Thus Kidinnu's system remains to us a torso. Furthermore, our calculations must be based on the rough approximations of the tables, since Kidinnu's textbook, unlike that of Nabu-rimanni, has not survived, and the one Greek quotation from it proves much greater exactness. But, even without his more theoretical exposition, his fame is secure.

If the accuracy of Nabu-rimanni's calculations is amazing, that of Kidinnu's is almost beyond belief. The moon-sun relation is only $1''$ too great; the sun-node $0'',5$; the moon-node $1'',5$; the moon-moon's perigee $9'',7$; the sun-equinox $15''$; sun's perigee-equinox $18''$; and sun-sun's perigee $3''$ too small. His true greatness best appears when compared with modern astronomers. Hansen, most famous of lunar astronomers, in 1857 gave the value for the annual motion of sun and moon $0'',3$ in excess; Kidinnu's error was three times greater. Oppolzer in 1887 constructed the canon we regularly employ to date ancient eclipses. It is now recognized that his value for the motion of the sun from the node was $0'',7$ too small per annum; Kidinnu was actually nearer the truth with an error $0'',5$ too great. That such accuracy could be attained without telescopes, clocks, or the innumerable mechanical appliances which crowd our observatories, and without our higher mathematics, seems incredible until we recall that Kidinnu had at his disposal a longer series of carefully observed eclipses and other astronomical phenomena than are available to his present-day successors.[30]

EUDOXUS OF CNIDUS, PRECURSOR OF EUCLID

Eudoxus of Cnidus began life as a physician. He visited Athens and there found a teacher in Plato, who, following his return from Egypt, had set up as a philosopher. Eudoxus then secured a letter of introduction from Agesilaus to King Nekht-har-hebi and set out for Egypt soon after the pharaoh's accession.[31] There he spent sixteen months with shaved beard and eyebrows under the tutelage of the Memphite Chonuphis. His observatory between Heliopolis and Cercesura—a watchtower with reference to which he took notes on the heavenly bodies—could still be pointed out more than three hundred years later.[32]

[29] J. Epping, *Astronomisches aus Babylon* (1889), pp. 93 ff.

[30] Cf. Fotheringham, *op. cit.*, pp. 38 ff.   [31] Plut. *De gen. Socr.* 7.

[32] Diog. Laert. viii. 86 ff.; Strabo xiv. 2. 15; xvii. 1. 29–30; Vitruv. ix. 6. 3; 6. 1; Philostrat. *Vit. Phil.* i. 484.

For the greater part the stories told about Eudoxus are puerile and too often flatly misleading. They are unnecessary, for Eudoxus was a great man in himself. Modern scholars acclaim his work as marking "the beginning of scientific astronomy."[33]

That such a belief has grown up is not difficult to understand. Though Eudoxus' *Phainomena* is itself lost, it was embodied in essentials in the versified edition by Aratus;[34] and this *is* the first *Greek* treatise on astronomy preserved. But the very title *Phainomena* is borrowed from Democritus, and we have already learned from the Chaldaeans what its contents must have been. The picture of the heavens found in Aratus is undoubtedly based on Eudoxus, but the picture is essentially that already borrowed by Democritus from Nabu-rimanni and his colleagues. Unlike Democritus, Eudoxus did not visit Babylonia, and no evidence can be shown that he knew anything of the improvements made by his Babylonian contemporary Kidinnu.

No doubt Eudoxus deserves all the credit which is his due for his ingenious but too complicated scheme of twenty-seven concentric spheres to explain the outlandish apparent motions of sun, moon, planets, and fixed stars. But a slight glance is enough to show that it is based, not primarily on his own observations, but on mathematical logic. The terminology employed by Nabu-rimanni and transmitted through Democritus, is all there—spheres, orbits, ecliptic, inclination, celestial equator, poles, circular motion, revolutions, resting-places, retrogressions, moon's highest north and south latitude. The problems raised by Nabu-rimanni's knowledge that the motions of the heavenly bodies are retarded and then accelerated in different portions of their orbits are solved by Eudoxus through a bewildering number of individual circular cycles, tied together by individual poles rotating along variously inclined axes. We may judge the system by its result; as new difficulties were encountered, epicycle was piled on epicycle until the medieval Ptolemaic system with all its involutions was attained. Nabu-rimanni's system was accurate so far as it went, for it was based first on sound, minute, and long continued observation, aided by a mathematical system quite as able—though in many respects quite different in method—as that employed by the Greek; ultimately, a successor of Nabu-rimanni, Seleucus from Seleucia by the Persian Gulf, was to discover that all these cycles and epicycles were unnecessary once it was realized that the earth went around the sun.

[33] Heath, *op. cit.*, p. 193.   [34] Arat. 19–732.

SCIENCE TRUE AND FALSE 459

But if Eudoxus was not so great an astonomer as Democritus, his fame is secure because he was the immediate precursor of Euclid. To what degree he was anticipated by Egyptians or even Babylonians it is at present difficult to say. Our discovery of oriental mathematicians is so recent that we are still in a state of amazement at their triumphs, and a history of oriental mathematics, much less an appreciation of their contributions to the Greeks, must be well in the future.

Like Democritus before him, Eudoxus was a polymath, who took almost the whole field of knowledge as his province. He paved the way for the outstanding scientific genius of antiquity—Aristotle. If in his own writings and those of his pupils the whole knowledge of his predecessors is summed up, Aristotle's greatest contribution is the firm basis he afforded for the still greater discoveries of the early Hellenistic age.

Chapter XXXII

RELIGIONS DYING AND LIVING

RELIGIOUS SYNCRETISM

NABU-RIMANNI and Kidinnu deserve first rank in the history of pure science, but we should not ascribe to them a modern "scientific philosophy." Such an attitude was possible only among agnostic Greek philosophers who, even so, were ahead of their times. Conservative Athens in reaction forced out Anaxagoras for teaching astronomy. In revulsion against his former heterodoxy, Socrates declared that astronomical information was useless, that it was impiety to investigate what the god had not intended man to understand, and that an attempt to explain the mechanism of the gods was sheer insanity.[1]

Babylonia was even more conservative—so conservative, in fact, that it never realized that there might be a possible conflict between science and theology. Nabu-rimanni and Kidinnu were, first of all, priests, their lives devoted to the service of moon-god, sun-god, or the other divinities embodied in the celestial beings. They worshiped these gods through a ritual prescribed in the dim ancestral past. When they turned to more practical problems of "scientific" astronomy, they, at least, were never conscious of "impiety"; their sole purpose was to explain this very mechanism of the gods which Socrates condemned and thus quite literally to justify the "ways" of gods to men.

Great as was the scientific advance, Babylonian religion continued apparently static. Letters, administrative decrees, and business documents show us the temples going their way unchanged, troubled only by an increasing control of their properties by the government. Ancient religious literature was copied by the temple scribe and to the letter. Bel Marduk retained his ancient honors until Xerxes destroyed Esagila for inciting Babylon's rebellions; within a generation, worship had been restored, though with more limited resources. Anu and the Lady of Uruk, Shamash of Larsa and Sippar, Enlil of Nippur, and Nabu of Borsippa were honored with something of their former mag-

---

[1] See above, pp. 446–49.

nificence. The same gods were invoked by the same formulas in the monotonously repeated names of the great families.

The Nile Valley shows the same picture, intensified only by the fact that Egypt was longer politically independent and that Egyptian rulers were eager and able to rebuild the temples and to restore the cult. The archaizing tendencies which first appeared with the Saites continued, and hitherto neglected divinities like Neith of Sais resumed their honored status. More scanty references to other portions of the vast empire indicate a like situation for the other ethnic religions. Yet the uneasy thought persists that the apparently static picture is due only to our own ignorance—that we have not yet recognized hints of new underground movements which were soon to emerge and to fix their mark on a later world.

Personal names have their story to tell of syncretistic developments. As early as the reign of Artaxerxes I, we find Babylonian documents which show us numerous inhabitants honoring strange gods. Among them are the Persian Mithra and Baga, the Aramaean Shemesh, the Jewish Yahweh, and the Egyptian Isis and Harmachis. In the majority of cases, no doubt, these gods accompany their *émigré* worshipers, but there are other cases in which definite religious changes are suggested. When a Jewish merchant substitutes Nabu or Marduk for Yahweh, this may be mere syncretism—identification of one god with another. When it happens repeatedly, or when an Egyptian father who honors Harmachis names his son by a Babylonian divinity, it begins to look something like proselytism. Again, a father recognizes Yahweh, the son a Babylonian deity, and the grandson bears a noncommittal Iranian name; here is clear enough evidence of how the national religions were being interfused.

There is no indication in Egypt that the natives had as yet abandoned their ancestral gods, but they did intermarry. When, for example, Ashor took to himself the rich Jewish heiress Mibtahiah, it was expected that she would leave her own people and swear by her husband's gods; later, to be sure, she divorced Ashor and returned to her people, at which time she transferred her inherited wealth to the second husband, who was a fellow-Jew.[2]

Up and down the Nile Valley we find ostraca, papyri, and grave stelae of Syrian merchants. Herodotus knew of a Camp of the Tyrians near the temple of Hephaestus (as he called Ptah) in Memphis. Later documents know much of Ashur, the regular term for Syrian, such as

[2] A. E. Cowley, *Aramaic Papyri of the Fifth Century B.C.* (1923), Nos. 15, 20, and 25.

their island and their district.[3] The names of the merchants themselves betray the syncretism of the period. Hadad-ezer, for instance, still worships the Syrian weather-god, but Hori now reverences Egyptian Horus, though the father who named him bore the good Persian epithet of Bagabaga; another is called Bagadat.[4] That these Aramaean traders have actually been converted is proved not merely by their names; although Anan son of Elisha was a citizen (*baal*) of a Syrian town named after the Semitic god Baal, he had become a priest of Isis. Sheil or Saul, whose home was Syene, was a priest of Babylonian Nebo. Herem-shezab was also a priest—presumably of the divinity commemorated in his name. When, therefore, we have other names commemorating Anat (the great Syrian goddess), Ashima, Bethel, or Babylonian Marduk, we may expect some day to find the priests and temples of these deities along the Nile.[5]

All these last have been found in the special cemetery of the Aramaeans southwest of Memphis, where they were buried in clay, more rarely stone or wooden sarcophagi imitating the anthropoid forms of those used by the natives. Mostly the bodies are mummified, though the embalming is poor; the viscera are wrapped in a packet (which is sometimes laid in a wooden box painted with the traditional funeral attendants), and placed on the body. Names, paternity, and titles are written in ink or rudely scratched in, after which the sarcophagus may be surrounded or even vaulted over by bricks.[6]

Wealthier Aramaeans buried here or around the tomb of Osiris at Abydos set up regular grave stelae which fully prove that these new converts were committed to the earth with the proper Osirid rites. The style may betray the unpracticed hand of the "barbarian," and so may the accompanying hieroglyphics; the Syrian dress is usually retained, but the ritual of Osiris is depicted in the accompanying scenes and shines through the translation into Aramaic. This is true, even when the old wine of Osirid doctrine is poured into new bottles of Aramaic poetry:

[3] Herod. ii. 112; list of sites, Noël Aimé-Giron, *Textes araméens d'Egypte* (1931), pp. 10–11; documentary references, F. L. Griffith, *Catalogue of Demotic Papyri in the John Rylands Library*, III (1909) 318; add from W. Spiegelberg, *Kêmi*, II (1929), 107 ff., "Nebankh, prophet of Amon in the Ashur settlement in the temple of Smendes" in the Ptolemaic period.

[4] *CIS*, Vol. II, Nos. 424–25.

[5] Aimé-Giron, *op. cit.*, pp. 98–99, 103, 107, 110 ff.

[6] *Ibid.*, pp. 93 ff.; G. Jéquier, *AS*, XXIX (1929), 155 ff.; XXX (1930), 111 ff.

> Blessed be Taba, daughter of Ta-hapi,
> The devoted worshiper of Osiris the god;
> Naught of evil have you done,
> Slander of no man have you spoken;
> There before Osiris be blessed,
> From before Osiris take water.[7]

The more elaborate of these grave stelae date from the late fourth or early third centuries and show a complete acceptance of the Osiris faith. An earlier stela, dated 482, is strange. Under a winged disk without the usual uraeus stand the dead man and his wife praying before Osiris, Isis, and Nephthys. In atrocious Egyptian we read: "A royal offering, which Osiris, first of westerners, the great god, lord of Abydos, gives. He gives a good burial in the necropolis and a good name on earth, which is with the great god, the lord of heaven, to the honored lady Akhtobu." But the dead man and his wife wear Syrian headdress and so do the mourners, the jars used in the ceremonies are Syrian, not Egyptian, and the priests do not appear to be natives. Foreign also are the funeral couches, in the form of lions with upraised tails; they are grasped by a figure between, who is also strange.[8] We begin to suspect that there is syncretism not only of gods but of rituals.

THE FIRST MYSTERY RELIGION

Our suspicions have recently been more than justified by a spectacular decipherment, as yet in its beginnings, of a fourth-century demotic papyrus. Although the characters employed are demotic—for the most part alphabetic though with a good sprinkling of determinatives and ideograms—the ductus shows a foreigner's hand. The language thus concealed turns out to be what we should expect—the universal language of the empire: Aramaic.

Difficulties are presented by the poverty of the demotic alphabet employed for the transliteration as also by numerous other signs used either as true ideograms or as their phonetic equivalents; in compensation, we are aided by a word- or group-divider, by determinatives for god, female, or foreign land, and by phonetic complements added to ideograms to indicate how they should end when read as Aramaic. Already we are sure that the language thus concealed is archaic Aramaic as it was spoken in the fourth century under the Achaemenids.

[7] *CIS*, Vol. II, No. 141; cf. No. 142.   [8] *Ibid.*, No. 142.

For the first time we can read this archaic stage of the language with the approximately correct pronunciation. Here and there the consonants *y* and *w* have been added—exactly as in our manuscripts of the Hebrew Bible—to indicate that an *i* or a *u* or an *o* vowel is to be recognized; virtually all the *a* vowels, so frequent in Aramaic, are regularly made sure by another sign.

Enough has been translated in context to obtain surprising results. The long extract preserved—twenty-one columns with a total of well over two thousand words—hides a secret cult ritual. The hierophant gives directions for the miracle play, and then the mysteries are acted out. Poetical structure (both "parallelism of members" and actual rhythm) can be detected; vocabulary and content frequently recall the similar older literature of Ras Shamra recently excavated but written down in a cuneiform alphabet.

Over the whole composition hangs a funeral pall, lightened however by the firm hope of a blessed future life. Already we have seen how many Aramaean exiles by the Nile had abandoned their Semitic view of a drab and hopeless existence after death for a blessed life with Osiris; it is significant that the author of our ritual has taken over the familiar judgment scene before Osiris only to transfer it for the use of his own "Lady" Anat.

Full syncretism is everywhere present. While the great heroes celebrated are this Lady Anat and Baal, Mut or Death is the enemy. His temporary triumph over Baal, and Anat's restoration of her beloved to vigorous life, is the theme of the miracle play. Another god often mentioned is the Syrian Baal Shamain, "Lord of the Heavens," as his name is translated. A trinity of consorts once appears: Baal Saphon (the Lord of the north) and Padry of the Ras Shamra texts; Bel of Babylon and the Lady of Shingal (Esagila); Nabu of Borsippa (Bar Sap) and Nana of Eanna (Aiaku); to each divinity is added the consolation: "He (or she) will bless you."

Despite the close resemblance to the ritual poems of Ras Shamra, there is one outstanding difference. This is a *foreign* cult in an alien land and the ritual is *secret*. Egyptian or Babylonian ritual could be understood by anyone sufficiently well educated to spell out the writing; only secrets of practical knowledge such as astrology or liver divination, reserved for the use of the royal family, were written with unusual values for the key characters and with a specific warning against communication to the unlearned. Our papyrus, on the contrary, was composed in an elaborate cryptogram which neither the

Egyptian scribe nor his Aramaic colleague could decipher without a difficulty almost impossible to surmount unless he held the key. Here, then, we have our first known example of a genuine "mystery religion."[9]

RELIGIOUS EVOLUTION AMONG THE JEWS

Among other peoples of the Orient, then, we may glimpse underground movements beneath the apparently quiet surface; but only among three peoples—the Persians, the Greeks, and the Jews—can we trace definite religious evolution. In their years of precarious independence, the kingdoms of Israel and Judah had retained some shreds of autonomy only by playing off neighbor Egypt against Assyria or later against Chaldaea. Culturally, the Hebrews were a part, and on the whole a satisfied part, of the world civilization to be found alike on the Nile, the Tigris, and the Euphrates, as well as in the more insignificant states on the borders of the great empires. Only in the matter of religion had the Hebrews in recent years tended to go their own ways.

Arrival of the Iranians at first seemed to make little difference. For the most part, Iranian culture was based on that of the older empires. The religion of the Iranians was fundamentally monotheistic, and they must have felt a certain sympathy for a religion of a minor people who likewise believed in a unique divinity. It may not have been due to political considerations solely that we find so many illustrations of Persian interference in behalf of Jewish orthodoxy. In matters religious, Persia was tolerant, even beyond the example of her predecessors; there was no persecution of alien cults, unless they were combined with nationalistic threats of revolt. The natural result was that new concepts entered easily and found lodgment in even the most orthodox Jewish circles.

Yet, despite Persian tolerance, an increasing unity of religious culture was enforced by the political situation. Under the rule of the Achaemenids, the civilized world came nearer to being under one political control than ever before or since. In the case of the Jews, the whole oriental world, throughout which they were even now so widely scattered, recognized a common master. The importance of this factor in the religious evolution of the Jews cannot be overestimated.

Long since, the Jewish Diaspora had begun. We may start with Palestine itself. Half that country was occupied by thoroughly alien

[9] Raymond A. Bowman, "An Aramaic Religious Text in Cryptogram," *JNES*, III (1944), 219 ff.

peoples, Philistines who gave their name to Palestine, Phoenicians whose seaboard extended far south of the former Israelite back country, Aramaeans pushing down from the north, Arabs from the east, and Edomites from the south. Colonists deported by Assyrian monarchs occupied the capitals of the Israelite kings. Naturally, they worshiped the "God of the land" as well as their Mesopotamian divinities and wished to become a recognized part of the restored Jewish community. Rejected through Zechariah's prophetic influence and still more emphatically spurned by Nehemiah, they, too, joined the other enemies of restored Zion.

The majority of the Jews, the peasants, had been alienated by Josiah's "reforms" and especially by the insistence upon one legitimate sanctuary.[10] By the Exile they had been cut off from their natural leaders. They resented Zionist claims, clung to their peasant customs, and often worshiped old Canaanite deities quite like those of their pagan neighbors. When they found that the returned Zionists were not too pious to refrain from taking advantage of the mounting taxation, though they dubbed them slightingly "People of the Soil," far the greater number relapsed into a more or less open paganism.

Many Jews had found refuge in Egypt; during the Achaemenid period, they willingly served as Persian mercenaries and thereby did not win the love of the natives. When the Egyptians were long in successful revolt against their Persian paymasters, the fate of these mercenaries cannot have been happy.

No aid was given by Jerusalem, for these Jews were unorthodox. Against the one unique temple of Josiah's reform they set up a rival at Elephantine and worshiped other gods and goddesses than Yahweh.

Jews of the "captivity" in Babylonia, on the other hand, were far more "orthodox" than Jerusalem itself, which must every now and then be urged to recant by men like Ezra and Nehemiah. But, at that, only a few of the Babylonian Jews were truly orthodox. In Babylonia, as in Egypt, the wealthiest Jews intermarried with Gentiles and gave their sons names which honored foreign deities. In Palestine the bankers did not hesitate to plunder their fellow-Jews under the very shadow of the Holy City. Such hopes of nationalism as survived the disappearance of Zerubbabel must center about the high priest, but *he* became ever more worldly as he was accepted by the powers that be as

[10] Olmstead, "The Reform of Josiah in Its Secular Aspects," *American Historical Review*, XX (1915), 566 ff.

the sole representative of his people. Equally worldly was the higher priesthood, quite content to practice the cult along former lines.

Had these elements of Judaism controlled the future, the Jewish fate would have been that of the other ethnic groups. Fortunately, the same stirrings of spirit which were to result in a revived Zoroastrianism among the Persians and in the mystery cults imported from the Orient by the later Greeks were present in yet greater degree among certain truly spiritual Jews. Jewish priests and businessmen played their part in the political and economic history of the days after the collapse of Achaemenid rule, but Jewish history would have been that of the Gentiles had not new parties been formed.

We can see that these parties represent three widely different ideals dimly recognized in the later Achaemenid period. On the one side were the "Pious," deeply religious, faithful to the temple service, but at heart more concerned with a proper observance of that Law of Moses introduced by Ezra. To them salvation was possible only through complete separation (whence their later name of the "Separated," Pharisees) from all who did not agree with their doctrine, whether lukewarm priests or "People of the Soil." Marriage with Gentiles was anathema. Scribes learned in the Law like Ezra gave them direction, and their triumph was to come after the destruction of the Second Temple.

Another wing represented the broad church. In their own fashion members of this party were quite as religious as the so-called "Pious." Perhaps they were even more devoted to the temple and its ritual and to all that they considered true Judaism. In sharp contrast to the "Separated," they would extend these privileges to the whole world.

While the Pious were definitely pacifistic and never opposed foreign rule so long as religious freedom was allowed, an equally well-defined nationalism had shown itself in Haggai, Zechariah, and Malachi. In the writings of Zechariah, apocalypse made its first appearance among the Jews. But Zerubbabel disappeared and Malachi had no successor. Persian taxation diverted all thought to the problem of merely keeping alive. Nationalism and apocalyptic seemed to be dead among the Jews, but, as so often happens, appearances were deceptive.[11]

ORIENTAL CULTS AMONG THE GREEKS

Long before these new religious movements began to develop in the Orient and before a reverse movement from Greek lands slowly passed

[11] Olmstead, *History of Palestine and Syria* (1931), pp. 625 ff.

eastward, oriental religious thought powerfully influenced the Greeks. We start with Hesiod, who thus early knew Adonis as son of Phoenix, the "Phoenician."[12] Among the fragments of Sappho we read: "Woe to Adonis!" "Dying, Cythera, is the delicate Adonis, what can we do? Beat, maids, your breasts and rend your chitons." "Woe for Adonis of the four months' sojourn" in the underworld.[13] Timocreon of Rhodes, a comedian who was the open rival of Themistocles and of Simonides, tells us how, after Adonis had been honored by Aphrodite at the funeral rites, the Cypriotes continued to throw into his pyre live doves which flew away but then fell into another pyre and died.[14] According to the hymns of Praxilla of Sicyon, when Adonis was asked by the shades below what was the most beautiful thing he had left behind, he replied: "The most beautiful thing I left is the light of the sun; second, the shining stars and the moon's face; then also ripe cucumbers, apples, and pears."[15] Antimachus knew that Adonis ruled particularly over Cyprus.[16]

Well before the end of the fifth century, metics of Phoenician birth had introduced the cult of Adonis to Attica. Aristophanes brackets together the mysteries of Demeter at Eleusis, of Zeus at Olympia, and of Adonis. He speaks of the rites of Sabazius and of Adonis held on the roofs at the moment when the ill-fated expedition to Sicily was about to sail; later authors found ominous the fact that the funeral ceremonies for Adonis, whose images were paraded through the Piraeus amid the wailing of women, coincided with the departure of Athenian youth, few of whom would return.[17]

References to Adonis pile up during the fourth century. Cratinus would not have his principal train a chorus, even for the Adonis festival,[18] though Dionysius, tyrant of Syracuse, composed a tragedy under the name of the god.[19] Pherecrates wrote: "We shall carry on the Adonis rites and bewail Adonis."[20] Antiphanes composed an *Adonis*, and in his *Corinthian Women* he told of swine sacred in Cyprus to Aphrodite.[21] Eubulus explained why lettuce was food of the dead;

[12] Hesiod. *Cat.* 21.

[13] Sappho, Frags. 25, 103, 136 (Edmonds).   [15] Praxilla, Frag. 1 (Edmonds).

[14] Timocr., Frag. 5 (Edmonds).   [16] Antimachus, Frag. 14 (Edmonds).

[17] Aristophan. *Pax* 420; *Lysistrat.* 389–90; Plut. *Nic.* 13. 7; *Alcibiad.* 18. 3.

[18] Cratin, *Bucoli*, Frag. 15 (in T. Kock [ed.], *Comicorum Atticorum fragmenta*, Vol. I [1880]); cf. Frag: 376.

[19] Dionys., Frag. 1 (Kock).   [20] Pherecrat., Frags. 170, 198 (Kock).

[21] Antiphan. *Adonis*, Frags. 13 ff.; *Corinthia*, Frag. 126 (Kock).

in it Cypris laid out Adonis.[22] The *Adonis* of Araros, however, ridiculed the foreign divinity, for "the god is turning his snout toward us."[23] Philetaerus brought out an *Adoniazousae*, a play about the female members of a cult devoted to Adonis, while Philiscus celebrated the *Marriage of Adonis*.[24] Diphilus in his *Zographus* tells of Samian courtesans celebrating the Adonia in brothels.[25] The comic writer Plato in his *Adonis* gave an oracle to Cinyras, king of the Cyprians, to the effect that his son would be destroyed by Aphrodite and Dionysus.[26] Demosthenes himself referred to Adonis.[27] To no other oriental divinity do we have so many references, and we are not surprised to learn that in the year 333 the metics from Citium were at last given permission to build a temple for their own Aphrodite.[28]

Reception of Attis and of his mistress—the Phrygian Mother of the Gods, Cybebe or Cybele—was equally early. Already in the sixth century, Hipponax of Ephesus mentions her under the form Cybelis.[29] Soon after the great Persian War there was a state cult of the Mother in Athens, for the oracle of Apollo bade the citizens to appease her wrath, and they built the Metroön near the Agora. Her statue within, the work of Agoracitus, a pupil of Pheidias, showed her enthroned with her lions, a tympanum in her hands; she appears also on a contemporary relief.[30]

Pindar dedicated to her a shrine under her name Dindymene; her throne and her statue of Pentelic marble were sculptured by the Thebans Aristomedes and Socrates. Pausanias, author of the Greek guidebook, saw her shrine near the ruins of Pindar's house.[31] Euripides connects the bacchanal rites with the orgies of the Great Mother Cybele and is apparently followed by Diogenes of Athens in his *Semele* when he refers to Cybele, Phrygia, Lydia, Tmolus, Halys, Bactria, and the Persian law.[32] Early in the fourth century there was a Metroön at Olympia.[33] Theopompus in his *Capelides* says: "I also cherish your

[22] Eubul. *Astyti*, Frag. 14 (Kock).

[23] Araros *Adonis*, Frag. 1 (Kock).

[24] Kock, *op. cit.*, II (1884), 230, 443.

[25] Diphil., Frag. 43 (Kock).

[26] Plat. Comic., Frags. 1 ff. (Kock).

[27] Demosthen. *Crit.* 259–60.

[28] *IG*, Vol. II, No. 168.

[29] Hipponax, Frag. 121.

[30] *IG*, Vol. I, No. 4; Plin. xxxvi. 17; Arr. *Periplus* 11; Julian. *Orat.* v. 159B.; cf. Ad. Michaelis, *Mittheilungen des deutschen archäologischen Institutes in Athen*, II (1877), 1, n. 2; H. W. Roscher, *Lexikon*, II, 1663.

[31] Paus. ix. 25. 3.

[32] Eurip. *Bacch.* 78 ff.; Diog. Athen., Frag. 1 (Nauck).

[33] F. Adler *et al.*, *Baudenkmäler von Olympia* (1892), pp. 39–40.

Attis."[34] Antisthenes, however, when alms were demanded by a priest of Cybele, answered: "I don't support the Mother of the Gods, whom the gods themselves should support!" When taunted with his Thracian mother, the same Antisthenes retorted: "Even the Mother of the Gods comes from Mount Ida."[35] Antiphanes in his *Metragyrtes* dealt with a begging priest of Cybele, through whom one of the characters bought ointment from the goddess.[36]

With Attis and Cybele came Sabazius and his corybants. In his *Hours* Aristophanes brought to trial the Phrygian flute-player Sabazius with the other foreign divinities and banished them from Athens.[37] Sositheus placed the scene of his *Daphnis* or *Lityerses* at Celaenae, the ancient city of Midas.[38] Already Sappho had sung of Linus and Adonis.[39]

Ammon was somewhat a latecomer through the Greeks of Libya. After he had praised the god through his Libyan patrons, the Ammonians, Pindar dedicated a temple to him at European Thebes, with a statue made by Calamis.[40] Euripides knew the dry abodes of Ammon, longing for rain.[41] Aristophanes, this time no scoffer, places his oracle second only to that of Delphi.[42] When Athens sent an official mission to Ammon[43] and Hellanicus wrote a guidebook, an "Anabasis," to his shrine,[44] the Spartan Lysander followed suit and also visited the oracle.[45] Abuse of Ammon is conspicuously missing from the comedians.

This is the more remarkable because the comedians were definitely hostile to the cults imported from the Orient. Aristophanes blamed the women for adopting foreign cults, while his *Telmessians* ridiculed the superstitions for which its oraclemongers were notorious.[46] By 355 Isocrates contrasts the splendor of the celebrations at the festivals to honor alien gods with the neglect of the native deities.[47]

[34] Theopomp., Frag. 27 (Kock).

[35] Seneca *De constant*, 5; Elem. Alex. *Strom.* vii. 64; Diog. Laert. vi. 1.

[36] Antiphan. *Metragyrt.*, Frag. 154 (Kock); cf. Aristophan. *Aves* 876.

[37] Aristophan. *Lysistrat.* 388; *Aves* 872; *Vespae* 8 ff.; *Horae*, Frags. 566 ff. (Kock); Cic. *Leg.* ii. 37.

[38] Sositheus, Frag. 2 (Nauck).

[39] Paus. ix. 29. 8.

[40] *Ibid.* 16. 1.

[41] Eurip. *Troiad.* 734 ff.; cf. *Alcest.* 116.

[42] Aristophan. *Aves* 619.

[43] Plut. *Nic.* 13. 1.

[44] Athen. xiv. 652a.

[45] Plut. *Lysand.* 20: 4; 25. 3; Ephor., Frag. 126(J).

[46] Aristophan. *Lysistrat.* 387 ff.; *Telmesseis* (Kock, I, 525–26).

[47] Isocr. *Areop.* 29.

RELIGIONS DYING AND LIVING 471

THE DILUTION OF ZOROASTRIANISM

Darius I grew up under the influence of Zoroaster. He seems to quote from a Gatha in his tomb inscription, and other writings show clear traces of Zoroaster's thought and language. It is equally clear that Darius did not always follow his master's teachings; it is quite possible that he did not truly apprehend them. Not only did he and his successors invoke by name foreign gods—in their homelands this might be merely a matter of policy—but the official inscriptions intended for the empire did not even speak of Ahuramazda as sole god. Rather, he was the "greatest of the gods," and by his side they called upon "the other gods who are."

Banned by Zoroaster, Mithra persisted in men's affections. From every reign and in most of the languages of the empire, we find proper names which prove how many fathers placed their sons under the protection of the old pagan sun-god. We have previously mentioned references which indicate his worship. By Artaxerxes I, Mithra is officially placed next in honor to Ahuramazda himself. A hymn to Mithra, composed in the days of pagan ignorance, was preserved and was now revived, though in a dialect not employed by the prophet. Again revised in Parthian times, it has been preserved in its later form for use in present-day Parsee ritual.[48]

Artaxerxes II was especially devoted to Anahita, "the Immaculate," generally identified with Artemis by the Greeks.[49] Of the Persian monarchs, he first erected statues for her and set them up in Babylon, Susa, Ecbatana, Parsa, Bactra, Damascus, and Sardis.[50] Such a statue obviously lies behind the description of the goddess in the Yasht sung in her honor.

Here, the good Ardvi Sura Anahita is seen by her devotees as a beautiful maiden, very strong, full grown, high girdled, noble, of illustrious descent. On her head she has bound a golden crown with a hundred stars of eight rays—the star of Babylonian Ishtar—with outstreaming fillets. Square gold earrings she wears in her ears, and a golden necklace encircles her lovely neck. A robe embroidered with gold covers her body, but her undergarment is of soft beaver skin from three hundred animals who have borne four young (for then the pelts are at their best). Her waist is tightly girdled that her breasts may be

[48] Yasht 10. [49] Plut. *Artox.* 23.

[50] Berossus, Frag. 56(S); called Hera, Plut. *Artox.* 23. 5; Anaitis of Ecbatana, *ibid.* 27. 3; Anaitis, Strabo xv. 3. 15; Paus. iii. 16; of Aena temple at Ecbatana, Polyb. x. 27. 12; Anea, Strabo xvi. 1. 4; Nanaea, II Macc. 1:13, 15.

well shaped. In her hand she grasps the *baresma*, the holy bundle of twigs. Gleaming gold-incrusted shoes are on her feet.

From the region of the stars she is thus summoned by Ahura-Mazdah: "Come down, Ardvi Sura Anahita, from the stars above to the god-created earth; there shall the mighty rulers, the lords of the lands and their sons, worship you. The mighty men of valor shall beg of you swiftness of horses and overwhelming Glory; the Athravans, in their recitations, and the priests shall beg for knowledge and wisdom. Maidens with wombs as yet unfruitful shall beg for a lord to be a powerful husband, women about to bring forth shall beg for an easy delivery. All this will you grant them, Ardvi Sura Anahita, since it is in your power."

Anahita descends at the call of the Creator. Beautiful are her white arms, thick as a horse's shoulder. She needs all her strength, for Ahura-Mazdah has created for her four chariot steeds, tall, swift, and white—the wind, the rain, the cloud, and the sleet. Holding the reins, she drives down in her chariot; her horses crush those who hate the faithful, whether daevas or men, Yatus or Pairikas.

From the peak Hukarya, surrounded by precipices of gold a hundred times a man's height, Anahita leaps down. Then she becomes the mighty river which brings water both summer and winter to spread over the seven world regions (Karshvares). By day and by night she sends down a flood of waters as great as the whole of the waters which run along the earth.

Anahita possesses a thousand gorges and a thousand water channels, each a ride of forty days for a man on a good horse. By each channel stands a house, alight from a hundred windows, well built with a thousand columns, made firm by ten thousand beams; in each is spread a well-laid bed, well scented and decked with pillows. Thence she rushes on to the sea Vourukasha, the ocean surrounding the earth; all the shores of the sea boil over when she streams down.

On earth Anahita has other functions. She prepares the seed of men and the fruit of the womb for all women ready to bring forth. She causes all women to bear safely, and into their breasts she puts milk in due quantity at the proper time. She gives man health and increases his water channels, his fields and his herds, his possessions and his land. Anahita hates the daevas—once her partners—and obeys the precepts of Ahura.[51]

[51] Yasht 5; Fritz Wolff, *Avesta* . . . . (1924), pp. 166 ff.; H. Lommel, *Die Yäst's des Awesta* (1927).

A quite different picture of religious evolution is given by other writings now incorporated within the sacred Avesta, and specially named the Seven-fold Yasna (Haptanghati), which, like the authentic words of Zoroaster, are preserved in the Gathic dialect, though in prose. In them we may perhaps find the official ritual of the Achaemenid Empire; at least there is no direct reference to the great Iranian prophet, and the teaching is not by any means the same as his. As introduction we read: "We worship the holy Ahura-Mazdah, Lord of Righteousness. We worship the Amesha Spentas, who rule aright, who dispose aright. We worship the entire spiritual and temporal creation of Righteousness, according to the ritual of the good Mazdayasnian Faith." The latter term appears early, for shortly before 410 the Jewish community head at Elephantine, Jedoniah, tells his correspondent that the official set over the nome of No or Thebes is a Mazdayasnian.[52]

Now begins the Yasna proper:

That would we choose, Ahura-Mazdah and Righteousness the Beautiful, so that we may think and speak and do whatever is the best of deeds for both worlds. For the reward for the best deed we strive, that security and fodder be preserved for the Kine, whether we be instructed or uninstructed, whether rulers or subjects. Truly to the best of rulers is the Kingdom, for we ascribe the Kingdom to Ahura-Mazdah and to Best Righteousness. As a man or a woman knows what is right, with fervor let him execute what is right, for himself and for whomsoever he can bring to understanding. For to bestow on you, Ahura-Mazdah, honor and praise, and fodder on the Kine, we believe to be the best. For you we would labor and bring understanding to others as best we may. In the companionship of Righteousness, in the company of Righteousness, count every understanding person with the best comfort for both worlds. These revealed words, Ahura-Mazdah, with better ponderings of Righteousness would we proclaim; to you, however, we submit ourselves as their enjoiner and teacher. By the desire of Righteousness and of Good Thought and of the good Kingdom, there shall be for you, Ahura, praises upon praises, maxims upon maxims, and prayers upon prayers.[53]

Zoroaster's abstract manifestations of the deity are here anthropomorphized, and the six most outstanding have become the Amesha Spentas with an actual cult of their own. But other ancient Indo-Iranian gods have returned as accepted deities little inferior to Ahura-Mazdah himself. First of all stands Atar, the fire-god, who is honored by one entire prayer:

[52] Cowley, *op. cit.*, No. 38.   [53] Yasna 35.

Through the action of this Fire we draw near first to you, Mazdah-Ahura, through your Holiest Spirit, who is also torment to him for whom you have hastened torment. As the most joyful may you come to us, Fire of Mazdah-Ahura, with the joy of the most joyful, with the honor of the most honorable for the greatest of ordeals. As Fire are you the joy of Mazdah-Ahura, as Holiest Spirit are you his joy; what name of yours is most propitious, Fire of Mazdah-Ahura, with that would we draw near to you. With Good Thought, with Good Righteousness, with good deeds and words of the Good Doctrine would we draw near to you. We do obeisance to you, we thank you, Mazda-Ahura; with all good thoughts, with all good words, with all good deeds we draw near to you. The most beautiful body of bodies we bespeak you, Mazdah-Ahura: here the light and there that highest of the high, which is called the sun.[54]

Darius honored the god "who made this earth, who made yonder heaven, who made man, who made welfare for man." Our psalmist worships Ahura-Mazdah, who created the Kine and Righteousness, the water and the good trees, the light, the earth, and everything good, for his sovereign power and greatness and beneficent deeds. Him also would the psalmist worship with the collection of prayers dealing with the Kine, with the holiest names derived from Ahura and pleasing to Mazdah, with his flesh and his life.

For the spirits of dead ancestors, revered from earlier ages, Zoroaster had substituted the more spiritual concept of the Selves; the older belief in the Fravashays returned: "We worship the Fravashays of the believers in Righteousness, both men and women," as Best Righteousness himself, the Most Beautiful Spenta Amesha, Good Thought and Good Kingdom, the good existence, the good reward, and good Piety.[55]

Still more of the old nature worship appears in the next Yasna:

We worship this Earth who bears us, and those your wives, Ahura-Mazdah, so excellent through Righteousness, their zeal for the faith, their activity, their independence, their piety, along with the good blessing, the good desire, the good fulfilment, the good character, the good luxuriance. We worship the outspurting, coming-together, and flowing-off Waters, which, derived from Ahura, are Ahuras, who do good deeds, you who are easy to ford, good to swim, and good for bathing, a reward for both worlds. With the names which Ahura-Mazdah gave you, as Giver of Good, he created you, with them we worship you, with them we beseech your grace, with them we do obeisance to you, with them we thank you. And you, Waters, we beseech as the pregnant ones, you as the Mothers, and you as the

[54] Yasna 36.　　　　　　[55] Yasna 37; cf. Yasna 5.

milch Cows, who care for the poor, giving suckle to all, best, most beautiful.[56]

The stern, aloof Ahura-Mazdah of Zoroaster has become again an oriental monarch with a harem full of mother-goddesses.

No longer is the Ox Soul a subordinate of Ahura-Mazdah, for he, too, has become an object of worship: "And now we sacrifice to the Soul of the Kine and to her created body. Also we sacrifice to the souls of cattle which are fit to live." This is not all:

We worship the souls of those beasts which are tamed and broken, of wild herbs, and the souls of the holy wherever they were born, both of men and of women, whose good consciences are conquering in the fight with the daevas. We worship the Bountiful Immortals, both those male and those female. Thus we draw near to you, together with the good kinship of our kinsmen, with that of Righteousness and the blessed, and the good law of thrift and energy and the good Piety, the ready mind.[57]

At these allotments, Mazdah-Ahura, remember and bring to pass our request which you have ordained as reward for the Self of such as I. Grant it for this life and for the spiritual to come that we attain to fellowship with you and with Righteousness forever more. Grant that the warriors long for Righteousness, that the herders be fitted for continuous fellowship, and that they be zealously subservient to us! Thus may the nobles, the peasants, and the priests, with whom we are in fellowship, thus may we all, Mazdah-Ahura, as followers of Righteousness and just, persuade you to grant us what we desire.[58]

Praises and hymns and adorations we offer to Ahura-Mazdah and Best Righteousness. To your Good Kingdom may we attain forever, and a good King be over us. Let each man and woman of us so abide, most beneficent of beings, and for both worlds. Thus do we render you, the helpful Yazad, endowed with good devotees, their friend, with the ritual; so may you be to us our life and our body's vigor. By your grace and will, may we attain long life, may we be powerful. Lay hold of us to help, for a long time and with salvation. Your praisers and Manthra speakers may we be called; thus do we wish and to this may we attain. What reward most fit for our deserving you have appointed for the Souls, that bestow upon us for this life and for that of Mind so that we may come under your protecting guardianship and that of Righteousness forever.[59]

Noble as much of this truly was, nevertheless the teachings of Zoroaster had been diluted, and not a little was gross paganism. In some quarters a purer faith had survived, as we learn from the "Three Pray-

[56] Yasna 38.
[57] Yasna 39.
[58] Yasna 40.
[59] Yasna 41.

ers"—Ahuna Vairya, Ashem Vohu, and Airyema Ishyo—perhaps the oldest document after the Gathas. Here Zoroaster is very much in the picture: "As He (Ahura) is the longed-for Lord, so is he (Zoroaster) the Judge according to Righteousness, the creator of life's deeds of Good Thought to Mazdah and of the Kingdom to Ahura, he whom they have granted as shepherd of the poor."[60] "Righteousness is the greatest good; according to our desires it shall be, according to our desires it shall be to us, Righteousness for the greatest happiness."[61] "Let the longed-for priestly brotherhood come to support the men and women who are taught of Zarathushtra, to the support of Good Thought, whereby the conscience [self] may win the precious reward. I pray for the dear prize of Righteousness which Ahura-Mazdah can bestow."[62]

Zoroaster was not mentioned in the "Seven Chapters," for apparently they did not come from the circle of his immediate followers. When they were affixed to his Gathas, a supplement was needed:

You we worship, Bountiful Immortals, with the whole collection of this Yasna, the Seven Chapters. We sacrifice to the fountains of waters and to the fordings of rivers, to the forkings of highways and the meetings of roads. We sacrifice to the hills running with torrents and we sacrifice to both protector and creator, to Zarathushtra and the Lord. [Here Zoroaster is at last named, not as the prophet, but as a divine being worthy of honor with Ahura-Mazdah himself.]

To earth and heaven we sacrifice, to the stormy wind that Mazdah made, to the peak of high Haraiti, to the land and all things good. We worship Good Mind and the spirits of the holy, we sacrifice to the fish of fifty fins and to the sacred beast which stands in Vouru kasha, and to that sea of Vouru-kasha where he stands, and to the Haoma, golden flowered, growing on the heights, the Haoma drinks that restore us and aid this world's advance.[63] We sacrifice to Haoma that drives death afar [strange reversal of Zoroaster's condemnation of the "filthy drink"] and to the flood streams of the waters, to the great flights of birds, and to the return of the Fire Priests, as they go from afar to those who seek Righteousness in the lands.[64]

When this was written down, Alexander had come and gone. No longer was the Zoroastrian religion, even in its modified form, a recognized sect of the orthodox faith, supported by the power of the state. The story that Alexander himself destroyed the master-codex of the sacred writings is an invention to explain to later generations how

[60] Yasna 27:13.   [61] Yasna 27:14.   [62] Yasna 54:1.

[63] Already in 459 a standard at Elephantine was commanded dy Haomadata, "Haoma-given"; cf. Cowley, op. cit., Nos. 8:2 and 9:2.

[64] Yasna 42.

those writings almost perished. But Zoroastrianism was now merely one of many private sects. Against it were ranged all the subtle attractions of Greek religion, supported by magnificent temples and a gorgeous if empty ritual, as well as the destructive forces of Greek philosophy, both subsidized as Hellenizing influences by alien Macedonian kings.

For Zoroastrianism there remained only the formulation of the "General Confession," a setting-forth of the fundamental doctrines of the Masdayasnian faith in the hope of damming the ever rising tide of Hellenism.[65] Then it was time to recognize that the Gathic dialect had become a dead sacred tongue, and the canon was closed.[66]

GREEK KNOWLEDGE OF THE PERSIAN RELIGION

Greeks of the fourth century knew Persian religion much better than Herodotus.[67] About 390, Plato could tell of the *mageia* of Zoroaster, son of Oromasdes. Obviously, the *mageia* had by his time ceased to be Magian religion. Since the term is now applied to Zoroaster's Gathas, which have been collected into a ritual, the Masdayasnian religion must have become the official cult, though it is surprising that even this early the great prophet has been made a literal son of Ahuramazda.[68] Some have even seen in Plato's opposition of the Kingdoms of Good and Evil[69] a trace of Zoroastrian dualism.[70]

A good knowledge of contemporary Persian religion is shown by Xenophon in his *Education of Cyrus*. By order of the Magi, Cyrus first sacrifices to ancestral Hestia, then to King Zeus, and last to the other gods.[71] Thus we learn that, in the fourth century, Anahita was ranked even before Ahuramazda. There are purifying sacrifices accompanied by libations to Earth, and other sacrifices to the heroes who occupy the Median land, the Fravashis.[72]

By Magian rule, bulls are to be sacrificed to Zeus and to the other divinities, but horses are reserved to the sun. There is a chariot, drawn by white horses with golden yoke and garlanded, sacred to Zeus; in the procession next comes a chariot for the sun, then a third chariot

---

[65] Yasna 12; Wolff, *op. cit.*, pp. 40–41.   [66] Yasna 58; Wolff, *op. cit.*, pp. 58–59.

[67] The sources are collected by Carl Clemen, *Fontes historiae religionis Persicae* (1920); cf. "Mazdaismus," *PW*, Supplementband V (1931), cols. 679 ff.; E. Benveniste, *The Persian Religion according to the Chief Greek Texts* (1929); G. Messina, *Der Ursprung der Magier und die Zarathustrische Religion* (1930); H. S. Nyberg, *Die Religionen des alten Iran* (1938).

[68] Plato *I Alcibiades* 121; cf. Benveniste, *op. cit.*, pp. 16 ff.

[69] Plato *Leg.* x. 89E.

[70] R. Reitzenstein, in *Vorträge der Bibliothek Warburg 1924–1925*.

[71] Xen. *Cyrop.* vii. 5. 57; i. 6. 1.   [72] *Ibid.* iii. 3. 21–22.

with purple trappings whose purpose Xenophon evidently does not know, and, last of all, men carry fire on a great portable fire altar. When the procession reaches the sacred inclosure, the worshipers sacrifice to Zeus and make a holocaust of bulls; they also burn bulls to the sun (but they sacrifice to Earth as the Magi command) and then to the local heroes,[73] for the Magi take charge of that part of the booty which is assigned to the gods.[74] Sacrificial omens, celestial signs, flights of birds, and ominous words are the basis of Persian actions. As Cyrus felt death approaching, he returned to Persai (Persepolis) and sacrificed the sacred victims in one final ceremony to ancestral Zeus, the sun, and the other gods, upon the acropolis.[75]

Xenophon knew that the oath was taken by Mithra,[76] whose yearly festival was also known to Ctesias and Duris.[77] Deinon explains that the Magi sacrifice under the open sky because they believe that fire and water are the only emblems of divinity.[78] With the Platonist Hermodorus, he sought the meaning of Zoroaster's name from the Greek and interpreted it as "star-worshiper."[79]

Plato, as we have noted, understood that Zoroaster was the son of Ahuramazda himself. A few Greek scholars never forgot that the great prophet had been a contemporary of Darius' father Hystaspes, but the native Persians had invented for him a quasi-divinity, and so late a date was quite impossible on this thesis. The tradition now prevailed that Zoroaster had been born in prehistoric times. Greek credulity accepted the oriental chronology and sought only to fix it into their own. Hermodorus and Hermippus soon after set him five thousand years before the fall of Troy. The author of a *History of Lydia* ascribed to Xanthus dated him six thousand years before the expedition of Xerxes and listed among his many successors (down to the destruction of Persia by Alexander) the Magi Ostanas, Astrampsychus, Gobryas, and Pazatas; but, for the date, he may have been only copying Eudoxus.[80]

Aristotle wrote a book, now lost, the *Magian*, though he denied that the Magi practiced what was already coming to be known as "magic." He does not meekly swallow the claims of the Egyptians for a high antiquity, as did Herodotus and Plato; but, with equal credu-

[73] *Ibid.* viii. 3. 10–11, 24.   [75] *Ibid.* viii. 7. 1 ff.

[74] *Ibid.* iv. 5. 14.   [76] *Ibid.* vii. 5. 53.

[77] Ctes. *Pers.*, Frag. 55; Duris *Hist.* vii, Frag. 5(J).

[78] Deinon, Frag. 9 (Müller); Clem. Alex. *Cohort.* v. 56.

[79] Diog. Laert. i. 8.   [80] *Ibid.* 2; Plin. xxx. 1. 3–4.

lity, he accepts those of the Magi. The beginnings of true philosophy he traces instead back to the Magi and the Babylonian or Assyrian "Chaldaeans." With Hermippus, Eudoxus, and Theopompus, Aristotle states that the Magi believe in two principles: the good spirit, who is Zeus or Oromasdes, and the evil spirit, Hades or Ariemanius. Theopompus and Eudoxus add the Magian faith in an afterlife for men and their reliance on the continued existence of the world through their invocations. Finally, it is Theopompus who first describes to the Greeks Persian eschatology: For three thousand years one of the gods rules the other; then for three thousand years more they fight each other. In the end, Hades is defeated; men are happy, need no food, and cast no shadow. The god who brought about these blessings rests for a time.[81]

INFLUENCE OF THE PERSIAN CULTS

The temples of Anahita founded throughout the empire by Artaxerxes II appear soon to have been merged into the cult of other fertility goddesses. Toward the close of the Hellenic period the "Magian" religion became known to Greek thinkers. Thereafter, the Persian religion might have been confined to Iranian lands had not certain factors intervened.

After their defeat of the Sacae in Armenia, we are told, the Persians founded the walled city of Zela. There a temple of Anaitis and of the gods who shared her altar—Omanus and Anadatus—was established; its annual festival, the Sacaea, was celebrated down to the Christian Era. The city was small, inhabited mostly by temple serfs,[82] but from it Persian religion worked its westward way into Cappadocia, then south to Cilicia, where the pirates took over the cult of Mithra, and centuries later the sun-god dominated Roman armies and became a rival to the oriental Christ.

During these centuries also Zoroastrian thought was to make its most important contributions to a world religion. Semitic belief in existence after death was illuminated by true immortality. Satan the Accuser became the Devil. Egyptian apocalypse imported into Jerusalem was transformed into genuine eschatology, the doctrine of the *last* things, resurrection and the last judgment. Through the Jews, Zoroastrianism entered Christian theology.

[81] Eudoxus *Periodos*, Frags. 38–39 (see F. Gisinger, *Die Erdbeschreibung des Eudoxos von Knidos* [1921], p. 21); Deinon v (Frag. 5 [Müller]); Theopomp. *Philip.* viii. 64(J); Hermippus Callimach. *De mag.*, Frag. 79 (Müller); Aristot. *Philosoph.* i. 6; Plut. *De isid.* 369F ff.; Diog. Laert. i. 1. 8–9.
[82] Strabo xi. 8. 4; xv. 3. 15.

Chapter XXXIII

FRESH BREEZES FROM THE WEST

OVER the whole of the Achaemenid Empire new winds were blowing, and they came from the lands of the Greeks. Most significant were the shifts in language. The attempt to write the official Persian in a cuneiform alphabet had proved a failure. No monarch after Darius the Great had attempted a long composition, much less an autobiography. The language of Xerxes' much fewer inscriptions shows the beginning of linguistic decay, and the rare official records from the fourth century indicate almost complete ignorance of grammatical structure. Cuneiform Persian was rarely adapted for use on clay tablets and never after the first Darius.

Long before Cyrus, hymns to the pagan Aryan gods had been composed in another dialect. For a time they were officially subordinated to the Gathas of Zoroaster, recited in yet a third dialect. As the ancient gods were restored to royal favor, so were their hymns, though others of the pious continued to revise the Zoroastrian faith in the prophet's own dialect, but now only in prose.

At the beginning of the fifth century, Elamite cuneiform was employed, not only as one of the three official languages of the royal inscriptions, but as the ordinary speech of business documents at home and of the archives at Persepolis itself. In the fourth, the Elamite of the trilinguals became an almost senseless reproduction of a debased Persian original. Only the Babylonians among the peoples of western Asia continued to employ cuneiform on a large scale, but an almost complete break in the series of administrative and business documents at the middle of the fourth century implies that its use was more and more confined to the learned. Similar tendencies toward disuse of hieroglyphic, hieratic, and demotic were completely checked by the revival of Egyptian independence.

The triumph of the alphabet was almost complete. After centuries when the Sinaitic was seen only in rough graffiti from North Arabian oases, suddenly it blossomed forth in superb inscriptions from the high cultures of the southwestern peninsula. The mother-alphabet on the other line of descent, Phoenician, was regularly employed for inscriptions and coins at home and on Cyprus and found new life at Carthage and among other western colonies. At the beginning of our period, Jews still wrote excellent Hebrew; at its end, Hebrew was no longer in everyday use. When efforts were made to reproduce it as a sacred language, the date of the compositions is admitted by an abundance of Aramaic words and locutions.

In actual fact the future belonged to the Phoenician alphabet, as adapted by Aramaeans, and to the Aramaic language itself. From the days of Cyrus onward, official decrees from the Persian chancellery and diplomatic correspondence were generally in Aramaic. Hundreds of tablets from Persepolis marked in ink witness its archival use at the heart of the empire. It is found written by pen on clay tablets incised with Babylonian characters, and serves as an easily read label for the more difficult cuneiform. Inscriptions in Aramaic are common in North Syria and Cilicia and are met less frequently in Cappadocia, Paphlagonia, Mysia, Lydia, and Pamphylia. Greek mercenaries accepted coins bearing Aramaic legends, and, when the Great King wrote the Greeks, his letters must be translated from the regular official language. For a time, Aramaic threatened Egypt, but the revival of Egyptian nationalism turned the tide. As the cuneiform alphabet died out in Parsa itself, the Gathas and hymns tended to be reduced to writing, and the character employed was a variant form of the Aramaic. That the earlier sacred books had been committed to writing before Alexander is recalled by the legend that the invader had burned the master-scroll.[1]

GREEK LANGUAGE AND ART IN THE ORIENT

Aramaic never dominated Asia Minor, where, as in Egypt, nationalist feeling retained the Lydian and Lycian characters and languages for inscriptions. But here an increasing use of Greek foreshadowed the coming Hellenistic world. Carian had disappeared in favor of Greek. Lycian tomb records now and then added a brief Greek version. Coins minted by Persian satraps for Greek mercenaries sometimes have only Greek legends.

Independent Egypt under its last great dynasty remained free from any clear trace of Greek artistic influence. So did Palestine, for a few sherds from Greek pots imported for wine and oil by Greek mer-

[1] A. V. Williams Jackson, *Zoroaster, the Prophet of Ancient Iran* (1899), pp. 97, 224; *Persia Past and Present* (1906), pp. 306-7.

cenaries[2] do not give evidence to the contrary. Strato of Sidon was a Philhellene; we are not surprised to uncover anthropoid sarcophagi whose heads are certainly copied from Greek originals dating from the sixties down,[3] though others from the same date are as clearly Egyptian.[4] Coins from western Asia are almost without exception struck by Greek diemakers, as the blundered oriental legends prove to our discomfort. Their motifs are pure Greek virtually without exception and, when oriental, are treated in Greek fashion. Deities undoubtedly of oriental origin cannot be distinguished from their Greek congeners as to appearance, and the few oriental traits are at least given a Greek tinge. At first sight, Baal of Tarsus, for example, might be a truly Hellenic divinity, despite his Anatolian origin and his Aramaic name. Tyrian Melqart rapidly evolved into a Greek Heracles. Ahuramazda might retain his Persepolitan form, but the treatment was entirely Greek.

The western coast of Asia Minor was superficially Hellenized. Lycian art preserved a few indications of its native rock-cut character, but Greek sculptors or their able pupils produced an art so fine that it is accepted as Hellenic without question. The Mausoleum at Halicarnassus, adorned by four of the most famous sculptors of its day, represents the apex of pre-Hellenistic art. In contrast, for the first time, the Iranian regions show the primal development of a truly popular art.

During these last years the west coast of Asia Minor remained admittedly a part of the Achaemenid Empire. Our sources mention Persian satraps and officials as well as mercenary captains and tyrants. Though they often speak of internal troubles and raids from without, they should not mislead us. The Greek cities of Asia flourished under Persian rule—no doubt because it was so often nominal.

For proof we need look no further than the temples. The great structure of the period was the Artemis temple at Ephesus. After it had been deliberately fired by Herostratus in 356, it was rebuilt still more magnificently by the citizens through the thrifty sale of the old pillars and the women's ornaments; the architects were Demetrius and Paeonius. Its whole altar was filled with statues and reliefs by Praxiteles. Thrason made the chapel of Hecate and a wax image of

[2] J. H. Iliffe, "Pre-Hellenistic Greek Pottery in Palestine," *Quarterly of the Department of Antiquities in Palestine*, II (1933), 15 ff.

[3] C. C. Torrey, "A Phoenician Necropolis at Sidon," *Annual of the American Schools of Oriental Research*, I (1920), 1 ff.

[4] O. Hamdy Bey and T. Reinach, *Une nécropole royale à Sidon* (1892).

Penelope and the old woman Eurycleia. In the service of the many-breasted goddess were eunuch priests, who bore the Persian name Megabyzi, with their virgin associates.[5]

The almost equally famous temple of Didymene Apollo at Miletus, destroyed by Darius I after the Ionian revolt, rose from its ashes through the labors of Ephesian Paeonius and native Daphnis.[6] Pythius built the great shrine of Athena at Priene.[7] Still extant remains of these and similar buildings exhibit the wealth and good taste of Greeks in the last days of Persian rule.

Asiatic Greeks and Hellenized barbarians were patrons of the fine arts. Maussollus of Caria we have already met, as well as the great sculptors who decorated the Mausoleum. Scopas is said to have made many other statues in Caria and Ionia.[8] In addition, we have mention of one of Apollo Smintheus at Chryse and another of Leto and her nurse in the grove of Ortygia near Ephesus.[9] Praxiteles carved an Aphrodite for an unidentified city in Caria, later known as Alexandria by Latmos.[10] At Patara, Bryaxis set up a group of Zeus, Apollo, and lions.[11] Sthennis of Olynthus made for Sinope a figure of its hero-founder Autolycus.[12] All these were Europeans working in Asia; native sculptors were Pharax of Ephesus and Myagrus of Phocaea, who specialized in bronze athletic statues.[13]

European sculptors were also called upon to prepare dedications for European sites. The Milesians employed Satyrus the Parian when they set up the statues of Idrieus and Ada at Delphi. An unknown disciple of Scopas carved reliefs of the same rulers for Tegea.[14] "Mithradates the Persian, son of Rodotates, dedicated to the Muses a portrait statue of Plato which Silanion made" according to a copied inscription; the father was probably the satrap Orontobates, and the dedication made in the Academy at Athens, Silanion's native city.[15]

The lesser arts were not neglected. While Iranian lands were producing superb vases in bronze, the poorer Greeks worked mostly in clay; their artistic genius triumphed over their poverty and made each individual vase a treasure to be preserved. Polite literature ignored the names of these truly great artists, which must be collected from their

---

[5] Vitruv. iii. 12. 7; vii praef. 12, 16; x. 2. 11–12; Strabo xiv. 1. 22–23; Plin. vii. 125; xxxvi. 95.

[6] Vitruv. vii praef. 16.

[7] Ibid. 12.

[8] Paus. viii. 45. 4.

[9] Strabo xiii. 1. 48; xiv. 1. 20.

[10] Steph. Byz. s.v. "Alexandreia."

[11] Clem. Alex. Protrept. iv. 47.

[12] Strabo xii. 3. 11.

[13] Vitruv. iii praef. 2; Plin. xxxiv. 91.

[14] Cf. p. 436.

[15] Favorinus Memorabilia i, in Diod. Laert. iii. 25.

signed productions, and, even at that, many fine artists remain anonymous. For instance, a fragment from the "Chicago Vase-painter" has been recognized in Palestine.[16]

Although still confined mostly to Greek lands, the vases were sometimes exported and assist in dating foreign sites. One group from the beginning of the century has a special interest. It is generally called the Kertsch group because so many have been found at the ancient Panticapaeum in the eastern Crimea, but examples of its peculiar style have been recovered throughout the Mediterranean. Because one such vase is signed by Xenophontus the Athenian, the headquarters of this school has been thought to be Athens. What distinguishes this group is their interest in the Persians. Long notable has been the great vase which represents Darius and his court. In general, vase paintings of the early fourth century show draperies beginning to employ oriental ostentation.

Vase-painters were not the only Greek artists patronized by Scythian princes, who were rich in gold. Many of their vases and not a little jewelry betray the Greek touch. The motifs, however, are almost exclusively Iranian, and the greater part evidently was made by native Scyths with their own ethnic peculiarities. True Iranian jewelry is found throughout the empire. Numerous examples come from Egypt, quite a few from Cyprus, and there is a scattering from other countries. A collection of this very significant phase of Iranian art is yet to be made.[17]

Antiquity's greatest painter was said to have been Apelles of Ephesus. Among the stories told of him was how he took down a high Persian official named Megabyzus who visited his studio and attempted to talk learnedly on light and shade; pointing to boys grinding the colors, Apelles remarked that they had been greatly impressed by the noble's purple garments, but now they were laughing at him because he tried to talk about a subject he did not understand.[18] Almost equally great was Parrhasius, also from Ephesus. Other painters were Androcydes—the rival of Zeuxis—Polycles of Cyzicus, and Theon of Magnesia, who painted the madness of Orestes.[19]

[16] So recognized by Cleta Margaret Olmstead.

[17] Cf. for the present O. M. Dalton, *The Treasure of the Oxus* (2d ed., 1926).

[18] Strabo xiv. 1. 25; Plin. xxxv. 79; Plut. *Quomodo adulator* 15 (58D–E); cf. 472A; Herodas iv. 72–73; Athen. xii. 543C.

[19] Vitruv. iii *praef.* 2; Plin. xxxiv. 91; xxxv. 64. 144.

GREEK AUTHORS IN THE ORIENTAL WORLD

Among the historians were Ephorus of Aeolian Cyme and Anaximenes of Lampsacus. Deinon of Colophon and Heracleides of Cyme wrote Persian histories. A Lydian history had been written in Greek by Xanthus, but he was a native of the interior. Philiscus of Miletus, a pupil of Isocrates, wrote romantic Milesian tales. In answer to Isocrates, Amphyctionicus prepared a *Rhetorical Art*. Aristippus, the founder of the hedonistic philosophy of the Cyrenaics, once lived in Asia, where for a time he was a prisoner of the satrap Artaphernes.[20] Eubulides of Miletus, the pupil of Euclides, was said to have been the teacher of Demosthenes and an opponent of Aristotle; he enjoys the dubious honor of introducing many of the dialectic trick questions which helped so much to make sterile later philosophies, such as the Liar, the Disguised, Electra, the Veiled Figure, the Sorites, the Horned One, and the Bald Head.[21]

But Greek literature was coming to be written by "barbarians." From the Greek border came Theodectes of Phasaelis, a pupil of Isocrates and friend of Aristotle, who began as a writer of speeches and graduated to tragedies, of which he composed over fifty. Among them was the *Mausolus* to be recited at the funeral of the Carian prince. He also wrote an art of prose and a work on the parts of speech.[22] Another pupil of Isocrates, the rhetorician Crates, came from interior Tralleis.[23]

The writings of these once distinguished authors have been lost, all but a few words. To our ears the list of their names connotes little. The paintings, reliefs, and statues of the artists have also been lost, save as they are recovered through the work of late copyists. But other statues have been recovered in the ruins of the temples and public buildings. Enough has been preserved to reveal how wealthy and important was this portion of the Achaemenid world just before the dawn of the Hellenistic period.

[20] Diog. Laert. ii. 79.   [21] *Ibid.* 108.

[22] Dionys. Halicarnass. *Demosthen.* 48; Quintil. i. 4. 18; Plut. *Alex.* 17; Paus. i. 37. 4; Athen. x. 451E; xiii. 566E; Suid. *s.v.*

[23] Diog. Laert. iv. 23.

Chapter XXXIV

PHILIP AND THE START OF THE CRUSADE

THE INEFFICIENCY OF PERSIAN ADMINISTRATION

PERSIAN reconquest of Phoenicia and Egypt was a terrible shock to Macedonia and to the pro-Macedonian Greeks of Europe. Phoenician and Egyptian triremes once more gave Persia command of the seas, and their enormous wealth was again at the disposal of her diplomats, who knew only too well how to utilize it. To all appearances, the empire was stronger than it had been for an entire century.

Philip had been toying with the idea of the crusade preached by Isocrates. The thought was for the moment set aside, and Philip hastened to dispatch envoys with orders to negotiate a treaty of friendship and alliance with the Great King.[1] The revolting kings of Cyprus, together with Hermeias of Assos and other rebels who had depended on the assistance of Macedonia, were incontinently abandoned to the royal vengeance.

Thus deserted, there was nothing left for the Cypriotes but surrender to the suddenly increased power of their former master. Within a year after the reconquest of Egypt, all the cities of Cyprus—with the exception of Salamis, where Pnytagoras still held out, though he was compelled to stand siege—had made their peace. Evagoras II was recalled from his Carian exile and was promised his father's vacant throne—when Salamis was captured—but soon he was accused to the king and so fell into disfavor; thereafter Pnytagoras was left in peace.[2]

Mentor had been rewarded for his treachery at Sidon and for his assistance in reconquering Egypt by a gift of a hundred talents and by the command of the Aegean coast of Asia Minor. Through his influence, his brother Memnon and his brother-in-law Artabazus were pardoned and recalled from their refuge at the court of Philip, for the moment in professed friendship with Ochus. Hermeias was rightly accused of his former intrigues; lured to a conference, he was seized and crucified (341). Aristotle escaped and honored the memory of his late

---

[1] Plut. *Alex. virt.* 342B; Arr. *Anab.* ii. 14. 2; Diod. xvi. 45. 7.

[2] Diod. xvi. 46. 1-2.

host by writing a paean and an inscription for the statue which Hermeias had set up in Delphi.[3]

With forged letters bearing his seal, Mentor secured Hermeias' city. The former officials were allowed to retain their offices until, relaxed by their feeling of security, they brought out what they had hidden or sent to other places; then Mentor arrested them and took everything. Shortly thereafter, Mentor died and was succeeded by his brother Memnon, who married Barsine, the daughter of Artabanus.

Memnon captured Lampsacus and found himself in need of money; with typical cynicism he enforced a heavy contribution from the wealthiest citizens, bidding them to recoup their fortunes from the less prosperous, who in turn were promised restitution at some indefinite time in the future. For another contribution, Memnon pledged the revenues; when the revenues did come in, the pledge was coolly transformed into a promise of future payment with interest. He even tricked his mercenaries, saving a full month's pay by refusing to give wages or even rations for the "omitted days" of the twenty-nine-day month. Another mercenary leader, Stabelbius, general of the Mysians, found himself in debt to his soldiers; his trick was to promise the officers their pay if they would dismiss their men and raise new levies, but then he drove out the officers also. Through this constant imposition of financial trickery upon subjects and mercenaries alike, the Near East was being prepared to accept any invader who offered a firm and efficient administration.[4]

After the death of Idrieus, his sister-wife Ada ruled Halicarnassus until expelled by her younger brother Pixodarus (341–335). From the latter we possess a bilingual decree at Xanthus concerning a tithe of some tax for the men of Xanthus, Tlos, Pinara, and Candayda.[5]

ALLIANCE WITH ATHENS AGAINST PHILIP OF MACEDON

Early in 341 Demosthenes urges the Athenians to send an embassy to Ochus. His opponents claim that, by so doing, he is betraying the Greeks, but do they really care for the interests of the Greeks living in Asia? Every Athenian general enforces contributions from them under the name of "benevolences"; but what these Greeks really are

---

[3] *Ibid.* 52. 1 ff.; Theopomp., Frags. 250, 291(T); Callisthenes *Hermeias*, Frags. 2–3(J); Anaximenes *Epist. Philip.* 7; Didym. vi. 61; [Plato] *Epist.* vi, to Hermeias; Apollodor., in Diog. Laert. v. 4 ff.; Strabo xiii. 1. 57; [Demosthen.] *Philip.* iv. 32; Ovid *Ibis* 319–20.

[4] [Aristot.] *Oeconom.* ii. 2. 28–29, 40; Polyaen. vi. 48; Plut. *Alex.* 21. 4.

[5] *TAM*, Vol. I, No. 45.

paying for is to secure for their merchant princes protection against robbery on the high seas![6]

The Thracians, whom the king trusts and has called "benefactors," are fighting against Philip. The agent of Philip, who was plotting with Hermeias, has been captured, and now the king knows Philip's plans; let the ambassador who is to be sent urge Ochus to take common action against him. Ochus must realize that, after Philip has taken Athens, his advance against the king will be much less difficult. Let his auditors forget their stupid "barbarian, common foe of all Greeks," and face the facts. They claim that they are afraid of a man living in distant Susa or Ecbatana because he is plotting evil against them; in actual fact he once restored Athenian power and is now offering to do so again. If the Athenians have voted not to accept his aid, that is not the king's fault; it is the fact that the Athenians think there is no danger from Philip which makes the orator afraid.[7]

The embassy was sent, and Ochus was urged to break the treaty of friendship and to make war on Philip.[8] The Great King himself was busy putting down yet one more Cadusian revolt,[9] but Arsites sent mercenaries from Phrygia under command of the Athenian Apollodorus, and thus Philip was kept out of Perinthus (340).[10] The speech of Demosthenes had been justified.

Philip complained to the Athenians. Their action was strange, he pointed out, since but recently Athens had passed a decree inviting Macedonia to unite with the other Greeks in preventing Ochus from regaining Phoenicia and Egypt.[11] Demosthenes replied by reminding his hearers that the satraps of Asia had sent their mercenaries to keep Philip, the enemy of their own city, out of Perinthus; if, after this, Philip should conquer Byzantium, then his friends could ask financial support from Ochus, the richest of them all. If, however, the Great King sided with Athens, then it would be easy for him to defeat the Macedonian.[12]

[6] Demosthen. Cherson. 24 ff.; also in Philip. iii. 71, of the same year, omitted in the later edition edited by the orator himself!

[7] Demosthen. Philip. iv. 31 ff. Why this oration should be generally refused to Demosthenes when it fits so exactly what we should expect him to say in advocacy of an embassy which was admittedly sent is difficult to understand.

[8] Aeschin. Ctes. 238; Anaximenes Epist. Philip. 6–7.

[9] Diod. xvii. 6. 1; Just. x. 3. 2 ff.; Arr. Anab. iii. 8. 5; 11. 3; 19. 3; Curt. iv. 12. 12; 14. 3.

[10] Diod. xvi. 75. 1; Paus. i. 29. 10; Arr. Anab. ii. 14.5.

[11] Anaximenes Epist. Philip. 6–7. Since Anaximenes was a contemporary, the speeches in his history should fairly closely follow the facts.

[12] Demosthen. Ad Epist. Philip. 5–6.

PLATE LVII

Sardis (courtesy Turkish Press Department)

Halicarnassus (courtesy Turkish Press Department)

SATRAPAL CAPITALS

PLATE LVIII

Statue of Nekt-hor-hebt

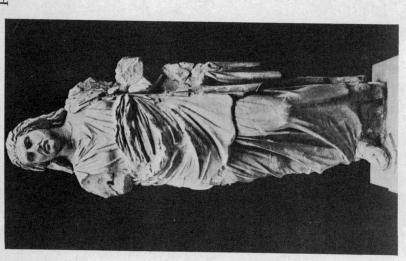

Statue from Mausoleum (from Brunn-Brückmann
Denkmäler, Pl. 241)

CONTEMPORARY FIGURES

PLATE LIX

Bull Capital from Palace (courtesy Beirut Museum)

Sarcophagus of Mourning Women (courtesy Istanbul Museum)

PERSIANS AND GREEKS AT SIDON

PLATE LX

Plain of Megalopolis

Phillippeum at Olympia

NEW CENTERS IN GREECE

PLATE LXI

Fourth Century (from *Marbles and Bronzes in the British Museum*, Pl. 14)

Achaemenid

Fifth Century

SCULPTURES FROM TEMPLE OF ARTEMIS AT EPHESUS

PLATE LXII

GREEK INTEREST IN PERSIA

Darius Vase (from Furtwängler-Reichhold, *Denkmäler*, Pl. 88)

PLATE LXIII

Golden Armlet with Griffin
(courtesy Iranian Institute)

Gilt Handle with Ibex (courtesy Iranian Institute)

Silver Bowl of Artaxerxes (courtesy Iranian Institute)

MINOR ARTS IN ACHAEMENID PERSIA

PLATE LXIV

Lion at Chaeroneia

Phillippi

THE IMPORTANCE OF PHILLIP OF MACEDON

CONSTRUCTIONS OF ARTAXERXES III

Ochus erected at Ecbatana the stone columns of the apadana under the protection of Mithra.[13] At Susa he completed the front and rear of the Darius palace whose restoration had been started by his father.[14] No Achaemenid seems to have erected elaborate constructions at Persepolis since Artaxerxes I; it is even uncertain if any had long resided in the antiquated buildings of the older capital. We need not be surprised if the deserted buildings strewn over the platform had a certain appeal for the gloomy Ochus, who appears to have constructed his own palace on the highest point of the terrace,[15] from which he would overlook the whole field of ruin.

ACCESSION OF ARSES; INVASION BY PHILIP

Just as Philip was destroying Greek independence at Charoneia (338), Ochus was poisoned by his physician on the order of the eunuch Bagoas and was apparently buried in the cliff behind the Persepolis platform, north of his father's tomb. Before his own were terraces of rough stone to protect from the vulgar herd the dead monarch as he slept high above the ruins he had loved.

Bloodthirsty as Ochus had shown himself to be, he was an able ruler, and it is not too far wrong to say that, by his murder, Bagoas destroyed the Persian Empire. The eunuch kingmaker placed on the throne Arses, son of Ochus by Atossa, who on his coins appears with huge beaked nose, broad face, and long, sharp beard.[16]

The assassination of Ochus changed the whole international situation. When an opportunity was presented for a renewal of the crusading idea, Philip was not the man to be slow in taking advantage. Late in this year 338 a Greek league was formed at Corinth, and Philip demanded reparation for the aid given to Perinthus. Arses' refusal to consider the demand was treated as a cause for war, and near the end of 337 Philip was chosen commander-in-chief for the now popular crusade. That year also, Timotheus (345–337) was followed at Heracleia

13 E. Herzfeld, *Archäologische Mittheilungen aus Iran*, IV (1932), 85; *Altpersische Inschriften* (1938), No. 25.

14 V. Scheil, *Inscriptions des Achéménides à Suse* ("Mém.," Vol. XXI [1929]), pp. 99–100; J. M. Unvala, in A. U. Pope (ed.), *Survey of Persian Art*, I, 34–35.

15 Schmidt notes that clues of the existence of a palace have been detected beneath the mass of loose chips at this point.

16 Diod. xvii. 5. 3–4; Trog. x; Arr. *Anab.* ii. 14. 5; Aelian. *Var. hist.* iv. 8; Chron. Oxyrhync. 4; Babelon, *op. cit.*, p. 626.

by his brother Dionysius (337–305), and Ariobarzanes (365–337) was succeeded in Cius by Mithridates (337–302).[17]

Philip's crusade began at once. Ten thousand Macedonians, led by Attalus and Parmenion and supported by a fleet, appeared early in 336 in Asia and announced that they had orders to "liberate" all the Greek cities under rule of the Persians. They found a warm reception in Cyzicus, and also in Ephesus—now dominated by Heropythes—where a statue of Philip was set up in the market place. Pixodarus assumed that the invasion was an accomplished fact and to protect himself offered Ada, his daughter by the Cappadocian Aphenis, in marriage to Arrhidaeus, Philip's illegitimate son. Alexander, the rightful heir, scenting a plot which would lead to his own loss of favor, hurried off the tragic poet Thessalus to suggest himself as a preferable son-in-law. The Carian was delighted at the better offer, but Philip had no intention of prejudicing the crusade by an inopportune alliance with a Persian vassal and put an end to the intrigue. Alexander was out of favor.[18]

ACCESSION OF DARIUS III

Arses objected to the tyrannical control exercised by the eunuch kingmaker and attempted to poison him, but he himself fell a victim to the draught after reigning less than two full years (November, 338, to June, 336). All his children were slain, and Bagoas presented the empty throne to the forty-five-year-old Darius. That he was only a son of Arsames, son of Ostanes, the brother of Artaxerxes II, shows how completely the main line of the royal house had been wiped out by Ochus and Bagoas.

The new king had already proved his martial ability by defeating a Cadusian rebel in single combat; for this feat of arms, he had been rewarded with the difficult satrapy of Armenia. His coins depict a strong mature face with aquiline nose and short beard, and he might have proved a good ruler had conditions been normal. At any rate, he quickly found an opportunity to show his mettle; alarmed at the intractability of his new appointee, Bagoas attempted to add him to those poisoned, but Darius forced the eunuch himself to drink the fatal cup.[19]

[17] *IG* (ed. minor), Vol. II, No. 236; Dittenberger, *Syl.*[3], No. 260; Arr. *Anab.* ii. 15; Diod. xvi. 88. 5; 89. 2–3; 90. 2.

[18] Diod. xvi. 91. 1–2; xvii. 7. 3; Just. ix. 5. 8; Trog. ix; Strabo xiv. 2. 17; Plut. *Alex.* 10; Arr. *Anab.* i. 17. 10–11; ii. 14. 2; iii. 2. 5; Curt. vii. 1. 3; Polyaen. v. 44.45.

[19] Diod. xvii. 5. 4 ff.; 6. 1–2; 7. 1; Trog. x; Just. x. 3. 2 ff.; Plut. *De Alex. fort.* 326E, 340B; Chron. Oxyrhync. 5; Arr. *Anab.* ii. 14. 5; Curt. vi. 3. 12; 4. 10; Johan. Ant., Frags. 38–39; Babelon, *op. cit.*, pp. 63 ff.

THE TROUBLES OF ALEXANDER

Shortly thereafter, in July of 336, Philip was murdered—some thought not without the guilty knowledge of the disgraced Alexander or of his mother, the fiery Olympias. The young king himself blamed the assassination on the agents of Darius, who had boasted of the deed in intercepted letters.[20] Whether the boast was true or not, some of the conspirators did seek refuge with the Persians.

The twenty-year-old Alexander found himself in no position to carry on the crusade at once. Greece was threatening to rise in rebellion, and there was imminent danger of attack from the barbarians to the north. Nor were matters going too well with the Macedonian troops in Asia. Memnon, now admiral of the Persian fleet, defeated them in a pitched battle near Magnesia. Summoned by the oligarchs, he then entered Ephesus; the great temple of Artemis was looted, Philip's statue was cast down, and the tomb of the liberator Heropythes in the market place was dug up. Parmenion won a fleeting success when Gryneium across the gulf from Pitane was captured and the citizens sold as slaves; but, when he attempted the siege of Pitane itself, Memnon forced its abandonment. Then Parmenion was recalled to fight in Europe. Memnon failed in an attempt to occupy Cyzicus under pretense that he was Parmenion's successor Calas, but he defeated Calas himself in the Troad and forced his retreat to Rhoeteum. So sure was Pixodarus that Persia would be the victor that he married Ada—once offered to Arrhidaeus—to the satrap Orontobates in sign of return to Persian allegiance.[21]

PERSIAN LOSS AND RECAPTURE OF EGYPT

Meanwhile Bagoas' murder of Ochus had brought quick reaction in Egypt. As Petosiris tells us, "the south was in disorder, the north was in revolt." A certain Khababasha, whose name suggests an Ethiopian origin, made his appearance in the south late in 337.[22] His year one, month Athyr (beginning January 14, 336), dates a marriage contract with Teos, the pastophorus of the Amon of Karnak in western Thebes; the document is complete with witnesses, all of whom write their autograph signatures.[23] A slingshot bearing the demotic name of Khaba-

---

[20] Arr. *Anab.* ii. 14. 5; cf. Curt. iv. 1. 12.

[21] Polyaen. v. 44. 4–5; Diod. xvii. 7. 9–10; Arr. *Anab.* i. 17. 9 ff.; 23. 8; Strabo xiv. 2. 17; for possible coins cf. Babelon, *op. cit.*, p. 123.

[22] Arses came to the throne before April 19, 337; it is rather improbable that Khababasha followed Persian practice and counted his first year from November 15, 337 (but see R. A. Parker, "Persian and Egyptian Chronology," *AJSL*, LVIII [1941], 285 ff., esp. pp. 298–99).

[23] W. Spiegelberg, *Papyrus Libbey* (1907).

basha, found among the ruins of the palace of Apries at Memphis,[24] suggests that the rebel had taken the ancient capital by assault. Memphis was well treated. Khababasha possessed sufficient resources to prepare a magnificent sarcophagus of polished black granite for the Apis calf which died prematurely in the second regnal year, during the month beginning January 12, 335, and which he then buried in the neighboring Serapeum.[25]

Khababasha visited the Delta and, in order to ward off the Asiatic fleet from Egypt, inspected every branch of the Nile which flows into the sea. On this visit, he reached Pe-Dep, the two quarters of Buto, and came to the marshland called the "land of Buto." Then said His Majesty to his attendants: "Inform me about this marshland."

Now they related before His Majesty: "The marshland called the land of Buto belonged to the gods of Pe-Dep from of old, before the wicked Khshrish [in reality it was Artaxerxes Ochus, not Xerxes] confiscated it. He offered in it no sacrifices to the gods of Pe-Dep." Then said His Majesty: "Bring the priests and the great ones of Pe-Dep." They were brought to him quickly. Then said His Majesty: "Let me know what the spirits of the gods of Pe-Dep did to the wicked man on account of his wickedness. Behold, they relate that the wicked Xerxes acted wickedly against Pe-Dep in taking away its property." Then they said before His Majesty: "Prince our lord! Horus, son of Isis and son of Osiris, prince of princes, king of the kings of Upper and Lower Egypt, avenger of his father, lord of Pe, the beginning and the end of the gods, whom no king resembles, he has expelled the wicked Xerxes from his palace with his eldest son. This has become known this day at Sais, the city of Neith, at the side of the mother of the god." (News has just reached the Delta that in the spring of 336 Arses has followed Ochus in death, and the deeds of Bagoas are attributed to the wrath of the Egyptian king-god!)

But the king realizes that he is actually no Horus: "O thou god who art mighty among the gods, whom no king resembles, lead me on the way of His Majesty Harendotes that I may live for him." Then said the priests and great ones of Pe-Dep: "May your majesty command that the marshland called the land of Buto be restored to the gods of Pe-Dep with bread, beverages, oxen, geese, and all good things." The king of Upper and Lower Egypt, likeness of the god Tenen, chosen of Ptah, son of Ra, Khababasha, living forever, presented the

[24] W. M. F. Petrie, *Palace of Apries* (1909), pp. 11, 16.

[25] B. Gunn, *AS*, XXVI (1926), 86-87.

marshland to the gods, the souls of Buto, and with it many royal gifts.[26]

While Alexander was quieting the tribes on the northern border and while Thebes and Athens were plotting revolt, Darius undertook the reconquest of Egypt. Khababasha sought to guard the Delta against the Asiatic fleet; all was in vain, however, for Darius was accepted as king of Egypt before January 14, 334, when a demotic document witnesses in his name an exchange of property,[27] and Khababasha all but disappears from history. To be sure, the first Ptolemy recognized him as a legitimate ruler, but Manetho, writing under the second Ptolemy, refused to insert his name in the royal lists, and he was quite unknown to the Greeks. The newly appointed satrap was Sabaces, who issued a large satrapial coinage in preparation for the approaching Macedonian invasion of Egypt; he then went off to die for Darius at Issus.[28]

BUILDING ACTIVITY OF DARIUS III AT PERSEPOLIS

In the breathing-spell thus afforded him, Darius returned to Persepolis, where he at least began his tomb and apparently threw together some sort of palace. The latter he erected in the only space remaining on the terrace: in the section bounded on the north by the palace of Darius I, on the east by that of Xerxes, and on the west and south by the edge of the high terrace. In ground plan his palace imitated that of Xerxes, but there were significant variations. It was smaller, and, instead of a great double stairway to the north, its only entrance was a short and narrow flight of steps in the northwest corner beyond the courtyard wall. These steps led into a northern portico like that of Xerxes, but the substitution of a court wall for the double stairway cut off the fine front view. There was no space for the centrally arranged interiors which his predecessors had built, and thus the large reception hall to the west, filled with sixteen columns, does

---

[26] Satrap Stele of Ptolemy I: H. Brugsch, *ÄZ*, IX (1871), 1 ff.; J. P. Mahaffey, *History of Egypt under the Ptolemaic Dynasty* (1899), pp. 38 ff.; U. Wilcken, *ÄZ*, XXXV (1897), 81 ff.; Sethe, *Urkunden des aegyptischen Altertums*, II (1904), 38 ff.; for dating, see Spiegelberg, *op. cit.*, pp. 2–3.

[27] F. L. Griffith, *Catalogue of the Demotic Papyri in the John Rylands Library*, III (1909), 32; cf. E. Revillout, *Notice des papyrus démotiques archaiques* (1896), pp. 480 ff. H. W. Fairman, in R. Mond and O. H. Myers, *The Bucheum*, II (1934), 3, publishes the stele of a Buchis bull which was born under Darius III and buried in 330–329 under Alexander.

[28] Arr. *Anab.* ii. 11. 8. For the coinage of Sabaces, see J. P. Six, *Numismatic Chronicle*, VIII (3d ser., 1888), 132 ff.; Edward T. Newell, *Numismatic Notes and Monographs*, No. 82 (1938), pp. 62 ff.; cf. M. Rostovtzeff, *The Social and Economic History of the Hellenistic World* (1941), pp. 89 and 1326, n. 20, Pl. XI, No. 7.

not balance the two small retiring rooms to the east, one with only four columns. Reliefs decorate the court wall along the front of the north portico. Together with other fragments in this most westerly courtyard they prove the absence of artistic integrity new at this site, for they were removed from elsewhere; also reused are sculptured blocks on the adjoining corner to the east—before the prolongation of the stairway which connects the courtyard in front of the palace of Xerxes to the courtyard between the palaces of Darius I and Darius III. These figures show what we have lost of a still virile art through the looting of Darius III at Persepolis. As for the reliefs on a tomb he had started to the south, they are rough and coarse, even if we attempt to excuse them as being merely blocked out; they mark the end of the marvelous Achaemenid art.

Chapter XXXV

ALEXANDER, HEIR TO THE CRUSADE

THE START OF THE CRUSADE: THE BATTLE ON THE GRANICUS

ATHENS requested financial aid from the Great King for its proposed revolt against Alexander, but Darius, after his recovery of Egypt, was so confident that there could be no danger from the youthful Macedonian that he replied: "I will not give you gold; do not ask me, for you will not get it!"[1] Alexander returned victorious from the north, the Greek revolt was put down, and Thebes was wantonly leveled to the ground in punishment. Nevertheless, the young conqueror was recommissioned by the league to carry on the crusade of civilized Greeks against the Persian barbarians. Awake at last, Darius sent off three hundred talents to Greece. Officially, Athens refused the gift, though Demosthenes took seventy for himself; Sparta was less reluctant. The great orator also wrote the generals in Asia, calling Alexander a boy and a fool. Charidemus fled to Darius.[2]

As his father's successor, Alexander was now the leader of the great crusade. Including allies and Greek mercenaries, he had at his disposal some thirty-five thousand troops, but the core was the Macedonian phalanx, and the most important single element was the native cavalry. Greek culture was equally well represented on the crusade. Private secretaries, Eumenes of Cardia and Diodotus of Erythrae, were ready to compile ephemerides, day-by-day accounts of the progress of the expedition. Professional historians, like Callisthenes, the nephew of Aristotle, and Onesicritus, a pupil of Diogenes who had already written a treatise on Alexander's education, were also present, ready to adorn the dull reports from the war front with all the rhetorical tricks demanded of contemporary historiography. The roads were measured by surveyors: Baeton, Diognetus, Philonides, and Amyntus. Botanists, geographers, and other scientists increased the staff.[3]

[1] Aeschin. *Ctes.* 238–39.

[2] *Ibid.* 156, 173, 209, 239–40, 257; Deinarch. *Demosthen.* 10, 18; Plut. *Demosthen.* 14. 2; 20. 4–5; 23. 2; *De Alex. fort.* 327D; 848E; Arr. *Anab.* i. 10. 6; Aelian. *Var. hist.* iv. 8. Justin (xi. 2. 7) ascribes the fall of Athens and Thebes to Demosthenes' Persian gold.

[3] Fragments of Callisthenes in F. Jacoby, *Die Fragmente der griechischen Historiker*, II B (1927), 631 ff.; cf. W. K. Prentice, "Callisthenes, the Original Historian of Alexander," *Transactions of*

In 334, shortly after the reconquest of Egypt by Darius, the crusade was inaugurated with all due ceremony. Xerxes had made it clear that his expedition was the Trojan War in reverse; Alexander therefore in turn reversed the details of this most famous of all oriental attacks. Xerxes had crosssed the bridge at Sestus; Parmenion, with his transports guarded by a hundred and fifty triremes, was now assigned the task of ferrying the army from Sestus across the Hellespont to Abydos. Xerxes had sacrificed at the crossing; Alexander sacrificed a bull to Poseidon and from another bowl poured a libation to the sea-goddess. His progress was halted by Lampsacus, which remained loyal to its Persian master; for such anti-Hellenic action, Alexander threatened complete destruction, but the citizens sent as ambassador the historian Anaximenes, who tricked the invader into granting them pardon.[4]

Ilium, now sunk to a mere village with a poverty-stricken temple, was the first stop. As the Magi of Xerxes had poured libations to the *fravashis* of the Trojan heroes, so Alexander poured libations to the heroes from Greece and ran nude around the traditional tomb of their greatest, Achilles. Sacrifices again honored the local Athena; in her temple Alexander dedicated his own armor and took in exchange the armor said to have belonged to the Greek victors. But sacrifices of aversion were offered to the shades of Priam, with the prayer that he be not angry with a descendant of Neoptolemus. Thus the world was informed that this was the second Trojan War, like the first, a crusade of enlightened Greeks from Europe against Asiatic barbarians.[5]

Experienced generals—Arsames, Reomithres, Petines, and Niphates —led the Persian armies. These were assisted by local levies; some were raised by Spithridates, satrap of Lydia and Ionia and brother of the former satrap Roesaces (whose coins were minted at Lampsacus and Cyme); others by Arsites, cavalry commander of Hellespontine Phrygia. Increased by twenty thousand Persian cavalry and almost the same number of Greek mercenaries under Memnon, the huge force collected at Zeleia, a few miles southwest of Cyzicus.

Memnon wisely advised retirement and the burning of cities and crops, but Arsites bombastically announced that he would not permit a single house to be destroyed in *his* satrapy. The Persians, suspicious

---

the American Philological Association, LIV (1923), 74 ff.; for the Ephemerides see Jacoby, *op. cit.*, II B, 618 ff.; cf. C. A. Robinson, Jr., *The Ephemerides of Alexander's Expedition* (1932). For the road surveyors cf. Jacoby, *op. cit.*, II B, 622 ff.; cf. Arr. *Anab.* i. 11. 3; Diog. Laert. vi. 84.

[4] Diod. xvii. 17; Arr. *Anab.* i. 11. 6–7; Paus. vi. 18. 3.

[5] Diod. xvii. 17. 6–7; 18. 1; Just. xi. 5. 12; Plut. *Alex.* 15. 4; Arr. *Anab.* i. 11. 7.

of Memnon as a Greek, supported the policy of Arsites. The army then marched west to the Granicus, behind whose high banks the troops drew up.

An immediate battle was just what the Macedonian strategists desired. In May, Alexander marched out to meet his opponents. Although the Persian troops were not too greatly superior in numbers, the first attempt to cross was a failure. When at last Alexander himself forded the stream, he was assailed on all sides by the Persian nobles; his helmet was smashed, and he barely escaped death at the hand of Spithridates. His effort, however, turned the tide. The long list of Persian dead—the generals Niphates and Petines, the satraps Spithridates and Mithrobarzanes, the nobles Arbupales, Mithridates, and Pharnaces (the son, son-in-law, and brother-in-law of Darius, respectively), and Omares, leader of the native mercenaries—showed how Persians could yet sacrifice themselves for their king. Rightfully blamed for the catastrophe, Arsites committed suicide.[6]

No effort was made to pursue the native cavalry, and Persians who surrendered were sent home. Instead, the whole vengeance of Alexander was poured out upon the unlucky Greek mercenaries, who, to the excited crusaders, were traitors to the cause of Hellenism, since contrary to the common desire they had fought for barbarians against the Greeks! Although they begged for quarter, nine-tenths of them were slaughtered, leaving only two thousand to expiate their sins as slaves on Macedonian estates. Their relatives back home in Greece would not forget such savagery, and Greek mercenaries in Persian pay had their warning: against Alexander they must fight to the death.[7]

ADAPTATION OF PERSIAN METHODS OF ADMINISTRATION

But already the veneer of Greek thought given him by Aristotle was beginning to wear thin. Already Alexander was coming to realize that his future subjects would include Orientals as well as Macedonians and Greeks. Immediately after Granicus, he initiated one policy which more and more was to be observed as time passed on. Ilium, alien though it was to Greece according to current thought, was constituted a free city under a restored democracy; the Persian tribute was remitted, new buildings fit for its ancient glory and its new significance were ordered constructed, and Alexander himself made a dedication to

[6] Arr. *Anab.* i. 13 ff.; list of dead, i. 16. 3; Diod. xvii. 19 ff.; Strabo xiii. 1. 11; Just. xi. 6. 10 ff.; Plut. *De Alex. fort.* 326F; *Alex.* 16; Marmor Parium B, 3; Frag. Sabbaticum (Jacoby, *op. cit.*, II B, 819); Chron. Oxyrhync. 5 (*ibid.*, p. 1153); Pap. Oxyrhync. 1798 (*ibid.*, p. 816).

[7] Arr. *Anab.* i. 16. 6; Plut. *Alex.* 16. 7.

Athena Polias.[8] This was to be the first of many city foundations, intended to recommend Greek city institutions and Greek culture to the natives of the interior.

With this effort at Hellenization went, however, the adoption of Persian administration for the satrapy as a whole. Calas was appointed satrap and ordered to collect the same taxes as under the Persians. Parmenion occupied abandoned Dascyleium, once the capital of the satrapy. The citizens of Zeleia were forgiven, since they were not responsible for the battle; such clemency paid, for on his march Alexander was met by Mithrines, garrison commander of the Sardis acropolis, and by the whole body of citizens, who, in return for his promise to allow the Lydians to follow their ancestral customs, surrendered the accumulated treasure stored in the citadel. A thunderstorm over the palace of the Lydian kings was an omen for the restoration of the temple of the native god now identified as Zeus Olympius. In the citadel he found other treasure: correspondence between the king's generals and Demosthenes to indicate how much money had been sent to the orator.[9]

With the organization of Lydia, Alexander took another step in his imitation of Persian administration. Asander, son of Philotas, a Macedonian, was appointed satrap; unlike Calas, he was not permitted to collect the taxes, contributions, and tribute, a task assigned to the Greek Nicias. Again following Persian custom, still another Macedonian, Pausanias, was made citadel commander in Sardis. Thus the Persian division of satrapal authority between three different officials, each directly responsible to the king, was retained, but it was an innovation to place the satrapal finances in charge of a Greek.[10]

Long-deserted Smyrna was the second of Alexander's city foundations. The Greek mercenaries fled from Ephesus; the exiles were restored and the government turned back to a democracy. Riots against the pro-Persians, however, were put down. The Artemis temple was ordered rebuilt by the taxes the citizens had paid to their former masters. Alexander, it was said, offered to pay the entire expense if an inscription regarding his generosity was carved on the temple; diplomatically the citizens replied that it was improper for a god to dedicate offerings to other divinities. Thereafter he extended the limits of

[8] Diod. xviii. 4. 5; Strabo xiii. 1. 26; Arr. *Anab.* i. 12. 1–5; Dittenberger, *Syl.*³, No. 277.

[9] Callisthen., Frag. 29(J); Diod. xvii. 21. 7; Plut. *Alex.* 17. 1; *Demosthen.* 20. 5; Arr. *Anab.* i. 17. 2 ff.

[10] Arr. *Anab.* i. 17. 7.

the refuge zone about the temple by a stade, sacrificed in person to Artemis, and led his troops in the sacred procession.[11]

CONQUEST OF THE AEGEAN

Parmenion was sent to receive the submission of Magnesia on the Maeander and of Tralleis. Lysimachus proceeded to the Aeolian and Ionian cities with orders to restore the democracies and the ancient laws but only on payment of the former taxes. The mercenaries in garrison at Miletus offered to submit when Nicanor arrived off Lade with one hundred and sixty ships. Three days later the superior Persian fleet of four hundred vessels anchored off Mycale and changed the situation. Hegesistratus had already surrendered the outer city by letter, but when the Persian fleet arrived and offered the hope of assistance, he determined to fight for the inner city. The citizens declared their intention to remain neutral. At daybreak, Alexander stormed the walls, while his fleet held off the awaited Persians. The greater number of the mercenaries were again slaughtered, but this time they fought to the last. A few escaped to the island; there they were enrolled by Alexander, who had been brought to realize his mistake, and thus another ideal of the crusade yielded to stern necessity! Alexander then exposed himself to a terrible risk by disbanding his own fleet; his justification was that he did not possess sufficient funds to keep up an expensive navy, and he was quite sure that there would be little danger once he had captured the shore bases of Memnon's fleet. Miletus had now surrendered, and its long-silent oracle of Apollo at Branchidae was, in reward, once more brought into action. Priene was freed of contribution and Erythrae from tribute.[12]

Pixodarus had died, and his son-in-law Orontobates had been ordered by the king to assume charge of Halicarnassus. His claim, through marriage to Ada, daughter of Pixodarus, was resisted by another Ada, the widow of Idrieus, who held out in the strong Carian fortress of Alinda, southwest of Alabanda. On the road she met Alexander and adopted him as her own son.

Halicarnassus had been well fortified by Memnon and filled with Persians and mercenaries. An attack on Myndus, following a proposal to surrender, was a failure, and Alexander returned to the siege of Halicarnassus. Orontobates and Memnon fired the city and retired

[11] Strabo xiv. 1. 22–23; Arr. *Anab.* i. 17. 9 ff.

[12] Callisthen., Frag. 30(J); Diod. xvii. 22; Strabo xiv. 1. 7; xvii. 1. 43; Arr. *Anab.* i. 18. 3 ff. C. T. Newton (ed.), *The Collection of Ancient Greek Inscriptions in the British Museum*, Part III, Sec. 1 (1886), No. 400; C. Michel, *Recueil d'inscriptions grecques* (1900), No. 37. 22–23.

into the citadel. Alexander completed the destruction of the unfortunate city and left three thousand mercenaries to garrison Caria, which
he granted to Ada with the title of queen; soon after, Ada brought
about the surrender of the citadel.[13]

By this time, winter was approaching, and Alexander prepared to
reduce the warlike hill tribes. First, he took Hyparna, again granting
terms to the mercenaries. Telmessus, Xanthus, Pinara, and Patara surrendered. Perhaps the reason is found in the last inscription we possess
in the native Lycian character. Here Ekowa, son of Epraseda, is a descendant of the well-known Arttompara the Mede; he is, however, a
general of the Lycian army under Alakhssantra, in whom we recognize Alexander!

Milyas was destroyed to open the defiles; its territory, though belonging to greater Phrygia, was counted to Lycia. The great fortified
rock of the Marmareis in the far interior was captured. Phasaelis sent
the conqueror a golden crown. Alexander assaulted a Phrygian out-
post which endangered the Lycians.[14] The whole west and southwest
coast had submitted. The abandonment of the fleet appeared to have
been justified, for by land operations alone Alexander had captured all
the naval bases on the mainland, and the Persian navy must abandon
the Aegean.

When Amyntas had deserted to the king, he had brought a letter
from a certain Alexander, son of Aeropus, whose brothers had assisted
in the murder of Philip. Darius ordered Sisines to go to Atizyes, satrap of Phrygia, and through him to inform this Alexander that if he
would assassinate his greater namesake he would be placed on the
Macedonian throne with the gift of a thousand talents of gold. Parmenion, however, captured Sisines, and learned the plot; the arrest of
the would-be pretender followed.[15]

INLAND TO PHRYGIA

With the Aegean believed safe, Alexander could advance toward
Perga, a stiff north wind permitting a march along the very shore at
the notorious "Ladder," in water up to the waist. An embassy from
Aspendus promised surrender but requested that the city be spared a
garrison; the request was granted in return for fifty talents in support
of the army and the transfer of the horses bred for the Great King.

[13] Diod. xvii. 24 ff.; Strabo xiv. 2. 17; Plut. *Alex.* 22. 4; Arr. *Anab.* i. 23. 7–8.
[14] *TAM*, Vol. I, No. 29; Strabo xiv. 3. 9; Diod. xviii. 28; Arr. *Anab.* i. 24. 4 ff.
[15] Arr. *Anab.* i. 25. 3 ff.

Along the coast, he marched as far east as Side, then turned toward the interior, where he vainly assaulted Syllium; at this point, he learned that the Aspendians had determined to fight. Abandoning the lower city, they had collected on the steep hill overlooking the Eurymedon, but when Alexander returned they offered surrender on the former terms. Their offer was rejected, and they found that now they must pay an indemnity of a hundred talents instead of the fifty, must promise obedience to the satrap and pay a regular tribute, and must undergo an investigation as to their right to hold the territory their neighbors asserted they had stolen.[16]

To reach Phrygia, Alexander again turned north. The Telmessians blocked the road between two heights, on one of which was their city. When the Macedonians pitched camp, the greater number abandoned the spot and the light-armed secured the road. An embassy from the Selgians and other Pisidians hostile to the Telmessians was granted friendship. Telmessus was abandoned entirely, and the natives retired to Sagalassus, occupied by the most warlike of the Pisidians; when their combined forces were defeated, Sagalassus was taken, and with it other Pisidian towns. More fortunate than his Iranian predecessors, Alexander had tamed—for the moment—these wild mountaineers.[17]

By Lake Ascania, where salt was gathered, Alexander reached Celaenae, whose steep acropolis was garrisoned by the satrap of Phrygia. The city was occupied, but the garrison, having retired to the citadel, promised to surrender if not relieved by a certain day. To watch the Persian satrap, Antigonus, son of Philip, was left behind with fifteen hundred soldiers as Alexander's own satrap.[18]

BRIEF SETBACK ON THE AEGEAN COAST

Meanwhile, the tide of war had turned again in the Aegean. The Persian fleet had indeed been rendered ineffective by Alexander's possession of the continental bases, but he had believed also that his land army could sufficiently guard his communications. This belief now proved to be almost entirely wrong. Memnon, instead of falling back on Cyprus and Phoenicia, seized Chios through treachery and occupied Lesbos—all but Mitylene, which was undergoing siege. Many other islands were sending him friendly embassies. In Europe, the

---

[16] Callisthen., Frags. 31–32 (J); Strabo xiv. 3. 9; 4. 1; Joseph. *Ant.* ii. 348; Arr. *Anab.* i. 26–27; Frag. Sabbait. 2.

[17] Strabo xii. 7. 3; Arr. *Anab.* i. 27. 5 ff.; 28.   [18] Curt. iii. 1 ff.; Arr. *Anab.* i. 29. 1 ff.

Spartans willingly received his gold. From these new bases, directly athwart Alexander's thin life-line back home, there was even greater danger of his communications being cut, and now he had no fleet!

But the Fortune in which his age so completely trusted had not yet forgotten Alexander. Just at this crucial instant Memnon died, and his tactical skill and energy were lost to Darius, though the loss was not immediately evident. Autophradates and Memnon's nephew, Pharnabazus, continued the blockade of Mitylene, which at last surrendered on terms: the pillars on which was engraved the treaty with Alexander must be removed; the exiles must be restored (which meant that pro-Persians were again in authority) and must be given half of their former possessions; and the Mitylenians must become allies on the terms of the King's Peace. Lycomedes of Rhodes was made commander of the imposed garrison, the exile Diogenes became tyrant, and the rich had to pay a fine and the commoners a general tax.

Pharnabazus transported the mercenaries to Lycia to recover Alexander's conquests. Autophradates won over some of the remaining islands which hitherto had continued loyal to Alexander. The crusader was facing imminent destruction when Darius made his next mistake, his dispatch of Mentor's son Thymondas to take over command of the mercenaries from Pharnabazus and to lead them direct to the king. Although Pharnabazus was officially assigned Memnon's position, loss of the mercenaries seriously weakened his chance of cutting off Alexander from Macedonia and reinforcements; nevertheless, he joined Autophradates and compelled Tenedos, still closer to Alexander's base, to destroy the treaty pillars and to accept the king's peace. Datames was dispatched to the Cyclades, but Proteas won over the majority of his ships and drove him off. Memnon's plan had failed when the guiding mind of the great strategist no longer functioned. Once more Fortune had intervened in behalf of Alexander.[19]

ON TO CILICIA

In the spring of 333, unmindful of the threat to the crusade, Alexander was in Gordium, the oldest Phrygian capital. In the temple of Zeus on the acropolis he cut with his sword the knot which bound the wagon of Midas and thus, according to traditional belief, won by unorthodox practice the lordship of Asia.[20] At Ancyra an embassy from Paphlagonia offered surrender but requested him not to enter their land with an army; they were ordered to obey Calas, the satrap of

---

[19] Diod. xvii. 29; Plut. *Alex.* 18. 3; Arr. *Anab.* ii. 1–2; Curt. iii. 1. 19 ff.; 3. 1–2.

[20] Just. xi. 7. 3 ff.; Plut. *Alex.* 18, 1–2; Arr. *Anab.* ii. 3; Curt. iii. 1. 12 ff.

Phrygia, but no tribute was imposed. Cappadocia also made a distant submission and was placed under the satrap Sabictas; there is no mention at this time of Ariarathes, who had succeeded Abd Susim as Persian satrap the year before.[21] But after Alexander passed on he was to return. Just before entering Cilicia, Alexander received five thousand infantry and eight hundred cavalry from Macedonia; the life-line back home was still in operation. The Cilician Gates had been occupied, but the defenders fled on the Macedonian approach, and the almost impassable gorge was open. It was reported that Arsames, the satrap of Cilicia, intended to plunder and abandon Tarsus; cavalry and light-armed were rushed ahead and prevented serious damage. Further advance from Tarsus was delayed by a dangerous, almost fatal, illness of Alexander, induced by a bath in the ice-cold waters of the Cydnus.[22]

Parmenion hurried eastward to occupy the Syrian Gates, while Alexander at his leisure visited the tomb of Assyrian Sardanapallus at Anchiale. Pro-Persian Soli was fined two hundred talents, and the Cilicians who occupied the heights were driven off. News arrived that Halicarnassus had at last surrendered. Returning to Tarsus, Alexander marched through the Aleian plain to the Pyramus, sacrificing at Magarsus to the local Athena and at Mallus to the local hero Amphilochus. Internal dissensions in the two cities were ended and their tribute was remitted, for Mallūs was an Argive colony and Alexander claimed to be a descendant of the Argive Heraclidae.[23] Soon thereafter, Balacrus, son of Nicanor, was appointed satrap of Cilicia and remitted the hostages and the fine of fifty talents imposed upon Soli.

Alexander had now traversed Asia Minor. His zigzag route has been given in some detail, since it affords one last full glimpse of the country under the rule of the Persian Empire. For the coming Hellenistic age, the picture is equally significant.

THE BATTLE AT ISSUS

At Mallus, Alexander first learned that the huge army brought together at Babylon by Darius was now at Sochi in northern Syria, two days from the Amanus Gates. While Darius was traversing these Gates, Alexander followed Parmenion through the Syrian Gates a few miles to the south and advanced eastward toward Sochi. Thus, when Darius himself reached the exit from the Amanus Gates, he dis-

[21] Diod. xxxi. 19. 4.

[22] Diod. xvii. 31. 4 ff.; Just. xi. 8. 3 ff.; Plut. *Alex.* 19. 1; Arr. *Anab.* ii. 4. 1 ff.; Curt. iii. 1. 22 ff.; 4 ff.; Frag. Sabbait. 6.

[23] Callisthen., Frag. 34(J); Diod. xvii. 32. 2; Strabo xiv. 5. 16; Arr. *Anab.* ii. 5; Curt. iii. 7. 2 ff.

covered that he was squarely planted across Alexander's line of retreat and could either attack him from the rear or cut off his communications with Macedonia. The Macedonian deserter, Amyntas, son of
Antiochus, rightly advised Darius to remain at this point and watch
the outcome of events.

But the Fortune of Alexander still was on guard, and the same evil
star which had ruined Xerxes and his generals yet hovered over
Darius. He listened to his obsequious courtiers, telling him that
Alexander was delaying in Cilicia through fear. The same report
reached Athens: Darius had come down to the seacoast with all his
troops; Alexander was shut up in Cilicia and was in want of everything. Darius therefore cut in behind Alexander and took Issus, killing or mutilating the sick Macedonians left in camp. The Persian
camp was fixed at the Pinarus—an excellent position, since the plain
was a mile and three-quarters wide from sea to foothills; diagonally
across it ran the Pinarus, which could be easily crossed only where it
left the slopes, while the upper course was through hills difficult to
climb.

Alexander retraced his road back through the Syrian Gates a distance of twelve miles—the phalanx in front, then the cavalry, and
last the baggage train. Reaching the plain at daylight, he deployed
the phalanx, first thirty-two deep, then sixteen, and then eight.
Darius formed his battle line at the camp with the Pinarus as protection. By the sea he placed his thirty thousand cavalry, next along the
river a similar number of Greek mercenaries, and the light-armed
along the hills.

The mercenaries were the first to be attacked. Darius, halfway
down the line, summoned the mercenaries to come to his aid from their
wing. Cavalry from his right attacked the Macedonian cavalry, who
made a countercharge. The mercenaries long resisted until Darius fled,
abandoning his mother, his sister-wife, his daughters Stateira and
Drypetis, his infant son Ochus, as well as his chariot, bow, shield, and
cloak. Among the dead were Arsames, Reomithres, Atizyes, Bubaces,
and Sabaces, satrap of Egypt. The battle had been fought with reversed fronts, a situation always fatal for the defeated; the greater
part of the Persians were killed in their flight up the gorges of the
many streams descending from the hills.[24]

[24] Callisthen., Frag. 35(J); unfair criticism of his account, Polyb. xii. 17 ff.; Chares of Mitylene,
Frag. 6(J); Cleitarch., Frag. 8(J); Diod. xvii. 32. 2 ff.; 35 ff.; Just. xi. 9; Plut. *Alex.* 20. 1 ff.;
Arr. *Anab.* ii. 6 ff.; Curt. iii. 8. 12 ff.; Marmor Parium B, 3; Chron. Oxyrhync. 6; Frag. Sabbait.
3 ff.

Chapter XXXVI

THE ORIENTAL GOD-KING

CONQUEST OF PHOENICIA

ISSUS meant the capture of the western half of the empire. The next step in the crusade was to be the occupation of abandoned Syria and Egypt. Menon, son of Cerdimmas, was appointed satrap of Coele-Syria. The Macedonian deserter, Amyntas, fled to Tripolis, and then by Cyprus to Memphis, where he was put to death by Mazaces, the new satrap of Egypt. Gerostratus, king of Arvad, had gone with the other Phoenicians and Cypriotes to serve with the Persian fleet under Autophradates; now that they were cut off, his son Straton met Alexander with a golden crown and surrendered the island city as well as the mainland cities of Marathus, Sigon, and Mariamne.[1]

At Marathus, a great and flourishing city, Alexander received a letter from Darius. He recalled how Philip and the last Artaxerxes had professed friendship and alliance. Only when Arses was made king had Philip taken the first unfriendly action. When Darius ascended the throne, Alexander had sent no embassy to renew the friendship and alliance. It was Alexander who had invaded his country; Darius had fought only defensive actions. As king to king, let Alexander return his family and establish the former friendship and alliance.

Alexander went still farther back into history. The king's ancestors had wantonly invaded Greece; as commander-in-chief of the Greeks, he intended to take vengeance through the new crusade. Coming down to the present, Darius himself had begun the troubles by siding with Perinthus, which had already injured Philip, and had sent his troops into Macedonian Thrace. Philip had then been murdered by conspirators suborned by Darius—of this he had boasted in his letters. With the aid of Bagoas, he had slain Arses and wrongly usurped the throne. He had urged the Greeks to war on Alexander; he had given money to the Spartans, and they had accepted it while others did not. Henceforth Darius must address him as king of Asia.[2]

Darius had sent his treasures to Damascus in care of Cophen, son

[1] Arr. *Anab.* ii. 13. 7–8; Curt. iv. 1. 1 ff., 27 ff.
[2] Arr. *Anab.* ii. 14. 1 ff.; Curt. iv. 1. 7 ff.

of Artabanus, but they were seized by Parmenion, whose letters to Alexander list the booty. Mention is made of gold cups weighing (in Babylonian measure) 73 talents, 52 minas, or about 4,500 pounds, and of other cups inlaid with precious stones weighing 56 talents, 34 minas, or about 3,400 pounds.[3] Ambassadors to the king from Thebes, Sparta, and Athens were taken prisoner—an excellent indication of exactly how "Greek" the crusade was considered in Greece itself.[4] Here also was captured Barsine, daughter of Artabazus and widow of Memnon, whose beauty and Greek education so appealed to the young king that she is said to have become his concubine who bore him a son named Heracles.[5]

Advancing from Marathus, Alexander received the submission of Byblus and an invitation from the anti-Persian Sidonians; in place of the Persian nominee, another Strato, Abdalonymus was granted the kingship. Kings of Cyprus and ambassadors from Tyre also promised submission; not quite sure of the latter's honesty—for Tyre had prospered after the destruction of Sidon by Ochus—Alexander announced that he would visit their island and sacrifice to their Heracles. They replied that it would be more proper to sacrifice in the ancient temple of Baalmelqart on the mainland at Old Tyre; when he insisted that he must visit the island, they declared that they would admit neither Persian nor Macedonian into their city.[6]

Alexander determined on a siege, for by the capture of Tyre the Persian fleet would be cut off from its last Phoenician base. He began the construction of a mole. Tyrian fire ships burned its towers, but new ships were collected from rival Sidon. Gerostratus of Aradus and Enylus of Byblus, informed that Alexander held their cities, deserted Autophradates and returned home. On news of Issus, the kings of Cyprus had brought in their navy of a hundred and twenty ships to the victor; only Pnytagoras of Salamis assisted Tyre. Eighty more vessels from Sidon and ten from Rhodes, Soli, and Lycia were also at the disposal of Alexander.

While the siege was being pressed, Alexander made an excursion toward Arabia into Mount Antilibanus, where fresh hordes of Arabs were forcing their way into the cultivated lands; parts of the country

---

[3] Athen. xi. 781F; xiii. 607F.
[4] Plut. *Alex.* 24. 1; Arr. *Anab.* ii. 15. 1 ff.; 11. 10; Curt. iii. 13; Polyaen. iv. 5.
[5] Just. xi. 10. 2–3; Plut. *Alex.* 21. 4.
[6] Just. xi. 10. 8, 11; Plut. *Alex.* 24. 2; Arr. *Anab.* ii. 15. 6–7; Curt. iv. 1. 15; 2. 4; Marmor Parium B, 4.

surrendered voluntarily and other towns were taken by assault, but he stayed only ten days, and the Arab threat remained for the future.[7] During the siege there arrived other envoys from Darius who offered a ransom of ten thousand talents for his family, cession of all the empire west of the Euphrates, and his daughter in marriage in return for friendship and alliance. Naturally, Alexander again refused.[8]

With his two hundred and ten ships, Alexander now blockaded Tyre from the sea also. The Tyrians were unable to break through. King Azemilchus fled for asylum to the temple of Heracles and was pardoned, but the remaining inhabitants, thirty thousand in number, were sold as slaves. At last Alexander could sacrifice to Heracles in his long-inviolate island home. He could march his army in procession and give a naval review for the god, could hold torch races and games in the sacred inclosure as proof that Baalmelqart was thoroughly Hellenized, and could dedicate the engine which broke the wall and consecrate the captured sacred ship. The enslaved Tyrians were unable to discover why Alexander's Hellenism was to be preferred to the savage treatment of Sidon by barbarian Ochus.[9]

Abdalonymus, just appointed king of Sidon, was now made king of Tyre also. The conquest of Tyre in 332 was taken as a new era of Alexander in Phoenicia. Pnytagoras was sent home, and next summer Salamis was ruled by his successor Nicocreon (331-311).[10]

Palestinian Syria made its submission[11] with the exception of Gaza, which had been fortified by the eunuch Batis and garrisoned by Arab mercenaries, for Gaza was now the sea terminal of the spice trade through Nabataean Petra. Gaza proper lay two and a half miles inland and was separated from the shore by deep sand; it was a large city with a strong wall along the edge of the high mound which covered the debris of much earlier predecessors. First Alexander ordered a counterwall against the south side of the city; after he had been

[7] Chares of Mitylene., Frag. 7(J), in Plut. *Alex*. 24. 6; Strabo xvi. 2. 23; Arr. *Anab*. ii. 17; 20. 1 ff.; Curt. iv. 2. 24; 3. 1; Polyaen. iv. 3. 4.

[8] The date is disputed: Arr. *Anab*. ii. 25. 1 ff. and Curt. iv. 5.1 ff. place the envoy at this time; Diod. xvii. 39. 1; 54; xxxv, 4; Frag. Sabbait. 5, already at Marathus; Just. xi. 12. 1 ff. and Plut. *Alex*. 29. 4; *Reg. imp. apophtheg*. 180B, not until after the return from Egypt.

[9] Diod. xvii. 40 ff.; Just. xi. 10. 12 ff.; Plut. *Alex*. 24. 3 ff.; Arr. *Anab*. ii. 20 ff.; Curt. iv. 2 ff.; Polyaen. iv. 13; Chron. Oxyrhync. 7; Frag. Sabbait. 7.

[10] Chares of Mitylene., Frag. 7(J); Duris vii, Frag. 4(J); Marmor Parium B, 4; Diod. xvii. 46. 5; Athen. iv. 167C-D; J. Rouvier, *Revue des études grecques*, XII (1899), 362.

[11] The story of Alexander's visit to Jerusalem and his reverence of the high priest Jaddua (Joseph. *Ant*. xi. 322 ff.) is unhistorical.

wounded, he completed the circumvallation by a wall a quarter of a mile broad and two hundred and fifty feet high. Engines and tunnels employed by the defense proved of no avail; at last the walls were scaled and the gates opened from within. The garrison still fought on, and all died at their posts. With the usual barbarity, the women and children taken were sold as slaves. The site was handed over to the neighbor tribes, but Gaza itself remained uninhabited. Hundreds of talents of myrrh and frankincense were carried off as loot, a heavy loss to Nabataean merchants.[12]

DISAFFECTION IN ASIA MINOR

In the interval the Persians who had escaped from Issus had retreated northward and had recovered Paphlagonia and Pontic Cappadocia. At their head was their former satrap Ariwarat (Ariarathes), who had already set his name in Aramaic on coins which imitated the nymph of Sinope and the eagle grasping the dolphin in its claws, a motif employed by his predecessor Abd Susim. After Alexander had passed on, Ariwarat repeated the oriental griffin devouring the Greek stag. Encouraged to advance into the Taurus, he added southern Cappadocia to his kingdom. Some of the coins newly minted at Tarsus by Mazdai fell into his hands, and from their design he copied the Greek half-nude Zeus for his own Baal of Gazur (Gaziura),[13] which he was to make his capital of a Cappadocian kingdom after Darius, his former master, was no more.[14]

Ariwarat is then worthy of remembrance as the first of a dynasty of Iranian kings of Cappadocia who were to preserve that country's independence throughout the whole of the Hellenistic period.[15] With his fellow-satraps, after their return, he attacked Alexander's general Antigonus in Phrygia. They were defeated, and Antigonus again pacified Lycaonia. Calas, now satrap of Hellespontine Phrygia, won back for the moment Paphlagonia, only to be driven off by another Oriental, Bas, Anatolian king of Bithynia. Once more the news was ominous for the future.[16]

[12] Hegesias Magnes., Frag. 5(J); Diod. xvii. 48. 7; Strabo xvi. 2. 30; Plut. *Alex.* 25. 3 ff.; *De Alex. fort.* 2; Arr. *Anab.* ii. 25. 4; 26–27; Curt. iv. 6. 7 ff.

[13] Strabo xii. 3. 15; Dio Cass. xxxvi. 12.

[14] E. Babelon, *Traité des monnaies*, II, Part II (1910), 431 ff., Pl. CX, Nos. 17–19; E. T. Newell, in *Numismatic Notes and Monographs*, No. 46 (1931), pp. 13 ff.

[15] Strabo xii. 3. 15; Arr. *Anab.* ii. 12. 2.

[16] Memnon xx. 2; Curt. iv. 1. 34–35.

Ignoring these signs of disaffection in his rear, Alexander pressed on his crusade. Gaza, the portal to the desert, was left a waste, and after but seven days' march he was at Pelusium, where he was joined by his Phoenician fleet. Pelusium was garrisoned, and by way of Heliopolis he reached Memphis. Only two years had elapsed since Darius had recovered Egypt, and this was too short a time to put its defenses in order; Sabaces had fallen at Issus, and his successor, Mazaces, could only welcome Alexander and turn over the palace and eight hundred talents. Greeks had long been allies of rebel Egyptians, even though their paid assistance was not always appreciated; it was barely a decade since Ochus had desecrated the sacred utensils, killed the holy animals, and initiated so harsh a rule that—no wonder—the Persians were hated and Alexander welcomed with enthusiasm. Soon the natives were boasting that the new king was actually the true-born son of Nectanebo, who had visited his mother Olympias in the form of a serpent; thus Alexander could be crowned at Memphis as Pharaoh with all the ancient ritual. For the natives, he worshiped the bull Apis and the other gods, but he also held literary and athletic contests to which came the most famous champions from Greece.[17]

To take the place of destroyed Tyre as the great commercial center of the eastern Mediterranean, Alexander determined to found a new capital which should bear his own name. Naucratis, the old emporium, was not well situated for this purpose; a better site was discovered a little west of the Canopic mouth of the Nile, which from the days of the Greek heroes was the usual entrance of sea-borne trade from the Greek world. Its predecessor, Racotis, had been nothing but a fishing village or a guard post against Greeks and Phoenicians, which held quiet the ever unruly herdsmen. It lay on a limestone ridge between the sea and Lake Mareotis and was therefore dry and healthful; the three-mile-long island of Pharos shut off the dangerous winds and afforded behind its lee an excellent harbor. A short canal brought potable water and furnished direct communication with the Nile; but, quite as important, the site offered the shortest route across the sea from Egypt to the lands of the Greeks, not only to Greece in Asia and on the mainland but even more to the colonies of the west which were about to enjoy their greatest prosperity.

Deinocrates, Rhodian architect of the temple of Artemis at Ephesus,

[17] Diod. xvii. 49. 2; Arr. *Anab.* iii. 1. 1 ff.; Curt. iv. 7. 1 ff.; Malal. vii. 189.

had followed Alexander, and was commissioned to lay out the long
narrow site; he employed the checkerboard pattern recently imported
from the East by Hippodamus of Miletus, whose shift in orientation
to due east-west perhaps justifies the attribution of the whole system
to him by the Greeks.[18] The line of wall, the market place, and the site
of temples for the Greek divinities and for Isis were marked out, and
a feast dated to Tybi 25 (January 30), 331, commemorated the foundation.[19] Hegelochus arrived with the news that Tenedos had come over,
that Pharnabazus had been taken prisoner at Chios, and that Lesbos
and Cos were Macedonian.[20]

During the centuries immediately preceding, the oracle of Ammon in
the Libyan oasis of Siwah had supplanted—at least in the eyes of foreigners—the more ancient temple at "hundred-gated Thebes." Croesus
of Lydia was the first outsider known to have consulted the oracle,
though Greek legend found predecessors in Perseus and Heracles.
Cambyses failed to plunder its oasis, but Greeks of Libya made the
oracle their own, and through them the god Ammon was made known
to the mainland. Pindar dedicated to him a temple at Boeotian Thebes,
and his statue by the famous sculptor Calamis might still be visited
in the second century of our era. Pindar also wrote a hymn for the
Ammonians of Libya. Euripides knew that men went for advice to
the "rainless seat" of Ammon, while, to a citizen of Cyrene, Ammon
was "our god." Aristophanes rated his oracle second only to Delphi.
During the Peloponnesian Wars the Athenians sent the god an official
mission, and Spartan Lysander countered with a visit of his own. Hellanicus prepared an itinerary, an *Anabasis*, through the desert to the
oasis shrine. Just before, Athens had paid for a new temple and had
lengthened the name of the sacred trireme to be Salaminia Ammonias.
There was good reason why Alexander should announce publicly his
intention to make the visit, especially as the shrine had been consulted
by his ancestors Perseus and Heracles, and he himself could claim descent from Ammon![21]

[18] Aristot. *Polit.* ii. 5. 1; vii. 10. 4.

[19] Diod. xvii. 52 (after the return from the Amon oasis); Vitruv. ii *praef.* 4; Strabo xvii. 1, 6;
Arr. *Anab.* iii. 1. 5; Marmor Parium B, 5; Frag. Sabbait. 11; Amm. xxii. 16. 7.

[20] Arr. *Anab.* iii. 2. 3 ff.; Curt. iv. 5. 19 ff.

[21] Herod. i. 46; ii. 32, 42, 55; iii. 25–26; iv. 181; Eurip. *Troiad.* 734 ff.; *Alcest.* 116; Aristophan.
Aves 619; Ephor., Frag. 127; Callisthen., Frag. 15(J); Plut. *Nic.* 13. 1; *Cimon.* 12. 5; *Lysandr.* 20. 4;
Arr. *Anab.* iii. 3. 1–2; Paus. ix. 16. 1; Athen. xiv. 652A.

In full array, Alexander led his troops along the bare coast to Paraetonium, which later claimed him as founder. Thence he turned south and followed the desert track used by the men of Cyrene to reach the oasis. Unseasonable rain assuaged the army's thirst, two crows and two talking serpents directed its march—at least according to the story. At its widest, Ammon's oasis was only five miles; it existed because of a spring, which changed its temperature—so it was said—with the hour of the day. Salt, the only product the oasis exported, was carried to the Nile in palm-leaf baskets, because it was purer than the salt of the sea.

Amid palms and olives, Alexander saw before him an isolated hill on which stood the famous temple within a squared-stone inclosure fifty by forty-eight yards in size. His attendants were bidden to change their garments in reverence and to stand without in the courts and colonnaded halls while he alone in ordinary garb entered the inner shrine at the far end of the inclosure, only thirteen by thirty feet. Under the roof of huge blocks, adorned by strange figures and stranger hieroglyphics, he dimly beheld on the altar the golden bark within which was kept the divine figure of varied precious stones. Inspired by the god himself, the prophet caused the image to give response through nods and signs and thus proclaimed to Alexander that he was the son of the god.

Through the prophet, Ammon had saluted Alexander as a father recognizes his son. Misunderstanding the salutation, Alexander thought his father Philip was speaking and inquired whether any of his murderers had yet escaped vengeance. He was warned by the prophet against use of such language; his true father was no mortal, and Alexander must change the form of his question. Letters to his mother Olympias were later quoted to the effect that he received secret responses about which he would tell her on his return; whether the letters are authentic may be questioned, but there can be no doubt that he was told he was actually the true son of Zeus Ammon. It was also reported that one of his questions was whether he would become lord and master of all mankind; the god made answer that all this would be granted to him. Through the native "philosopher" Psammon, who, according to the Greeks, taught that all mankind is under God's kingship, he learned that Zeus Ammon ruled the world which he had given to his newly discovered son.[22]

[22] Callisthen., Frag. 15(J); Craterus letter in Strabo xv. 1. 35; Plut. *Alex.* 27. 3 ff.; *Reg. imp. apophtheg.* 180D; more briefly, Diod. xvii. 49 ff.; Just. xi. 11; Arr. *Anab.* iii. 4. 5; Curt. iv. 7, 5 ff.;

KING WORSHIP

Alexander had been accepted as a legitimate Pharaoh. As such, he was the physical son of the god. The divine birth could be seen depicted on the walls of the temples for all to behold, and the Pharaoh himself was often called the "good god." In his earthly form, Alexander was "king of the south and north, Setep-en-Amon-meri-re, son of the sun, lord of risings, Arksandres."

Although he never visited Thebes in person, his figure became familiar to its inhabitants. In the Luxor sanctuary, four columns were removed and though the relief of Amenhotep III was left on the walls, a chapel open at both ends was erected in the vacant space; in it was placed the bark of the Theban Amon, and both interior and exterior were filled with Alexander's repeated figure before the various gods of Thebes. At Karnak the door of the fourth pylon was restored in his name. To the right of the inner sanctuary, in a chapel built by Thutmose III, were a few reliefs presenting that king in the act of sacrifice; the blank walls were covered with similar scenes in which Alexander officiated. The execution is well done, for the artists of the Thirtieth Dynasty were still available, and the brilliant colors are well preserved to this day. Similar restoration was done at the temple of Khonsu.[23] No doubt Alexander himself was shown the same reliefs, now lost, in Memphis and the Delta. Alexander recognized that to the native Egyptians it was a matter of course that the reigning monarch should be acclaimed as a god. Also, he was still a youth, but his conquests had been so extraordinary that divine assistance must be postulated. It was therefore easy for him to become fully aware of his own divine kingship. Thus king worship entered the Greek world.[24]

Chron. Oxyrhync. 7; Frags. Sabbait. 9–10. For the temple see M. Jomard and F. Cailliaud, *Voyage à l'oasis de Syouah* (1823); G. Steindorff, *Durch die Libysche Wüste zur Amonsoase* (1904); C. D. Belgrave, *Siwah* (1923); G. E. Simpson, *The Heart of Libya* (1929). See J. A. O. Larsen, "Alexander at the Oracle of Ammon," *Classical Philology*, XXVIII (1932), 70 ff.

[23] C. R. Lepsius, *Denkmaeler aus Aegypten und Aethiopien*, Abteilung III, Pls. 32, 82–83; Abteilung IV, Pls. 3–5; Sethe, *op. cit.*, pp. 6–8.

[24] Calvin W. McEwan, *The Oriental Origin of Hellenistic Kingship* (1934).

Chapter XXXVII

PERSEPOLIS—THE CRUSADE ENDS

SATRAPAL ORGANIZATION OF WESTERN ASIA

HAILED as the son of Zeus-Ammon, Alexander returned through the Nitrian Desert straight to Memphis, where another gymnastic and literary festival was celebrated to prove that he had not yet forgotten the Hellenic crusade. But he could not ignore the strength of the Nile Valley, rich in resources and so isolated from the rest of the world. It would be unsafe, he realized, to place a land so strong under the sole rule of any one man. Two former nomarchs, Doloaspis and Petisis, were promoted; he divided the civil control between them, while the other nomarchs were left in their respective nome capitals. Cleomenes of Naucratis, a native-born Greek, was placed in charge of the strategically important nome of Arabia about Heroopolis; in addition, he was to collect the tribute from all the nomarchs throughout Egypt. Apollonius, son of Charinus, was assigned oversight of Libya.

Although natives were given a surprisingly prominent share in the civil administration, the large military force demanded for so outstanding a satrapy was selected exclusively from Macedonians or Greeks. Polemon, son of Theramenes, commanded the fleet, while the army was divided between Peucestas, son of Macaratus, and Balacrus, son of Amyntus. Pantaleon of Pydna was appointed garrison commander in Memphis, and Polemon, son of Megacles, in Pelusium. Lycidas the Arcadian was set over the Greek mercenaries; their scribe was Eugnostus, son of Xenophantes; their overseers, Aeschylus and Ephippus of Chalcis.[1]

While Alexander was busy dividing the responsibility for Egypt, the Samaritans had burned alive Andromachus, satrap of Syria. In the spring of 330 Alexander hurried back to Syria, punished the rebels, and installed Menon as successor to Andromachus. Another athletic and literary contest was held at Tyre.[2]

The satrapies were now regrouped into larger units for taxation purposes under the general oversight of Harpalus, son of Machatas; in

[1] Arr. *Anab.* iii. 5; Curt. iv. 8. 5.   [2] Arr. *Anab.* iii. 6. 1; Curt. iv. 8. 10.

513

addition to Cleomenes in Egypt, Coeranus of Beroea was to collect the
taxes in Phoenicia, and Philoxenus in Asia beyond the Taurus. The
kings of Cyprus—Nicocreon of Salamis and Pasicrates of Soli in particular—were assigned regular choragic duties. Nearchus became satrap of Lycia and of the lands as far as the Taurus; Menander became
satrap of Lydia; and Asclepiodorus, son of Eunicus, was appointed satrap of Syria in place of Menon, who had proved too slow in gathering
supplies for the projected eastern expedition. Thus Alexander was
slowly feeling his way toward a more efficient organization of his
empire.[3]

GAU GAMELA

Mazaeus with three thousand cavalry had prevented the completion
of two bridges across the Euphrates at Thapsacus. On the arrival of
Alexander with seven thousand horse and forty thousand foot, he retired, wasting the country before him. Crossing the river, the army
followed the lower slopes of the Armenian Mountains because here
it was cooler and here also forage was easier to secure. A report came
in that Darius was holding the far bank, but in the actual crossing
the only difficulty met was the swiftness of the current.

For some strange reason, Darius had made up his mind not to contest the strong Tigris bulwark. Instead, he encamped on a smaller
stream, the Bumodus, four days' journey eastward, where he ordered
the ground leveled for the deployment of his enormous force; only too
obviously he knew nothing of tactics and expected to overwhelm the
Macedonians by sheer weight of numbers.

Safely across the unguarded river, Alexander's troops gazed in awe
at the high mound of Nineveh. This city, they were told, had been
built by Sardanapallus, as was proved by a column inscribed in Chaldaean writing; after a siege, it had been destroyed by Founder Cyrus.
With the Tigris on their left and the Gordyaean Mountains to their
right, the army marched four days through Aturia (Assyria) until
scouts reported the presence of the enemy. Alexander rested his men
four days and on the fifth marched out at dawn. That day the advance
was through rolling country which effectively shut off enemy view until close at hand. Once contact was established, the Macedonians were
ordered into camp and thus secured a good night's rest, while Darius
kept his soldiers all night under arms, guarding the leveled plain already prepared for the coming battle. The plain itself was known as

[3] Arr. *Anab.* iii. 6, 4 ff.; Plut. *Alex.* 29; Diod. xvii. 6. 26; Dittenberger, *Syl.*[3], No. 302.

Gau Gamela, the "grazing place of the camel," while on the low foot-hills to the north might be recognized a hamlet whose ruined mound still preserves its memory as Tell Gomel. [4]

A clear picture of the battle (October 1, 331) is possible because the victors captured both the imperial army list and the orders for dis-posal of the various corps. As in the similar army list from the reign of Xerxes, each satrapal contingent was under the command of its own satrap. On the extreme left were the Bactrian cavalry under Bessus, who was also in charge of the Indians and Sogdians. Next came the Scythian Dahae, and then the Arachosians and hill Indians led by Barsaentes. Persian cavalry and infantry were intermingled, after which were stationed the Susian and Cadusian contingents, apparent-ly detached from their proper commanders.

In the center was Darius himself, surrounded by the loyal kinsmen, the Persian Immortals (whose spears were butted with golden apples), and other detachments of Indians, deported Carians, and Mardian archers. At the side of the king and on either flank of the Persians were Greek mercenaries. Behind the center was the reserve; this consisted of Uxians, who, together with the Susians, should have been led by Oxyathres, son of Abulites; of Babylonians and Sittacenians under Bupares (from whom the Carians had been detached); and of tribes-men from the Persian Gulf under Ocondobates, Ariobarzanes, and Otanes.

On the right wing were, successively, the Albanians and Sacesinians (who, like the Cadusians, should have been under Atropates); the Tapurians and Hyrcanians, led by Parthyaeus; the Medes, under that Atropates who in early Hellenistic times was to give his name to Media Atropatene and so indirectly to the modern Adhorbaigan; the Parthians and Sacae; and, finally, the levies from Syria within the riv-ers and Hollow Syria which Mazaeus had brought with him on his retreat.

This was the main line of battle. Before it was thrown a deep caval-ry screen commanded by Phratophernes. On the left were the allied Sacae, the mounted archers led by Manaces, other Bactrians, and a hundred of the dreaded scythed chariots. In the center were the still more dreaded elephants and fifty additional chariots. On the right, supported by yet another fifty chariots, were the Armenians under Mithraustes and Orontes (the son of a more famous satrap of that

---

[4] Strabo (xvi. 1. 3) translates "Gaugamela" as "Camel's House," but actually *gau* means "grazing place." For the Nineveh episode see Amyntas *Stathmi* iii, Frag. 2(J); Athen. xii. 529E ff.

name), and the Cappadocians whom Ariaces, like Mazaeus, had withdrawn.

Many of these satraps bore honored names, long known in the famous families. There is no indication that they were less brave than their fathers, but they had learned nothing of contemporary tactics. We may detect some evidence of an attempt to break away from the old satrapal levy, but this alone was not enough to win the battle.

In contrast to our almost too full account of the battle arrangement, we know little of the struggle itself, which was fought on October 1, 331. An effort on the part of Darius to outflank the Macedonians was a failure. The scythed chariots and elephants did not, as expected, terrorize their opponents. Instead, Alexander broke through the line directly opposite the king; Darius fled as at Issus, but his subordinates fought so bravely that the Macedonians were in great difficulties, and Alexander himself was needed to save the day. He crossed the Lycus and encamped while Parmenion was clearing the camp of the Persians. By midnight, Alexander was again hurrying his cavalry on to Arbela, seventy-five miles away; when he arrived, it was to discover that Darius had a second time escaped, once more leaving—as at Issus—his chariot and weapons. With the Bactrian cavalry, the kinsmen, and the Immortals, Darius fled through the mountains to Ecbatana.[5]

A good picture of the wild flight after the battle is given by Semtutefnakhte, an Egyptian priest-physician in attendance on Darius at the time. He thanks his god Harsaphes: "You protected me in the battle of the Greeks when you hurled back the Asiatics. They killed many at my side, but no one raised a hand against me. I saw you afterward in a dream. Your majesty said to me: 'Hasten to Ehnas, behold, I am with you.' I passed through the foreign lands, I was alone, I reached the sea and feared not. I came to Ehnas and no hair of my head was taken away." In the temple of his god at Ehnas, he set up a stele to him, and he expressed the hope that the reader would pronounce the name of the dedicator. The prayer was granted in a way Semtutefnakhte could scarcely have dreamed: under an early Roman emperor the stele was carried off to Italy and used to authenticate the gingerbread temple of Isis at Pompeii![6]

---

[5] Callisthen., Frags. 36–37(J); Amyntas *Stathmi* iii, Frag. 2(J); Eratosthenes, Frags. 29–30(J); Diod. xvii. 55 ff.; Strabo xvi. 1. 3; Just. xi. 13–14; Plut. *Alex.* 31 ff.; *De Alex. fort.* 329F; Arr. *Anab.* iii. 7 ff.; Curt. iv. 9–10; v. 1 ff.; Marmor Parium B, 5; Chron. Oxyrhync. 7.

[6] A. Erman, *ÄZ*, XXXI (1893), 91 ff.; H. Schäfer, *Aegyptiaca: Festschrift für Georg Ebers* (1937), pp. 92 ff.; P. Tresson, *Bulletin de l'Institut Français d'Archéologie Orientale*, XXX (1931), 369 ff.

PLATE LXV

Artaxerxes III Stairway (West of Palace of Darius at Persepolis) (courtesy Oriental Institute)

Relief (courtesy New York Metropolitan Museum)

LATE ACHAEMENID SCULPTURE

PLATE LXVI

"Alexander" Coins Found at Persepolis (courtesy Oriental Institute)

The Last Tribute-bearers at Persepolis (courtesy Oriental Institute)

THE OLD ACHAEMENID AND THE NEW GREEK

PLATE LXVII

"Alexander" Portrait (from *Marbles and Bronzes in the British Museum*, Pl. 33)

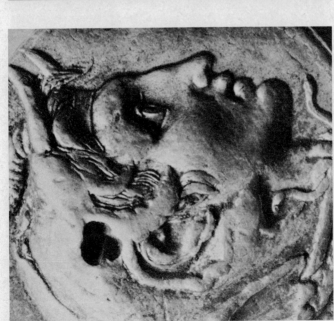

"Alexander" Coin (from K. Lange, *Herrscherköpfe, des Altertum*, Pl. 42)

THE DEIFICATION OF ALEXANDER

PLATE LXVIII

Near Syrian Gates

Cilician Gates

ALEXANDER'S CAMPAIGN

PLATE LXIX

Alexander in the Sanctuary at Luxor (courtesy Oriental Institute)

Darius on His Unfinished Tomb

OPPONENTS OF THE EAST AND WEST

PLATE LXX

Ruins at Persepolis (courtesy Oriental Institute)

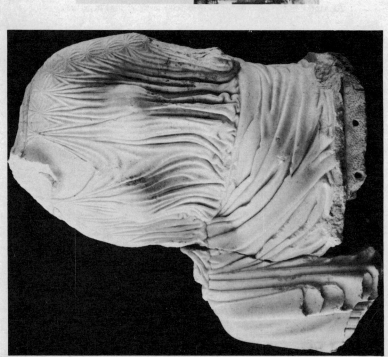

The Greek Lady at Persepolis (courtesy Oriental Institute)

THE END OF ALEXANDER'S CAMPAIGN

Gau Gamela was truly a decisive battle. By his flight Darius had surrendered all claim to the Persian throne. To be sure, months would elapse before his death could be announced and his corpse find burial— not in the half-finished tomb he had begun to the south of the Persepolis terrace, but high up the cliff in the graves of his predecessors. Other months must elapse while Bessus the Bactrian satrap fought on to confirm his claim to the title of the fourth Artaxerxes. It would be years before the Iranian Plateau was pacified. But the great war was ended, and Alexander would be accepted as himself a great Persian monarch by the majority of his subjects.

One final scene was needed to round out the crusade. Arbela was the capital of the region in which the decisive battle had been fought; although seventy-five miles distant from the field, it was generally assigned the honor of naming the battle, for Gau Gamela was an unknown hamlet. The near-by mountain was called Nicatorium, "Mount Victory." From Arbela—named, the Greeks said, from its founder Arbelus, son of Athmoneus—the army turned southward. The Caprus or Lower Zab was crossed, and the naphtha font in the land of Artacene—where today the Mosul oil fields are an object of dispute and where to our own time the fires leap up when the soil is slightly scratched—was visited. Then came the shrine of Anaea or Anahita, Sandracae, where was a palace of the first Darius, Cyparisson, and the crossing of the Gyndes or Diyala on the road to Babylon.[7]

THE SURRENDER OF BABYLON AND SUSA

As he neared the city, flourishing again after its ruin by Xerxes, the conqueror was met by priests and nobles, bringing their gifts of welcome and promising to surrender Babylon's treasures. After such a demonstration, the Persian satrap Mazaeus could only ratify formally the submission already accomplished. The garrison commander, Bagophanes, came out from the citadel in which the royal treasure was guarded; he ordered flowers for the streets and crowns to honor the new Great King. Frankincense and other costly perfumes burned on the silver altars, Magi chanted hymns, and Chaldaeans and Babylonians followed their example. To the joy of the whole population, Alexander commanded that the temples be rebuilt, above all that of Bel Marduk, which had lain waste since its destruction by Xerxes.[8]

Following the precedent established in Egypt, where two natives

[7] Strabo xvi. 1. 3–4.

[8] Arr. *Anab*. iii. 16. 3; Curt. v. 1. 19 ff.; Marmor Parium B, 6.

had been given a divided civil control, Alexander rewarded Mazaeus for his prompt submission by renewal of his satrapal office, while Bagophanes was continued in his oversight of the treasure. Military control, however, as in Egypt, was in the hands of Macedonians— Apollodorus of Amphipolis and Menetas of Pella; the latter was also made general overseer of the satrapies as far west as Cilicia. Agathon guarded the citadel, and Asclepiodorus, son of Philo, collected the taxes. Mithrines, who had surrendered the citadel at Sardis, was appointed satrap of Armenia, but he seems never to have brought it under effective control.[9]

Alexander's old master Aristotle had requested his royal pupil to send home to him anything of scientific interest. Callisthenes accordingly forwarded to his uncle the Chaldaean "observations" over a period of thirty-one thousand years; presumably they were calculations made by Kidinnu or by members of his school. At any rate, we may compare the thirty-one thousand years of these "observations" with the thirty-four thousand years which, according to the earlier Babylonian king lists, were supposed to have elapsed since the universal flood. With Aristotle was Calippus, who utilized the "observations" to extend his own in deriving values for the length of the year and of the synodic month; despite this aid, his value for the synodic month was farther from the truth than even those calculated three centuries earlier from the saros cycle.[10]

From Babylon an easy road across the plain led almost due east to Susa. On the way through Sittacene, Alexander met the son of Abuletes, satrap of Susa, and received a letter from Philoxenus, whom he had sent ahead direct, reporting that the inhabitants had surrendered the city with its treasure. Twenty days out from Babylon, Alexander arrived in person and found that the treasure in the palace of Darius I amounted to forty thousand talents of silver and nine thousand talents of gold in coined darics.[11] This palace was then abandoned (as excavations prove), but the palace of Bagoas was handed over to Parmenion for residence. Abuletes was retained as satrap and Mazarus as garrison commander, but the general was Archelaus, son of Theodorus; Zenophilus was over the citadel, and Callicrates over the treasure. At this

[9] Diod. xvii. 64. 5–6; Plut. *Alex.* 39. 6; Arr. *Anab.* iii. 16. 4–5; Curt. v. 1. 43–44.

[10] Porphry, in Simplicius *Ad Aristot. De caelo ii. 12* (ed. Heiberg [1894], p. 506); Hipparchus, in Theon (cf. Abbé Rome, *Annales de la Société Scientifique de Bruxelles*, XLVI [1926], 9); J. K. Fotheringham, *Quellen und Studien*, B, II, 40.

[11] So Diod. xvii. 66. 1–2. Other estimates: Just. xi. 14. 9; Plut. *Alex.* 36. 1; Arr. *Anab.* iii. 16. 6 ff.; Curt. v. 2. 8 ff.

time also, Menes was commissioned satrap over a united Syria, Phoenicia, and Cilicia. Sacrifices and athletic contests, including a torch race, introduced Susa to Hellenic customs, and Alexander was ready to move on.[12]

PERSEPOLIS

The Coprates and Pasitigris were crossed, and the Uxians who lived in the low country and had been subject to the Persians quickly made their submission. Hillmen Cossaei, ruled by Medates, refused to grant passage save on the terms permitted the Persian king, who paid them good money every time he moved from Susa into Persis. Alexander considered such payment blackmail and beneath his dignity; guided by Susians, he advanced by an unsuspected trail, plundered the Cossaean villages, and killed many of their inhabitants; then he seized the pass leading to Persepolis. His fleeing opponents finally returned to promise a yearly tribute of a hundred horses, five hundred pack animals, and thirty thousand sheep—expecting, no doubt, that Alexander would never return to make the collection.[13]

Parmenion was sent by the main road to the east, while Alexander followed the hills into Persis. Ariobarzanes, the satrap, had blocked the Persian Gates by a wall, but, guided over a rough path by a Lycian who knew both Greek and Persian, Alexander outflanked him while the main force attacked and broke through the wall. Thereupon the garrison of Persepolis shut out the retreating Ariobarzanes, and its commander Tiridates sent to Alexander, urging him to hurry before the city was destroyed. A bridge across the Araxes was hastily completed, and the Macedonians rushed on to occupy Persepolis before the garrison could plunder it for themselves. The capital was reached by the first of February, 330.[14]

Long since, the conqueror appeared to have forgotten the crusade. Everywhere he had posed as the legitimate successor of the Achaemenid monarchs. Persian satraps—Mazaeus of Babylon and Abuletes of Susa—had within the past few months been retained at their posts. When, therefore, Tiridates urged Alexander to hasten the occupation of the city and thus save the treasure, he had good reason to expect that he, too, would be rewarded: like Bagophanes in Babylon, with

---

[12] Plut. *Alex.* 39. 6; Arr. *Anab.* iii. 16. 9; Curt. v. 2. 16–17.

[13] Diod. xvii. 67; Strabo xv. 3. 6; xi. 13. 6; Curt. v. 3. 1 ff.; Arr. *Anab.* iii. 17.

[14] Diod. xvii. 68–69; Strabo xv. 3. 6; Arr. *Anab.* iii. 18. 10; Curt. iv. 4. 1 ff.; v. 5. 2–3. For the date cf. C. A. Robinson, Jr., *The Ephemerides of Alexander's Expedition* (1932), p. 81.

the oversight of the treasure, or, like Mazarus in Susa, with permission to retain his position as garrison commander.

His justified expectations were disappointed. At Susa, Alexander had forgotten the crusade, even when he was shown the gorgeous colors of the palace from which Artaxerxes II had dictated the notorious King's Peace and to which Greek ambassadors so often had traveled to learn the king's will and to accept his subsidies. Persepolis, on the other hand, had remained almost unoccupied during the last century. Its name was not associated with any of the events of Greek history which the most ardent crusader might consider disgraceful; in fact, the name seems to have been virtually unknown in the western part of the empire. Yet it was at Persepolis that Alexander formally ended the crusade.

That Alexander should have confiscated the huge treasure of gold and silver, valued at one hundred and twenty thousand silver talents,[15] might have been expected, for there was precedent. Equally proper, according to current practice, was the emptying of the "king's cushion," a large chamber filled with five thousand talents of gold at the head of the royal bed, and of the "king's footstool," a smaller chamber with three thousand talents at the foot. Proper also was the carrying-off of the golden vine, its clusters of the most costly jewels, which extended over the bed.[16] But that the entire settlement (with the exception of the palace inclosure) which had grown up at the foot of the terrace should have been handed over to the soldiers for plunder needs explanation.

Their loot was enormous. Persepolis—subsequent reports declared—was the richest city under the sun; even the private houses were filled with all sorts of precious objects accumulated during the long years of its existence. The men were all slain without mercy, the excuse being the crowds of horribly mutilated Greek captives the soldiers had freed; the women, of course, were enslaved, and the Macedonians fought one another over the plunder. Had Persepolis been taken by sack and not freely surrendered by its garrison commander, it could not have received worse treatment. To add to his evil reputation, Alexander even boasted in his letters how he had ordered the Persian captives to be massacred![17]

---

[15] Diod. xvii. 71. 1; Curt. v. 6. 9.

[16] Amyntas *Stathmi*, Frag. 6(J); Chares of Mitylene. *Hist. Alex.* v, Frag. 2(J); Athen. xii. 514E.

[17] Diod. xvii. 70; Just. xi. 14. 10 ff.; Plut. *Alex.* 37. 2; Curt. v. 5. 5 ff. Note how the whole unsavory episode is omitted by Arrian!

During his residence in the city[18] Alexander made an excursion to Parsagarda, where again as of right he expropriated the treasure accumulated by his great predecessor, the elder Cyrus, and made Cobares satrap of this oldest Persian settlement.[19]

The barbarities at Persepolis were followed by an act of sheer vandalism—the burning of the marvelous palaces on the platform. When Alexander made public his intention to destroy the mighty structures of Xerxes at Persepolis in vengeance for the latter's destruction of Athens and the burning of the Greek temples, Parmenion urged the young crusader to spare them. It was not right, he insisted, for Alexander to destroy his own property; the Asiatics would not wish to join him—from his mature wisdom Parmenion made clear—if he gave the impression of merely traveling through and of not wishing to retain the sovereignty of Asia. This came so close to the brutal truth that Alexander refused even to listen.[20]

Later historians attempted to extenuate the crime. Some declared that the burning was indeed premeditated but that Alexander soon repented and in vain ordered the fire extinguished.[21] More commonly the blame was transferred to a woman, Thaïs, mistress of General Ptolemy, who, it was said, took advantage of a drunken feast to persuade Alexander to cast the fatal torch.[22]

At Persepolis itself the ruins continue the story. Burned beams of the roof still lay their print across stairways and against sculptures. Heaps of ashes are all that remain of the cedar paneling. Mud-brick walls, deprived of their cover by the burning roofs, have flowed down with the rains into the sunken courts. The triple line of circumvallation, also of mud brick, has disintegrated, leaving only the foundations laid in hard stone. The bronze gates in each of the four sides[23] have disappeared.

So thorough was the search for loot that only a handful of coins have been unearthed by the excavators. A few more scraps of gold leaf

[18] Four months according to Plut. *Alex.* 37. 3, but Robinson, *Ephemerides*, pp. 74 ff., has proved that the stay could not have been half so long.

[19] Arr. *Anab.* iii. 18. 10 and Curt. v. 6. 10 place the visit to Persagada (thus spelled by Curtius) *before* the burning of Persepolis; for Cobares see Curt. v. 6. 10; for Parsagardae see Arr. *Anab.* iii. 18. 10 and Strabo xv. 3. 7.

[20] Strabo xv. 3. 6; Arr. *Anab.* iii. 18. 11–12.

[21] Plut. *Alex.* 38. 4.

[22] Cleitarchus, Frag. 11(J); Diod. xvii. 72; Plut. *Alex.* 38. 1 ff.; Curt. v. 7. 3 ff.; Athen. xiii. 576E.

[23] Diod. xvii. 71. 4 ff.

are all of this precious metal that have rewarded their labors. Hundreds of vessels carved from the most varied and most beautiful stones were carried out into the courts and deliberately smashed. A marvelous seated female statue, carved in marble just before the date of the Parthenon sculptures, had been carried from Phocaea or some near-by city to Persepolis during the troubles incident to the Spartan expeditions which professed to liberate Asia. Placed in the museum hall of the Persepolis treasury, it had remained safe until Alexander's occupation. Then the Macedonian soldiers knocked off and destroyed the head and tossed the torso into a near-by corridor, leaving only a mutilated hand to indicate the room in which it originally stood.[24] Alexander could not have shown more plainly how thin was his veneer of Greek culture.

The burning of Persepolis was a symbol to the world that the great crusade had reached its destined end. Unfortunately, both symbol and crusade were equally out of date. His first conquests were organized by Alexander on the model of a Persian satrapy. In Egypt he had learned that he was son of a god and therefore himself a divine king. More and more he came under the influence of oriental beliefs, and soon he was to take over Persian pomp and circumstance. At the end he was to dream of unifying Persian and Greek peoples and cultures. The Orient had conquered its fierce conqueror.

The much-vaunted "Fortune of Alexander" turned against her favorite even before his premature death. By their incessant wars, his successors destroyed the empire he had received virtually intact from the last Darius, and even the Romans proved unable to restore it. His dream of a fusion of cultures remained a vision for the distant future.

While historians have increasingly emphasized the significance of the Hellenistic Age which immediately followed, the reign of Alexander has sunk back in retrospect to its true status as a prelude. Today we are less interested in Alexander's personal character than in his anticipations of the new era. But Alexander looked not only forward but backward as well; his reign was both a prelude *and* an epilogue. With the burning of Persepolis, the older age of the independent oriental empires came to an end.

Persepolis was never again occupied, but its fate had its compensations. The Macedonia of Alexander has disappeared, almost without

---

[24] Erich F. Schmidt, *The Treasury of Persepolis and Other Discoveries in the Homeland of the Achaemenians* (1939), pp. 65 ff.

trace. Its older capital Aegae is a malaria-ridden site and nothing more; when its alternate name Edessa is mentioned, we think at once of the great Mesopotamian capital. The tombs of the Macedonian rulers, where Alexander had thought to be gathered to his fathers, have never been found; his own capital, Pella, is a mass of shapeless ruins. Philippi, his father's foundation, enjoyed its greatest prosperity under Roman sway, but, at that, its few ruins are late. Nothing has been preserved of the original Alexandria; the city of his successors, the Ptolemies, must be sensed through its modern successor, eked out by a few freestanding monuments and by buried ruins marked only on a plan.

But Persepolis stands to this day, preserved for posterity by its very burning. The palaces of Darius and Xerxes still tower above the plain, a marvel to the passing wayfarer. So nearly complete are their rooms that at sunset it is not difficult to evoke the departed ghosts. Far from completing their destruction, Alexander's intended holocaust has preserved for us virtually unscratched magnificent reliefs whose beauties at last may rival the Greek. The smashed vases inscribed with the name of Xerxes have been pieced together by the patient archeologist, who has also collected numerous bits to illustrate the daily life. If Alexander's fires destroyed many invaluable parchments, the majority would in any case have perished through the mere passage of time; unwittingly he did us the priceless service of baking the tablets hitherto preserved only on the crude clay so easily disintegrated. The stone slabs uncovered by the archeologist have been deciphered by the philologist and have been proved to contain the royal records; Darius and his successors now tell their own story in their own language.

For the whole empire period, archeologist and philologist have come to the aid of the historian. Like Persepolis, Susa has been excavated and its Elamite literature made known, though the mound at Ecbatana awaits its turn. The mounds of Babylonian cities have afforded thousands of business documents which are dated in the reigns of Persian monarchs and have for the first time made possible a sketch of economic life within their empire. Egyptian temples erected by Persian kings, or more numerous shrines built by native rulers in successful rebellion against them, may be visited by the most casual tourist. Hieroglyphic inscriptions and demotic or Aramaic papyri have been deciphered and add to our knowledge. No longer are we entirely dependent on the Greek "classics" for the story of Persia, even in its relations with the West; new excavations in Greek lands have rewarded us with valuable inscriptions and have shown us how Asia prospered in the last days of Achaemenid rule. As for the biblical story of the Jews, it has become a vitally new history when viewed against the contemporary background. Close to twenty-three centuries have elapsed since Alexander burned Persepolis; now at last, through the united effort of archeologist, philologist, and historian, Achaemenid Persia has risen from the dead.

TOPOGRAPHICAL INDEX

NAME INDEX

Abd (Arab), 295

Abd Susim (satrap, Dar. III), 422, 503, 508

Abd Susin (Sysinas, *q.v.*), 422

Abdalonymus (king of Sidon, Alex.), 506–7

Abdashtart (Strato, *q.v.*), 411

Abdemon (Phoenician king in Cyprus, Dar. II), 367

Abdmanat (Arab), 295

Abiyada Yathi, son of Ilyafa Yathi (Arab), 443, 445

Abrocomas (satrap, Arta. II), 374, 398

Abrocomes, son of Dar. I, 252

Abuletes (satrap, Dar. III and Alex.), 378, 515, 518–19

Abulites; *see* Abuletes

Achaemenes (Hakhamanish), 23, 107, 450

Achaemenes, son of Dar. I (satrap, Xer. and Arta. I), 235, 244, 246, 303

Achaeus (Gr. writer), 348

Achilles (Hakhlaza), hero, 350, 496

Achoris of Egypt (Arta. II), 397 ff., 401–2

Ada (Carian queen, Arta. III), 436, 483, 487, 499

Ada, daughter of Pixodarus (Dar. III), 490–91, 499–500

Adad, god, 294

Adad-shum-usur (administrator, Dar. I), 73

Adonis, god, 207, 450, 468 ff.

Adrastus, son of Gordias, Phrygian, hero, 322

Adrata (Dar. I), 193

Aeaces, son of Syloson, tyrant of Samos (Dar. I), 156

Aegyptus (Arta. III), 425

Aena (Anahita, *q.v.*), 471 (n. 50)

Aeropus, son of (Philip), 500

Aeschines of Athens (orator, Arta. III), 426

Aeschylus (overseer, Alex.), 513

Aeschylus (writer), 109, 143, 173, 199 (n. 12), 232, 266, 270–71, 363

Aeshma, demon, 18

Aesop (writer), 325, 333

Afrasiab, demon (Frangrasyan, *q.v.*), 22

Agamemnon, hero, 44, 382, 387

Agathon (commander, Alex.), 518

Agbaal of Phoenicia, 243

Agesilaus (Spartan commander, Arta. II), 382–90, 413, 417, 419–20, 457

Agoracritus (sculptor), 469

Ahasuerus (Artaxerxes, *q.v.*), 395

Ahiqar (Ahiqar, *q.v.*), 323

Ahiqar, 323–27, 332–33

Ahmose (Amasis, *q.v.*), 227

Ahmose sa Neith (Egyptian architect, Dar. I), 223

Ahmosi (Egyptian prophet, Dar. I), 220–21

Ahqqade (Lycian prince, Arta. II), 391

Ahura, god, 24, 28, 94 ff., 97, 99 ff., 103–4, 197, 233, 472 ff., 476

Ahuramazda: Ariayaramnes, 24, 29; Cyrus, 61; Zoroaster, 94–98, 102–5; Dar. I, 101, 108, 110, 116 ff., 119, 122–23, 125–28, 132, 146, 168–69, 171, 175, 182, 184, 195–99, 214–17, 225, 229, 471; Xer., 231–34, 247, 274–75, 285; Arta. II, 423, 471; on Carian coins, 409; on Cypriote coins, 399; late, 472–78, 482

Akhtobu, goddess, 463

Alakhssantra (Alexander, *q.v.*), 500

Alcaeus (poet), 208

Alcibiades (Dar. II), 361, 367 ff., 372–73

Alcides of Caunus (Arta. I), 344

Alcmaeonidae (Dar. I), 160–61

Alexander, son of Aeropus (Alex.), 500

Alexander, son of Amyntas (Dar. I), 149

Alexander (Commander, Arta. II), 377

Alexander the Great (Aksandres, Alakhs-santra): accession of, 490 ff.; Battle of Gau Gamela, 514–17; and Asia Minor, 493, 495–505; and Babylon, 517–18; and Egypt, 431, 509–13; and India, 381–82; and Persia, 17, 66, 125, 162, 169–70, 188, 216, 219, 274, 371, 445, 478, 481, 517–24; and Phoenicia, 505–8; as student of Aristotle, 435

Alexander of Macedon (Xer.), 250, 253, 256

Alilat, god, 295

Allah, god, 295

Alman, son of Ammikarib (Arab), 443

Alogune (Babylonian concubine, Arta. I), 355

Alyattes of Lydia, hero, 208

Amasis (Ahmose) (general, Dar. I), 227

Amasis of Egypt, 39, 57, 88–92, 142, 208 ff., 219, 223, 448

Amasis the Maraphian (Dar. I), 149

Amazons, 207

Amel-Marduk, son of Nebuchadnezzar (king of Chaldea), 35, 57, 136

Amenemhet of Egypt, 8

Amenhotep III of Egypt, 512

Amestris (daughter of Dar. II), 357, 364

Amestris (daughter of Otanes, wife of Xer.), 239, 267, 285, 290, 308, 312, 344–45, 355, 449

Ammikarib (Arab), 443

Ammisadiq, son of Hamathat (Arab), 444–45

Amon, god, 2, 8, 12, 220 ff., 223, 269, 271, 294, 349, 393, 404, 431, 450, 462 (n. 3), 470, 491, 510–13

Amorges (Homrkhkha), son of Pissuthnes (Dar. II), 359–60

Amos, 14

Amphiaraus, hero, 296

Amphilochus, son of Amphiaraus, hero, 296, 503

Amphyctionicus (writer), 485

Amurtis (Amyrtaeus, *q.v.*), 374

Amyntas, son of Antiochus, Macedonian (Dar. III), 500, 504–5

Amyntas of Macedonia (Dar. I), 149

539

SUBJECT INDEX

Ablution, 176
Abode of Good Thought (Zor.), 101
Abortion, 133
Abu (astron.), 201
Acacia, 165
Academy, Athens, 483
Academy of Plato, 211
Accuser (Satan), 479
Acharnians (Aristophanes), 354
Aconite, 414
Acorns, 348
Acropolis: Antandria, 363; Athens, 253, 308–9, 353; Celaenae, 501; Gordium, 502; Persepolis, 478; Sardis, 40, 42, 153, 498; Scepsis, 378; Susa, 45
"Actinography" (Democritus), 333, 336
Ada (money), 348
Addaru (month), 201, 206, 329, 454–55
Administrator of temple (*leshoni, shatammu*), 75, 134, 220 ff., 225
Adonia, 469
Adoniazousae (Philetaerus), 469
Adonis (Antiphanes), 468
Adonis (Araros), 469
Adonis (Plato the comic writer), 469
Adukanish (month), 177
Adultery, 289
Agate, 220
Agora, Athens, 460
Agriculture, 4, 16, 23, 68, 78, 81, 98, 187, 396, 442
Ahuna Vairya (Zor.), 197, 476
Aiaku (Eanna), 464
Airu (month), 202
Airyaman (class), 23
Airyema (Zor.), 197, 476
Alabaster, 184, 219, 230, 237, 353
Almanac, 329, 337, 342
Almonds, 348
Alms, 470
Alpha (astron.), 337
Alphabet, 4, 10, 13–14, 480–81; (Aram.), 116, 178, 464; (Car.), 269, 296, 391; (Egypt.), 463; (Gr.), 206–7, 296; (North Arabic), 294, 442, 480; (Pers.), 24, 68; (Phoen.), 481
Altar: (Arab.), 443; (Babyl.), 517; (Egypt.), 319, 399, 402, 404, 418, 511; (Gr.), 265, 482; (Jew.), 136, 305, 365–66; (Pers.), 28, 61, 105, 196, 229, 478–79; (Phryg.), 347; (Scyth.), 148
Altar (astron.), 335
Alum, 82
Ambassadors (Plato the comic writer), 394
Ambrosia, 26
Ameretat (Immortality), 96
Ammatu (measure), 82
Amulet, 90
Anabasis (Hellanicus), 470, 510

Anabasis (Xenophon), 299
Andromeda (astron.), 334
Angareion (intelligence), 299
Animal, 81, 85, 98, 183, 519; holy, 72, 509; representation of, 163, 223, 268, 277, 279 ff., 386; sacrificial, 75, 386
Ankh, 235
Anklet, 365
Ant, 18, 292
Antelope, 244, 279
Antidemonic law (Videvat), 16 ff., 130, 132
Antonia, tower of, Jerusalem, 315
Anu (Mars) (astron.), 334, 452–53
Apadana: at Babylon, 162; at Ecbatana, 226, 423, 489; at Persepolis, 170, 188, 225–26, 273–87, 353; at Susa, 170, 225, 422
Apis bull; *see* Bull, Apis
Apocalypse, 138, 467, 479
Appadanna; *see* Apadana
Apple, 180, 468, 515
Apprentice, 70, 76–77, 87
Apricot, 166
Archaism, 461
Archer, 227, 387
Archer (astron.), 334–35, 338, 453–54
"Archer" coins, 189, 387, 409
Architect, 223, 230, 432, 482, 509
Archives: at Babylon, 121; at Elephantine, 244–45; at Persepolis, 176–94, 219, 272, 281, 480; at Susa, 69–70, 176
Arcturus (astron.), 334
Ardabs (measure), 245, 366
Areopagus, Athens, 253
Argo (astron.), 335
Aristocracy, 44, 74, 152, 154, 372, 414, 441
Arithmetic, 210, 448, 454
"Arithmetic" (Democritus), 333
Armaiti (Piety), 96
Armor, 174, 217–18, 239 ff., 258
Armor-bearer, 364
Arrow, 65, 70, 174, 217, 239–44, 253, 258, 267, 409
Arrow (astron.), 334
Artaba (measure), 293, 418
Artichoke, 212
Artisan (*huiti*), 23, 76, 168, 189, 273–74, 277, 412
Asceticism, 382
Asha (Righteousness), 96
Ashem Vohu (Zor.), 197, 476
Ashir (Destiny), 96
Asphalt, 81, 161
Ass, 81, 132, 165, 183, 241, 246, 325–26, 351, 450
Assassination, 22, 57, 105, 110, 112, 148, 283, 289, 355–56, 371–72, 378, 409, 489, 491, 500
Assault and battery, 131
Assembly of citizens (*puhru*): (Babyl.), 54, 72,

556

PHOENIX BOOKS *Titles in print*

THE UNIVERSITY OF CHICAGO PRESS

30